Girl Culture

An Encyclopedia

Volume 1

Edited by
Claudia A. Mitchell
and
Jacqueline Reid-Walsh

GREENWOOD PRESS
Westport, Connecticut • London

Library of Congress Cataloging-in-Publication Data

Girl culture : an encyclopedia / edited by Claudia A. Mitchell and Jacqueline Reid-Walsh.
    p. cm.
  Includes bibliographical references and index.
  ISBN: 978–0–313–33908–0 (set : alk. paper)
  ISBN: 978–0–313–33909–7 (vol. 1 : alk. paper)
  ISBN: 978–0–313–33910–3 (vol. 2 : alk. paper)
  1. Girls—United States—Social conditions—Encyclopedias. 2. Teenage girls—United States—
Social conditions—Encyclopedias. I. Mitchell, Claudia. II. Reid-Walsh, Jacqueline, 1951–
HQ798.G523   2008
305.235'2097303—dc22   2007040517

British Library Cataloguing in Publication Data is available.

Library of Congress Catalog Card Number: 2007040517
ISBN: 978–0–313–33908–0 (Set)
        978–0–313–33909–7 (Vol. 1)
        978–0–313–33910–3 (Vol. 2)

First published in 2008

Greenwood Press, 88 Post Road West, Westport, CT 06881
An imprint of Greenwood Publishing Group, Inc.
www.greenwood.com

Printed in the United States of America

∞™

The paper used in this book complies with the
Permanent Paper Standard issued by the National
Information Standards Organization (Z39.48–1984).

10 9 8 7 6 5 4 3 2 1

Contents

List of Entries

Guide to Related Topics

Beauty and Body Issues

Abstinence Bracelets
Anorexia
At Twelve
Beauty Pageants
Binge Eating
Body Modification
Bulimia
Children's Beauty Pageants
Disordered Eating
Fat Girl
Henna
Lipstick and Lip Gloss
Menstruation
Sex Bracelets
Thin Ideal

Books

Anne of Green Gables
Are You There, God? It's Me, Margaret
The Baby-sitters Club
Blume, Judy
Caddie Woodlawn
Career Novels
Cherry Ames
Chick Lit
Coming-of-Age Memoirs
Crossover Literature
Fairy Tales, Modern
Fairy Tales, Traditional
Forever . . .
Ginny Gordon
Hinton, Susan Eloise (S.E.)
Little House on the Prairie
Little Women
Lolita
Nancy Drew
"Other" Girlhoods in Teen "Reality"
    Fiction
Pippi Longstocking
Ramona
Series Fiction
Sweet Valley High
Trixie Belden
See also Part 1, Studying Girl Culture

Celebrities and Icons

Barbie. *See* Part 1, Studying Girl Culture
Beyoncé

Calamity Jane
Celebrity Bad Girls
Disney. *See* Part 1, Studying Girl Culture
Duff, Hilary
Hello Kitty
Hilton, Paris
Holly Hobbie
Lohan, Lindsay
Lopez, Jennifer
Madonna
Miss Piggy
Oakley, Annie
Olsen, Mary-Kate and Ashley
Pink, the Color
Raven
Spears, Britney
Unicorns

Clothing and Fashion

baby phat
Bikini
Bobby Sox
Bra
Hijab
Hot Pants
La Senza Girl
Midriff Tops
Poodle Skirt
Recycled Clothing
Schoolgirl Uniform
Shopping
Style. *See* Part 1, Studying Girl Culture
Thong

Comics

Batgirl
Betty and Veronica
Catwoman
Comics
Little Lulu
Little Orphan Annie
Poison Ivy

Romance Comics
Wonder Woman

Digital Culture

Avatar
Blogging
Cell Phones
Girl Gamers
gURL.com
Lara Croft
MySpace
Sims, The
Social Networking
Web 2.0
Web sites
See also Part 1, Studying Girl Culture

Dolls and Toys

American Girl
Barbie. *See* Part 1, Studying Girl Culture
Blythe
Bratz
Cabbage Patch Kids
Doll Culture. *See* Part 1, Studying Girl
    Culture
Dollhouse
Dream House
Easy-Bake Oven
Flava Dolls
Jem and the Holograms
Holly Hobbie
Ken
Mattel
Midge
Muslim Dolls
My Little Pony
My Scene
Paper Dolls
Polly Pocket
She-Ra: Princess of Power
Skipper
Strawberry Shortcake

Preface

Girl Culture: An Encyclopedia has been written as an authoritative guide to contemporary girl culture—inasmuch as it is possible to chart an ever-changing terrain. Although the primary focus of the encyclopedia is on girl culture in the United States, the fading of borders that has accompanied the increasing profile of a television, film, and the Web now means that issues of concern and relevance to one country or culture are subjects of cross-national, if not universal, significance.

For example, t.A.T.u., the two girl singers who became popular in Russia in the early twenty-first century, also became popular in North America. And the most popular girls' fashion doll of all, Barbie, is available in 150 countries, though the meaning of Barbie may differ from one cultural context to another. But even before television and the Internet, there were classic texts about girlhood, such as *Anne of Green Gables*, written by the well-known Canadian author Lucy Maud Montgomery. Anne is just as popular among readers in the United States as she is among readers in Canada, and it's quite possible that, in proportion to the population, she is even more popular among readers in Japan.

This encyclopedia of girl culture is intended for a broad audience, so that it may serve, we hope, as an authoritative reference tool for high school and university students. Because of the diversity of the target audience, we have encouraged contributors to include a variety of references, ranging from Web sites to scholarly books to journal articles.

One problem that we have discovered in our own research is that, too often, girl culture (and the study of childhood and adolescent culture more generally) is dismissed as not being very important; somehow, the academic integrity accorded to other areas of study is often absent in the context of girlhood. As a consequence, even basic facts are sometimes difficult to obtain. For example, a number of years ago, when we were involved in a study of the relationship between the Stratemeyer Syndicate and the ghostwriters of the *Nancy Drew* series (particularly the contribution of the first ghostwriter, Mildred Wirt Benson), we discovered in a university card catalog entry that the author was listed as Harriet Adams, the daughter of the Stratemeyer Syndicate founder and the person who had publicly claimed to be the author. Clearly, the facts had not been checked. The lack of academic rigor in relation to girlhood and popular culture makes the challenge of doing research in the field both frustrating and oddly fascinating.

The time frame for the encyclopedia spans the early 1920s through the second half of the first decade of the twenty-first century. In focusing on contemporary girlhood, however, we have, where appropriate, noted the historical antecedents. The time frame turned out to be one of the fascinating issues. Somehow it was easier to generate a large number of topics from the past couple of decades than from the 1940s through the 1970s. In part, this is because girl culture, like many other aspects of popular culture, has been a burgeoning area, primarily in the past 30 years.

We are often asked, "How did you come up with these topics?" and "Where does one start on a project like this?" The start of the encyclopedia actually occurred around our respective dinner tables and over coffee with friends, colleagues, and relatives. "If you were putting together an encyclopedia on girl culture," we would ask, "what would you include and why?" In no time at all, we had amassed a list of several hundred topics, and these we posted on a dedicated Web site (http://girlculture.mcgill.ca). We then invited potential contributors to consult the Web site to see if they could think of other topics to add.

That was the easy part! *Everyone* had ideas on what should go into an encyclopedia on girl culture. The next question we came up with, though, was a much harder one: Who wants to write an entry on X or Y? Through our students, the Internet, and our many colleagues who are already working in the area of girl culture, we managed to put together a list of potential contributors. We were particularly indebted to the many authors who had already contributed to a previous edited book on girlhood, *Seven Going on Seventeen: Tween Studies in the Culture of Girlhood* (Mitchell and Reid-Walsh 2005), many of whom were keen to extend the work that they had begun in that book.

What fascinated us in the process was the three-part response of people: (1) "Easy. I would love to write about Cabbage Patch dolls. I had the lovely Petronella!" Then, with the realization that this was not a memoir-writing exercise, but an encyclopedia-writing exercise, (2) "Oh, no. Where do I start? How do I locate sources?" Finally, (3) came a sense of pride and accomplishment from writing a 535-word entry on a topic that had not been covered previously in such an informational way: "Did you know . . . ?"

The scope of the book, we think, is broad and representative of a wide range of topics within girl culture, involving different material and media forms: fashion, television, film, the Internet, music, toys, dolls and games, slogans, social issues represented in popular culture, and girl culture issues examined within girlhood studies. Although it is probably a bit of an exaggeration to say that this encyclopedia is exhaustive, it is, we trust, comprehensive. One of the challenges in producing an encyclopedia that has three types of entries—critical essays of more than 5000 words, mid-length entries of 1500–2000 words, and very short entries, some as brief as 400 words—is to decide which topics warrant a heavier treatment than others and whether a broader topic can best be covered through a series of very short entries with cross-referencing. As much as possible, this encyclopedia covers the more complex issues and topics in several ways: this holds for both the long essays and the short entries.

In some cases we ended up combining several entries into one, with the idea that a single, more coherent entry would result. We speculate, however, that most readers actually prefer to see a wide range in the A-to-Z section, and so for the most part we have preferred the "see also" approach over combining topics.

The process of naming the entries was difficult. Given that the whole encyclopedia is about girl culture, we have, of course, avoided as much as possible the formulation "Girls and . . ." as headings. It is critical that readers be able to find what they are looking for, and we hope that, if all else fails, readers will find the comprehensive index at the end valuable and easy to use.

In some cases we ran into the problem of deciding what the real focus of an entry should be: Are we talking about the person or about the show or music related to the person? In some cases, as with Annie Oakley, are we studying the person as she was in real life or as she was characterized in a television show or in a fiction or nonfiction book? In other cases there may also be a doll or other tie-in artifact. As more and more trans-media merchandising takes place, this kind of intertextuality becomes even more complicated. As much as possible, we have encouraged contributors to deal with the full range of manifestations of a particular phenomenon, though we also discovered along the way that even the specialists with regard to a topic often see it primarily as one type of manifestation and may not even know of all of the different dimensions that apply. A good example of this is *Buffy the Vampire Slayer*: both film and television show, but also the focus of novels and a long line of fan fiction.

Finally, we want to make reference to the coverage of the topics. As most scholars of cultural studies will agree, girl culture, like the broader topic of women's culture, is far from neutral territory. Barbie, for example, as we ourselves have explored in other writing (e.g., Mitchell and Reid-Walsh 1995, 2002), is probably one of the most controversial subjects within the popular culture of childhood, with parents, teachers, and feminists variously lamenting her negative influence on girls. Even the history of Barbie is contested in terms of whether someone is to be blamed for Barbie or credited. At other points, though, there has been a revisiting; once Bratz dolls came on the scene and seemed far more sexualized than Barbie, some critics began to see Barbie as more benign. Thus, while we have ensured that the entries offer denotative information (dates, names, places), we recognize that rarely do these discourses exist without some sort of connotative meaning; in fact, in terms of their importance to the study of girl culture, it is the connotative meanings that are critical. Where possible, then, we have encouraged authors not to shy away from these debates, but to address them in a balanced manner. What we also recognize, though, is that connotative meanings can and will change, and it will be up to the new scholars who use this encyclopedia to contribute to a deepened understanding of the issues. The entries as they exist at this particular time and in this particular context, we hope, will contribute to the long-term study of girl culture.

HOW TO USE THIS BOOK

The encyclopedia starts with an introductory chapter, which gives an overview of the overall area of girl culture. The encyclopedia ends with a comprehensive index. The index is followed by profiles of close to 150 contributors, who in and of themselves represent a "who's who" in writing about girl culture.

At the heart of the encyclopedia are two main sections, "Studying Girl Culture: A Reader's Guide" and "Girl Culture A to Z." The first, and shorter, section offers a series of full-length critical essays that serve to map out the cultural terrain of the larger area of girlhood studies. These are chapters written by well-known scholars in the area of girl culture who, because of their own research in the area of girlhood studies, are well qualified to provide a reader's guide to key issues and contemporary topics in the area. Some, such as Valerie Walkerdine, have been publishing in the area of girl culture since the 1980s and continue to research and write about new issues of girlhood, bringing to this work several decades of in-depth study. Other scholars, such as Shelly Pomerantz, are relatively new in the area, conducting research in a new era of girlhood studies.

From a consideration of the topics, ranging from the contribution of Disney to girl culture, to girls' reading practices, to growing up girl in the age of AIDS, to changing constructions of girlhood in the context of the "mean girl" phenomenon, to a "how-to" of studying girl culture, it is clear that the area is multifaceted and multidisciplinary in scope. The authors of these chapters have tried to make their work as accessible as possible to a variety of audiences, but in doing so, retain an awareness of the importance of seeing the study of girl culture as a critical area of cultural studies more broadly.

These chapters also provide an overarching frame for the more than 250 entries covered in "Girl Culture A to Z." They are chapters that readers are likely to return to over and over again as they engage in their own research in this important area of scholarship.

The second, longer section of the book, "Girl Culture A to Z," offers readers a more conventional, encyclopedic treatment of girl culture. From abstinence bracelets to zines, these entries of varying length are designed to give readers quick, authoritative accounts covering more than 200 topics. The focus is on topics relatively contemporary interest, from the early 1920s through most of the first decade of the twenty-first century.

Wherever possible we have included a *See Also* list of associated entries to illuminate the links between topics. Many of the shorter entries, as noted above, are given more in-depth analysis in the "Studying Girl Culture" section. Thus, short entries such as those on Ken, Skipper, Dream House, and "Math class is tough" refer the reader to the full-length essay on Barbie in the first part of the book.

Each of the short and medium-length entries also includes a number of key references in the Further Reading list. Wherever possible, we have directed readers to useful and relevant Web sites, but because this encyclopedia is meant to expand the possibilities for scholarship in the area of girl culture in general, readers are also referred to more scholarly books and articles.

Although there are other encyclopedias of girlhood, to the best of our knowledge, this is the first time that girl culture—from playful topics such as dolls, makeup, television shows, fashion, magazines, music, games, and toys to such serious issues such as dieting and girls' voice—has been covered in such a comprehensive way. Girl culture has too often been an area associated with apology. The well-known British novelist Jane Austen expressed this inclination so brilliantly several centuries ago in *Northanger Abbey*, when she wrote: "And what are you reading, miss? Oh it is only a novel!" We regard girl culture as more than "only a topic," and we invite the reader not only to join in the investigation and critiquing of the study of girl culture, but also to celebrate it as a fascinating area of study that is continuously in flux.

Further Reading

Mitchell, Claudia, and Jacqueline Reid-Walsh. (1995). "And I Want to Thank You Barbie: Barbie as a Site for Cultural Interrogation." *Review of Education/Pedagogy/Culture Studies* 17, no.2, 143–155.

———. (2002). *Researching Children's Popular Culture: Childhood as a Cultural Space.* London and New York: Routledge, esp. chap. 6, "Historical Spaces: Barbie Looks Back."

———. (2005). *Seven Going on Seventeen: Tween Studies in the Culture of Girlhood.* New York: Peter Lang.

Acknowledgments

The production of this two-volume encyclopedia on girl culture would never have been possible without the commitment and enthusiasm of a great number of people. From the nearly 150 contributors to the encyclopedia to those who were willing to offer suggestions for topics to those who advised us on a particular date or other detail, the project has been very much a collaborative one.

We would particularly like to acknowledge, however, the complete dedication of Lindsay Cornish, our editorial assistant on the project. Her passion for and expertise in the whole area of girl culture, along with her ability to track down contributors and to contribute her own entries, have been truly outstanding.

We would also like to acknowledge Meaghan Robertson, for getting us started on mapping out the encyclopedia and for constructing our girl culture Web site; Theresa Dejmek, for her work with contributors in the first stage of the encyclopedia; and Lesley Cohen and Maija-Liisa Harju, for their editorial assistance toward the end of the project. We thank Fiona Wilson for her advice on contemporary girl culture entries.

Our families have been wonderfully supportive about this project and have either contributed entries or offered advice. We are particularly grateful to our daughters, Krista, Dorian, Sarah, and Rebecca. Additionally, we thank Zac Campbell, Marcus, Jakob, and Devon Peterli for their input into girlhood culture.

Finally, we thank Kristi Ward of Greenwood Press for keeping us focused and for ensuring that the encyclopedia was ready for publication.

Introduction

The scene is a hotel deck overlooking a remote bay on the Island of St. Lucia in the Caribbean Sea. If you look closely you can see a popular emblem of girl culture sweep by and stop offshore. It is the *Black Pearl*—the ship used by Johnny Depp and his crew in the Disney film series *Pirates of the Caribbean*. Black and remarkably small—though sturdy—it looks authentic (but has a motor for easy maneuvering). Tourists on board gaze at the spectacular scenery and seascapes that are part of the "on location" scenes featured in the film series.

This image was chosen for the introduction to this encyclopedia of girl culture for several reasons. The most obvious is that there are several entries in these volumes that refer to the film itself, to the production company, and to the heroine, Keira Knightley—not to mention pertinent entries concerning key concepts in girl culture and popular media. But another reason for starting with this image of the pirate ship is that it is an instance of how girls in the twenty-first century have appropriated and modified key emblems of boy culture and made them their own. The *Pirates of the Caribbean* films are adventure tales, but the increasingly visible swashbuckling heroine shows how the classic adventure story has changed. Initially the genre was the province of teenage boys who read the classic novels of Robert Louis Stevenson and later Rudyard Kipling. Only secretly was the adventure genre enjoyed by girls.

In the twenty-first century the archetypal boys' genre is being revised and adapted by popular media to appeal to girls and boys. Not only are Johnny Depp and Orlando Bloom heartthrobs, in the classic Hollywood sense, for a range of girls and young women, but the heroine Elizabeth Swann (played by Knightley) is presented not as a passive damsel in distress but as a swashbuckling figure herself, a role model for girl viewers. Knightley's "action hero" behavior in these films nicely cross-references the film that made her famous—the British *Bend It Like Beckham* (2002). This film was immensely popular with teen and tween girls on both sides of the Atlantic and appealed to multicultural audiences.

Knightley played a white, teenage (in a film cast mostly with South Asian women), single-minded tomboy whose passion is soccer. Her active roles establish her as a "new" type of heroine in popular girls' films: the athletic girl.

WHAT IS A GIRL? IDEAS OF GIRLS AND GIRLHOOD

The terms included in an encyclopedia about "girl culture" or "girls' culture" at first sight seem self-evident, in no need of definition or elaboration. Upon a closer look, however, each entry seems less clear. To begin thinking about what a girl is we initially have to think about issues of age, and a number of questions need to be posed. How old is a girl? How has the age range defining girlhood changed over time in Western culture? What implications do earlier ideas of girls and girlhood have on our view? What delimits girlhood? Is it age or the preclusion of sexuality?

To understand ideas of girls and girlhood, we may find it useful to examine the concepts historically. From an inspection of early materials it is apparent that the terms "girl" and "girlhood" are usually presented in opposition to "boy" and "boyhood"—yet the ages and behaviors for the corresponding groups are not parallel. For example, the idea of the "seven stages of mankind" (and womankind) has been promoted in the West since the Middle Ages. In a famous Renaissance school text considered a precursor of the picture book, *Orbis Sensualism Pictus*, translated from Latin into English by Charles Hoole in 1659, John Amos Comenius drew upon a long pictorial tradition in his enumeration of "the ages of man (and woman)." Although the terms "girl" and "boy" are used narrowly and in a chronological sense, we will focus on the first four states since they encompass the entire stage of infancy and youth in each sex. "A man is first an Infant, then a Boy, then a Youth, then a Young-Man, then a man. . . ." "So also in the other Sex there are, a Girl, A Damosel, A maid, a woman . . ." (cited in Demers 2004, p. 40). In the accompanying illustration the infant is set apart in its cradle, while the other ages, in balanced pairs, move up and down the stairs of life stages, so males and females are represented equally. It is interesting to note that the infant's being set off by itself can be interpreted two ways: either it is sexless and genderless or, because it is mentioned only once, and not repeated in the female list, it can perhaps be considered male. Also, the imprecision or ambiguity of the English translation becomes apparent when it is seen that the girl is presented as the first stage of womanhood while the boy is identified with the stage after infancy. As a result, the impression is given that there are six ages for woman but seven for man.

Medievalists who study childhood up through the Renaissance, such as Shulamith Shahar (1990) and Nicholas Orme (2001), elaborate the three stages of childhood in such a manner that they introduce ambiguity into the definitions in different ways. Shahar introduces her discussion of medieval ideas of age and stage by quoting the work of child developmental psychologists Jean Piaget and Erik Erikson (Shahar 1990, pp. 21–22) and considering them as continuing the medieval approach. She notes that in medieval thought the upper end of the second stage of childhood, *pueritia*, was ages 7 to 12 for girls and ages 7 to 14 for boys (p. 22). The second stage was defined in terms of the ability to articulate oneself. Before this, in infancy, *infans*, the child was considered incapable of true comprehension, only speaking in imitation of adults. Some authors even believed there was a substage in the second phase of childhood that began around the age of 10 or 12. By the second half of the twelfth century, although a child could be betrothed at the age of 7, it was not considered binding. By the end of the second stage, however (age 12 for girls and 14 for boys), a betrothal or contract of marriage was considered binding, and children began to bear criminal liability. The upper limit of this stage was determined by puberty (Shahar 1990, pp. 24–26). The entry into the third stage, *adolescentia*, was connected with the ability to sin and readiness to receive the sacrament. Depending on gender and class, the activities associated with this stage differed: for a peasant boy it might be tending one's own flocks; for a noble boy it might be training to become a knight; for girls, there was the option of marriage.

Shahar notes in her comments about the first stage of childhood that girls and boys were usually treated the same, but in analyses of the second stage girls and boys were discussed separately, although the focus was on the education of boys. In commentaries on the third stage, which started earlier for girls than for boys, girls were almost completely overlooked. The change from childhood to married life seemed to occur "without the transitional stage undergone by young men from the nobility and urban class before they married and settled down." Even Dante was interested in only the "rational soul" of boys. She states that "it was no accident that authors felt no need to attend at length to girls when discussing adolescentia and the transition to full adulthood" (1990, pp. 29–30).

Moving forward in time to the eighteenth century, we will tell an anecdote to illustrate the ideas of girlhood and boyhood during this period. A few years ago, when we first visited the Victoria and Albert's Museum of Childhood in London, we were struck by how the exhibits of clothes and accessories on one floor and the toys on the other floors seemed gendered or even sexualized in different ways, evocative of gender distinctions in contemporary toys and fashion. On the toy floors the toys "for boys" from the eighteenth century onward—for example, hoops, hobbyhorses, and optical toys—seemed neutral or sexless compared with the shapely three-dimensional dolls and paper fashion dolls, based on an idealized woman's body, for girls. On the clothing floor, the fashion for boys similarly seemed sexless or androgynous, while girls' fashions, which adopted women's dresses to the unformed girl's body, appeared to be sexed not in terms of the body shape but in the implied lack of mobility in the constraining garments—both undergarments and clothes for wearing outside the home. Looking at girls' fashion today, especially that of tween girls, which similarly adapts clothing associated with a woman's developed body—such as bustiers or, in particular, the notorious example of thong underwear—to an unformed shape, we asked ourselves: what are the similarities and differences between now and then in the ideas of a girl's childhood being implied or contained in these garments? What is different and similar in the two eras' sexualizing of young girls? Is the phenomenon of "kids growing older younger" (KGOY) unique to the present day, or are we in some part of a long cycle spiraling back into another re-working of earlier phenomena, including fashion?

WHAT IS GIRL CULTURE?

In the twentieth and twenty-first centuries, a number of paradoxes have emerged in the scope of the term "girl": on one hand, teen girl culture seems to be moving progressively downward in age to touch upon even the lower limits of girlhood. Younger and younger girls are playing with Barbie dolls, and the lower edge is defined only by the skill in hand manipulation and the danger of swallowing small parts. Perhaps the word "tween" itself, as suggested by the insertion of the diminutive consonant "w," will come to mean simply a variation or miniaturization of teen culture. On the other hand, because teen culture and girl culture is extending also at its upper end—up to age 25 or 30—youth culture potentially encompasses much of childhood, all of adolescence, and all of young adult-hood. This can be seen, for example, in young women's practice of deliberately appropri-ating icons of young girls' culture, such as Hello Kitty merchandise, as a playful way of reusing artifacts they may or may not have played with when young, re-imaging them in deliberate, tongue-in-cheek ways by talking on Hello Kitty cell phones or using Hello Kitty screen savers on their computers. Even older women far beyond any definition of girlhood—such as baby boomers—shop at the Gap or Old Navy, struggling to keep fit; females of all ages dye their hair to such a broad extent that it has become the norm; and makeover shows abound on cable television, including a show about extreme makeovers involving plastic surgery. All these activities and popular culture phenomena center on a reconstruction of youth (Mitchell and Reid-Walsh 2002).

This elongation of the state of girlhood raises a number of questions about femaleness and age. With young women and older women acting younger than their chronological age, are we trying to engage in a process opposite to KGOY, "adults growing younger older"? It appears that Western society may be trying to construct a simplified process of aging composed of two negligible stages (infancy and old age, which are insignificant because of the lack of physical autonomy or the stigma associated with them) and one viable one: youth—or at least people who can access youth culture. Because women are living longer, a female can be a girl by participating in girl culture for almost a third of her life! What is the larger significance of this extended time frame? Perhaps this phenome-non can be understood as emphasizing how unnatural or, rather, how "constructed"—artificial and fabricated—the nature of youth is. In some ways, the present North American understanding of girls and girlhood can be seen as a logical outcome of a process that started in the West hundreds of years ago.

UNDERSTANDING GIRL CULTURE

Another approach to thinking about girl culture is in the way it might be categorized. While the categories below are by no means exhaustive—and might seem stereotypical—they nonetheless give a sense of the range of ideas that might be seen to make up the cul-ture of girlhood, providing a way to think about how girl culture is organized, at least within popular culture and popular representations of girlhood.

Social practices. One way to think about girl culture is to consider the social practices (what girls do) that are often associated with (and marketed to) girls. These social prac-tices overlap with particular objects and things. In conventional popular culture of the 1950s and 1960s, teenage girls were represented as talking on the phone—particularly a pink Princess telephone. In issues of the *Betty and Veronica* magazine (in association with *Archie* comics), as well as in teen fiction and teen movies, a recurring image is that of the teenage girl who cannot be separated from her phone; of course, the worst punishment she can imagine is to be "cut off" from the phone or forced to go on a camping trip with family members (and separated from her "lifeline" to the outside world). The introduction of the cell phone has inaugurated a set of new social practices centered around the ideas of text messaging, airtime, social messaging, and specific models of cell phones as signifi-cant in girl culture (such as Motorola's RAZR Pink phone). Another social practice asso-ciated with girl culture is getting ready for prom. For decades *Seventeen* magazine has devoted its March issue to the prom, popular culture is full of scenes of shopping for the perfect prom dress, and girl talk is all about what happens after the prom (Best 2000). Other social practices associated with girlhood include shopping (including particular brands and retailers), cheerleading (encompassing clothing and popularity), diary writing (with associations of "Dear Diary," secret diaries, hiding diary only to have it discovered by siblings or parents), and babysitting. Beginning in the late 1990s, an increasing number of girls' social practices speak to the idea of girls as cultural producers within what might be described as a DIY (do-it-yourself) movement: girls as filmmakers, girls as DJs, and girls designing their own Web sites.

Material culture. We might also look at girl culture in relation to material culture. As noted above, clearly social practices such as talking on the telephone are associated with particular objects of material culture. Some ways of categorizing girl material culture include clothing, accessories, and play objects. Girl-related clothing, for example, might include items of lingerie (crinolines, thong underwear), shoes (saddle oxfords, penny loafers, sling backs), specific garments (twin-sets, poodle skirts, bubble skirts, hot pants), as well as school uniforms that span several eras. Play objects can include the vast range of dolls (Barbie, Bratz, Cabbage Patch Kids, Blythe, Jem, wedding dolls) and doll play paraphernalia (Easy-Bake Ovens, Fisher-Price kitchens, doll carriages).

Media. We might categorize girl culture in relation to specific media texts ranging from books to films to music to television shows. Books can include *Sweet Valley High*, *The Baby-sitters Club*, the romances of the 1950s, series fiction such as *Trixie Belden* and *Nancy Drew*, and the chick lit or junior chick lit of the twenty-first century. Another category could be girls' films—particularly those from the mid-1990s on.

Space. Girl culture is also associated with specific spaces. In the mid-1970s, the idea of girl bedroom culture was introduced in the work of Angela McRobbie and Jenny Garber (1976, 1991). In their work they noted that girls were largely absent from the "street-corner society" associated with adolescent boys. They observed that, although the social world of boys was more likely to be on the street (or perhaps later, in video arcades), girls were using their bedrooms to establish their own social world (pajama parties, telephone conversations, and testing out various identities by trying on clothing and changing hair-styles). From the 1960s on, the shopping mall has also been represented as a girl space, particularly within popular culture. Since the late 1990s, girls have become associated with virtual spaces and "digital bedrooms." Virtual spaces can refer to girls' Web sites, online communication, and, in the twenty-first century, social networks such as Facebook, MySpace, and YouTube. Yet, in marked contrast with the seemingly infinite virtual space, girls' spaces can also be found in the miniaturized play worlds of the Barbie Dream House and Polly Pocket.

Rites of passage. From the Bat Mitzvah to the Quinceañera, we can observe formalized rites of passage for girls embedded within particular religious or cultural practices. Other rites of passage represented in girl popular culture might include the first bra, ear piercing, menstruation, Sweet Sixteen parties, debutante balls, proms, dating, and so on.

Girls' bodies. The body is also important in girl culture. The ideas associated with the body can include, for example, all of the implications of menstruation (including the related products and advertising), breast development (getting a first bra, concealing breasts, breast enlargement, breast reduction), hair (products associated with hair, hairstyles—ponytails, beehives, and backcombing—hair dryers, hair dyes), and beauty (beauty pageants, beauty products, beauty and fashion magazines). Girls' bodies are also associated with weight (anorexia, thinness, obesity, binge eating, bulimia, dieting), mental illness (bipolar disorder, cutting), and addictions and social habits (smoking, drugs, and alcohol).

People. Girl culture is made up of people ranging from teen idols (such as popular singers, musicians, dancers, and other performers) and sports figures to models, movie stars, fashion designers, and sometimes even political figures. Within the category of "people" we can include fictional girls who seem to possess individual identities beyond their original texts—characters in books, movies, comic strips, and television shows—ranging from Anne of Green Gables and Nancy Drew in books to Lisa Simpson in cartoons and Little Lulu in comics.

Social relations. Girl culture can be read through the lens of social relations. These can include friendships (girlfriends, best friends, breaking up with friends, social networking), hostile relations (bullying—including cyber-bullying—meanness, social aggression, gossip), and heterosexual relations (dating, crushes, breaking up with a boyfriend, date rape, sexual relations, birth control, unprotected sex, HIV and AIDS, STDs). Social relations and girl culture can also be explored through alternative cultural practices such as lesbianism and gay identity, as well as girls as tomboys.

Theoretical and social concepts about girl culture. Within girl culture is an emerging girlhood discourse about popular culture made up of a number of key terms. This discourse can include such terms as "innocence," "moral panics," and "KGOY," all of which speak to how adults "construct" girls, as well as terms such as "compulsory heterosexuality" and "hetero-normativity," which refer to the kinds of social worlds that construct girls' lives. Additional terms are "feminist nostalgia," "covering over," and "social forgetting," which refer to relationships between womanhood and girlhood. Terms such as "texts of desire" and "cumulative cultural text" speak to ways of theorizing media and material culture associated with girlhood.

OVERARCHING THEMES IN GIRL CULTURE

There are a number of key themes in the treatment of girlhood within girl culture as represented in the media, popular culture, and everyday events. While these themes recur in the alphabetical section of this encyclopedia, they represent the types of issues that can be found within girlhood studies more generally.

Sexuality. As noted in previous sections, it is difficult to escape the fact that girl culture is often linked to sexuality. Somehow, there is something about the term "girl" itself that is not only gendered (girl, not boy) but also sexualized in ways not normally associated with either boys or boyhood. Much of girl play is often regarded as sexualized—from Barbie to Bratz in doll play to girls' clothing, which in the late twentieth and early twenty-first centuries may be linked to older adolescent girls (e.g., such items of apparel as thong underwear) and also to sexuality in music, movies, and even illnesses associated with reproductive health ("a girl thing"). It is interesting to note that a group in India working with pre-adolescent girls (known as *balkishori*) made it their mission to try to recover childhood for girls, diverting attention away from reproductive health and emerging sexuality as the main focus of their work with girls in favor of playing sports and having fun (Vacha 2005).

Devaluing girls' culture. A second theme is the devaluing of girls' culture. Traditionally, girls' literacy practices (reading novels—especially romance fiction—and writing in diaries and autograph books), girls' play (for example, dolls), and girls' interests (friend-ships, domestic relationships) are often seen not as very serious or equal to the demand-ing business of reading nonfiction or engaging in boys' play. It is worth noting that although girls may play with boys' toys (and even if players are regarded as tomboys, the activity in and of itself is not devalued), boys who play with toys associated with girls may earn the term "sissy." Much of this work on the devaluing of feminine culture has been addressed in the work on women's culture found in Janice Radway's now-classic study on reading romance novels (1994), as well as in Joke Hermes' work on women's magazine reading (1995).

Ephemerality. In a similar way, girls' culture is often regarded as ephemeral, just a pass-ing fad that is not to be taken seriously. This phenomenon is fascinating, because so many of the texts of girls' popular culture that are dismissed as ephemeral have been around for decades. *Seventeen* magazine has been in existence since 1944 and Barbie since 1959; and while on one hand the ephemerality might be seen as "girls growing up and out of" cer-tain fads and interests—something poignantly depicted in the film *Toy Story 2* when Emily grows up and outgrows Jessie the cowgirl doll, whom she then discards—it is inter-esting to note that, somehow, texts associated with boys' culture are not so easily dis-missed. Studies of adult male readers of the *Hardy Boys* suggest that they do not "outgrow" the books in quite the same way that adult female readers outgrow *Nancy Drew* (Mitchell and Reid-Walsh 1996).

Lost girlhoods. Another recurring theme might be described as "lost girlhoods," or social forgetting. This theme refers to the practice of covering over the past, either through apology ("Oh, that was when I was just a girl") or through actually forgetting the pleasures of girl play. Adolescent girls may feel the need to dismiss their previous play with Barbie or may try to discourage young girls from playing with Barbie or Bratz even though they themselves played in the same ways and were not negatively affected. Feminist memory groups, as seen in the work of Frigga Haug et al. (1987) and June Crawford et al. (1992), have devoted much of their work to recovering some of the memories of girlhood that have been "covered over" (see also Mitchell and Reid-Walsh 1998). In the work of Lyn Mikel Brown and Carol Gilligan (1992) are many references to the idea of girls losing themselves or their voice at adolescence—as well as the related idea of recovering voice. In their work they also frame the idea of the nice girl or the good girl.

The themes noted above may suggest that much of girls' "growing up" amounts to just survival (and escape). That, however, is not the only story of girlhood, as we see in the following themes.

Agency. The theme of agency has become a key concept within girls' culture since at least the early 1990s, suggesting a side of girls' culture that is all about empowerment. The concept of girl power itself, some suggest, is all about agency. Some of the work centering around girls' interactions with play and popular culture suggests that they are not simply "dupes" who are taken in by advertising, but have minds of their own—which means that the meanings they make of romance novels, fashion magazines, and doll play are neither unitary nor fixed. The shifting meanings girls bring to their engagement with popular cul-ture must be respected. Erica Rand, in *Barbie's Queer Accessories* (1995), argues that, by playing with Barbie in non–Mattel-sanctioned ways—whether by making their own clothes, constructing alternative tableaux, cross-dressing, or maiming limbs—the girl players have subverted or "queered" Mattel's intentions (see Reid-Walsh and Mitchell 2000). Girls in these cases make their own meanings of Barbie.

Young girls (as opposed to female children or adolescent girls) suddenly constitute an economic force all their own; there is now no shortage of public data on the dollar figure attached to the purchasing power of 9- to 13-year-old girl consumers of clothing, hair products, CDs, concert tickets, and so on. Tween culture has also been growing at a rapid pace. New dolls and accessories, such as My Scene, Flava, and Bratz; clothing (such as Bratz clothes and Hilary Duff fashions); films about young adolescent girl culture, such as *13 Going on 30*; and novels ("junior chick lit") have appeared on the scene.

Girls just want to have fun. Alongside the idea that girls have minds of their own (albeit consumer-oriented, girl power minds of their own) is the theme "girls just want to have fun," made popular in the 1990s and continuing into the twenty-first century. In newer manifestations of this theme, we see that girls not only want to have fun, but they also want to be bad (a counter to themes of the nice girl, the good girl, and the girl-next-door). The "bad girl" phenomenon is associated with images of incarcerated icons such as Paris Hilton.

THE GIRL CULTURE TIMELINE

In the spirit of an imaginary board game devoted to girls' culture, such as a special, pink edition of the popular Trivial Pursuit game, let us imagine a card with the following question:

When did girl culture begin?
1944
1959
1930
1533
1617
1697
1790
None of the above
All of the above

The correct answer is "all of the above." Each of these dates represents a milestone in the history of girls' culture and girls' popular culture: in order, these dates refer the initial publication of *Seventeen* magazine, the emergence of the Barbie doll, the publication of the *Nancy Drew* mysteries, the first use of the term "tomboy," the first use of the term "debutante," the publication of Perrault's fairy tales, and the invention of the paper doll. These are only a very few of the key dates in the history of girls' popular culture. If we were to select a "Top Ten" among the significant dates preceding the second half of the twentieth century, these might include 1921 (beauty pageants), the 1870s (sororities), and 1693. The last is the date of John Locke's *Some Thoughts Concerning Education*, where he posited that children's minds and characters are analogous to blank slates. By believing that children are not innately evil, as claimed by Reformed Christian theology, Locke paved the way for later philosophers—such as Jean Jacques Rousseau and the Romantic theorists—who believed in the innocence of children and in childhood as a separate state.

If we compare the many dates associated with girls' culture with the many meanings of "girl" and "girlhood" across the centuries, we can observe the parallels. In each case, the history of girls and their popular culture is much longer than is commonly imagined. It is interesting to observe that all the terms, texts, and artifacts referred to so far are valid today. This suggests both that, if one were to develop a timeline of girls' popular culture, it would be a lengthy chart and that many of the ideas, practices, texts, and artifacts associated with girls have achieved longevity. These are not examples of "dead culture," found only in museums. Some terms seem to have existed for hundreds of years with slightly different meanings, such as "innocence." Other terms have faded in and out of fashion, such as "debutante." These aspects of flow and continuity are somewhat ironic—for in popular culture the "new," or apparently new, is the order of the day. Yet Nancy Drew has reinvented herself successfully for over 75 years and *Seventeen* for over 60 years—to name only two examples.

If one were to examine a timeline of girls' popular culture, it would become immediately obvious that certain periods are associated with more texts and artifacts than others. Only a few items would originate in the seventeenth, eighteenth, and nineteenth centuries, and the largest number of girl culture texts and artifacts would be from the twentieth century. Indeed, most popular culture texts that are mass-produced and/or copyrighted—such as Barbie, Mattel, the Little Mermaid, Disney, lipstick, bobby sox, and miniskirts—are twentieth-century inventions. It is equally apparent that, as the twentieth century progressed, more and more items were associated with girl culture—like an engine gaining steam. This is partly because of the crossover of girls' texts and artifacts into different material forms. The invention of plastic and new mass production methods made it possible for objects such as dolls, dollhouses, kitchen sets, and other toys formerly made of wood to be produced more cheaply. Another type of expansion is the crossover of girls' texts into different media forms, enabled by the invention and popular adaptation of media in the twentieth century; thus, narratives such as *Little Women, Anne of Green Gables*, classic fairy tales, or *Harry Potter* exist not only as paper texts but also as television programs or films. Books and stories can be repackaged as tie-ins to multimedia texts, because most girls have been exposed to the latter first.

In the second half of the twentieth century, in addition to the broadcast media of television, radio, and film, girls' texts and artifacts crossed over into new, digital media. Polly Pocket, the Bratz dolls, and construction toys such as the Dream House now exist in material form as well as in digital form on Web sites or in computer games. Types of play may also flow between media, existing both on paper and in digital media—girls can play with paper dolls as they have for centuries, but they also have access to virtual paper dolls on the Barbie Web site or on CD-ROM. Because girls can also print dolls and their clothes out on paper, they are playing with multiple media simultaneously. Of course, many products have been invented only by recent capitalist production methods or have become possible only because of technological innovations such as the computer, CD-ROM, the Internet, social networking spaces such as MySpace and Facebook, cell phones, text messaging, iPods, and iTunes. Girl celebrities and singers such as Britney Spears, Lindsay Lohan, and Hilary Duff exist not only as people on film or television, as did Shirley Temple and Annette Funicello, but on all media platforms. This crossover and proliferation of media forms also promises a strong "afterlife" for early, pre–digital media stars associated with girls' popular culture, such as the Spice Girls and Olivia Newton-John. Since we are presently still in the midst of this flurry of development, the end is not in sight. Girls' popular culture is still in development, adapting and changing. Like Web sites, and like ideas of girls and girlhood, girls' popular culture is continually "under construction"!

Further Readings

Best, Amy. (2000). *Prom Night: Youth, Schools and Popular Culture*. New York: Routledge.

Brown, Lyn Mikel, and Carol Gilligan. (1992). *Meeting at the Crossroads: Women's Psychology and Girls' Development*. Cambridge, MA: Harvard University Press.

Crawford, June, et al. (1992). *Emotion and Gender: Constructing Meaning from Memory*. London: Sage.

Demers, Patricia, ed. (2004). *From Instruction to Delight: An Anthology of Children's Literature to 1850*. Toronto: Oxford University Press.

Haug, Frigga, et al. (1987). *Female Sexualization: A Collective Work of Memory*. Trans. Erica Carter. London: Verso.

Hermes, Joke. (1995). *Reading Women's Magazines*. Cambridge: Polity Press.

McRobbie, Angela, and Jenny Garber. (1976). "Girls and Subcultures." In Stuart Hall and Tony Jefferson, eds. *Resistance through Rituals: Youth Subcultures in Post-War Britain*. London: Hutchinson. Rpt. in Angela McRobbie. (1991). *Feminism and Youth Culture: From Jackie to Just Seventeen*. Houndsmills, UK: Macmillan, pp. 1–15.

Mitchell, Claudia, and Jacqueline Reid-Walsh. (1995). "And I Want to Thank You Barbie": Barbie as a Site for Cultural Interrogation." *Review of Education/Pedagogy/Culture* 17, no. 2, 143–155.

———. (1996). "Reading on the Edge: Serious Series Readers of Nancy Drew and the Hardy Boys." *Changing English* 3, no. 1, 45–55.

———. (1998). "Mail-Order Memory Work: Towards a Methodology of Uncovering the Experiences of Covering Over." *Review of Education/Pedagogy/Culture* 20, no. 1, 57–75.

———. (2002). *Researching Children's Popular Culture: The Cultural Spaces of Childhood*. London and New York: Routledge.

Orme, Nicholas. (2001). *Medieval Children*. New Haven, CT: Yale University Press.

Radway, Janice. (1984). *Reading the Romance: Women, Patriarchy, and Popular literature*. Chapel Hill: University of North Carolina Press.

Rand, Erica. (1995). *Barbie's Queer Accessories*. Durham, NC: Duke University Press.

Reid-Walsh, Jacqueline, and Claudia Mitchell. (2000). "'Just a Doll?': Liberating Accounts of Barbie Play." *Review of Education/Pedagogy/Culture* 22, no. 2, 175–190.

Shahar, Shulamith. (1990). *Childhood in the Middle Ages*. London: Routledge.

Vacha. (2005). "Reclaiming Girlhood: Understanding the Lives of Balkishori ibn Mumbai." In Claudia Mitchell and Jacqueline Reid-Walsh, eds. *Seven Going on Seventeen: Tween Studies in the Culture of Girlhood*. New York: Peter Lang, pp. 135–147.

PART 1

Studying Girl Culture:
A Reader's Guide

Introduction to Part 1

The "Studying Girl Culture" section of this encyclopedia offers a collection of critical essays that serve to map out the terrain of contemporary girl culture within the larger area of girlhood studies. These are essays written by well-known scholars in the area of girl culture who, because of their own research in the area of girlhood studies, are well qualified to provide a reader's guide to key issues and contemporary topics in the area. In particular, these essays show the importance of theory in studying girl culture.

These essays also offer comprehensive coverage of some of the best-known texts and practices within girl culture, ranging from girls and fashion, Disney, doll culture, literacy, and, of course, within the twenty-first century, new media and technologies. Another set of entries in the collection highlight representations in girl culture, ranging from an entry on the study of girl culture through film—particularly since the 1990s, when girlhood became popularized—to depictions of race and presentations of HIV and AIDS as a critical theme in the lives of young people since the early 1990s. Through their examples the authors of these essays make their work as accessible as possible to a variety of audiences. They also, however, emphasize the importance of treating the study of girl culture as a critical academic area within cultural studies and gender studies more broadly. The Further Reading section at the end of each essay points to a range of information in the area.

ABOUT THE ESSAYS

The first essay, "What Does It Mean to Be a Girl in the Twenty-first Century? Exploring Some Contemporary Dilemmas of Femininity and Girlhood in the West," is an appropriate place to start the study of girl culture. The essay is co-authored by Jessica Ringrose and Valerie Walkerdine (one of the world's most cited and most respected authors on girl culture). While the authors note some of the issues that have dominated the study of girl culture in the past, this essay highlights the ways in which a new culture of girlhood is emerging. The authors take up, for example, the contemporary work on "mean girls" and girls' aggression (topics that are covered as well in shorter entries in Girl Culture A to Z) as themes that are in contrast with the focus on girls' self-esteem in the literature of the late 1980s and early 1990s.

The second essay, "How to Study Girl Culture," is meant to give an overview of some of the contributing (and confounding) factors in the study of girl culture. The authors, Claudia Mitchell and Jacqueline Reid-Walsh, refer to this work as "girl-method." From acknowledging the difficulty of defining "who is a girl, anyway?" to such issues as "how are the voices and experiences of girls themselves represented?" this essay acknowledges that what we know about girls' culture is defined by who is asking and who is answering.

The third essay, "Doll Culture," by Juliette Peers, highlights the ways that aspects of girl culture can be studied "through history" and "in history." There is a long-standing association between girls and dolls. Thus, as Peers points out, playing with dolls, engaging in fantasy through dolls, playing out traditional roles through dolls, and collecting dolls all contribute to a deeper understanding of girl culture.

An essay on "Barbie Culture" by Catherine Driscoll takes the most famous and best-selling doll of all and shows how Barbie is much more than "just a doll." In particular, the essay highlights the links between Barbie (and her empire of products), the producers of Barbie, and the girls who play with/consume Barbie. As Driscoll concludes, "But whether in doll play or across the broader range of what now comprises Barbie, Barbie is a territory filled with the practices of knowing and being a girl. From the 1959 slogan, 'Barbie, you're beautiful,' through to the leisure-packed home page of 'everythinggirl,' Barbie negotiates images of ideal and actual girlhood, stretching the idea of the girl to encompass past, present, and future possibilities and exploring which borders and which desires simultaneously define girls and girl culture."

Like Barbie, Disney—particularly in association with such popular animated films as *Cinderella, Beauty and the Beast, Mulan,* and *Pocahontas*—has often been regarded as synonymous with the contemporary culture of North American girlhood. The essay by Hoi Cheu offers a fascinating treatment of a critical aspect of girl culture by drawing attention to the world of the producers alongside the resulting films.

The sixth essay, "Romance in Teen Publications," by Naomi Johnson, is an overview of several types of texts avidly read by teen and tween girls—fashion magazines, teen romances, and teen novels such as *Gossip Girl*—and one type of text created by girls themselves: zines. Those in the first group are discussed as ways to inculcate the conventions of femininity, beauty routines, shopping, and heterosexual romance, while the latter form of expression is a place where girls can question and challenge the status quo.

Style, as the next essay points out, is a critical feature in understanding the identity formation of adolescent girls. The essay points at ways in which identity is shaped, in terms of how others wish to represent us and how we wish to represent or define ourselves to others. Shauna Pomerantz draws on the work of the French theorist Michel Foucault to explore the idea of how girls are looked at and how their behavior is monitored in relation to style. This essay is important for the "how-to" of studying girl culture because it shows the application of a particular theoretical position, that of Foucault.

The next essay, by Juliette Peers, provides an historical overview of ballet as a presence in girl culture as both leisure and work. She begins with the nineteenth century, when ballet dolls were played with by elite girls and other girls worked as ballerinas; describes the twentieth century, when ballet became a popular subject for books, films, and dolls and ballerinas came to be seen as role models for girls; and discusses the flourishing and contested presence of ballet today in its positive and negative aspects as both a practice and a play activity.

Meredith Cherland's essay on girls' literacy practices takes the overall area of girls' reading and writing practices (and now technology practices) and embeds this work within the study of girls' lives more broadly. Some of the earliest work in the study of girlhood, dating back to the late 1980s and early 1990s, focused on this important area, taking up such questions as whether girls "resist" the dominant images in romance texts, for example, or whether these books simply reinforce particular stereotypes. As Cherland points out, this is a rich field for investigating a variety of theoretical concepts related to desire and fantasy.

Given the significance of new media and digital technology, it is critical to understand girls' participation in this culture. As Katynka Martínez, the author of the essay "Girls, Digital Culture, and New Media" points out, the gendered digital divide and the ways in which girls seem to have been left out of new media is an interesting subject. She writes, "To better understand the relationship between girls and digital technology/new media it is essential to recognize how gendered technological orientations have created a gendered digital divide." She looks at some of the ways girls have drawn on their bedroom culture to engage digital technology "on their own terms." Martínez also looks at how these practices have led to girls' online communities and girl-oriented activism.

In their essay "Girl Gamers," Suzanne de Castell and Jennifer Jenson highlight the fascinating terrain of marketing, the gaming industry, gender inequalities, and girls' social practices. They offer a brief history of girls and gaming along with an analysis of the popularity of such games as The Sims (and Sims 2), the best-selling game of all time. Their essay is particularly critical to a deepened understanding of the ways in which traditional attitudes toward girlhood and girl culture continue to infuse the industry. In a hopeful vein, the authors note, "Change may come, however, through technological innovation, rather than ideological transformation."

Margaret Tally's essay "Representations of Girls and Young Women in Film as an Entry Point to Studying Girl Culture" looks at the ways in which girlhood has become popular culture in and of itself through the phenomenon of girl-focused films, which have dominated the film scene since the mid-1990s. She then uses the popularity of girlhood to develop an analysis of girls in the context of feminist issues, including friendships, domestic life, and growing up.

Elaine Correa's essay "Whose Girlhood? Race, Representation, and Girlhood" takes us back to some of the questions posed in the essay "How to Study Girl Culture." Correa reminds us of the ways in which the North American girlhood scene has been dominated by particular images of "white" and "middle class" and the ways in which such images construct what it means to be a girl (and whose lives are left out).

Finally, Nancy Lesko and Elisabeth Johnson's essay "Girlhood in the Time of AIDS: Popular Images, Representations, and Their Effects" applies close reading methods in analyzing popular-culture representations of heterosexuality and HIV/AIDS. As the authors point out, girlhood of the late twentieth century and beyond has been complicated by the threat of HIV and other sexually transmitted infections. Their analysis reminds us that the theoretical perspectives and analytical tools of girlhood—girl-method—have a great deal to offer not just to the study of girls' lives, but to the preservation of girls' lives.

What Does It Mean to Be a Girl in the Twenty-first Century? Exploring Some Contemporary Dilemmas of Femininity and Girlhood in the West

How are girls constructed into categories such as successful girls, mean girls, bad girls, and violent girls? How are major concerns over girls' aggression and meanness related to current gender anxieties over middle-class "girl power" and girls' success? How are girls pathologized into such oppositional categories as the successful but mean "Supergirls" and the counterpart to this type, the failed, deviant, abject, violent nonfeminine girls who must be transformed? These are some of the core dilemmas foisted on girls within contemporary girlhood in the West. They are dilemmas that are constructed in the media, in popular culture, and through psychological and educational debates about girlhood.

SUCCESSFUL GIRLS

In opposition to the largely liberal feminist concerns used as a reference point to address issues of self-esteem and vulnerability in "girls" during the 1980s and 1990s, in the new millennium there has been a "postfeminist" onslaught of talk and writing about "girl power" and the increasingly commonsense "presumption" of gendered equality in education and work (Foster 2000; Gonick 2006; Harris 2004; McRobbie 2004; Taft 2004). It has been widely argued (see Adkins 2002; Francis and Skelton 2005) that education, work, and the labor market have been "feminized." The British Labour Party think tank Demos went as far as to say that the "future is female." They argued in 1997 that women are set to enter the labor market in huge numbers. In one sense, then, feminism has come of age, giving women choices in work as never before. Changes in Western countries mean that manufacturing and farming are in decline while communications and service are dominant. The latter are the kinds of work that stress qualities ascribed to femininity: service, empathy, communication, nurturance, looked-at-ness.

At the same time, the educational rhetoric of "failing boys" has directly promoted the notion of overly "successful girls" (Ringrose 2007). This educational debate over failing boys draws on specific measures of girls' superior exam achievements and makes claims that girls have reached unparalleled levels of success and that feminist interventions into schooling may have gone "too far." Girls' achievements are consistently positioned as won at the expense of boys, contributing to the larger postfeminist gender anxiety referred to as the "crisis of masculinity" (Epstein et al. 1998).

In the discourse of "successful girls," girls are imagined as model neoliberal citizens, "climb[ing] the techno-rationalist ladder to success" (Benjamin 2003), somehow balancing ideals of masculinity with femininity in postfeminist formations such as the supergirl, supermom, and yummy mummy (Ringrose 2007; Walkerdine and Ringrose 2006). An international media frenzy keeps these anxieties alive with headlines like "Girls top of the class worldwide: Women have overtaken men at every level of education" (BBC News 2003, para.1) and "Girls beat boys at school, now they get higher pay" (Blair 2006). The cover story "The new gender gap: From kindergarten to grad school, boys are becoming the second sex" in the U.S. periodical *BusinessWeek* suggests that "girls have built a kind of scholastic Roman Empire alongside boys' languishing Greece" (Conlin 2003).

However, Lisa Adkins's (2002) study shows that this version of a female future, with a labor market operating on feminine values, is far too simplistic, and the same can be said for the thesis in which feminization is said to have contaminated schools and universities (Reay 2001; Ringrose 2007). Adkins argues that it is, in fact, easier for men to perform or act out femininity and therefore to enter the new labor market than it is for women to perform or act out masculinity in professional and business domains. We can think of how this is mirrored in education by considering Walkerdine's research on girls and mathematics (1998b), which demonstrated that girls in mathematics classrooms in the 1980s were singled out for failure to display behavior considered "brilliant," which was taken to be a sign of using concepts rather than following rules; yet the small number of girls who displayed what would have counted as brilliance in boys were equally pathologized as being unfeminine and overassertive. One teacher called one girl displaying this kind of performance a "madam." It was both easier and more difficult, it seems, to be one of the girls than one of the boys. Yet now girls are more likely to be required to display both characteristics—those ascribed to femininity as well as those ascribed to masculinity—apparently with ease: welcome to the world of the supergirl!

THE ANATOMY OF A SUPERGIRL

On April 1, 2007, the *New York Times* carried the headline for a story on the "super-girl phenomenon" "AMAZING +: Driven to Excel; For Girls, It's Be Yourself, and Be Perfect, Too" (Rimer 2007). The story exposes "the trend that girls are under enormous pressure to be smart, demonstrate leadership, get into the best college, all while being thin, pretty and wearing expensive jeans" (p. 1). It would seem that *the* central issue facing middle-class girls is navigating the contradictory markers of masculine rationality and feminine wiles. The supergirl is meant to balance contradictory subjectivities with ease. For instance, Rimer talks about two girls, Colby and Esther:

> The [girls] say they want to be both feminine and assertive, like their mothers. But Colby made the point at lunch that she would rather be considered too assertive and less conventionally feminine than "be totally passive and a bystander in my life."
>
> Esther agreed. She said she admired Cristina, the spunky resident on *Grey's Anatomy*, one of her favorite TV shows.
>
> "She really stands up for herself and knows who she is, which I aspire to," Esther said.
>
> Cristina is also "gorgeous," Esther laughed. "And when she's taking off her scrubs, she's always wearing cute lingerie." (Rimer 2007, p. 1)

The U.S. television hit *Grey's Anatomy* follows the lives of three beautiful female surgical interns, Meredith Grey, Christina Yang, and Izzy Stevens, in their battle to find time for men and romance and to succeed as surgeons. The title plays on the central character Meredith Grey's anatomy/embodiment as a woman cum surgeon. The central story line is Grey's turbulent, illicit affair with her married supervisor, Dr. Sheppard. The final episode of season 2 saw Izzy Stevens's character give up her surgical career for a heart transplant patient, as the weight of balancing romance and medicine had become too intense. Christina Yang's positioning by the girls in the *New York Times* article as the ideal representation of supergirl, as embodying both masculine assertiveness and feminine sexiness, is fascinating. Christina's character is an emotional cripple who doesn't cook or clean and is a surgery "junkie." A recent episode featured her falling asleep during sex after two orgasms before the handsome Dr. Burke could achieve his own climax. But Christina is still slim, sexy, and desirable. Her femininity is emblazoned upon her body through lingerie. The thong, it would seem, is a stand-in for the absent behavioral markers of passivity. As Rosalind Gill (2007) suggests in her analysis of porno-chic media and "raunch culture," a hyper-feminine, sexualized embodiment (the focus of the numerous body and clothing makeover television shows aimed at women and girls) (Walkerdine and Ringrose 2007) becomes a marker granting the girl/woman a form of sexualized power without which she is in danger of slipping into dangerous forms of androgeny and masculinity. But is balancing the masculine (assertiveness) and the feminine (desirability/passivity) this easy? Drawing on Aapola, Gonick, and Harris's (2005) analysis, isn't the "supergirl phenomenon" yet another manifestation of femininity in crisis under the weight of opportunity and power? How *are* assertiveness and femininity to be reconciled and navigated?

In Walkerdine's research on young girls playing classic video games (2007), girls found a number of ways of managing the contradiction between being caring and supportive toward other girl players while trying to cope with winning. Not one girl in the study, however, managed this without problems. Classic strategies involved subterfuge, such as engaging in caring and soothing talk to the other player while trying to win unnoticed; presenting oneself as abhorring violence and being afraid of being killed in the game while encouraging the other girl players to "kill him, kill him!"; and continually struggling to develop game skills because of lack of access to games often accorded to boys or brothers. For example, four girls playing a game of Super Smash tacitly agree not to harm the avatar of one of the girls who claims to be afraid of being killed ("Don't hurt me. I'm innocent," often expressed in an affected whisper or an exaggeratedly "girly" "loser" voice). In another example, girls display caring behavior to each other in the group while their avatars struggle to kill each other. This dynamic is subtle and often shifts from moment to moment in game play. Positions sometimes also shift between girls, as in the following example, in which Katie explicitly encourages Rosa to kill: "Try and kill that frog." "Kill the frog. Scootch him. Smooch him. Smooch him." "Kill him. Kill him." But she also protests, "I can't watch. I can't watch." Thus, when Rosa follows her entreaty to kill, Katie hides behind her hands, arms, or turns away, maintaining her position as "scared." Despite the requirement of the game that the player proceed by killing, Katie resists this by either playing cautiously to protect herself or asking someone else to do the killing for her, encouraging the other to kill when she is the observer. The contradiction/ambivalence between this simultaneous disavowal and engagement is masked by the feminized performance of "being scared" and "hiding."

Ringrose's research on aggression and bullying (forthcoming) among racially marginalized and white, working-class girls in Wales (ages 13 and 14) shows that masculine assertiveness or direct confrontations among girls at school, at the playground, at home, and on MSN were quickly recouped by demands to "get along" and "talk it out nicely" rather than engage in open conflict. Responding to constant imperatives to be good and nice, girls described learning to downplay conflict and to hide disputes and emotions from teachers and parents. During one incident where a friendship group was disciplined through an anti-bullying intervention, after a public schoolyard dispute with a girl Katie, who—as Elizabeth put it—"thought she was better than us," the head teacher's (highly astute) advice during the disciplinary meeting with all the girls was to "just be friends." The phrase "just be friends" at once trivializes and obscures the competitive heterosexualized economy of the school and re-marshals the girls into "heteronormative femininity" (Youdell 2006), deflecting responsibility for coping with, and ultimately negating, conflict back to the girls. It is no wonder that secrecy and repression (read as manipulation and meanness) prevail, as Gwyneth noted that the lesson of this experience was: "We learned to . . . like . . . talk to girls quietly by themselves."

Indeed, the more research that is done, the clearer it appears that feminine assertiveness is tolerated only in particular, often peculiar, manifestations. This raises important questions. Is the rhetoric of girls as mean one way that traditional qualities of femininity as indirect, passive, repressed, and pathological can be *reconciled* with the new, unsettling claims of girl power and success and assertiveness? As Gonick has suggested, "the vulnerable girl has recently been replaced by the 'mean girl' in public consciousness" (2004, p. 395). How is the moral panic or media frenzy over girls' "increasing" aggression and meanness connected to fears and anxieties over girls' success? Is meanness a pathological offshoot of girl power?

MIDDLE-CLASS MEAN GIRLS, OR THE NEW PATHOLOGIES OF GIRL POWER

In 2002 the *New York Times Magazine* featured the cover story "Mean Girls: And the New Movement to Tame Them" (Talbot 2002). The article suggests that "mean girls" are "an amalgam of old-style Queen Bee–ism and new style girls' empowerment, brimming over with righteous self-esteem and cheerful cattiness" (p. 4); it tells us it is girls' cleverness that makes them "like sharks," dangerous, "crafty" and "evil" masters of "intricate rituals of exclusion and humiliation"—practices boys are "not smart enough" to engage in (p. 6). A spin-off of this article, also titled "Mean Girls," appeared in the UK *Observer* (Hill and Hellmore 2002) and documented the "insidious and sophisticated" cruelty that groups of clever girls are exacting on one another. In the Canadian documentary series *It's a Girls' World*, there is a universalizing narrative of ruthless girls working in covert ways to create cultures of exclusion. The final installment outlines the long-term "costs" of girls' pathological nature:

> New evidence suggests that women pack up their social baggage from childhood and tote it to the office with their briefcases. Professional relationships among women at work are mired in the same dynamics that propelled them into hurtful behaviours in their younger years. Now the stakes are higher—their career is on the line. More than that, the male-dominated organizational structures of the workplace may actually foster resentment, cut-throat competition and power struggles among female bosses and their employees. After four decades of feminist efforts and hard won parity with men, a woman's success may well come at the expense of her own sex. (Canadian Broadcasting Corporation 2007, para. 6)

These are distinctly postfeminist narratives where feminism is actually held accountable for the fostering of girls' aggression in what has become a dominant story of girls/women who want power at all costs, with other girls/women their primary victims. In these stories, meanness is the logical extension of a naturalized, white, middle-class feminine subject traversing the rational worlds of school and work, where feminine pathology is bound to express itself through repressive, coercive, and masochistic tendencies.

As Walkerdine's (1993, 1998a) work shows, normative, Western girlhood has always been organized around nice/mean, good/bad, binaries and their complex chains of signifiers. Meanness is becoming a dominant motif for contemporary Western girlhood—one that does not disturb the traditional boundaries of appropriate femininity, but rather entrenches them. Meanness (either to others or to oneself) lies within the boundaries of normative, repressive femininity. Meanness shores up the lack of fit experienced by the girl/woman trying on masculine subjectivity in the realms of school, office, and personal relationships—girls' incapacity for rational fraternity. Girl power folds back into the age-old story of femininity claiming that girls and women cannot express their newfound opportunities for success in normative, positive ways and that they are plagued by pathology and lack, and at risk of slipping into cruelty and/or violent excess.

It is the belief of some leading feminist researchers that the drive for perfection, for supergirlhood, involves attempting to manage an impossible contradiction, that is, by performing or taking up positions usually ascribed to femininity (care, nurturance, emotionality) and simultaneously performing those ascribed to masculinity (assertiveness, cleverness, rationality), all the while presenting oneself unambiguously as a woman. As was remarked with respect to *Grey's Anatomy*, it is the sexy underwear beneath the scrubs that is important. The rational and scientific doctor is also the femme fatale, the vamp. While popular culture presents for us performances through which the maintenance of both roles might appear to be accomplished without any problems, thus making the formerly impossible possible, the examples given here demonstrate that it is far from straightforward to attempt both performances at once. This is further illustrated by a study of transition to womanhood (Walkerdine et al. 2001) in which middle-class British teenage girls were simply expected to do well at school as well as be good looking, sexually attractive, and so on. But what these girls revealed in interviews were deep anxieties about themselves, demonstrated as eating disorders and various forms of anxiety about not being good enough. After all, perfection is impossible, and the production of a fiction that perfection may indeed be attained, that oppositions between masculinity and femininity may easily be crossed, that being assertive, clever, and "drop-dead gorgeous" is easy to maintain, mean that most girls are likely to experience anything less than perfection as failure—their failure, their pathology.

Ringrose's research (forthcoming) also suggests the impossibility of this imperative for feminine perfection (see also Renold and Allan 2006). As with the biblical story of Adam and Eve, the ideal sets up the fall. With nurturing comes the possibility of rejection, with niceness comes the possibility of cruelty and betrayal. There is a knife edge to be traversed in attempting to occupy the normative structures of femininity throughout child and adult culture, where meanness, bitchiness, and secret manipulation are repeatedly produced and legitimated as truth claims.

Unfortunately, little critical inquiry concerning the symbolic bounds and constraints of idealized femininity (the impossibility of being a supergirl) is evident in the developmental psychology and school psychology research on girls that dominates public discussion and educational debates on girls' behavior. Developmental psychology has constructed girls as indirectly and/or relationally aggressive in counterpoint to normal masculine direct aggression (Crick and Rose 2000). In previous work Ringrose has explored how the research on girls' indirect and relational aggression is highly suspect because it presents this behavior as natural and as a universal phenomenon, representing the feminine as repressive and pathological, obscuring larger structures or discourses of gender, sexuality, and power (Ringrose 2006). As it is reconciled so neatly with commonsensical stereotypes of the feminine, it is not surprising that research on indirect aggression dominates popular culture through the figure of the "mean girl" (Ringrose 2006) and is increasingly taken up in educational policy and practice about bullying in North America and the UK. This, as has been emphasized, positions the problem as a pathology within the girl to be corrected and is thus highly problematic.

The Mean Girl as the Norm

The mean girl dominates an American School Board report on the "quiet violence in your school." Vail (2002) paints a picture of indirect aggression as follows:

> Look at the pretty girl with the honey-blond hair, the one always in the middle of an adoring orbit of friends, the one with the seemingly endless supply of outfits from Abercrombie and Fitch. She has everything, all right, but popularity isn't always what it seems. She and other adolescent girls live in a world where best friends can become enemies overnight, where one look from another girl can mean the difference between isolation and belonging. It's a world where no one tells you why you can no longer sit at the lunch table with your friends, where secrets are traded like currency.

In this account it is proximity to idealized middle-class, feminine characteristics that guarantees girls' indirectness, cruelty, and repressed rage. While class tends only to be implied in the colorblind and class-evasive discourses that dominate North America, in the British context this meanness is identified as a product of middle-class parents' indulgence in stories like "Little-Miss Perfect: The Latest Tyrant in the Playground," where we learn "Little Miss Sunshine was often a well-dressed middle-class girl who did her school work. Her parents had bought her designer clothes and a television of her own, but left her emotionally neglected" (Blair 2006, para.5). Such stories foster a culture of individualized blame upon parents for unleashing the new monsters of girls' success. There have been hysterical reactions from schools, including mass suspensions, in the UK, where girl culture is demonized as "mob rule" (BBC News 2004a, para.4). There are also major charities producing sensationalist reports, such as the recent YWCA (2002) UK report *If Looks Could Kill*, where the logical transition between meanness and violence is obvious.

One effect of these narratives, as pointed out by U.S. criminologists Chesney-Lind and Irwin (2004), is a focus on middle-class mean girls as the new culprits of schoolyard bullying, a postfeminist backlash where neoliberal imperatives for success and normative regimes of heterosexualized competition are ignored in favor of an individualizing focus on pathological girls. In this context of "crisis," new therapeutic techniques, educational texts, and psychological strategies are increasingly popularized for privatized, individual consumption by middle-class parents through Web sites by sponsors such as the Ophelia Project (www.opheliaproject.org), as well as books like Simmons's (2002) *Odd Girl Out* and Wiseman's (2002) *Queen Bees and Wannabes*. The Hollywood blockbuster film *Mean Girls*, which is based on Wiseman's book, presents this commercialized narrative of pathological meanness for an even wider, mass audience. Through such media, meanness becomes glamorous and erotic. Competition, aggression, and sabotage of one another and oneself become the dominant ways of describing girlhood. In its intensified presentation, meanness also becomes banal, a predictable by-product, a predictable perversion of girl power. Another effect of the mean-girl discourse pointed to by Chesney-Lind and Irwin (2004) is to direct attention away from increasing discipline and criminalization of those girls who do not fit the "successful mean girl" mold. Indeed, what this essay concludes is that while the middle-class mean girl is constructed as pathological, this profile is also constituted as the expected norm. Indirectness and meanness reaffirm conventional femininity, repression, and pathology and is central in the regulation of the boundaries of normative girlhood and appropriate models of neoliberal subjectivity. These normative boundaries are constitutive of "others," deviant and failed femininity, in danger of slipping into unmanageable excess—for instance, hyper-sexuality, pregnancy, dropping out of school, or delinquency and violence.

TRANSFORMING THE VIOLENT NON-GIRL

A UK example illustrates how girls' behavior continues to be regulated through class- and culture-specific symbols, and shows also how those girls who transgress dominant models of white, middle-class femininity—whose behavior can be equated with deviant masculinity—are under increased scrutiny as objects of failed femininity and increasing discipline and criminalization (Worrall 2004). The front-page headline of the *London Metro* newspaper on February 17, 2004, read, "The 13-Year-Old Girl Who Terrorized City." Ellen Moore is described as a "glue-sniffing school girl who led a gang of 50 young thugs" in Leeds (BBC News 2004b, para.1). Not indirectly mean to other girls or herself, but directly aggressive to the public at large, Moore is said to have "led a vicious campaign of intimidation and abused shoppers, workers, residents and police in Leeds." The reporter tells us, "In a bid to curb her reign of terror, Moore was made the subject of a five year anti-social behavior order . . . banned from the city centre unless accompanied by a parent." Her sister, 15, who was also in the gang, was said to have laughed when a magistrate imposed a 5-year ban on her the previous year. Of Moore's parents, we are told only that "her mother was in court to see [Ellen] punished."

Moore, who is pictured in a baggy track suit, was also "barred from wearing a hooded top over her head to obscure her identity." We might see this as an effort to stop her masquerading as male. Moore is the classic "laddette," girl turned boy, a bad girl who leads other youth into criminal acts, a specter of gender ambiguity in a postfeminist narrative of state retribution for bad mothering. Moore's case is also illustrative of what feminist criminologists describe as a shift from the "welfare route" to the "justice route," reflected in the rapidly increasing criminalization of marginalized girls through new disciplinary regimes such as the "anti-social behavior orders" (ASBOs) in the UK and other mechanisms of criminalization in the United States and Canada (Chesney-Lind and Brown 1999; Worrall 2004).

In the UK ASBOs are increasingly common. Indeed, one of the most recent reality TV hits there is *ASBO Teen to Beauty Queen* (FiveTV), where young girls with ASBOs from working-class neighborhoods in Manchester compete to become the UK's first entrant to the Miss Teen International beauty pageant held in Chicago. The girls are to transform from resistant troublemakers—bad girls, utterly defiant of middle-class feminine propriety—into subjects who can perform as appropriately passive-aggressive competitors for the title of beauty queen. This show follows on the heels of those such as *Ladette to Lady* (ITV1), concerned with the transformation of working-class, "chav" girls (those who smoke and drink, are single mothers, and depend on welfare benefits) into something viewed as more respectable, palatable, and *productive* by a middle-class public (Skeggs 2005; Walkerdine and Ringrose 2007). The point here is that Ellen Moore, and the ASBO girls on the show, signify the criteria of girls' abject failure and must be transformed. The violent ASBO girl defies the image of neoliberal success and adaptation, refusing to perform the tightrope balancing act of modeling masculine productivity and success on the one hand and feminine passivity and sexual desirability on the other. Criminalization is possible and increasing because of the slippage into the wrong sort of masculinity, that of irrational violence (Worrall 2004). The ASBO girls are deviants, whose qualities cannot be reconciled with the newest version of successful, neoliberal feminine subjectivity, the successful but mean supergirl.

CONCLUSION: RE-REGULATING FEMININITY

Many authors remain concerned that the sensationalism around these various depictions of girls in "crisis" (Aapola et al. 2005)—the supergirl, the mean girl, the violent girl—are not contributing to the provision of greater resources for addressing girls' everyday emotional needs at school, particularly those girls at risk of violence and criminalization (Chesney-Lind and Irwin 2004; Cruddas and Haddock 2005; Worrall 2004). Discourses of mean girls are being fed into educational policy and practice concerning bullying in North America, the UK, and Australia, in ways that obscure the political problems of postfeminist, neoliberal, neoconservative, "Third Way" cultures of school neglect and massive disparities in schooling provision across economic and social divisions. Continuing gender inequalities, boys' sexual harassment and bullying of girls, and sexist school and classroom practices (Francis 2005) are eclipsed by a seductive high drama of "girl on girl" cruelty, masochism, and pathology (Jiwani 2000). Postfeminist media and educational policy moral panics (or, some might say, anti-feminist backlashes) over "failing boys" (see Hoff-Somers 2000) continue to funnel the bulk of resources into addressing issues of boy's literacy and their behavioral needs (Ali et al. 2004; Bouchard and Proulx 2003; Davinson et al. 2004; Foster 2000). A range of international research in the Western English-speaking contexts of Australia, Canada, the UK, and the United States indicates that issues impacting girls such as self-harming, anorexia, bulimia, sexual bullying, school truancy, and (self-) exclusion are repeatedly deflected and neglected by policymakers (Chesney-Lind and Irwin 2004; Eyre et al. 2004; Lingard 2003; Osler et al. 2002; Woods 2005).

What is revealed is ample evidence that in the cultural and representational terrain of contemporary girlhood in the West there is heavy regulation of femininity and the promotion of enduring, impossible contradictions surrounding girls' relationships to success, aggression, and violence. These are heavily contested affective sites that girls must continuously navigate. Because femininity cannot easily be reconciled with either rational self-hood (Hey 2006) or overt expression including aggression, new narratives about the indirect pathological malady of relational aggression and a host of new imperatives to manage these implications of the (passive-aggressive) feminine that plague the supergirl (who is successful but mean in her drive for perfection) have emerged. Lest feminine lack slip into excess or direct, externalized expressions of rage, heavy regulation is applied to any femininity that transgresses its strictures and bounds. Fears about the return of the repressed into girls' violence and retribution express themselves through heightened anxieties over failed, deviant femininity that must be carefully regulated. This regulation is organized around class- and race-specific categories of the feminine that continue to produce normative and deviant girls, in new editions that bound the limits of the feminine once again.

Further Reading

Aapola, S., M. Gonick, and M. Harris. (2005). *Young Femininity: Girlhood, Power and Social Change.* Basingstoke: Palgrave.

Adkins, L. (2002). *Revisions: Gender and Sexuality in Late Modernity.* Buckingham and Philadelphia: Open University Press.

Ali, S., S. Benjamin, and M. Muthner. (2004). "Introduction." In S. Ali, S. Benjamin, and M. Muthner, eds. *The Politics of Gender and Education: Critical Perspectives.* Basingstoke: Palgrave.

BBC News. (2003). *Girls Top of the Class Worldwide.* [Online June 2007]. BBC News Web site http://news.bbc.co.uk/1/hi/education/3110594.stm.

———. (2004a). *Schoolgirls in Mob Brawl over Boy.* [Online June 2007]. BBC News Web site http://news.bbc.co.uk/2/hi/uk_news/england/dorset/4042281.stm.

———. (2004b). *City Terrorised by Teenage Girl.* [Online June 2007]. BBC News Web site http://news.bbc.co.uk/2/hi/uk_news/england/west_yorkshire/3496117.stm.

Benjamin, S. (2003). "What Counts as 'Success'? Hierarchical Discourses in a Girls' Comprehensive School." *Discourse* 24, no. 1, 105–118.

Binder, Patti. *Stressed Out Super Girls* [Online June 2007]. What's Good for Girls blog http://whatsgoodforgirls.blogspot.com/search?q=the+trend+that+girls+are+under+enormous+pressure+to+be+smart.

Blair, Alexandra. (2006). *Little Miss Perfect: The Latest Tyrant in the Playground.* Times Web site http://www.timesonline.co.uk/tol/news/uk/article715634.ece.

Bouchard, I. B., and M. C. Proulx. (2003). *School Success by Gender: A Catalyst for Masculinist Discourse.* [Online March 2003]. Status of Women Canada Web site http://www.swc-cfc.gc.ca/pubs/pubspr/0662882857/index_e.html.

Canadian Broadcasting Corporation. *Join Host Paul Kennedy IDEAS: It's a Girl's World* [Online June 2007]. CBC Website http://www.cbc.ca/ideas/features/girls_world/index.html.

Chesney-Lind, M., and M. Brown. (1999). "Girls and Violence: An Overview." In D. J. Flannery and C. R. Huff, eds. *Youth Violence: Prevention, Intervention, and Social Policy* Washington, DC: American Psychiatric Press.

Chesney-Lind, M. and K. Irwin. (2004). "From Badness to Mean-ness: Popular Constructions of Contemporary Girlhood." In A. Harris, ed. *All About the Girl: Culture, Power and Identity.* New York: Routledge, pp. 45–56.

Conlin, M. (2003, May 26). "The New Gender Gap." Business Week Online Web site http://www.businessweek.com/magazine/content/03_21/b3834001_mz001.htm.

Crick, N., and A. Rose. (2000). "Toward a Gender-Balanced Approach to the Study of Social-Emotional Development—A Look at Relational Aggression." In P. Miller and E. K. Scholnick, eds. *Toward a Feminist Developmental Psychology.* New York: Routledge, pp. 153–168.

Cruddas, L., and L. Haddock. (2005). "Engaging Girls' Voices: Learning as Social Practice." In G. Lloyd, ed. *Problem Girls: Understanding and Supporting Troubled and Troublesome Girls and Young Women.* London: Routledge-Falmer, pp. 161–171.

Davinson, K. G., T. A. Lovell, B. W. Frank, and A. B. Vibert. (2004). "Boys and Underachievement in the Canadian Context: No Proof for Panic." In S. Ali, S. Benjamin and M. L. Muthner, eds. *The Politics of Gender and Education: Critical Perspectives.* Basingstoke: Palgrave.

Epstein, D., J. Elwood, V. Hey, and J. Maw. (1998). *Failing Boys? Issues in Gender and Achievement.* Buckingham: Open University Press.

Eyre, L., T. A. Lovell, and C. A. Smith. (2004). "Gender Equity Policy and Education: Reporting on/from Canada." In S. Ali, S. Benjamin, and M. L. Muthner, eds. *The Politics of Gender and Education: Critical Perspectives*. Basingstoke: Palgrave.

Foster, V. (2000). "Is Female Educational 'Success' Destabilizing the Male Learner-Citizen?" In M. Arnot and J. A. Dillaough, eds. *Challenging Democracy: International Perspectives on Gender, Education and Citizenship*. London: Routledge-Falmer.

Francis, B. (2005). "Not Knowing Their Place: Girls' Classroom Behaviour." In G. Lloyd, ed. *Problem Girls: Understanding and Supporting Troubled and Troublesome Girls and Young Women*. London: Routledge-Falmer.

Francis, B., and C. Skelton. (2005). *Reassessing Gender and Achievement: Questioning Contemporary Key Debates*. London: Routledge.

Gill, R. (2007). "Supersexualize Me! Advertising and 'the Midriffs'" In F. Atwood, R. Brunt, and R. Cere, eds. *Mainstreaming Sex: The Sexualization of Culture*. London: I.B Tauris.

Gonick, M. (2004) "The 'Mean Girl' Crisis: Problematizing Representations of Girls' Friendships." *Feminism & Psychology* 14, no. 3, 395–400.

———. (2006). "Between 'Girl Power' and 'Reviving Ophelia': Constituting the Neoliberal Girl Subject." *NWSA Journal* 18, no. 2, 1–23.

Harris, A. (2004). *Future Girl: Young Women in the Twenty-first Century*. New York: Routledge.

Hey, V. (2006) "The Impossibilities of Polymorphous Sociality? Living between Representations, Desire and Performativity in Girls' Social Worlds." Paper presented at ESRC Seminar on Girls and Education, 3-16: Continuing Concerns, New Agendas. Lancaster University, Lancaster.

Hill, A., and E. Hellmore. (2002, March 3). "Mean Girls." *Observer: Guardian* [Online August 17, 2004]. Guardian Unlimited Web site http://observer.guardian.co.uk/focus/story/0,6903,660933,00.html.

Hoff-Somers, C. (2000). *The War against Boys (How Misguided Feminism Is Harming Our Young Men)*. New York: Simon & Schuster.

Jiwani, Y. (2000, May). "Deconstructing the Myth of 'Girl' Violence: The Denial of Race in the Murder of Reena Virk." *Kinesis*, 7–14.

Lingard, B. (2003). "Where to in Gender Policy in Education after Recuperative Masculinity Politics?" *International Journal of Inclusive Education* 7, no. 1, 33–56.

McRobbie, A. (2004). "Notes on Postfeminism and Popular Culture: Bridget Jones and the New Gender Regime." In A. Harris, ed. *All about the Girl: Culture, Power and Identity*. New York: Routledge, pp. 3–14.

Osler, A., C. Street, M. Lall, and K. Vincent. (2002). *Not a Problem? Girls and School Exclusion*. London: NCB Enterprises for the Joseph Rowntree Foundation.

Reay, D. (2001). "The Paradox of Contemporary Femininities in Education: Combining Fluidity with Fixity." In B. Francis and C. Skelton, eds. *Investigating Gender: Contemporary Perspectives in Education*. Buckingham: Open University Press.

Renold, E., and A. Allan. (2006). "Bright and Beautiful: High-Achieving Girls, Ambivalent Femininities and the Feminisation of Success." *Discourse: Studies in the Cultural Politics of Education* 27, no. 4.

Rimer, Sara. (2007, April 1). "AMAZING +: Driven to Excel; For Girls, It's Be Yourself, and Be Perfect, Too." *New York Times*, 1. New York Times Web site http://select.nytimes.com/gst/abstract.html?res=F10912FD35540C728CDDAD0894DF404482.

Ringrose, J. (2006). "A New Universal Mean Girl: Examining the Discursive Construction and Social Regulation of a New Feminine Pathology." *Feminism and Psychology* 16, no. 4, 405–424.

———. (2007). "Successful Girls? Complicating Post-feminist, Neo-liberal Discourses of Educational Achievement and Gender Equality." *Gender and Education* 19.

———. (forthcoming). "'Just Be Friends': Exploring the Limitations of Educational Bully Discourses and Practices for Understanding Teen Girls' Heterosexualized Friendships and Conflicts." *British Journal of Sociology of Education* 29.

Simmons, R. (2002). *Odd Girl Out: The Hidden Culture of Aggression in Girls*. New York: Harcourt.

Skeggs, B. (2005). "The Making of Class and Gender through Visualizing Moral Subject Formation." *Sociology* 39, no. 5, 965–982.

Taft, J. (2004). "Girl Power Politics: Pop-Culture Barriers and Organizational Resistance." In A. Harris, ed. *All about the Girl: Culture, Power and Identity*. New York: Routledge, pp. 69–78.

Talbot, M. (2002, February 24). "Girls Just Want to Be Mean." *New York Times Magazine*, 24–26. [Online August, 12, 2004]. New America Foundation Web site http://www.newamerica.net/index.cfm?sec=Documents&pg=article&DocID=752&T2=Article.

Vail, K. (2002). "How Girls Hurt: The Quiet Violence in Your Schools." *American School Board Journal* 189, no. 8. [Online August 17, 2004]. American School Board Journal Web site http://www.asbj.com/2002/08/0802coverstory.html.

Walkerdine, V. (1991). *Schoolgirl Fictions*. London: Verso.

———. (1993). "Girlhood through the Looking Glass." In M. de Ras and M. Lunenberg, eds. *Girls, Girlhood and Girls' Studies in Transition*. Amsterdam: Het Spinhuis, pp. 9–25.

———. (1998a). *Daddy's Girl*, 2nd ed. Cambridge, MA: Harvard University Press.

———. (1998b). *Counting Girls Out*, 2nd ed. London: Taylor and Francis.

———. (2007). *Children, Gender, Video Games: Towards a Relational Approach to Multimedia*. London: Palgrave.

Walkerdine, V., H. Lucey, and J. Melody. (2001). *Growing Up Girl: Psychosocial Explorations of Gender and Class*. London: Palgrave.

Walkerdine, V., and J. Ringrose. (2006). "Femininities: Reclassifying Upward Mobility and the Neo-liberal Subject." In B. Francis and C. Skelton, eds. *Gender and Education Handbook*. Thousand Oaks, CA: Sage.

———. (2007, forthcoming). "Abjection, Shame and the Makeover: Regulating Working Class Femininities." *Key Words: A Journal of Cultural Materialism*, 4.

Wiseman, R. (2002). *Queen Bees and Wannabes: Helping Your Daughter Survive Cliques, Gossip, Boyfriends and Other Realities of Adolescence*. New York: Crown.

Woods, M. (2005). "The Victimization of Young People: Findings from the Crime and Justice Survey 2003." *Home Office Findings*, 246.

Worrall, A. (2004). "Twisted Sisters, Laddettes, and the New Penology: The Social Construction of 'Violent Girls.'" In C. Alder and A. Worrall, eds. *Girls' Violence: Myths and Realities*. New York: SUNY, pp. 41–60.

Youdell, Deborah. (2006). *Impossible Bodies, Impossible Selves: Exclusions and Student Subjectivities*. London: Springer.

YWCA. (2002). *If Looks Could Kill: Young Women and Bullying*. Oxford: YWCA.

JESSICA RINGROSE AND VALERIE WALKERDINE

How to Study Girl Culture

Since the early 1990s increasing attention has been given to the study of girlhood, girls' lives, and girls. One of the consequences of this work is the emergence of research methodologies and research tools that take into account a new "girl culture terrain." In a sense this new area brings its own "how to," focusing specifically on age (girls, not women), gender (girls, not boys), and the social value of the texts (often regarded as having little value as in the case of fashion magazines, soap operas, diary writing, and romance reading as opposed to classic texts). The work on the study of girl culture has led to what has been termed "girl-method," a shorthand way to refer to the range of methodologies and techniques for gathering and analyzing evidence in girl-centered research (Mitchell and Reid-Walsh 2005).

WHAT IS GIRL-METHOD?

"Girl-method" as an overarching term for the "how to" of researching girl culture speaks to the politics of doing research and refers to the following:

1. Working *with* girls (participatory), *for* girls (advocacy), and *about* girls
2. Taking into account who the researchers are (and what their relationship to girlhood is)
3. Including the girls themselves as participants (so that they are agents and not subjects)
4. Addressing the cultural contexts of the girls in terms of race and class: *whose* girlhood?

As is obvious from the range of methodological issues raised in the various studies of girl culture, the notions embedded in ideologies of girls and young women choosing to research their own lives, or of researchers working *with* girls, *for* girls, and *about* girls, are complex. They cross generations, cultural contexts, and disciplinary boundaries, and interrogate lines between the researcher and the researched.

WHERE DOES GIRL-METHOD COME FROM?

In seeking to define methodologies that are specific to studying girl culture, researchers are treating as a precedent the rich body of work on feminist methodology and the study of women's lives. They are also drawing on childhood research involving young children. These areas provide a background to girl-method. Feminist theorist Sandra Harding states, for example, that while there is no *unique* feminist method, there is a distinctive methodological perspective or framework that challenges the implicit male-centered bias in research. Although this statement has been modified in subsequent work by feminists occupying different marginalized positions according to race, ethnicity, class, sexuality, and geographical location, girls—too often—still seem to be subsumed under the category of women, or are seen as some monolithic category. It is as though a very young (preschool) girl and a mature adolescent are both "girls" in the same way.

Thus, it is useful to think about the types of feminist approaches to doing research that allow for greater specificity. This work includes the studies of collective memory work of Frigga Haug and her colleagues in Germany and of June Crawford and her colleagues in Australia. It also includes the work of Ann Oakley, who highlights the contradictions inherent in women interviewing women—noting, for example, the ways in which women's autobiographies (of both the researcher and the researched) may overlap, but also may differ significantly in relation to power (who is the researcher and who is being researched?). In working in girlhood studies, with a very few exceptions, power and age dynamics, as well as the intersectionality of race, class, ethnicity, and gender and sexuality need to be foregrounded in self-reflective ways.

Another methodological area relates to the use of the visual (film, photography, art-making) as part of what Carson and Pajaczkowska (2001) call feminist visual culture. In particular, researchers and activists such as Jo Spence, Brinton Lykes, and Caroline Wang have employed visual methods such as photography with women not only to see "through the eyes" of other women, but also to study the ways in which visual methods as research tools can contribute in a democratic way to policy change.

Within the work in childhood and youth studies, particularly the emerging body of literature within the "new social studies of childhood," are other method areas linked specifically to girl-method. In these studies, attention has been drawn to the need to recognize the power differentials between adult researchers and child participants as a result of differences in status and size (Jenks et al. 1988). In addition, increased attention has been given to participatory methodologies and ways of getting at the perspectives of children using, for example, the visual. Wendy Ewald and James Hubbard have used photography with groups of marginalized children all over the world to obtain a "through the eyes of children" perspective. The role of children as photographers was also highlighted in the Academy Award–winning film *Born into Brothels*. The photo-voice work of Caroline Wang noted above has been adapted to work with children in South Africa (Mitchell et al. 2006). Other studies with children have employed drawings (Weber and Mitchell 1995). Mitchell and Reid-Walsh (2002) and Mitchell and Weber (1999) have also used memory work as a way to study childhood by looking at life after childhood. In these studies adults recall, for example, their own childhood play (playing school, playing cowgirl) and through these memory work activities use the past to try to understand the present and future.

GIRLS' EXPERIENCES AT THE CENTER

To date there is a limited body of literature that attends to methodologies for work *with* girls or for facilitating research *by* girls, even though the literature on girlhood is replete with references to participation and the need for girl-centeredness.

Heather-Jane Robertson's "A Capella Papers" represent a girl-method that focuses on group work with girls. In 1990 Robertson published a series of papers based on studies conducted with groups of high school girls in various parts of Canada. Drawing on the ideas of feminist consciousness-raising groups of the 1970s, she investigated the ways in which girls' collective experiences helped shed light on girl culture and on some of the particular challenges of looking at girls' identities, self-esteem, and "speaking out." Robertson's project with girls was one of the first to "make explicit" a girl focus as central to the method itself and not just to the findings.

Lyn Mikel Brown and Carol Gilligan's (1992) "listening guide" was one of the first research "tools" specific to the study of girls' lives. Noting the complexity of hearing girls' "real" voices in interviews, Brown and Gilligan worked out a four-step approach for listening to the audio recordings of the interviews with girls. In this approach, which they describe as "voice centered," they regarded the process of meaning-making as involving an understanding of the relational world of girls. To understand girls' relationships, however, it is necessary to get an idea of the types of relationships (with teachers, parents, peers, and so on) as well as a sense of the girl and her relationship to herself. The fist time they listened to a tape, their attention was on the story that the girl was telling. The second time the objective was to get at the "self" or "the voice of the I." When they listened the third and fourth times, they focused on how girls talk about relationships. They observed; "In working with girls and women, we are particularly attentive to their struggles for relationships that are authentic or resonant, that is, relationships in which they can freely express themselves or speak their feelings and thoughts and be heard" (p. 29). What was also particularly significant about the work of Brown and Gilligan was their attention to the links between women (as researchers) and girls (as researched), serving as a model of women researchers engaging in self-reflexivity as part of a project involving work with girls.

A third girl-method, developed by a team of women researchers in the UK, is the transcript analysis work of Janet Holland et al. (1999), who studied girls' sexuality. Like that of Brown and Gilligan, the work of Holland and her colleagues takes into account the links between the lives of women researchers and the lives of girl participants. They use the term "unraveling" to describe the process of working with the variability in young women's accounts of negotiating and decision making in discussions of condom use. They point out the difficulty of relying solely on the personal accounts of respondents as a tool of interpretation, as well as the need to start with the everyday experiences of girls and young women. Speaking about the difficulty of exploring with young women the centrality of gendered power relations as a feature of their lives when they are not yet even aware of "gender" as a construct, the authors observe that "women's personal experiences are not a sufficient means to explain social practices and processes . . . there is a complex process of negotiation between data and analysis. Personal experience can be valid as a source of knowledge, but circumscribed by the limits of personal ideas and practices" (p. 466). They are particularly interested in the fact that when, as women and as researchers, they read through the transcripts from the interviews, they often disagreed on the interpretation of the data because of their own girlhood experiences. In other words, they recognized that they were bringing their own background experiences and subjectivities to their research with girls. Rather than gloss over their differences, they realized the importance of making their different interpretations central to their work, often using them as the "entry point" to their work on girls' sexuality.

Finally, Gerry Bloustien's (2003) work on "girl-making" through video might be regarded as an explicit girl-method tool for giving voice to girls through the visual. In working with girls to document their everyday lives through video recordings Bloustien draws attention to the "constructedness" of girls' identity and the ways in which producing video narratives is not just recording what is happening but is in fact shaping the events of the girls' lives.

MAPPING OUT CRITICAL ISSUES IN GIRL-METHOD

Four themes within research methodology are key to contributing to the development of a practical girl-method "map" for researching girl culture: age disaggregation, participatory process, intergenerationality, and historical context.

"How Old Are You?" Age Disaggregation

Age disaggregation refers to the practice of refining a term such as "girl" to specify separate yet often overlapping age categories, such as "very young girls" (i.e., preschool), "tween girls" (from the age of 6 or 7 to 12 or 13), "very young adolescent girls" (age 10 to 14), "adolescent girls" (age 13 or 14 up to 16 or 17), and so on, rather than simply seeing the term "girl" as all encompassing. How and when do we disaggregate girlhood according to age, and what do we lose when we do not? The category "girl" can refer to the baby girl sexually abused by a man who believes the myth that having sex with a baby can cure AIDS. It can also refer to the little girls in Walkerdine's (1998) *Daddy's Girl* or the tween "whistle blower" girls that Lyn Mikel Brown and Carol Gilligan write about. "Girl" can also be a category in youth studies, defined by UN agencies as being female and between the ages of 15 and 29. Cynthia Fuchs (cited in Mitchell and Reid-Walsh 2002) points out that there are at least five different generations of females who might classify themselves or be classified as girls. These include 55-year-old women who are Gap shoppers with their Baby Gap granddaughters; girl rock bands from Generation X; Gwen Stefani, claiming that she is "just a girl"; the commodification of girlhood nostalgia through American Girl branding aimed at tween girls; and finally baby girls (and "It's a girl").

Age disaggregation provides a useful auditing tool for taking stock of the research area, for identifying gaps, and for self-monitoring in the study of girl culture. To what extent, for example, does the overall area of girlhood studies privilege one set of girl experiences over others, and why? In an audit of studies that claim to be girlhood studies or girl centered, how is girlhood defined and what are the dominant issues? How many of the studies are about adolescent girls, or girls and young women in their early 20s, or about girls between the ages of 5 and 8, and so on? If researchers were to engage in an audit of girlhood studies, to what extent does an age bias privilege some issues over others (for example, dating or the sexual identities of teenage girls, issues over girlhood play, and the early social identities of very young girls)?

Girls' Voices through the Participatory Process

The notion of "girls' voices" is a critical one in the study of girl culture. Although many adult researchers working in the area want to claim that the voices of all the girls are heard, the participation of those who are usually marginalized is an area of research that is burgeoning, both in terms of appropriate methodologies and also in terms of "fraughtness" in relation to ethical issues, levels of participation, tokenism, privileging/romancing the voices of participants, putting our own interpretations on the words of our participants, and so on. When it comes to the participation of minors, the area becomes even more contested. Hart's (1997) discussion of "ladders" of child participation is a useful one for monitoring levels of participation on a scale of 1 to 9. A "1" might refer to children placed on a stage in front of a "children's rights" group of adults to sing "We Are the World." A "9" category might be one where no adults are present at all, where children have defined the issues (violence in schools, their right to hold an event) and have taken action themselves to consult with adults to bring about change. Most research studies, particularly those that are funded (and hence require adult participation), lie somewhere in the middle. After acknowledgment of the power differentials between adult researchers and children "participants," how do adult researchers minimize the presence of the former and maximize the presence of the latter?

Equally important are the challenges of working with girls as co-researchers on topics such as popular culture that come with some form of "built in" devaluing, with the devaluing of women's culture (e.g., romance reading, watching soap operas) often carried over to the devaluing of girls' culture (e.g., playing with Barbie, reading fashion magazines). Girls and young women are often put in the position of apologizing for romance reading (see Radway 1991) or magazine reading, and even for reading novels generally (Mitchell 1982). As Gannett (1992) and many others point out, certain writing genres such as journal and diary writing, when they are associated with girls and women, are often seen to have little value. Even the status of girls' blogging and other computer use may be under scrutiny. Understanding girls' play, and in particular the links between girls' play and many aspects of identity, through the "authentic voices" of girls may be complicated. As Buckingham and Sefton-Green (1994) and others have pointed out in their work on children's television viewing, children have usually figured out what they "should" say to adults. This self-censoring might be reconfigured as "what they can't say to adults," or even worse, the children might interpret the intrusiveness of the adult questioner to indicate that play activities must be engaged in secretly. For older girls, this might mean not admitting to having had a Barbie (or to still playing with Barbie or My Little Pony after the age of 9), buying *Sweet Valley High* books, and so on. The point is not that these spaces cannot be negotiated, but that there is a further devaluing of the genuine participation of girls if researchers fail to make the actual status of the texts explicit, or if they don't take the low status of texts into account in invoking the voices of girls.

The Lives of Girls and Women: Intergenerationality in the Unraveling of Girlhood

Intergenerationality is also a feature of research related to girl culture since the research itself is usually initiated by adults and often by women (and former girls). Intergenerationality here refers to the links between the lives of women and the lives of girls. Although intergenerationality may be interpreted in a number of ways in the context of researching girl culture, memory work is a particularly useful tool. Far from seeing memory as "useless longing" (hooks 1994), various researchers are using memory work as a way to interrogate the past: Why do we remember things a certain way? What (or who) is left out of the memory? How can the past inform the future? Retrospective accounts do not have to extend far into the past; indeed, in one study (Mitchell and Weber 1999) 10- and 11-year-old girls in the fifth and sixth grades looked back at their first-grade school photographs as a way to talk about their own experiences of schooling.

Retrospective accounts in the context of lost photographs can be revealing. The black feminist author bell hooks, for example, writes of a lost photograph of herself as a small girl in a cowgirl outfit and the ways in which the loss of the photograph is associated now with a loss of "that girl." In other work, women have written memory accounts of particular items of clothing in what Weber and Mitchell (2004) call "dress stories." In their collection *Not Just Any Dress* are a number of retrospective accounts of girl culture told through the "conduit" of a story of having to wear a communion dress, a school uniform, little-girl Polly Flinders' dresses, and even being dressed by her mother as a Barbie doll.

In other memory work studies the attention has been on girlhood play, as in the case of women's memories of playing with Barbie (Reid-Walsh and Mitchell 2000). There the point is that although Barbie is often regarded as a "feminist nightmare" in terms of emphases on body, beauty, fashion, and consumerism, women talk about Barbie as being the first doll they ever had with which they didn't have to engage in conventional domesticity: feeding the baby (doll), changing the diaper of the baby (doll), and so on. In memory work involving former readers of Nancy Drew books, it is again interesting to note the ways in which participants revise their girlhood experiences through an adult woman lens. In one case, a woman who is now a police officer credits Nancy's amazing feats at solving mysteries as central to her career (Reid-Walsh and Mitchell 1995). The point is not that memories should be taken at face value or correspond to "the" truth. Rather, the focus is on understanding why we remember girlhood in a certain way and what this now tells us about girl culture and women's identities. As Kathleen Weiler (1992) observes in her study of retired women teachers looking back at their choice at age 18 to go into teaching as "free choice" or as "a calling," most women wishing to enter a profession at the time had three choices: teacher, nurse, or secretary.

Barbie in the Seventeenth Century? Girl History

Working back through history to study girl culture may seem like a non–girl-centered approach and one better left to historians. However, there is often a tendency in work focusing on popular culture and on contemporary issues to disregard the past. This "presentist" approach, however, may obscure some of the possibilities for understanding why Barbie as a fashion doll is regularly trashed in the media or how girls and women for centuries have been "claiming a space" for themselves through diary writing. Feminist literary critic bell hooks has long emphasized the need for historical approaches in feminist work, particularly if the history is a negative one (1994). She points this out in the context of relations between black and white women in the United States and in North America generally in order to highlight the challenges for collective feminist projects today in crossing boundaries of race and class. This is necessary so that girls and girlhood can be studied in a scrupulous manner, whether the topic is of urgency, such as girls and AIDS, or whether on the surface it appears trivial, such as work on girls' popular culture, which in fact is far from trivial. To take an example from the latter, one might look at the Barbie doll within a historical context. The fashion doll of seventeenth-century Britain might be regarded as a precursor to Barbie. The moral panics surrounding Barbie or Bratz dolls might also be read within a historical context. Too often researchers operate under the influence of some form of amnesia. Girl history, then, as an approach invites research that "looks back." It can be intergenerational, so that one can look at long-lasting girl culture texts such as Nancy Drew, which has been around since 1930, or *Seventeen* magazine, which has been around since 1944. Or it can lead to studies that look at "long-term history," asking questions about pillow books as precursors to twentieth-century diary writing or, again, the seventeenth-century fashion doll as a precursor to Barbie.

GIRL-METHOD: EXTENDING THE LIMITS
OF STUDYING GIRL CULTURE

Some might argue that what is mapped out here as girl-method is simply a version of "good method" within women's studies. At the same time, researchers are recognizing that within women's studies girls, particularly pre-adolescent girls and younger, have remained on the margins over the last 30 years. Others might argue that girlhood studies (and girl-method) simply complement boyhood studies, and that there is nothing unique to working with girls other than seeing them (and possibly working with them) as a distinct and separate grouping based on age. While there are important overlaps between boyhood studies and girlhood studies, they have their respective "parent" groups—feminist studies and masculinity studies—that inform the emerging research areas and also inform one another theoretically and in terms of method. Methodologically, certain things are unique to girls and women studying girl culture, with the idea of girl-centeredness and girls' voices being critical. The articulation of the idea of girl-method offers a platform for action that includes particular tools and approaches, particular orientations that acknowledge in a rights-based way the unique historical and contemporary contexts for girls and young women, the position of women studying girlhood and ways of taking action.

See also Video Play; Voice

Further Reading

Bloustien, G. (2003). *Girl Making: A Cross Cultural Ethnography of Growing Up Female*. New York: Berghahn.

Brown, Lyn M., and Carol Gilligan. (1992). *Meeting at the Crossroads: Women's Psychology and Girls' Development*. Cambridge, MA: Harvard University Press.

Buckingham, David, and Julian Sefton-Green. (1994). *Cultural Studies Goes to School: Reading and Teaching Popular Media*. London: Taylor & Francis.

Carson, Fiona, and Claire Pajaczkowska, eds. (2001). *Feminist Visual Culture*. London and New York: Routledge.

Crawford, June, Susan Kippax, J. Onyx, U. Gault, and P. Benton, eds. (1992). *Emotion and Gender: Constructing Meaning from Memory*. London: Sage.

Drotner, Kristen. (1992). "Modernity and Media Panics." In Michael Skovmand and Kim Christian Schroder, eds. *Media Cultures: Reappraising Transnational Media*. London: Routledge.

Gannett, Cinthia. (1992). *Gender and the Journal: Diaries and Academic Discourse*. New York: SUNY Press.

Harding, Sandra, ed. (1987). *Feminism and Methodology*. Bloomington: Indiana University Press.

Hart, Roger. (1997). *Children's Participation: The Theory and Practice of Involving Young Citizens in Community Development and Environmental Care*. London: Earthscan.

Haug, F., et al. (1987). *Female Sexualization: A Collective Work of Memory*. E. Carter, trans. London: Verso.

Holland, Janet, Caroline Ramazonuglu, Sue Sharpe, and Rachel Thomson. (1999). "Feminist Methodology and Young People's Sexuality." In Richard Parker and Peter Aggleton, eds. *Culture, Society, and Sexuality*. London: UCL Press/Taylor & Francis, pp. 457–472.

hooks, bell. (1994). *Teaching to Transgress: Education as the Practice of Freedom*. London: Routledge.

Jenks, Allison, Chris James, and Alan Prout. (1998). *Theorizing Childhood*. Cambridge: Polity Press.

Mitchell, C. (1982). "'I Only Read Novels and That Sort of Thing': Exploring the Aesthetic Response." *English Quarterly*, 67-77.

Mitchell, C., R. Moletsane, and J. Stuart. (2006). "Why We Don't Go to School on Fridays." *McGill Journal of Education* 41, no. 3, 267–282.

Mitchell, Claudia, R. Moletsane, Jean Stuart, Thabisile Buthelezi, and Naydene De Lange. (2005). "Taking Pictures/Taking Action! Using Photo-Voice Techniques with Children." *ChildrenFIRST* 9, no. 60, 27–31.

Mitchell, Claudia, and Jacqueline Reid-Walsh. (2002). *Researching Children's Popular Culture*. London: Routledge.

———. (2005). *Seven Going on Seventeen: Tween Studies in the Culture of Girlhood*. New York: Peter Lang.

Mitchell, C., S. Walsh, and R. Moletsane. (2006). "Speaking for Ourselves: A Case for Visual Arts–Based and Other Participatory Methodologies in Working with Young People to Address Sexual Violence." In F. Leach and C. Mitchell, eds. *Combating Gender Violence in and around Schools*. London: Trentham Books.

Mitchell, Claudia, and Sandra Weber. (1999). *Reinventing Ourselves as Teachers: Beyond Nostalgia*. London: Falmer Press.

Oakley, Ann. (1981). "Interviewing Women: A Contradiction in Terms." In Helen Roberts, ed. *Doing Feminist Research*. London: Routledge & Kegan Paul, pp. 30–61.

Radway, Janice A. (1991). *Reading the Romance: Women, Patriarchy, and Popular Literature*. Chapel Hill: University of North Carolina Press.

Reid-Walsh, Jacqueline. (1992). "A Female Interrogative Reader: The Adolescent Jane Austen Reads and Rewrites (His)story." *English Quarterly* 24, no. 2, 8–19.

Reid-Walsh, Jacqueline, and Claudia Mitchell. (1995). "Romancing Nancy: Feminist Interrogations of Successive Versions of Nancy Drew." *Review of Education/Pedagogy/Cultural Studies* 17, no. 4, 443–455.

———. (1996). "Reading on the Edge: Serious Series Readers of Nancy Drew and Hardy Boys Mysteries." *Changing English* 3, no. 1, 45–55.

———. (2000). "Just a Doll? Liberating Accounts of Barbie-Play." *Review of Education/Pedagogy/Cultural Studies* 22, no. 2, 175–190.

———. (2001). "The Case of the Whistle-blowing Girls: Nancy Drew and Her Readers." *Textual Studies in Canada: Canadian Journal of Cultural Literacy* 13/14, 15–24.

Robertson, Heather-jane (1990). *A Cappella: A Report on the Realities, Concerns, Expectations and Barriers Experienced by Adolescent Girls in Canada*. Ottawa: Canadian Teachers' Federation.

Walkderdine, V. (1998). *Daddy's Girl*, 2nd ed. Cambridge, MA: Harvard University Press.

Wang, Caroline. (1999). "Photovoice: A Participatory Action Research Strategy Applied to Women's Health." *Journal of Women's Health* 8, no. 2, 85–192.

Weber, Sandra, and Claudia Mitchell. (1995). *That's Funny, You Don't Look Like a Teacher: Interrogating Images of Identity in Popular Culture*. London and New York: Falmer.

———, eds. (2004). *Not Just Any Dress: Narratives of Memory, Body and Identity*. New York: Peter Lang.

Weiler, Kathleen. (1992). "Remembering and Representing Life Choices: A Critical Perspective on Teachers' Oral History Narratives." *Qualitative Studies in Education* 3, no. 1, 39–50.

CLAUDIA A. MITCHELL AND JACQUELINE REID-WALSH

Doll Culture

One of the most characteristic examples of girls' material culture, the idea of the doll as a small representation of a human and as a popular toy, unravels under closer scrutiny. Some doll-like figures have a functional existence that extends beyond play, such as the artist's lay figure or the small mannequins sold along with miniature cutout patterns to teach girls the basic skills of home dressmaking in the 1930s and 1940s. Dolls have also found a serious place in the educational curriculum. Dressing a doll circa 1900 frequently replaced the task of making a sewing sampler so that girls in rudimentary public schooling could learn sewing skills. Dolls from other countries or dressed in national costumes have often been employed in the schoolroom to encourage children's interest in different cultures. Such activities continue today often at an informal level or supplemented with picture books and other learning materials. However, this use of dolls was particularly widespread in the 1920s and 1930s, extending to collections of dolls housed in publicly run children's museums and in museum "education," "community," and "outreach" programs. In the era between the world wars the exchange of "friendship dolls" between North American and Japanese school children, at a time of heightened international tensions, serves to indicate the role of diplomatic agency that dolls were seen as filling at the level of everyday culture. Many of these dolls were demoted from their cherished positions in classroom displays and were summarily and publicly "executed" when hostilities broke out. Functional dolls may be misread later in history as having been play dolls, and vice versa. Likewise, misreading across cultures may misidentify religious and ritual figures as toys. Even Christian figures from the Roman Catholic tradition before early modern times, with their elaborately sewn garments reflecting fashionable, courtly dress and accessories, can be mistaken by collectors and dealers for play dolls.

Although it is assumed that women will put aside dolls upon leaving their girlhood years, there are myriad male and female interactions with dolls, from work-based to leisure, from closeted secret activity to hobby to commercial enterprise. Buying and selling dolls at "doll fairs" and on the Internet is a significant business in North America and elsewhere. Dolls also overlap into the category of decorative figurines and statuettes for children and adults, especially the many types of non-jointed dolls and dolls with elaborate porcelain, resin, or plastic detailing. Academic literature that addresses issues related to the quality of childhood experiential and material culture and the appropriate role of capitalism in childhood, often ignores the irony and sophistication of adult reactions to and engagement with dolls and their extension downward into girlhood.

Aside from their use in play narratives and activities, dolls can play many other roles in the material culture of girls' lives. Dolls can function as aspects of their room decor, housewares, accessories, and even jewelry. In the latter context one may include the small figures on beaded chains and tassels popular for decorating mobile phones and also pens and pencils, South American worry dolls, and certain Mattel Liddle Kiddles of the 1960s, which could be worn as necklaces. There are eras when the preferred representational aspect of doll formats is decidedly naturalistic and other times, as in the 1960s and the present, when abstract and distorted doll formats appeal to buyers.

A human identity for a doll is not necessarily a given. Since the early 1900s soft animal toys and teddy bears have shared many of the play and comfort functions of dolls. Hello Kitty, internationally famous, has a feline head but an essentially human body form and wears many different clothes and takes on a variety of looks. Similar cat and dog dolls were produced throughout the twentieth century, starting with porcelain versions, including those by Heubach. The Five-in-One doll (1912) was dressed as a middle-class girl, with a girl's body and a set of interchangeable heads, including a molded celluloid cat head with glass eyes, made in Germany. Trolls and German Mecki Hedgehog dolls are other anthropomorphic dolls that have enjoyed great popularity in the last half-century. In recent years many toy horses, cats, and dogs marketed explicitly at girls have featured long nylon hair that allows for Barbie-style "hair play." These animals are supplied with many accessories, including garments and hair ornaments, by their manufacturers, following the Mattel pattern of aggressively marketing a wide range of desirable add-ons without which the doll or doll play would not be complete. My Little Pony is a perennial example of this genre. These animal toys are closely related to modern dolls and doll products.

DOLLS 1900–1945

The predominant doll formats around 1900 were German bisque dolls, with cheaper dolls of glazed porcelain, wood and papier-mâché. Bisque, matte glazed porcelain, was particularly prized for its ability to subtly capture the texture and toning of human skin. No material used in subsequent years has matched this mimetic capacity, and perhaps this led to the return of bisque dolls as ornaments of girls' lives in the 1980s. The illusionistic potential of bisque was apparent in even in relatively cheap models, giving it a popularity that more than compensated for its capacity to shatter. Celluloid dolls were also produced around 1900. Like all early plastic items, they closely imitated more expensive and highly regarded materials; thus these plastic dolls, which resembled bisque dolls, were fixed to kid leather or jointed composition bodies as were bisque heads. These German dolls were generally fashioned as images of little girls, frequently bearing a solemn, calm expression and a slightly slimmer, longer figure than was the norm for later dolls. The most favored body type was the ball-jointed composition and wood strung with elastic. Thus these dolls were both more fragile and far more flexible than typical dolls later in the century.

The majority of these dolls came from two cities in east central Germany. The trade was split roughly into two parts: Sonneberg was known for the ordinary but thoroughly acceptable grade of doll, and Waltershausern produced the more expensive models, although Sonneberg also exported a small number of extremely fine dolls. The general quality level of the Sonneberg dolls is far superior to the cheap plastic dolls produced in the second half of the twentieth century. Although assembly and shipping were concentrated in factories, the majority of steps needed to complete a doll, including the modeling of individual components and limbs, wig making, shoe making, and box construction, were broken down into small segments and performed by thousands of home-based workers living around the main centers, who brought their items to a central factory and received pay and materials for the next week's work. Porcelain head making required kilns and heavy equipment, and so it was generally concentrated in the factories. Doll production was engaged in by all family members to maximize the income stream. The sad irony that German doll producers employed girls who were the same age as the girls in other countries who played with the exported dolls did not go unnoted in the press at the turn of the century. Even children nominally enrolled in public schools worked after hours on doll production. The trade was international in its scope, and prior to about 1940 most girls born into families from the prosperous end of the working class and higher in any urban center around the world, race and cultural context notwithstanding, owned at least one German bisque doll.

There were smaller numbers of bisque dolls made in other countries, including the United States, but most notably France, which had supported a luxury doll industry over the previous half-century. By around 1900 this industry was in serious decline due to German companies' ability to provide product of solid quality at much lower price. The French dolls' personae were elegant and overtly sensuous—even ecstatic—in expression, foreshadowing the imbrication of dolls and sexuality often attributed to Barbie and, more recently, Bratz, and blurring the adult/child boundary. The French doll look also predated the melding of provocative sophistication of grooming with children's physical proportions exemplified by the child beauty pageant queen by about a century, albeit in a far less tawdry context. This precedent may not excuse these sexualized, "prostitot" representations, but it does suggest that these cultural idioms have a far longer history in narratives of taste and styling than is usually assumed and are not expressions specific to late American capitalism.

The first significant change in the market was the appearance of baby and character dolls by around 1910. The character doll was modeled to express a certain emotion, from pensiveness to glee, depending upon the model. Some were actual portraits of living children, including relatives of the dollmakers and celebrities such as Princess Juliana of the Netherlands. On occasion notable sculptors, such as Levin-Funke, created the face model, and the design was publicly credited to them. The baby doll made its first substantial impact on the market at this time and reflected the gender roles that were standard in modern industrial-military states. An urban myth claims that one doll is the portrait of a member of the German imperial family, although accounts differ as to which one, with the candidates spanning three generations. This so-called Kaiser Baby was among the most popular of the character dolls, while the sweet-faced My Dream Baby perhaps was the longest-surviving, widely produced throughout the 1920s and 1930s. Kammer and Reinhardt's mold 126 also established a doll type that remains highly visible 80 years later, that of a laughing, chubby baby or toddler (depending on the body configuration). A similar product is now produced in plastic rather than bisque, but the persona is identical.

World War I prompted a major upheaval and shift of power in the doll world. German doll products became harder to find in 1914–1916, although dolls were still being produced as a major source of foreign income from neutral countries, often in the face of extreme supply shortages (dolls' eyelashes were made of sewing cotton rather than bristle or sable, for example). With the entry of the United States into the war in 1917, new German dolls became impossible to obtain. The United States came to the forefront as a new site for the mass production of dolls and there were dramatic changes to the formats available. U.S. doll makers preferred unbreakable materials and favored a chubby toddler-infant form with simplified jointing and hair and eye detailing. Many dolls had cloth toddler bodies with swinging legs that gave the effect of walking when the doll was swung from side to side. Other dolls from the United States referenced early newspaper comics characters such as the Yellow Kid and the Katzenjammer Kids. They featured the exaggerated shapes and characterizations of these cartoon characters. France, Italy, South Africa, and Australia also were forced to make substitute products during the war.

North American dollmakers' chosen formats also were more in keeping than were European doll formats with changes in the cultural placement of dolls. The emerging disciplines of psychiatry and psychology made pronouncements upon dolls and endorsed dolls that were unbreakable and allowed for hands-on training in "mothering" activities, such as washing and feeding. Rubber and celluloid were now seen as more suitable for doll production than porcelain as they allowed for practical mothering activities in play. Advertisements for dolls in 1920s North America offered quasi-psychological literature to assist adult buyers in making the correct doll purchase. One advertisement suggested that the baby doll was an antidote to "race suicide" (Peers 2005), a reference to Oswald Spengler's theories about the growing power of inferior races with higher birth rates over whites. According to pseudo-scientific discourse, the white races were also being depopulated by selfish feminists refusing to have babies. This change in doll usage reflected middle-class women's changing roles in the home after the war, when servants for housekeeping and child rearing duties were less affordable than in the early 1900s, and domestic drudgery was therefore represented as essential rather than as insulting to the female image.

As dolls were becoming closely identified with medicalized norms of girls' behavior, many adult doll-type products began production in the 1920s and 1930s. Some of these, such as the Lenci felt dolls from Italy, crossed over from adult mascot or living room decorations into the realm of children's toys. Others—such as the pincushion dolls and porcelain dolls in the shape of hair tidies, bookends, perfume bottles, vases, powder bowls, powderpuffs, lamp bases and face brooches—would have been familiar items to the younger teen at least in their personal home environment and their mother's room, if not standing on the girl's dressing table or decorating her bedroom. During the 1920s, it was trendy for adult women to carry dolls in public, especially in urban areas, as a fashion accessory, and perfume flasks, purses and handbags were produced with doll or teddy bear faces. The Nancy Ann Story Book Company of California produced small dolls in series that encouraged young girls to collect the whole set. The Nancy Ann dolls crossed over from the younger play audience to a young adult audience, who regarded them as mascots and ornaments. Because the Nancy Ann dolls were extremely popular, the company had to switch to locally produced dolls when the supply sources in Axis countries became unavailable during World War II.

German bisque dolls continued to be produced into the war years, and the industry remained a crucially important one to the national economies of the Second and Third Reichs as well as the Weimar Republic. The doll trade halted due not to lack of infrastructure, but to lack of manpower because of military conscription. Despite popular belief, the doll factories were neither bombed by the Allies nor substantially looted by the Russians for plant and equipment in the postwar years. Only after the post-1989 reunification were the production lines stripped and the buildings razed for property speculation and other newly arisen opportunities for short-term capital gain, and only then was the capacity for doll production rendered apparently unfeasible. There is a persistent myth that some factories resumed production—even during the Eastern bloc years—with their output directed to the adult collector market, not to girls, which now floods eBay and antique auctions and fairs in the United States and elsewhere. As these items are sold as "antiques," their corporate and craft network origins are generally denied, with the products claimed to have emerged from pre–World War II "hidden storehouses." Thus the seemingly irrelevant child's doll has become part of the complex, unstable experience of the Eastern bloc's adaptation to capitalist processes and values. If the old doll factories were manufacturing "antiques" for cash-laden United States buyers, then the doll played its part in economically supporting the East German state, just as it did the previous German regimes. Likewise, the extensive cultural and economic capital contributions of the doll and toys generally to the United States throughout the middle and late twentieth century should not be overlooked.

During World War II, dolls in military dress reflected the times and notably included the new female service personnel. In the United States dolls again performed functions in adult as well as in play cultures as they featured prominently in domestic "shrines" to service personnel on active duty overseas, serving as a more tangible, three-dimensional touchstone to the absent relative than a photograph. Paper dolls became popular due to wartime shortages of materials. Just as in the Depression when their price made paper dolls the only dolls that poorer families could afford for their daughters, they were often the only new doll product that was freely available. In both Allied and Axis countries, older nineteenth-century porcelain dolls, with or without fashionable makeovers such as shorter haircuts and modern dress, were given to girls as compensation for the lack of new product or the limitations on purchases due to rationing. Small dolls also were used as good-luck mascots to protect against injury, as they had in the previous world war by both civilians and combatants. In World War II such dolls as well as teddy bears were favored by pilots and rode in many a warplane.

DOLLS 1945–1950s

Soon after the war, dolls became part of the plastic revolution. By 1950 plastic—first hard plastics and later softer plastics such as vinyl—was the preferred material for commercial dolls. Synthetic materials now also provided doll wigs, as they do to this day. Plastic also replaced glass as the preferred material for dolls' eyes. Likewise, leather shoes were replaced by plastic ones as the doll became even more of an industrial object. The norm for the doll product at mid-century was set by Ideal, Horsman, and Effanbee of the United States; Pedigree, Roddy, and Rosebud of the UK; and Regal of Canada. Despite the different geographical locations, the product was often remarkably similar in format and style. For many people these dolls are the quintessential form—plain and childlike, with a sweet, generalized expression and wearing girls' fashions, often in the form of printed cottons. This postwar concept of the doll obscures the many different and alternative doll formats that were produced. These solid, plain little-girl dolls have generally disappeared from production a half century later; an exception is the UK Amanda Jane Company, which has moved from a bourgeois to an elite style due to its old-fashioned aura. A similar development has occurred with U.S-based Vogue's Ginny, who was a star of the postwar doll world, as well as the products of the Terri Lee Company, also were widely popular. Both companies' dolls remain in production six decades later. Madame Alexander of New York catered to a more upscale market, as did the UK's Chiltern and, later, Sasha dolls. Sasha dolls are renowned for possessing a solid intellectuality, despite their bizarre origins as representations of Holocaust victims.

The development of adult fashion dolls with high-heeled shoes and molded breasts in the mid-1950s led to an explosion in dolls of this format, though slightly larger than the 11.5-inch norm of today. The earliest was undoubtedly Madame Alexander's Cissy in 1955. Cissy was presented as an upper-class debutante or glamorous model/magazine icon, a depiction of those women who in the interwar period and up to the late 1940s/early

1950s in the top end of the market were as often society women as paid professionals; the latter finally took over as models for fashion photography in the middle to late 1950s. When Madame Alexander's New York childhood as a poor east-end immigrant is factored into the equation, Cissy becomes even more complex. An enterprising, highly gifted woman, Bertha Alexander as a child had watched, from the pavement in 1890s New York, white upper-class beauties wearing feathered hats drive by in carriages, and she declared— to the surprise of her family—that she wanted to be one of those ladies. Fashions and lifestyles changed, and the adult Bertha acquired neither her carriage nor her feathered hat, but she became a wealthy woman by marketing and retailing, under the more aristocratic name and persona of Madame Beatrice Alexander, a hybrid of upper-class (white) beauty with an Old Testament vision of the strong Jewish heroine, such as Esther or Judith, in the form of a doll product. Her dolls were stylish and yet encoded with a feminist intent, paying tribute to women of *virtu* and self-reliance—Queen Elizabeth II, Margot Fonteyn, Louisa May Alcott, and the tempestuous yet resourceful Scarlett O'Hara, the survivor of male-instigated war and disorder.

Barbie was a late entrant into this market, appearing in 1959 and drawing her form from a popular European doll, Bild Lilli, which was originally marketed as an adult novelty but was rapidly commandeered by children. Barbie was a runaway success, going through three editions in the first year, with the third edition produced in extremely large quantities, firmly establishing the singular popularity that she would enjoy for the next four years and beyond. This success was undoubtedly supported by the glamorous and chic television campaigns launched by Mattel in the 1950s, indicating how closely the company was attuned to new formats and processes of marketing. These stylish television advertisements ratified the position of dolls within the postwar dream and used the familiar imagery of the perfectly groomed and poised woman that appeared in many commercials of the 1950s. Toys and dolls were a sign of U.S. postwar prosperity and the spending power of families, as baby boomer children amassed more toys than even the elites of previous generations. In the 1950s Italian papier-mâché dolls were extremely expensive and beautifully designed, and were among the few alternatives to plastic dolls and dolls of U.S. origin. They were often taller than the usual doll, between 3 and 4 feet high and usually dressed in Victorian crinolines and picture hats. Because they were physically impressive, they were used as parlor and living room decorations as well as being girls' toys.

DOLLS 1960s–1970s

The 1960s were dominated by manufacturers' desperate attempts to decrypt or improve on the seemingly undefeatable Barbie formula—including the British Sindy, who was the most successful of these rival dolls. She was consciously developed to counter the explicit U.S. cultural references in the Barbie narrative and is still celebrated among Britons as an icon of resistance to the global reach of North America. Mary Quant, the most internationally successful British designer of the early 1960s, is believed to have provided advice about Sindy's wardrobe. Sindy's boyfriend, Paul, is believed to have been a reference to Paul McCartney of the Beatles—again a nationalist entry in the contest of the world's public cultures.

There were Barbie clones from many different nations in both Europe and Asia. Some of these dolls were directly copied after Mattel products and often were offered at a lower price, because authentic Mattel products in the early days of Barbie were extremely expensive outside of the United States. Thus such dolls were not always regarded as "cheap" or tawdry. Barbie's cost, which was seen as beyond the reach of ordinary families, and the urgent pleas girls made to their parents to buy them a Barbie were also read as part of a pernicious plot by America to destabilize the family unit and the economies of countries beyond its shores. In the last 20 years Mattel has marketed its product at a more accessible price as the dolls have lost their luxury status and presentation.

Technology began to be applied in earnest to novelty doll products of this period. There were innumerable battery-powered dolls, both iconic branded products and unnamed. Typical novelty dolls of the period were Chatty Cathy, Dancerina, Tiny Thumbelina, and Giggles. Inevitably these dolls would break and were too expensive to be replaced. From Tressy to Chrissy, the growing-hair doll, whose hair was wound and unrolled on spindle inside her head, was a very popular novelty of this period. Simpler mechanisms, such as crying (e.g., Ideal's Tearie Dearie) and drinking/wetting dolls, were also very popular. Parents and adults may have seen in these dolls admirable images of maternal care and devotion, while children may have enjoyed the more prurient implications of the "wetting" dolls and their soaked panties.

Bizarre-shaped dolls were also popular among designers of the middle to late 1960s and into the 1970s, including Flatsy, Blythe, Little Sophisticates, Little Miss Sad Eyes, and the Liddle Kiddles. Another high-profile, strangely shaped doll format of the 1960s were the rag dolls with extremely long legs and dolls made of cord and strung-together puffs of material, often taking the form of clowns but also girls and women. These dolls were often seen lounging on beds and chairs. For teenage girls of the period the beautiful, large-eyed, anime-inspired Bradley rag dolls (made in Japan), which had hand-painted organza faces over molded (plastic) masks and were sometimes mounted on lamp bases and music boxes, were standard bedroom fixtures. Often they wore exotic international costumes or Victorian and Marie Antoinette styles. Another successful manifestation of this interest in novelty doll formats conceived to counter Barbie were the miniature Dawn dolls, which outsold Barbie until 1977, a few years later, when Superstar Barbie won back most girls. These dolls had an extensive, but tiny, wardrobe of mid-1970s fashions.

Troll dolls of various sizes, with their wildly colored long hair, were a massive doll fad of the mid-1960s that extended to boys and adults. Small trolls were made to fit on the end of a pencil and often invoked school teachers' wrath in this era, when play was still seen as suspect in the primary school curriculum. It was popular to keep collections of different-size trolls as a family—although the dolls were genderless, as they had no genitals and generally wore no clothes. Their faces were masculine and wizened, but friendly and good-hearted. Troll hair featured bright colors, and although the first dolls were made of flesh-colored plastic, the later, cheaper trolls came in many bizarre combinations of hair and body colors. Thus they could be seen as an aspect of the questioning of gender and other conventionalities of the later 1960s. The original dolls came from Scandinavia but most were copied in Hong Kong and other cheaper markets. Like the other bizarre-shaped novelty dolls, trolls brought visual signifiers of the unstable, psychedelic, spaced-out world of late 1960s San Francisco into the culture childhood. Cereal box toys, exported in the millions from Australia to United States breakfast food manufacturers in the late 1960s and early 1970s, although often regarded as "boys' toys," were also cherished by girls and shared with trolls the androgynous, indefinable body and mind-blowing range of unnatural colors in representing a small figure.

The most beautiful and conventional dolls of this period were the stylish Ideal dolls of the Chrissy family, including Velvet and Tiffany Taylor. The sculpting made their faces and bodies seem assured and appealing, with a strong evocation of an individualist persona. The dolls' dressing was an elegant reflection of early 1970s fashion: miniskirts in chocolate-colored velvet and coarse orange lace, which make the dolls perfect documents of the design values of the period. On the other hand, the early 1970s was a down period for Mattel as Ideal came to the forefront (until Superstar Barbie restored the former hierarchy). This oeuvre of beautiful, quality Ideal dolls marks the end of a fairly straight and formal vision of doll making that had dominated since the renaissance. One can easily track the pedigree of this solid and predictable definition of the doll trade back to early nineteenth-century Germany, and certainly earlier, with—sadly—far less material evidence. After the 1970s, doll production ceased to be a solid central point of reference in marketing products to and for girls, becoming increasingly diffused amid a white noise of both competing—and therefore diverse—and similar—and thus indistinguishable—products. Also, the increasing decline in both price and production values in some ways debased the doll, although dolls were now being seen more widely and in greater numbers than previously in their history. More little girls had more dolls than ever before.

SHIFTS IN DOLL CULTURE: 1970s–1980s

Although this essay focuses on the material culture of the doll, by the 1970s there appears to have been a diffusing and debasing in girls' play and personal relationships to the doll. It is impossible to comment with certainty about doll play activities of the past due to the general neglect of children as sources of historic witness. The picture is also distorted somewhat by a strong preference in the few academic treatments of dolls toward tracking historical evidence of a 1970s-style, second-wave refusal of the doll as a constriction, rather than a celebration, of femaleness, as is found in the writing of nineteenth-century British novelist George Eliot. Given these cautions about evidence, significant changes in the attitudes toward dolls appear to have taken place around the 1970s. Frances Hodgson Burnett's novel *A Little Princess* (1905) can be taken as epitomizing an earlier view. It focuses on Emily, a singularly large and expensive doll engaged in an imagined dialogue with her owner, Sara, notable in her persona and her possessions. Sara nearly forfeits her angelic status when she meanly accuses Emily of indifference and lack of concern. Burnett assumed that Emily could supply both concern and empathy for her owner perhaps because of her elegance and status as lovely object—bypassing puritanical fears of physical beauty and of the chimeric, seductive qualities of material objects. Many other Victorian and Edwardian doll stories similarly imaged the doll as a persona in her own right, a mature but small-scale being.

By the 1970s and 1980s most dolls belonged to a range of cheap consumer items, thousands of plastic toys bought cheaply, discarded promptly, broken easily, and prone to becoming physically damaged and dirty. Anyone who has been to garage sales, church fairs, and thrift shops is familiar with the grubby doll bodies piled, concentration camp style, in what North American poet Denise Duhamel has called the "mass grave of a toy chest." Discarded dolls are now merely so much industrial pollution and space taken up in landfill. Naked dolls with unruly hair in dreadlocks are carried by their ankles by girls through shopping malls, rather than being wheeled in prams or dressed up in hat and gloves for a promenade. This change should not be read only as a sign of cultural decline.

It indicates the greater educational and lifestyle opportunities offered to girls, who once were expected to dress, to maintain, and to entertain their dolls as a demonstration of female responsibility, as a reflection of either the class and social consciousness of the Victorian era or the approved mothering activities of the psychologized 1920s–1960s. Cheap, disposable dolls mean that doll products are available to virtually every child in any industrialized society in the world.

The diffusion and debasing of the doll also illustrates the modern capitalist shifting of production out of industrialized and into developing nations, particularly those of Asia. This process of moving doll production out of the United States to cheaper facilities abroad (while keeping the same price point) was begun by Mattel. The loss of an idea of value being associated with an individual item also can be seen as relating to the manner, during the last two decades or so, in which *virtu* resides no longer in a specific object, but in the media and discourse surrounding it—the value-added-ness of marketing, graphic design, branding, and communication that has become the core metaphor of current society. Not surprisingly, these changes were substantially brokered once again by Mattel, which regained the centrality of doll production with Superstar Barbie in 1977 and has flooded the world with constantly changing Barbie products ever since. Constant change keeps the products at the forefront of the market and ensures that the buyer never has enough products. Even Barbie's origins now seem somewhat conservative, with the one cherished doll and the wardrobe of haute couture outfits carefully stored in the dollcase. The wide range of original items still available for vintage Barbie collectors is a testament to the love and care given by so many girls nearly half a century ago to their Barbie dolls. There is now a Darwinian hierarchy of Barbies in most middle-class homes from the pristine collector Barbie on the dressing table or the bedroom shelf to the dirty, scribbled upon, limbless Barbies for bath play in the bathrooms.

As for the more nostalgic dolls that have been produced especially since the 1970s, they are also conscious constructs and, in some ways, are essentially meaningless—from the various evangelical and Protestant Christian symbols of newly devised, trivial sentimental traditions and "precious moments," to the intellectualizing, even slightly left-wing, but upper-class, American Girl dolls. Real middle-class girls, especially older ones, may not be playing with dolls at any given time. They could be doing anything, from playing soccer to making money through a soft porn real-life blog.

Following the general swing in the 1970s toward nostalgia in middle-range product design, from Laura Ashley, to Crabtree and Evelyn, to Royal Albert, to the *Little House on the Prairie* television series, a strong market emerged for sentimental dolls such as Holly Hobbie, Matilda, Penny Brite, and Strawberry Shortcake. These were self-consciously "girlie" dolls, but they represented only a pastiche of Victorian style and said more about conservative Christian values in the United States than about any intellectually credible interest in design history. Both Holly Hobbie and Strawberry Shortcake also had their own series of greeting cards, plaques, and posters, with sweet homilies, produced by companies such as Hallmark, indicating the imbrication of another major U.S. company with girlhood—as well as the linkage between card producers, publishers of religious material, and girlhood. Though these products may seem to celebrate girlhood, Strawberry Shortcake, with her metaphor of pastries and desserts as naming devices, served to remind women that they were items to be consumed—eaten—and that they had to mask their natural bodies and environment with scented products. This suggests an overlapping of the doll industry with the petrochemical industry, the household cleaning product industry, the cosmetics and fragrance industries, and even the vast middle-class vanilla sex toy and marital aid industry—which should not be read as disjunctive to an ordered social structure. Strawberry Shortcake inducts girls to be consumers of all these many governing agencies of everyday life. In this way, these dolls can be considered as disturbing as the continually maligned Barbie.

Although different in tenor, another core doll product of the 1970s were Mego's celebrity dolls, depicting a wide range of performers from Donny and Marie Osmond to Cher to *Charlie's Angels* to Brooke Shields. Celebrity dolls have remained a staple of doll making to the present. In the late 1970s a variant of the celebrity doll, Star Wars figures as a marketing product of the first three Lucas films in this series, established another crossover between boys' and girls' toys. They also allowed doll-type products to be marketed to boys while leaving them free of any anxieties about their future sexual orientation. Lord of the Rings figures, Harry Potter, and images of various soccer stars are later manifestations of this trend. Star Wars figures also established the booming secondary market for modern toys and dolls at inflated prices and the concocted "collectible," again at an inflated price, that is an important aspect of the overall doll market of the late twentieth century. Collectible dolls are often given as presents to girls by doting parents and grandparents, as well as being bought as personal items by adult women.

Mattel regained market dominance, as noted earlier, with Superstar Barbie in 1977; it then established the hot pink format for doll packaging that has remained to the present day. Superstar Barbie, whose name derives from the aesthetic of Andy Warhol, brought the spirit of disco and 1980s visible excess to the world of dolls through her looks and her personal styling. Barbie was also firmly reinvented as camp—a fact that is often piously overlooked by the family market—although Mattel ensured that there were both bourgeois and queer Barbies available in any given range of releases. In 1981 the African American version became Barbie and no longer Christie—a Barbie friend and secondary character. Mattel has a long history of employing a racially diverse staff, and many white Barbies have in fact been styled by non–white-bread designers, which raises the question of whether she is a parody as much as a celebration of white dominance.

Very different were the Cabbage Patch Kids dolls, which went from a cottage industry in 1976 to a national brand in 1983, when they were commercially licensed to Coleco, later to be taken over by Mattel. Cabbage Patch dolls were a publicist's dream, with their public ritual of being born and named in the Babyland General Hospital of Cleveland, Georgia, and the purchaser's "adoption" of the doll, with the appropriate papers. They also had a lively presence in North American urban mythologies. In addition, these dolls were an embodiment of vernacular, working-class, rural American life—in contrast to the New York and Long Island Madame Alexander dolls and Californian Barbie—with their self-consciously white trash names and their weird, presumably inbred physicality that highlighted and critiqued prejudicial stereotypes by making them absurdly prominent. At first the doll was a folk product affectionately imbued with social satire and commentary, a good-natured traveler from the lowest level of white society throughout the United States. The name suggested subsistence farming and lack of gastronomic sophistication, but they in fact constituted a subversive act of revenge by the defeated South, the backwoods hicks, first against their colonizer and next the world. The familial and craft origins were lost, however, once the concept was sold to larger commercial concerns when demand far outstripped local production. My Child was Mattel's "homely doll," with wide appeal to middle-class girls in the 1980s, and it is again collected by them now as adults.

Their features were less distorted than those of the Cabbage Patch dolls, with whom they were intended to compete. Though My Child is loved by collectors and now commands four-figure sums at auctions, its base substance of fluffy flocked plastic is among the least attractive of all late–twentieth-century doll materials—a somewhat remarkable achievement given the wide scope of the field of potential rivals for this distinction.

DOLLS 1980s–2000s

The 1980s witnessed a substantial revival of porcelain dolls in the retail market. Most of them were cheaply made in Asia and included male dolls, Pierrots, and Charlie Chaplins, as well as girls and women in Victorian dress. Simultaneously there was a demand for a range of expensive European and nostalgically designed porcelain dolls in elaborate dresses, such as those by Annette Himstead and Hildegarde Gunzel. Also in the 1980s there was a crossover between girls' bedroom ornaments and adult decorating culture and collectible dolls. Again this indicates a linkage between dolls and the overall pattern of design history in relation to the spirit of play and the sense of *Homo Ludens* in general 1980s design from architectural toys to Memphis products. Fantasy and lowbrow Celtic revival culture brought us Jem—the glam punk rock doll with a mystical capacity to self-transform, change shape, and heroically right wrongs—and She-Ra: Princess of Power— a fantasy/classical-style swordfighter predating *Xena Warrior Princess*.

Barbie dominated the market until the early 2000s through continued novelty of function and dress. All other doll product designers scrambled to keep up; even Sindy, the most persistent of all rivals, finally imploded after having been "surgically altered" bit by bit over two decades to more closely resemble her nemesis. She is no longer available internationally and has been through about three makeovers in the last decade in the British market. Throughout the later twentieth century there were attempts at "anti-Barbies," from Happy to Be Me to Get Real Girls, but with the exception of the American Girl line, none has captured the public's fancy to any significant degree.

American Girl dolls of the 1980s and 1990s were a means of intellectualized resistance to Barbie, with their lessons about crucial periods and events in U.S. history and their imaginative reinsertion of girls into the narrative of national development. Sadly, few other nations have endeavored to assemble a similar narrative to this one, which, though undoubtedly faux, is intriguing insofar as one can conceive of rebuilding the polis and the national agora with a little girl as informed witness, if not player. Effanbee in the late 1930s produced a historical series that also envisioned the development of the United States through doll-girls—most wearing crinolines. Thus Madame Alexander's Scarletts also stand as reminders that the nation was made by women as much as men and that males' narratives of nation building through noble conflict are as fabricated and shaky as women's romantic narratives. Yet what was certainly most successful about the American Girl narrative was the expensive fantasy, retail, tea-party, exhibition, and theatre venue developed as the central command center, the American Girl Place. The first branch was in Chicago. Smaller American Girl Places, minus the theatre space, are starting to open in major regional centers across the United States. This elitist aspect is not much different from the doll salons of the second Napoleonic empire or the whimsical neo-rococo chateaux in Japan, Korea, and now California, where currently Asian ball-jointed dolls priced at US$1000+ are presented to new owners. Of course, these doll headquarters also copy the deep South Cabbage Patch doll birthing facility, where the dolls of the same name emerged to greet their new owners amid applause 20 years earlier. The American Girl Place is an extremely complex facility purpose built to serve the needs of young girls and those buying essentially play dolls for them. Ironically, the American Girl brand ended up as a Mattel subsidiary.

Throughout the 1980s and 1990s the market for Madame Alexander staples—ballerina, *Little Women*, and *Gone With the Wind* dolls—remained strong. Concurrently, Baby Born and other European-style baby dolls kept alive older doll paradigms as well as the doll's function as facilitating correct mothering even though the fascist and imperial societies that created the baby doll were supposedly long defeated. Many baby dolls now were gendered anatomically. Mattel increasingly cross-marketed dolls with other major corporate names during the 1990s. The partners were not only couture houses for the collectors' market and the upper-class market, but also various suburban brands, like Little Debbie, Avon, Disney World, McDonald's, the "Got Milk?" campaign, and Coca-Cola. Mattel was not the only cross-marketer of dolls. McDonald's cross-marketed with Takara Corporation in Japan the much-loved Jenny and Licca (wearing McDonald's uniforms). In the United States Happy Meals of the 2000s feature miniature jointed Madame Alexander dolls covering the company's history and entirely overturning the upper-class reputation of the dolls. Dolls from My Scene, Bratz, and *Dora the Explorer*—often cited as a Hispanic breakthrough into middle-class girls' lives—as well as the Japanese animé-styled *Powerpuff Girls* are additional actual or expected McDonald's cross-marketing products of the 1990s and 2000s.

Bratz entered the toy buying market for dolls in 2002–2003 and quickly surpassed Barbie in the doll market. The Bratz dolls have also cornered the European and Australian doll buying markets. They could do nothing wrong in interpreting the fashion trends of the early 2000s and provided an index of popular fashion as on-target as the documentary evidence of teen magazines such as *Mademoiselle* and *Sixteen* on the one hand and MTV on the other; however, they seem to have lost momentum as of 2007, likely a consequence of moving too close to the juvenile market and losing their competitive fashion edge. This is representative of a general slowdown and lack of insight characterizing the present state of the doll market. The Bratz have normalized themselves into conventional toys, with grooming animals and the French Bebe-styled large Bratz and girl Bratz. The punk-inspired anti-baby dolls, the fierce and streetwise Bratz Babies who look like infant biker molls (and whose bottles are, no doubt, filled with bourbon) and ride around in hotted-up prams, are perversely sinister, fascinating, but they no longer necessarily make for good fashion copy. However, they do represent an unexpected female incursion into the hyper-masculinized realm of biker imagery.

Disney Princesses were built up as a brand throughout the later 1990s into the 2000s. They are no longer periodical products incidental to film releases, but have remained ongoing offerings. Their marketing appeal is also buoyed by glaring presence of Disney videos/DVDs in every household—in contrast to former times, when the Disney classics would disappear from the screen and, therefore, from family and child consciousness for several years at a time. Disney Princess dolls are distinguished by their color schemes and now feature a range of subsidiary merchandise. They appear impossibly together on a joint product, cut loose from their originating narratives. The doll license was transferred from Mattel to the German company Simba during the past decade. Royal Doulton of England produces porcelain figurines of the Disney Princess characters. The Disney Fairies expanded from the slight stardom of Tinkerbell in Peter Pan to command various non-cinematic videos of their own. The demand for fairy products in the new millennium is such that Bratz and Mattel have been obliged to develop subgenres as well as generic and "knock-off" fairies. These ladies are, of course, sanitized fairies—not the anarchic, society-destroying, baby-stealing, food-spoiling, hair-pulling, valiant hero–kidnapping fairies of uncensored folk myth. Girl-related videos from studios other than Disney, such as *Anastasia*, likewise have generated vast quantities of associated doll products in the past decade. Mattel dominates the overlapping doll–computer game market and in fact established this genre of girls' toys.

The last decade has seen the revival of 1960s and 1970s dolls, including funky rag dolls as well as Blythe. More Blythes have probably been made in the twenty-first century than were ever made during the era of her first appearance. Bratz clones of all levels of quality and price point have emerged. Another trend that is currently extremely popular are anthropomorphic dolls such as the Fashion Kitties, which are, of course, *unheimlich* and disturbing images of women as atavistic and animalistic, signaling a return to old concepts of social and racial hierarchy that positioned women, children, imbeciles, and the non-white at the lower levels of civilization. Hello Kitty—in fact, a somewhat upper-class London cat according to her life narrative—is perhaps the most popular of all human-animal hybrids. She has traveled the world to establish an appeal that now may be more secure than Barbie's, now encompassing more than three decades, since her debut on products in 1975 (the character was developed in storyboards a year or so earlier) but currently lacking the "crisis" of Barbie. Hello Kitty's licensed-product range is generally considered to be the largest of all girls' toys. In addition to her Japanese markets there are product lines specifically developed for girls' and women's markets in both Europe and North America. Their quantity and range make it hard to track Hello Kitty products outside their originating territories; like the Bratz line, they include references to established adult brands such as Chanel and Vuitton. The crossover indicates that the brand is being marketed to adults as well as children (as do adult-size Hello Kitty clothing and Hello Kitty electrical goods) even with the strictly juvenilizing tendency dominant in today's doll market in Western cultures. Hello Kitty's genial, high-spirited, open personality makes it sound blasphemous to mention social Darwinism and racial atavism in her presence.

DOLL CULTURE IN THE 2000s

Certainly the doll play market is shrinking and preschool girls (or their parents and guardians) now form the core market for dolls. The later part of the millennium's opening decade is dominated by fairy and princess lines, which are distinctly repetitive and self-referencing. This steady infantilization of the play doll market with its stress on princesses and fairies is reducing the "fashion" elements. At the same time, interest in weird toy/ornament/mascot concepts is growing in older teen markets, thanks to the growing Asian influence in fashion consumption. This teen market does not currently cross over into that for conventional dolls.

Asian influences are opening up an older market as exemplified by Hello Kitty accessories for mature customers. One notes the ongoing focus on antique doll looks in Japanese fashion, especially the Sweet Lolita fashion subculture, which consciously imitates Victorian French dolls. The Lolita look (the name is taken from the novel but has remarkably purged the masculine sexuality inherent there) has placed dolls in a far more central position of culture than they usually are permitted to assume. Outside Japan teenage and early 20s Lolitas must possess a special degree of courage, especially those whose public persona and styling include such details as Mary Pickford or Shirley Temple wigs. Due to the scorn for the extremely feminine in mainstream Western society (unless mediated by the male authority and authorizing persona of drag and transexuality), it is socially more acceptable to dress in clothing that is sexually explicit or that expresses violent rejection of the state, such as fashion characteristic of punk culture, than in Lolita "girlie" and doll styles. In many countries the Lolita spirit is reduced to a few doll-inflected gestures—lace gloves or Mary Jane shoes. In some countries (e.g., Ireland) the Lolita look is virtually nonexistent on the streets; in other countries, such as Australia and Britain, the look has been assimilated into more established fashion subcultures such as punk or Goth, which uphold rather than critique the fear of the excessively feminine as a sign of dependence and inappropriate citizenship. Although fashion forecasting agencies have been pushing both the Lolita look and images of late–nineteenth-century French dolls (and other elaborate and finely crafted dolls) as a suitable direction for the late "noughties," customers have not responded. Forecasting is not quite the all-powerful conspiracy that it is assumed to be. If the doll is too radical a female concept to embrace, the Marie Antoinette look in the wake of Sofia Coppola's film seems to have been taken up. This narrative successfully launches the idea of girlhood and pleasure, and its lush visual culture, pitted against the responsible white male state, although with the final implied warning that the state will destroy girlhood in the name of the people and their rights.

However, the exciting character of the edges of the doll market have not yet penetrated the center. The funky art-toy Blythe market does not meet the staid adult collector market, with its current obsession with the "rebirth" of baby dolls, a poignant and sinister indication of the limited roles of women in a neoconservative vision of society. Nor does the funky art-toy market touch fairy and princess child consumers. In some cases the current failure of Mattel is due not to inability within the firm but to the customers' inability to move as quickly or see as broadly as does Mattel. The collector market is highly conservative and the family market seems to want a limited, predictable range of products. Mattel's sophisticated urban dolls the Magic Circle disappeared, as did their social opposites, the Flavas. The doll apotheosis has yet to happen, and boys' toys such as train sets and digital war games or do-it-yourself cardboard Eiffel Towers still have more currency as social metaphor than girls' toys. Both a core sample of the specific nature and experience of girlhood and a metaphor of girlhood universal in its resonances, the doll speaks of the—often overlooked—importance of girls' culture within a wider social context.

Further Reading

Coleman, D. S., E. A. Coleman, and E. J. Coleman. (1986). *The Collector's Encyclopedia of Dolls* (2 vols.). New York: Crown.

King, Constance Eileen. (1977). *The Collectors' History of Dolls*. London: Robert Hale.

Peers, Juliette. (2004). *The Fashion Doll: From Bébé Jumeau to Barbie*. New York: Berg.

———. (2005). "Doll History and Fashion Theory." In Suzie Plumb and Jackie Lewis, eds. *Guys 'n' Dolls: Art, Science, Fashion and Relationships*. Brighton: Brighton Museum and Art Gallery/Hove.

JULIETTE PEERS

Barbie Culture

The "Barbie" doll was introduced by Mattel, Inc., in 1959. Although the doll was initially considered innovative for being a "teenage" doll, it was not truly representative of a grown-up infant figure; in actuality, Barbie was no more teenage or adult than any other doll. Fashion dolls, including three-dimensional ones, had been popular with youth for centuries. For her part, Barbie was modeled to some degree on the famous German comic/burlesque doll "Bild Lili"—but Barbie also represented a set of discourses about adolescent girlhood and will always be referred to in the feminine, rather than neutral, pronoun. Although the figure of the girl caught between childhood and womanhood, and positioned in that way as both an ideal and a problem, developed its recognizable contemporary form in the late nineteenth and early twentieth centuries, its visibility dramatically expanded with new and more widely disseminated forms of popular culture after World War II, with the teenager continuing as one of the dominant icons of the United States in the 1950s. Barbie appeared in the wake of this massively popular concretization of the idea of the teenager, the teenybopper, and the teen.

Unlike previous incarnations of the fashion doll, Barbie was crafted for long-lasting play, for which her fashion accessories would always be secondary to the doll herself. In this sense, she resembled the new post–World War II consumer, around whom proliferating commodities could endlessly circulate. Unlike the previously more popular baby dolls, Barbie was not a game about motherhood, but a game about gender in a broader sense, where—like the ideal of the teenage girl—she is a participant in the debates about gender roles that emerged after the women's suffrage movements and amid ongoing changes to women's labor practices.

If Barbie is thus a product of political and popular cultural changes that reached a degree of institutional stability in the United States of the 1950s, she is also a product of technological and transnational economic changes following World War II. She was always a global product in some sense. Although first seen at the 1959 American Toy Fair, Barbie's mass-produced form was molded in Japan. Even more significant, the history of Barbie's production parallels the expansion of transnational commodity marketing that established not only the manufacturing, distribution, and sales of the dolls themselves, but also the gender norms Barbie spoke to. Barbie's American-ness is not just about maps of ethnicity dominated by idealized whiteness, and maps of gender dominated by commodity circulation on the one hand and the open-ended process of youth consumption on the other, but also about factories. The raised plastic on Barbie's body traces a history of exploitation and "modernization": from "Made in America" to "Made in Japan," and then on to Hong Kong, Korea, Taiwan, and ultimately China. From the beginning, Barbie was produced in durable plastic from advanced molding techniques in a compact and thus portable 11.5-inch format. Each of these elements of Barbie's design brands her as something unique—something that could not have worked at any other time. Most important, Barbie's changing form (as much as her changing representation of gender) demonstrates that if Barbie is a product of her time, she is a product not just of 1959, but of *all* the times and places in which she is and has been produced.

THE BARBIE DOLL

Ruth Handler, the central figure in Barbie's design, claimed that she based the idea for Barbie on what she saw in the doll-play practices of children. Apparently, much of this interaction was overlooked by others—probably because of the dominance of baby dolls on the toy market. Handler noticed that girls were using dolls "to reflect the adult world around them. They would sit and carry on conversations, making the dolls real people. I used to watch that over and over and think: If only we could take this play pattern and three-dimensionalize it, we would have something very special" (Lord 1997, p. 30). However, Barbie was never merely a three-dimensional paper doll. Important design dimensions separate her from earlier fashion dolls, given that both the static and the movable parts of Barbie were assembled in such a way as to maintain a glamorous pose, however she was positioned. This design not only was complex and modern in a technical sense but was also a visualization of the fashion model that relied on the everyday recognizability of glamorous movie poses.

Although it is crucial to think about Barbie's form when talking about the uses and meanings of the dolls, it is equally important to recognize that Barbie's highly successful form, despite its apparent homogeneity over decades, has never been fixed. Changes to Barbie began almost immediately, when her heavy makeup was removed in 1961. Barbie's face alone can be used to map a series of telling changes to the image Barbie is designed to convey. Beginning in 1971, with Malibu Barbie, the doll began to look straight ahead rather than coyly to one side; and with the mid-1970s superstar face mold, Barbie gained as a permanent standard feature a dazzling smile rather than cupid's-bow lips. But across these changes to the standard face, we can also trace the proliferation of minor variations. By the superstar period, we can clearly see the diversification of Barbie into a standard but gradually changing "playline" and its variation in multiple supplementary novelty marketing lines. The same trajectory can be seen in Barbie's bodily form, where some changes are short-lived—for example, the introduction in 1970's "Living Barbie" of jointed ankles, which allowed the doll to wear flat shoes as well as high heels. Others, such as bendable knees and a swivel waist, became part of the standard playline model. The history of Barbie's physical form is one in which gradual design changes mark out the expected parameters of Barbie play, all of which tend toward making her lifestyle play more flexible.

Such variations are always something more than marketing gimmicks. The twisting body that made the sixties Barbie more groovy may have remained, even though her flexible elbows have come and gone. And the bizarre narrative of adolescence in 1975's "Growing Up Skipper" (you wind her arm, and she grows height and breasts), or the various mechanical gimmicks that allow Barbie to have facial movement or be attached to various accessories, are even more transient. But Barbie's variations are always statements about the dominant and possible forms of femininity at a given time. When standard Barbie's exaggerated attached eyelashes were replaced by less pronounced, painted-on eyelashes, this signaled, in part, changes to the role of makeup in dominant images of female beauty as well as changes to the presumed normative relationship between childhood play and adult gender roles. Even novelty changes to Barbie say something about dominant and emergent gender narratives of the time, as with Busy Barbie's (1972) "holding hands" for grasping her accompanying TV, record player, suitcase, and a tray with glasses, reflecting fresh access to newly diverse material goods marketed at adolescents. Changes to Barbie's hair are exemplary in this regard. The move from ponytail Barbie to "bubble cut" Barbie is a story about the displacement of the "teenybopper" by the "mod" as an icon of cool girlhood, and a subsequent model like "Growing Pretty Hair Barbie" (1971) allows girls to play games with the way different hairstyles comprise different—however partial and transient—modes of femininity.

WE GIRLS CAN DO ANYTHING, CAN'T WE BARBIE?

The Barbie doll was never only a "fashion doll," but always a set of opportunities for adding to an image of girlhood. Originally, Barbie appeared with her trademark striped swimsuit, a fashionable ponytail, and optional extra clothes and accessories. In 1961 the Ken doll arrived. Then, in 1963, best-friend Midge was introduced, followed a year later by a little sister, Skipper. By that time, Barbie had clearly left her role as three-dimensional paper doll behind. Fashion continued to be crucial to Barbie, but sometimes she was a girl with her finger on the pulse of the latest style, sometimes there was no more than a fashionable undercurrent to some other role she was portraying, and sometimes fashion was her profession. With each change, Barbie became part of a social network referencing her future, and games about the future perhaps comprise Barbie's most important accessory. If Barbie's form and Barbie's production have changed, they pale in significance next to Barbie's constant renegotiation of ideals about girlhood. Barbie's form, Barbie's narrative, and Barbie's material accessories are all caught simultaneously between images of sexy womanhood, images of adolescent experimentation with gender and identity, and the open-endedness of child's play.

The importance of specific life narratives for Barbie has waxed and waned. For a time in the sixties, she even had parents and a last name (Barbara Millicent Roberts); but the story of "Swan Lake Barbie" can hardly be reconciled with that of "Barbie in Hawaii" or any of the various career Barbies. There are obviously sound commercial reasons for the cast of characters who are all linked to Barbie, but the types of relationships involved in Barbie's characterized accessories are not arbitrary. Barbie has had a brother and no fewer than five little sisters (from Skipper in 1964 to Krissy in 1999), and occasionally "cousins." She has had even more "friends," both boys and girls, either visually and culturally similar to her or different from her, and sometimes with relatives or other life narratives of their own. She has, then, a girl's social networks. It is especially important to understanding Barbie's ongoing changes that Ken's role in her life is sometimes crucial and sometimes peripheral. In 2004 plans were in the offing to make Ken entirely obsolete. But he is still around. And although Ken is only another characterized Barbie accessory, he also stands in for the necessity of the boyfriend accessory to ideal girlhood.

The Ken-and-Barbie question thus becomes part of the debates about the kind of role model Barbie presents that have always been part of Barbie's metamorphosis. Barbie has become an apparatus, in a sense, for thinking about what girls can and should do and want. The contentiousness over 1991 "Teen Talk Barbie"—speaking, among 270 other "teen talk" lines, "Wanna have a pizza party?" and "Math class is tough!"—exemplifies this function of Barbie. On the one hand, this Barbie appeared at the same time as a report critical of inadequacies in girls' education and was criticized by women's groups; on the other hand, the culture-jamming group calling itself the Barbie Liberation Organization emerged to circulate instructions for swapping Barbie's voice box with the vengeance- and violence-laden voice box in Hasbro's talking GI Joe. Both groups used Barbie to mark out a place for public conversation as much as they pointed to the effects Barbie might be thought to have on girls and the dominant images of girls in popular culture.

The impact of feminism on gender norms in the United States has continually been mirrored in Barbie, who has always responded to changing ideas about gender and its implications. Both Prom Queen Barbie and Astronaut Barbie, as well as all of the "forcibly liberated" Barbies produced to counter Mattel's presumed public image, are part of the Barbie girl. Barbie is composed of contradictory images of girls' experiences, pleasures, and aspirations. Although she began as a fashion model, Barbie soon took a turn as a fashion designer (1960). She's been a flight attendant (1961 and 1966) and a pilot (both commercially and in the Air Force). She's had many incarnations as a teacher, since at least 1965. She's been a nurse (1961) and a number of doctors of different types since 1973 (including a surgeon and an Army medic). More than once she's been an ice-skater (beginning in 1975) and a ballerina (first in 1961), but she's also been a football player, a gymnast, an equestrian star, and a NASCAR driver. She's been a club singer (1961) and a rock star with her own band (1987), and she has reincarnated various pop stars, like Beyoncé Knowles (2006). As noted earlier, Barbie has been an astronaut—indeed, far more often than one might expect (1965, 1986, and 1994). She's been a police officer (1993) and a firefighter (1994), as well as a presidential candidate (1991) and even a president (2000). However, Barbie has usually been a more down-to-earth working girl—presented as everything from an office girl to an executive and back again to a "Working Woman," complete with laptop (1999).

Long before the "everythinggirl" slogan of the Barbie Web site, Barbie participated in a discourse on the ongoing expansion of girls' possibilities. Although Barbie as a mode of consumption raises a range of questions about the influence of producers over consumers, the Barbie Web site has also been an important meeting place for consumer subversion since the feminist critiques of the late 1960s. The expansive contradictions of Barbie's careers and the marketing of a public, active, and more independent life for Barbie in the wake of the impact of feminism on girls' expectations are crucially important elements of why Barbie became so famous; Barbie was not only resilient in the face of feminist critique; she also managed to accompany the emergence of feminism as a powerful component of the public sphere and attempted to embrace feminist concerns about girlhood's interaction with gender norms and identities. Feminism and Barbie have thus become interwoven in the cultural economies that circulate ideas about girlhood. Thus the commercial Barbie slogan of the mid-1980s, "We Girls Can Do Anything," can be redeployed as the title of a small-circulation art and text zine—*We Girls Can Do Anything, Right Barbie?*—produced by ten U.S. high school girls in 1997. And it can be done without in any way being outside the reach of girls' Barbie play because the continual making over of Barbie's lifestyle has become entrenched in critical debates about gender roles.

EVERYTHINGGIRL

The dominance of Barbie among girls' toys is not consistent, and changes to Barbie often result from the efforts of Mattel to keep her popular. It's crucial to Barbie's relation to girl culture that Barbie does not embody and does not wear the fashions of her girl users. Barbie enters girl culture as a form of aspirational marketing, presenting ways in which the tween girl can use, produce, or respond to images of adolescence and womanhood that are offered to her from many different sources—sources in addition to Barbie. To no one's surprise, some of these other sources are also dolls, because Barbie has many imitators and descendants. At the present time, Bratz dolls come closer to Barbie's success than any previous alternative fashion doll. In comparison to Barbies of recent years, the Bratz girls may indeed look like, as they claim to be, "The Only Girls with a Passion for Fashion!" because they appear to have a passion for just that one thing. Bratz dolls are modeled, as are the franchised accessories for the girls who play with them, on Barbie's claim to a strong identification between girl and doll—an identification with the doll as a girl rather than as a girl's toy. The legal action between MCA Entertainment and Mattel that is taking place at the time of this writing signals the importance of the Bratz dolls as competitors of Barbie by its evident parallels with the early 1960s lawsuits between Mattel and other companies seeking to capitalize on Barbie's success. In the popular media as well, Bratz dolls have begun to inherit some of Barbie's notoriety, although at present they lack Barbie's capacity to address a long history of debates about and images of femininity. In fact, Bratz dolls may never have that capacity because they are directed less toward the future of their girl users than to a more immediate set of real-life possibilities.

Although countercultural Barbies may be the products of artists, children, and culture jammers, Barbie's mainstream has become increasingly complex, in part because she has come to address very diverse audiences. Barbie was always a multimedia success and has long had a loyal transnational audience, keeping pace with the popular technologies circulating images of her and other "girls" in the expanding field of popular girl culture. She was sold by television from the outset, advertised during *The Mickey Mouse Club* and thus directly to girls in 1959. In 1965 the Mattel Club, whose membership soared in the wake of Barbie's popularity, claimed to have had more members than any other club for girls except the Girl Scouts. And despite predicted or actual declines in Barbie's sales and popularity (which do not necessarily mean the same thing), and with whatever amount of longevity, Barbie's history has been one of media and medium diversification. Across DVDs, computer games, dolls and their accessories, clothing, and other items for Barbie fans to wear and use—from pencils to surfboards to NASCAR helmets—Barbie aims to keep pace with the changing norms, fields, and practices of girl culture.

In the early twenty-first century, in the era of Web 2.0, what "Barbie" encompasses is sold as "everythinggirl." On Barbie.com, a pixel-based version of her now-iconic figure, adapted to look more lifelike, proclaims, "Hi, Barbie Girl!" She is represented in a "home" space dominated by old and new media—from pop-star wall posters to computers. The cross-media expansion of the Barbie franchise is spectacularly evident here, where "girls" can click on online Barbie movie samples, watch previews of Barbie computer games, set up Barbie-narrated "home pages," play interactive online games in which they dress or situate Barbie as they wish, and identify and circulate themselves as Barbie Girls. Barbie's alignment here with computer know-how as much as fashion looks and less historically specific ideals for Barbie continues the long trajectory of keeping Barbie up-to-date with the latest trends in girl life. Nevertheless, even in online formats, it is lifestyle games that still dominate. However technically different it might be to backyard dressmaking or bricolage Barbie homes, dressing Barbie online and reordering her living space continues a set of certainties about girl play and Barbie play.

Networks of discipline and powerful ideologies of gender, body, and self are inseparable from questions of taste and style for today's modern girl. (Although this is also true of today's modern subject-citizen, the girl consumer has long been seen as exemplifying the entanglement between self and commodities.) On the one hand, her long success has inspired commentators to insist that Mattel has "correctly assessed what it means to a little girl to be a grown-up" (Morgenson 1991, p. 66), and on the other hand she has focused ongoing public and popular debate about girls' body images and social expectations. Even before the institutionalization of feminism and its enormous impact on Barbie's role as an aspirational figure, Barbie was never a stable, closed image of mature womanhood. She always stopped before reaching any closure on what it was she could aspire to or achieve. She always stopped, for example, at being a bride: Barbie may have had a "steady," but she was never Mrs. Ken, and her life was the life of an (as yet) single girl. Ken was always an accessory who functioned more as an optional narrative anchor for Barbie than as a doll in his own right; he was an accessory much after the style of Barbie's houses, cars, or horses, and never as crucial as her clothes.

FAB FASHION LOOKS AREN'T JUST A GIRL THING!

As the "most popular woman for sale in all the world" (Lord 2004, p. 300), Barbie now extends from shampoo and bikes for Barbie girls (rather than Barbie dolls) to doggy beds and the "Hot Tub Party Bus" for the Barbie girl's Barbie. But if Barbie computer and online games, for example, still center on the assemblage and the makeover as ways of compiling a complete picture of a girl's life (or of crucial elements of a girl's life), in the menus of Barbie.com a crucial change to the Barbie universe is evident. More subtly positioned between the frames of everythinggirl's options are links that indicate Barbie has other audiences than those who want to play at identifying with Barbie's ideal life. The "Collector" menu tells a rather different story about the *now* of Barbie than does the reproduction of the same Barbie site and same Barbie games in languages other than English under the menu item "Global Barbie."

One of the most complicated elements of Barbie's iconic role, particularly in the last two decades, is the way her representation of girlhood pushes at the limits of, and sometimes clearly exceeds, girl play at being a girl. Mattel's BarbieCollector.com presents an entirely different version of "The Barbie Fan Club" from that produced by Mattel for girls' consumption. Although the two sites are not entirely distinct, as the quiz assessing how well you know Barbie history on Barbie.com attests, the portal for Barbie.com is focused on girl-doll play, while the portal for Barbie Collector frames Barbie as quite a different link between gender and commodification. Whereas Barbie on Barbie.com needs things, and is associated with successful commodification of gender in multiple ways that all articulate gender through commodities, including Barbie herself, Barbie Collector positions Barbie as a history of commodified femininity—from new lines indexing that history, such as the Hollywood glamour dolls styled on old movies, to reproductions of old Barbie dolls.

Barbie collection relies on reference to an archive of images of femininity rather than on any activity that would intervene in the role of these dolls as indexing an archive. That is, whether understood as memorializing ideal femininity or as commercial (bankable) objects, the collector's dolls lose value with any attempt to modify them, even by handling, whereas the Barbie of girl-doll play gains its value precisely from the possibility of being used. Most telling, perhaps, is that the Barbie collection locates Barbie as able to speak to a history that Barbie herself does not need to have been part of. Although "Sleepytime Gal Barbie Doll" reproduces a 1966 costume (despite, as any avid collector would note, introducing some variation on the 1966 doll itself), "Barbie Doll Learns to Cook" is a "vintage repro" doll only in the sense that she reproduces the gesture toward idealized past femininity. This Barbie was never produced before, with her "set of adorable cooking accoutrements—including a 'toaster' and 'toast' slices—[that] add a little bit of humor and a whole lot of fun to this truly whimsical set!" (BarbieCollector.com). She is a 2007 reference to a vision of 1960s femininity that Barbie would never have participated in during that period. Barbie did have outfits suited to domestic chores in the sixties, and there was even—although not presented as glamorous images of womanly life—an idealization of domestic labor in the early Barbies, with aprons and kitchenalia. But there was never a Housewife Barbie in this whimsical sense.

Barbie collecting was always part of Barbie play, as the cast of Barbie characters and the range of Barbie manifestations anticipated. If Barbie is placed on a pedestal/shelf by collectors, then she is equally unattainable for the girl invested in girl-doll play, but the unattainability of Barbie works very differently for girl play than for collectors. In the 1980s, with the Barbie doll's original fans reaching their second or third decade, and early Barbie dolls now old and rare enough to classify as both collectibles and oldwares, Mattel responded to the rise of Barbie collecting with a porcelain doll collector line. Although it is important to recognize that Mattel, from the outset in 1959, always catered to adult consumers as those who might buy Barbie for children, since the 1980s Barbie has been explicitly marketed in two directions: to tween girls, and to consumer groups for whom either the ideal of the tween girl who loves Barbie or the ideal of the adolescent girl Barbie represents for tweens is highly desirable. Even when consumed nostalgically, as an erotic object, as a historical text, or as an object for feminist and other cultural criticism, Barbie represents girls playing with gender.

READING (ABOUT) BARBIE

If no other object marketed as a children's toy has generated as much media interest as Barbie, it is because she has become an icon not only of the importance of what girls aspire to—whether that is to have a dream date and then a dream home, to be impossibly slender, or to be president—but also of the irresolvable openness of girlhood itself. Thus Barbie has become a standard for scholarly discussion of the relations between popular culture, dominant ideologies, and childhood development as much as she has always been a centerpiece for the popular media. No product for girls, no dominant toy of any year, no feminist account of popular culture, and no transnationally marketed representation of the body can entirely escape its relation to Barbie in the Western public sphere; nor can any contribution to intellectual inquiry about girls, girlhood, feminism, embodiment, or commodity culture entirely avoid Barbie.

In academic scholarship about Barbie, there is both widespread concern about the effects of girls playing with Barbie and equally widespread enjoyment in the long spectacle of the Barbie archive; and this notion not only is consistent with the concerns of the mainstream media—if those concerns are articulated differently—but also mirrors the two dominant modes of Barbie consumption. Concern over Barbie play rests on the presumption that gender play is more telling and influential on identity development than other kinds of games, on the simultaneous presumption that girls are more vulnerable to such influence than boys, and on Barbie's special claim to identification between girls and dolls—that girls playing Barbie are indeed "Barbie girls." The reasons why the "action figure" G.I. Joe is not the same kind of doll serve as an apt summary of these arguments: It doesn't matter what G.I. Joe wears, and his "career" or other lifestyle choices are never in question. Plus, there is no sense of there being dramatically different ways of being a G.I. Joe. G.I. Joe references a specific type of action in the world as well as secondary identities associated with that action. A doll is something the player interacts with and does something to—whether dressing up or nurturing or hacking to pieces. An action figurine is, instead, a summary of a set of actions circumscribed by the narrative built into it, and anything else done with G.I. Joe is a counter-narrative. Although Barbie may seem to be similarly constrained by ideal and normative femininity, both her declared and played-out lives are far more open, from president to fairy to office worker to diva to disembodied head for grooming games.

Scholarship on Barbie tends toward either psychological evaluation of Barbie play or cultural studies analysis of the interplay between Barbie, Mattel, Barbie's audiences, and Barbie's cultural contexts. Recent cultural analysis of Barbie is often historiographically inflected, but the emphasis is less on assessing the dangers of Barbie play than on the indeterminacy of Barbie and Barbie play. In this way, such critics participate in the diversification of Barbie that has arisen contemporarily with such scholarship. For example, Erica Rand discusses the openness of Barbie as a sexual image and object in her book *Barbie's Queer Accessories*. Crucial to this, Rand argues, is Mattel's move in the 1970s to divest Barbie of all narrative fixity, including her name, parents, and a clear context for her age or "developmental" position (1995, pp. 58–64). Anne Ducille's (1994) analysis of "ethnic" Barbie friends foregrounds an important example of the complexity that arises from this claimed lack of fixity, considering how "colored" but otherwise standard-playline Barbies like Colored Francie (1967) were displaced by the umbrella Barbie, who could be any ethnicity at all and still be "Barbie," and then supplemented by specialist ethnic body molds. Whereas Rand stresses the openness enabled by Barbie's diverse and contradictory identity, Ducille sees Barbie diversification as an attempt to eschew the stability built into Barbie. The two authors, then, agree that the key characteristic of contemporary Barbie is her multiplicity.

Barbie's variation does, of course, have real limits. Not only are certain kinds of Barbies made, involving choices about whether "Veterinarian Barbie" and "Princess Pink Barbie" represent Barbie in the way Mattel wants, but certain Barbies are *not* made, like "Feminist Barbie" or "Pregnant Teen Barbie." Each of these choices entails a set of predictions and prescriptions about Barbie play. Some kinds of play are not "Barbie" play, even if they involve Barbie dolls. In order to remain Barbie, Barbie will always be a girl, and she must not cross the important sexual boundaries stretching from puberty to the edge of a stabilized image of mature womanhood. But whether in doll play or across the broader range of what now comprises Barbie, Barbie is a territory filled with the practices of knowing and being a girl. From the 1959 slogan "Barbie, you're beautiful" to the leisure-packed home page of "everythinggirl," Barbie negotiates images of ideal and actual girlhood, stretching the idea of the girl to encompass past, present, and future possibilities and exploring which borders and which desires simultaneously define girls and girl culture.

Further Reading

Driscoll, Catherine. (2002). *Girls: Feminine Adolescence in Popular Culture and Cultural Theory.* New York: Columbia University Press.

———. (2005). "girl-doll: Barbie as Puberty Manual." In C. Mitchell and J. Reid-Walsh, eds. *Seven Going on Seventeen.* New York: Peter Lang, pp. 217–234.

Ducille, Anne. (1994). "Dyes and Dolls: Multicultural Barbie and the Merchandising of Difference." *Differences* 6, no. 1, 46–68.

Lord, M. G. (2004). *Forever Barbie: The Unauthorized Biography of a Real Doll*. New York: Walker.
Mattel. [Online March 2007]. Barbie.com Web site http://barbie.everythinggirl.com/.
Mattel. [Online March 2007]. Barbie Collector Web site http://www.barbiecollector.com/.
Morgenson, Gretchen. (1991, January 7). "Barbie Does Budapest." *Forbes*, 66ff.
Rand, Erica. (1995). *Barbie's Queer Accessories*. Durham, NC: Duke University Press.

CATHERINE DRISCOLL

Disney and Girlhood

DISNEY: THE ARTIST AND THE CORPORATION

As an animation artist and a film producer, Walt Disney (1900–1966) was a major contributor to shaping girl culture. Preceding "Steamboat Willie" (1928), which introduced Mickey Mouse to the world, his first success was "Alice's Wonderland" (1923), a comic short film about a live-action little girl interacting with a cartoon world. For the next four years similar shorts, under the collective title *Alice in Cartoonland,* were the focus of Disney's work. From his first full-length feature, *Snow White and the Seven Dwarfs* (1937), to his studio's mature works, which include animated and live action—*Cinderella* (1950), *Alice in Wonderland* (1951), *Sleeping Beauty* (1959), *Pollyanna* (1960), *Mary Poppins* (1963)—Disney always paid close attention to girl culture. Even in films like *Pinocchio* (1940) and *Bambi* (1942), the male protagonists were constructed to appeal both to boys and to girls.

It was not just good business sense that made Walt Disney a success. His passion for the art of animation was the foundation of his work. When asked to make another *Mary Poppins,* he replied, "By nature I'm a born experimenter. To this day I don't believe in sequels. I can't follow popular cycles." During World War II, when his company was shut out from its foreign markets, Disney insisted on experimenting with high-cost technologies and epic-scale masterpieces. Even though the release of *Pinocchio* and *Fantasia* in 1940 had proven that high-budget production was a risky wartime venture, he didn't fold up shop. He produced the film *Bambi* and released it in 1942. Despite the film's high-quality artistic achievements and domestic success, the cost of running the studio, in light of a stock market crash, a labor dispute, and a worldwide depression, took their toll and nearly drove the studio into financial ruin. Not until eight years later, with the release of *Cinderella,* did Walt Disney return to the feature-length animation market.

In 1950, for $1 million, Walt Disney was asked to sell his 350 cartoon shorts to his television sponsor. He refused the offer on the basis that his films were "timeless" for the theater (Maltin 1973, p. 20). But Disney did not reject the new medium. After he turned down the offer, he produced a special one-hour Christmas program to be televised by NBC, but only on the condition that the show would not be interrupted by any commercials. In the meantime, he started a new company, Buena Vista, which would be used to distribute his full-length films. Beginning in 1954, Disney hosted the *Disneyland* TV series in collaboration with ABC. The 1950s also marked the beginning of Disney's live-action productions: *Treasure Island* (1950), *The Story of Robin Hood* (1952), *20,000 Leagues under the Sea* (1954), and others. Although these films were based on well-known boys' adventure stories that were considered classics of children's literature, the adaptations appealed to girls as well.

During this period, Disney diversified further by creating true-life fantasies in amusement parks, beginning with Disneyland, which opened on July 16, 1955, in Anaheim, California. " [Walt] Disney is dedicated to the ideals, dreams, and the hard facts which have created America," California Governor Goodwin Knight said in his speech during the opening ceremonies, "with the hope that it will be a source of joy and inspiration to all the world" (Holliss and Sibley 1988, p. 70). Today "Disney" is an international cultural producer, with film studios, movie distribution companies, cable networks, specialty TV channels, book publishing companies, newspapers, radio stations, amusement parks, resort hotels, cruise lines, clothing lines, and toy outlets—all of which are interconnected.

Especially relevant to girl culture is the fact that the corporation has identified the tween girl market as its primary target since the late 1990s. The culture under the Disney label has had so much influence on the feminine imagination and children's perception of life for so many generations that it is not possible to study girl culture and women's formation of identity without taking "Disney" into serious consideration.

DISNEY CLASSICS

Early Disney experimental shorts are prankish. Free of didacticism, they are about child's play. The main goal of their production is to create laughter, for Walt Disney was hired by sponsors to produce a little humor of the day for the theater. As Disney began to identify with the children's market, his style began to change. By studying Mickey Mouse's change of appearance over time, paleontologist Stephen Jay Gould demonstrated that Disney unconsciously discovered the evolutionary principle of "neoteny" (Gould 1980, p. 104). Because we mammals require parental care for an extended period of time, we developed a natural affection for the baby face (big head, large eyes, bulging craniums, weak chins—in short, the "cute" look) so that we remain attracted to our young. As Gould pointed out, in over 50 years of gradual transformation, Mickey's appearance has grown backward, from adult to baby (pp. 95–107). Walt Disney might not have known the scientific principle, but his identification with the family market was conscious. Not only does Mickey Mouse gradually grow "younger," but he also becomes increasingly better behaved. The use of juvenility in Disney's house style is developed out of a prolonged process of experimentation; it is connected to Disney's role as a perpetuator of the American dream in the family setting.

The mature Walt Disney played the role of educator and cultural guardian. This role was not very different from that of the Grimm brothers and Hans Christian Andersen. Disney's storytelling—original as well as adaptive—had the same motivation as that of the collectors and writers of nineteenth-century fairy tales, who believed these stories should be a tool of domestic education. Their view led to the "refinement" of the old wives' tales: removing coarse language, minimizing sexual and excremental references, and so on (Carter 1990, p. xvii); similarly, Disney's classic tales carry this sense of "refinement." Disney's classic stories are references for life's many challenges, yet also cast a sweetened reality for the wives and children of the traditional household.

At the same time, Disney's masterpieces can indeed underscore a reality that tastes more like dark chocolate than candy. When Disney's classics have happy endings, they do so only in the context of greed (*Snow White*), social discrimination (*Dumbo*), the destructive nature of humanity (*Bambi*), sacrifice (*Old Yeller*), the cycle of life and death (*Perri*), and cruelty (*Cinderella*). As the narrator of *Perri* explains, "Death is a necessary evil; some die that others may survive." Or as *Bambi*'s theme song reveals, "[L]ife may be swift and fleeting; hope may die." *Bambi* can be regarded as Disney's response to a time of darkness, even though it was conceptualized, based on Felix Salten's book, before World War II. The film preserves Salten's themes of life and nature while spinning a poetic realism to portray human destruction. In *Bambi* nature, represented by a harmonious animal world, is set against a common enemy—namely humanity. As film critic Leonard Maltin described it, "The drama in *Bambi* is one of understatement, and its effectiveness is great. Dialogue, which is kept to a minimum, is used in a quiet way to contrast the vociferous nature of the film's climaxes. Man is never shown in the film, yet the simple statement by Bambi's mother, after a frenzied chase with dozens of deer running for shelter, that 'man [pause] was in the forest' creates an impact no literal device could accomplish" (Maltin 1973, p. 56). Although Bambi survives the forest fire caused by the faceless humans—a happy ending, one may suggest—the film is overshadowed by environmental destruction and anguish. Its ending is cathartic, bringing about a release of negative emotions rather than providing a lighthearted, "happy" resolution. In this context, the adorable portrait of the animals in Disney's house style is an effective tool for teaching children about the love of nature as well as the nature of love. Love can be defined as a necessary good that motivates one to confront death for the sake of others' lives. It is an engine of survival.

In general, Disney classics demonstrate a balance between entertainment value and artistic quality, revealing life's various challenges and expressing the diverse emotions that a child might feel. They seem to follow certain thematic patterns, some appealing to children generally and others relating specifically to girls. These themes are addressed individually in the discussion that follows.

Alice's Wonderland

The Alice theme involves the exploration of an imaginary world that is full of illogical wonders. From a child's point of view, the world is magical and strange, often overwhelmingly incomprehensible, so this theme is an attempt to identify with children's confusion and to encourage them to go on with life's journey. Obviously, the entire *Alice in Wonderland* is about meeting strange people in strange places. But the Alice theme also recurs in many Disney classics: the visit to the whale's stomach in *Pinocchio*, the dream of the pink elephants in *Dumbo*, the Never-Never Land in *Peter Pan*, the "Jolly Holiday" episode in *Mary Poppins*, and so on. The journey to the strange world always provides a new perspective on life. Most of the time, Disney's adventurer does not return to reality, concluding, as Dorothy does in *The Wizard of Oz*, that "there is no place like home." The protagonist in Disney's classics gains new insights about life through the magic of fantasia. Figuratively, Walt Disney's version of Alice's wonderland is Disneyland itself.

The Pinocchio Symptom

The Pinocchio symptom is also a key element in *Alice in Wonderland*. Instead of the strangeness of the world, this theme refers to the strangeness of the fast-growing, constantly transforming body of a child. The Pinocchio theme is about coping with growth and socialization. It identifies with children's feelings of being out of control in both body and mind, best represented comically when Pinocchio is partially turned into a jackass. Usually accompanying the Pinocchio symptom is the realization that things will turn out all right in time—that is, when the potential of the character's humanity is fully realized. Beneath the Pinocchio symptom is the promise of the ugly duckling's transformation into a swan (the motif of the ugly duckling being best known through Hans Christian Andersen's fairy tale of that name).

Bambi's Lament

Perhaps because he identified closely with the tradition of fairy tales in great literature, Walt Disney was not afraid of discussing the loss of loved ones with children through stories. The death of Bambi's mother is certainly the most memorable moment in all of Disney's tales. But the theme also has many variations—for example, the imprisonment of Dumbo's mother, Old Yeller's rabies infection, and the entire cursed kingdom in *Sleeping Beauty*. Most of the time in children's films, the loss of a loved one is implied rather than portrayed. The loss of the natural mother in *Snow White* and also in *Cinderella* is a good example. This theme is a main ingredient in the fairy tale tradition. Years ago, as Angela Carter explains, "The maternal mortality rates were high and a child might live with two, three or even more stepmothers before she herself embarked on the perilous career of motherhood" (1990, p. xix). Even with the present-day low rates of maternal mortality, the danger of the world and the unpredictability of life remain. Storytelling is a human way of coping with the hardship and complexity of life; the theme of loss and the cycle of life are crucial to children's mental health.

Dumbo's Flight

Dumbo's flight is particularly fascinating. In contrast to European literary themes that Disney inherited through the tradition of children's literature, it is the most "American" in terms of its social and political assumptions. It dramatizes the idea that, if one finds one's own individuality and strength, one can rise above hostile circumstances and become successful. It encourages children to pursue their dreams and live up to their potential. Structurally, Dumbo's flight requires a character who is socially unpopular and/or emotionally confused. Like Dumbo, not knowing what to do with his life, the character will go through a painful process of self-realization. When the dream is realized, the character will surprise the crowd in triumph. Dumbo's flight does not recur very often in Walt Disney's films because Disney's mantra is more about "never giving up your dream" than about actually "realizing your dream." Nevertheless, this theme will eventually become central to contemporary Disney girl culture.

The Cinderella Fantasy

Similar to Dumbo's flight, the Cinderella fantasy is about coping with hostile circumstances; however, unlike Dumbo, Cinderella finds love rather than a career. Like Snow White and Sleeping Beauty, Cinderella is passive. She has a good heart but no ambition. Escape, not success, is the incentive. Unlike the case with Alice, the ordinary little girl who finds self-control in dreamland, Cinderella's journey is incomplete without her Prince Charming. Although this theme has been heavily criticized for presenting a passive model of femininity to girl viewers, in Walt Disney's defense, he did not produce many princess stories in his lifetime, even though the box office receipts suggested that they had universal appeal. Loved by the public, the Cinderella fantasy is a dream of glamour, a fantasy about transcending the meritocracy of modern life through wish fulfillment in the imaginary space.

DISNEY IDEOLOGY

Entertainment, including a child's bedtime story, is never just entertainment. Cultural products always reinforce or resist (and sometimes both at once) a society's collective social values and belief systems. A film's ideological meanings refer to the ideas that the film conveys about its world's social relations, economic structures, and political institutions. Disney classics are not as timeless as Walt Disney would have liked to think; they all carry the ideological baggage of their time.

Dumbo, for example, is an icon of the American dream; his story takes America's capitalist sociopolitical system for granted. In a socialist context, realizing one's dream to become a star would not be a positive story; like the horse in George Orwell's *Animal Farm*, a socialist hero would sacrifice his or her life for the community without wanting glamour or financial benefit in return. Dumbo's success is measured by a Hollywood contract and a cheering crowd. The irony is that capitalism is ashamed of its own materialist measures, so its stories always add an extra layer to cover the economic drive. Robin Wood calls this surplus "the Rosebud syndrome" (2004, p. 719), a reference to Orson Welles's famous movie *Citizen Kane*. After a lifelong pursuit of power and wealth, Kane, on his deathbed, longs for Rosebud, his childhood sled. Disney's Rosebud may be best represented by the kite of the unemployed father at the end of *Mary Poppins*: it symbolizes the sentiment of family love—one can be poor and happy at the same time.

In a traditional patriarchal American family, the father is the protector and breadwinner, and the mother is the nurturer and caregiver. Consequently, classic Disney male heroes fight for survival and success, while the female protagonist is preoccupied with love and marriage. If she has a job, it is usually babysitting or teaching. This division explains the gender distinction between Dumbo's flight and Cinderella's fantasy. Beneath *Cinderella* is the domestication of women—girls being socialized by their stories to wait in their tower, like Rapunzel for Prince Charming.

That which is rarely represented or altogether hidden can also be ideological. White-male centered, Disney classics rarely feature other races and cultures. If they are represented, they are often stereotyped: the blacks sit by the railway to sing while foreign or aboriginal cultures are locked in their past, romanticized or demonized. For example, the crows in *Dumbo* are one notable representation of African Americans. Seemingly uneducated and unemployed, they nonetheless are happy (Rosebud syndrome).

Similarly, homosexual relations are taboo. Critics like Eleanor Byrne and Martin McQuillan argue that the "brotherhood" of the Merrie Men in *The Story of Robin Hood* and the "friendship" of the Seven Dwarfs project "homosocial desire" (1999, p. 137), but such interpretation may be overdriven by the political scope of the critics. Nevertheless, the difficulty in connecting Disney classics to homosexual themes proves that Disney has a schema of compulsory heterosexuality. Even today, when the issue of gay and lesbian relationships has become an open social discourse, Disney's representation of non-heterosexual orientation remains in the dark, with only an occasional portrait of a womanly man (such as Hannah Montana's stylist) or a comic moment of gender transgression (such as the cross-dressing scene in *Mulan*).

DISNEY REVISION

Rather than being static across time, a society's ideology is constantly changing. Especially in social relations, American ideology has changed a great deal since Walt Disney died in 1966. Our society has been vastly altered by the civil rights movement and the anti-establishment movement of the 1960s as well as by the second-wave feminist movement of the 1970s. Accordingly, the Disney corporation has had to make adjustments.

Decades ago, at a time when fewer than 0.2 percent of Hollywood films involved women as writers or directors, Disney employed Mary Rodgers to write the screenplay for *Freaky Friday* based on her 1976 book. Although *Freaky Friday* appears to portray the stereotypical white middle-class household of its time, the writing exhibits Disney's first feminist critique of North American patriarchy. In the film, Annabel swaps bodies with her mother for a day. After the swap, she immediately sees gender inequality. As her father is leaving home for work, he gives her (presumably his wife) a list of errands to do, saying, "I do my job; you do yours, right?" Annabel thinks to herself, "Oink, oink, Daddy." Later, she comments, "Iron this, polish that, go here, go there—as a dad, you're super. As a husband, you're more like a traffic cop." In the end, when the mother and daughter switch back to their own bodies, Annabel's mother worries that Annabel will be angry about cutting her hair. "How do you like yourself?" she asks. "Well," Annabel replies, "I don't know." Then her mother apologizes. But Annabel responds, "I wasn't talking about the way I look; I was talking about the way I am. . . . I am so much smarter than I thought, and so much dumber." Thus the epiphany of self-knowledge quickly makes Annabel a changed woman. Although that moment of ideological rupture is brief and ambiguous, *Freaky Friday* is the beginning of an era of Disney revision.

However, Disney's revision is not always about incorporating progressive ideas or revolutionary political views. Particularly in the Reagan years (1981–1989), ideological revision often meant taking one step forward and two steps backward. More than those of other major Hollywood studios, Disney pictures tended to stay away from any heated political debate of the time and stood firm in its objective to produce "wholesome" home entertainment.

The new Disney rapidly expanded during the Reagan years. Tokyo Disneyland opened in 1983. At the same time, the Disney Channel (called the Family Channel in Canada) was endorsed by the National Parent Teacher Association and Reagan as "informative, entertaining and wholesome family entertainment." Home video also began to flood into average households. In contrast, Disney's feature films performed poorly in the early 1980s, which led to the establishment of Touchstone Pictures to release films with adult themes such as *Splash* and *Pretty Woman*. Although Disney was busy expanding throughout the globe and re-issuing classics to video stores during the Reagan years, the corporation did not produce as many great animated films as it had in the past. A handful of titles like *The Fox and the Hound* (1981) simply were not up to fulfilling Walt Disney's legacy.

Toward the end of the Reagan era, Disney returned to the children's animation market with *The Little Mermaid* (1989). This film marks a decade of transformation and restructuring. *The Little Mermaid* was the first manifestation of the new Disney, a multinational corporation with an integrated internal marketing strategy for transmedia franchising. At the time, EuroDisney was under construction in Marne, France. Not surprisingly, *The Little Mermaid* and the next major animated feature, *Beauty and the Beast* (1991), were taken from European literary sources. (A similar strategy was employed when Disney entered the Chinese market with *Mulan* in 1998 to bolster Disneyland in Hong Kong.) The new Disney is an integrated corporate cultural producer rather than a focused storyteller. Unlike Walt Disney, who refused to "follow popular cycles," the new Disney is always prepared to remake old classics or direct sequels straight to TV or DVD. Also, the choice of subject in its grand production is carefully coordinated with Disney's theme park development, fashion line, CD release, or even the route of its cruise package. Due to its worldwide expansion, Disney films of the 1990s adopted a broad variety of cultures into the Disney family: Arab (*Aladdin*), African (*The Lion King*), French (*The Hunchback of Notre Dame*), Native American (*Pocahontas*), Chinese (*Mulan*), Greek (*Hercules*), and so on. With a multinational agenda, Disney enfolds the world into its "happy family."

DISNEY WORLD AND GIRL CULTURE

Around the time of *Pocahontas* (1995) and *Mulan* (1998), a new force in the consumer market had been identified—"tweens," a group that fits somewhere between children and teens. The film and entertainment business did not have much of a model for this market, except for a few Japanese TV shows aimed at tweens, such as *Sailor Moon* and *Pokémon*. Disney was in a good position to enter the tween market. First, its strong background in the children's market ensured a smooth transition. Second, stylistically and strategically, it already had a working relationship with the Japanese. The big-eye style of Osamu Tezuka (*Astro Boy*) that defines Japanese animation, for instance, was greatly inspired by Mickey Mouse; in turn, *Kimba the White Lion*, Tezuka's series in the 1960s, inspired Disney's *The Lion King*. Stylistically, Disney animation was ready to make the transition. After the success of *Princess Mononoke* (1999), Disney adopted the distribution rights to Hayao Miyazaki's epics (*My Neighbor Totoro, Kiki's Delivery Service, Whisper of the Heart, Castle in the Sky, Nausicaä*, etc.). Miyazaki is a natural associate for Disney. The Japanese master even is nicknamed "the Japanese Walt Disney." Thematically, films like *Spirited Away* and *Howl's Moving Castle* are essentially more complicated tween re-imaginings of *Alice in Wonderland*.

Miyazaki's female-oriented films provide a sensible echo to the new Disney because, as the company entered the tween market, it soon realized that its competitors (e.g., the Cartoon Network and Nickelodeon) had already captured the boys. The studio soon decided to concentrate on tween girls. A story that appeals to tween girls does not necessarily have to have a female protagonist. Instead, it has to relate to tween girl issues. Of course, male-oriented stories are still made (e.g., *Pirates of the Caribbean* [2003]), but the new focus led to a significant reduction in male-centered adventure movies. In the animated world, most of Disney's male-oriented films are out of Pixar, a studio that thus far has concentrated on films with male protagonists (*Toy Story; A Bug's Life; Monsters, Inc.; Cars;* etc.). The best Disney animations after the year 2000 are female-oriented stories. *Lilo & Stitch* (2002), for instance, is a powerful comedy about a Hawaiian girl from a broken family who turns an alien monster into a loving family member. The portrait of Lilo and her sister's struggle with poverty is so powerful, indeed "edgy," that many critics wonder whether the crew had forgotten that it was making a "Disney" film. But the film is in fact in tune with Disney's new agenda. As Gary Marsh (Disney Channel's entertainment president) revealed, there are five ingredients to successful tween programs: "[T]hey should contain humor, optimism and depict real kids in real-life situations. They should tell an age-appropriate emotional story with situations preteens can relate to. And they should have navigational tools for life that kids can learn from" (Bauder 2007).

Disney's tween girl culture, of course, is modified from its classic themes. In fact, the series of Anne Hathaway films (*The Princess Diaries I & II* and *Ella Enchanted*, from 2001 to 2004) can be seen as the studio's active revision of its past. In these films, Alice's wonderland is replaced by a schoolyard full of everyday struggles with bullies and friends. Entering the school, as shown in the opening scene of *The Princess Diaries,* becomes a standard introduction that is not unlike Alice's fall into a strange new world filled with crazy people. In contrast, the imaginary kingdom of Genovia is sane and controlled, embodying adulthood.

Bambi's lament is habitually hidden in families headed by single parents. Single parenting is normalized. In the case of *The Princess Diaries,* the death of the father, because of a divorce, does not cause any grief, although the father's voice is a determining factor in the princess's actions. But the pattern is not without exceptions. Although neither is about parental death, *Tuck Everlasting* (2002) openly explores the issue of human mortality, and *Bridge to Terabithia* (2007) is a cathartic drama based on a young adult novel about coping with death and grief.

The Pinocchio symptom is a key issue because the emergence of tween culture is overshadowed by the sociological and psychological realization that in some cases children appear to be growing up too fast and too soon. When Mia is told that she is a princess and she can rule a country, she responds, "My expectation in life is to be invisible and I'm good at it. . . . I am no princess; I am still waiting for my normal body parts to arrive." The obedience spell in *Ella Enchanted* also carries the Pinocchio theme. At one point Ella has so little control over her body that she ties herself to a tree in order to avoid committing a murder. For tween girl culture, of course, this comic moment also challenges the society's patriarchal values. Contrary to traditional teaching, disobedience is desirable.

To enhance career-oriented ambitions, Dumbo's flight is now the norm of Disney girl fiction. In a peculiar way, it is combined with the Cinderella fantasy. In *The Princess Diaries,* being a princess is a "job," and Mia accepts the job in the end: "If I were princess of Genovia, then my thoughts and the thoughts of people smarter than me would be much better heard and just maybe those thoughts could be turned into actions." *Ella Enchanted,* an explicit rewrite of *Cinderella,* also characterizes Ella as a social activist. Prince Charmont, the revised Prince Charming, is his uncle's oblivious political puppet. Ella has to transform the prince and save him from his evil uncle. The new figure of Prince Charming—and "love at first sight" in other films such as *The Lizzie McGuire Movie* (2001) and *Read It and Weep* (2006)—is like the prince in Robert Munsch's "The Paper Bag Princess": "You look like a real prince, but you are a bum." Also, a new theme is modulated from the Dumbo-Cinderella merge. In many of the recent "dreams come true" movies, the main characters become overnight sensations about one-third of the way through the story. They then abandon their loyal friends (usually one of whom has a romantic interest) and go out with their love "at first sight." In the end, not only do they learn that Prince Charming (or Princess Smart in *Skyhigh*) is not worthwhile as a person, but they also have to repent, apologizing to their friends for acting like a "jerk."

Nevertheless, Disney's "postfeminist" revision may not be as liberating as it seems. In a DVD interview for the reissue of *Freaky Friday,* Jodie Foster looked back to her role in 1976 and presumed that a remake of the film would give a greater inspiration to women: the daughter might realize that she would have to learn to be independent and become the president of the United States. In reality, the coming-of-age girl in the 2003 remake of the film only wants to be a rock star. On the surface, it may seem that we are in a new age—women's liberation has been achieved. The mother is now an independent psychotherapist instead of a housewife. But, according to Disney, she is incomplete without a man. Unlike Jodie Foster's Annabel, Anna in the 2003 *Freaky Friday* gains no critical understanding of her society; exchanging bodies with her mother only helps her realize that she should accept her new stepfather.

Cinderella's new dream is stardom, and the new magic is fashion design and hair-styling. *The Lizzie McGuire Movie, Ice Princess,* and *High School Musical* all fit into this category. Although these productions appear to be about real kids in real-life situations, they are in fact modernized fairy tales. The new Cinderella dream may be best represented in the three-part Disney Channel production *That So Suite Life of Hannah Montana* (2006). The series melds three popular sitcoms into one master plot that contains all the ingredients of the new Cinderella: Raven (fashion), Zack and Cody (models), and Hannah Montana (pop star). The meeting of the great stars generates the hype, and the sentimental surplus of Rosebud symptom is the game. Miley (the ordinary girl who lives the dream of Hannah Montana) learns that her father might have sacrificed his own dream to be a singer so that she could have hers, and therefore she tries to help her father reclaim his stage. Once again, glamour and success are not everything. For the average viewers to sustain an almost impossible dream of star life, they have to let the star dream for them. Consequently, the star must address the ordinary lives of people. As Hannah Montana sings, "I got everything that I always wanted/Is it always what it seems?/I'm a lucky girl/ Whose dreams came true/But underneath it all/I'm just like you." Such is the fairy tale of the new Disney.

See also Fairy Tales, Modern; Fairy Tales, Traditional; KGOY

Further Reading

Bauder, David. (2007). Disney Hopes to Hit the Tween Jackpot Again. [Online February 6, 2007]. Globe & Mail Web site www.globeandmail.com.

Byrne, Eleanor, and Martin McQuillan. (1999). *Deconstructing Disney.* London: Pluto Press.

Carter, Angela. (1990). "Introduction." In Angela Carter, ed. *The Virago Book of Fairy Tales.* London: Virago Press, pp. ix–xxii.

Cheu, Hoi F. (2007). "Feminist Film Theory and the Postfeminist Era: Disney's *Mulan.*" In *Cinematic Howling: Women's Films, Women's Film Theories.* Vancouver: UBC Press, pp. 1–20.

Gabler, Neal. (2006). *Walt Disney: The Triumph of the American Imagination.* New York: Knopf.

Gould, Stephen Jay. (1980). *The Panda's Thumb: More Reflections in Natural History.* New York: W. W. Norton (reprinted in 1992).

Holliss, Richard, and Brian Sibley. (1988). *The Disney Studio Story.* New York: Michelin House.

Maltin, Leonard. (1973). *The Disney Films.* New York: Bonanza Books.

Tally, Peggy. (2005). "Re-imagining Girlhood: Hollywood and the Tween Girl Film Market." In Claudia Mitchell and Jacqueline Reid-Walsh, eds. *Seven Going on Seventeen: Tween Studies in the Culture of Girlhood.* New York: Peter Lang, pp. 311–329.

Wood, Robin. (2004). "Ideology, Genre, Auteur." In Leo Braudy and Marshall Cohen, eds. *Film Theory and Criticism,* 6th ed. New York: Oxford University Press, pp. 717–726.

HOI F. CHEU

Romance in Teen Publications

One of the most vivid memories of many a young tween girl is trying to figure out how to be "pretty," especially if, by the standards of the day, she is not attractive. As a result, she may subscribe to a teen magazine at the age of 10 and pore over articles that outline makeup strategies to "correct" eyes placed too far apart or too close together, or promote clothing styles designed to conceal bodies that are too pear-shaped, too square, or otherwise "wrongly" shaped. The stakes are high, for she believes that, by purchasing the "right" beautifying products and clothing, she will be more popular at school—and even find a little romance. By the age of 12 she may have added romance novels to her reading repertoire, gossiping with her friends about who had "done it" while passing around a copy of Judy Blume's classic teen romance story, *Forever* . . . in which the well-read portions of the book automatically open to the steamy scenes. These magazines and novels were an important influence on many North American girls' understandings of what it meant to be girls, and on our dreams for our lives as women.

Publications created for adolescent girls are incredibly popular. For instance, the classic teen romance *Sweet Valley High* stories and their offshoot series were distributed internationally in 25 languages with 250 million copies printed (Schoenberger 2002). *Seventeen* magazine will distribute over 4 million magazines in 2007, according to the latest semi-annual publication numbers (SRDS 2006). In schools, girls socialize by circulating and discussing storylines, advice, and fashion found in adolescent publications (Cherland 1994; Durham 1999). Although they are marketed toward women, teenage girls also read publications such as *Cosmopolitan*, *Mademoiselle*, or *Glamour* (Currie 1999).

If simply because of the number of adolescent girls purchasing and reading them, these publications deserve scrutiny. Although dismissed by some as mindless entertainment, these pieces of literature have ideological implications. Millet (1970) stated that the way women are represented in literature influences how they define themselves as subjects in their own lives. Readers often do not critically evaluate these texts or question the patriarchal, capitalistic premises upon which dating and clothing advice is based (Buckingham and Bragg 2004; Christian-Smith 1994; Currie 1999; Durham 1999; Finders 1997; Steele 1999; Willinsky and Hunniford 1986). Therefore, this essay will discuss how mass media serves as an important communicator of social norms by reviewing themes related to sexuality, romance, and consumption that commonly appear in Western publications created for and by adolescent girls.

One important goal of feminist scholarship is generating knowledge of how gender is defined through cultural practices. Dow (1996) argued that critical media analysis is not an effort to create the correct, best, or most widely accepted audience interpretations of a text. Rather, ". . . criticism is an argumentative activity in which the goal is to persuade the audience that their knowledge of a text will be enriched if they choose to see a text as the critic does" (Dow 1996, p. 4). Understanding themes within teen publications increases knowledge of how gender and consumer norms are produced, reproduced, and challenged.

Many scholars have conducted analyses of novels and magazines marketed to and created by adolescent girls. These researchers work under the assumption that these publications *inform*, rather than dictate, readers' understandings of personal identity and social values. Although mass media may not always create ideas, they reconstruct and broadly circulate particular systems of meanings pertaining to gender and consumption. Feminist-inspired media challenge some of these ideas. Therefore, textual critics examine what role media play in both facilitating and opposing dominant ideologies. Given this, textual analyses can provide insight into prevailing ideas of femininity and, equally important, spaces of resistance.

LANGUAGES OF DESIRE

In studies of mainstream teen publications ranging from romance novels to magazines, researchers have found that girls are encouraged to prioritize heterosexual romantic relationships above other interests—and that the ability to obtain a boyfriend or maintain a romantic relationship is directly related to female appearance and consumption of beautifying products (Carpenter 1998; Christian-Smith 1988, 1994; Durham 1996; Garner et al. 1998; Gilbert and Taylor 1991; Mazzarella 1999; McRobbie 1991; Pecora 1999). Articles or storylines written for teens tend to focus on heterosexual sex only, describing it paradoxically as both something to be desired and something to be feared, while primarily focusing on male pleasure and leaving female sexual desire unacknowledged.

Adrienne Rich (1986) has stated that "compulsory heterosexuality" norms are maintained as women receive daily messages through societal myths and conventions. Indeed, in Carpan's (2004) comprehensive listing of over 1600 teen romance novels, a mere 20 books feature gay, lesbian, or transgendered protagonists. A diverse selection of teen romance stories is not widely available (Christian-Smith 1988). Similarly, Carpenter (1998), Durham (1996), and Garner and colleagues (1998) all found a presumption of heterosexuality to exist in popular teen magazines, including *YM*, *Teen*, *Seventeen*, *Glamour*, *Cosmopolitan*, and *Mademoiselle*, published between the 1970s and 1990s. In her analysis of sexual scripts in *Seventeen* magazine over three decades, Carpenter (1998, p. 164) observed that "normative" sex was presumed to be vaginal, heterosexual intercourse, an "either/or decision" rather than a continuum of possible activities. Lesbianism and masturbation were increasingly discussed over the decades, but editors described these as less satisfying than heterosexual sex.

Mainstream publications typically privilege heterosexuality in specific ways. Through editorial advice and storylines, writers promote rigidly circumscribed circumstances for sex, which is depicted as something to be both feared and desired. Furthermore, writers typically focus on only masculine pleasure during sexual encounters.

TEEN MAGAZINES

Durham (1996), Carpenter (1998) and Garner et al. (1998) found that readers were warned that males would pursue sex aggressively and counseled how to avoid it. Recreational sex for feminine pleasure was rarely addressed (Carpenter 1998). Advice column editors and feature stories regularly depicted sex as dangerous for girls by highlighting the risk of hurt feelings, sexually transmitted diseases, pregnancy, and sexual violence (Carpenter 1998). Significantly, one magazine broke from other magazines in its depiction of feminine sexuality. *Cosmopolitan*, a magazine founded during the 1960s sexual revolution, described women as having strong sexual appetites and advised them of assertive sexual strategies (Durham 1996).

Ironically, while most magazine editorial content encouraged girls to be wary of sex, it also encouraged girls to consent to sex once they had established a committed, heterosexual, loving relationship (Carpenter 1998; Durham 1996; Garner et al. 1998). However, in sex-related content, girls' own sexual desires were downplayed; instead the articles focused on how to sexually satisfy a male partner. Durham (1996, p. 24; her emphasis) exemplified this with *Cosmopolitan* articles, which advised readers to convey "genuine interest in *his* pleasure" or "experiment with your lover to find out what thrills *him*." So, despite a more progressive stance toward female sexuality, *Cosmopolitan* still upheld traditional standards of women's primary sexual focus as satisfying male desire. Garner et al. (1998, p. 71) asserted that editorial content ". . . reflected more graphic sexual content rather than sexual agency on the part of women. Overall, male pleasure oriented and drove the advice."

ROMANTIC FICTION

Teen magazines were not the only publications that portray feminine sexuality as something to be tightly controlled and that focus on male pleasure exclusively. After analyzing popular teen romance novels published between 1942 and 1982, Christian-Smith (1988, 1994) found that the storylines promoted feminine sexuality as acceptable in committed, romantic relationships but fraught with dangers such as unplanned pregnancy or rejection. Christian-Smith (1988, 1994) argued that heroes *control* the heroine's sexuality. To be properly feminine, a heroine should "capitulate" to the "masterful" hero. When she "receives" her first kiss, her sexuality is "awakened" by the boy.

Furthermore, the primary focus was on the heroine's emotional reactions rather than physical ones. For instance, in *P.S. I Love You*, the heroine relayed that the hero's touch "had created a tiny tingle of electricity that reached the insides of my heart" (Conklin 1981, p. 213). Similarly, McRobbie (1991) found that romantic fiction printed in the British teen magazine *Jackie!* did not describe sexual desire in terms of female physiological responses. Rather, "the girl's sexuality is understood and experienced not in terms of a physical need or her own body, but in terms of the romantic attachment" (McRobbie 1991, p. 102). In these stories, sexuality for heroines was presented as emotions related to a relationship rather than physical pleasure.

In a study of recent adolescent romance novels, Johnson (2006) found some changes from earlier teen fiction storylines of a completely passive heroine awaiting a hero's kiss. In the contemporary best-selling series *Gossip Girl*, heroines initiated sexual encounters, but only in a narrow set of circumstances. Johnson (2006) stated that, with one exception, female characters in the first three novels of the series initiated sex if they either were under the influence of drink or drugs or were "in love" with their partner. Therefore, some current teen romances retained the relational focus of sexuality present in earlier romance stories (Christian-Smith 1988, 1994; Gilbert and Taylor 1991) and teen magazines (Carpenter 1998; Durham 1996; Garner et al. 1998).

In addition, sexuality was still depicted in terms of male, rather than female, physiological responses, even though the stories were relayed from the female characters' points of view. When characters Vanessa and Dan had sex, Dan noted the "electric current . . . running between them, pinging out of [his] toes, his knees, his belly button, his elbows, and the ends of his hair" (von Ziegesar 2003a, pp. 30–31). However, Vanessa's response to the lovemaking was never revealed. Similar to findings from popular teen magazine studies (Carpenter 1998; Durham 1996; Garner et al. 1998), female sexual agency for personal physical desires was ignored in this adolescent romantic fiction.

ROMANCE AND CONSUMPTION

Numerous researchers have asserted that both adolescent romantic fiction and teen magazines describe romance as an imperative part of being feminine (Durham 1996; Garner et al. 1998; Gilbert and Taylor 1991; McRobbie 1991; Pecora 1999) and even necessary as part of the growth from girl to woman (Christian-Smith 1988; Gilbert and Taylor 1991). Significantly, particular strategies were promoted as routes to obtaining a romantic relationship, which were directly related to the need to create a particular feminine appearance through beautifying products.

Teen publications often included narrow portrayals of an "ideal" physical appearance. Sengupta (2006) stated that ads in *Teen Vogue*, *Seventeen*, and *Fashion 18* supported a white beauty ideal by primarily featuring white women in beauty advertisements. In editorial content, teen magazines explicitly advise readers how to alter their appearances to find romance. For instance, Mazzarella (1999) found that publishers promoted commodities as a route to feminine power in her review of prom sections of issues of *Seventeen*, *Teen*, and *Your Prom*. In order to achieve a successful prom night (and thus a boy's love), a girl must purchase numerous products: teeth polishers for a white smile, enhancing undergarments, purse contents adequate to handle any beauty emergency, and, of course, the "perfect" dress. By following these steps, girls were led to believe they could influence their actual or desired boyfriends through the limited resource of physical desirability, which was achieved through purchasing power.

Teen romances also featured beautifying products and clothing as the route to love. Alloy Entertainment, a marketing company subsidiary, has "developed" best-selling teen novel series that include *Gossip Girl*, *The Clique*, and *The A-List*. In the July 3, 2005, article "Alloy Entertainment behind Girl Book Craze," published in the *Lawrence Journal-World*, Associated Press reporter Colleen Long stated, "Alloy Entertainment operates more like the romance novel industry than a traditional trade publisher. It has a New York staff of about 10 editors who diligently research what's hot in the teen world—what girls are wearing, the music they like, the TV shows they Tivo." Staff members then developed storylines, found writers, and sold books to publishers, but kept the marketing rights (Long 2005). Although Alloy has not publicly acknowledged product placement in their novels, Johnson (2007) found a preponderance of brand names in them.

In an analysis of the first three books in the *Gossip Girl* series, Johnson (2007) found 580 actual brand name references in 643 pages of text. The storylines made specific links between products, romantic relationships, and sexuality. For instance, a character named Vanessa stopped at Victoria's Secret and mused, ". . . Maybe, just maybe, a Very Sexy rose lace plunge demi bra and matching lace tanga were just the type of thing [sic] she needed to make herself . . . irresistible to Dan . . ." (von Ziegesar 2003b, pp. 86–87). In addition, the storylines glamorized the high school–age heroines' uses of particular brands of cigarettes and alcohol. Overall, the use of products in mainstream teen magazines and adolescent romantic fiction modeled a narrow and unhealthy ideal femininity.

While mass media may communicate widely traditional, restrictive norms of femininity, these discourses are neither absolute nor unchanging. For instance, Rosa Guy's *Ruby* featured empowered lesbian protagonists (Bowles-Reyer 1999) and won the American Library Association's Best Book for Young Adults award in 1992 (Carpan 2004). A greater challenge to heterosexual norms comes from adolescent girls themselves, rather than the mass media producers, who often take moderate stances to avoid alienating advertisers and parents.

GIRL-PRODUCED ZINES

Publications produced by adolescent girls, rather than industry, offered alternatives to a commercialized, narrowly defined beauty standard. Kearney (2006), Wray and Steele (2002), and Green and Taormino (1997) illustrated how "grrrl zines" and "gURL e-zines" challenge norms of femininity, including the expectation of heterosexuality. Publications with feminist-inspired themes produced counter-discourses, highlighting a variety of possibilities. Kearney (2006) stated that grrrl zines regularly criticized the "body fascism" promoted by ultra-thin fashion models and the cosmetics and clothing industries. For instance, in the zine *Bikini Kill #2* Allison wrote, "Is being a strong and sexy woman the most powerful form of subversion? Maybe the most powerful for those who are born that way but being a strong and 'non-beautiful' or 'ugly' or 'fat' woman and declaring openly that you like the way you are is the most *defiantly powerful* form of subversion . . ." (Kearney 2006, p. 183; emphasis in original). In addition, zine writers challenged a white beauty ideal by chronicling experiences of girls of color who resisted racial assimilation. Grrrl zines questioned beauty routines and dominant norms of consumption (Green and Taormino 1997; Kearney 2006).

IMPLICATIONS

Adolescent publications can help girls define themselves and dream of potential futures. Given that we live in a traditionally patriarchal, capitalistic society, repeating themes in mainstream publications favoring male-centric sexuality and the necessity of crafting a particular female appearance through purchase are hardly surprising. Writers and publishers, the texts they develop, and adolescent girls' negotiations of meanings from these texts all operate within cultural belief systems. However, cultural norms are not fixed. This fluid nature points to competing discourses as a route to political change through transformation of normative values and behaviors. Grrrl zines and other feminist-inspired publications challenge dominant norms and are an important part of changing social expectations of femininity.

See also Chick Lit; Romance Comics

Further Reading

Bowles-Reyer, Amy. (1999). "Becoming a Woman in the 1970's: Female Adolescent Sexual Identity and Popular Literature." In Sharon R. Mazzarella and Norma Odom Pecora, eds. *Growing Up Girls: Popular Culture and the Construction of Identity.* New York: Peter Lang, pp. 21–48.

Buckingham, David, and Sara Bragg. (2004). *Young People, Sex and the Media: The Facts of Life?* New York: Palgrave Macmillan.

Carpan, Carolyn. (2004). *Rocked by Romance: A Guide to Teen Romance Fiction.* Westport, CT: Libraries Unlimited.

Carpenter, Laura M. (1998). "From Girls into Women: Scripts for Sexuality and Romance in *Seventeen* Magazine, 1974–1994." *Journal of Sex Research* 35, 158–168.

Cherland, Meredith Rogers. (1994). *Private Practices: Girls Reading Fiction and Constructing Identity.* London: Taylor and Francis.

Christian-Smith, Linda K. (1988). "Romancing the Girl: Adolescent Romance Novels and the Construction of Femininity." In Leslie G. Roman and Linda K. Christian-Smith, eds. *Becoming Feminine: The Politics of Popular Culture.* London: Taylor & Francis, pp. 76–101.

———. (1994). "Young Women and their Dream Lovers: Sexuality in Adolescent Fiction." In Janice M. Irvine, ed. *Sexual Cultures and the Construction of Adolescent Identities.* Philadelphia: Temple University Press, pp. 206–227.

Conklin, Barbara. (1981). *P.S., I Love You.* New York: Bantam. Quoted in Christian-Smith, Linda. K. (1994). "Young Women and Their Dream Lovers: Sexuality in Adolescent Fiction." In Janice M. Irvine, ed. *Sexual Cultures and the Construction of Adolescent Identities.* Philadelphia: Temple University Press, pp. 206–227.

Currie, Dawn H. (1999). *Girl Talk: Adolescent Magazines and Their Readers.* Toronto: University of Toronto Press.

Dow, Bonnie J. (1996). *Prime Time Feminism: Television, Media Culture, and the Women's Movement since 1970.* Philadelphia: University of Pennsylvania Press.

Durham, Meenakshi Gigi. (1996). "The Taming of the Shrew: Women's Magazines and the Regulation of Desire." *Journal of Communication Inquiry* 20, 18–31.

———. (1999). "Girls, Media, and the Negotiation of Sexuality: A Study of Race, Class, and Gender in Adolescent Peer Groups." *Journalism and Mass Communication Quarterly* 76, 193–216.

Finders, Margaret J. (1997). *Just Girls: Hidden Literacies and Life in Junior High.* New York: Teachers College Press.

Garner, Ana, Helen M. Sterk, and Shawn Adams. (1998). "Narrative Analysis of Sexual Etiquette in Teenage Magazines." *Journal of Communication* 48, 59–78.

Gilbert, Pam, and Sandra Taylor. (1991). *Fashioning the Feminine: Girls, Popular Culture, and Schooling.* North Sydney, Australia: Allen and Unwin.

Green, Karen, and Tristan Taormino, eds. (1997). *A Girl's Guide to Taking over the World: Writings from the Girl Zine Revolution.* New York: St. Martin's Press.

Johnson, Naomi. (2006, November). "'All I Want Is Everything': Feeling and Framing Rules for Sexuality in a Best-Selling Young Adult Romance Series." Paper presented at the annual meeting of the National Communication Association, San Antonio, TX.

———. (2007, February). "'All I Want Is Everything' (Expensive): A Feminist Analysis of Product Placement in the Teen Romance Series *Gossip Girl*." Paper presented at the annual meeting of the Western States Communication Association, Seattle, WA.

Kearney, Mary Celeste. (2006). *Girls Make Media.* New York: Routledge.

Long, Colleen. (2005, July 3). "Alloy Entertainment Behind Girl Book Craze," *Lawrence Journal-World,* 5.

Mazzarella, Sharon R. (1999). "The 'Superbowl of all Dates': Teenage Girl Magazines and the Commodification of the Perfect Prom." In Sharon R. Mazzarella and Norma Odom Pecora, eds. *Growing up Girls: Popular Culture and the Construction of Identity.* New York: Peter Lang, pp. 97–112.

McRobbie, Angela, ed. (1991). *Feminism and Youth Culture: From "Jackie" to "Just Seventeen."* Boston: Unwin Hyman.

Millet, Kate. (1970). *Sexual Politics.* New York: Doubleday.

Pecora, Norma. (1999). "Identity by Design." In Sharon R. Mazzarella and Norma Odom Pecora, eds. *Growing Up Girls: Popular Culture and the Construction of Identity.* New York: Peter Lang, pp. 49–86.

Rich, Adrienne. (1986). *Of Woman Born.* London: Virago.

Schoenberger, Chana. R. (2002, October 28). "A Valley Girl Grows Up." *Forbes,* 114.

Sengupta, Rhea. (2006). "Reading Representations of Black, East Asian, and White Women in Magazines for Adolescent Girls." *Sex Roles* 54, 799–808.

SRDS. (2006, Winter). *SRDS Consumer Magazine Advertising Source.* Des Plaines, IL: SRDS.

Steele, Jeanne Rogge. (1999). "Teenage Sexuality and Media Practice: Factoring in the Influences of Family, Friends, and School." *Journal of Sex Research* 36, 331–341.

von Ziegesar, Cecily. (2003a). *All I Want Is Everything: A Gossip Girl Novel.* New York: Little, Brown.

———. (2003b). *Because I'm Worth It: A Gossip Girl Novel.* New York: Little, Brown.

Willinsky, John, and Mark R. Hunniford. (1986). "Reading the Romance Younger: The Mirrors and Fears of a Preparatory Literature." *Reading-Canada-Lecture* 4, 16–31.

Wray, Jennifer, and Jeanne Rogge Steele. (2002). "Girls in Print: Figuring Out What it Means to Be a Girl." In Jane D. Brown, Jeanne Rogge Steele, and Kim Walsh-Childers, eds. *Sexual Teens, Sexual Media: Investigating Media's Influence on Adolescent Sexuality.* Mahwah, NJ: Lawrence Erlbaum Associates, pp. 191–208.

NAOMI R. JOHNSON

Style and Girl Culture

A girl's style includes anything that embellishes, covers, or decorates her body. Articles of clothing, such as jeans, hoodies, tank tops, T-shirts, dresses, and skirts, are a part of girls' style. Accessories, such as jewelry, belts, hats, scarves, backpacks, purses, bags, and shoes, are a part of girls' style. Bodily adornments, such as hair color, makeup, piercings, and tattoos, are a part of girls' style. Accoutrements, such as buttons, iPods, earphones, Discmans, cigarettes, and even books and CDs, are a part of girls' style. But, beyond these individual items, style and girl culture refers to the way in which all of these elements interact and come together to create an overall "look." A girl's look is the effect she achieves through her style, whether goth, punk, skater, preppy, dressy, sophisticated, sporty, random, gang, Hip Hop, alternative, mainstream, hippy, straight-edge, grunge, club, skid, metal head, or other expressions that girls might use to describe their look, such as "pretty normal," "just regular," or "totally average." But this list is not exhaustive. A complete taxonomy of girls' style is impossible given the permutations and combinations that exist. Style is ultimately a form of creative expression unique to each girl.

While style is something that exists on the surface of the body, it carries enormous depth. Style functions as an accessible and malleable form of embodied subjectivity and expression for girls, becoming a marker of gender, race, ethnicity, class, sexuality, age, and even nationhood. It is an integral part of how girls insert themselves into the social world as both individuals and members of groups. Style enables girls to signal belonging, friendship, conformity, religious beliefs, politics, resistance, rebellion, ambivalence, anger, desire, cultural and lifestyle affiliations, individuality, image, and personal taste. As a result of these complex and overlapping articulations, style is always more than "just fashion." It is a tool for identity construction and negotiation ("Who am I?"). It is a form of power. Style is also a form of bodily discipline or control and is an essential part of how girls engage in and create culture. It is inextricably entwined with global capitalism and constructions of girlhood within the marketplace. It is also one of the primary ways that girls make meaning in their everyday lives.

STYLE AND EXPLORING: "WHO AM I?" "WHO AM I BECOMING?"

While the idea of identity has traditionally been seen as something stable and unchanging, new definitions of identity incorporate the idea that identity can be "in progress" and "in flux." Stuart Hall, a well-known cultural theorist, defines identity as the suturing or stitching together of two things—how we have been represented by others and how that positioning affects how we might represent ourselves. This way of thinking about identity is contextual and relational. Identity is not felt as the same in all situations, but shifts and adapts within a given social setting. For girls, identities might change in different contexts: school, home, mall, work, friends' houses, and elsewhere—as well as in relation to different people: teachers, parents, peers, boys, siblings, best friends. Not only are girls constructed differently in each of these contexts, but they engage in different performances of girlhood. They are positioned by others ("this is my little girl," "act your age") and they seek to reposition themselves ("I am not a little girl any more"). Girls become attached to particular storylines of the self, but when the context changes, other storylines become prominent and identity shifts yet again.

Style operates as a tool for playing with identity precisely because it enables girls to shape how they have been positioned by others. Their embodied self, or embodied subjectivity, as scholars call it, suggests that the mind and body are not split, but rather operate in tandem as a single unit. The mind (on the inside) and the body (on the outside) work in the formation of conscious expression. Yet the body is never naked in society; it is always dressed. As such, style is an elaboration of the body, adding dimensions and details that would otherwise not exist. As an unavoidable feature of social existence, style operates as a vital locus of embodied subjectivity enabling girls to shape how they have been positioned by gender, race, ethnicity, class, sexuality, age, nationality, and other constituting forces.

Style operates as a type of social skin. As social skin, style is more than an extension of the body—it *is* the body in public space. Style grants not just visibility but meaning to the body, revealing and releasing it, cloaking and confining it, shaping it and giving it definitions, borders, and folds. Style fashions the body into a social text that can be "read." When girls dress for a given situation or social event, such as a trip to the mall or getting ready for the prom, they do so knowingly and with forethought about how they wish to represent themselves. Girls' style announces to others how they want to be seen, treated, and experienced as embodied subjects. Girls' social visibility is wrapped up in style; their identities are contingent upon it.

Nowhere is the connection between style and identity more apparent for girls than in the school. As the place where girls spend the majority of their time, the school functions as a central social world where belonging and the cultivation of an image are often seen as crucial features of survival. The school is also a key site for the construction of girlhood through discourses that describe, define, and restrain how girls "should" act and look. The school is therefore the stage upon which a particular performance of identity is rendered, one that relates specifically to how a girl wishes to be seen. Sometimes this is called a "symbolic economy of style." A symbolic economy of style refers to the linking of specific items of clothing to specific lifestyle affiliations. For example, girls who wear a particular brand of jeans may be seen as popular, girls who wear particular sneakers may be seen as skaters, girls who wear dog collars may be seen as punks, girls who wear baggy track suits may be seen as hip hoppers, girls who wear bandanas of a certain color may be seen as gang bangers, and girls who wear particular brands may be seen as belonging to various racial and ethnic groups. As Julie Bettie (2003, p. 62) writes in her high school ethnography of girls' raced and classed identities, "Hairstyles, clothes, shoes, and the colors of lipstick, lip liner, and nail polish, in particular, were key markers in the symbolic economy that were employed to express group membership as the body became a resource and a site on which difference was inscribed."

Group membership is based on an understanding of the symbolic economy of style that operates within each school context—a context that shifts from city to city, neighborhood to neighborhood, and even from school to school. What is cool in one school is not what is cool in another, causing the same item of clothing to operate quite differently in different contexts. While a girl cannot become "anything" or "anyone" just by changing her clothes, style serves as a visible code that enables girls to understand each other as the same. This process of identification is a central one for group formation and membership. If identity is the public performance of "who" a girl is in a given context, then identification is the private struggle for belonging that makes that performance possible. Identification is often based on desire, longing, acceptance, and feeling connected to others. If a girl identifies with a particular social group, it means she recognizes herself in them and sees herself as one of them. Conversely, a girl experiences "dis-identification" when she feels no affinity for a social group and does not recognize herself as one of them. Style is one of the key ways in which identifications and dis-identifications occur in the school. Girls forge social groups based on the recognitions that take place through style. Style thus plays a key role in the struggle for inclusion and exclusion in the school.

As social skin, style acts as a bridge between public performance and private thought, between action and emotion, between the body and the mind, between the self and the social. Because of these powerful convergences, style can be viewed as a porous covering enabling girls to transfer something of themselves into the social world, as well as enabling the social world to transfer something of itself to girls. Style is thus an entrance into and an exit out of girls' "in flux" identities, affecting how they understand themselves in relation to the social world and to each other.

STYLE AS AGENCY AND POWER

Style can also be viewed as a form of agency. Agency is related to the decisions we make and actions we take *within*, and not outside of, discourse's affect. In other words, girls make decisions within a range of possibilities. This way of thinking about agency suggests that girls' choices of style are not without limitation; they are not entirely "free" choices. Girls are constrained by a host of factors that may impact how they choose to dress: parental control, economic resources, peer and media pressure, cultural and religious restrictions, racial and ethnic codes, body type, homophobia, and gender normativity—among many others. While girls may see themselves as fixed within narratives beyond their control, they may also feel that they have the power to modify how they are positioned within and by those narratives—particularly through style.

Style as a mode of agency can offer girls the power to make either subtle or explicit changes to their images. An image is dependent upon a girl's "look" to showcase her personality, interests, and affiliations. A girl may try on a variety of images throughout her schooling or may develop one specific image over a period of years. But however a girl chooses to play with her image, its cultivation highlights the identity materials made available to girls within their specific positioning. This active engagement enables girls to gain some measure of control over how they have been shaped by structures beyond their control. In this way, not only are modification and transformation possible, but a form of power is made available to girls who might otherwise feel lost or trapped in the narratives that govern their lives. Using style to craft an image enables a girl to inscribe herself, rather than simply being inscribed by others—to use her own voice to speak back to how she has been spoken to. Girls may spend a great deal of time cultivating, renovating, and re-inventing their images while simultaneously laboring to ensure that they appear authentic and not posed. Images are staged representations of identity, but ones that must appear "natural" and "organic" if they are to be believed.

As a form of agency, style is used to purposefully shape how a girl is seen by others. For instance, a girl who is known to be quiet at school can use elements of style to become more socially visible; a girl with a religious background can use style to showcase another side to her personality, such as music lover or athlete; a social outcast can use style to forge an unforgettable image; a preppy girl can seek to become less mainstream by wearing clothing deemed to be unfashionable; an academic girl can be seen as sporty by wearing a "real" track suit and "real" sneakers; a girl who feels like one of the crowd can distinguish herself as alternative by wearing facial piercings or by dyeing her hair a different color; a girl can cultivate a laid-back image by refusing to care about what she wears and by doing her own thing; a girl can become affiliated with a different race or ethnicity by engaging in particular elements of style that signify her belonging to that cultural group. A girl may also use style to complicate her image, to keep others from guessing "who" she is, or to engage in what might be described as hybrid forms of identity, where several identities are tried on at the same time. For example, as noted above, a girl might test out being sporty and academic at the same time.

The cultivation of particular images offers insight into the ways that girls may seek explicit forms of power and authority in their own lives. They may cultivate an image from a particular subculture such as punk, goth, hip hop, skater or rave—to name just a few. Doing this may offer a particular form of power that enables girls to critique mainstream girlhood. While little has been written specifically on girls in subcultures, Lauraine Leblanc's (1999) study of punk femininity explores the ethos of DIY, or a do-it-yourself attitude. Girl punk style resists uncomplicated, sweet, and innocent femininity and takes up instead the more complicated bricolage, or combinations of "looks"—aimed at critiquing not just parental or corporate culture but also the masculine edge of the punk subculture, often viewed as misogynist and anti-female. Creating their looks from "found objects," used clothes, and a bondage gear aesthetic, girl punks use style to forge an image of resistance, intimidation, and anger. Using fashion against itself, girl punks often put traditionally feminine items, such as skirts, makeup, and fishnet stockings, together with harder-edged items, such as dog collars, chains, combat boots, and facial piercings. Marked by irony and parody, girl punk style plays with traditional gender norms and pushes the boundaries of what is and is not acceptable for girls in the social world.

While subcultural affiliations can offer counter-cultural examples of style as a form of power, the most common kind of power that teenage girls seek to generate through style is one based on a dominant view of female sexuality. Sexual power within a heterosexual matrix is perhaps the most utilized form of power that teenage girls enact through style, triggering a long-standing feminist debate. In second-wave feminism, pro- and anti-sex camps have debated the issues surrounding sexual power since the mid-1960s. Pro-sex feminists see sex and sexuality as sources of empowerment for women, and anti-sex feminists see sex and sexuality as forms of heteronormative control used to objectify women. More recently, third-wave feminism has addressed sexual power as a tool for independence, liberation, and pleasure. The personal enjoyment of sex and sexuality has also become associated with postfeminism, where individual power ("It's all about me") has superseded a collective politics ("United we stand"). Using sex and sexuality as forms of power has thus been dubbed "do-me," "lipstick," or "babe" feminism and conflates the pursuit of sexual pleasure with the end of gendered oppression. Girls' style has mimicked this conflation with T-shirt slogans such as "hottie," "dream on," "sex fiend," "slut," "porn star," and "pay to touch."

But sexual power through style is not available to just anyone. A teenage girl must fit into a particular mold of heterosexual beauty and be seen as conventionally "sexy." To be conventionally "sexy" is to emulate the mainstream pop and film stars of the day. In the early twenty-first century, such stars include Britney Spears, Christina Aguilera,

Jennifer Lopez, Lindsay Lohan, and Paris Hilton. The styles made popular by these stars include low-rise jeans, visible thongs and bra straps, exposed cleavage, midriff-revealing T-shirts and tank tops, and pants that fit tightly, showing the outline of a girl's figure. Despite their controversial nature, it is hard to ignore the ways in which teenage girls use these items of apparel to cultivate their images. Such an image may offer teenage girls power in the school's symbolic economy of style, where conventionally "sexy" dress might equal popularity, attractiveness, thinness, preppiness, status, and the ability to get boyfriends. While this kind of influence has been critiqued within certain feminist circles, it is the one power girls are taught to utilize from a very early age. Though girls are told that using sexy modes of dress to gain attention is empty and shallow, they see ample evidence of this power in magazines, on television, and in films. Given this contradictory message, it is not surprising that teenage girls view a sexual power attainable through conventionally "sexy" styles as a quick way to garner attention and status.

UNDER THE GAZE 24/7: STYLE AS CONTROL

While style offers girls opportunities for testing out different identities and for agency and power, it can also function as a form of control and as a way of disciplining the body. The French philosopher Michel Foucault (1977) theorizes that those who are always under the gaze will start to regulate themselves and internalize forms of bodily discipline. In Foucault's examples, such populations include prisoners, mental patients, and students, whom those in authority may at any and every moment be watching from covert locations. Never knowing when the gaze will fall upon them, Foucault suggests that members of such populations become their own disciplinarians and learn to govern themselves. As a result, it is not the constant surveillance that disciplines the body, but rather the *threat* of constant surveillance. Foucault sees this threat as an "unequal gaze"; one never knows when or from where the gaze will come, only that it is out there, lurking in the shadows. Foucault calls this form of surveillance the panopticon, named after a prison design with a central tower that enables guards to peer into any cell at any time. Never knowing when they are being watched, prisoners must always be on their best behavior.

Like prisoners in the panopticon, girls are under constant scrutiny in North American society. Even in moments when the gaze of boys, other girls, security guards, sales people, teachers, school administrators, and parents does not fall upon them directly, girls may still feel the gaze as a result of having internalized its constant presence in their lives. Girls become used to being looked at and begin to see surveillance as a natural feature in their lives. As a result, girls gaze upon themselves, wondering if they are thin enough, pretty enough, smart enough, sexy enough, well dressed enough, or ritzy-looking enough for those who would gaze upon them. Girls patrol the borders of their own bodies in anticipation of the judgment of others. Girls thus exist in a perpetual panopticon where they are observed, if not by others, then by themselves as a form of self-regulation and control that can feel like a self-imposed prison.

Style is one of the most immediate ways for boys to scrutinize and judge girls. While not all boys will make comments about how girls look in their clothes, such judgment is often a common feature of girls' experiences of schooling. For example, boys may comment on how a girl looks in her jeans: "You look hot in those jeans," "you look fat in those jeans," "you look disgusting in those jeans," "you should *not* be wearing those jeans," or "those jeans make your ass look big." Such comments may become internalized by girls, who hear what boys will say even before they say it and judge themselves accordingly when trying on clothes in a store or getting dressed for school. As dressed bodies, teenage girls are inspected, dissected, rated, ogled, praised, lusted after, and overlooked by boys. Girls may anticipate this judgment, wait for it, cringe at it, dish it back, or pay little attention to it. While the male gaze can be resisted and, to some extent, ignored, it still holds powerful sway over how girls think about themselves and their dressed bodies.

But the male gaze need not be confined to the school. It is a gaze that exists in North American society generally. Emanating from a culture that demands perfection from the female form, girls are literally soaking in surveillance, not just in their "real" lives, but in the forms of popular culture that surround them. On reality TV shows, such as *America's Next Top Model* and *Pussycat Dolls Present: The Search for the Next Doll*, young women must withstand constant scrutiny en route to celebrity. Style as bodily discipline is a major component of these shows, from fashion makeovers to photo shoots to the cultivation of just the right image. Dressed bodies are then posed, inspected, insulted, remade, picked over, stripped down, and rebuilt. From these popular texts, girls learn how to dress in a way that is pleasing to the judges based on styles that are conventionally "sexy." They also learn to endure surveillance of their dressed bodies as a normal feature of femininity.

Perhaps just as influential, however, is the policing of girls by their peers. Girls' observation of other girls' styles is part of the internalization of the male gaze. Rivalries are fostered among girls, who are forced to compete with each other for boys' attention. Girls thus use criteria that boys would use on them in order to scrutinize other girls' dressed bodies. The most common example of this judgment is the "slut" label. Girls call other girls "sluts" or "skanks" as a means of "othering" them. In the school, the "slut" label pertains more to how a girl dresses than to any sexual activities in which she might engage. A girl may be called a "slut" for wearing conventionally "sexy" styles as a means of controlling her popularity or social status. A girl may be called a "slut" for wearing clothing that is considered to be "trashy" or "hoochie," drawing on racial and ethnic discourses. A girl may also be called a "slut" for wearing clothing that is considered to be "dirty" or "poor," drawing on class-based discourses. These labels have the power to link specific modes of dress to specific forms of girlhood and femininity, signaling which girls have disciplinary power in the school and which girls do not. In making fun of how a girl dresses, other girls can cause her to feel panic about her body, her image, and her performances of gender, race, ethnicity, class, and sexuality.

Aside from these forms of policing the dressed girl's body, no example highlights the disciplinary nature of style more than school dress codes. Dress codes appear to be a neutral school policy, but actually function as what Foucault (1978) calls a "regulatory ideal." This ideal is often based on a white, middle-class, heterosexual form of femininity. Sexual, racial, and ethnic differences that may inform how girls dress are often overlooked in the writing of this formal school policy. Consequently, dress codes form what Nancy Lesko (1988) calls a "curriculum of the body" that teaches girls how to see styles—and thus the people inside of them—as either normal or abnormal.

Recently, a new generation of dress codes was written in schools across North America in order to address the "hyper"-sexual styles that have come into vogue in the early twenty-first century. Items that have been banned from many schools include low-rise jeans that show a girl's underwear, micro mini-skirts, midriff-revealing tops, shirts that show cleavage, and spaghetti-strap tank tops. The focus on controlling girls' bodies makes transparent the power that dress codes have to regulate femininity and sexuality by banning particular performances of girlhood. Instead, dress codes offer a singular view of girl-hood marked by whiteness, heteronormativity, and a denial of sexual desire in the school.

STYLE AS CONSUMER GIRL CULTURE

Girls have been identified as one of the largest markets in today's global economy. Girls engage in more discretionary spending than any other generation before them, making them not just a large market, but a much-targeted one as well. In the hopes of tapping into girls' needs, marketers have labored to understand what girls want, what they buy, and what they wear. This emphasis on consumer girl culture has created a frenzy around the North American girl, making her the object of competition, curiosity, and intensive research. As a result, more and more products have become available to girls, marketed directly at them in venues that have been created for the express purpose of capturing the attention of the tween and teen girl consumer. Such venues include *Teen Vogue*, *Cosmo Girl*, and *La Senza for Girls*. Not coincidentally, the term "tween" has recently come into use, defining and grooming a market that previously did not exist. A tween is a girl between the ages of 9 and 13—no longer a child, but not yet a teenager. The creation of cohorts, generations, and groups is a standard theme in the marketing world as stores and advertisers strive to create common denominators in order to attract the widest possible array of girl customers.

Because style is one of the primary elements of consumer girl culture, the mall is one of the most popular girl hangouts. Due to age constraints and parental regulations, girls do not always have access to the streets or other public places. But the mall provides girls with a safe venue for socializing, hanging out, and having fun. It also provides girls with ample access to stores that will allow them to emulate their favorite pop and film stars. Girls interested in emulating Jennifer Lopez might purchase a velour track suit. Girls interested in emulating Paris Hilton might purchase a baby doll dress. Girls interested in emulating the Olsen twins might purchase oversized sunglasses or items of apparel from their popular clothing line. Girls interested in emulating Avril Lavigne might purchase black Converse high-top sneakers or a studded belt. These styles are made famous by stars but retailed to girls by marketers, who carefully package the cultural ideals that such stars represent.

But the question remains, who is influencing whom? Do girls drive consumer girl culture through their interests? Or do marketers tell girls what they want to buy, thus creating the illusion of need? In the *Frontline* documentary *The Merchants of Cool* (Goodman 2003), this cycle is called the feedback loop, meaning that it is impossible to determine who sets trends in motion. Styles become trendy when girls take them up en masse, seeing them as necessary purchases. But marketers also create trends by telling girls that one particular item of apparel or look is the must-have of the season: Ugg boots, crocs, skinny jeans, peasant skirts, crop tops, b-Ts, 80s retro, kimono dresses. But beyond these individual trends, girls' style has become a feature of global capitalism, where everything is inter-connected through multimedia conglomerations. Bratz dolls sell girls' clothing. *Seventeen* magazine sells girls' clothing. MTV sells girls' clothing. *America's Next Top Model* sells girls' clothing. Music companies sell girls' clothing. As a result, girlhood itself has become the product. Packaged as an outfit, a song, a video, an ethos, girlhood is now a commodity sold to girls as new and improved versions of themselves.

Because girls spend a great deal of money in the global marketplace, consumer girl culture has been viewed as nothing more than passive engagement with mass cultural domination. Girls are often constructed as the ultimate dupes who will buy anything that marketers tell them is "cool." But as Catherine Driscoll (2002, p. 186) notes, just because something is connected to girlhood does not mean that it should be thrown on the "scrap heap of mass culture" and deemed insignificant. The devaluing of consumer girl culture suggests that "girl things" are not taken seriously as cultural forms. It also suggests that girlhood itself is unworthy of any "real" attention. This perspective constructs girls as "clueless" consumers, rather than participants in popular culture; but popular culture is an arena of consent and conflict, where power must be won rather than assumed. While girls certainly spend their money in the global marketplace, they also have a tremendous amount of authority in selecting their purchases. If girls choose not to buy a particular item, marketers have no choice but to respond. Girls and marketers thus exist in mutual tension as girls exert the power to shift marketing expectations by simply refusing to buy what marketers assume they will want.

STYLE AS FUN AND FANTASY

For many girls, style is a form of pleasure, whimsy, and entertainment. Girls use style as a feature of socializing. Girls pore over magazines together, looking at and talking about style. Girls discuss their own styles with each other, asking for counsel and feedback from trusted friends. Girls try on clothes together and engage in conversations about how they want to look. Girls shop together, looking for outfits for specific events or unspecified amusements. These conversations open up spaces for discussions related to body image, constructions of gender, advertising and marketing, the production of trends, and the pressure girls feel to look and dress certain ways. Such conversations have the power to create rapport, friendship, and community as well as critical and feminist thinking. While not all girls enjoy talking about clothing, those who do can forge intimacies over style, strengthen relationships with others, and engage in both lighthearted and deep conversations. Style also provides girls with a venue for fantasy that allows them to play with alternative ways of performing girlhood. When looking at clothing in stores, girls can talk through their desires to dress differently with friends and test out new ways of embodying subjectivities. In these discussions, girls may recognize ways of being that they had yet to think about, or gain approval for an idea that they had only been toying with in secret.

Girls can also use style to fantasize about desires, sexualities, and lifestyles without having to give them public voice. In their imagination, girls can try on outfits that they would never wear in public for fear of ridicule or risk. Girls can employ infinite styles in make-believe scenarios. Style as imagined costume opens doors for fantasies that might otherwise seem impossible, dangerous, or intimidating. Alone in her room, a girl might use style similarly, enacting performances of girlhood in clothing borrowed from friends, siblings, and parents. It is here, in private space, where girls can gather the courage to debut an image at school or elsewhere, practicing how to look and be in clothes that could open new doors for identity.

Clothing as a creative cultural expression allows girls to adorn and adore their bodies, to feel good about themselves, to feel "sexy"—however a girl may interpret that word—to feel professional, to feel smart, to feel strong, to feel athletic, to feel a sense of belonging and pride, and to see themselves differently—not just through the eyes of others, but in their own minds' eye. Style can change how a girl walks, talks, and carries herself. It can instill confidence and bring delight. It can enable girls to create their own world and make their own mark. It can offer cohesion like sports uniforms, gang insignia, or recognizable features of racial or ethnic groups do. It can offer a form of fun to girls in public or private. While easily critiqued by adults who may not always understand its purpose, style is anything but a superficial consideration in the lives of girls. Though riddled with complexities that evoke critique, style is a serious issue for girls, who use it to infuse their lives with significance and meaning.

Further Reading

Bettie, Julie. (2003). *Women without Class: Girls, Race, and Identity*. Berkeley: University of California Press.

Driscoll, Catherine. (1999). "Girl Culture, Revenge and Global Capitalism: Cybergirls, Riot Grrls, Spice Girls." *Australian Feminist Studies* 14, no. 29, 173–195.

———. (2002). *Girls: Feminine Adolescence in Popular Culture and Cultural Theory*. New York: Columbia University Press.

Foucault, Michel. (1977). *Discipline and Punish: The Birth of the Prison*. London: A. Lane.

———. (1978). *The History of Sexuality: An Introduction*. Robert Hurley, trans. New York: Vintage Books.

Goodman, Barak. (2003). "The Merchants of Cool." *Frontline*.

Hall, Stuart, and Paul Du Gay. (1996). *Questions of Cultural Identity*. London and Thousand Oaks, CA: Sage.

Leblanc, Lauraine. (1999). *Pretty in Punk: Girls' Gender Resistance in a Boys' Subculture*. New Brunswick, NJ: Rutgers University Press.

Lesko, Nancy. (1988). "The Curriculum of the Body: Lessons from a Catholic High School." In Leslie G. Roman, Linda Christian-Smith, and Elizabeth Ellsworth, eds. *Becoming Feminine: The Politics of Popular Culture*. London and New York: Falmer Press, pp. 123–142.

Pomerantz, Shauna. (2006). "'Did You See What She Was Wearing?' The Power and Politics of Schoolgirl Style." In Yasmin Jiwani, Candis Steenbergen, and Claudia Mitchell, eds. *Girlhood: Redefining the Limits*. Montreal: Black Rose Books, pp. 173–190.

———. (forthcoming 2007). "Cleavage in a Tank Top: Bodily Prohibition and the Discourses of School Dress Codes." *Alberta Journal of Educational Review* 53, no. 4.

———. (forthcoming 2008). *Girls, Style & School Identities: Dressing the Part*. New York: Palgrave.

SHAUNA POMERANTZ

Ballet and Girl Culture

Ballet has been ubiquitous in girls' cultures of leisure, imagination, and even work throughout the twentieth century and earlier. Although material and written cultural evidence about girls' interaction with ballet as an ideal self-image or wish fulfillment is fragmentary up to the turn of the twentieth century, this central focus of girls' life has much deeper roots than is usually thought. The sketchbook and doll collection of Queen Victoria when she was a young girl, from about 1830 until she was around 10 or 11 years old, both include detailed representations of ballet stars and their costumes in two and three dimensions. The frequent appearance of ballet themes in the young Victoria's creative art suggests the great impression that the art form made upon her; she replicated images of the dancers in the tedium of ordinary days following her trips to the theater. Victoria's high social status (although the physical setting for her childhood was respectable and almost middle-class rather than lavish and indulged—her dolls were among the cheapest on the market) may have influenced the collection only to the extent of providing a later impetus for the preservation of material culture elements that would be otherwise regarded as trivial or childish and be thrown away in bourgeois households.

Ballet affects girls' cultures in many ways. Most apparently, it is an after-school and weekend activity for uncounted thousands of girls in ballet classes and schools across the suburbs of most large cities in many countries. Second, ballet frequently provides narratives of self-development and self-fulfillment, or even instruction about female identity, available through novels and films. Third, motifs of ballerinas in two and three dimensions are constantly found on products intended for girls' consumption. Ballet themes and motifs are so widespread in the material culture of girls' lives as to be taken for granted and hardly given any scholarly or critical notice, and yet they are a universal sign of an appropriate style of femininity—couth and graceful, yet disciplined and regulated—or that of femaleness itself. Cinema historian Adrienne L. McLean outlines the "identifying symbols of the ballerina" as "her tutu, toe shoes, tights, and, most importantly, her image as an inhuman, delicate and dangerous creature with wings. At once victim and wielder of supernatural power, the ballerina and her roles come to embody the tension implicit in the Romantic, and hence modern, view of life" (McLean 1991). Casting aside the existential meaning of the ballerina as symbol of modern angst and the individual psyche, the ballet "Giselle" (1841) may be freely said to predate Sigmund Freud by half a century with its linking of girls' physical and mental equilibrium to healthy and well-regulated heterosexual relationships and acceptance of public social and gender roles and responsibilities. In the way of ornaments for girls' bedrooms and personal accessories for girls, the ballerina's signifiers are repeated endlessly as decorative motifs. The consumers of girls' culture and ballet characteristically jettison the negative associations in favor of a lyrical and positive reading of ballet as a sign of girlhood and femaleness.

GIRLS AS BALLERINAS

Girls have always been involved in formal dance performances and activities centered around professional dance. In the nineteenth and early twentieth centuries ballerinas often started class as girls under age 10 and were performing on stage by their early adolescence.

Even before they had finished their training or attained the teenage years, girls would appear on stage as supernumeraries, pages, cupids, angels, pixies, and other beings where a small scale had some thematic or representational relevance in performances. Little girls dressed to match older performers would sometimes be placed at the back of the stage or suspended above it on wires or elevated platforms to create a sense of exaggerated perspectival illusion in set piece spectacles or transformation scenes. The well-known Degas statuette *Little Dancer Aged Fourteen* (1878–1881) is a reminder of the myriad girls of junior teen years and younger employed as dancers in the days before legislation kept children out of the visible workforce in Western democracies. Augusta Maywood, the first North American to attain fame as a ballerina in Europe, made her debut at age 12 in Philadelphia in 1837. Some ballet companies, such as the Viennese Children's Ballet, which toured Europe and the United States to much acclaim, featured only highly trained child and adolescent ballerinas. This tradition of a troupe of child dancers lingered in some European opera houses until the Second World War. Likewise, in the commercial theater, child dancers in corps and as soloists with some balletic inflection to their performances featured in vaudeville, music halls, and the British pantomime—again up to the Second World War.

When discussing European opera houses and music halls, subsequent historians have often emphasized the working-class origins of dancers, but the recent revisionist study *Degas and the Dance* (De Vonyar 2002) brings these generalities into closer focus and reveals the multilayered context of these girls' lives and the professionalism to which they aspired in the nineteenth and early twentieth centuries. Research demonstrates that ballerinas came from a wider range of class backgrounds than was previously assumed. Some came from professional theatrical families with long associations with the stage. Others came from white-collar families and considered themselves part of the middle class, often moving in musical and literary circles that Degas frequented. Nor were these dancers all illiterate or uneducated; some shared expert discussions on art and cultural matters with the artist and other colleagues, and some even owned his paintings. These hitherto-overlooked, though recorded, facts about the girls painted by Degas, whose images have been central to the explosion of ballerina-themed cultural materials of the past half century, provide important commentary upon the subculture of girls as professional ballerinas a century ago. The girl professionals at the turn of the twentieth century and later can be seen as avatars of the explosion of interest in ballet classes among the middle classes during the second decade of the twentieth century.

A HISTORY OF THE REPUTATION OF THE BALLET AND BALLERINA

Despite (or perhaps because of) its position as an exalted, genteel—if bloodless and effete—art form, and also as a site of quintessentially female culture, ballet has had a checkered historical reputation over the past two centuries. The interaction of girls and dance, as well as the vision of women that is engendered by dance, is colored by this checkered history. The ballerina has at times epitomized the perfect, admired woman and at other times represented a dangerous underclass of frivolous and disorderly women. However, the ballerina's reputation since at least the second decade of the twentieth century has been securely positive. An important question is when the pragmatic vision of the ballerina as quasi-prostitute and sexually available proletarian was overwritten by the luminous vision of the ballerina as ideal woman and of ballet as an appropriate career path or wish-fulfillment for girls. In nineteenth-century literature, the absent ballerina mothers of Becky Sharpe in *Vanity Fair* and Adele Varens in *Jane Eyre* made them performative outsiders with tainted, non-womanly natures. Both Becky and Adele were marked as different in their respective narratives, forward, pert, aware of an audience and "the gaze," and, above all, extremely self-centered—all in opposition to that era's norm of girlhood and vision of women as Christian and self-sacrificing. Here the ballerina is not an image of the perfect woman. There is also an implied malignant agency in these girls' shadowy mothers. Certainly by the 1950s, if not a decade earlier, a parallel transformation turned the acidic, clear-eyed vision of Degas into textile and wallpaper prints, ideal decor, and soft furnishing must-haves for female children's bedrooms—not to mention their greeting cards. These Degas-inspired motifs were in conscious polarity with the Wild West–, car-, and rocket-themed motifs of boys' bedrooms of the period.

In the late nineteenth century and early twentieth centuries, these contradictory images of ballet dancers co-existed, and some girls, who were known to be dedicated to dance as a "art," worked alongside those looking for a wealthy patron to pay their—and their families'—bills. This dichotomy could be found even in one family. In the van Goethem family, for instance, three sisters trained as ballerinas in Paris. One sister, Antoinette, was arrested for theft; one, Marie, modeled for Degas; and the third, Louise, danced at the Paris opera and was appointed a soloist in the 1890s, working as distinguished dance teacher until the 1930s (one of her pupils, Yvette Chauviré, possibly the best-known French dancer of the mid-twentieth century, is still alive as of 2007). Marie van Goethem, the "Little Dancer," has in recent years become the subject of a children's picture book, *Degas and the Little Dancer* (2003), by Laurence Anholt; a young adult novel, *Marie Dancing* (2005), by Carollyn Meyer; and a tragic ballet with a self-consciously darker and more sexual take on Marie's story, *La Petite Danseuse de Degas* (2003), choreographed by Patrice Bart. Sadly, nothing is recorded of Marie's life after she was mysteriously dismissed from the Paris opera ballet at age 17, although the persistent popularity of her story, in both sanitized and eroticized versions, demonstrates the ongoing cultural fascination with the idea of "the girl ballerina." *Degas and the Little Dancer* tells of young Marie's dream of being remembered as the most famous ballerina in the world coming true a century later, when her statue becomes the most popular exhibit at an imaginary art museum. This book is today a favorite children's title in gallery and museum gift shops.

In another dichotomy, an opposition has often been established, especially in popular films of the 1930s and 1940s, between "European" ballet—portrayed as decadent and formal—and American tap dancing, or musical comedy, represented as spontaneous and joy-filled in performance and believed to reflect more down-to-earth concerns compared with the otherworldly ballet. Images of Stan Laurel dancing as a sylph in a long tutu and floral wreath in the *Dancing Masters* (1943) and the dancing hippopotami in *Fantasia* (1940) are typical of the skepticism that surrounded ballet in North American popular culture of the time. However, the consolations and escape offered by dance classes and the image of the ballerina held their own against such strictures throughout the twentieth century, though more for girls than for boys, for whom the shadow of differentness—as well as the legend of Nijinsky as both genius and doomed, ultimately insane victim of Diaghalev—provided particularly strong disincentives to take up professional dance. Simplistic interpretations of the Nijinsky story still inform films about women and dance. The conflict between a spouse—representing normalcy and family life—and a possessive, charismatic impresario over a dancer, who is finally driven insane, forms the basis of *The Red Shoes*; and a dancer whose artistry is overcome by insanity is also the theme of *Spectre de la Rose*.

Academic analysis of ballet has often been sharply divided between those who see it as an essentially conservative celebration of male power and sexual desire—with the ballerina as a fantasy fetish and even a hard, upright phallus—and those who read it as a site of consolation, subversion, and agency for women and girls. The thousands of suburban girls who flock to dance classes perhaps serve to validate the latter interpretation. Historically, the dancing body is the most active and expressive of all female bodies whose existence is regularly subject to social permission and approval. Concurrently, this permission is sometimes hotly contested and even virtually revoked when ballet is seen as a nonrespectable art form. The desire to control or surveil the freely dancing female body can be traced from nineteenth-century speculation about dancers' sexuality and "availability" to current analyses that focus on dance schools as fermenters of unhealthy body image and eating disorders.

Comments, especially from France and England, about the corps de ballet girls as quasi-prostitutes should also be regarded as belonging to the ongoing phallic fantasy of the avant-garde and the ongoing sexist vision of traditional nineteenth-century bohemia, where women were cast only as sexual doormats, elements of which remained as late as the postwar era in much of European cinema. Viewing the dancer as mere sexual agent also conforms to the patterns of the de-voicing and belittling of women in high art fora tracked by feminist art historians in the United States during the 1970s. From the 1830s to the 1860s among the top echelon were ballerinas—including Marie Taglioni, her niece Marie Taglioni II, Amalia Geltser Taglioni, Lucile Grahn, and Katti Lanner—whose artistic integrity, manifest talent, and intelligent and pleasing social personae positioned them as singular female virtuosos who made their own livings and were accepted in polite society. Fanny Elssler was granted an audience at the White House when she toured the United States. These ballerinas forged a new independent paradigm within the canons of female respectability that was unparalleled for its era and predated the emergence of a formal feminist demand for equality in work opportunities by nearly a generation. In the next generation of overt feminist striving, ballet was regarded as a cultural expression performed by women but generally directed at a male audience.

BALLERINAS AS "SUPERSTARS" AND ROLE MODELS FOR GIRLS

The changing social status of ballerinas offers a useful means for tracking the role of ballet in girls' lives. Thus the class and respectability of ballerinas also indicate the wider social acceptability of ballet as an art form appropriate for girls. Ballet had regained its mid–nineteenth-century status by 1910, if not a few years earlier. More detailed research by Alexandra Carter and Jill Devonyer reveals continuing care by some ballerinas to project the image of a skilled and dedicated professional even when the a priori assumption was that the ballet's main goal was to entertain men. Such dancers include sisters Blanche and Suzanne Mante, sisters Eugene and Louise Fiocre, Rosita Mauri, Rita Sangalli, Adeline Genée, and Phyllis Bedells, along with many of the solo dancers of the Imperial Russian ballet, who lived in considerable style in St. Petersburg and Moscow. Tamara Karsavina was always viewed as a woman of great intelligence, sophistication, and beauty, unquestionably a lady and never a slattern. Albertina Rasch, the most widely acclaimed ballerina in the United States before the modern revival of ballet, was likewise regarded as a person of taste, musicality, and intelligence. She was seen as more cultured and refined than chorus girls or tap dancers, and her dance was always regarded as a class act—above mere vaudeville or musical comedy. Moreover, Rasch was renowned as a businesswoman, theatrical agent, and dance director of her various troupes—not just a ballerina in her own right. Her versatility was celebrated as a demonstration of the entrepreneurial spirit of American women and girls.

Undoubtedly, Anna Pavlova established both the desirability and the intensity of the ballerina image for the twentieth century. The ghost of her ladylike gracefulness both on and off the stage, as well as her nearly manic and quasi-monastic dedication to her career and the "spirit of the dance," still haunt popular visions of ballet. Dreams and images of ballet as a career are still built around the base elements of the Pavlovan image. Pavlova toured the United States repeatedly throughout the 1910s and 1920s, inspiring thousands of American girls with the desire to dance, while imposing a degree of frenetic neuroticism on the dream as well, reflected after her death in the image of the ballerina in films such as *Waterloo Bridge* and *The Red Shoes*. Images of Pavlova in elegant dress among a group of Campfire Girls during World War I fundraising campaigns in the United States (around 1917–1918) showed her as a welcome guest at an unlikely tea party around the band's campfire, attesting to the admirable nature of the renowned dancer as a role model for young girls. This story is told more artfully by the publicity photographs probably from a similar date in which Pavlova, in full costume, dances en pointe for an admiring Mary Pickford. Although Pavlova was dressed in a professional costume of tutu and point shoes, the mature Pickford was dressed down to represent an ordinary girl in her print frock and ringlets; her role as the distillation of the ideal American girl, an American "everygirl," as it were, should be noted here. Pavlova was poised and confident before the earthbound Pickford, who was posed in an attitude of homage and adoration. Pavlova also astutely manipulated the value systems of progressive America, selling her image to innumerable advertisers and product designers and thus spreading it wider and wider throughout everyday life in America. Remarkably, she also managed to hide the possibly de facto nature of her marriage and obliterated the strangeness of her lack of household or children, as well as her foreign status, in order to appear to adoring North American audiences as the perfect woman. Among the myriad young girls inspired to dance by Pavlova was Agnes de Mille, who was later one of the key figures responsible for establishing an identifiably North American cultural idiom in ballets such as *Rodeo*, and who also reached an audience of millions with the dance/dream scenes in films of Rodgers and Hammerstein musical productions.

The predominance of middle-class girls as professional dancers began to rise in the teens of the twentieth century. In the 1880s, Marie Taglioni trained highly respectable English girl Margaret Rolfe in pointe work, leaping, and pas de deux passages with a retired male dancer, far beyond the requirements of social dance, which was the nominal focus of her teaching. Cleo de Mérode, a star of the 1890s who toured internationally, successfully sued feminist Simone de Beauvoir in 1955 for wrongly describing Cleo in public as a prostitute who had taken an aristocratic-sounding stage name as self-promotion. Cleo's defense was that she was a professional dancer and member of the old, noble, and distinguished de Mérode family. Sergei Diaghilev's recruitment of upper- and middle-class girls for his corps de ballet opened this career path for women around 1910. Ballet became extremely popular in interwar Britain as a career in which a girl could be seen to be an independent professional without risking the essential characteristics of femininity or being tainted by the rough-and-tumble of the corporate or political world. Diaghalev accepted wealthy girls into his company for various reasons, particularly to gain sponsorship and social attention as well as for their attractive appearance in the corps. Possibly his vision of ballet as art, not titillation, as well as his placement of ballet alongside other high arts, encouraged him to employ members of society. His dancers freely socialized with the top echelons of society. Olga Khoklova was the daughter of a colonel and Romola de Pulsky was of socially prominent status. Her desire to take classes with the Diaghalev company was accepted by its other employees. Alice Marks, of middle-class British origins, danced with Diaghilev. In the years after Pavlova's death, it was Markova who spread the image of the intelligent, socially couth ballerina throughout the United States and England. Marks was only 14 when she debuted, rechristened as the Russian Alicia Markova. The story that her father owned the Woolworth's-like department store chain Marks & Spencer is an urban legend. When it was obvious that the Sadlers Wells—later Royal—Ballet favored the blander Fonteyn, Markova left Britain to work in the United States, becoming the most prominent and gifted ballerina based there in the 1930s and 1940s, before the emergence of North America–trained stars and the establishment of major companies such as the New York Ballet.

The direct identification of ballet with girlhood was strengthened with the Baby Ballerinas, Tamara Toumanova, Irina Baronova, and Tatiana Riabouchinska, in the early 1930s. The Russian Revolution meant that impoverished women from formerly leisured and refined families had to earn incomes in exile. Many girls from "white Russian" families received dance tuitions in refugee communities, particularly in Paris, where three stars of the Imperial Ballet had settled. The three girls in their early teens, supported by phenomenal natural abilities and Hollywood-style publicity machines, toured internationally and were constantly presented on stage in the roles of women twice their age. Toumanova was dancing in major productions at age 9. The aura of Hollywood-like glamour around these girls made them a very modern image of girlhood. They were more vibrant and cultured than the performing girls offered by Hollywood such as Shirley Temple, Judy Garland, and Deanna Durbin, with whom they did, however, share very clear affinities.

The Ballets Russes in the 1930s were truly cosmopolitan, auditioning dancers from many countries and backgrounds as they toured, many dancing under Russian stage names. Dancers left the company at various legs of the international tours and stayed at their points of embarkation to open ballet schools around the world, further spreading the popularity of ballet as a glamorous pastime and, with luck, a career. Local dancers auditioned and joined the company. There is no greater demonstration of the extraordinary power of ballet over girls' imaginations and the opportunities that it offered girls—who often were totally riveted by their first ballet performance, during the period roughly from 1910 to 1940, by Pavlova's company or the Ballets Russes—than the cultural diversity of some of the prominent American members of the Ballets Russes in the 1930s to 1950s. American stars of the Ballets Russes included Sono Osato, a Japanese Canadian born in Nebraska, who joined the company at age 14; Alicia Alonso, a Cuban; the Tallchief sisters, Maria and Marjorie, daughters of a chief of the Osage nation; Rosella Hightower, from the Choctaw nation; Yvonne Chouteau, from the Cherokee nation; and Raven Wilkinson, an African American. Most of these dancers later moved to Europe and received star billing with major companies. Wilkinson was often forcibly stopped from performing with her peers during tours south of the Mason-Dixon Line by civic authorities and police, even being physically removed from the stage during rehearsals, to the distress of her friends and colleagues. There were serious anxieties about Wilkinson being onstage alongside white women, dressed similarly to them as swans, fairies, ladies in period costume, crinolines, and other such signs of "refinement," which inflamed local cultural mythologies. These concerns referenced older ones about Diaghalev's United States tour, where *Scheherazade*, with its corps de ballet of white girls and "blacked-up" men, became the subject of frequent requests for removal from scheduled performances, especially in Southern states. Wilkinson later, like many mid-century North American ballerinas, auditioned successfully for European companies, where she never met with such discrimination but was instead acclaimed.

However, in the second and third quarters of the twentieth century, the cultural fascination with the ballerina coalesced around Margot Fonteyn. Like Pavlova, she was seen as a perfect woman, but she also added a uniquely British reserve to the dance: sexless, cold, and *über*-respectable. She was celebrated as the embodiment of English hauteur and coolness. Despite her well-hidden affair with Australian Constant Lambert and her later marriage to a Panamanian diplomat and politician—certainly not the expected consort of a British de facto princess—Fonteyn also communicated the idea of the ballerina as a couth and regulated woman. She loomed large in the public memory of the United States by the late 1940s, thanks to impresario Sol Hurok, who managed the Royal Ballet's appearances in that country and whipped up a considerably frenzy for the company. Her name even inspired the Margot ballerina doll of Madame Alexander.

BALLET DOLLS

Ballerina dolls are a good index of the fortunes and profile of dance in girls' worlds. A number of dolls unquestionably represented ballerinas in the early to middle nineteenth century, but ballerinas merged with fairy dolls in nineteenth-century doll dressing, and even with some of the more fanciful interpretations of angels. Tutus and ballet shoes—which were of course virtually indistinguishable from girls' everyday footwear between 1830 and 1860—sometimes were worn by angelic attendants, personified by dressed dolls, in mid-nineteenth century homemade tableaux on Roman Catholic devotional themes. These dolls, of course, bought into the fascinating question of the shifting gender of the supposedly intersex, asexual, or gender-neutral angel from generation to generation. Some dolls in tutus lack either angelic or large fairy wings, suggesting that they are dancers. The many commercial mid–nineteenth-century paper dolls sold with sets of ballet costumes, and sometimes even named for specific stars such as Marie Taglioni and Fanny Elssler, suggest that there was a place for images of ballerinas in the homes and play rituals of respectable mid–nineteenth-century girls. There is certainly an oeuvre of dressed Jenny Linds, Adelina Pattis, and other singers in costume suggesting that middle- and upper-class women and girls were engaged enough by the appearances and costumes of stage performers to own dolls and dress them to represent the stage stars of the second and third quarters of the nineteenth century. Madame Alexander, since the 1940s, and Mattel, since the mid-1970s, have issued annual ballerina dolls.

Although Barbie had a ballet tutu in her annual wardrobe releases from 1961 on, the Ballerina Barbie of 1976 was the first of the annual Barbies issued solely as a dancer. She could also perform some ballet moves when set on her stand. Dancerina was an earlier Mattel ballerina—a battery-powered dancer who could balance en pointe and dance several steps unsupported—a near-miracle in 1969. A number of other Mattel battery-powered dancers used the same mechanism. Various threads through the popular culture of ballet unite in such dolls. Not only did Margot Fonteyn inspire the name of a Madame Alexander ballet doll, but also there are a number of "Degas" ballerinas by both Madame Alexander and Mattel, the latter in the form of Barbie dolls. Mattel provides an index to popular American conceptions of ballet. Ballerina Barbie releases over the past three decades focus on ballets with high profiles among United States audiences, such as *The Nutcracker* and *Swan Lake*. *The Nutcracker* has been, especially in the United States, a Christmas ritual for the last six decades—just like the even older tradition of the pantomime in the United Kingdom, where the fairy queen is sometimes a danced role.

The *Nutcracker* was also the subject of Mattel's first Barbie animated feature film, which has had a huge impact in domestic video and DVD sales. Many of Mattel's other films for girls have ballet themes, such as *Swan Lake*, or balletic associations, such as the *Twelve Dancing Princesses*, which promotes a whole cast of ballerinas that includes some mechanical twirling dolls. The Mattel animated films also provide a point of crossover between ballet themes and the burgeoning popularity of fairy culture, representing another core theme of Mattel films and associated products. Another close crossover genre of imagery with Mattel ballet dolls are ice-skating Barbies. Ice-skating dolls have been popular in the United States and Canada since the 1930s, with the introduction of Sonja Henie dolls. The Barbara Ann Scott dolls continued that trend in the 1950s, referencing girls' leisure time classes and competitions in pursuit of this dance/sport. The most elaborate ballet Barbies have musical stands similar to that key ornament of girls' bedrooms, the musical jewel box with mirrored interior and twirling ballerina, made by the million in Japan and, later, China.

BALLET TEXTS

Ballet books are another means of popularizing ballet to girls. Ballet themes were ubiquitous in mid–twentieth-century girls' and young adult fiction. Much of this writing came from British authors, especially Noel Streatfield and Lorna Hill, but Elizabeth Enright also occasionally presented prominent ballet themes in her American fiction. In *Four Storey Mistake* (1942), the key subplot concerns wealthy heiress Clarinda Cassidy, who eschews the life of a New York socialite to tour as a ballet star under a Russian stage name—not Bulova, because that is the watch; and not Popover, because that is the donut—remarked one character. Another strong text image of dance are the ballet scenes in the autobiographical *Save Me the Waltz* by Zelda Fitzgerald, although this book has become only relatively freely available in recent years despite being released commercially in the 1930s. *Save Me the Waltz* emphasizes the link between feminist ambition and dance but also engages the idea of the ballerina as the superior girl who is later tamed and delimited, if not destroyed, by mental illness and forced to accept the responsibilities and lesser status of women in everyday life.

Children's picture books of the last few decades frequently feature ballet. Angelina Ballerina—the dancing mouse—proved to be a very popular character with very young girls in the 1990s through her storybooks and associated merchandise. Many preschoolers love Angelina and want to be like her, and thus go to dance classes. Ballet memorabilia, including ballet annuals and glossy albums, attaché cases, ballet shoes, ballerina motifs, ballerina playing cards, statuettes, music boxes, and porcelain ballet shoes, has burgeoned in the past half century, focusing on products marketed to girls and their mothers. Ballet is the dominant theme in many girls' bedrooms, from the comforter on the bed to the titles on the bookshelves.

Ballet is a major locus of female mythology and life narratives from girlhood on. Ballet films also promote the idea of the ballerina as an eloquent metaphor for the status and travails of females and their life journeys. These films are often directed at older women—but are certainly available to younger girls. Ballet films often feature a suffering heroine and extreme, life-making or -breaking decisions; in a number of these films, the dancer, cast as a figure of extraordinary beauty and skill, finally dies to enable the continuation of the flatter, everyday life narratives of those around her. These films include *Waterloo Bridge*, *Turning Point*, and *Pavlova: A Woman for All Seasons*. *Pavlova*, in particular, ascribed beauty and masochism to women and included the child Pavlova and her later pupils as witnesses to the journey of growing up. In the early 1980s *Flashdance* and *Fame* made dance wear a mainstream, daytime fashion for girls. An aberrant dancer was the central plot of Hans Christian Andersen's story, "The Red Shoes," which was adapted to film in 1947. The hero pursued a capricious ballerina who resisted male suitors. The fairy tale plot was linked with a real-life narrative conveying two important messages about family and home. First, there was a straightened version of the Diaghalev-Nijinsky narrative, in which the doomed victim escapes from the amoral, perverse possessiveness of the evil Other, only to lose access to the talent that defined her, leaving her no escape except insanity. Second, there was the message that a woman's true place lies in domestic bondage as wife and mother. Although there is an escape from the forced encoding of woman as domestic in the postwar era, the ending allows for an ambiguous validation of the amoral, if not gay, spirit of art against the Cromwellian repression and the ultimately violent, destructive impetus of heterosexual social responsibility. *The Red Shoes*, watched by girls as well as women, was the foundational narrative of women's role and limitations in the postwar period. Here individual self-expression and professional specialization opposed and finally became incompatible with the role of wife and homemaker. It is a phenomenally successful film even to this day, ironically because of the seductive, artificial beauty of the ballet scenes and the veracity of the female power and talent that, on the surface, it seeks to condemn.

Lola Montes, by Orphuls, is—like "The Red Shoes"—a meditation on female status and identity in the postwar period. The performer/dancer is identified as the key to female nature for a 1950s audience. Pitched as an avant-garde, art house film but surely loved by popular audiences for the circus and ballet elements that were so much a part of 1950s popular taste, its fantasy elements and many plotline diversions to circus performances made it amusing and accessible to all ages despite the often scandalous details of Lola's life.

A recent reference to ballet is found in the musical film *Chicago*. The Hungarian prisoner provides an ongoing prima ballerina reference in gesture and styling throughout the popular musical comedy, invoking the old opposition of hoofer versus ballet dancer, along with tensions between the classes, which were common in films of the 1930s and 1940s. The ballet/acrobatics image telescoped, as in *Lola Montez*, and the ballerina is revealed yet again as a foreign exotic with an implied couth class status, but again is ultimately doomed.

Montez is also an important figure in the narrative of girls and dance. A respectable young British army wife during the early to mid-1840s, she remarkably broke free of middle-class Victorian constraints to become an internationally famous dance star. Old drawings and photographs show that, though she was billed as a Spanish dancer, she had totally absorbed the inflections of ballet in both gesture and costume. Montez not only demonstrates the agency that professional dance offers to women, but prefigures early–twenty-first century media celebrities in that sexual allure, as much as actual performing talent, underpinned her fame. Montez's self-transformation from respectable wife to international star is a precise foreshadowing of the major girlhood dream narratives that would be offered in the media age a century or more later. Perhaps Montez is a melancholy artifact of the lost cultural potential of women in a Victorian bourgeois context—a rare survivor and determined personality like the Brontës and Emily Dickinson.

One of the ultimate images of filmed ballet as female life narrative is the dream ballet from *Oklahoma*, which links a dance narrative to the important issue of female identity and behavior as Laurie is with the nightmare vision of cancan dancers and Jud's non-domestic, predatory sexuality in opposition to the bourgeois life promised by Curly—surely a cautionary tale during the conservative postwar era. This story is still reinforced in miniature in the many high school performances of the musical. This sense of negotiation and working through a future life is a common theme of ballet for female viewers. Dance has frequently occupied itself with plots involving marriage. Early ballets were associated with royal weddings, and many narrative ballets offer meditations about choices in love and the melancholy outcomes of love gone wrong, as well as the near-universal theme of male betrayal—or at least male failure in understand and support. Another curious feature in romantic and classical ballet is the predominance of female communities—without men. The plots often present communities of young women and the marital passage out of the otherworldly enchantment—the "fairytopia" as Mattel names it—of those cloistered "feminine microcosms" into a wider, mundane, patriarchal world. Domesticity in general—life after marriage—which features in many narrative interior scenes in the visual arts—rarely appears in ballets, although *Appalachian Spring* is one exception. Ballet themes often negotiate courtship and marriage choices and validate true love versus the political, economic, or social expediency of arranged alliances. Thus girls are given an inkling of the shape of the responsibilities they will face when they grow up, even while being granted a pleasurable vision of an alternative world.

In recent years there has been a diffusion of the ballerina image throughout girlhood. She is now even more visible than in the mid-twentieth century. However, she is not necessarily associated with professional dance companies such as the Royal Ballet or Russian companies (which retained their high reputation in the West even through the Cold War years). Girls are no longer content to endure years of discipline, and—despite any misgivings—suburban ballet classes frequently allow younger pupils to attend classes in full ballerina rig of tutu, wings, and tiara without having earned these symbols by demonstrating exceptional talent. It is socially acceptable for little girls to appear on the streets with their mothers just as if they were dressed for class in dance wear that includes ballet shoes, leotards, crossover jackets, the "Kirov" chiffon tunic—and, of course, tutus. Neither tutus nor the Kirov tunic appeared in the 1980s' habitual referencing of ballet wear. Tutus also correspond to the "fairy" and "princess" styles also frequently worn in public by very young girls, especially preschoolers. The ballerina image also coincides with the development of extremely elaborate children's themed birthday parties as an expensive sign of status in middle-class suburbia. The piñata—seen outside North America as a sign of European culture and class that lends distinction to a suburban party—often features ballerinas and fairies. In England, retired ballerina stars complain that ballet has been devalued by the suburban classes and exhibits an increasing devaluation of effective professional training. For much of the middle class, classical music has replaced ballet as the ideal female career, implying monastic discipline and self-regulation, but with a higher class status and without problematic discourses of "body image" or sexuality. The British educational system validates musical training but not professional dance training.

At a more popular level since the mid-1970s, gymnastics, in the wake of the reconfiguration of the sport by star Eastern European gold medalists, has provided a high-profile, public frame for publicly displaying the pre-pubescent female, or even the androgynous "Balanchine," body. The latter ideal is generally blamed for propagating cultures of body image disorders among young, aspiring dancers, such as anorexia and bulimia. The gymnast has proven to be a serious challenge to the ballerina. She is no sylph or fairy, but practical, sporty, active, and modern, providing the image of an ideal girl. Moreover, the gymnast as graceful and immature has exorcised the specter of the man-woman possessed of both aesthetic and sexual lifestyle implications that has haunted other professional female sports stars, including swimmers, golfers, tennis players, and even players of team sports. The female gymnast has integrated women into the media and made public validation of sports a core cultural metaphor.

Ballet appears to have slipped behind opera to some degree in the public imagination in Britain, Europe, and Australia in the early twenty-first century. Opera has captured a chic, radical market and presents, especially in Europe, extreme manipulations of the visual style of the classics while leaving the original music still intact. The frequent— even mandatory—referencing of bizarre, strongly masculinist and sexist imagery and violence in such productions is readily accepted as "avant-garde." Classical ballet productions that attempt a similar contemporary engagement and reimaging often involve a deconstruction of the ballerina persona with strongly masculinist outcomes, such as the obliteration of the feminine from Matthew Bourne's all-male *Swan Lake* or the violent— presumably sexual—attack upon Clara by a battalion of rats in Red Army uniforms in Graham Murphy's *Nutcracker*. The latter scenes evoked public anger from mothers taking their children to the ballet with the expectation of a visit to the magical kingdom of sweets where the sugar plum fairy reigns. Certainly Murphy's Diana-Camilla-Charles reworking of *Swan Lake*—which has been substantially hindered in public circulation by the iconic status of the male *Swan Lake*—does present a more female-orientated vision of contemporary heterosexuality. Although as in traditional *Swan Lake*, and, ironically, in real life, the only trajectory imaginable for Diana/Odette is a high-profile, premature death. In the late twentieth century, Princess Diana was like Anna Pavlova—an instance where the ballerina mythos incarnated into a living figure. There have been at least two balletic imagings of Diana in the decade since her death.

Traditional interpretations of ballet classics may survive more effectively in North America, where a cohesive image of elaborately staged narrative ballet is projected through private school performances, regional companies, and university-based ballet companies into a relatively vernacular and community-level consciousness and clearly cherished by everyday audiences—and even by performers. Even more remarkably, despite the relative cultural neglect in Europe and Australia, a strict interpretation of narrative ballet flourishes in Asia from communist Shanghai to capitalist Singapore, as well as in Japan, where a strong amateur ballet scene exists for adults in addition to girls. The conventionality of these interpretations is striking, with references to the obvious ethnic and cultural differences of the performers totally avoided. Classical ballets with clear regional content such as *Red Detachment of Women* or *Yugen: Tsukiyomo the Moon Goddess* are in the minority compared with Asian-produced *Swan Lakes* and *La Sylphides*, costumed precisely as in the West. Nor do any political or postcolonial references emerge from the performers' negative experiences with ballet's predominantly Eurocentric imagery. This alone suggests that the art form is far more culturally complex and less monolayered than the current intellectual degree of disdain for it suggests.

The ritual of the elaborate annual recital brings ballet into the daily fiber of North American child and family life. Classical ballet is ubiquitous in this context, either as isolated turns and divertissement or as the interpretation and adaptation of a well-known classic. High school musicals and recitals may well include a cancan and other dances with some historic or balletic association—such as the cancan featured in Gaite Parisienne, one of the most popular productions of the Ballets Russes in the United States—as well the interpolated, extended balletic numbers of vintage musical comedies. A vast selection of this performance material has been uploaded to YouTube, again demonstrating that ballet is more resilient and diverse as an art form than is usually believed. Parents are often expected, to their chagrin or joy, to take part as stage crew, set builders, tailors, and dressers. Thus the ballet comes to resemble the more contemporary, often mocked, and generally less esteemed phenomenon of the children's beauty pageant.

A central song in the film and Broadway show *A Chorus Line* pays homage to the thousands of girls in suburban dance classes every weekend and after school around the world, as well as to the symbolism of beauty and romance that sustains them beyond their sometimes dysfunctional family lives. The reality of unsuccessful relationships and heterosexual miscommunications is placed against the escape provided by ballet—where every prince finds his swan.

Further Reading

Banes, Sally. (1988). *Dancing Women: Female Bodies on Stage*. London: Routledge.

Carter, Alexandra. (2004). *Rethinking Dance History: A Reader*. London: Routledge.

———. (2005). *Dance and Dancers in the Victorian and Edwardian Music Hall Ballet*. Aldershot: Ashgate.

De Vonyar, Jill. (2002) *Degas and the Dance*. New York: Harry N. Abrams.

Foster, Susan Leigh. (1996). *Choreography & Narrative: Ballet's Staging of Story and Desire*. Bloomington: Indiana University Press.

McLean, Adrienne L. (1991, Summer). "The Image of the Ballet Artist in Popular Films." *Journal of Popular Culture* 25, no. 1, 1, 19.

Stoneley, Peter. (2002). "Ballet Imperial." In *The Yearbook of English Studies, Volume 32: Children in Literature*, 140–150.

JULIETTE PEERS

Girls' Literacy Practices

Literacy is a social practice. Reading and writing (and *all* the processes that allow people to make meaning from images and print) used to be understood as a set of psychological skills. But for the past 30 years researchers have been making it clear that literacy "skills" are also the *social practices* of a certain historical moment, produced by people whose identities are marked by race, class, ethnicity, religion, sexual orientation, age, and gender. *Girls'* literacies differ from the literacy practices of boys and older people, because girls occupy a different social position in the world.

Within the category of girls is a wide variety in the ways girls live and practice literacy. North American girls vary in race, class, ethnicity, and religion. These social identities influence the ways girls interact with popular culture and new technologies, as well as the ways girls read and write both in and out of school. Girls are individuals. Still, we can make these general observations: Most girls use literacy to participate in a North American culture of girlhood that they themselves help to create, to interact with popular culture and media, and to explore possibilities for adult womanhood (Greer 2003).

Any discussion of girls' literacies must define "gender" as well as "literacy." The idea that literacy is a set of social practices is consistent with the idea that gender is more than biology. Gender also is a set of social practices, something people *perform* in their daily lives. People "construct" their gender identities in interaction with the cultural messages that surround them. Gender is something people *do* (West and Zimmerman 1987), and literacy is something people *do* (Cherland 1994; Finders 1996). People use literacy, as they use everything else that comes to hand, to perform as the people they believe themselves to be, and girls are no exception. Literacy is, among other things, a way to do gender—a means of being a girl. It is also a way for a child, otherwise limited by age, to participate in society. Examining girls' literacy practices provides insight into what girls believe about being a girl today, and about their futures.

Some recent research and scholarship on gender and literacy is psychologically framed and experimental in approach, but this essay will provide an overview of other research that examines the ways girls *perform* literacy, linking girls' literacy practices to the popular culture and media discourses of our time. This entry will also reflect on the meanings girls' literacy practices have for girls themselves as well as for society today. It is organized into three sections: girls' *reading* practices, girls' *writing* practices, and girls' literacy practices *online* with electronic texts.

GIRLS' READING PRACTICES

In 1984 Janice Radway published *Reading the Romance: Women, Patriarchy and Popular Literature,* a study of adult women and their reading of romance novels. Radway found that the women she studied were not passive absorbers of formulaic plots with happy endings. They did not read romances simply to escape their ordinary daily lives. They read to imagine themselves as more powerful people, capable of changing their lives and acting on their desires. Since *Reading the Romance,* researchers have been keenly interested in the social psychology of *girls'* reading. Linda Christian-Smith (1990), for example, studied the reading of working-class teen girls who escaped to a more satisfying fictional world even as they internalized cultural messages about the narrow possibilities for their futures.

Cherland (1994) studied younger girls and their reading of fiction both in and out of school, finding that the affluent lower–middle-class white girls she studied used their fictional reading to act out their culture's beliefs about girlhood, time, and consumerism. The girls learned to read fiction, including popular series novels like *The Baby-sitters Club*, in ways that enabled them to form and maintain friendships with other girls their age, and to educate themselves about the intricacies of human relationships. Growing up in a culture that required them to be busy, but denied them practical work, they filled their time with fictional reading. Growing up in a culture that encouraged them to consume, these girls spent their money on paperback books and collected series novels in the same way they collected stuffed animals and clothes. Girls exercised *agency*, the ability and the will to act on the world around them, through their reading. And yet they struggled with cultural messages from popular genres (like the horror stories in novels, music videos, and films) that portray girls as sexual objects and helpless victims. At the same time, instructional practices in schools neither acknowledged nor valued female experiences of the world and led girls to expect that others would be more powerful in daily life. Cherland found that the girls she studied were encouraged in school to be passive, but that they resisted by using their reading to experience vicariously much more than what was culturally approved for them.

It seems that in girls' reading the psychic and the social intersect, as Valerie Walkerdine (1990, 1997) demonstrates by using psychoanalytic concepts such as *fantasy* and *desire* to understand girls' cultural lives and their interactions with print, film, and other artifacts of popular culture. Walkerdine sheds light on the psychic struggles girls face as they grow up in a culture that uses and devalues them. She describes a "psychology of survival" (1997) that allows girls to think and endure even as they receive cultural messages that may threaten and demean them, messages that they resist while creating more positive meanings of their own.

Over the past 10 years, much of the research on girls' reading has continued to explore this kind of complex psychological interaction with cultural messages that takes place as girls form their identities—in part through reading. Sally Smith (2000), for example, studied an after-school book club whose members were prosperous middle-class 11-year-old girls, Latina and African American as well as white. Smith found that these girls read to imagine themselves as independent, daring, and courageous agents in their worlds. They read to engage with both the intimidating and the fascinating aspects of sexuality and to explore in safety their own desires and dreams for the future. Harper (2007) analyzed young adult novels, finding that many of the fictional texts girls read did offer a wide range of life possibilities for female characters, but that rigid expectations of girls' behavior commonly reassert themselves and make independent girls seem aberrant. In and out of school, girls continue to struggle with the texts they read; but many manage to be "resistant readers" nevertheless (Fetterley 1978). They do not necessarily identify with the messages they encounter, but instead turn them around them by imagining themselves as active agents of their own desires.

Yes, girls do resist. Even when adults attempt to alter the messages in children's texts to make them more positive, girls resist. Bronwyn Davies, for example, found that some girls read *against* feminist stories and continue to position female and male characters along conventional gender lines (Davies 1991). Recent research continues to support

Davies's findings. Children fit feminist stories into conventional frames. They often focus on the importance of female beauty and are even less accepting of nontraditional male characters than of nontraditional female characters (Rice 2000, 2002). Fortunately, teaching interventions through drama and critical discussion have been found to improve children's acceptance of nontraditional gender roles (Davies 2003; Rice 2000). There is hope. While research has revealed a myriad of ways in which school practices continue to disadvantage girls and young women (AAUW 1993; Fishman 1996; Orenstein 1994; Sadker and Sadker 1994), today's teachers and parents are working to find ways to read *with* girls, to show them they are valued, to acknowledge patriarchy and undermine its hierarchies of power so that girls through reading might have better chances for healthy lives.

There are, of course, alternative spaces outside the reach of adults where girls can read the world independently. One of these spaces is popular culture. A growing number of studies have offered analyses of pop culture products and events as well as ethnographic studies of children's and youth's engagement with them. Some of these studies focus on girls (Best 2000; Cherland 2005; Finders 1996; Lemish 1998; Mazzarella and Pecora 2001) and their readings of prom night, the Spice Girls, teen magazines, the *Baby-sitters Club* series, and the stories implied in music videos. Girls read popular culture to read the world around them as well as to reconstruct it.

GIRLS' WRITING PRACTICES

Kathleen Rockhill (1993) argues that literacy can be about "empowerment" for girls if they learn to think and read and write critically. She suggests that culture (the media, the church, the school, and so on) manipulates girls' desire to be good, appropriate, feminine people who (it sometimes seems) are not supposed to be independent, intelligent, or educated. Many literacy researchers study girls' reading and writing as contexts where girls "construct" their identities through interaction with many cultural messages. Reading and writing are two sides of the same coin, so to speak, and the work of Margaret Finders (1996) considers them together. She conducted a year-long ethnographic study of young girls' literacy practices in and out of school in which she followed two groups of seventh-grade girls (age 12) in a junior high school considered one of the finest in the American Midwest. Although the school population was almost exclusively white, there was a stark division between students from affluent homes and the working-class students who lived in trailer parks. Finders followed the girls in two social cliques, "the Tough Cookies" and the "Social Queens." The "Tough Cookies" were a loosely connected group of girls from the trailer parks who managed heavy responsibilities at home; the "Social Queens" were a tightly organized group of affluent and popular girls. Finders studied the girls' writing and reading experiences at school and at home during one school year. She found that, through their writing and reading practices, both groups of girls organized their lives and their alliances with other girls, their teachers, and their parents.

Finders was disturbed to see that the progressive literacy program offered at their school failed to provide a transformative or liberating education for any of these girls. The program was less authoritarian than a traditional literacy program. It allowed for greater student choice, more personal response, and greater and more intense collaborative reading and writing experiences. Yet the Cookies (the "trailer park girls") were alienated by this program and the middle-class assumptions that shaped it. The Queens, on the other hand, were alienated by the program's interference in their social agenda. Rather than freeing students, the actual effect of the program (and of junior high in general) was a constriction of the girls' time, movement, and conversation so that "only through a literate *underlife* [of passing notes and secret diaries] were these girls provided any opportunity for more freedom, independence, or responsibility" (Finders 1996, p. 129). Both sets of girls were never provided with the means to rewrite the traditional gender and class messages that organized both their lives and the literacy program in which they and their teachers were engaged. Both groups of girls were left vulnerable. The affluent Social Queens were prepared by teen magazines to be consumers and competitors for men's desires. The Tough Cookies were silenced and alienated, having neither political clout nor economic resources: "While the Social Queens rehearsed their roles to secure their place in society through romance and commodities, the Cookies were reminded again and again [through their literacy practices] that there was no place for them" (p. 128). Finders repeats the call, made by other feminists engaged in literacy education, for a more critical school literacy program for all children. "I advocate a pedagogy that situates reading [and writing] not simply as an aesthetic experience [or a means for self expression], but as a political act as well. . . . Such a pedagogy would acknowledge the ways in which texts serve to enable and constrain social roles" (pp. 127–128). Finders places considerable responsibility on teachers. "If we deny our power as educators, we deny our students the opportunity to rewrite cultural and social scripts" (p. 128).

Heath Blair (1996, 1998, 2001), who also researches *boys'* literacy practices, has provided an urban study of Canadian Aboriginal girls' constructions of gender identity in middle school (grade 8). Blair's study, like Cherland's (1994) and Finders's (1996), is a year-long ethnographic study of classroom life. But the girls Blair studied lived in an economically depressed neighborhood, where children of several different races and ethnicities came together at school. Some of Blair's findings have to do with the girls' writing, which Blair found to be "infused with the multiple realities of their lives" and especially reflective of the girls' gender. Blair found that the girls chose to write in different genres than the boys in the same classroom, also choosing different topics. The girls wrote names, symbols, greetings, lyrics, reminders, and love tags on their clothing, arms, and hands, using writing as decoration and identification.

The girls also wrote intimate private notes and passed them to one another in class as a means of building and maintaining relationships with other girls; and they used diary entries to express their feelings and fears, reflecting on the pain and violence of their lives. Neither genre was sanctioned in the school literacy curriculum.

The literacy curriculum for Blair's girls included daily free writing time, which the girls used to write stories and poetry. The Aboriginal girls' writing was marked by culturally different ways of seeing, thinking, and being explicit, but their teacher did not try to understand the intercultural realities of their lives. Blair's study is brilliant in its portrayal of girls disadvantaged by their race and class, who explore meanings of both gender and ethnicity in their writing as they construct their gender and ethnic/racial identities through writing.

In another interesting study of difference and identity construction in children, Elizabeth Moje (2000) studied graffiti writing and the other literacy practices of seventh-graders in Salt Lake City, Utah. The young people she studied were not white, not middle class, and not Mormon. They were the children of Latina, Laotian, Cambodian, and Somali immigrants, marginalized by both their color and their poverty. Excluded at school, they became "gangstas" (affiliated with gangs) in order to belong somewhere. They learned to use alternative, unsanctioned literacy practices as a way to be "part of the story," as a way to claim space and to take up a social position in the world. While more boys engaged in "tagging" and graffiti writing, some girls did as well. Tagging is a form of graffiti—the act of writing letters and images to label something. Tagging is done very quickly, under dangerous conditions, in unsanctioned, highly visible public locations. The girls (and boys) Moje (2000) studied practiced their "tags" in special art notebooks at school before attempting them in public. It is the elements of speed and danger that distinguish "tagging" from other forms of graffiti. However, "gangsta" *girls* were more likely to use poetry, prayer parodies, notes and letters to friends, journal entries, word plays, and alternative spellings to position themselves as gang members, to find a voice and some social power, and to position others as friends or enemies. Almost all of these literary practices were vilified and devalued by adults at school and in the community, but they offered these girls (and boys) ways of changing the meanings of their lives.

Other research has looked at the writing practices of girls who are the children of refugees and immigrants to North America. Ellen Skilton-Sylvester's (2002) case study of Nan, a Cambodian teenager living and going to school in Philadelphia, followed from a larger study involving three years of observation in the homes and at the school of seven young Cambodian girls, all children of refugee families (Skilton-Sylvester 2002). The larger study found that there were important differences in what these girls wrote at home and what they wrote at school: differences in genres, in the social and academic prestige of writing, in the functions of writing, and in the volume and quality of written texts. At the school the girls attended, being good at literacy had negative peer group consequences. As the children of Khmer refugees who had escaped from the genocide of the Pol Pot regime, which had murdered people for being literate, the girls were culturally Cambodian. They were growing up within a transplanted Cambodian culture in which women had traditionally been given little formal schooling. But in spite of many social, historic, and cultural reasons why Cambodian girls might have turned their backs on literacy after moving to North America, these girls enjoyed an active writing life at home that was nearly invisible at school (p. 62). Nan was a prolific writer at home, producing plays, fictional and nonfictional stories, captioned pictures, and letters. But at school Nan struggled with academic literacy, and her teachers were doubtful of her ability to read and write in English.

Skilton-Sylvester (2002) describes the ways in which Nan's home literacy practices were oral, visual, and creative. At home, her strengths as a speaker, artist, and storyteller were assets, but they did not help her at school, where the written word was more valued and formal accuracy mattered more than meaning. Nan's opportunity to express herself through writing was constrained in school. Skilton-Sylvester (2002) concludes that if Nan had learned to write in her native Khmer, she might not have fallen so far behind her native English–speaking peers in school in her ability to understand and create texts in English. Nan was not unintelligent or uncooperative. She was complex, diligent, and committed to learning. Nan had strengths and cultural preferences, and she used all the resources available to her to develop academic literacies at school. But she failed, and the possibilities for her future were curtailed. Skilton-Sylvester argues that teachers at school must allow their students who are learning English as a second language to use all of their multimodal resources to perform literate acts in the classroom so that they can use literacy to convey meaning, build relationships, "do social work," and succeed. Girls' out-of-school literacy resources (their first languages, their histories, their home communities) "can be a foundation for school literacy" as they use writing to do the social work of school (p. 88) and form their adult identities.

GIRLS' LITERACY PRACTICES ONLINE

Since 1970, girls have been appropriating new technologies to participate in the social world for their own purposes, and this participation has extended their repertoires of reading and writing practices. For those girls who have access to computers, technology has increased their options for creativity and self-definition through literacy, for creating more extended communities through literacy, and for blurring or sharpening the lines of age and gender (Schrum 2003). Girls' uses of technology for doing gender and literacy have taken some fascinating forms.

Many girls use computer technology to extend and maintain friendships with other girls. Girls have long used traditional forms of reading and writing at home and school to maintain friendships (see Cherland 1994; Finders 1996; Smith 2000). Now those who have access to computers can use electronic forms of reading and writing to do the same. Online book clubs and media chat rooms, blogs, MySpace, Live Journal, and other interactive Web sites all require reading and public writing, and all provide ways for girls to meet other girls (and sometimes boys) with similar interests.

For some girls with access, using interactive media to meet boys can be dangerous. "MySpace: A Place for Friends" is an interactive Web site that invites the reader to create her own profile, upload her digital picture, and write her own blog about her personal life and special interests. Some young girls, it seems, have been posting nude and semi-nude pictures of themselves to attract male interest. The creators of MySpace have tried to act responsibly by developing new ways of detecting pictures that include too high a proportion of flesh tones! While MySpace may *feel* safe and private to the girls who post nude pictures, it is a public site, available to anyone with an Internet connection and the Web address. There have been many cases of dangerous encounters between predatory men and young girls seeking attention that were initiated on the Internet. Girls (as well as boys) need adult supervision and support as they read and write online.

Girls are also using e-mail, text messaging and instant messaging to stay in touch with the friends they already have—even those they see every day (Greer 2003). These messages are most often brief and filled with abbreviations and codes, but they do involve composing (writing) for specific social purposes. While there has been some speculation that these forms of writing may interfere with children's ability to spell and write in standard English, there is no real evidence that this is so. On the contrary, some teachers believe that online writing outside of school may increase writing fluency in school. It is of interest that more girls spend more time on e-mail and text messaging than do boys (Roberts and Foehr 2004).

Greer (2003) suggests that blogs and other forms of online journals may have changed the genre of "diary" from a private form of writing to a public one. Live Journal, for example, is a Web site with the tagline "A place where you can share your thoughts with the world." Greer points out that older Americans and Canadians are used to thinking of diaries as private documents, but that diaries have now come full circle. Young female diarists of the eighteenth and nineteenth centuries knew that their diaries were public documents that would be scrutinized by their parents and other authority figures. Only in the late nineteenth century did diaries become private documents, kept under lock and key. Today, through blogging, diaries have become public again. And today's online diaries are interactive. Online diaries typically consist of a "front page" where the diarist introduces herself to readers. A title/date list of entries allows visitors to choose which parts of the diary they would like to read. There is also an opportunity for visitors to leave notes and responses. But diaries are still, as they always have been, performances of girlhood, composed in complex cultural contexts that both enable and constrain what can be read and written.

Zines are another fascinating genre of writing that North American middle- and upper-class girls use to express themselves and to exercise agency. Zines are self-published, so computer technology and desktop publishing software are required for their production and distribution. They are alternatives to popular culture magazines and a form of independent media. They are not new (having first appeared in the 1930s), but the technologies being used to produce them today are relatively new.

Zine writers also include boys, but the international movement of zining today is most popular among girls who use writing and editing creatively to express themselves on a variety of topics and in a number of ways (Guzzetti 2002). Zines may publish the author's poetry, present articles on a topic that the popular media ignore, or express political views. Barbara Guzzetti (2004), for example, has studied adolescent girls who publish their own zines by writing against gender, race and class stereotypes, confronting homophobia and racism, speaking their minds in ways that are not culturally approved for girls, and attempting to inspire social activism through their writing. She found that these girls were supported in their zining by their parents, who shared their anger at social injustice, who encouraged their desire to think and write critically, and who had the economic resources to provide the computers, the software, and the supplies needed for their daughters' zine production. It is interesting to note that social class is an important factor in zine production. It may also be a factor in creating the confidence that girls require for speaking out both online and in the classroom. Hartman (2006) has found that white working-class girls are much less likely to speak out because they have found that their silence is approved in school—and that it is in their academic best interests to refrain from expressing their ideas and opinions.

Sometimes a passion for popular culture intersects with available technologies to inspire girls to create *new genres* for their writing. Chandler-Olcott and Mahar (2003), for example, investigated girls' "fan fiction" writing in a seventh-grade classroom in upstate New York. Two girls, marginalized by the upper–middle-class peer culture of their school, used their interest in *animé* (Japanese animation) to design personal texts written for their own social purposes. Working on the Internet at home in the evenings, the girls enjoyed *animé* online. They also collected *animé*-related videos, comics, and other memorabilia to support their recreational writing of *fan fictions*, stories they produced for themselves and other "insiders" familiar with the *animé*-inspired source material they had found online.

Chandler-Olcott and Mahar observed that, although much of this writing occurred at school, teachers were never made part of the audience of the girls' fan fictions; furthermore, the writing of fan fictions was neither acknowledged nor sanctioned by school literacy instruction in any way. Chandler-Olcott and Mahar understood the girls' writing of fan fictions as a construction of meaning in which the girls used popular culture to remake themselves. As they composed their fan fictions online, the girls integrated various visual, linguistic, and audio designs into one text. The girls' fan fictions were illustrated stories that borrowed from *animé* cartoons certain elements that the girls chose to incorporate into the Web pages where their fan fictions were posted (for other *animé* fans to read). The girls' complicated and sophisticated fan fictions were *hybrid* texts, woven from a variety of discourses and genres. They linked a variety of cultural texts to produce their work, relying on their readers' knowledge of popular culture to help them understand. They combined characters from more than one television show, for example, drawing on a variety of messages about heterosexual relationships that play out in many of the media and print texts of our time. All this allowed the girls to do identity work around female heterosexuality and issues of power. And all of this was invisible at school.

Chandler-Olcott and Mahar (2003) ask teachers to acknowledge these invisible forms of students' online literacies in order to understand and know their students (and their lifeworlds) better, helping them do a better job of overt instruction and critical framing in literacy instruction. Teachers need to be aware of these hidden online processes and multimodal designs so that they can provide classroom teaching that will engage *all* students in literacy learning. Students need to control many forms of literacy, some of them online literacies, to achieve full, equitable social participation in public, community, and economic life.

CONCLUSION

There is little doubt that girls today who have access to new interactive media enjoy them and find many uses for them, including new ways to be creative, new ways to maintain friendships, and new ways to extend their communities and enter the wider world. But girls can and do still read books and discuss them with their friends. They still write notes in the classroom and poetry and research reports for their teachers. Girls use literacy today in a wide variety of ways to participate in a North American culture of girlhood that they themselves help to create, to interact with popular culture and media, and to explore possibilities for adult womanhood (Greer 2003). Girls use literacy to perform girlhood—to be girls.

Further Reading

AAUW Educational Foundation. (1993). *How Schools Shortchange Girls*. New York: Marlowe.

Best, A. (2000). *Prom Night: Youth, Schools, and Popular Culture*. New York: Routledge.

Blair, H. A. (1996). "Gender and Discourse: Adolescent Girls Construct Gender through Talk and Text." Unpublished doctoral dissertation, University of Arizona, Tucson.

———. (1998). "They Left Their Genderprints: The Voice of Girls in Text." *Language Arts* 75, no. 1, 11–18.

———. (2000). "Genderlects: Girl Talk and Boy Talk in a Middle Years Classroom." *Language Arts* 77, no. 4, 315–323.

———. (2001). "On the Margins of the Middle: Aboriginal Girls in an Urban Middle School." In A. Ward and R. Bouvier, eds. *Resting Lightly on Mother Earth: The Aboriginal Experience in Urban Educational Settings*. Calgary, AB: Detselig Enterprises Ltd., pp. 63–81.

Chandler-Olcott, K., and D. Mahar. (2003). "Adolescents' Anime-Inspired 'Fanfictions': An Exploration of Multiliteracies." *Journal of Adolescent and Adult Literacy* 46, no. 7, 556–566.

Cherland, M. R. (1994). *Private Practices: Girls Reading Fiction and Constructing Identity*. London: Taylor & Francis.

———. (2005). "Reading Elisabeth's Girlhood: History and Popular Culture at Work in the Subjectivity of a Tween." In C. Mitchell and J. Reid-Walsh, eds. *Seven Going on Seventeen: Tween Studies in the Culture of Girlhood*. New York: Peter Lang, pp. 95–117.

Christian-Smith, L. K. (1990). *Becoming a Woman through Romance*. New York: Routledge.

Davies, B. (1991). *Frogs and Snails and Feminist Tales: Preschool Children and Gender*. Sydney, Australia: Allen & Unwin.

———. (2003). *Shards of Glass: Children Reading and Writing beyond Gendered Identities*. Creskill, NJ: Hampton Press.

Fetterley, J. (1978). *The Resisting Reader: A Feminist Approach to American Fiction*. Bloomington: Indiana University Press.

Finders, M. (1996). "Queens And Teen Zines: Early Adolescent Females Reading Their Way toward Adulthood." *Anthropology in Education Quarterly* 27, no. 1, 236–253.

Fishman, A. R. (1996). "Getting What They Deserve: Eighth-Grade Girls, Culture, and Empowerment." *Voices from the Middle* 3, no. 1, 25–32.

Gilbert, P. (1994). "And They Lived Happily Ever After: Cultural Storylines and the Construction of Gender." In A.H. Dyson and C. Genishi, eds. *The Need for Story*. Urbana, IL: NCTE.

Greer, J., ed. (2003). *Girls and Literacy in America: Historical Perspectives to the Present*. Santa Barbara, CA: ABC-CLIO.

Guzzetti, B. J. (2002). "Zines." In B. J. Guzzetti, ed. *Literacy in America: An Encyclopedia of History, Theory and Practice, Volume 2*. Santa Barbara, CA: ABC-CLIO, p. 699.

Guzzetti, B. J., and M. Gamboa. (2004). "Zines for Social Justice: Adolescent Girls Writing on Their Own." *Reading Research Quarterly*, 39, no. 4, 408–436.

Harper, H. (2007). "Reading Masculinities in Books About Girls." *Canadian Journal of Education*.

Hartman, P. (2006). "'Loud on the Inside': Working-class Girls, Gender, and Literacy." *Research in the Teaching of English* 41, no. 1, 82–117.

Lemish, Dafna. (1998). "Spice Girls Talk: A Case Study in the Development of Gendered Identity." In Sherrie A. Inness, ed. *Millennium Girls: Today's Girls around the World*. Lanham, MD: Rowman & Littlefield, pp. 145–167.

Mazzarella, S., and N. Pecora. (2001). *Growing Up Girls: Popular Culture and the Construction of Identity*. New York: Peter Lang.

Moje, E. B. (2000). "'To Be Part of the Story': The Literacy Practices of Gangsta Adolescents." *Teachers College Record* 102, no. 3, 651–690.

Orenstein, P. (1994). *School Girls: Young Women, Self-esteem, and the Confidence Gap*. New York: Doubleday.

Radway, J. (1984). *Reading the Romance: Women, Patriarchy, and Popular Literature*. Chapel Hill: University of North Carolina Press.

Rice, P. S. (2000). "Gendered Readings of a Traditional 'Feminist' Folktale by Sixth Grade Boys and Girls." *Journal of Literacy Research* 32, no. 2, 211–236.

———. (2002). "Creating Spaces for Boys and Girls to Expand Their Definitions of Masculinity and Femininity through Children's Literature." *Journal of Children's Literature* 28, no. 2, 33–42.

Roberts, D. F., and U. G. Foehr, with V. J. Rideout and M. Brodie. (2004). *Kids and Media in America*. Cambridge and New York: Cambridge University Press.

Rockhill, K. (1993). "Gender, Language and the Politics of Literacy." In B. V. Street, ed. *Cross-Cultural Approaches to Literacy*. Cambridge: Cambridge University Press, pp. 156–175.

Sadker, M., and D. Sadker. *Failing at Fairness: How America's Schools Cheat Girls*. New York: Simon & Schuster, 1994.

Schrum, K. (2003). "'That Cosmopolitan Feeling': Teenage Girls and Literacy, 1920–1970." In J. Greer, ed. *Girls and Literacy in America: Historical Perspectives to the Present*. Santa Barbara, CA: ABC-CLIO, pp. 103–120.

Skilton-Sylvester, E. (2002). "Literate at Home but Not at School: A Cambodian Girl's Journey from Playwright to Struggling Writer." In G. Hull and K. Schultz, eds. *School's Out! Bridging Out-of-School Literacies with Classroom Practice*. New York: Teachers College Press, pp. 61–92.

Smith, S. A. (2000). "Talking about 'Real Stuff': Explorations of Agency and Romance in an All-girls' Book Club." *Language Arts* 78, no. 1, 30–38.

Walkerdine, Valerie. *Daddy's Girl: Young Girls and Popular Culture*. Cambridge, MA: Harvard University Press, 1997.

———. *Schoolgirl Fictions*. London: Verso, 1990.

West, C., and D. H. Zimmerman. (1987). "Doing Gender." *Gender and Society* 1, no. 2, 125–151.

MEREDITH CHERLAND

Girls, Digital Culture, and New Media

Children and adolescents are often the first populations to begin using new forms of media. Ownership of information and communication technologies, such as computers and video game consoles, is more prevalent in households with children. This especially holds true for new media devices that are small, portable, and have been marketed especially to youth (for example, iPods and PSPs). Nevertheless, girls' exposure to and engagement with digital technology and new media have been impacted by traditional gender roles that have been re-inscribed in the technology and media itself. This has resulted in a gendered digital divide marked by higher rates of male participation in programming courses and lower numbers of women pursuing degrees in the fields of information technology and computer science. To better understand the relationship between girls and digital technology/new media, it is essential to recognize how gendered technological orientations have created a gendered digital divide. Yet girls have drawn from aspects of their bedroom culture to engage with digital technology on their own terms. In response to this, creators of new media have targeted girls as a special market, and moral panics have arisen regarding girls' unsupervised use of digital technologies. Still, girls have found diverse ways of using digital technology and new media to develop community, engage in self-empowerment, and pursue online routes toward girl-oriented activism.

THE GENDERED DIGITAL DIVIDE

The disproportionately high rates of male participation in programming courses and low numbers of women pursuing degrees in the fields of information technology and computer science can be traced back to gendered technological orientations. From an early age, boys are encouraged to view computers as toys to use at their leisure. At the same time, girls are more likely to approach a computer as a tool that will help them finish specific tasks. Most times these tasks are cast as feminine clerical activities, such as data entry and word processing. Thus, boys approach computers with a tinkering mentality and are enthusiastic about taking apart a device, whereas girls often experience feelings of unease when they receive error messages while working with computers. A study on mothers' and daughters' use of computers found that mothers tended to use computers for word processing and did not engage in programming, tinkering, pirating, or game playing. Although daughters use the computer more than their mothers, tinkering has consistently been found to be a male leisure-time activity.

The gendered digital divide has been a reality since the introduction of digital technologies. The first sign that this divide was narrowing came with female teachers' use of e-mail and Web browsers. Since then, computer courses have become more common in grade schools. However, when asked to identify factors that led to their interest in digital technology, very few female Web site creators refer to in-class instruction. Participation in online message boards and exposure to computer-savvy female characters in popular culture, such as Willow in *Buffy the Vampire Slayer*, are more often cited as factors that encouraged girls to view themselves as active participants in the world of digital technology.

Positive tech-savvy female role models may exist on television, but they are harder to find in video games. Women usually appear only as helpless victims who must be rescued or as eye candy that is ultimately obtained by a male character after the completion of a mission. The earliest examples of female characters that broke free from this mold, Ms. Pac-Man and Mama Kangaroo, were not even human. A recent study by the Children Now organization found that 64 percent of platform game characters are male, 19 percent are nonhuman, and only 17 percent are female. The majority of the characters controlled by players are male (73 percent), and only 15 percent are female. The female characters in video games are routinely objectified: 20 percent expose their breasts and more than 10 percent reveal their bottoms. Violence against these female characters is also common. Moreover, the violence is racialized: 90 percent of black female characters serve as victims of violence, but only 45 percent of white female characters are victimized.

While video game players can choose their own characters, it is in the realm of Massively Multiplayer Online Games (MMOG) that these characters interact with others. A MMOG is a computer game played simultaneously by hundreds or thousands of people logged on to an online host that connects them to the game. Players are allowed to design their own characters, or avatars, and determine whether they will mimic the objectified female characters of traditional video games. Choosing a female avatar has numerous repercussions in the online world. It is more common for male players to assist female avatars by guiding them through stages of the game or providing them with items that are useful for completing missions in the online game. Nevertheless, just as female characters in video games are routinely victimized, female MMOG avatars are more likely than their male counterparts to be targets of verbal harassment. And although MMOGs enable players to inhabit different body types, wear new hairstyles, or become supernatural creatures, male players are often preoccupied with determining the "real gender" of a female avatar. Interviews with female MMOG players indicate that women often encounter a hostile reception upon entering an online game but are met with more congenial attitudes if introduced via an existing relationship with a male player.

GIRLS' DIGITAL BEDROOM CULTURE

Researchers have argued for the existence of gendered technological orientations by pointing to the fact that boys are attracted to "new" media while girls spend more time consuming media available on "old" formats like television and radio. Even female members of a school's computer club will more often refer to movies and music in their casual conversations. However, girls have used their interest in these "old" media to enter the realm of new digital technologies. For example, young female fans of the ABC teen drama *My So-Called Life* regularly posted their thoughts and comments on an online bulletin board dedicated to the show. When the show was put on hiatus in 1995, the girls maintained contact through the bulletin board and acted together to put the show back on the air. They placed full-page ads in the entertainment trade magazines *Variety* and the *Hollywood Reporter*, calling for the return of their favorite show. This is just one example of how the Internet has enabled girls to engage with old media in a new environment. It is also an example of how girls' intimate conversations and romantic fandom have moved beyond the confines of their bedroom walls and are now being shared with others online. Bedrooms have historically been the space in which girls have been able to develop their own subculture even as their mobility is being hindered by parental restrictions. The "bedroom culture" associated with girls is to a large extent dependent on girls' access to media in their rooms. Thus, fashion magazines, a radio, and a telephone have become synonymous with the typical teen girl's intimate living quarters. The growing presence of computers within girls' rooms has recently created a "girls' digital bedroom culture." With access to computers and the Internet, many girls have replicated their bedroom culture in an online environment.

Early home pages created by boys and girls were often markedly different. Contests and competitions were usually the focus of boys' Web sites while girls encouraged interactivity and presented an idealized version of their bedrooms. For example, the wallpaper, graphics, and images often replicated what already existed in their rooms (pop stars, stuffed animals, and cartoon characters). In addition, many of the activities that the girls engaged in while in their rooms were easily transferable to the online environment. Thus, sending letters and creating a photo album took the form of signing a guest book and posting pictures. Girls' experience in keeping diaries served indirectly as a training ground for creating Web site entries, and their penchant for talking on the phone prompted them to include interactive elements on their sites, including chat functions, surveys, and advice columns.

The popularity of the social networking site MySpace has resulted in a remarkable rise in the number of what can be considered youths' personal Web sites. Although MySpace users are, to a large extent, dependent on the Web design that is built into the system, they still personalize their profile by adding photos of themselves and their friends, musicians, celebrities, cartoon characters, and so on. The features of a MySpace profile are remarkably similar to those cast as feminine in early personal Web sites. Blogs often function like diaries, surveys are routinely forwarded on the site, photos are uploaded on a regular basis, and posting comments is the most essential feature of the site. When girls were first establishing an online presence, there was a hope that online anonymity might empower them to assert ideas and opinions they were hesitant to voice in face-to-face encounters. The growing presence of girls online that has been enabled by MySpace holds this open as a possibility. Through their photos, surveys, and blogs, girls are producing a self-narrative in a public arena. However, many times they continue to privilege boys in this "self"-narrative. For example, a profile name like "adamschik43ver" is a new and unique identification but one that is ultimately dependent on a girl's connection to a boy.

The popularity of MySpace has been so widespread that youth use it in place of e-mail. Yet text messaging has remained an important part of digitally mediated communication. Studies have shown that girls send more text messages than boys. Often girls send messages with the intent of simply keeping in touch rather than communicating any particular bit of information. Such messages have been referred to as methods of establishing an "ambient virtual co-presence." The growing use of camera phones has resulted in a similar phenomenon termed "intimate visual co-presence." In both cases material is being shared and "full-time intimate communities" are being created. By sending text messages and photos, girls engage in a process of self-narration and continue the conversation that was once limited to the phone calls made from their bedrooms.

MARKETING TO GIRLS

Some researchers have claimed that girls do not gravitate toward video games because they are more oriented toward narrative genres and storytelling as opposed to acts of shooting and competition. This claim is a bit misleading since most video games that boys play are in one way or another connected to other media sources like comic books, movies, or cartoons. Therefore, without consciously thinking about it, boys may be creating their own narratives and piecing together the histories of the characters in the game. Nevertheless, many of the first computer games created for girls were viewed as markedly different for their emphasis on a narrative structure (these include *American Girl*, the *Purple Moon* titles, *Barbie Storyteller*, HerInteractive's *McKenzie & Co.*, and *Chop Suey*). *Barbie Fashion Designer* sold more than 500,000 copies in its first two months of release, making it the first best-seller within the girl video game market. Many of the games marketed to girls have tended to focus on stereotypically feminine activities such as applying makeup and changing hairstyles. However, some of the best-selling games of all time have taken a gender-neutral approach, appealing to both boys and girls. *The Sims* has had large male and female audiences. Likewise, *World of Warcraft* has been hugely popular with male and female gamers partially because players can choose from among diverse character roles that range from healers to warriors.

During the mid-1990s, prior to the release of *The Sims* and *World of Warcraft*, major game companies reworked their marketing and design approaches with an eye to potential female consumers. Media studies scholar Henry Jenkins refers to these trends as the "girls' game movement" and identifies five factors that shaped the movement. The first is purely economic: gaming companies were looking to expand their market by focusing on casual gamers, older gamers, and women. Jenkins identifies the second factor as a political move to try to develop girls' interest in science and engineering by introducing them to the gaming function of computers. Technology was the third factor. The home computer's new capability of hosting CD-ROM games meant that the barrier to entry was lower than it had been when games were limited to specific platform systems like Sega and Nintendo. Fourth, Jenkins credits the rise of female entrepreneurs who were launching female-oriented businesses during this time. The fifth factor that shaped the girls' game movement was a change in aesthetics that privileged more psychologically nuanced characters, softer color palettes, more richly layered soundtracks, new interface designs, and more complex stories.

At approximately the same time that game companies were courting girls, the Pokémon media franchise was released in the United States. The Pokémon video game was originally popular solely among adolescent boys but soon the video games, animé, manga, and trading cards were being enjoyed by elementary school children, preschoolers, and girls. Part of Pokémon's appeal among girls is credited to its manifestation as a virtual pet. The hand-held mini-computer Tamagotchi had already exposed girls to the responsibilities that caring for a virtual pet entails. When girls were introduced to Pokémon they found that making sure it ate, slept, bathed, and exercised was part of its allure. Pokémon's popularity among both boys and girls resulted in large audiences for the animated television series and moved the Kids WB (the Warner Bros. block of morning and afternoon programming) to the top of the cable ratings.

MORAL PANICS AND NEW MEDIA

Pokémon's multiple platforms as video game, animé, manga, and trading cards enable what cultural anthropologist Mimi Ito refers to as a "hypersocial" form of peer-to-peer social organization. The rarity of particular Pokémon media objects gives these objects a high exchange value that only kids and collectors recognize. Their understanding of the monetary value of particular items and their use of these items to establish social status has generated a new form of social organization based neither on adult rules nor on expectations for children. This has prompted many adults to try to monitor hypersocial behavior by banning Pokémon and Yu-Gi-Oh! trading card games.

Moral panics surrounding girls' use of new media have also been prompted by the existence of pro-ana and pro-mia Web sites. These Web sites and online communities approach anorexia and bulimia as lifestyle choices rather than physical or mental illnesses. These sites enable the development of bonds among a national and international community of anorexic and bulimic girls by providing tips for weight loss or purging and offering advice on how to avoid the surveillance of those who view anorexia and bulimia as diseases. Most pro-ana and pro-mia Web sites and online communities have been deleted by Internet service providers. However, the anthropomorphized "Ana" for anorexia and "Mia" for bulimia suggest an attempt to create a type of intimacy that is enabled through the communities that form online. This intimacy and friendly jargon is reminiscent of teen girls' bedroom culture and an indication that such conversations and attempts at establishing community existed long before the rise of the Internet.

The most widespread moral panic surrounding new media has arisen in relation to a fear of sexual predators targeting youth through the Internet. A study of five major daily newspapers' articles on teen girls and Internet crime found that girls are usually presented as the victims but rarely given a voice in these articles. Law enforcement officials are usually the main sources in these articles, and girls are positioned as needing to be protected not only from sexual predators but also from technology itself. The Deleting Online Predators Act of 2006 (DOPA) takes a similar approach to dealing with crimes in an online environment. The proposed U.S. federal legislation would require all schools and libraries that receive federal funds to restrict access to online communities. Internet filters would be used to block access to chat rooms and commercial social networking Web sites like MySpace. The supporters of the legislation reference a Crimes Against Children report stating that one in five children receive a sexual solicitation online. However, DOPA supporters overlook the fact that 76 percent of the unwanted solicitations came from fellow children. Most of the discussion surrounding DOPA and sexual predators continues to position youth, and especially girls, as helpless victims of adult men and new technology.

ACTIVISM, SELF-EMPOWERMENT, AND DEVELOPING COMMUNITY

The Riot Grrrl movement of the 1990s was organized in opposition to patriarchy and aimed at challenging the media's representation of girls as helpless victims. Distros (small, independent distribution companies that sell handcrafted goods, such as zines and buttons and stickers carrying names of bands and feminist slogans) used to function as mail-order companies. As the technology became more accessible, distros began to make use of computers and the Internet to distribute their productions. While they were used as sites of distribution, the distros' Web sites also linked to topical sites related to their interests, and some even advertised for fellow distros.

The ability of Web sites to link to other, related sites has enabled the use of archives and has also allowed for the distribution of fan fictions. Fan fiction and fanzine groups, even those associated with boys' content, are usually an arena inhabited by girls and women. Many of these fan fictions are based on animé (Japanese animation) series.

Animé is often characterized as either shonen animé or shoujo animé. Shonen animé consists of series that feature action, adventure, explosions, big robots, and battles. Boys are the target audience for these series. Shoujo animé tends to focus on the emotions and relationships between boy and girl characters. These series usually include strong female heroines and, not surprisingly, have strong female followings. In the early 1990s, the U.S. television industry realized that most of its programming was either for children or adults, and decided to import programming from Japan that would resonate with tween audiences. *Sailor Moon*, a shoujo animé about teen female superheroes, filled this gap and was the first shoujo animé to be officially licensed for distribution in the United States.

Sailor Moon provided many girls with their first exposure to the type of cultural artifacts that are consumed by *otaku*, or obsessive fans, especially of Japanese popular media. Since then, animé conventions have become more popular in the United States, and diverse animé series have been distributed online. However, a girl's decision to not simply consume animé but also actually create her own *manga* (Japanese comic) continues to be wrought with tension. Limiting one's otaku sensibility to reading manga and occasionally drawing a character is considered normatively feminine. However, the reality is that female participation within the realm of animé fan fiction stems from the 1970s and 1980s, when women began creating their own *doujinshi* (manga created by amateurs). Most of these doujinshi were fan fictions written for women by women and created romantic couplings between *bishounen* ("pretty boy") characters from mainstream manga. Since then, the production and sharing of doujinshi has been facilitated by the rise of the Internet. The producers of doujinshi post their stories online and receive validation from peers who are familiar with the original mangas that they draw from. The relationship between the doujinshi creator and the reader of the manga is reciprocal, with Web site creators often asking visitors to submit their own fan-written stories and fan-drawn pictures.

School-age creators of animé fan fictions have admitted that their personal writing is more important to them and of higher quality than the work they complete for classes. This is partially because they are writing for vastly different audiences. When developing fan fictions, they are writing for peers who are quite familiar with the characters and have a passion for the original text. On the other hand, when they write for school they are simply writing for a teacher or test scorer who is not necessarily invested in the subject of the essay. These differences are highlighted in *The Daily Prophet*, an online school newspaper created for Hogwarts, the magic school in the *Harry Potter* book series. *The Daily Prophet* was created by Heather Lawver, a teen girl living in rural Mississippi. She has hired columnists and outlined recommendations for how teachers can use her template to create their own version of a Hogwarts school newspaper. Many educators have welcomed the popularity of the *Harry Potter* book series because it has made kids excited about reading. However, youth like Lawver are not simply reading the books but are engaging more deeply with the world within the book and using online environments to seek out other fans and build on shared interests. Many U.S. media education initiatives and media literacy programs during the late 1990s focused on having girls protect themselves from media representations that might negatively affect their self-esteem. A common approach was to have girls keep a media journal in which they would make note of everything they consumed. The girls were also expected to create entries in a private journal. Very few of these programs actually encouraged girls to create their own productions. The growing accessibility of digital media allows for the possibility of girls creating their own self-narratives and sharing these with diverse communities.

Further Reading

Buckingham, David, and Rebekah Willett. (2006). *Digital Generations: Children, Young People, and New Media*. London: Lawrence Erlbaum Associates.

Cassell, Justine, and Henry Jenkins, eds. (2000). *From Barbie to Mortal Kombat: Gender and Computer Games*. Cambridge, MA: MIT Press.

——. (forthcoming). *Beyond Barbie and Mortal Kombat*.

Ito, Mimi. [Online February 2007]. Mimi Ito Weblog http://www.itofisher.com/mito/.

Jenkins, Henry. *Confessions of an Aca/Fan: The Official Weblog of Henry Jenkins*. [Online February 2007]. http://www.henryjenkins.org/.

Kearney, Mary Celeste. (2006). *Girls Make Media*. New York: Routledge.

Mazzarella, Sharon R., ed. (2005). *Girl Wide Web: Girls, the Internet, and the Negotiation of Identity*. New York: Peter Lang.

Sefton-Green, Julian. (1998). *Digital Diversions: Youth Culture in the Age of Multimedia*. London: UCL Press.

Seiter, Ellen. (2005). *The Internet Playground: Children's Access, Entertainment, and Mis-Education*. New York: Peter Lang.

KATYNKA Z. MARTÍNEZ

Girl Gamers

Girl culture has always had a somewhat uneasy relationship with digital games; and, reciprocally, digital games have had an uncomfortable relationship with girl culture. On the one hand, girl games occupy a marginal status in a world of computer games dominated by violent entries such as *God of War, Manhunt,* and *Stalker.* On the other hand, girls who play digital games are targeted directly by "pink box" titles like *Rocket's New School, Barbie: Horseshow,* or *Mary Kate and Ashley: Sweet 16.* This is not to say that girls have not played, or do not now play, digital games. Rather, their relationship with gaming—the access that they have to technology that allows play, and the kinds of games that they choose to play—depends on a broader cultural engagement with this new media form. Since the late 1990s girls and digital game play has received increasing—if erratic—attention from scholars and the gaming industry alike.

A HISTORY OF GIRLS AND DIGITAL GAMES

The Early Years

It was not until the appearance of *Barbie Fashion Designer* on the video game scene in 1996 that the industry first noticed a potential, as-yet-untapped market for games aimed at a female audience. The success of *Barbie Fashion Designer* (which stayed at the top of the game charts, beating out boys' games *Duke Nukem* and *Quake*) meant that a culture traditionally focused on the play patterns and preferences of men and boys was left asking, "What do girls and women want?" This sudden shift of industry focus led to the creation of many pink box titles—more from the Barbie franchise as well as Nancy Drew game titles and the development of the Purple Moon series. Purple Moon games were created by Brenda Laurel, formerly of MIT, who meant to target girls' interests directly by consulting real girls on the design of the game. As far as the industry was concerned, though, initial forays into the girls' game movement were unsuccessful: Mattel, who bought the Purple Moon series, soon stopped its development, and no Barbie computer game title since has been as successful.

At the same time, academics were beginning to take note of the public attention given to girls and game play. In 1998 Henry Jenkins and Justine Cassell produced an edited collection, *From Barbie to Mortal Kombat,* that explored some of the more pertinent issues of the girl gaming movement. One of the first concerns was that, while the Internet seemingly had a democratizing potential, if not carefully guided it could easily result in the marginalization of women and girls, whose voices would be minimized by the sheer dominance of male interests. It was argued that fewer women and girls were online than men, that they had fewer "safe places" to gather, fewer reasons to access the Net, and fewer communities to participate in online. Moreover, women and girls were largely underrepresented in technological fields. Socially, then, women and girls were seen to be less technologically skilled and less competent than their male counterparts. Key papers in the collection also focused on the potential of digital game play for engendering girls' technological abilities. For example, de Castell and Bryson provided a thoughtful discussion of the gendered nature of game play and detailed "player preferences," uncovering the kinds of games girls were drawn to. For instance, they noted that girls were drawn to games that were collaborative and exploratory, but that they avoided games that required confrontation and violence. The collection still represents the strongest commentary on girls and game play to date. In the intervening years, however, there have been new developments in the field and a shift in focus.

Contemporary Approaches to Girls and Gaming

In 2000 *The Sims* was released, and its follow-up, *Sims 2*, has become the top-selling PC game of all time. Along with traditional gamers, girls and women were buying and playing the game in record numbers. *The Sims* and its franchise, it has since been argued, is successful as a crossover hit for a number of reasons: its design team includes women, the game is based on the premise of an elaborate dollhouse, it provides varying and frequent interactions that appeal to a female audience, and it is essentially nonviolent. Ironically, the success of *The Sims* did not lead to a broadened market release of more appealing games for girls and women; these gamers continue to be radically underrepresented in the industry. The success of *The Sims*, however, did renew interest in the design of games for girls. For example, Sheri Graner Ray's recent *Gender Inclusive Game Design: Expanding the Market* (2004) tackles the question of design in video games for this nontraditional market through a simplified and stereotyped account of male and female players' differences and preferences. The author further makes suggestions on how designers can more effectively capture the attention of a female audience.

Scholars, on the other hand, have begun to move away from universalized and stereotyped accounts of girls and their game play. While girls certainly are less visible as gamers, they are still an integral part of the gaming community (Bryce and Rutter 2003; Carr 2005; Taylor 2006). They often now find support and encouragement in their play from their male relations (brothers, uncles, fathers, boyfriends, husbands) and are beginning to create communities of their own (e.g., Frag Dolls, Quake Grrls, Riot Grrrls, and numerous all-female Counterstrike communities). Rhetoric concerning preferences, moreover, has moved from denoting simple binaries (violence/no violence, collaborative/competitive) to recognizing that games are highly contextual and depend on social, cultural, and other everyday factors; game preference is not based simply on what a girl might like or dislike at a given moment (Carr 2005; Krotoski 2004). It is becoming clear that, while girls *do* play, what and how they play is always negotiable and context dependent; girl gaming does not necessarily occur only in the company of other girls or women.

RESEARCH ON GIRLS' GAME PLAY

It is relatively difficult to find rich, reliable data on the play practices of girls, primarily because studies include gender in game play for its statistical relevance alone. In quantitative surveys of video game ownership and play, for example, data is separated by gender to show that women and girls *are* playing games, but the information collected in no way accounts for the kinds of games they play, the duration of their gaming, or how these relate to the game play of their male counterparts. This account serves only as a kind of checkmark, glossing over what may be very different play patterns, preferences, and possibilities. Two large, oft-cited surveys that publish data on video game players in North

America are the Kaiser Family Foundation (http://www.kff.org/entmedia/) and the Entertainment Software Association (http://www.theesa.com). According to Kaiser's large survey of media and children (including over 2000 respondents and over 600 seven-day media use diaries), 33 percent of girls surveyed reported having a video game console in their bedrooms (compared with 63 percent of boys), while 48 percent of girls owned handheld video games (vs. 63 percent of boys). What these statistics do not provide is a clear picture of the kind of video game consoles respondents had access to in their bedrooms. The surveyors did, however, ask respondents to indicate the approximate time spent playing console and handheld games, concluding that there is a marked gender difference in terms of time spent on video game play:

> Boys are much more likely than girls to play video games on any given day (63 percent versus 40 percent, respectively), and to spend more than an hour daily with video games (31 percent versus 11 percent). Boys spend almost three times as much time as girls playing video games (1:12 versus 0:25). . . . Similarly, boys spend triple the time that girls spend playing console games (48 minutes versus 14 minutes), but just double the time for handheld games (24 minutes versus 11 minutes). (Kaiser Family Foundation 2005, p. 33)

The statistics of the Entertainment Software Association are much more general and report on gender only as it relates to number of players. Although they account for players by age, they do not report gender and age together, so it is difficult to surmise where girls fit into the picture, other than that they represent an unknown portion of the 38 percent of female game players.

REPRESENTATIONS OF FEMALE GAME CHARACTERS

Small steps have been taken by the industry to attract more female players by providing more varied female character choices in games. Lara Croft (*Tomb Raider* series) and Samus (*Mortal Kombat*) are no longer the only girl characters; players can now choose from a range of female characters in most role-playing games, in nearly all Massively Multiplayer Online Games (MMOGs), and in a range of other titles from *Mario Kart* to *Digimon Racing*. Sports games, however, continue to focus on male teams and players—the one exception being the new Wii "Sports" title that rotates between male and female non-player characters (NPCs).

At the same time, while the possibilities for choosing a female character in a video game have certainly increased, females are still highly underrepresented in digital games and tend to be more sexualized than male characters. Prominent female protagonists, like Lara Croft of the *Tomb Raider* series and Samus Eran from the *Metroid* series, are often referred to as examples of a changing tide in the video game industry toward less passive, more powerful female characters. Though there may be more active roles for female figures in games, they are still highly sexualized, depicted with oversized breasts and lips and very little clothing. Furthermore, they are almost exclusively white.

GIRLS AS GAME DESIGNERS

The first wave of public interest in, and research on, girls and gaming addressed game play as a way for girls to develop confidence and competence with new technologies. The second wave of social criticism addresses girls' roles as game designers. Designing games is thought to facilitate general computer use and proficiency in various levels and kinds of programming. Yasmin Kafai's (1995) groundbreaking research on children as game designers, along with the work of Valerie Walkerdine et al. (1998), neglect, however, to account for the contexts in which girls design games. They presuppose that, for girls and boys, the video game arena is a level playing field; they do not address particular issues of access to, and restrictions on, experiences that girls have as gamers. Until scholars take prior differences and contextual factors seriously, one cannot expect to find much deviation from the kind of gender stereotyping that has thus far dominated theory and research concerning girls and gaming.

THE ROAD AHEAD

Future Girl Gamers and the Industry

The video games industry has been widely criticized for not creating games that appeal to girls and women as well as for not hiring and retaining more female employees in key game design positions. A recent survey by Electronic Arts (a leading game design company), for example, found that only 40 percent of teenage girls play console games (compared with 90 percent of boys), and most of those leave behind their game playing after a year (http://news.bbc.co.uk/2/hi/technology/5271852.stm). In an effort to encourage girls in the design and development of games, a number of intervention-focused research projects have been carried out in North America to help give girls programming skills. These include the Rapunsel project, Alice and Storytelling Alice (open-source software that allows users to create 3D games) to teach programming, and Jill Denner's work with middle-school girls and digital game creation (Denner et al. 2005).

Contemporary girls' digital game designers promise greater attention to: "casual" games (easily interrupted or quick-play mini-games), "serious" games (games for education and training), and possibly also mobile games, using cell phones as primary platforms. These industry goals reflect deeply entrenched ideological assumptions about girls' future gaming desires, play styles and preferences. They presume that girls and women will prefer games that they do not have to invest much time in, games that have socially redeeming value (as opposed to those designed for entertainment only), and games that they can integrate with activities that allow them to engage with others (as opposed to solitary play). These attitudes toward girls and gaming reinforce inequitable experiences, conditions, and attributions that have thus far defined and delimited what and how girls play. Change may come, however, through technological innovation rather than ideological transformation.

Hope in Hybrid Games

The first video game success for girls was a hybrid of gaming and production. *Barbie Fashion Designer* did not encourage players to generate high scores on a screen; it allowed girls to design and produce real patterns for making Barbie clothes. The second hit, *The Sims* (alternatively characterized as a "sandbox" and a "dollhouse"), was also an amalgam of fixed-form game and free-form play. Most recently, another major crossover hit has emerged, *Guitar Hero*, which offers players the chance to star, alone or with another player, as either a male or female performer. Players utilize a plastic guitar controller that takes them through a variety of song choices at four levels of difficulty. A player who reaches expert levels (as the manufacturers encourage) might as well take up the real instrument since the skills involved are equivalent to those required for real guitar playing. Another new interactive game that girls tend to excel at is *Dance Dance Revolution*. This digital game combines music with dance; an actual floor dance pad registers players' abilities, matching them with dance steps projected on the screen. In terms of popularity, various versions of karaoke games—*Singstar*, *Karaoke Revolution: Country*, *American Idol*, and others—lie somewhere between these two options. These games encourage players to develop rock star–level vocal skills, providing solo or multiple singers with microphones with which to record their voices over a full musical backdrop. As a further development, the latest console from Nintendo, Wii, demands full-body physical engagement from players: they must actively go through the moves required in real sports games such as tennis, baseball, or bowling. Players engage "virtually" through their "Mii" avatar. What is important to note about the new hybrid game forms, which bridge traditional game and toy constructs, is that they are presumed to encourage and develop gamers' "real-world" abilities.

The defining obstacle marking the boundary between "real gamers" and those who merely dabble in video gaming has for many years been the game controller, known as the *joystick*. Much has been discussed regarding the disincentives in mainstream video game narratives—in characters, artwork, and the level of technological experience required. Little attention has been paid to the actual tool used for game play and its suitability for female players. Over time, the functional limitations of this ideologically unassailable command-and-control stick have become more apparent, and controller design has changed greatly, along with its terminology (references to joysticks are becoming increasingly scarce).

Current controller technologies are moving away entirely from manual controls like the "Thrustmaster" joystick—taking new forms such as microphones, dance pads, and guitars. These devices move the player from an eyes-to-screen relation into a fully embodied world of vision, sound, and activity—a notable advancement from the hand-on-joystick requirements of early video game play.

New game technologies, therefore—and specifically new game controllers that propel girl gamers beyond simply accepting what is made for them in gaming (reflected in so-called girl-friendly narratives, game types, and characters)—may lead to a rich future for female gamers.

Further Reading

Bryce, J., and J. Rutter. (2003). "The Gendering of Computer Gaming: Experience and Space." In S. Fleming and I. Jones, eds. *Leisure Culture: Investigations in Sport, Media and Technology*. Eastbourne, UK: Leisure Studies Association, pp. 3–22.

Carr, Diane. (2005). "Context, Gaming Pleasures and Gendered Preferences." *Simulation and Gaming* 36, no. 4, 464–482.

Cassell, Justine, and Henry Jenkins, eds. (1998). *From Barbie to Mortal Kombat*. Boston: MIT Press.

de Castell, Suzanne, and Mary Bryson. (1998). "Retooling Play: Dystopia, Dysphoria, and Difference." In Justine Cassell and Henry Jenkins, eds. *From Barbie to Mortal Kombat*. Cambridge, MA: MIT Press, pp. 232–261.

Denner, Jill, Linda Werner, Steve Bean, and Shannon Campe. (2005). "The Girls Creating Games Program: Strategies for Engaging Middle School Girls in Information Technology." *Frontiers: A Journal of Women's Studies* (special issue on Gender and IT) 26, no. 1, 90–98.

Ivory, James D. (2006). "Still a Man's Game: Gender Representation in Online Reviews of Video Games." *Mass Communication and Society* 9, 103–114.

Kafai, Yasmin B. (1995). *Minds in Play: Computer Game Design as a Context for Children's Learning.* Hillsdale, NJ: Lawrence Erlbaum Associates.

Kaiser Family Foundation. *Kids & Media @ The New Millennium: Program for the Study of Media and Health.* [Online April 2007]. Kaiser Family Foundation Web site http://www.kff.org/entmedia/1535-index.cfm.

Krotoski, Aleks. (2004). *Chicks and Joysticks: An Exploration of Women and Gaming.* London: Entertainment and Leisure Software Publishers Association.

Ray, Sheri Graner. (2004). *Gender Inclusive Game Design: Expanding the Market.* Hingham, MA: Charles River Media.

Taylor, T. L. (2006). *Play between Worlds: Exploring Online Game Culture.* Boston: MIT Press.

Walkerdine, Valerie. (1998). "Children in Cyberspace: A New Frontier?" In Karin Lesnik-Oberstein, ed. *Children in Culture.* London: Macmillan, pp. 231–247.

Walkerdine, Valerie, Angela Thomas, and David Studdert. (2007). *Young Children and Video Games: Dangerous Pleasures and Pleasurable Danger.* [Online April 2007]. University of Salford, Creative Technology Graduate Course Web site http://creativetechnology.salford.ac.uk/fuchs/projects/downloads/young_children_and_videogames.htm.

Suzanne de Castell and Jennifer Jenson

Representations of Girls and Young Women in Film as an Entry Point to Studying Girl Culture

Films offer a window into culture and, more generally, into our society's perceptions of gender, family, and social life. At the same time, films offer a means by which we understand who we are and how we should behave. Films, then, reflect as well as shape our images of ourselves and others. For girls and young women, this function of films assumes a special importance. While there have been representations of girls in film since the days of child star Shirley Temple in the 1930s—and even earlier—the representations of girls in films in the mid-1990s up to the early twenty-first century are particularly relevant both as girl culture and as an entry point to the study of girl culture. Indeed, films made about girls during this period have portrayed the changing nature of girls' experiences with an eye toward possible profits to be made in the production of films about young women—which ultimately become an integral part of girl culture.

In films since the early 1990s, teen girl audiences emerged as one of the most powerful demographic groups. This can be seen in the success of a range of genres from low-budget romantic comedies such as *Clueless* (1995), to nostalgic films such as *Now and Then* (1995), to slasher parodies such as *Scream* (1996), and finally to big-budget films like *Titanic* (1997), whose female film audience contributed to its unprecedented success. Television, too, has offered a rich variety of strong, young female characters in such shows as *Charmed* (1998–2006), *Dawson's Creek* (1998–2003), *Felicity* (1998–2002), and *Buffy the Vampire Slayer* (1997–2003). These kinds of cultural representations of young women are mirrored in the music industry by performers from Britney Spears to Lindsay Lohan to Britain's Spice Girls. What is shared by many of these cultural icons and film and television characters is a sense of their social power as young women—what came to be known as Girl Power.

GIRL POWER AND SECOND-WAVE FEMINISM

While many of the girl films of the 1990s could be said to represent Hollywood's attempt to tap into the growing girl consumer market, these films also represent a kind of postfeminist response to the original ideals of the women's movement from the 1960s; this is often referred to as the "second wave" of feminism. These new representations of girls take for granted that equality has been achieved and that female empowerment, or Girl Power, includes a healthy dose of ironic deployment of female sexuality. Girls in these contemporary films are viewed as free agents who can make choices, and when they must do battle, it is often viewed as a response to threats from other, competitive females. Sisterhood becomes understood as finding your few true girlfriends in a social landscape peppered with female competitors.

Film scholar Kathleen Rowe Karlyn argues that young women today no longer see the past struggles of their mothers as part of their own social landscape. This new landscape distances young women from a more collective sense of their lives as part of a larger struggle at the same time as it privatizes any conflicts or ambivalences they may have in trying to live up to the tight strictures of, say, femininity (dieting, for example, is a private response to the desire to live up to the prevailing cultural norms of beauty). As she writes, "Brought up during a period of social conservatism, young women today are reluctant to identify themselves with any social movement and instead more likely to place their faith in free-market individualism."

For scholars such as Judith Butler, the new cultural representations of young women assume that freedom and ambition are part of young women's lives. In fact, for Butler, this new freedom has led to a new kind of subjection to larger cultural norms, or what she calls the "ethic of freedom." Writing about this burden for young women, cultural studies scholar Angela McRobbie goes on to note that "[t]hese popular texts normalize post feminist gender anxieties so as to reregulate young women through recourse to administrations of freedom . . . these forms successfully drive a wedge between women, which set off the mother, the teacher, and the feminist into the realms of a bygone age. By these means post feminism undoes feminism, on the basis that it is 'always already known.'"

INTERGENERATIONALITY

Relationships between mothers and daughters in contemporary films often personify intergenerational struggles, to the point where the daughter is often shown as more mature and grown-up than the parent. In the film *Anywhere But Here* (1999), Susan Sarandon plays a neurotic, flighty mother who drags her thoughtful, intelligent daughter, played by Natalie Portman, off to California to fulfill her own needs. Even in relatively gentle fare, the mother is more often than not portrayed as a peer who is herself in need of counsel, as in such shows as *Gilmore Girls* (2000), where the daughter must often assume the role of "bff," or "best friend forever." Describing the characters' relationship, one viewer writes, "Lorelai Gilmore, 32, has such a close relationship with her daughter Rory that they are often mistaken for sisters. Between Lorelei's relationship with her parents, Rory's new prep school, and both of their romantic entanglements, there's plenty of drama to go around."

Often in these intergenerational representations, the mother is portrayed as simply too narcissistic to know how to parent. For example, in *Titanic* (1997), the mother is so consumed with protecting and improving both her own and her daughter Rose's social status that she will not even acknowledge the working-class character played by Leonardo DiCaprio, who saves Rose's life. In another film explicitly directed to girl audiences, *The Parent Trap* (1961, remade in 1998), the mother and father are both so selfish that they choose to split up their twin daughters—one for each parent—when they divorce during the children's infancy, rather than work together to co-parent. It is only when the two girls meet at a summer camp by accident that each realizes she has an identical twin.

SISTERHOOD AS TOXIC

In recent girl films more generally, some swipes are taken against the most sacred tenets of second-wave feminism. For example, the whole notion of girls being supportive of other girls, or "sisterhood is powerful," becomes deeply problematic in many recent films directed at girls. In fact, Girl Power becomes a kind of double-edged sword, something that unites girls but at the same time can destroy or harm them. While the notion of power can imply strength, it can also imply danger; in the case of Girl Power, this means that girls can be each other's worst enemies.

For example, in *Mean Girls* (2004), the lead girl character, played by Lindsay Lohan, finds herself in a social jungle that she must wade through in order to survive her high school years. Similar to this scenario are those presented in other recent films directed at girls, including *Jawbreaker* (1999), *Clueless* (1995), *13 Going on 30* (2004), and *The Princess Diaries* (2001). In these films, girls find themselves at the mercy of the "mean girls" in their school and are tormented by these young predatory females. In some of the films, such as *Clueless*, the girl characters themselves possess an inordinate social power; their bond is what solidifies this power in the high school social hierarchy, at the same leading to internal conflicts between them. In fact, in the film *Jawbreaker*, the popular girls actually find themselves "eating their own," as their friendship leads to one of them being choked to death by a jawbreaker candy. Here is how one viewer describes the film: "Meet Liz Purr: Friendly. Pretty. And popular. Flash-forward to the morning of her 17th birthday, and you'll find her being taken out of her bed, tied-up, and taken to the trunk of the car that her three best friends (Courtney, Julie, and Marcy) are riding [in] while being gagged with a jawbreaker. Everything goes terribly wrong as the 3 girls pop the trunk to find Liz dead, from choking on the rock hard candy."

Alternatively, in *The Princess Diaries* (2001) and *Never Been Kissed* (1999), the lead girl characters find themselves isolated, and it is another girl who befriends them and serves as an emotional salve against the cruelties of the other girls. Whether they are shown as socially powerful or powerless, however, the social world is peopled with "Alpha Girls" who are out to knock other girls down in the social hierarchy. In either case, it is a far cry from the earlier feminist credo "sisterhood is powerful." While the girls in these films try to find other girls to bond with and to help them feel less isolated, this often takes place within the context of a social world filled with predatory, hyper-competitive females.

DOMESTIC AND WORKING LIFE

In those films for girls where the original ideals of feminism are dealt with directly, such as women's right to have meaningful careers, there is commonly the implicit assumption that women have always been able to hold high-profile jobs, but there is also the inevitable cautionary tale of how these careers are themselves problematic for the female characters. In other words, when a female character is shown pursuing a career, it is simply assumed that she would be able to be a high-profile editor, emergency room physician, head of a modeling agency, and so on. At the same time, these prominent women are shown to be unhappy or unable to have meaningful relationships outside of their jobs; and upon realizing this they often give up their careers to be with the romantic male lead.

Three actresses who are often cast in films for younger female audiences are Reese Witherspoon, Jennifer Garner, and Kate Hudson. These young female stars themselves are often portrayed in film and gossip magazines as being contented with their new roles as first-time mothers in "real life." They are invariably photographed with their children in "ordinary" activities such as going to the beach or shopping for food or baby clothes. In the world of gossip magazines, these young female stars represent the wholesome embodiment of the new wave of motherhood in Hollywood more generally. Girls identify strongly with these positive role models who are both glamorous, fitting back into their pre-pregnancy bikinis within weeks of giving birth (with the help of personal trainers) and relentless in affirming their belief that motherhood is the best thing that ever happened to them. That they are celebrities who can command millions of dollars per film for light romantic comedies directed toward increasingly younger female audiences seems almost incidental to their lives, for they are more often portrayed as engaging in family activities outside the vortex of Hollywood superstardom.

Perhaps not surprisingly, then, these young female actresses are often cast as workaholic young women who must learn the painful lesson that they have nearly managed to sacrifice true happiness by putting too much emphasis on their work, to the exclusion of finding true love and motherhood. By the end of these films, however, female viewers witness their transformation, as they end up choosing the nice guy and the family and live happily ever after. The larger message for girls is that, as in the real lives of their film star heroines, true happiness lies not in the competitive working world of Hollywood, but in the realm of the family.

This lesson is brought home in several recent films directed toward younger female audiences. In the Reese Witherspoon movie *Just Like Heaven* (2005), for example, Witherspoon portrays an overworked attending physician who had no life until she became a coma patient.

In *Raising Helen* (2004) Kate Hudson portrays a young, career-obsessed woman whose sister dies unexpectedly and leaves her to take care of her three young children. By switching roles and replacing her sister as a full-time parent, she realizes what she has been missing in life, which in turn allows her to get together with the handsome pastor who runs the school that her nieces and nephew go to.

Finally, in *13 Going on 30* (2004), the female character played by Jennifer Garner is a high-profile editor who loses consciousness, literally, of the important things she gave up along the way, including the crush she had on Mark Ruffalo's character when she was 13. In her desire to be a grown-up, she forgets that as a young girl she had to dump the younger Mark in order to run with the "Alpha Girls"—in other words, to achieve popularity in high school, she launched herself into a trajectory of soulless careerism. In fact, the actor Mark Ruffalo ends up in several of these light romantic comedies, playing the low-key, hip, urban, anti-macho "nice guy," whom the young women mistreat until they realize the error of their careerist ways and discover where true happiness lies.

This stereotype of the nice guy and careerist young woman who almost loses her only chance at real happiness is echoed in the recent comedy *View from the Top* (2003), starring Gwyneth Paltrow, another young actress who recently gave birth (to her second child) in real life. In this film, Mark Ruffalo once again appears as the nice boyfriend jettisoned by Paltrow's character, who is so focused on getting to the top of the airline attendant food chain and becoming a stewardess on international flights that she almost loses him forever—as well as, by implication, the opportunity to be grounded, in a good way, with a man who will love her.

SEX AND POWER

Another area where films aimed at girls challenge earlier views of feminism is in the equating of girls' social power with their newly found sexual power. In the 1960s, the treatment of women as sexual objects was perceived as one of the primary forms of oppression of women in society. In critiques of everything from advertisements, to films, to sexual harassment in the labor force, and all the way to incest and rape, women's sexuality was viewed as something exploited by men and used to keep women effectively in a permanent underclass, exploited and unsafe. For young women today, however, the demonstration of their sexuality, via everything from clothing, to music, to explicit forms of overt sexual behavior, is portrayed as something that increases their social power.

These sexual displays are often portrayed as "innocent," as when Jennifer Garner excitedly grabs her newfound breasts in 13 Going on 30, and proudly shows them off to "another" 13-year-old. Since she is supposedly a 13-year-old trapped in the body of a 30-year-old, we are meant to be happy for her now that she has these grown-up breasts that are not really hers.

Even more common than this innocent view of female sexuality as a surprise to the young girl is the idea that her newly discovered sexuality is a source of social or even physical power, as is the case with such television shows as Buffy the Vampire Slayer and Charmed, both of which routinely depict beautiful young women in tiny costumes displaying superhuman powers. These young women demonstrate their sexuality not only through their clothing but also by using it as a form of empowerment and strength as they battle all kinds of human and superhuman evil forces.

A third view of girls' sexuality as empowering can be seen in the myriad Cinderella-type films in which the girl undergoes a transformation from ugly duckling to sexy swan. In Never Been Kissed (1999), Drew Barrymore is portrayed as a beautiful, sexy twenty-something who goes undercover to a high school and identifies with the supposedly ugly-duckling nerd Leelee Sobieski. We know that Drew will finally be kissed, a feat that could never have happened in high school, when she herself was nerdy and not sexy. In The Princess Diaries, the character of Anne Hathaway becomes socially powerful only when she undergoes the transformation from sexless ugly duckling to sexually desirable princess. However, she still remembers her nerdy friend when she becomes a beauty and in the end, her friend similarly undergoes a cosmetic transformation, mirroring television reality shows such as Extreme Makeover.

In film after film directed to girl audiences, sexual power and beauty are inextricably linked as the means of social acceptance. The only wrinkle is the fact that these young women are still "themselves" underneath; the message presumably is that what is inside is more important than what is on the outside. At the same time, however, it is clear that what was inside was not enough to make it in the social hierarchy, so the subliminal message is that looks do matter, and that sexual power is the means by which social acceptance is achieved.

BEYOND BLONDE

This message is most clearly articulated in the Reese Witherspoon film Legally Blonde (2001), which was a huge commercial success with young female audiences. In this film Witherspoon plays Elle, a young, ditzy girl from Southern California who is crushed when her boyfriend breaks up with her because he is going to Harvard Law School and does not think she is smart enough to be part of his new life. The character, Elle, finds herself in the position of fighting for him by studying for the law boards herself and, to everyone's surprise, gaining admittance into Harvard also, where she is continually subjected to the other students' perception of her as another "dumb blonde." Through the course of the film, however, a transformation occurs as she is shown using her knowledge of fashion, girl culture, and tenacious hard work, which allows her to both excel in law school and realize that she does not want to be with the boyfriend after all.

In *Legally Blonde*, then, are all the trappings of the "new" or ironic postfeminism: the female character realizing with dismay that she is considered a "dumb blonde," yet at the same time having the audience in on the joke that her looks are really a source of her ability to outwit those around her. In fact, this version of postfeminism asserts that Elle's intelligence is derived, at least in part, from her ability to use her feminine intuition to gain an advantage in the legal world. She also uses her knowledge of the fashion world—the world of looks—to beat out those around her who would simply dismiss her as a dumb blond. The audience is supposedly in on the fact that, of course, you can be a "dumb blonde" and at the top of your class at Harvard Law School. These are not mutually inconsistent positions, but proof of the new kind of Girl Power, one based, at least in part, on playing into the earlier trappings of femininity.

There have been several comparisons made between *Legally Blonde* and recent films directed at girls that play on this idea of using feminine wiles as a means of empowering the female protagonist. Writing about the hip, ironic stance that these movies adopt, film scholar Cynthia Fuchs goes on to observe, "And if you pay money to see it, *Legally Blonde* presumes, you get the joke: all this foofiness is really just a way to sugar-coat Elle's steely resolve, admirable ingenuity, and fabulous moral fiber, and—more importantly—to indict the entrenched gender/class/race systems that put her in her place (on top, sort of)" (http://popmatters.com/film/reviews/l/legally-blonde.shtml).

This, then, is the way feminism is served up in many contemporary films directed to girls: when sexism is explicitly recognized, it is countered with a kind of self-conscious, hyper-feminine awareness that becomes a means of combating the sexism. The use of irony and being in on the joke allows girls to both laugh at and identify with the use of feminine wiles to overturn the entrenched order.

CONTEMPORARY GIRL CULTURE THROUGH A HISTORICAL LENS

For the most part, contemporary films directed toward girls take the gains of feminism for granted and seldom question them, particularly when it comes to their portrayals of the world of work for women. The big exception to this formula lies in those contemporary films that explicitly deal with period representations of young women. For example, in the film *Ever After* (1998), Drew Barrymore plays a Cinderella character who demonstrates a kind of proto-feminism embodying the ideals of second-wave feminism. As one viewer describes her character:

> Andy Tennant's film *Ever After* tells the "real" story of Cinderella. In this film version, Cinderella is Danielle De Barbarac, played to perfection by Drew Barrymore. Our heroine does have a wicked stepmother and stepsisters, but in no way is she in need of rescuing. Contrary to other adaptations of Cinderella, Danielle rescues herself from her horrible family and the prince from gypsies. With help from her fairy godmother Leonardo da Vinci, Danielle overcomes hardship, marries Prince Charming, and lives happily ever after.

In another historical film, *Joan of Arc* (1999), the idea that a young woman not only could stand up for herself, but could lead her nation forward, is given life. In this television film, the young actress Leelee Sobieski portrays the historical figure of Joan of Arc not simply as victim, but as a young woman from humble beginnings who is able to defy the great powers and stand up for what she believes in. Here is how one young female viewer described her reaction to seeing this film in her history class:

> I saw this movie in my history class, and it was great! It makes her an extreme role model that says that girls can do anything guys can, and sometimes in this case, much better. I still think it was sooooo unfair that this wonderful hero had to die in the end but it really makes you believe that she is the Maid of Larine! It really shows the pain that Joan had to go through, whether the information was real or not, this was still a wonderful historical movie.

Yet another period film, the remake of *Little Women* (1994), features several young female stars in a vehicle that radically questions traditional roles for women. In addition, the film allows for a historically accurate portrayal of a mother figure, who is depicted as neither a "best friend" nor a narcissistic or weak character.

In these three films, young women are portrayed as struggling against their traditional roles and demonstrating bravery in the face of these restrictions. Period and historical films for young women can be said to open up a kind of cultural space that actually allows for a reconciliation of the generational conflicts between the second-wave feminists and their postfeminist daughters.

This attempt at reconciliation is most explicitly confronted in the film *Mona Lisa Smile* (2003). During the 1950s, Katherine Watson (played by Julia Roberts) accepts a job as an art professor at Wellesley College. At this all-girl school, the free-spirited Watson guides her students through the limitations that society places on them and fosters their intellectual and personal growth. The film itself includes many A-list young Hollywood stars, including Kirsten Dunst, Julia Stiles, and Maggie Gyllenhaal, who are portrayed as biding their time while they wait to get married.

The film emphasizes the differences between "then" and "now" and includes some unique DVD special features, among which are sections titled "College Then and Now" and "What Women Wanted: 1953." In these clips, historical footage is shown of young women from the early 1950s, the stores they shopped in, and the cars and other consumer items they were encouraged to buy. Interspersed with this footage are statistics that include the percentages of women working, who took full-time jobs upon graduation, and who claimed to be virgins, then versus today.

Despite the emphasis on difference, the movie also demonstrates the relevance of the issues faced by young women in the 1950s to girls today. Because the film depicts a pre–sexual revolution vision of how women lived, it can play to both second-wave feminists and their postfeminist daughters with its depiction of the "before" time—before the women's rights movement of the 1960s. Interestingly enough, the persona Julia Roberts adopts in her other films is partly that of a woman who is railing against the social structures women find themselves in, also presented in such films as *Erin Brockovich* (2000) and *Mystic Pizza* (1988). In *Mona Lisa Smile*, however, the character must confine herself to challenging her young charges to look beyond marriage after college.

The more general point is that, in *Mona Lisa Smile*, the question of women's place is explicitly raised. In this way, it resembles other period films for young women that use history as a backdrop to make the point that women's freedom is something that was not always a given, but is rather the result of struggles on the part of the female characters. The character played by Julia Roberts is effectively a voice from the future, exhorting her

1950s students to wake up from their cultural slumber. By the end of the film, the young women do indeed question what was behind Mona Lisa's smile. At the same time, however, the character played by Julia Stiles admonishes Julia Roberts's character to honor her own choice to marry and have children—since Roberts had told them that they should be free to choose—even though Stiles's choice is not one Roberts's character would herself make.

This theme of Roberts herself being hypocritical is echoed by the handsome Italian professor who, upon being exposed as a fake war hero, in turn challenges Roberts's character for running away from happiness and "burying" herself in work. This condemnation of the character's use of her job to bury her ambivalence about her personal life underscores the fact that the film raises the specter of women's careerism in the same way that lighter, contemporary romantic comedies do. Whereas women's careerism becomes a familiar trope in many films directed toward girl audiences, in period and historical films it is raised within the context of an entire culture that held women's labor force participation to be deeply suspect and that would eventually be challenged by the women's movement of the 1960s.

Though a review of recent films aimed at girls reveals a kind of amnesia with regard to the struggles of the second wave of the women's movement, there are exceptions, including period films in which young women are portrayed as questioning the strictures of their time. In these films, the point is not so much that the young women are ahead of their time as that their lives and the limitations they faced are something that young women of that time were forced to fight against.

GROWING UP

Also in contrast to the spate of Girl Power films are those films that explore the conflicts and issues girls face in navigating the road to adulthood. For example, the "sisterhood is powerful" theme of recent films has too often been presented as a kind of bulwark against other girls in the social landscape of high school. There are signs, however, that portrayals of young women bonding together in the face of the larger, adult issues they face represent a renewal of the idea that girls can draw strength and sustenance from one another.

One example of the kind of film where young women negotiate the pains of becoming adults together is *Sisterhood of the Traveling Pants* (2005), which portrays four young women who provide emotional support for one another by sharing a pair of jeans that magically adapts its size to fit the wearer. One viewer notes:

> This is NOT a chick flick, this isn't a teeny-pop film, and there's NO Hilary Duff or Lindsay Lohan anywhere in sight. The *Sisterhood of the Traveling Pants* is about the fears and insecurities that all young people feel as they enter adulthood, boys and girls. We all have to deal with our bodies, with our parents, with love, and with death, and this film deals with all of these issues with honesty, sensitivity, and maturity. And most importantly, this movie reinstates the fact that none of us has to deal with these issues alone. (http://www.imdb.com/title/tt0403508/usercomments)

The film *Now and Then* (1995), which has been accused of being a female version of Rob Reiner's *Stand by Me* (1986), also shows young women bonding together and facing all kinds of coming-of-age issues, as does the British film *Bend It Like Beckham* (2002), starring Keira Knightley.

Both *Mona Lisa Smile* and *Little Women* portray young women serving as emotional anchors for one another as they cope with the adult world. It may be in the portrayal of permanent, sustaining friendships between girls—in the face of so many other changes in young women's lives—that the earlier feminist message that "sisterhood is powerful" is most clearly discerned. In recent films directed toward older women the theme of female friendships also resonates. For example, *Sisterhood of the Traveling Pants* has been referred to as a young adult version of *Divine Secrets of the Ya-Ya Sisterhood* (2002) or *Waiting to Exhale* (1995), and it is clear that such films tackle the issues of the second wave of feminism most directly.

Girl culture and interrogations of feminism are alive and well in contemporary Hollywood films featuring girl protagonists. The number of films focusing on girls released between 1995 and 2005 gives a sense of the range of issues to be taken up through exploring girlhood as well as an insight into the marketability of girl culture itself.

Further Reading

Gateward, Frances, and Pomerance, Murray, eds. (2002). *Sugar, Spice, and Everything Nice: Cinemas of Girlhood*. Detroit, MI: Wayne State University Press.

Karlyn, Kathleen Rowe. (2003). "*Scream*, Popular Culture, and Feminism's Third Wave: 'I'm Not My Mother'." *GenderOnline*, no. 38, http://www.genders.org/g38/g38_rowe_karlyn.html.

Kramer, Peter. (1999). "Women First: *Titanic*, Action-Adventure Films, and Hollywood's Female Audience." In Kevin S. Sandler and Gaylyn Studlar, eds. Titanic: *Anatomy of a Blockbuster*. New Brunswick, NJ: Rutgers University Press, pp. 108–131.

McRobbie, Angela. (2004). "Notes on Feminism and Popular Culture: Bridget Jones and the New Gender Regime." In Anita Harris, ed. *All about the Girl: Culture, Power, and Identity*. New York: Routledge, p. 12.

Tally, Peggy (2002). "Re-imagining Girlhood: Hollywood and the Tween Girl Film Market." In Claudia Mitchell and Jacqueline Reid-Walsh, eds. *Seven Going on Seventeen: Tween Studies in the Culture of Girlhood*. New York: Peter Lang, pp. 311–329.

MARGARET TALLY

Whose Girlhood? Race, Representation, and Girlhood

Is "girlhood" a collective experience? At perhaps many different levels there are aspects of "being a girl" that can be considered part of the broader context of "girlhood." However, the question of "whose girlhood?" immediately necessitates a shift in perspective in how we consider categories of race and representation as well as how racial images of girlhood are reflected, examined, and understood in society. The social construction of girls' identity within a Western perspective may reflect the similarities of those experiences that affect how girls are generally viewed and treated within society. These collective experiences can offer some threads within, or common features of, girlhood that are based on gender identity or gender association. Through a sense of shared gender identity, developmental stages in girlhood can provide bases from which girls come to know what it means, or feels like, "to be a girl." But does this mean that shared moments of "girlhood identity" are the same, regardless of how race and representation are constructed in society?

The intersection of difference from the vantage point of race and representation must generate critical questions about how difference is understood within images of girlhood. Whether as a member of the dominant culture (usually implying an "insider" status) or as a member of a subordinate group (generally associated with minority status as an "outsider"), the interplay of identity and power is evident in how girlhood is defined. A good example can be found in the creation of the social cliques that emerge in high school. For many girls, these cliques may operate in defining who is accepted as part of the "in group" and is subsequently able to exert some control or power over what is viewed as "cool" or "trendy." The insider status of the dominant members of society operate in the same way by permitting those individuals to define what counts and what should be valued.

From the perspective of visible minority group members, the images of "girlhood" that have often received recognition tend to reflect the "typical" experiences of being a girl from the perspective or viewpoint of the dominant culture. These images of girlhood are often expressed through images of whiteness. Debutante balls—or social parties or gatherings—held among the social elite or upper-class members of society are examples of how the dominant group exerts control or power in defining universal images of girlhood. Similar to these exclusive social parties, which require certain levels of economic wealth for one to participate, the images of whiteness produced by the dominant or social elite are considered as typical experiences to be encountered by average white girls. Although many young white girls may not participate in all of these so-called defining events, barred by monetary and other restrictions (such as differences in parental rules or geographic location, or pure denial of opportunity), the underlying assumption is that these aspects of life are what constitute a general sense of girlhood in Western society. From the stereotypical assumptions of sleep-over parties, dating, and hanging out with friends, to talking on the phone or text (and instant) messaging, the emphasis on traditional notions or images of girlhood permeates how girlhood has been defined, and continues to be viewed, in North America.

The emphasis on these experiences as normative behaviors of girls is further re-defined and legitimized by the reflections of "white identity" that saturate the various media—in television programs, including *Full House*, *Seventh Heaven*, and *Gilmore Girls*; magazines directed at specific audiences, such as *Tiger Beat*, *Teen*, and *Cosmo Girl*; and toys and games, including Barbie, cosmetics kits, and dollhouses. The sense of shared or common experiences of girlhood may position girls differently depending on how they are viewed as "other" or "different from" those who constitute or reflect the so-called norm. Young girls who experience differences in girlhood outside the representations of whiteness may internalize their experiences as being less important or undervalued because there are no visible traces of these experiences within popular contemporary notions of girlhood in society. Notably, very few television shows focus on girlhood from any perspective other than that of typical, middle-class white households. There are very few moments when the traditional Bat Mitzvah of Jewish girls is celebrated or even represented—just as there are few moments in which young Latina girls' Quinceañeras are made visible within popular representations of girlhood. Even fewer toys, games, and magazines are available with non-white representations of girlhood. Thus, for these girls, the sense of belonging or experiencing girlhood as represented and defined in Western society is contingent upon participating in events that are distant, if not remote, from their own cultural practices or traditions. For young Muslim girls, having boyfriends and dating are not cultural practices or traditions generally endorsed in their religion. Thus, as a mere consequence of being "other," some girls may comprehend their differences as aspects of their identity that deny them the collective, anticipated, and—most important—socially sanctioned experience of girlhood, particularly within a North American context.

For those girls whose experiences are not recognized as part of the collective identity of girlhood, the recognition of being "other" may become internalized as another aspect of life in which their identities as members of society are erased, silenced, or simply denied. These young girls may view their differences as preventing them from fully participating in socially ascribed activities, removing them still further from feeling embraced and accepted as part of the larger culture. The paradox of this type of thinking is that, despite their desire and will to belong, those who are viewed or represented as "other" cannot reconstruct themselves sufficiently to fit into the representations of girlhood as defined by the dominant culture.

The recognition and politics of being "different" as understood from multiple perspectives is relevant to any discussion of girlhood in contemporary society. Thus it is crucial to probe further, questioning how race and representation affect the experiences of those defined as other in relation to "normal" girlhood. Preliminary questions in reflecting on "whose girlhood" include: How do representations of girlhood become fixed within our cultural discourse? How powerful is the media in constructing and deconstructing images of girlhood? What impact do consumers have in restructuring how girlhood is defined?

ADVERTISING GIRLHOOD

The impact of the media as a means of representing girlhood is a major contributor to the selection of girlhood images available in society, as well as in how girlhood is defined, accepted, and replicated. Through advertising, the media has successfully created a sense of "normality" that anyone can purchase by consuming products. The institutional structure of our consumer society has oriented our culture (and its attitudes, values, and rituals) even further toward the world of commodities (Jhally 2003). Because advertising presents consumption as a way of life, consumers must be able to think for themselves, learning how to analyze not just the *meaning* of advertising but also the influence of the advertising industry in our society and in our lives.

Sut Jhally, in "Image-Based Culture—Advertising and Popular Culture" (2003), indicates that advertising is a communication system "through" and "about objects," for it does not merely tell us about things but rather relates to us how things are connected to important domains of our lives. As members of society, girls not only see through various media forms (such as television programs and magazines) images of what constitutes girlhood but are also reinforced with ideas of girlhood as experiences that all girls encounter regardless of their race, ethnicity, social class, physical ability, or sexuality. These representations of girlhood are worrisome—and, some researchers would even say, dangerous—not only to those who do not conform to them but also to those girls who are part of the dominant culture and view these images as reflections of what girlhood should be for them. The way teen fiction series represent "first love" relationships between young teenagers is a good example. Often love relationships are situated in a triangle that includes two girls interested in the same boy. Worthy of the love and affection of a male character, the "good" girl is portrayed as virtuous and somewhat naïve, with the other girl portrayed as "bad" and willing to do whatever she must to capture his affections. Television shows like *Dawson's Creek*, *Seventh Heaven*, and *Degrassi: The Next Generation* all use this device. Many times, the male will trap himself by participating in intimate acts with the bad girl, only to learn later that she used or misled him. In the meantime, the good girl is pressured to engage in intimate ways with the male character, thinking that this is the only way to keep his attention and affections.

The notion of the audience participating in their own manipulation is what Tony Schwartz has coined "partipulation." Schwartz argues that advertisers are most successful when the audience participates in its own manipulation by unquestioningly accepting what the media offers, presenting no challenge or criticism. If representations of girlhood are produced and reinforced in the same manner, without any question or challenge, are not consumers then participating in the manipulation of the image of girlhood as a commodity? Take, for example, consumers' wishes to purchase toys, games, or videos such as Barbie dolls, *Tomb Raider* computer games, or Madonna CDs. What are the associations made with the purchase of such items—other than their retail costs or purchase prices? When consumers first think about the value of an item, they often justify their purchase by claiming that the item is "useful," "cool," "fashionable," "trendy," "desired," or "needed—since everyone has one." If consumers assign value to an item solely in reference to the discourse of the advertisers, then they have actually participated in their own manipulation, in complicity with the media

STEREOTYPICAL REPRESENTATIONS OF GIRLHOOD

Every image embodies a way of seeing (Berger 2002). The ways people see things are affected by what they know or believe; one's perception or appreciation of an image thus depends upon a way of viewing. This suggests that viewers can exercise some control over what is seen and how it is understood. If girls are able to view representations of themselves in terms of what constitutes girlhood, then when they are prevented from viewing or situating themselves in these representations, are they not simultaneously being deprived of contributing to a form of knowledge that belongs to all girls? Who benefits from the deprivation, denial, erasure, or silencing of their representations? For example, how much do girls learn about the differences in their experiences of girlhood? How do girls understand each other in terms of the differences among them as members of a collective grouping (girls) and in terms of shared affiliations based on culture (ethnicity), race, sexuality, or ability? If only a few images are identified as representative of girlhood, then these representations remain static and not inclusive of all girls.

"While popular description of life in the information age seems to dwell on state-of-the-art computer systems and communication links, it is clear that much, if not most, of the information people have comes from nothing fancier than television screens and daily newspapers" (Wresch 2002, p. 323). Yet it is at this important juncture, where information starts and too frequently ends, that the power of the media is profound. As indicated previously, the media determines daily agendas, interprets meaning, confers status, and at worst, endorses destructive behavior. What is disturbing for our society, according to researchers Tait and Burroughs (2002), is that the media's most powerful impact is on children who frame definitions of, and draw conclusions about, the world through the messages they receive.

Some researchers, such as Jean Kilbourne (2003), believe that there may be a connection between the rise in various social and health problems among young girls within society and the increase of media and information accessible to girls. According to Kilbourne, images projected in the media of the "perfect" female body type, along with peer pressure, contribute to the development of eating disorders and other unhealthy behaviors in adolescent girls. While Kilbourne acknowledges that it is impossible to speak accurately of girls as a monolithic group, much of her work does address issues of an "ideal" body image as portrayed within a predominantly Eurocentric framework. Here again, the vulnerability and silence surrounding images of various groups of girls dealing with these issues are not reflected in the representation of girlhood concerns.

In addition to the experiences that they may encounter as part of girlhood, Kilbourne contends that young girls enter adolescence facing a series of losses. She discusses these representations of girlhood as existing in a framework wherein aspects of diverse identities are dominated by standard notions of whiteness that have become pervasive and normalized in society. She refers to these losses as ranging from loss of self-confidence and sense of efficacy and of ambition to the loss of girls' "voice" as well as of their sense of being unique, powerful individuals as they were when children. Although these losses may not be experienced by all girls, the assumptions of girlhood are framed by the dominant group membership, which defines how girls experience "growing up in a toxic cultural environment, at risk for self mutilation, eating disorders and addictions" (Kilbourne 2003, p. 259). She concludes that "the culture, both reflected and reinforced by advertising[,] urges girls to adopt a false sense of self, to bury alive their real selves, to become 'feminine,' which means to be nice and kind and sweet, to compete with other girls for the attention of boys and to value romantic relationships with boys above all else" (Kilbourne 2003, p. 259)

MEDIA OBSESSION WITH WEIGHT AND SIZE

Advertising's obsession with size and weight continues to receive tremendous support in popular magazines as well as air time on several television talk shows. Many contemporary girls' magazines, such as *Seventeen* and *Cosmo Girl*, focus readers' attention on improving body shape and size through the diet secrets of the stars or weight programs endorsed by selected celebrity spokespersons. The commercial success of these programs suggests that average young girls believe they may be able to redefine their bodies with ease over a short period of time. Along with an emphasis on weight reduction, many training programs or exercise routines are readily available, accompanied by home delivery of food and personal trainers for those who can afford these expensive lifestyle additions. The illusion that weight loss and redefinition of the body can be achieved at will by following certain routines, often unsupervised by medical professionals, is misleading and potentially dangerous. The promise of a simple "quick fix" for dietary issues may lead many young girls down a destructive path in which over-the-counter medication, diet pills, or starvation may culminate in other serious health complications. Today, several Web sites and chat rooms are dominated by young girls who communicate to each other about eating disorders such as anorexia and bulimia. These discussions by young girls about their experiences provide chilling evidence of the serious problems that can result from poorly regulated or irresponsible advertising concerning body weight and size.

Notably, a great deal of attention in the celebrity news has recently focused on the eating disorders of young stars, including Lindsay Lohan, Kate Bosworth, and Mary Kate Olsen. In various forms of popular entertainment, these young girls are often classified as reflecting the beauty ideal. Although the attention on beauty as measured by thinness and size is a commonplace of mainstream representations of girlhood and beauty, several young celebrities of color have recently drawn attention to other forms and representations of beauty contextualized by racial identity or culture. Notably, supermodel and talk show host Tyra Banks (*America's Next Top Model*) was photographed on vacation in a one-piece bathing suit, with shocking headlines indicating that she had drastically increased in size because of weight gain in her thighs (as depicted in the photo). Although Banks responded to the photo and the impropriety of the comments, she also dedicated several of her talk shows to confronting "size-ism" in the media. Banks (like Oprah Winfrey and many other black women) contends that, from a cultural standpoint, images of beauty associated with size are not valid for non-white groups in terms of what constitutes the beauty ideal (*People* cover story, January 27, 2007, "You Call This Fat?"). Similarly, many Latino/Hispanic popular culture texts endorse a full-figured body as a sign of beauty and desirability. Celebrities such as Jennifer Lopez, notorious for her full-size posterior and curvaceous figure, as well as many popular non-white singers such as Jennifer Hudson, India Arie, and Norah Jones continue to redefine beauty within cultural and racial lines.

The notion that larger proportions in women are synonymous with attractiveness is reinforced by some contemporary celebrities in Hollywood. Large women with hourglass figures are often depicted in rap music videos as well as in sitcoms. Although issues of size are more closely associated with beauty as defined by white standards, some young non-white celebrities, including Nicole Richie, Brandy, Beyoncé, and Janet Jackson, reflect the impact of the industry and changes embedded in mainstream culture regarding representations of non-white young girls. Several other celebrities acknowledge beauty as defined by culture and race and openly tackle the commercialization of beauty by integrating beauty ideals with healthy living. Raven Symoné (of the *That's So Raven* television show), America Ferrara (*Ugly Betty*), and Kim Fields (*Facts of Life*) were child or young actresses who literally grew up on television or in film, challenging stereotypical, often Eurocentric images of beauty.

Outside the Western/Eurocentric sphere of influence, other images of beauty are embraced. For instance, in many African nations larger women are viewed as more attractive. Among the Maori (the indigenous people of New Zealand) as well as the First Nations/Aboriginal peoples of North America, large women are equated with beauty, prosperity, and desirability. In India, concepts of beauty are linked to individuals with voluptuous figures, representative of the various iconic images and representations of female deities (Wolf 1991).

MEDIA INFLUENCES ON CHILDREN

People cannot help but construct notions of themselves that are drawn, at least in part, from the media images that surround them, as Kellner (2003) has argued. Because advertisers use idealized images of people to sell their products, most people think themselves woefully inadequate in comparison with such images. In fact, the images that are "staged as representations of 'real' people are really representations of people who 'stand for' reigning social values such as family structure, status differentiation, and hierarchical authority" (Jhally 2003, p. 250). Hence the stereotypical representations of girlhood that position girls as a common category are as problematic for girls from the dominant culture as they are for girls from minority groups.

Various studies have been conducted of what children conclude from the images they view on television, as well as how they interpret these representations. Researchers have repeatedly indicated that children from all races tend to associate positive characteristics with white characters they have viewed on television, and negative characteristics with minority characters they have seen. These studies confirm the pervasive conscious and unconscious impact that the media has on race-based representation, as well as the influence of media in creating negative perceptions of those viewed as "different." In *The First R: How Children Learn Race and Racism*, Van Ausdale and Feagin (2001) indicate that children learn race roles just as they learn sex roles—from all that they observe around them. They suggest that children re-create racial power roles, as they do gender roles, by their categorization either as oppressor or as oppressed.

Although children may believe that all races are represented as participating in appropriate and inappropriate behaviors and actions, they agree that the news media *tends* to portray both African American and Latino people more negatively than it does white or Asian individuals.

> African American children feel that the entertainment media represents their race more fairly than the news media (47 percent to 25 percent). For example, daily in news reports, when crimes are committed by people of African American descent, the description of the individual is often noted in the report. These racial descriptions occur less often when the crimes are committed by white members of society. Asian children feel the opposite, favoring the news media (36 percent to 28 percent) while White and Latino children are split between the two. (Tait and Burroughs 2002, p. 103)

There are numerous reports daily on television that demonstrate the way different racial groups are represented in news reports versus entertainment programs. More television shows feature African American characters than feature either Asian or Latino/Hispanic groups. Given this division between representations of minority groups, it seems logical that African American people would prefer television programs over news reports for their positive forms of representation. Likewise, in news reports, people of African American backgrounds are more often cited and identified racially in association with criminal activity than other minority groups. However, children of all ages and races expressed faith that the media could help bring people together by showing individuals of different races interacting. For example, Disney programming promotes diversity of representation (as in *That's So Raven* and *Lizzie McGuire*), and other television companies also promote the learning about socially acceptable behaviors through their portrayal of different ethnic and racial groups (e.g., *Degrassi: The Next Generation* and *Seventh Heaven*).

"MONEY TALKS": SHIFTING THE FOCUS OF REPRESENTATION

While the dominant culture can exert power by how it racially defines others, the role of a capitalist economic enterprise in maintaining dominant representations of girlhood must also be acknowledged. Attempts at economic gain, whether packaged in magazines (*Cosmo Girl*, *Teen Beat*) or television shows (*Gilmore Girls*, *Laguna Beach*, *Dawson's Creek*), are oriented toward white audiences because Eurocentric media executives are well aware of the steady growth of marketplace demands for goods and services. However, although traditionally the Eurocentric media has focused predominantly on representations of girlhood through a lens of whiteness, the promotion and distribution of products for consumption is becoming more color conscious as new consumers emerge from diverse ethnic and racial groups. The underlying objective of this capitalist enterprise, despite its traditional alignment with the Eurocentric media, is to create and maintain consumers of all ages and races.

Today, advertising images of "non-white" people can be more varied than in the past, partly because of political pressure to change the monolithic representations that once dominated the media and also because of the realization that it is in the economic self-interest of companies to appeal to all target markets. In "Advertising and People of Color," Wilson and Gutierrez (2003) provide an important historical perspective on racialized representations in advertising texts, suggesting that, after years of neglect and demeaning stereotypes of blacks (Aunt Jemima selling syrup), Latinos (Juan Valdez selling coffee), Native Americans (chiefs featured in Lakota ads), and Asian Americans (endorsing technology or computer products) in advertising aimed at white audiences, social protest (including boycotts) and target marketing led to significant changes to these once-common practices. Wilson and Gutierrez (2003) also discovered, especially in the cases of blacks and Latinos during the 1970s, that significant gains in visibility and in respectful representations in mass audience advertising occurred. This shift means that black and Latino consumers are now courted with the use of "prestige imagery" of themselves. However, when the media targets specific minority audiences (as in Spanish-language broadcasts or magazines, and cable stations directed at African American viewers), the potential for growth is evident, as is the possibility of community costs associated with this new advertising imagery.

> The slick, upscale lifestyle used by national advertisers is more a goal than a reality for most Blacks and Latinos. It is achieved through education, hard work, and equal opportunity. Yet, advertisers promote consumption of their products as a short-cut to the good life, a quick fix for low-income consumers. The message to

their low income audience is clear: "You may not be able to live in the best neighborhoods, wear the best clothes, or have the best job, but you can drink the same liquor, smoke the same cigarettes, and drive the same car as those who do." (Wilson and Gutierrez 2003, p. 291)

These manipulations of targeted groups for increased revenue position minority consumers as easily lured by material signifiers of popular, dominant culture. Likewise, when advertisers embrace forms of representation either of the dominant culture or of the constructed minority culture, the actual value of cultural practices and traditions of minority groups or dominant group members is trivialized for profit. In the same way, representations of girlhood as dictated by the dominant white culture hold the potential for manipulating experiences of girlhood through desire formulated by customer consumption. This can be seen in the way some celebrities have reconstructed themselves to be more marketable; several pop singers, including Alicia Keyes, Rianna, and Ashantee, have avoided association or classification by their racial identity—unlike India Arie and Tracy Chapman, whose music and lyrics are linked to their racial identities. Similarly, the static nature of representations of girlhood produced by dominant white culture fails to reflect the diversity of experiences of white girls based on class, religion, geographic location, physical ability, access to opportunities, and family obligations or restrictions. Hence representations of girlhood, like representations of the dominant cultural identity, can become pawns in the economic game of buy-and-sell.

RACE AND REPRESENTATION

The differences evident in social constructions of identity (often affiliated with racial/ethnic, gender, linguistic, sexual, physical, and class differences) are also aspects of identity that are relevant to the question "whose girlhood?" As Kendall (2006) has discussed, "separating whiteness and white privilege is a bit like trying to unscramble an egg—pulling apart the yolk and the albumen" (p. 41). Although the parts are different from one another, when mixed they become inseparable. Therefore it is essential to recognize that the "demand for representation or recognition of group identities often rests on a deeply problematic view of difference as fundamentally bounded and separate rather than multiply constituted and inextricably linked"(Abu el-haj 2006, p. 166).

In relation to the interplay of race and representation, a framework of recognition is often identified as essential to reconciling the way race has been erased from the representation that reflects the dominant group's political, social, and economic agendas. Unfortunately, the manner in which this has been promoted often positions race, ethnicity, gender, or culture as a static possession of a distinct group. Furthermore, this view of difference fails to inquire whether all of the people who identify with a particular group participate in or encounter the same experiences. There is little acknowledgment of the ways in which individuals experience multiple group affiliations (Abu el-haj 2006). Thus, this framework of recognition fails to make visible the ways in which all systems of communication are co-produced and the fact that their production constitutes power relations. If we were to treat the traditional representations of girlhood as simply the dominant culture's documented record and view it as one perspective among multiple bodies of experience, then perhaps girls would be able to understand the relationship between domination and oppression as it exists in their own as well as in other representations of girlhood. The production of divergent representations of girlhood necessitates that different representations constructed according to race not simply coexist but challenge each other.

Contemporary notions of whiteness are sometimes expressed as "illuminating the invisible" (Marx 2006) because whiteness incorporates so much of what white people and many people of color consider to be normal and thus neutral. According to Chennault, as cited by Marx (2006), since whiteness is perceived by whites as the status quo and as a "normal" experience, it manifests as "raceless" (p. 314). This notion of racelessness and imperviousness has been linked to colonialism. According to Helms, as cited by Marx (2006), "the development of White identity in the United States is closely intertwined with the development and progress of racism in the country" (p. 49), and thus, "when whiteness is deconstructed, it clearly can be discerned that racism lies at its heart" (p. 46). Extending this logic further, representations of girlhood that are constructed and reproduced by the dominant white culture will inevitably transmit notions of racial superiority in practice. These representations are harmful not only to people from historically oppressed groups, who already suffer the effects of monolithic, misrepresentative discourses about themselves, but also to those people from the dominant groups who are trapped by these visions and thus become unable to cross boundaries to fight against the embedded oppression these representations offer.

The representation of girlhood must reflect images of girlhood that are inclusive. It is important that the media portray differences of experiences that emerge from diverse perspectives, understandings, and positions of girls in society. Representations of girlhood should account for those living within, outside, and in between the spaces in which identity and difference are constructed and contested. The incorporation of these images and experiences will broaden the representations of girlhood as well as inform new understandings of girlhood. This will enable critical challenges to the question "whose girlhood?" to be addressed in a meaningful way, beyond the level of tokenism or practices of "partipulation" that pervade contemporary media.

Further Reading

Abu el-haj, Thea Renda. (2006). *Elusive Justice: Wrestling with Difference and Educational Equity in Everyday Practice*. New York: Routledge.

Berger, John. (2002). "Excerpts from Ways of Seeing." In Inderpal Grewal and Caren Kaplan, eds. *An Introduction to Women's Studies: Gender in a Transnational World*. Boston: McGraw-Hill, pp. 278–281.

Dines, Gail, and Jean M. Humez. (2003). *Gender, Race, and Class in Media: A Text-Reader*. Thousand Oaks, CA: Sage.

Hall, Stuart. (2002). "From 'Routes' to Roots." In Inderpal Grewal and Caren Kaplan, eds. *An Introduction to Women's Studies: Gender in a Transnational World*. Boston: McGraw-Hill, pp. 458–459.

hooks, bell. (2002). "Race and Gender." In Herb Boyd, ed. *Race and Resistance—African Americans in the 21st Century*. Cambridge, MA: South End Press, pp. 61–65.

Jhally, S. (2003). "Image-Based Culture—Advertising and Popular Culture." In Gail Dines and Jean M. Humez, eds. *Gender, Race, and Class in Media: A Text-Reader*. Thousand Oaks, CA: Sage, pp. 249–257.

Kellner, D. (2003). *Media Spectacle*. New York: Routledge.

Kendall, Frances E. (2006). *Understanding White Privilege*. New York: Routledge.

Kilbourne, J. (2003). "The More You Subtract, the More You Add: Cutting Girls Down to Size." In

Gail Dines and Jean M. Humez, eds. *Gender, Race, and Class in Media: A Text-Reader*. Thousand Oaks, CA: Sage, pp. 258–267.

Marx, Sherry. (2006). *Revealing the Invisible*. New York: Routledge.

Tait, Alice, and Todd Burroughs. (2002). "Mixed Messages: Race and the Media." In Herb Boyd, ed. *Race and Resistance—African Americans in the 21st Century*. Cambridge, MA: South End Press, pp. 101–108.

Van Ausdale, Debra, and Joe R. Feagin. (2001). *The First R: How Children Learn Race and Racism*. Lanham, MD: Rowman & Littlefield.

Wilson, C., and F. Gutierrez. (2003). "Advertising and People of Color." In Gail Dines and Jean M. Humez, eds. *Gender, Race, and Class in Media: A Text-Reader*. Thousand Oaks, CA: Sage, pp. 283–293.

Wolf, Naomi. (1991). *The Beauty Myth: How Images of Beauty Are Used Against Women*. Toronto: Vintage.

Wresch, William. "World Media." (2002). In Inderpal Grewal and Caren Kaplan, eds. *An Introduction to Women's Studies: Gender in a Transnational World*. Boston: McGraw-Hill, pp. 322–327.

ELAINE CORREA

Girlhood in the Time of AIDS: Popular Images, Representations, and Their Effects

The popular media plays a crucial role in representing images of social groups and propagating taken-for-granted beliefs about social phenomena. HIV/AIDS is one of these social phenomena the media works with and through as we read about and watch characters affected by this condition in magazines and on screen. In the 1980s the public was bombarded by campaigns to support medical research for a cure for, and to protect ourselves from, a disease that seemed to target drug abusers, blood transfusion recipients, and sexually active people who did not "protect" themselves. In the early part of the twenty-first century, the media is focusing more on how HIV/AIDS kills people in Africa. Relatively little attention is paid to the ways rates of HIV infection and related sexually transmitted infections (STIs) are affecting young women. According to the Kaiser Family Foundation and the Centers for Disease Control and Prevention, the share of AIDS cases among women in the United States has risen from 8 percent in 1985 to 27 percent in 2004. Though men still constitute the majority of persons diagnosed with the AIDS virus, cases in women have decreased at a much slower rate (13 percent) than have cases among men (35 percent) (as of July 20, 2006, http://www.kff.org/hivaids/upload/7525.pdf). In light of such statistics, and in the context of the media's role in constructing and propagating popular knowledge about HIV and AIDS, it is critical that we know and understand the popular representations of HIV and AIDS that appear in girl culture, as well as the media's representations of girls dealing with HIV and AIDS.

IMAGES OF HIV AND AIDS IN POPULAR CULTURE

Popular texts for teens are clearly an important "information point" on sexuality. In an April 2006 *ELLEgirl* sex survey of thousands of girls averaging 16 years of age, 23 percent reported that they get the majority of their information about sex from TV and magazines, whereas 12 percent go online (Dunlap and Bothorel 2006, p. 2). However it is not easy to track down specific articles or other media texts, such as television programs, that deal with HIV and AIDS, because the issues are often embedded in intricate storylines, such as that concerning Robin, a character in *General Hospital* who tested positive for HIV. Over the past 25 years stories, characters, and information centering on HIV and AIDS have steadily trickled into teen mainstream media texts (magazines, movies, television shows, and Web sites). While HIV/AIDS is not often the subject of the feature story in a teen girls' magazine or the lead article on a girls' health Web site, it is often mentioned in association with other STIs, emerges in an advice column, appears mid-issue amid other articles mentioned on the cover, is referred to throughout the site, or appears as a character's dilemma.

Though the topic of HIV/AIDS looms in the background in popular teen girls' texts, its presence carries significance for the girls who are the intended audience. Linda Christian-Smith (1993) explains the central role these texts play in girls' crafting of selves and identities and development of knowledge of social power differentials: "through literacy, young women construct and reconstruct their desires and gender subjectivities, as well as their awareness of social differences and power relations" (Finders 1996, p. 72). But such texts are not only important to the construction and reconstruction of female identities. Popular texts also contribute to "commonsense" notions of what it means to be a girl in the time of HIV and AIDS. Blumenreich and Siegel (2006) caution that "books serve as another cultural means through which particular ways of talking and thinking about HIV and AIDS come to be treated as true and unproblematic" (p. 87).

There are a number of recurring, troubling messages and scripts surrounding HIV/AIDS and girlhood in media and popular culture: girls should embrace abstinence, lest they fall prey to HIV-positive male predators; girls should learn a lesson from their promiscuous female peers who contract the virus through their deviant lifestyles; and girls should rescue the "innocent victims"—those suffering the effects of the virus through no fault of their own (e.g., AIDS orphans). Rarely encountered are uncensored, complicated portraits of girls living with and beyond HIV, teen experiences that suggest imaginative possibilities and meanings not signified in the media texts reviewed.

GIRL CULTURE AND HIV/AIDS IN THE MOVIES

Kids

In 1995 Larry Clark directed *Kids*, a drama shot in cinema verité style ("shaky-cam" faux documentary) portraying 24 hours in the lives of some Manhattan teens and pre-teens. In the film's early scenes Jennie, an adolescent girl protagonist played by Chloe Sevigny, learns that she is HIV positive. She quickly links her diagnosis to her only sex partner, Telly (played by Leo Fitzpatrick), an adolescent boy obsessed with having sex with young virgins. Throughout the film, Jennie wanders Manhattan, at times in a drugged-out haze, at other times leaning forlornly against a taxicab window looking for Telly—who, simultaneously, is wooing Darcy, the 12-year-old virgin sister of his friend Bennie.

The film projects a male/female dichotomy, drawing stark gender lines between attitudes about HIV. To illustrate and frame this dichotomy, Clark opens and closes the film with scenes of Telly deflowering willing 12-year-old virgins. While Clark portrays kids of both sexes as sensual beings equally interested in sex, girls are depicted as responsible clinic goers while boys dismiss the sex-ed and health class discourses about sexually transmitted diseases and responsible sexual behavior. This is evident in an early film segment that cuts back and forth between "girl talk" and "guy talk." Jennie talks with her girl-friends about sex, desire, and prowess; they also discuss going to the clinic to determine if one of their friends contracted any diseases from a one-night stand of unprotected sex. This conversation is interspersed with cuts from a conversation between Telly, his friend Casper, and other boys. They banter about diseases being "made up," remarking that "no one I know died from that" and "I'm gonna go out f***ing."

Immediately after her diagnosis as HIV positive, Jennie becomes passively distraught. She spends the remainder of the film staring sadly out the window of a cab, wandering through a club, or loafing on the sidewalk while Telly's and Casper's actions and attitudes propel the narrative. Quite literally, Jennie spends the film's duration perpetually one step behind Telly as he moves in pursuit of another virgin conquest.

The insight into Telly's and Jennie's lives is strongly biased toward male subjectivity. We visit Telly's house. We meet his mother. We hear about his philosophies, desires, interests, and loves. We, and most of those in the film, learn little of Jennie beyond her HIV diagnosis. When Jennie does speak, she is typically inquiring about Telly's where-abouts. Her sheer determination leads the audience to believe that when she finds Telly, she will do or say something, that a change or moment of climax will occur. This tension peaks when Jennie arrives at Telly's location—the aftermath of a house party. Wading through and tripping over the unconscious young bodies strewn everywhere, she opens a door and sees Telly having sex with the virgin Darcy in the master bedroom. There Jennie stands, unable to muster the will to interrupt his sex with Darcy or to confront him with her diagnosis. She is too late, too stunned, too high, to do anything. Instead Jennie closes the door and passes out on a couch in the living room, silent. As she slumbers, Casper takes her clothes off and sexually penetrates her limp body. She sleeps through the sex, moaning occasionally and stirring, still sleeping.

Jennie fails to "rescue" or "protect" Darcy from Telly's infection, and she never tells anyone that she has HIV. Any confrontation she may have had or will have with Telly is left to the audience's imagination, off screen. Jennie instead ends the film as Casper's pas-sive infector and possibly the victim of a rape. The film's focus on a twenty-four-hour period limits the depth of Jennie's role as a person living with HIV. The audience is con-fronted with her shock as she wanders, but learns little else of the life that likely stretches before her—a life infected by HIV. This effectively renders *Kids* nothing more than a movie about the initial shock of diagnosis.

Rent

A contrasting image to this "day in a life" representation of HIV and AIDS is the year-long profile of life and death involving multiple HIV-positive characters in *Rent*, the 1996 Broadway musical hit adapted to film in 2005. *Rent* remained among the top ten box office hits for three weeks after its release and has been a popular DVD rental. Among this film's cast are four main characters living with HIV and AIDS. They, along with their other bohemian friends, reside in New York's lower east side and work to make ends meet through performance art, filmmaking, music, teaching, and acting. One of the four char-acters is Mimi, played by Rosario Dawson. She works as an exotic dancer, spends time with friends, injects heroin privately, and is partnered for the majority of the film with Roger, an unemployed but aspiring musician striving to pay the rent. He, too, is HIV positive.

While *Rent* portrays HIV-positive characters having different experiences, coping mechanisms, lifestyle choices, sexual preferences, and opinions toward the diagnosis and its effects, Mimi, as the film's central female character living with HIV, offers an interest-ing portrait of young women and HIV and AIDS.

Themes of silence, deviance, and living the "right way" with HIV and AIDS inscribe Mimi's character. The film is evasive in terms of the characters' infection stories. Roger finds out that Mimi carries HIV/AIDS when her AZT beeper goes off. They then burst into song, proclaiming, "I Should Tell You"—never telling each other or the audience anything. Such silence surrounding the terms of the disease recalls past centuries' hushed whispers in the context of words such as "consumption" and the disconcerted looks that resulted from someone "infected" entering the room. While the musical did break ground by bringing a racially diverse cast to Broadway and centering around characters with mul-tiple sexual identities, its approach to the discourse surrounding HIV/AIDS and girls still seems close-lipped and moralistic. As a woman infected with HIV/AIDS, the only character addicted to heroin, and the only character who is an exotic dancer, Mimi's sends the message that female persons with HIV and AIDS are drug-abusing, sexually promiscuous social misfits. Mimi's work as a stripper subtly underscores old stereotypes of the sexually promiscuous female as the agent of her own infection. These messages suggest that girls and women infected with HIV and AIDS are in some way socially deviant, thereby constructing an image of HIV and AIDS that cannot so easily be mapped onto the general female population. Mimi's life before meeting Roger (working, living, taking heroin) is further rendered "at odds" when placed against her simultaneous decisions to stop using heroin and to start attending an HIV and AIDS support group. In the film sequences that show her smiling with her group and working through night sweats with Roger's encouragement, she seems to be undergoing a conversion to embrace Roger's monogamous love, a drug-free life, and a psychically healthy support group culture—the "right way" to live with her disease. Her later relapse, disappearance, and near-death experience cement this dichotomy between the right and wrong ways to live with HIV, as she almost dies after being discovered homeless, drugged out, and succumbing to sickness on the street. Rescued by her friends, she "sees the light." The audience is led to believe that she will return to clean living after the film's final frame.

The character of Angel in *Rent* offers possibility and complicates an otherwise clear-cut split between male and female characters living with AIDS. As a cross-dresser, or "drag queen," Angel signifies a feminine role in the film. This version of femininity contrasts with Mimi's character, as Angel is truly "an angel" who offers salvation and disappears at the same time. Angel saves Collins after he is beat up, shares her diagnosis with the audience, and invites everyone to join her at Life Support on Christmas—the regular gathering for people with and without AIDS. The time spent developing Angel's character focuses on her care for Collins (another of the film's characters living with AIDS), her financial stability (she is the one character typically able to pay the rent or pick up the tab for food), and her sense of innovation in difficult situations (breaking down the door when the group is locked out of their home, making a large sum of money playing drums to kill a dog). AIDS is a part of Angel, but she is not encapsulated in all the risk group markers of drug abuse and promiscuity that mire Mimi's character. Though Angel, as a transgender person, represents an HIV and AIDS "risk group," when compared with Mimi Angel's function in the film might be considered "a staging of otherness, of the divine, the feminine, and death, which makes the invisible visible, an enchanted illusion in a disenchanted world, an untimely understanding of history" (Lather 1997, p. 237). Angel's decline renders the physical pain and illness of AIDS visible. But more important, the film's plot and social network are in many ways contingent on both her life and death. She brings care, shelter, food, financial stability, and ingenuity to dire situations during the film's main action—uniting and preserving a cadre of friends. And as Angel moves into the hospital for her final days, friends long close but since estranged are reunited to care for her. Angel's death precipitates the unraveling of a previously tight-knit circle of friends as her funeral catalyzes the plot's speedy dissolution. It is apparently no accident that her name is "Angel."

On the surface, *Rent* and *Kids* draw two incredibly different portraits of girls and young women living with HIV and AIDS—one a white, pubescent, semi-virginal girl, the other a Puerto Rican–American stripper addicted to heroin; one grappling with diagnosis and the other struggling to live "la vie boheme." Nevertheless, the range of possible identities for girls and women living with HIV seems limited. Girls remain "constrained" as prey to male sexual predators, carriers of HIV, or agents of their own destruction who must sacrifice past lifestyle choices for new, clean, monogamous awareness. There is no escape from social scripts as Jennie and Mimi live as a wandering victim and a clean-living convert, respectively, in the time of HIV and AIDS. But these scripts are tempered by the possibilities presented in *Rent*'s Angel, whose range of character traits and whose plot centrality press the audience to explore a multi-dimensional female character living with and dying from AIDS.

GIRL CULTURE AND HIV/AIDS IN TEEN MAGAZINES

In 1998 *Teen People* became the first teen spin-off of an adult magazine to enter the mainstream periodical market (Brown 2001). While it boasts a 20 percent male readership, an anomaly in a teen magazine market that is notably gender specific, 8 million of its 10 million readers are girls between 12 and 21 years of age (Magic, online, July 20, 2006). The articles found in *Teen People* tend to be similar to the feature articles found in other teen magazines, such as *Seventeen* and *Sugar*.

A number of articles found in *Teen People* between 2002 and 2006 position girls as potential victims of knowing HIV-infected male predators and showcase HIV-negative activists fighting on behalf of the innocent victims of HIV/AIDS in Africa.

In 2002 *Teen People* included a profile of an HIV-positive girl who shares her story about contracting and living with the disease. In *"I Have HIV,"* Tei Rose shares an account strikingly similar to Larry Clark's portrayal of Jennie in *Kids*—another virgin infected during deflowering. Tei explains that at age 15 she lost her virginity and contracted HIV from 20-year-old Nushawn, a young man who knowingly infected "dozens of young women." In a first-person, confessional narrative, Tei relates how she had sex "in the moment," describing the emotionally devastating impact of testing positive and the process she went through to forgive Nushawn. The article ends with a classroom sex-ed style numbered list of directives: (1) "Don't Have Sex," (2) "Practice Safe Sex," (3) "Never Share Needles," (4) "Get Tested," and (5) "Find Treatment," to ensure that *Teen People* readers "Know the Facts."

Here, even harder lines are drawn between girls and boys with HIV, as Nushawn is constructed as a "serial" infector imprisoned for 12 years after passing HIV onto at least 13 young women. As his victim, Tei chooses to "not hate" Nushawn despite her emotional devastation. She instead turns blame back toward herself, dubbing her prior state "stupid" and proclaiming her new HIV-positive incarnation to be "more educated" (Rose 2002, p. 137). Tei, the naïve, violated, HIV-positive victim, offers Nushawn a path to redemption, placing the blame for her infection on herself. Thus the discursive moral of her tale is clear: sex is dangerous. First-time sex can be a death sentence, but the way to cope with a negative diagnosis is through mourning, forgiveness, and self-blame. This is further underscored by directive number 1 in the article's closing caution: "Don't Have Sex."

For teen girls who do not have sex, or at least do not have HIV but do want to "get involved" in a global "humanitarian" effort, *Teen People* directs their attention to the AIDS crisis in Africa. In 2002 and 2006 the magazine profiled two activist teen girls working to raise money for "AIDS orphans in villages across Africa," research, and treatment. In 2002 Abdul Majeed Arsala, a 16-year-old girl, made *Teen People*'s list of "20 Teens Who Will Change the World" for her work in founding Assisting AIDS Orphans. Though Abdul notes that "AIDS orphans aren't just in Africa, they're everywhere," the brief profile effectively locates the AIDS crisis in Africa and stays focused on the children orphaned by AIDS—the "innocent victims" whom it might be "safer" for teen girls to be working to save. The "innocent victims" discourse came to the media fore during the mid-1980s, when hemophiliac Ryan White contracted HIV from a blood transfusion. In 2006 Blumenreich and Siegel noted that "creating this category of 'innocent victims' only compounded the implicit guilt of those in 'risk groups'" (p. 99), such as *Rent*'s Mimi—drug users, the sexually active, and social deviants.

A more recent, 2006 article entitled "AIDS Walk in Africa" further contributed to *Teen People*'s portrayal of the HIV-negative activist girl. In an anonymous travel diary, we read about Chloe Lewis's missionary-like crusade through Tanzania, where she worked to raise money for AIDS research and treatment. The article describes Chloe playing with young children, distributing toys and school supplies to grateful inhabitants, crying with persons recently diagnosed with HIV, and getting to know an inspiring HIV victim who was infected by his mother. The piece concludes with a list of "Stars in Africa," framing Chloe's work with other AIDS Africa campaigns conducted by celebrities such as Angelina Jolie, Alicia Keys, and Jessica Simpson.

Along with reinforcing the "risk group"/"innocent victim" distinction, the activist discourse regarding HIV and AIDS in Africa also creates a comfortable distance that enables girls to join the cause without confronting some of the domestic facts about the spread of HIV and AIDS in the United States or the structural inequities that exacerbate the crisis in Africa. Chloe effectively leaves HIV and AIDS in Africa. The article ends with Chloe stating, "There's so much potential in these kids. I wish I could take them all home [to the United States] with me . . ." (Anonymous 2006, p. 109).

HIV/AIDS continues to spread among persons living in poverty, among people of color, and among women everywhere. Moreover, the politics surrounding the overpricing that maintains and drives up the cost of drug therapy, as well as the discriminating cost of health care, have a genocidal impact on the minority groups dying of AIDS at disproportionate rates here in the United States as well as in Africa. Nonetheless, the *Teen People* activist discourse evades discussion of such facts, instead highlighting the beauty of Tanzania and its people in comments like "I wonder if the people think this country is as beautiful as I do, and I wonder how they're dealing with HIV. They seem so carefree and kind. It seems like as long as they have music or a cold drink, they are happy and smiling" (p. 107). Although it is important to paint a tangible and balanced portrait of an African country grappling with HIV and AIDS, relating the dramatic travels of a teen girl watching the pain and happiness of people living with HIV and AIDS without exploring the context and conditions that inscribe individuals effectively shrouds structural inequities in need of interrogation. The causes of HIV and AIDS are silenced. The virus is instead rendered a specter to be experienced or escaped.

GIRL CULTURE AND HIV/AIDS ON THE INTERNET

Cyber options available to teen girls looking for information about HIV and AIDS on the Web range from HIV quizzes to hard-facts Web sites, discussion blogs, articles, and downloadable films. A follow-up piece to the April 2005 sex survey in *ELLEgirl* listed two Web sites recommended to adolescent girls for information about sexual health: www.teenwire.com and www.sexetc.org. These Web sites feature a range of genres, including iMovies and conventional articles.

Nightmare on AIDS Street, an iMovie written by 15-year-old Nicole Zepeda, is one screenplay of several produced by Scenarios USA, a nonprofit organization that sponsors a teen screenwriting competition. Teen authors compete to have their films shot by a professional film crew. Completed films are used to spawn discussion in classrooms across the nation on topics surrounding teen life and healthy decision making. *Nightmare on AIDS Street* is literally a nightmare (or daymare) Isobel Martinez experiences as she awaits HIV and AIDS test results in a doctor's office. A horror film–style soundtrack accompanies the roughly replayed events of a weekend party. Images of Isobel's teacher and her mother expressing harsh disappointment flash across the screen. Haunting most scenes is a younger Isobel wearing a ruffled white dress and two perfectly parted pigtails—dancing, giggling, staring, and consoling teen Isobel as she nervously awaits her diagnosis. Repeatedly we hear that Isobel "doesn't know what happened" as she queries a young man she paired off with at a party. At the film's close, we are left to assume that she was drunk, passed out on roofies, or date-raped.

Sex is portrayed as a completely forgettable, regrettable, and inevitably dangerous act, as Isobel is unable to recall the events of the evening and begs her suitor to detail them over the phone. Through her partner's refusal to recount the evening's events and scrambling to leave the phone, boys are painted as unconsoling, unrepentant, insensitive beings with little interest in postsexual relationships. It seems that girls are meant to be frightened into abstinence, and the movie offers no alternatives. Such messages are reinforced by the angry images of a teacher and a mother scolding Isobel for her partying and poor decision making. The moral appears to be quite simple: sex disappoints adults. Sex is something you will not even remember. Sex might put your life in danger. Never put yourself in a situation where you think you might need to take an HIV test. If you are awaiting HIV test results, you have probably gone too far. The viewer is left fearful of the nightmare that is a clinic visit.

"To Be Young, Smart and HIV-Infected: Living a Positive Life," an article written by 17-year-old Ben Cogswell hosted at www.sexetc.org, tells the story of 19-year-old Marvelyn Brown. Here he intersperses interview quotes with his own narrative to describe how the young African American woman contracted HIV from her "attractive" boyfriend during consensual, unprotected sex. Her personal experience is framed and interspersed with Cogswell's "straight-talking" delivery of facts and moral conclusions. The following statement is one example of this framing of experience with HIV protection advice: "Marvelyn now knows that not only do you have to be careful with contraception if you're having sex, but you also have to take measures to protect yourself from life-threatening diseases like HIV by getting tested and using a condom every time you have sex" (p. 1). This tone is heightened by Cogswell's repeated use of the second-person pronoun "you," effectively positioning the audience as recipients in need of the article's information to avoid future HIV contraction.

Cogswell's article does make several well-intentioned points as he frames Marvelyn's story with facts about the disproportionate impact HIV and AIDS on the African American community. Though Marvelyn was infected by a man, Cogswell spends more time discussing Marvelyn's experience as a consenting young woman (not a virgin) having sex with someone she was interested in than on focusing on any predatory details of her sex partner. This focus sharply contrasts with the images of virgins and sexual victims preyed on in *Kids*, *Teen People*, and *Nightmare on AIDS Street*. Cogswell also shares how Marvelyn's family has rallied around her, but complicates this rosy picture with their fear of community ostracism and Marvelyn's experience of peer rejection at school. Marvelyn's picture is neither tragic nor sugary sweet, but Cogswell does choose to end on a positive note with Marvelyn's discussion of the "positive role" HIV has played in her life, and rounding out the article with some final "tips" on how to avoid contracting HIV. While the piece seems balanced in its portrayal, Marvelyn's choice to "dedicate her life to educating youth about HIV and AIDS" (p. 2) does recall some of the activist messages rendered in *Teen People*, but this time from the perspective of a young HIV-positive woman. This raises questions about what career and life choices outside of HIV and AIDS activism might exist for girls living an HIV-positive life, as it seems certain that many persons would prefer not to define their lives through their experience with a disease.

CONCLUSION

The preponderance of teen texts represent girls as victims of male predators or of their own promiscuity, or as the Florence Nightingales of the twenty-first century, offering curative sanctuary and rescue to the disease's innocent victims in far-off countries. Such images propagate a narrow set of options for girls and convey reductive messages about life in relation to HIV and AIDS, although Cogswell's article "To Be Young, Smart and HIV-Infected: Living a Positive Life" makes some efforts to portray a more complicated and contextual vision of Marvelyn's life with and beyond HIV.

It is important to acknowledge, however, that media messages are always filtered through personal life experiences. And young people are hardly the passive recipients of projected facts, images, or information. Messages of the popular media never fall on inactive eyes and ears. Moreover, girls will have opportunities to identify with characters such as Angel in *Rent* or other performers of life experiences with and in relation to HIV and AIDS that are not necessarily female or exist outside of the popular media. In fact, powerful images and representations of HIV and AIDS circulate in our personal lives as we interact with and discuss what we know, wonder, and assume about its impact on our society. Noncommercial, independently produced media for youth and by youth, although less professional in terms of production quality, may be a forum where popular media discourses are contested. While youths' access to these media sources is hampered by nonprofits' limited budgets and infrastructures for dissemination, the growing popularity of YouTube, MySpace, and other collaborative Web 2.0 technologies may produce a "popular media" forum that is both accessible to a broad youth audience and open to their complicated portrayals of life with and in relation to HIV and AIDS.

None of these facts absolves the commercial media of their responsibility to propagate more diverse, nuanced representations of young girls infected by HIV and AIDS. However, they do suggest some hopeful venues for change as we work to place continual pressure on the popular media industry as it contributes to our social understandings of girlhood in the time of HIV and AIDS.

See also Abstinence Bracelets; Moral Panic

Further Reading

Anonymous. (2006). "AIDS Walk in Africa." *Teen People* 9, no. 4, 106–109.

Blumenreich, M., and M. Siegel. (2006). "Innocent Victims, Fighter Cells, and White Uncles: A Discourse Analysis of Children's Books about AIDS." *Children's Literature in Education* 37, no. 1, 81–110.

Booth, S., J. Braunschweiger, M. Hainer, C. Sittenfeld, and W. Wilson. (2002). "Fourth Annual Tribute: 20 Teens Who Will Change the World." *Teen People* 5, no. 3, 126–139.

Brown. J. (2001). *Trash Mags with Training Wheels*. [Online July 20, 2006]. About-Face Web site http://www.about-face.org/r/press/salon091001.shtml.

Christian-Smith, L., ed. (1993). *Texts of Desire: Essays on Fiction, Femininity and Schooling*. London and New York: Falmer Press.

Clark, L. (director/writer), C. Woods (producer), H. Korine (writer), and J. Lewis (writer). (1995). *Kids* [motion picture]. United States: Lions Gate.

Cogswell, B. (2006). *To Be Young, Smart, and HIV-Infected: Living a Positive Life*. [Online July 12, 2006]. Sex, Etc. Web site http://www.sexetc.org/story/2231.

Columbus, C. (director/producer/writer). (2005). *Rent* [motion picture]. United States: Sony Pictures.

Dunlap, L., and E. Bothorel. (2006, April). "*ELLEgirl* Reader Poll: Sex Survey." *ELLEgirl*, 114–116.

Finders, M. (1996). "Queens and Teen Zines: Early Adolescent Females Reading Their Way toward Adulthood." *Anthropology and Education Quarterly* 27, no. 1, 71–89.

Henry J. Kaiser Family Foundation. *AIDS at 25: An Overview of Major Trends in the U.S. Epidemic*. [Online July 20, 2006]. Kaiser Family Foundation Web site http://www.kff.org/hivaids/upload/7525.pdf. 2006.

Lather, P. (1997). "Creating a Multilayered Text: Women, AIDS, and Angels." In W. G. Tierney and Y. S. Lincoln, eds. *Representation and the Text*. New York: State University of New York Press.

Media Activities and Good Ideas by with and for Children. (n.d.). [Online July 20, 2006]. Unicef Web site http://www.unicef.org/magic/bank/case018.html.

R., T. (1996). *A Lesson I Learned about AIDS* on General Hospital. [Online July 18, 2006]. Teen Ink Web site http://teenink.com/Past/1996/6574.html.

Rose, T. (2002). "I Have HIV." *Teen People* 5, no. 8, 137.

Scenarios USA. (n.d.). [Online July 24, 2006]. Scenarios USA Web site http://scenariosusa.org/about.html. n.d.

Valdez, K., and A. Valdez (directors), A. Ludwig (producer), and N. Zepeda (writer). (2000). *Nightmare on AIDS Street* [motion picture]. [Online July 7, 2006]. Scenarios USA Web site http://www.teenwire.com/interactive/do-archive-movies.php.

NANCY LESKO AND ELISABETH JOHNSON

PART 2

Girl Culture A to Z

A

ABSTINENCE BRACELETS. Abstinence bracelets and other jewelry worn by girls proclaiming their chastity emerged as social artifacts in North America in the early 1990s. By that time it was well established that HIV and AIDS presented a lethal danger to the wider heterosexual population, rather than being confined to specific communities such as gay men and intravenous drug users. Simply by wearing a special bracelet, often made of silver or pewter, carrying a phrase such as "Worth Waiting For," girls (and to a lesser extent boys and young men) can signal their commitment to "saying no" to sex before marriage. Abstinence bracelets are of particular significance to girl culture because a young woman's virginity is sometimes regarded as a potential gift or cultural trophy for a future husband, particularly in evangelical and fundamentalist circles.

In the early 1990s groups began staging large-scale "chastity rallies" on school campuses across the United States, Canada, and, to a lesser extent, the UK, Australia, and New Zealand. At these rallies adult speakers, usually influential pop culture icons such as former Miss Americas or professional athletes, addressed youthful crowds using emotionally charged speeches and testimonials to urge the young people to save their virginity until marriage. Even if he or she was no longer a virgin, the speakers urged, an attendee could still promise to lead a chaste life before finding a life partner. Speakers encouraged attendees to sign pledge cards affirming their commitment to chastity, or to purchase branded merchandise with slogans such as "True Love Waits"™ or WWJD? (What would Jesus do?) to remind them of their public and collective promise.

Bracelets, rings, and necklaces communicating this message are sold at such rallies, in bookstores and other retail outlets, and through Web marketing. They range in price from about ten U.S. dollars to several hundred dollars for those made of precious metals. Despite the intended purpose of the jewelry as a marker of a *personal* commitment to virginity and chastity, such jewelry is also marketed as gifts to adolescents from adult relatives, who use them as objects of persuasion.

Abstinence brackets and abstinence-only messages can also be found in mainstream girls' **magazines** such as *Seventeen*. For example, in the July 2005 issue there is a four-page article on the virtues of abstinence, which not only tries to convince readers to practice abstinence using quizzes and citing statistics ("53 percent of high school students are virgins," "70 percent of sexually active teens say they had sex to try to make their relationship closer," "92 percent of teenagers agree that being a virgin in high school is a good thing," "Stop! Read this before you have sex"), but also aims to ally itself with the virginity movement ("one in eight teenagers has taken a virginity pledge") (*Seventeen*, July 2005, 84–88). The article also directs readers to several Web sites, such as candiesfoundation.org, which carries a strong abstinence message ("To be sexy you don't have to have sex"), and http:// teenpregnancy.org, which appears to promote a strong abstinence message as well. Abstinence bracelets are prominently featured in its online photographs with the message "I'll wait."

Complicating this issue is the interpretation of "abstinence." For some, the word implies a disciplined choice to abstain from any sexual behavior or thought; others consider abstinence to mean that all forms of sexual expression short of actually engaging in heterosexual intercourse are acceptable. Many critics note that reconciling what youth feel they are committing to with adult expectations of what abstinence actually means presents a considerable challenge for both educators and adolescents.

See also Sex Bracelets

Further Reading

Kempner, Martha. (2001). *Toward a Sexually Healthy America: Abstinence-Only-Until-Marriage Programs that Try to Keep Our Youth "Scared Chaste."* [Online June 2007]. Sexuality Information and Education Council of the United States Web site http://www.siecus.org/pubs/tsha_scaredchaste.pdf.

Legal Momentum. *Sex, Lies & Stereotypes: How Abstinence-Only Education Harms Women.* [Online June 2007]. Legal Momentum Web site http://legalmomentum.org/legalmomentum/files/ truthabstinenceonly.pdf.

LISA TRIMBLE

AFRICAN AMERICAN PRESENCE IN POPULAR CULTURE. The African American presence in popular culture is particularly notable for being *about* African Americans but not *for* them. The complexities of the African American presence in popular girl culture can be traced largely through dolls, which have long played an important role both in girl culture and, perhaps surprisingly, in national negotiations of race and inequality. As access to and control over a wide variety of media have broadened, the African American presence in popular culture has become increasingly prevalent, particularly in the areas of music and television.

Dolls, Race, and Popular Culture. One of the earliest African American girls to become an element of popular culture is the character of Topsy, a young slave girl in Harriet Beecher Stowe's abolitionist novel *Uncle Tom's Cabin* (1852). The novel itself became an important cultural touchstone, and dolls based on its characters Eva and Topsy likewise became widely popular. These "topsy-turvy" dolls featured the white Eva and the black Topsy as two parts of a single doll. Basically the doll had no legs and two heads, one at each end of the doll; the bodies of Eva and Topsy were joined at the waist. If the doll was held one way, she was Eva. Flip the skirt up, turn the doll over, and the doll would become Topsy. Interestingly, these early dolls suggested the intertwined nature of race relations by their very construction, which joined Eva's white body with Topsy's black one. As manufacturing and media developed, black dolls continued to be a staple of doll production.

The civil rights movement established an enduring connection with black dolls in the popular imagination through the work of psychologists Kenneth B. and Mamie Phipps Clark. In 1939 and 1940 the Clarks conducted what are referred to as "the doll studies," in which young children were presented with two identical dolls, one with brown skin and one with pink skin. The child subjects were asked a series of questions, such as "Which doll is the good doll?" and "Which doll would you like to play with?" The final question was "Show me the doll that looks like you." African American children, the Clarks found, tended to associate positive characteristics with the pink-skinned doll and negative ones with the brown-skinned doll. When asked which doll looked like them, children often became agitated, refused to choose, broke into tears, or chose the pink-skinned doll. These results, the Clarks argued, indicated that African American children understood that they lived in a society in which their race, and therefore they themselves, were not valued. This research is widely viewed as having made a key contribution to the 1954 Supreme Court decision that held segregated public schooling to be unconstitutional in the landmark case *Brown v. Board of Education of Topeka, Kansas*.

Influenced by social change and the civil rights movement, major toy producers began to make black dolls in large numbers in the 1960s. **Mattel** introduced its first black doll, Christie, in 1968. By the late 1980s, the African American middle class had grown in both size and buying power. During this period the African American popular culture presence made a marked shift toward representations of African Americans that they themselves produced. Pressured by disgruntled consumers who did not want dolls that were little more than brown plastic poured into the same molds used to make white dolls, toy manufacturers began to produce so-called ethnically correct dolls, which purported to more realistically represent the features of different racial groups. While in many ways problematic, this change nevertheless represented an attempt to embrace diversity in a broad and more democratic fashion than was previously the case.

Mattel's offering in the ethnically correct doll category was the Shani line—three African American dolls in light, medium, and dark skin tones. Among the more controversial aspects of these dolls was their hair, which remained long, silky, and easy to comb. In short, Mattel was unwilling to sacrifice what the industry calls "play value" for a version of African American hair that might be curly, kinky, or nappy. Moreover, it was rumored that Mattel had reshaped the dimensions of Shani's body—specifically, by giving her an enlarged rear end. Questions about Shani's hair and body dimensions reflect those at work more broadly for African American women and girls. They are simultaneously pressured to conform to dominant, white beauty norms but are defined by their race as being outside those norms.

More recently, the **American Girl** doll Addy has entered the scene. Addy is one of the original American Girl dolls, developed as an antidote to Barbie, who is viewed by many as a vapid, pointy-footed sexpot. Each American Girl doll is packaged with a story set in a different period of history. The dolls are designed with soft, cylinder-shaped bodies that deemphasize sexuality; their stories instead emphasize a can-do spirit, friendships, the ability to overcome challenges, and an interest in learning. American Girl dolls have been widely successful, but because of their $80 price tag, they are primarily marketed to middle- and upper-income families. Not surprisingly, Addy's story centers on her escape from slavery. Of the thirteen historical characters offered by American Girl, nine are white; Addy remains the only African American doll in the series. The message in these numbers could be interpreted as a statement that there are many ways to be white, but only one way to be African American.

Hand Clapping, Double Dutch, and Hip Hop. Popular culture is not synonymous with mass culture. The everyday games played by African American girls are important popular culture resources that have been passed down from girl to girl for generations. In these forms, created and generated by girls themselves, an image of African Americans emerges that is multifaceted and complex in ways that the American Girl version, for instance, is not. Girls' hand-clapping games test skill and competency as well as weave stories about romance, school, and other topics. Double Dutch, a form of jump rope, demands intense physical stamina and creativity in performing complex moves. Both of these vernacular forms mix music, singing, and dance in distinctively African American ways, and emphasize a fusion of dance, song, syncopation, and improvisation. It has been argued that these games—played intensively by inner-city girls—have made significant contributions to the emergence of **Hip Hop** music and break dancing. The relative invisibility of these forms may have much to do with the gendered way in which men versus women and boys versus girls are under surveillance in public space; focus is often given to men and boys, who are viewed as dangerous and threatening. Similarly, because boys and men have dominated the music industry, the debt owed by this mass cultural phenomenon to urban girls' popular culture is less likely to be recognized. Hip Hop songs, which graphically detail the trials of urban life, did not effectively describe girls' and women's experiences until girls and women started making their own music.

Queen Latifah is one of the first women to break into the Hip Hop scene as a rapper and musician. Much of what she has to say, in a nutshell, is "mind your manners, and watch while I beat you at your game." Similarly, such artists as TLC, **Missy Elliott**, and Salt-N-Pepa explore issues of romance, sexuality, poverty—the whole gamut—from the point of view of the women they are.

Media: Film, Television, and the Web. Queen Latifah's successful musical career is equaled by her forays into film and television. Like many African American celebrities, Queen Latifah has consistently challenged dominant notions of African American femininity and sexuality. She plays a lesbian bank robber in *Set It Off* (1996) and celebrates her large, curvy figure rather than trying to change it. In the film *Beauty Shop* (2005), Queen Latifah's character asks her daughter, "Does my butt look big?" When her daughter answers yes, Queen Latifah responds, with a satisfied smile, "Good!"

Still, breaking into various media has often required African American women and girls to break out of stereotypes. Until the 1980s portrayals of African American families, television tended to focus on poverty and the inner city. Janet Jackson, for instance, got her first big break in show business with a role in *Good Times* (1974–1979), a sitcom set in the Chicago housing projects. The groundbreaking *Cosby Show* (1984–1992) was the first to offer a prime-time view of a middle-class African American family in which both parents were working professionals. Two of the actresses who portrayed girls on that show went on to attain influential positions in girls' popular culture. Lisa Bonet played Cosby's daughter Denise, and went on to star in the spin-off series *A Different World*. This series was the first and only show to focus on an African American women's institution of higher learning, Spelman College. Born in 1985, **Raven**-Symone played Olivia on the *Cosby Show*'s final three seasons. Her career exemplifies those of more recent popular culture figures, and covers multiple media outlets. As popular girl culture has become more media-driven and increasingly dominated by cross-pollination among movies, television, and merchandising, stars have become brands themselves. Raven-Symone has a successful recording career, and starred in the Disney Channel series *That's So Raven* (2003–2006) and in the Disney movie *The Cheetah Girls* (2003), both of which spawned huge merchandising deals for a wide array of products, including a Raven-Symone perfume.

Today's girls face a world dominated by tightly coordinated media and merchandising, in which celebrities themselves are brands. It is tempting to view girls' popular culture as little more than a mass-marketing ploy. However, increased access to media, including cameras and the Internet, has opened opportunities for girls to share their perspectives more widely than ever before. Kiri Davis's short film *A Girl Like Me* (2006) examines notions of beauty and race. She interviews friends and conducts her own version of the Clark doll studies, with results not much different from those of the late 1950s. Shown in the Media That Matters Film Festival, Davis's film was viewed by more than half a million people and has since been viewed by hundreds of thousands more. On one hand it is disturbing that little may have changed for African American girls since the Clarks' time. On the other, the fact that at least one girl's exploration of these issues has reached so many is perhaps a positive sign of things to come.

See also Cross-Merchandising

Further Reading

Chin, Elizabeth. (1999). "Ethnically Correct Dolls: Toying with the Race Industry." *American Anthropologist* 101, no. 2, 305–321.

Craig, Maxine Leeds. (2002). *"Ain't I a Beauty Queen?" Black Women, Beauty, and the Politics of Race.* New York: Oxford University Press.

DuCille, Anne. (1996). "Toy Theory: Black Barbie and the Deep Play of Difference." In *Skin Trade.* Cambridge, MA: Harvard University Press, pp. 8–59.

Forman-Brunell, Miriam. (1993). *Made to Play House: Dolls and the Commercialization of American Girlhood.* New Haven, CT: Yale University Press.

Gaunt, Kyra D. (1998). *The Games Black Girls Play: Learning the Ropes from Double Dutch to Hip Hop.* New York: New York University Press.

Thomas, Sabrina Lynette. (2007). "Sara Lee: The Rise and Fall of the Ultimate Negro Doll." *Transforming Anthropology* 15, no. 1, 38–49.

ELIZABETH CHIN

AGUILERA, CHRISTINA (1980–). Christina Aguilera is a singer who gained popularity in the late nineties with **tween** and teen girls. She is a five-time Grammy award–winning artist with a four-octave vocal range. She was born on December 18, 1980, in Staten Island, New York, to an Ecuadorian father and an American mother. She appeared on *Star Search* at age 10 and joined the cast of *The New Mickey Mouse Club* in 1992, staying on the show for two seasons. Aguilera appeared on the show with **Britney Spears**, **NSYNC*'s Justin Timberlake, and *Felicity*'s Keri Russell, until the show ended in 1994. In 1998 she recorded "Reflection" for Disney's animated film *Mulan*, and she was later signed by RCA Records. Her self-titled debut album, released in 1999, included the hit single "Genie in a Bottle" and earned her a Grammy Award for Best New Artist. She followed the success of her first album with a Spanish album, *Mi Reflejo*, which reflected her Latina heritage and won her a Latin Grammy Award. In 2001 Aguilera collaborated

Christina Aguilera performs at the 2002 MTV European Music Awards in Barcelona. (Courtesy of Photofest.)

with **Pink**, Mya, and **Lil' Kim** in the song "Lady Marmalade," which earned her another Grammy. This also marked the introduction of Aguilera's new provocative image.

Her second official English album, *Stripped*, was released in 2002. Aguilera co-wrote a majority of the tracks, some of which address her father's physical and emotional abuse toward her mother and herself when she was a child. The music video for one of the tracks from this album, "Dirrty," was controversial for its sexually provocative images of clothing and dance. In 2006, she released her third English album, *Back to Basics*, earning another Grammy with "Ain't No Other Man."

Aguilera has been involved with various philanthropic campaigns, notably Aldo's "See No Evil, Hear No Evil, Speak No Evil" HIV and AIDS awareness campaign. Shortly after the release of *Stripped*, she posed nude or semi-nude for various photo shoots, dyed her hair black, and referred to herself as "Xtina," having the nickname tattooed on the back of her neck. She also got multiple body piercings. Her new image was accompanied by a candid and flamboyant outspokenness. Her unorthodox fashion sense was often met with disdain and resulted in her frequent appearance in celebrity "worst-dressed" lists. She has since embraced a mature glamour image and more conservative fashion choices.

See also Body Modification; Latina Presence in Popular Culture

Further Reading

Dominguez, Pier. (2002). *Christina Aguilera, A Star Is Made: The Unauthorized Biography*. Phoenix, AZ: Amber Books.

Scaggs, Austin. (2006). *Dirty Girl Cleans Up*. [Online May 2007]. *Rolling Stone* Magazine Web site http://www.rollingstone.com/artists/christinaaguilera/articles/story/11111757/christina_aguilera_still_dirty_after_all_these_years.

CASSANDRA WOLOSCHUK

ALL-AMERICAN GIRL.   *All-American Girl* is a half-hour sitcom that aired on ABC from 1994 to 1995 and starred comedienne Margaret Cho in the role of Margaret Kim, a young Korean American woman facing the challenges of transitioning into adulthood. Although criticized for various reasons, from uneven writing to questionable depictions of Korean American life, *All-American Girl* remains to date the only television show to cast a young woman of Korean heritage in the lead role.

On the show, Margaret Kim is a young woman in her early twenties who lives at home, works at a beauty counter of a local department store, and is pursuing a law degree.

Portrayed as a party girl, Margaret is constantly at odds with her mother, played by Jodi Long, who wants her to adhere to traditional Korean values and to marry a young Korean American man. Consequently, issues such as who Margaret dated and whether or not she should move out feature prominently in the show's episodes. Her older brother, played by B.D. Wong, is the very embodiment of his mother's values and does not support Margaret in her efforts to assert herself. Her father, played by Clyde Kusatsu, attempts to remain neutral during the heated mother-daughter feuds. Margaret's only ally is her grandmother, played by Amy Hill, who is portrayed as a zany old woman who loves American popular culture, and whose opinion is easily dismissed.

In early 1995, when the show's meager ratings began slipping even more, the writers drastically altered the premise of *All-American Girl*: by the final episode of the show, all of the actors who played Margaret's family had been fired with the exception of Amy Hill. Margaret was suddenly living in an apartment with three young men and pursuing a career in the entertainment industry. The episode, which was called "Young Americans," was intended to be the pilot of a new series of that name that would feature Cho as the star. However, that show was never produced.

Although the creator of *All-American Girl*, Gary Jacobs, earned a Media Achievement Award from the Media Action Network in 1994, the show was problematic on many levels. For example, most of the actors who were hired for the show were not in fact Korean American (of the main cast members, only Cho claims Korean heritage). Also, some of *All-American Girl*'s depictions of the day-to-day realities of Korean American life have been called a "confused blend of Asian cultures" or simply wrong (one focus group noted the inaccuracy of the language and accents used by the characters) (Orbe et al. 1998, p. 128). It has also been criticized for relying heavily on stereotypes for many of its laughs. These criticisms eventually led the producers of the show to hire an "Asian consultant" to ensure the show's Korean authenticity.

Cho's relationship with her *All-American Girl* producers was equally difficult. Concerned that she did not fit the image they had envisioned for the star of the show (they had a particular problem with the roundness of her face), the producers told Cho that she needed to go on a diet in order to secure the role of Margaret Kim. Cho then turned to diet pills, lost thirty pounds in two weeks, and subsequently suffered kidney failure. Cho was also criticized as not being "Asian enough" in her role as Margaret Kim. The irony of the situation was not lost on the comedienne: years later, in her stand-up show *I'm the One That I Want*, she joked, "I was too fat to play myself." The issue of creative control over the show persists even today: on the 2006 DVD release of *All-American Girl* Cho can be heard on the commentary track saying, "It is *not* based on my stand-up" every time the words "based on the stand-up of Margaret Cho" appear on the screen.

See also Stefani, Gwen; The Thin Ideal

Further Reading

Orbe, Mark P., Ruth Seymour, and Mee-Eun Kang. (1998). "Ethnic Humor and Ingroup/Outgroup Positioning: Explicating Viewer Perceptions of *All-American Girl*." In Yahya R. Kamalipour and Theresa Carilli, eds. *Cultural Diversity and the U.S. Media*. New York: State University of New York Press, pp. 125–136.

Prasso, Sheridan. (2005). *The Asian Mystique: Dragon Ladies, Geisha Girls, and Our Fantasies of the Exotic Orient*. New York: Perseus Group.

LINDSAY CORNISH

AMERICAN GIRL. Marketed primarily to preteen girls, the American Girl brand includes doll collections, books, a **magazine**, movies, **Web sites**, party supplies, theme stores, and the "Real Beauty" bath and body product line. At the core of the American Girl brand are two lines of dolls sold only through the company's catalog, Web site, and American Girl Place stores: the Historical Characters collection, which features eleven dolls, each with a story that situates her in a specific time period in American history, and the Just Like You collection, which allows customers to select a doll, sold in contemporary dress, with one of twenty-five prefabricated combinations of hair, skin, and eye colors. Packaged in jewel tones and marketed as girls' peers and as models of girlhood rather than as baby dolls or teen dolls, American Girl dolls connote wholesomeness and traditional social values while centering girls' lives within the fabric of America's past and present. The American Girl brand claims to celebrate girls' lives and contributions to American history as well as to promote a girlhood that revolves around curiosity and determination.

Acquired by **Mattel** in 1998, American Girl was the brainchild of Wisconsin-based educator and entrepreneur Pleasant Rowland. In the mid-1980s Rowland became frustrated while shopping for a doll to give to her niece. Feeling that Barbie (see the essay on Barbie in Part 1) was too sexualized for a little girl and that **Cabbage Patch Kids**, the other popular doll of the era, were just plain unattractive, Rowland began to conjure up her own doll. At the same time, she was captivated by a visit to Colonial Williamsburg, a living museum in Virginia. Linking these two experiences, Rowland created the American Girl Collection.

Rowland's goal was to create a collection of beautiful dolls that celebrated girls throughout American history. The collection was rooted in the fictional identities of three historically situated, 9-year-old American Girls: Kirsten, whose family emigrated from Sweden to the Minnesota frontier in the 1850s; Samantha, an orphan living with her wealthy grandmother who encounters the movement for women's suffrage at the turn of the century; and Molly, a suburban, middle-class girl on the home front during World War II. Subsequently, Rowland added eight dolls to the historical collection: Felicity, a spunky pro-independence girl living in Virginia just before the American Revolution, and her best friend, Elizabeth, who supports the king; Addy, an African American girl who flees from the plantation where she was enslaved; Josefina, a **Latina** girl coping with her mother's death in New Mexico in 1824; Kaya, a Native American girl growing up in 1764, who strives to be like the woman warrior she admires; Kit, whose family struggles to survive during the Great Depression; Nellie, a servant girl who is later adopted into Samantha's wealthy family; and Emily, a British girl who comes to live with Molly's family while her country is under attack during World War II. Each character-driven line includes an 18-inch doll and six stories that situate the girl within her historical period. In addition, each collection can be supplemented with various outfits, accessories, and doll-size furniture. Girls may also buy clothing in their own size to dress themselves like their doll.

The Just Like You collection of dolls, sold with contemporary outfits and accessories, was released in 1995 following the appearance of *American Girl* magazine three years prior. As with the historical collection, these dolls are meant to represent preteen peers of the doll owner. With the goal of representing the full range of American girls' identities and activities, outfits available for these dolls include **sports** attire for tennis, soccer, and basketball, in addition to dresses for parties and ballet recitals, and accessories include a computer armoire as well as a salon kit and a guitar.

American Girl products have been praised for their high quality and for putting girls in the center of their own world. In so doing, the company encourages girls to appreciate their youth, which some scholars would say is in contrast to such dolls as Barbie or **Bratz**, which encourage girls to adopt more adult-like behaviors and clothing. American Girl also recognizes a multiplicity of American girl identities.

However, critics of the company charge that the high price of the dolls, the characters' appearance, and the associated spin-off merchandise, such as hair and skin care products, outfits, accessories, and doll hair salons, encourage a traditionally feminine focus on grooming and fashion. Additionally, while American Girl stories involve tales of dynamic girls who participate in many activities, from cooking to training service dogs, some claim that the doll collection positions girls solely as consumers. The brand has also been criticized for its sanitization of American history, as well as its glossy multiculturalism, which fails to address racial, economic, and social inequalities and injustices.

See also KGOY

Further Reading

Acosta-Alzuru, Carolina, and Peggy J. Kreshel. (2002). "'I'm an American Girl . . . Whatever That Means': Girls Consuming Pleasant Company's American Girl Identity." *Journal of Communication* 52, 139–161.

Inness, Sherrie A. (1998). "'Anti-Barbies': The American Girls Collection and Political Ideologies." In Sherrie A. Inness, ed. *Delinquents & Debutantes: Twentieth-Century American Girls' Cultures*. New York: New York University Press, pp. 164–182.

EMILIE ZASLOW

ANNE OF GREEN GABLES.   L. M. (Maud) Montgomery's beloved tale of Anne Shirley was an instant best seller when it was first published in Boston in 1908. Although the novel was first marketed to readers of all ages, from the 1930s onward book covers featured increasingly younger girls, and it soon became recognized as a girls' classic. Anne has connected girls and girlhoods across space and through time.

The Novel. *Anne of Green Gables* is an inspired work. Anne Shirley arrives at Green Gables as the result of a mix-up: middle-aged brother and sister Marilla and Matthew Cuthbert intended to adopt a boy to help them on their farm but have been sent Anne instead. Gradually, through the power of her imagination and her infectious exuberance, Anne transforms Avonlea's conservative Scots-Presbyterian community. Set on Prince Edward Island in the late Victorian era, this novel evokes nostalgia for the simplicity of childhood in a small town. And yet its heroine exhibits all the attributes of a modern girl: her marked possession of intelligence, verbal dexterity, ambition, and education explains the novel's enduring popularity more than a century after its first publication. Iconic passages detail Anne's rebellious and insubordinate behavior. She stands up for herself—she cracks her slate over Gilbert Blythe's head in the schoolroom, and she confronts the town's moral authority, Mrs. Rachel Lynde, in a dramatic showdown. Anne's emotions run the gamut of adolescent feelings: readers experience rage, love, thrills, promises of eternal friendship, and expressions of the deepest despair through her. Anne's melodramatic grief over her red hair and freckles and her desire to rename herself, all speak to teenage preoccupations with body image and identity. The novel also dwells on girls' fashion rituals, as when Anne and her friend, Diana Barry, mark their transition to adulthood by putting up their hair and wearing long dresses. Montgomery's descriptions of these formative moments validate experiences that are particular to girls, and highlight elements of their culture.

The ending of *Anne of Green Gables* is filled with pathos. Matthew Cuthbert dies and Anne Shirley gives up her Avery scholarship to save Green Gables and stay home with Marilla, whose eyesight is declining. The conclusion has been criticized by some critics as being conventional, because it focuses on the heroine's sacrifice. Because Anne adamantly insists on delaying but not abandoning her ambitious dreams, the ending may rather reflect the author's ambivalence. *Anne of Green Gables* certainly speaks to a change in the social values of the time. The Victorian notion that a child should have a certain use value as a worker on the farm was being abandoned. Orphans were being adopted instead for the emotional benefits to both the child and the adoptive parents. The idea of providing children with support in a loving home versus institutionalizing them in a cheerless orphanage had reached its tipping point in the era's social and political conscience.

Montgomery's Influences. Montgomery's first novel was written over a brief period (spring to winter, 1905–1906) and was the culmination of a decade of short fiction. Supposedly based on an orphan girl in Cavendish in 1892, when Maud Montgomery was a 17-year-old schoolgirl, the novel's influences remained hidden until recently. In 1934 the author disclosed in her journal that she had based Anne's face on a picture clipped from a magazine. Montgomery was seemingly unaware that the photographic subject was Evelyn Nesbit, a 16-year-old model and Gibson Girl in New York (later associated with scandal and notoriety as the mistress of New York architect Stanford White). But Montgomery's Anne was also based on orphan literature inspired by James Whitcomb Riley's popular poem **Little Orphan Annie**. These formulaic stories provided Montgomery with a template that she would ultimately transcend, just as she parodied the Sunday school story tradition of the popular *Pansy* books by Isabella Macdonald Alden and *Rebecca of Sunnybrook Farm* (1903) by Kate Douglas Wiggin.

Anne of Green Gables was influenced by Montgomery's love of the British and American literary Romantics, such as Lord Alfred Tennyson, Sir Walter Scott, William Wordsworth, the Brontës, Henry David Longfellow, and Washington Irving. It possesses a magic similar to that found in Lewis Carroll's *Alice in Wonderland* (1865) and J. M. Barrie's *Peter Pan* (1904), the former an ode to dreaming and the latter an escape into the Neverland of childhood. Anne Shirley's habit of imagining glittering castles in Spain was inspired by the author's daydreaming and spiritual love of landscape. Modeled after Cavendish, Prince Edward Island, the novel's setting of Avonlea is like a lively character itself. Anne embellishes the landscape with descriptions of red soil and purple sunsets, canopies of white apple and cherry blossoms, woodlands of fir and fern, and the lull of the murmuring sea. Her renaming of the landmarks (Lover's Lane, Lake of Shining Waters, White Way of Delight, Dryad's Bubble, and the Birch Path) map a romantic geography that is portable and exportable across national, temporal, and cultural borders. The architecture of Green Gables was based on the unassuming gabled farmhouse owned by Montgomery's relatives. This house became the Green Gables Heritage site in 1937. It is protected by the Prince Edward Island National Park and attracts 200,000 visitors annually.

Socially Significant Readings in Different Times. The novel's social satire was an important basis for its popularity among readers of all ages in Montgomery's time, including master satirist Mark Twain, a devoted Anne enthusiast. Montgomery loved a good joke and could be quite irreverent. Through comedy, the Sunday school teacher and future minister's wife articulated religious and social criticism that she would never have dared to voice in any other context. Private and secretive, Montgomery always hid her true emotions in public; the people of Cavendish would have been shocked to hear some of her private thoughts (as many were when selections of her journals were first published in 1985). *Anne of Green Gables* poked fun at small-town life and parochial attitudes, including the author's own, depicting hilarious situations that many readers of the time, or those living in similar communities, could identify with.

Contemporary scholars have been prompted to undertake lesbian readings of the text because Montgomery's novel strongly emphasizes and idealizes girlhood and romantic female friendships. Anne's most intense relationship, for example, is with her "bosom friend," Diana Barry, to whom she confides her inmost thoughts and feelings. Their intimate friendship is an effusive, romantic affair and is said to be based on Montgomery's own erotically charged friendships with girls and women. The novel also explores and redefines nontraditional identities such as "the spinster" or "old maid" (Montgomery's own social position when she was writing the novel) and alternative relationships (such as single parenting in middle age). Profoundly subversive without being overtly feminist, the novel reflects a comic genius that relies on subtle gender play and gender reversal— as when gray-bearded, shy Matthew Cuthbert hitches the sorrel mare to the buggy and goes shopping for a fashionable dress with puffed sleeves for Anne's Christmas gift.

Anne's Legacy. In response to the young girls and adults clamoring for more stories about Anne, Montgomery spent a lifetime writing a series of sequels: *Anne of Avonlea* (1909), which details Anne's experiences as a teacher; *Anne of the Island* (1915), describing her college years; and *Anne's House of Dreams* (1917), in which Anne marries Gilbert Blythe. When Anne grows up and becomes a mother, she loses some of her spunk, although a new cast of characters supplies the spark that endeared the original to readers. Montgomery's novels outside of the Anne series, *Rainbow Valley* (1919) and *Rilla of Ingleside* (1921), reveal a darker, wartime vision. In her later years, the author returned to chronicling Anne's life in the epistolary novel *Anne of Windy Poplars* (1936), focusing on Anne's years as the principal of Summerside high school, and to Anne's growing family in the short story collection *Anne of Ingleside* (1939).

The Appeal of a North American Girlhood Here and Abroad. The novel has remained a best seller and has *never* been out of print. Within just five months of its publication, *Anne* sold 19,000 copies in the United States and Canada. When Montgomery visited her publisher, L. C. Page, in Boston in 1910, she was celebrated by the media as the "Canadian Jane Austen." In 1919 Anne Shirley made her film debut in a silent movie starring Mary Minter. A movie with a full soundtrack starring Dawn O'Day followed in 1934. More recently, Canadian director Kevin Sullivan's *Anne of Green Gables* films (1985, 1987, and 2000) have enjoyed remarkable popularity in many countries.

With over 50 million copies sold, translations into more than seventeen languages (including Braille), and biennial international conferences devoted to its interpretation, the tale of the talkative orphan girl has spread across the world. Anne has found friends throughout the United States and Canada, Sweden, Denmark, France, Italy, Iceland, Germany, Portugal, Japan, Korea, China, and many other countries. The novel and its sequels have spawned movies, television series, and musicals, as well as a worldwide industry of dolls, T-shirts, postcards, foods, and other businesses. The enduring classic has also influenced numerous other female writers, including Margaret Atwood, Alice Munro, Margaret Laurence, Kate Lawson, Helen Keller, and Swedish writer Astrid Lindgren. Its

1952 Japanese translation, *Akage no An*, created a cult following in Japan: approximately 6000 Japanese visitors travel to Green Gables annually. Today there are Anne fan clubs and e-mail discussion lists in Canada, the United States, Japan, and Germany, to name just a few places where "Anne mania" persists.

Anne is an iconic Canadian figure. As a girl "from away" who arrives at Green Gables to forge a new home for herself, Anne Shirley has been interpreted as the universal immigrant, who must adjust to a new place and who is able to transform her adopted homeland through courage and imagination. Anne's journey to self-knowledge is a story about gaining power; she is said to embody a pioneering spirit comparable to that of Huckleberry Finn. That so many diverse readers embrace and celebrate the particularities of Anne's girlhood, and are transformed by seeing their own experiences through her fantastic vision, is the true wonder of her legacy.

See also Hair, Stereotypes of; Pippi Longstocking; Series Fiction

Further Reading

Blackford, Holly. (forthcoming 2008). *Anne with an E: The Centenary* Anne of Green Gables. Metuchen, NJ: Scarecrow Press.

Gammel, Irene. (forthcoming 2008). *Looking for Anne: The Life and Times of* Anne of Green Gables. Toronto: Key Porter.

Montgomery, L. M. (1997). *The Annotated Anne of Green Gables*. Wendy E. Barry, Margaret Anne Doody, and Mary E. Doody Jones, eds. New York: Oxford University Press,

Reimer, Mavis. (1992). *Such a Simple Little Tale: Critical Responses to L. M. Montgomery's* Anne of Green Gables. Metuchen, NJ: Scarecrow Press.

Waterston, Elizabeth. (1993). *Kindling Spirit: L. M. Montgomery's* Anne of Green Gables. Toronto: ECW Press.

IRENE GAMMEL

ANOREXIA. Anorexia nervosa is an eating disorder characterized by self-starvation and extreme weight loss. Accompanying these symptoms is an extensive preoccupation with food and the body. Characterized as a psychiatric disorder, it is a disease influenced by social factors. Although anorexia has been present for many centuries, it occurs with higher prevalence today than ever before, and contemporary culture has shaped the disease in new and different ways. Estimates vary, but most reports suggest that between 0.5 and 3.7 percent of Americans suffer from anorexia, and an overwhelming majority of these anorexics (more than 90 percent) are girls and women. Anorexia can be fatal, with death resulting in 5–20 percent of all cases (National Eating Disorder Association 2006).

Biomedical explanations of anorexia classify it as an individual disease—a chemical imbalance that manifests as an obsession with the **thin ideal**. Some medical models extend their explanations to suggest that anorexia is linked to desires for control and perfection; however, few recognize the more complex ways in which anorexia is socially and culturally constructed or its effects that go beyond physical (and even psychological) symptoms.

Because North American popular culture frames the female body as something that requires careful maintenance to reach "perfection," anorexia is no longer understood as the strange behavior of a few sick individuals, but as part of a spectrum of behaviors—including dieting, exercise, and cosmetic surgery—that have become commonplace among females. Scholars have noted that although anorexia often begins as an internalization of external models of beauty, the struggle soon turns inward, and many anorexic girls would not even cite thin models or cultural images as motivations for their behavior.

Some have argued that anorexia is a form of resistance. For example, girls who **blog** about their experiences with anorexia talk frequently about how their eating behaviors are an attempt to resist those who seek to control their lives, including their food intake. Scholarly and popular debates often occur about whether and the extent to which anorexics are active agents who make their own conscious choices, or are victims caught in the throes of an all-consuming disease.

Online communities—often called pro-ana (pro-anorexia) communities—of girls and women (and a few boys and men) with eating disorders have recently begun to develop. The users' beliefs vary: some claim that anorexia is a lifestyle choice and not a disease, although the majority use the community space as a forum for open and honest exchanges about their experiences, and they receive support from others engaged in similar struggles. Often these communities take the form of individual online journals linked together by a blog ring. Whereas many in the popular media present negative aspects of these sites, others recognize the sites' potential to create a community of healing or support.

Recent events have moved anorexia into headline news. Such events include the ban in Spain on runway models whose body mass index (BMI) is too low (body mass index is a measure of body fat that compares height and weight; the "normal" range for BMIs is 18.5–24.9) (Centers for Disease Control and Prevention). Other events drawing media attention to the subject of anorexia were the public acknowledgments by celebrities **Mary-Kate Olsen** and Scarlett Pomers that they had struggled with the disorder. Certain magazines speculate on a weekly basis about the eating habits of various girl culture celebrities. This increased coverage has the potential to raise awareness about anorexia, and may encourage girls and women to be more open about their struggles. However, the portrayal of Olsen's and Pomers's recovery as seemingly quick and painless, the casual nature in which media refer to a diagnosis of anorexia, and the sometimes catty tone of such media coverage also have the potential to undermine the seriousness of the issue.

See also Social Networking

Further Reading

Bordo, Susan. (1997). "The Body and the Reproduction of Femininity." In Katie Conboy, Nadia Medina, and Sarah Stanbury, eds. *Writing on the Body: Female Embodiment and Feminist Theory.* New York: Columbia University Press, pp. 90–110.

Brumberg, Joan Jacobs. (2000). *Fasting Girls: The History of Anorexia Nervosa.* New York: Vintage Books.

Centers for Disease Control and Prevention. (2007). *About BMI for Adults.* [Online June 2007]. Centers for Disease Control and Prevention Web site http://www.cdc.gov/nccdphp/dnpa/bmi/adult_BMI/about_adult_BMI.htm.

National Eating Disorder Association. (2006). *Anorexia Nervosa.* [Online March 2007]. National Eating Disorder Association Web site http://www.edap.org/p.asp?WebPage_ID=286&Profile_ID=41142.

Spitzack, Carole. (1993). "The Spectacle of Anorexia Nervosa." *Text and Performance Quarterly* 13, 1–20.

KATRINA R. BODEY

ARE YOU THERE, GOD? IT'S ME, MARGARET.   *Are You There, God? It's Me, Margaret* is the title of **Judy Blume**'s third novel, considered to be the author's first book for adolescent readers. Published in 1970, it is the story of 11-year-old Margaret Simon, whose family moves from Manhattan to New Jersey right before Margaret is to begin sixth grade.

On her family's first day in their new house, Margaret meets Nancy Wheeler, a neighbor who is also 11 and who invites Margaret to her house. Through Nancy, Margaret meets Gretchen and Janie, two other girls who will be in their sixth-grade class. The four decide to form a secret club dubbed "The Preteen Sensations (PTS)," devoted to monitoring the physical signs of their maturity (to comparing **bra** sizes, for example, and wondering who will get her menstrual period first), and making lists of boys they like. At the end of each meeting, the girls engage in a round of breast-developing exercises during which each girl bends her arms at the elbows and moves them back and forth, chanting "I must—I must—I must increase my bust!" (p. 50).

Two opposing characters—God and a classmate, Laura Danker—figure prominently in the novel. Margaret, who is the only child of a Christian mother and a Jewish father, has not been raised in a religious household. Her mother's parents are determined that Margaret be Christian while her father's mother (and Margaret's favorite grandmother) always wants to know whether Margaret has met any nice Jewish boys. Caught in the middle and uncertain about which religion is hers, Margaret talks to God in private, beginning each monologue with the titular phrase, "Are you there, God? It's me, Margaret." While God hears Margaret's private wishes to dance with a boy she likes at the sixth-grade dance, to finally develop breasts, and begin having periods, Laura Danker seems to have already embodied these desires on her own. Laura looks more like a woman than any of Margaret's other classmates—especially when she wears a sweater—and is rumored to have "gone behind the A&P" grocery store with more than one boy. When Margaret is assigned to complete a group project with Laura, the two get into an argument and Margaret is allowed a glimpse of Laura's discomfort with her own physical development.

Blume has said that she based *Are You There, God?* on her own experiences as a girl. On her **Web site** she confesses: "When I was in sixth grade, I longed to develop physically. . . . I tried doing exercises, resorted to stuffing my bra, and lied about getting my period" (Blume 2001, para. 3). This frank, personal, and popular novel is included on the American Library Association's list of most frequently challenged books (meaning that numerous requests have been made to remove the book from school or library shelves). Blume recalls that when she made a gift of three copies of the novel to her children's elementary school, the books never reached the library shelves. The principal had decided that the novel's frank discussion of **menstruation** made it inappropriate for elementary school readers. In spite of this history of censorship, *Are You There, God?* remains a classic among Blume's fans.

See also Forever . . .

Further Reading

Blume, Judy. (1999). "Places I Never Meant to Be: A Personal View." *American Libraries* 30, no. 6, 62–67.

———. (2006). *Are You There, God? It's Me, Margaret.* [Online February 2006]. Judy Blume's Home-base Web site http://www.judyblume.com/margaret.html.

AMY S. PATTEE

ASIAN BEAUTY PAGEANTS.   Asian beauty pageants in North America are complex cultural constructs wherein the interrelated issues of racial identity, femininity, and transnationalism (i.e., the interacting flows of capital, people, and institutions across the borders of nation-states) converge. Young Asian girls living in North America often aspire to participate in these pageants. Understanding the convergence of racial identity, femininity, and transnationalism is integral to the study of North American girl culture in relation to the increasingly culturally pluralistic societies of the United States and Canada.

Miss America, the earliest national **beauty pageant**, was created in Atlantic City, New Jersey, in 1921. Since then the exposure of the U.S. and Canadian general public to pageant culture has been limited primarily to mainstream media coverage of the Miss America event, and of the Miss USA and Miss Universe pageants. However, over the last 20 years, beauty pageantry has maintained a fervent following among various Asian communities across the United States and Canada. Year after year, numerous young women of Chinese, Indian, and Filipina descent who were born and/or educated in North America congregate for competition in their respective communities. For the winner, an ethnic pageant title offers the chance to compete in the larger competition held in her parents' birthplace. For example, the Hong Kong–based Miss Chinese International Pageant features winners of the "Miss Chinese" title from around the world. For many, it provides the opportunity to attain fame in the "old country." For example, in the last six years several winners of the Miss India USA and Miss India–Canada pageants have flown to Mumbai in hopes of becoming the next stars of Bollywood, India's Hindi-language film industry. The allure for others is to seek validation of their personal appearance, which may not correspond with mainstream perceptions of the "perfect" beauty queen.

North America–based Asian pageants can be regarded as complex cultural constructs based on four main themes: (1) North America–based Chinese and Indian beauty competitions as launch pads to the Asian entertainment market; (2) North America–based Indian beauty competitions and their perpetuation of standards of "First-World exotica," or "First-World otherness"; (3) Miss Chinese Toronto as a transcultural popular form; and (4) North America–based Filipino beauty contests and their contrasting affiliations with feminine beauty, racial purity, and national pride.

The Significance of Ethnic Beauty Pageantry.   A number of unique qualities distinguish Asian ethnic pageants from mainstream beauty pageants. Asian American and Asian Canadian beauty pageants are transcultural forms through which Asian communities appropriate certain aspects from the dominant (i.e., mainstream North American) culture, and control or determine what they wish to absorb. They structurally emulate the model of mainstream pageants, including, for example, such components as a swimsuit competition, an interview segment, and a coronation. However, they look to imagined, archaic, or idealized images—some of which are evoked in folkloric dance routines and songs and traditional costumes—from the "old country." These pageants consequently bring into play complex identities for teenage girls and young women where notions of beauty, ideal femininity, and national pride are neither North American nor purely Indian, Chinese, or Filipina.

North America's Chinese and Indian Beauty Competitions: Launch Pads to the Asian Entertainment Market.   In the United States and Canada, the Miss Chinese and Miss India pageants are lavish, for-profit events that offer girls and young women the chance to seek fame and fortune—not in Hollywood, but in the film industries of Hong

Kong or Bollywood. For instance, the winners of the San Francisco-based Miss China-town USA and the Miss Chinese Toronto competition, two of North America's most large-scale and lucrative Chinese pageants, are eligible to participate in the Miss Chinese International pageant. At this "champion of champions" competition, the winners join holders of other "Miss Chinese" titles from communities around the world, and contend for the coveted "queen of queens" crown. The titleholder is guaranteed a chance to network with top talent scouts in the Cantopop (Cantonese pop) music, TV, film, and modeling industries. A major success story—one that many competing ABC (American-born Chinese) or CBC (Canadian-born Chinese) participants aspire to repeat—is that of Christy Chung. In 1994 Miss Chung won the Miss Chinese–Montreal crown. This success enabled her to compete at the Miss Chinese International pageant—which she won—to find herself on the flight path to land major roles in action comedy films opposite Jackie Chan.

Similarly, winners of the Miss India USA (based in New York City) and Miss India–Canada (based in Toronto) pageants—two competitions with direct ties to Bollywood—get the chance to visit Mumbai. There they can network with talent scouts from the world of MTV veejaying, modeling, acting, and infotainment reporting. In the past decade, numerous Misses India USA and Misses India–Canada have tried their luck in Mumbai, and a number of them have indeed become household names. For instance, Gita, a former Miss India–Canada, notes that although she did not become a Bollywood megastar, she did become a "mini starlet." She worked as the emcee of English-language TV serials, was cast as the female love interest in several Hindu music videos, and modeled for Indian fashion **magazines**.

Reasons vary for why North American-born and -educated Chinese and Indian pageant titleholders would seek an entertainment career in their families' homelands. Some Asian beauty queens still have difficulty finding adequate work in Hollywood, despite the roles for culturally diverse individuals recently created in TV and film. These pageant winners find that their title offers them the opportunity to find substantial, lucrative work in entertainment, even if it is situated in an East- or South-Asian milieu. Others, raised from a young age on imported Hong Kong or Bollywood films, TV series, and music videos in their parents' living room, fantasize about gaining entry to the industry that spawned such cultural commodities.

Indian Beauty Pageants and "First-World Exotica," or "First-World Otherness." "First-World exotica" and "otherness" are two notions that relate to the Miss India USA and Miss India–Canada pageants. When winners of these pageants return to India to try their luck in the entertainment world, a major alluring factor for Bollywood talent scouts is that although these titleholders may look Indian, their Western education, upbringing, and values—which can be grouped under the terms "First-World exotica" or "First-World otherness"—set them apart from their native-born female counterparts. Her First-World otherness is doubly beneficial if Miss India USA or Miss India–Canada is linguistically adept in her parents' native tongue.

Miss Chinese Toronto: Transculturated Popular Form. One interesting factor that differentiates the Miss Chinese Toronto competition from mainstream pageants is that the Toronto pageant serves as a venue for a popular transcultural form—the Cantopop music award show. Award show programming continues to be popular in Hong Kong and southern China, and Chinese expatriates and their children relish and consume it via satellite TV in Canada and around the world. The Miss Chinese Toronto pageant revolves around numerous musical numbers that integrate mainstream pageant components (like the evening gown competition) with elements associated with the Hong Kong pageant. These numbers involve elaborate sets and performers wearing outrageous costumes that pay postmodern homage to Chinese sword-fighting serials and American sci-fi films. The Toronto pageants also feature popular guest singers who lip-synch Cantonese versions to cover British and American pop songs. Whereas the Cantopop shows feature professional backup dancers, in the Miss Chinese Toronto pageant, it is the contestants who fill these roles. The contestants' presence, as an important part of the appropriated cultural form, is emphasized in song lyrics that integrate their names and promote their pageant personas. The pageant illustrates the complex transnational flows at work: the Cantopop music award show format, developed in the contestants' homeland to be consumed by national subjects and Cantonese expatriates, collides with the Miss Chinese Toronto pageant. The pageant, produced in Canada by Fairchild TV, a Cantonese-language network with stations in Toronto and Vancouver, caters especially to the local Chinese community and to viewers in Hong Kong, where it is also broadcast and produced (in Cantonese only).

Chinese beauty queens in the 2006 Los Angeles Chinese New Year Parade. (Courtesy of David Alexander Liu/Shutterstock.)

Filipino Beauty Contests and Their Contrasting Affiliations with Feminine Beauty, Racial Purity, and National Pride. Whereas the Miss Chinese and Miss India pageants in the United States and Canada are for-profit ventures, most Filipina pageants in North America (with the exception of Miss Filipina USA) are sponsored by local community organizations and feature a significant fundraising component. The contestant who sells the most pageant tickets receives a title and all funds raised go toward a charitable cause. Sometimes the recipient of the "Miss Popularity" title is also the overall first-place winner. This title had been the source of no small controversy; in fact, efforts were made to reduce the importance of fundraising in the crowning of Miss Philippines–Montreal 2004.

There exists an implicit preference for *mestiza* looks in Filipino beauty pageants across North America, where the ideal Filipina is represented by girls and young women whose beauty reflects their mixed ancestry. They must be tall, have light-brown hair, a "Western" nose, and—above all—fair skin. The beauty standards upheld by these pageants refer simultaneously to Caucasian body images and specifically Filipino beauty standards. Paradoxically this results in the desire at U.S. and Canadian Filipino beauty pageants to select a winner who represents a "racially authentic" Filipina American or Filipina Canadian woman. However, any standard of authentic beauty is very much in question, given the Filipino diaspora and long history of colonization and intermarriage in the Philippines.

Conclusion. In general, North America–based Asian pageants are not just framed in relation to Western standards of beauty and pageant culture. At the same time, these competitions address themselves to audiences "back home" and to the specific contexts of those national and transnational entertainment industries. The aspects of beauty and femininity to which they adhere reflect the multiflow negotiations between the local and the transnational.

See also Children's Beauty Pageants; The Thin Ideal

Further Reading

Banet-Weiser, Sarah. (1999). *The Most Beautiful Girl in the World: Beauty Pageants and National Identity*. Berkeley: University of California Press.

Cohen, Colleen Ballerino, Richard Wilk, and Beverly Stoeltje, eds. (1996). *Beauty Queens on the Global Stage: Gender, Contests, and Power*. New York: Routledge.

Mani, Bakirathi. (2006). "Beauty Queens: Gender, Ethnicity, and Transnational Modernities at the Miss India USA Pageant." *Positions—East Asia Cultures Critique* 14, no. 3, 717–747.

Tice, Karen W. (2006). "There She Is, Miss America: The Politics of Sex, Beauty, and Race in America's Most Famous Pageant." *Journal of Women's History* 18, no. 4, 147–156.

Watson, Elwood, and Darcy Martin. (2000). "The Miss America Pageant: Pluralism, Femininity, and Cinderella All in One." *Journal of Popular Culture* 34, no. 1, 105–126.

Wu, Judy Tzu-Chun. (1997). "Loveliest Daughter of Our Ancient Cathay! Representations of Ethnic and Gender Identity in the Miss Chinatown USA Beauty Pageant." *Journal of Social History* 31, no. 1, 5–32.

MONICA MAK AND JESSICA WURSTER

AT TWELVE. One of the best-known and most provocative sets of photographic images of **tween** girlhood can be found in photographer Sally Mann's collection *At Twelve: Portraits of Young Women*, produced in 1988. That same year, the collection was made into a book by the same name. *At Twelve* is an intimate glimpse into the contradictions of girlhood: the images offer a number of juxtapositions—from boyish to feminine, from sensual to innocent, from object to subject.

Sally Mann produced the collection of portraits of girls who were all around age 12 and who lived in the photographer's community in Virginia. Mann plays with the contradictions of girlhood through a group of portraits that defy standard representations of childhood. In the photograph titled "The Only Girl on the Boys' Summer Softball Team," a girl leans sensually against a brick wall. She dangles her bat behind her, eyes closed, hip outthrust in dirty baseball pants, hair stuck in sweaty curls around her face. She is a young girl whose androgyny, sensuality, and independence—her contradictions—arrest the viewer.

Mann is also known for her photographic work of her own young children, which has drawn both reverence and controversy. Tracing her own children's growth toward adolescence in sensual, large, black-and-white images, Mann has often had to justify whether her staged and sensualized approach to children is appropriate—in both the realm of art and the realm of parenting.

In *At Twelve* Mann's images of girlhood sit ambiguously between being staged and being captured moments of lives lived. Her portraits of tween girls are often unsettling and contest generally held views of girlhood. They speak to girls' toughness and defiance but also to their fears, burdens, and conflicts. As Mann writes in the introduction to the book: "What knowing watchfulness in the eyes of a twelve-year-old . . . at once guarded, yet guileless. She is the very picture of contradiction: on the one hand diffident and ambivalent, on the other forthright and impatient; half pertness and half pout" (Mann 1988, p. 14).

Art historians and those working in the sociology of childhood note that Mann's photographs evoke society's fear of representing girlhood as a time of sexuality, and raise questions about the appropriate positioning of photographer relative to subject, especially when the photographer is also the intimate friend, relative, or mother of the girl depicted. Mann's photographs are regarded as having disrupted a version of childhood in which children and preadolescents fill an idyllic, modern understanding of **innocence**, both psychologically and sexually. They have also been seen to confront society's expectations and stereotypes, and in so doing they force viewers to recognize in these depictions children who *are* sexual beings, tweens who *are* comfortable in their bodies, and girls who have not yet learned to turn their gaze away.

A major criticism of Mann's images of girls in particular is located within a type of **moral panic** in relation to the idea that she has been negligent in portraying children as sexual beings for all the world (and especially men) to see. Mann's view, however, is that these girls have not been created as passive objects but as active agents in their own depictions. The girls themselves have chosen to convey images that are sexualized—but images that are at the same time rugged, strong, beautiful, awkward, uncertain, and confident.

Some of Mann's work, including images from the *At Twelve* series, is shown in the permanent collections of New York's Museum of Modern Art, the Metropolitan Museum of Art, and the Washington, D.C., Corcoran Gallery of Art, among other galleries. In 2006 director Steven Cantor made a feature-length documentary film about Mann and her work called *What Remains*.

Further Reading

Higonnet, Anne. (1998). *Picturing Innocence: The History and Crisis of Ideal Childhood*. New York: Thames and Hudson.

Mann, Sally. (1988). *At Twelve: Portraits of Young Women*. New York: Aperture.

Townsend, Chris. (1998). *Vile Bodies: Photography and the Crisis of Looking*. New York: Prestel.

Walsh, Shannon. (2005). "'Losers, Lolitas, and Lesbos': Visualizing Girlhood." In Claudia Mitchell and Jacqueline Reid-Walsh, eds. *Seven Going on Seventeen: Tween Studies in the Culture of Girlhood*. New York: Peter Lang, pp. 191–205.

SHANNON WALSH

AVATAR.   In the digital world the term "avatar" refers to an image that represents an embodied self in a virtual environment. Two-dimensional icons are used in Internet forums, chat rooms, and other online spaces, whereas three-dimensional models are often used in computer games. For girls, avatars are important elements of play and interaction because they represent the girl in virtual environments and may therefore influence the formation of girls' personal identity and relationships and affect how girls construct and maintain their identity through the appearance and actions of their avatar.

In a virtual environment, girls typically choose from a predetermined list of avatars that they may be able to customize. However, some sites offer girls the possibility of creating an avatar completely of their own making. An avatar in a video game functions as the gamer's embodied character in the game. ***The Sims***, a popular computer game among girls, is an example in which much of the pleasure of play occurs through the customization of the avatar. When creating an avatar for game play, players are faced with a selection of physical characteristics—sex, body type, hair, and eye and skin color. In choosing the avatar's personality, a player can select varying attributes, such as degrees of shyness and intelligence and a sense of humor, and can determine the avatar's zodiac signs and life goals. Making choices for her avatar allows the creator to play with a range of possibilities that may not exist in her everyday life.

Users interact in a virtual environment through their avatars. For girls, these representations provide the possibility of interacting anonymously in spaces such as chat rooms. In this way, they are able to circumvent the social and physical restrictions typically placed on young girls, and are enabled to play as equals. Traditionally much of girls' play has occurred within domestic or supervised space to safeguard girls from such perceived dangers as strangers and from information deemed inappropriate by adults. Interaction through avatars may provide unprecedented opportunities for playing with identity, as girls can choose to assume roles that they may otherwise be discouraged from exploring in offline environments. For example, girls can choose to interact online using a male avatar or they can choose to be a warrior, barbarian, or villain—roles not typically encouraged in traditional girls' play.

See also Social Networking

Further Reading

Castronova, Edward. (2003). *Theory of the Avatar.* [Online February 2007]. Social Science Research Network Web site http://ssrn.com/abstract=385103.
Thomas, Angela. (2004). "Literacies of the Cybergirl." *E-Learning* 1, no. 3, 358–382.

SHANLY DIXON

B

BABY PHAT. baby phat is a brand of clothing created by former model Kimora Lee Simmons. The creation of the brand was her attempt to market urban luxury to girls and women. A former fashion model, mother, actress, and writer, Lee Simmons is also the wife of legendary hip hop producer Russell Simmons. He is the owner of Phat Farm, baby phat's male-oriented counterpart, and Def Jam Records.

Starting as a line of baby t's, T-shirts worn by models at a Phat Farm fashion show in 1993, the baby phat brand first appeared on the male-dominated urban wear scene in 1998. The women's brand has since expanded to include accessories, lingerie, handbags, footwear, beauty products, and swimwear. In 1999, the brand expanded to include clothing for younger girls. To date, the line includes clothing, shoes, and accessories for babies, girls, **tweens**, teens, and young women. Items that are particularly popular with tweens and teens are quilted black jackets, jeans, sneakers, rhinestone-studded **cell phones**, and **MySpace** page graphic décor that girls can download to customize their page. The brand's logo, which is a line drawing of a thin cat, features prominently.

Popular understandings of the term "baby phat" vary. Generally, it is a term used to describe a cute girl of any size, but typically one who is voluptuous. The baby phat women's line follows suit, ranging in size from extra small to XXXL, with a juniors' line that ranges from extra small to XL. Such offerings ensure that the brand is accessible to many girls and women, regardless of body shape and size. Moreover, models on the **Web site** reflect the same diversity of body shape and some diversity of ethnicities.

Critics have targeted Kimora Lee Simmons, claiming that she flouts publicly her wealth and celebrity status. Others have said that her overtly self-confident style is an integral part of the appeal of the baby phat line: girls and young women who wear baby phat clothing embody the luxury, beauty, and fame of Simmons and other girl culture celebrities who have been photographed wearing items from baby phat, including **Mariah Carey**, **Jennifer Lopez**, and **Lil' Kim**. For some girls and women, this is an act of empowerment; it may even be an act of transcendence of their own socioeconomic status.

baby phat has also been targeted by critics for the style of clothing that it offers for women, sometimes referring to it as "slutty." This appears to be a critique of the ultra-feminine styles that show off the wearer's curves, an argument that is frequently associated with **moral panics** and the sexualization of girls. However, the other side of the argument is that baby phat provides a line of urban clothing that is distinctly female in the male-dominated world of **Hip Hop culture**.

See also KGOY; Slut

Further Reading

Merskin, Debra. (2004). "Reviving Lolita? A Media Literacy Examination of Sexual Portrayals of Girls in Fashion Advertising." *American Behavioral Scientist* 48, no. 1, 119–129.

ELISABETH JOHNSON

BABYSITTERS.   The standard definition of a babysitter in *The Oxford Dictionary of Current English* (1987) is someone who looks after a child when the parents are away (p. 47). Babysitting became the primary form of adolescent part-time employment, particularly for girls, during in the 1920s. Since then, female babysitters have served as the object of adult anxieties about girl culture. A history of babysitting in twentieth-century America reveals that parents' fears and fantasies about teenage girls have found expression in the figure of the babysitter, who usually personifies adults' ideas of female adolescence. As the domain of girls, babysitting has largely functioned as a system of gender role socialization. However, it has also provided girls with the resources and opportunities to negotiate the demands of a first job, and, importantly, it has given female **tweens** and teens the financial means to either spend or save money.

Origins and Early History (1920s and 1930s).   During the 1920s, middle-class mothers were faced with two problems: a declining population of working-class "servants" and the spread of "scientific childrearing." Scientific childrearing was an idea advocating that traditional modes of birthing, raising, and educating children should be replaced with standardized methods based on scientific reasoning. Both of these trends left mothers with less time to spend with their children, and they therefore turned to middle-class high school girls to "mind the children." New needs for childcare had been generated by the decade's economic prosperity, middle-class expansion, suburban development, and leisure opportunities. These forces also shaped the lives of female adolescents as a newly emergent and "problematic" cultural group. By the mid-1920s, the authors of *Wholesome Childhood* (1924) had already issued a warning to mothers: steer clear of high-school girls who flirted with men on street corners in front of the children in their care.

Experts, educators, and parent-employers became uneasy about hiring middle-class teenage girls as babysitters. These girls, for whom high school had come to serve as an incubator of American girl culture, held "modern" beliefs and behaviors that openly challenged gender norms and traditional ideals of girlhood innocence. The increasing social and sexual autonomy of teenage girls disturbed many adults, who found themselves caught between their growing fear of adolescent girls and their increasing need for them. Instead of babysitting, however, most middle-class girls relied on weekly allowances for their "spending money." Experts believed that allowances, which were often rewarded on completing household chores, would instill adolescent girls with a sense of financial responsibility and would curb impulsive spending. However, girls in the process of shaping a new social identity that was both age- and gender-specific mostly spent their pocket money on **magazines**, makeup, and the movies—the building blocks of American teenage girl culture.

The collapse of the national economy and the loss of job opportunities during the Great Depression of the 1930s led girls to "mind the children" as babysitters, although the term was not in common use until after World War II. Age-segregated schools fostered the development of teen culture, especially among adolescent girls who used the money they earned babysitting to negotiate between old-fashioned gender identities and new cultural forms (such as clothing styles, magazines, and beauty products) that widened the gap between adults and adolescents. Often, both teenage girls' own parents and the parents who employed girls to babysit objected to their modern ways. Teenage girls—who wore makeup, donned new trend-setting fashions, talked on the telephone, and entertained friends while babysitting—provoked female employers to complain. They also caused experts to criticize girls' cultural practices that were perceived as threats to the social and sexual order.

By the end of the 1930s, an increase in the national birth rate was accompanied by more permissive child rearing practices by young parents. Despite this permissiveness, babysitters felt exasperated and exploited by their female employers, who often heaped housework onto already overwhelming childcare duties.

New Babysitters for a New Economy (1940s and 1950s). Women's entrance into the work force during World War II both heightened the demand for babysitters and reduced the number of adolescents willing to babysit. The war economy generated new employment opportunities for adolescents, and many teenage girls found jobs in stores and factories. Wage-earning girls also took advantage of widening opportunities for teen-centered entertainment. On the home front, modern American girl culture proliferated. Even the youngest teens gained a sense of economic and social independence, which led to the redefinition of the teenager as a social, sexual, and even political being. Although adults tolerated many aspects of girl culture, the sexual assertions of female adolescents provoked panic among those who feared the disintegration of traditional morality, the collapse of the nuclear family, and growing opposition to established gender roles.

In an effort to direct girls back into the home, where they could help ease the shortage of babysitters, organizations and schools nationwide promoted child care classes. But the "army" of babysitters was composed of preadolescents and elementary-school age children rather than teens, because these younger children had no other options for making money. Both working mothers and the babysitters they hired were inadequately supported and under-resourced while on the job, and mothers often paid youngsters to watch their own children as well as those from other less financially stable families. No matter how young they were or how many children were in their charge, wartime sitters were also expected to do the dishes and other housekeeping tasks.

Babysitting was again established as the primary means of employment for teenage girls immediately after the war, when they were again excluded from the formal economy. Girls were often faced with no other viable employment options but to babysit for the large (and continually growing) population of the generation that would later be called baby boomers—children born in the late 1940s and 1950s. Teen babysitters were still paid low wages, assigned many housekeeping tasks, and expected to care for large broods of babies. However, drawing on the wartime expansion of rights for women and youth, teenage girls began to reorganize the field of babysitting. Ideas of female empowerment joined with youth culture's claims to autonomy and gave rise to babysitter unions in high schools and colleges throughout the Northeast and Midwest.

Although the number of unions remained small in number in the late 1940s and early 1950s, babysitters claimed their rights in manifestos and codes of conduct and fought to standardize wages and eliminate housework. The success of their organizations was owing to the support provided by high school teachers, guidance counselors, community women, and mothers, who were now desperate for time off from the exhausting demands of full-time childcare and domestic work. However, fathers often criticized teenage girls, whom they perceived as rebels who undermined paternal and patriarchal authority with their unions and demands. In the postwar era, masculinity was unsettled by the social changes that had fueled girl culture and empowered women, especially in the workforce, during the war. It was in the years following the war that men began to criticize, satirize, and sexualize teenage babysitters in print, pictures, and popular movies.

The increasing commercialization of teen culture and the expanding market in teen goods motivated girls to babysit, but the job did not always seem worth it to girls, many of whom used slang to critique babysitting as "bratting." Contributing to a lack of sitters (particularly in the suburbs) were girls who turned down parents' pleas to babysit. The problem was particularly acute, given that low birth rates in the 1930s and soaring birth rates in the postwar era led baby boomers to outnumber babysitters until the end of the 1950s.

Irreverent Adolescents (1960s and 1970s). Prejudiced by exaggerated criticisms of teenage girls, parent-employers often perceived **"bobby-soxer"** babysitters as irreverent and irresponsible. Employers were anxious about the challenges that this new generation of girls were posing to gender norms and often suspected babysitters of overstepping their limits and violating moral codes. Parent-employer suspicions about the seemingly unstable, unsteady, and uncertain subculture of girls led many to turn to adult neighbors for childcare. Networks of adult sitters, or "babysitting co-ops," were established, largely by suburban mothers who were cut off from other family members. Parent-employers also began turning to the segment of the teenage male population, who were presented in popular culture as upstanding, trustworthy, reliable, and responsible.

As parents became increasingly dissatisfied with teenage girls' raiding refrigerators and being caught dancing to popular radio in the living room, educators and experts began to turn babysitting into a profession. Training classes sought to restrain girls' autonomy in their employers' houses and reduce parental anxiety by standardizing babysitting and dictating what was appropriate and inappropriate behavior. By the 1960s, states also passed legislation that restricted babysitters' rights to sue their employers.

The intent of popular girl culture in the 1960s was largely to turn unruly girls into obedient babysitters. Featuring teen girls as energetic and attentive babysitters, popular dolls, games, television shows, and movies reflected and reinforced but also restrained girls' growing independence. In cautionary urban legends told as "true" stories, pleasure-seeking babysitters were held responsible for catastrophes and horrors in the home. In the most enduring babysitter legend of the 1960s (and the basis of many horror movies since), the babysitter is victimized by a male murderer because she fails to "check the children." The relationship between the male killer and the female babysitter in this legend draws out adult anxieties about the social changes set in motion by youth culture, feminism, and the sexual revolution of the 1960s.

Made into the anti-heroes of 1970s horror movies, the male monsters of babysitting legends sought retribution for the rise of female empowerment and the decline of male privilege. The soaring rates of divorce, along with increasing female employment and declining fertility rates, created a sense of dread in adults who needed babysitters but feared teenage girls' power to subvert the social order.

The Rise of Tween Sitters (1980s and 1990s). In 1980 there were 33 million children in the United States of age to require a babysitter (under 10 years old) and only 21 million between the ages of 15 and 19 (Wee 1997). Attractive yet cunning teenage girls in popular movies continued to raise parental anxieties, as they embodied anti-feminist fears about female authority, empowerment, and autonomy. Although teen babysitters were portrayed in movies as vixens using persuasion and seduction to destroy their employers' marriages and families, preadolescent girls were being represented in the media as wholesome "super sitters" who helped, not harmed, families. The establishment of Safe Sitters, Inc. (1980) and other babysitting training programs nationwide taught girls vocational skills as well as domestic work by encouraging some aspects of girl culture and restraining others. The enormously popular ***Baby-sitters Club*** book series, for instance, aimed to familiarize elementary schoolgirls with babysitting and make **Girl Power** into a cultural product.

Despite the concerns of parent-employers about the inexperience of youthful sitters during the 1980s and 1990s, those who wanted an evening out often turned to tweens because of their prepubescent **innocence** and energy and because there were still too few teenagers around. Even when the teenage population grew, however, girls often preferred after-school activities, such as sports and music lessons, weekend socializing, and part-time employment, to babysitting. Low unemployment rates enabled girls to work in retail stores and fast food restaurants located in suburban malls. Although these "real" jobs might not have paid much more than babysitting, they required less patience and provided regular hours, higher status, the ability to socialize with other teens, and access to goods.

In contrast to the fictional babysitters in tween stories who love their jobs, young adolescent girls at the end of the twentieth century and the beginning of the twenty-first expressed many of the same complaints as the teens of a generation before them. Girls are committed to preserving their autonomy and sense of empowerment and still object to low wages and poor working conditions.

Further Reading

Forman-Brunell, Miriam. (2008). *Sitting Pretty: Girls, Grownups, and the History of Babysitting*. New York: New York University Press.

Margoin, Leslie. (1990). "Child Abuse by Baby-Sitters: An Ecological Interactional Interpretation." *Journal of Family Violence* 5, no. 2, 95–105.

Wee, Eric L. (1997, September 22). "Calling All Babysitters: Shortage Has Parents Trying Every Name and Trick in the Book." *Washington Post*.

MIRIAM FORMAN-BRUNELL

BABY-SITTERS CLUB, THE.   *The Baby-sitters Club* is a series of books written by Ann M. Martin and published by Scholastic Press between 1986 and 2000. The series centers on a group of middle-school girls, living in the fictional town of Stoneybrook, Connecticut, who create their own babysitting business. Four 13-year-old characters are introduced in book 1, *Kristy's Great Idea*: Kristy Thomas, a bossy yet appealing **tomboy**; Mary Ann

Spier, who is shy and sensitive; Claudia Kishi, a Japanese American who dresses with style; and Stacey McGill, who loves fashion and boys. During the 14 years of the series, the girls remain in seventh and eighth grades, competently handling the struggles they encounter through their babysitting, supporting each other, having crushes on boys, enjoying sleepovers, welcoming new members, and adjusting to changes in their lives. Each volume centers on one of the girls, who tells the story in her own voice.

The *Baby-sitters Club* books portray life in the white, middle-class American suburbs. The girls are all middle class, the children of parents with an assured income and a high standard of living. Even Claudia, the token visible minority, is a child of the dominant culture and the middle class. The girls who bought the *Baby-sitters Club* books were also generally middle class, and they tended to identify with the characters (Greenlee et al. 1996) and often came to see themselves, too, as capable young women with agency and influence (Cherland 2005).

The demand for **series fiction** books such as the *Baby-sitters Club* was socially created and regulated (Taxel 2002) by the children's publishing industry. When Scholastic and other publishers began to engage in market research in the 1980s, they were able to create several wildly successful series of books for a particular market, the female teenage reader. Characterized by formulaic plots and stock characters, series such as **Sweet Valley High** and *The Baby-sitters Club* were immensely profitable. When market research suggested that preteen girls were another potential market, Scholastic approached Ann M. Martin about doing a series for preteen girls. Martin wrote the first thirty-five books, and many of the subsequent books were outlined by Martin and then ghostwritten, including forty-three books by Peter Lerangis. Produced quickly with formulaic plots for a specific market, *The Baby-sitters Club* books were enormously lucrative. The series sold over 175 million copies and inspired many spin-off media texts, including *The Baby-sitters' Little Sisters* book series, a television movie, a TV series, the "Super Special" books (these were longer books, sold at higher prices, that concerned all of the characters from *The Baby-sitters Club* in one longer story), and a wide array of trademark merchandise, including lunchboxes and calendars.

Many teachers lamented their female students' preferences for series books such as *The Baby-sitters Club* over children's literature of higher quality. However, there is no doubt that millions of girls loved these books. They were a cultural phenomenon. There is today a generation of predominantly white middle-class American and Canadian women in their late 20s who remember Kristy, Mary Anne, Claudia, Stacey, and their friends with affection and gratitude and who recall fondly their reading experiences with *The Baby-sitters Club*.

See also Babysitters

Further Reading

Cherland, Meredith. (2005). "Reading Elisabeth's Girlhood: History and Popular Culture at Work in the Subjectivity of a Tween." In Claudia Mitchell and Jacqueline Reid-Walsh, eds. *Seven Going on Seventeen: Tween Studies in the Culture of Girlhood.* New York: Peter Lang, pp. 95–117.

Greenlee, Adele A., Dianne L. Monson, and Barbara M. Taylor. (1996). "The Lure of Series Books: Does It Affect Appreciation for Recommended Literature?" *The Reading Teacher* 50, no. 3, 216–225.

Taxel, Joel. (2002). "Children's Literature at the Turn of the Century: Toward a Political Economy of the Publishing Industry." *Research in the Teaching of English* 37, no. 2, 145–197.

MEREDITH ROGERS CHERLAND

BACKSTREET BOYS.   This boy band was from Orlando, Florida, and is arguably one of the most successful formations of this particular genre ever. Riding the coattails of previous boy bands such as Menudo, New Edition, and **New Kids on the Block,** the Backstreet Boys, featuring the singing talent of Nick Carter, Brian Littrell, Howie Dorough, A. J. McLean, and Kevin Richardson, were catapulted to success in Europe in 1993.

Several years after the band's 1995 debut on the European pop charts and the hype generated from interest, most notably in Germany, Jive Records decided to capitalize on the resurgence in the demand for pop music in North America by heavily promoting the boys' eponymous 1997 U.S. release, which compiled hit songs from their first and second international albums, *The Backstreet Boys* (1996) and *Backstreet's Back* (1997). At this point, considering the members' ages (ranging from 16 to 25) and the hole in the market for clean-cut pop heartthrobs to adorn the walls of girls' **bedrooms** across America, the target market of **tweens** and early adolescent girls embraced these pinups with open arms.

Combining choreography and catchy songs about young love, the Backstreet Boys toured extensively in America and Canada in the late 1990s and played to sold-out crowds, which were mostly composed of screaming prepubescent girls who were chaperoned by their parents. Although Nick Carter was definitely the star of the group, there was enough variety in the band to appeal to all young girls, whether they liked the wholesome all-American type, such as Carter and Brian Littrell, or the bad boy, such as bandmate A. J. McLean.

The singles released off the two first albums, namely "Quit Playing Games with My Heart" and "Backstreet's Back," were in such heavy rotation on commercial radio that the 1999 release of the Backstreet Boys' third album, *Millennium,* was a phenomenal hit that guaranteed the band the number 1 position on the worldwide billboard charts and the adoration of even more young female fans. The album featuring the hit single "I Want It That Way" went platinum eleven times and sold 30 million copies internationally.

The band cemented its success by traveling the world in 1999 on the "Into the Millennium" tour, even stopping in smaller American towns generally ignored by agents and record company executives. Furthermore, the band's management team signed deals with Burger King, and the endorsement assured that, on any given day, youth were constantly exposed to some form of Backstreet Boys paraphernalia.

In 2000 the band came out with another album, *Black and Blue,* which featured original material co-written by the members. In the years since the band's formation, its fame had grown exponentially. The hype was not only driven by strategic promotion and endorsement deals, but also became increasingly generated by the young fans themselves through fan club networks and the adeptness with which teen girls use the Internet to communicate with one another.

The Backstreet Boys, ca. 1998. (Courtesy of Photofest.)

Following the launch of *Black and Blue*, the Backstreet Boys compiled a greatest hits album, *The Hits: Chapter One*, in 2001. Despite the compilation's sales figures (totaling about 6 million), as a result of almost 10 solid years of touring, the engagements of several members, and the widely publicized drug abuse problem of A. J. McLean, the Backstreet Boys split up that year.

The band's star, Nick Carter, pursued a solo career; the other four members disappeared into relative obscurity. Carter's solo success was short-lived, and he was ultimately overshadowed in the tween and young adolescent community by the continuing success of the rival boy band *NSYNC, as well as by the success of his own younger brother, Aaron Carter. Most recently, however, the Carter family took advantage of their sons' fame and agreed to participate in a reality television program called *House of Carters*.

The Backstreet Boys briefly reunited in 2005 and launched a semi-successful comeback in the form of an adult contemporary album called *Never Gone*.

See also Fan Culture

Further Reading

Wald, Gayle. (2002). "I Want It That Way: Teenybopper Music and the Girling of Boy Bands." *Genders* 35, http://www.genders.org/g35/g35_wald.txt.

DORIAN MITCHELL

BARRYMORE, DREW (1975–).   Drew Barrymore is an American actress and film producer who is an icon of popular girl culture. Born into a family of famous actors, she began her acting career with small roles in commercials and made-for-TV movies. She has since appeared in more than forty movies.

When she was only 5 years old, Barrymore performed in her first movie role. She played Margaret Jessup, the daughter of a scientist who tests hallucinatory drugs on himself in the film *Altered States*. When she was 6, director Steven Spielberg chose her for the role of little Gertie in *E.T.: The Extra-Terrestrial*, released in 1982. In this film Gertie is a young girl who, with her two older brothers, secretly befriends a stranded alien. Spielberg's story of friendship and loss provided Barrymore the opportunity to prove her acting mettle. Beloved by children and adults alike, the movie surpassed *Star Wars* as the top-selling movie of the time and is currently ranked twenty-fourth on the American Film Institute's list of "100 Greatest Movies" (*Citizen Kane* Tops Great Movies List 2007). With her sweet and candid demeanor, Barrymore became an instant celebrity and made numerous television appearances, including a notable turn on *The Tonight Show Starring Johnny Carson* and a night as host of *Saturday Night Live* when she was 7 years old.

Barrymore earned critical acclaim for her subsequent work in such movies as *Firestarter* (1984) and *Irreconcilable Differences* (1984), for which she received a Golden Globe nomination for Best Supporting Actress. However, by age 9, Barrymore had begun a struggle with substance abuse; she was smoking cigarettes, drinking alcohol, and—by age 12—smoking marijuana and snorting cocaine. She quickly became a **celebrity bad girl** whose life was closely watched by the paparazzi. All the while, she continued to act in movies such as *Cat's Eye* (1985), *See You in the Morning* (1989), and *Motorama* (1991). By 1994 she had overcome her addictions and wrote the **coming-of-age memoir**, *Little Girl Lost*.

During her late adolescence and early adulthood, Barrymore acted in several roles that reflected her "bad girl" persona. For example, in *Poison Ivy* (1992) and the made-for-TV movie *The Amy Fisher Story* (1993), she played **Lolita** characters who manipulated men with their sexuality. During this period, she became the godmother of the only daughter of **Courtney Love** and Kurt Cobain, Frances Bean.

In 1995 Barrymore appeared nude in the January issue of *Playboy*. She guested on the *David Letterman Show* in April of that year; she climbed on top of Letterman's desk, danced around (showing off several of her tattoos), and flashed the host her breasts. That same year, she starred in *Mad Love*, playing the role of a wild teenage girl who battles depression. She appeared in *Boys on the Side*, in which her character leaves an abusive boyfriend and forges meaningful friendships with a group of supportive women. In 1996 she played the role of Casey Becker in the first installment of the satirical teen slasher film franchise, *Scream*.

In 1998 Barrymore starred with Adam Sandler in the romantic comedy *The Wedding Singer*—the first of many roles she played in this genre of film. In 1998 Barrymore also starred in *Ever After: A Cinderella Story*, a feminist retelling of the traditional **fairy tale**. That same year, she co-founded a movie production company called Flower Films. The company produced several movies, including *Never Been Kissed* (1999), a romantic comedy; ***Charlie's Angels*** (2000) and *Charlie's Angels: Full Throttle* (2003), which were remakes of the successful television show from the 1970s and 1980s; and *Donnie Darko* (2001), a psychological thriller that has earned a cult following. Barrymore has done voice work for children's films, providing the voice of the title character in the animated Christmas TV special *Olive, the Other Reindeer* (1999), and that of Maggie, the love interest of the man in the yellow suit in the movie version of *Curious George* (2006). Barrymore was also the subject of the documentary *My Date with Drew* (2005), in which director and producer Brian Herzlinger is given thirty days to get a date with Drew Barrymore.

In 2007, at age 32, Barrymore was named Ambassador Against Hunger for the United Nations World Food Programme, with the assignment of applying her celebrity to the promotion of feeding programs in schools in the world's poorest countries. Later in 2007 Barrymore was named the "new face" of CoverGirl cosmetics.

See also Temple, Shirley

Further Reading

Barrymore, Drew. (1990). *Little Girl Lost*. New York: Simon & Schuster.
CNN. (2007). "*Citizen Kane* Tops Great Movies List." [Online June 2007]. CNN Web site http://www.cnn.com/2007/SHOWBIZ/Movies/06/21/afi.movies.ap/index.html.

LINDSAY CORNISH

BAT MITZVAH.   The Bat Mitzvah is a ceremony that celebrates a Jewish girl's becoming an adult member of her community. Somewhat like **Quinceañera** and **debutante** balls, the Bat Mitzvah is a rite of passage for many Jewish girls, especially in North America. Its roots are religious in origin, but the practice is popular with Jewish people from across the religious spectrum, including many who would consider themselves secular. The celebration itself varies greatly, both historically and between different sects of Judaism. According to Jewish law, girls become Bat Mitzvah at the age of 12 or 13. Although the Bat Mitzvah is often understood as an extravagant birthday party (as in the 2006 film *Keeping Up with the Steins* or the 2005 episode of the television show *Entourage* entitled "The Bat Mitzvah"), Bat Mitzvah literally refers to the girl's becoming a "daughter of the commandments."

Origins and Evolution of the Rite. The Bar Mitzvah, a Jewish male's **coming-of-age** ceremony (literally, "son of the commandments"), is a rite of passage dating back to medieval times. The Bat Mitzvah, however, is a modern invention. It is said that Rabbi Mordecai Kaplan, founder of the left-wing movement known as Reconstructionist Judaism, developed the ceremony based on having seen a Bat Mitzvah on a trip to Italy; his daughter, Judith Kaplan, became the first American Bat Mitzvah in New York City in 1922. Since then, the Bat Mitzvah ceremony has become increasingly popular, especially in egalitarian Jewish communities where girls and women are regarded as having equal rights and responsibilities in religious practice as boys and men.

In Orthodox communities, Jewish girls may have ceremonies or other familial events to mark their coming of age. However, these generally do not involve reading from the *Torah* (Old Testament) or leading services, because these practices are not included in the religious participation of Orthodox women. Orthodox girls are not invited to have an *aliyah* (which literally means "ascent" and involves stepping up to the *bimah*, or stage, to recite a blessing over the *Torah* before it is read). Although the coming-of-age celebration for an Orthodox girl is more likely a small affair among family and friends, if she is to read from the *Torah* or conduct services in honor of becoming Bat Mitzvah, she does so exclusively in the presence of other women. It is in Orthodox communities that the differences between Bat and Bar Mitzvah ceremonies are most apparent; the ceremonies that mark a boy becoming Bar Mitzvah are much more public than are the ceremonies for girls.

The Bat Mitzvah Process. Bat Mitzvah ceremonies differ from place to place. In fact, in its most basic form, all that is required to become Bat or Bar Mitzvah is to be called up to the *Torah* for an *aliyah*—in theory, then, it is technically impossible for Orthodox Jewish girls to become Bat Mitzvah. In many denominations of Judaism today, the ceremony is increasingly marked by the full participation of the Bat Mitzvah in the entirety of a Saturday morning Shabbat (Sabbath) service. Usually the service is followed by a party (or sometimes several parties) and a *Seudat Mitzvah* (literally, a "commandment meal"), a celebratory feast.

In Conservative synagogues that support egalitarianism in the Bar or Bat Mitzvah ceremony, young women embarking on the Bat Mitzvah journey often begin with Hebrew lessons three times a week. A girl may begin these lessons as early as first grade and may then become Bat Mitzvah five or six years later. Over the course of these years, she learns about Jewish history, the Hebrew language, Israel, ritual, and prayer. She is working toward gaining the knowledge and confidence to lead her congregation in a full Saturday morning service (two to three hours in length) on the day of her Bat Mitzvah. At a Conservative synagogue, the service is likely to be in Hebrew and much of it is sung, so the Bat Mitzvah also needs to learn the words and be able to carry the tunes to the various songs and prayers.

A main event in the Bat Mitzvah ceremony is the reading of the *Haftorah*, a text selected from the book of Prophets (*Nevi'im*) and read directly after the reading of the *Torah* during the Saturday morning service. The *Haftorah* is also in Hebrew, and, like the *Torah* portion, it is chanted, but the notes (called *trope*) of this cantillation are different from those used for other parts of the service. Although some girls read all or part of the *Torah* portion that falls on the day of their Bat Mitzvah, the *Haftorah* portion is usually the piece that they focus on most diligently during preparation in the year leading up to the big event.

At the end of the service, the members of the congregation often throw candies at the Bat Mitzvah as a way of offering hope for a sweet future. After the service, there is usually a party. In a Conservative synagogue, the ceremonies for girls and boys are often exactly the same, as are the expectations for them as members of the community.

Another important part of many Bat Mitzvah celebrations is the *D'var Torah*, literally a "word of *Torah*." In this case, the Bat Mitzvah is invited to discuss the *Torah* portion that is read on her Bat Mitzvah day. Usually this involves giving a summary of the reading, selecting its key themes, and consulting relevant commentaries on the portion (many of which are now available online). In their *D'var Torah*, young people often tie their portion to themes that are close to their own life experiences, as well as those of their families and communities. Many look for ways to make the reading both personally meaningful and socially relevant. An interesting tradition one might encounter involves Bat or Bar Mitzvah youth who are using their celebrations as a way of remembering a young person who perished in the Holocaust, by symbolically sharing the *bimah* with her or him. In this way, the Bar or Bat Mitzvah takes on the adult responsibility of remembrance. It is also not uncommon to see young people use their Bar or Bat Mitzvah celebrations as a way of practicing *tzedakah* (literally, righteousness or justice, but generally understood to mean charity, which is considered an obligation given by God to all Jews) by earmarking a portion of the gift money they receive for a charity of their choice. In many synagogues today, individual or class *tzedakah* projects, usually involving some form of social justice, are an encouraged or even mandatory part of the preparatory curriculum.

Modern Incarnations of the Bat Mitzvah Rite. In recent years, criticism of the lavishness and excess of some Bar or Bat Mitzvah events has increased. In 2005, *Washington Post* reporter David Segal wrote that a New York businessman "reportedly spent millions on his daughter's Bat Mitzvah, renting out the Rainbow Room, which sits atop Rockefeller Plaza, and flying in the rapper 50 Cent, as well as Aerosmith, Tom Petty, and Stevie Nicks" (p. C-1). As Segal reports, this is an extreme case, but even more "average" events can include expensive dinners and live musicians or performers. In this respect, there is usually little difference between parties thrown for boys and girls. The focal point of the rite becomes the celebration, and, in a way, the individual child and her religious rite of passage is made peripheral, only the first chapter in a very long book of events organized around her becoming Bat Mitzvah. This certainly is not always the case; Bat Mitzvah ceremonies can be held at home with close family and friends, or they can be held in a synagogue filled with community members, followed by a modest lunch. Some girls travel with their immediate families to Israel to become Bat Mitzvah there. Indeed, there are probably as many ways to celebrate a Jewish girl's coming of age as there are girls themselves.

Critics of the lavish turn that many of these events have taken are particularly concerned with how they detract from the ceremony's significance (both religiously and symbolically, as a rite of passage). Indeed, the high visibility of Bat Mitzvah ceremonies has sometimes made young Jewish girls and boys the envy of their non-Jewish peers. Just as Jewish children have long envied Christmas and begged their parents for trees, Gentile children now demand "faux Mitzvah" parties. A 2004 *Wall Street Journal* article reported on one Methodist teen from Texas who had been to so many Bar and Bat Mitzvah parties that she insisted she was willing to learn Hebrew if it meant she could have one of her own. Her parents acquiesced to a party hosted by their daughter and two of her friends for 125 people at a country club, complete with all the nonreligious trappings she had come to associate with her Jewish friends' rites of passage. The teen was quoted as saying: "I wanted to be Jewish so I could have a Bat Mitzvah. . . . [H]aving the party fulfilled that." There have also been reports of "black Mitzvahs" thrown to celebrate a girl's African American heritage. Heralded by *USA Today* reporter Olivia Barker as the "Bar or Bat Mitzvah bloat," this idea represents a broader trend of holding increasingly elaborate teen celebrations, including **Sweet Sixteens**, debutante balls, and Quinceañeras.

Bat Mitzvahs in Popular Culture. Most people are more familiar with the Bar Mitzvah than the Bat Mitzvah, likely because the Bar Mitzvah has appeared much more frequently on film and in television. However, quite a few pop culture images of Bat Mitzvah girls exist. Young adult novels about Bat Mitzvahs include *You Are So Not Invited to My Bat Mitzvah* (2007), *The Bat Mitzvah Club: Debbie's Story* (2001), and *Pink Slippers, Bat Mitzvah Blues* (1994). Dozens if not hundreds of "how to" and "what is" books have also been published. Classic texts such as **Judy Blume's *Are You There, God? It's Me, Margaret*** (1970) have also tackled discussions of religion and identity, including the Bat Mitzvah.

Bat Mitzvahs have also been visible on television. In 1981, Archie Bunker celebrated his niece and adopted daughter becoming Bat Mitzvah on *Archie Bunker's Place*; in 1982, **mean** girl Muffy Tepperman (of *Square Pegs*) excluded her series' stars Lauren and Patty from her Bat Mitzvah celebration; and, in the third season of *Sex and the City* (2000), Samantha was hired to be the publicist for the Bat Mitzvah of a cunning New York teen, who calmly states, "We'll be lucky if we can swing this for under a mil." More recently, Delia Brown of *Everwood* became Bat Mitzvah (2006). This story arcs across the last season of a five-year series following the life of a New York City surgeon who moves to Colorado after losing his (Jewish) wife. Delia, his daughter, sees Judaism as a way of connecting with her mother, which makes her father a bit perplexed. He would like her to have a party but is discouraged by the obstacles of preparing Delia to become Bat Mitzvah in their somewhat remote Colorado community. It is through a chance connection with a patient, a Holocaust survivor, that Dr. Brown decides that finding a way for Delia to become a Bat Mitzvah is meaningful and worth struggling for.

One of the most interesting popular culture Bat Mitzvahs is certainly Grace in *Joan of Arcadia* (2003–2005). Grace is a whip-smart independent thinker who defies every stereotype about Jewish girlhood. After refusing to become Bat Mitzvah at the age of 13, much to the chagrin of her Rabbi father, she decides to go through with it at age 16. In episode 10 of season 2, Grace tells her best friend Joan: "It was a political thing and a daughter of the Rabbi thing . . . one last empty ritual and then I'm out of here. Then, when you handed me the *Torah*, it hit me. This is a genius way of attacking adulthood, this religion. There's no easy answers here. It's basically a book of questions . . . and I hope I'm up for it."

There is an enormous amount of information for and about Bat Mitzvahs on the Internet. Roughly thirty to forty groups directly relating to Bat Mitzvah celebrations are found on the **social networking** site Facebook; these groups are devoted to anticipating upcoming Bat Mitzvah celebrations ("If you are counting down the days until Emily's Bat Mitzvah"), reminiscing about those past ("Maddie's Bat Mitzvah was amazing"), and discussing silly facts or memories ("The majority of my pajamas I got at a Bar or Bat Mitzvah when I was 13"). There are also dozens of blogs by girls and their parents counting down to Bat Mitzvah celebrations. Searching online, one can hire a Rabbi or Cantor, sign up for Hebrew lessons, find (or register for) gifts, and rent a hall, band, or photographer. Many of these consumer sites specialize particularly in the Bat or Bar Mitzvah scene.

A popular **Web site** entitled "Bar Mitzvah Disco" launched a campaign encouraging people who became Bar and Bat Mitzvah in the 1970s, 1980s, and 1990s to send in pictures from their special day. The response was so overwhelming that the creators expanded the Web site, published a book, and are making a movie, all of which chronicle the festivities (in this case, quite dated) of this rite of passage in a forum that allows for both humor and critique.

See also JAP

Further Reading

Bennett, Roger, J. Shell, and N. Kroll. (2005). *Bar Mitzvah Disco*. New York: Crown.

Oppenheimer, Mark. (2005). *Thirteen and a Day: The Bar and Bat Mitzvah across America*. New York: Farrar, Straus & Giroux.

Segal, David. (2005, December 13). "13 and Counting: In N.Y., Bar and Bat Mitzvah Parties Add Up to Lavish, Theatrical Events." *Washington Post*, C-1.

MICHELE BYERS

BATGIRL.   Batgirl is a female crime-fighting superhero, originally created by DC Comics in 1961. She has been reincarnated many times in the medium of comic books, television, and movies. She is a great example of the various roles that girls take on in their daily lives: the "by day or by night" motif of many superheroes can easily be translated into "at school or at home" or "at work or at play" in girl culture.

Batgirl's outfit is fairly typical of those of female superheroes: a feminized version of her male counterpart's suit, it is tighter and shorter than Batman's. It consists of an eye mask, a head covering with pointed bat ears, a waist-length cape with pointed edges, a utility belt, gloves with gauntlet extensions, and high boots. Her bodysuit invariably has the "Bat" symbol across the front, and the color scheme varies depending on the era of the depiction: either black and gold, for older incarnations, or dark purple and gold, for more recent versions of the character.

The original Batgirl was Betty Kane, who made her first appearance in the comic book *Batman* #139. Betty Kane was the niece of Batwoman, Kathy Kane; the two fought crime together, often associating with Batman and Robin in crime-fighting and romantic capacities. Betty Kane appeared in the *Batman* comic series seven times between 1961 and 1964.

After Betty Kane came the second and best-known Batgirl, Barbara Gordon. She was the daughter of Gotham City Police Commissioner James Gordon, and she worked as a librarian by day. Her first comic book appearance was in *Detective Comics* #359 in 1967. Barbara (or Babs) Gordon becomes Batgirl after foiling a kidnapping attempt on Bruce Wayne, Batman's alter ego, at the hands of the villain Killer Moth. At the time of the accidental encounter, she was on her way to the policemen's masquerade ball, dressed as a female version of Batman. Barbara Gordon appeared in comic books numerous times between 1967 and 1988, and she continues to be seen in "flashback" comic book stories, in which newer issues reference older characters and plotlines.

Barbara Gordon's story continues in comic books beyond her role as Batgirl. Shortly after choosing to end her crime-fighting career, Barbara is shot in the spine by the Joker, a prominent villain. This injury causes her to take up crime fighting again, but not as

Batgirl—this time she takes on the superhero persona of Oracle. Oracle is wheelchair bound and supported by a team of various heroes. Because she can't physically fight crime anymore, her team carries out the crime-fighting tasks that she sets for them. Oracle works as a freelance information broker and expert hacker by day and as her crime-fighting self by night.

The third Batgirl was Helena Bertinelli, who appeared in comic books in the late 1990s. Helena Bertinelli was also known as the Huntress, before she took up the Batgirl uniform, but she soon learned that criminals feared her more as Batgirl. In Bertinelli's comics, Gotham City is leveled by an earthquake and Batman is nowhere to be found. When Batman finally returns to the city and learns of Bertinelli's new superhero persona, he tells her that any failure on her part will cause her to lose the privilege of wearing the Bat costume. When the villain Two-Face and his gang of over 200 criminals knock Batman unconscious and tie him up, Bertinelli comes to his aid as Batgirl. However, she fails to protect the city fully from Two-Face, which results in Batman denying her the role of Batgirl.

The most recent comic book version of Batgirl is Cassandra Cain. Cassandra (or Cass) is of Asian descent and has the blessing of both Batman and Barbara Gordon to become Batgirl. She is the daughter of assassin David Cain, and she was trained by him to be the ultimate assassin and martial artist. A consequence of Cassandra's arduous training is that she was not taught to speak; the speech center of her brain was instead trained to read the movement and body language of others to predict their next move with 100 percent accuracy.

Batgirl also has a long history of television appearances. In 1967, the same year that Barbara Gordon appeared as Batgirl in comic books, Barbara Gordon appeared on television in the final season of the live-action *Batman* television series. She was played by actress Yvonne Craig. Craig was not allowed the fighting skills of the comic book Batgirl; she mostly kicked or threw objects at criminals. In 1972, Craig took up the role of Batgirl once more for a television commercial promoting equal pay for women.

In 1968, Batgirl was animated for television for the first time. She was voiced by Jane Webb, and she made a series of appearances on *The Batman/Superman Hour*. In 1977, another animated Batgirl turned up in *The New Adventures of Batman*, voiced by Melendy Britt. The most recent cartoon incarnations of Batgirl have been on the following television shows: *Batman: The Animated Series* (voiced by Melissa Gilbert), *The New Batman Adventures* (voiced by Tara Strong), and *Batman Beyond* (voiced by Stockard Channing as a futuristic version of the Batgirl character, who has become Gotham Police Commissioner herself).

Finally, Batgirl has had some screen time in the movies. In 1997, the movie *Batman and Robin* included a Batgirl played by Alicia Silverstone. Interestingly, the writers chose to create another new persona for Batgirl in the movie: Barbara Wilson. Barbara was the niece of Bruce Wayne's butler, Alfred Pennyworth, and had many similarities to the Barbara Gordon character of television and comic books.

An examination of all of Batgirl's incarnations reveals a pattern in her character: her crime-fighting persona has been heavily influenced by her relationships with key people in her life who already fought crime. Over the years, Batgirl has been drawn to emulate their heroic ways and to fight alongside these characters, rather than standing alone as a leader, such as **Wonder Woman**. Ironically, only when she is cloaked in yet another alter ego, the Oracle, is she able to come into her own and lead a band of like-minded heroes.

See also Bionic Woman; Catwoman; Comics; Poison Ivy

Yvonne Craig (as Barbara Gordon/Batgirl) in 20th Century Fox Television/ABC's television series *Batman*. (Courtesy of Photofest.)

Further Reading

Daye, Kathleen A. (2003). "A Feminist Perspective on the Female Superhero in DC Comics: Soft Porn Spandex Queens or Real Heroes for a Troubled Universe?" Ph.D. diss., Roosevelt University.
Inness, Sherrie A. (2004). *Action Chicks: New Images of Tough Women in Popular Culture*. New York: Palgrave Macmillan.
Robbins, Trina. (1996). *The Great Women Superheroes*. Northampton: Kitchen Sink Press.

BROOKE BALLANTYNE

BEACH BLANKET BINGO.   *Beach Blanket Bingo* was one of a cycle of beach movies that began in 1963 with *Beach Party*. Like *Beach Party*, it starred **Annette Funicello** and Frankie Avalon. These films presented an idealized world of adolescent girlhood and boyhood, a world devoid of drugs, alcohol, social protest, or draft boards.

The *Beach* movies were part of a plan by two producers, Samuel Arkoff and James Nicholson, to capitalize on the potential profits from films catering to teens. Consequently, they formed American International Pictures (AIP), teamed up with producer-director Roger Corman, and began producing low-budget "B" films about drag racing and delinquency in the 1950s. Interest in delinquents began to decline by the early 1960s, and AIP turned its attention to the beach lifestyle of southern California that was celebrated at the time in the **surfer girl** music of Jan and Dean and the Beach Boys. The first offering, *Beach Party*, starred former Disney "mouseketeer" Annette Funicello, as Dee Dee, and pop singer Frankie Avalon, as Frankie. Other sequels included *Bikini Beach* (1964), *Pajama Party*

(1964), *Muscle Beach Party* (1964), *How to Stuff a Wild Bikini* (1965), and *The Ghost in the Invisible Bikini* (1966).

Although the plots of these beach films were interchangeable, often complex, and punctuated by musical numbers, they usually involved Frankie's efforts to get Funicello's character, Dee Dee, alone. His plans were always foiled because Dee Dee refused to capitulate. Notably, Dee Dee was one of the only girls who did not do the watusi dance, which was popular at the time, nor did she show her navel, because Funicello had contractual obligations to Disney. Although girls in the films were represented as scantily clad "beach bunnies" in the fantasy world of the beach movie, these unchaperoned teens nonetheless slept in separate rooms in their rented, summer beach houses. Through it all, Dee Dee was the beacon of purity and virginity, surrounded by sexy, nubile teens. The chaste Dee Dee clearly had marriage on her mind.

In *Beach Blanket Bingo*, directed by William Asher and produced by Arkoff and Nickelson, the characters take up skydiving. The manager, Bullets (Paul Lynde), of singing star Sugar Kane (Linda Evans) hires skydiving surfers Steve and Bonnie (John Ashley and Deborah Walley) from Big Drop's (Don Rickles) skydiving school to fake a skydiving stunt. Frankie, who mistakenly thinks he has saved Sugar, takes skydiving lessons from Bonnie, who uses Frankie to try to make Steve jealous. Dee Dee also decides to take up skydiving in an effort to show Frankie she can do whatever he can do. Sugar is kidnapped by the Malibu Rat bikers and their leader Eric Von Zipper (Harvey Lembeck). There is a subplot in which Frankie's friend Bonehead (Jody McCrea) falls in love with a mermaid named Lorelei (Marta Johnson). Buster Keaton even makes an appearance as himself.

In the 1987 film *Return to the Beach*, Funicello and Avalon took up their roles as Dee Dee and Frankie once again, playing the middle-aged parents of a surfer daughter. It was Funicello's last film role before she was diagnosed with multiple sclerosis.

See also Bikini; Dee, Sandra

Further Reading

Lisanti, Thomas. (2005). *Hollywood, Surf and Beach Movies: The First Wave 1959–1969.* Jefferson, NC: McFarland.

GEORGANNE SCHEINER GILLIS

BEAUTY PAGEANTS.   Beauty pageants are competitions for girls and women in which the contestants are judged based primarily on their physical appearance. These contests typically involve several rounds, which include swimsuit and formal wear competitions and talent competitions. A panel of judges votes for the winners of each round, until one winner of the pageant remains.

Beauty pageants emerged in the United States in the early 1920s as a promotional gimmick. The "National Beauty Tournament" was initially designed to keep tourists in Atlantic City after Labor Day. The concept of a beauty tournament revolved around a competition of the nation's most beautiful bathing beauties, with the winner to be crowned "Miss America." The first Miss America title was awarded in 1921 to Margaret Gorman, a 16-year-old school girl representing Washington, D.C. As the idea and popularity of beauty pageants flourished, accordingly the number of contestants and rules for these pageants evolved. Generally, contestants for beauty pageants in the United States were selected for competition based on marital status, size, age, physical ability, sex, and racial identity. Beauty pageants became synonymous with definitions of beauty exemplified by single, thin, able-bodied, young white women. In addition to these physical attributes, contestants who desired to compete were required to be residents of the states they represented.

Changes to the rules and regulations of beauty pageants mirrored historical, social, and political restructuring that occurred throughout the decades. For example, the Miss America contest was discontinued from 1929 to 1932 as a consequence of the Great Depression; the first Jewish Miss America was crowned in 1945 just after World War II; in 1960, the first African American woman to compete for a state title was Miss Iowa, Corrine Huff; and the format of the competition, along with the prizes, has shifted from a central focus on beauty to include social graces, talent, education, and activism.

The growing fascination and interest in beauty pageants has culminated in numerous beauty contests around the world. Many of these contests are aligned with corporate businesses and serve as potential platforms for young women to enter the glamorous world of Hollywood. Some of the most critical moments in defining beauty in pageants were the racial breakthrough of the first African American woman to win the coveted Miss Universe title in 1977, followed by the crowning of her successor, a white South African in 1978, as well as the first Eurasian to be crowned Miss USA in 1984, followed by her successor, the first Mexican American winner in 1985. Other milestones include the crowning of Miss USSR as Miss Universe in 1990 and the awarding of the first Miss Universe Botswana title in 1999.

Today beauty pageant competitions cover an array of individuals; many are redefining "beauty" to be inclusive and representative of a diversity of people. Feminist critiques have challenged the definition of beauty as represented by beauty pageant competitions and have encouraged a redefining of beauty beyond the international obsession with perfection and symmetry. As a result of controversy and debate, beauty pageants have witnessed significant restructuring and change, as evidenced by the existence of Drag Queen beauty pageants for men dressed in women's clothing and Digital World beauty contests for the most beautiful virtual woman or **avatar**. However, the premise of ideal beauty is that which is defined by the major beauty competitions such as Miss Universe and Miss America.

See also Asian Beauty Pageants; Children's Beauty Pageants; The Thin Ideal

Further Reading

Cromie, William. (2000, June 8). "The Whys and Woes of Beauty Pageants." [Online May 2007]. Harvard University Gazette Web site http://www.hno.harvard.edu/gazette/2000/06.08/beauty.html.

McElroy, Wendy. (2004). *In Defense of Beauty Pageants*. [Online May 2007]. Lew Rockwell Web site http://www.lewrockwell.com/mcelroy/mcelroy46.html.

ELAINE CORREA

BEDROOMS.   A girl's own room is a field for expressing the girl's character, activities, personality, style, and dreams as framed by particular historical periods. In the early twentieth century, parents were more likely to control the room's appearance, expressing who they wished the girl to be rather than how she saw herself. During the prewar period in the United States, culturally stereotypical images of girls often prevailed. More recently, girls have been allowed to decorate their own rooms and choose what they feel best represents who they are and what they like to do. Prescriptive literature often represents idealized girls' rooms and normative ideas about suitable behavior and decorating, but sometimes **magazines** give teenage girls the space to represent themselves, to show the rooms they have created, or to tell how they have modified their parents' ideas. These representations offer a survey of what has been created in twentieth-century girls' rooms and data for speculation on the meanings of these changes for girls in American culture.

The Turn of the Twentieth Century. At the turn of the twentieth century, children were defined as generic, not boys or girls, until they reached the age of 6 or so. They resided in nurseries, not bedrooms, which were decorated with plant and animal motifs and complemented by easily cleaned white paint for walls and furniture. Pictures chosen to appeal to a child's imagination included representations of castles, farm scenes with animals, or Noah's ark. The nursery was outfitted with toys—a large set of building blocks, toy animals and dolls, a rocking horse, wagons—intended for all of the children to play with. Rarely did nurseries include objects assigned to boys or girls; perhaps a tea set would not appeal to the boys, and boys might prefer heavy mission-style furniture. But clearly gendered colors, materials, and objects were typically reserved until a child got older and moved into his or her own room.

At somewhere between six and twelve years old, many girls could expect to have rooms of their own; by age 12 fully half of girls in poorer households and nine out of ten in wealthy homes had their own rooms in 1936, according to a survey conducted by the White House Conference on Child Health and Protection. Then the girls began to acquire objects and furnishings that would lead them toward womanhood. Dressing tables, for example, stressed the girl's appearance, and mirrors invited her to attend to her hair and clothing. Dressers, closets, and built-in shelves encouraged the girl to put her belongings away and become a neat housekeeper. Built-in window seats provided economical seating for girls who enjoyed reading there or playing with dolls. The style of the décor in a girl's room in the 1910s alternated between "**pink**-and-blue prettiness," the cliché for female adolescence and the idea that style should be keyed to the personality of the inhabitant: muslin frills and white-painted furniture suit some girls, but mahogany furniture and colorful walls suit another. Strikingly, a girl was expected to have a number of skills that would help her create her room. A girl of 12 or 14 was able to paint hand-me-down furniture, make her own curtains with a stenciled design, or sew her own pillow covers, perhaps embellished with embroidered images of her favorite flower. She could decorate her dressing table with a skirt, ornamenting it with strips of flower-printed fabric. By puberty, girls were expected to have an identifiable personality and the skills to represent their own tastes, not just by selecting, but also painting, sewing, or embroidering the objects for their own rooms. Her own room was a demonstration of a girl's skills as well as a space that framed her growing independence.

Older girls, who lived at home until marriage, decorated their rooms to establish aspects of maturing personality and taste. Preserved in a photograph of May Flaherty's room in her family home in Helena, Montana, c. 1900 is her decorative scheme—hundreds of cards, prints, and pictures hung from a molding near the ceiling and covering the wall behind her metal bedstead. These personal images were combined with pennants from school, a Turkish corner full of pillows, and large and small framed pictures. The sheer number of personal items ornamenting the walls is echoed in a description by Mark Twain of Julia Nast's room: Julia, at age 20, had covered her walls in "pictures, photographs, etchings, . . . Christmas cards, menus, fans, statuettes, trinkets, and knickknacks."

Twain estimated that there were 3,000 "pretty trifles" ornamenting Julia's room (Ruhling, p. 47). Although girls—even 20-year-olds—were not allowed the independence to create their own homes, they did create highly personalized spaces within the parental home, perhaps in complete contrast to the taste in which the rest of the house was decorated. Older girls' or young women's rooms were essential to them because respectable girls did not move into their own quarters until marriage, and thus they needed the equivalent of a studio apartment where all or most of life's activities could take place on their own terms.

Before World War II. In the era between the 1920s and World War II, girls' rooms took on a didactic function. Middle-class mothers hoped their daughters would grow up to have good taste and an appreciation of beauty so that they would know how to decorate their own homes when they married. These skills could be nourished early by giving daughters a well-decorated room with good furniture and fine fabrics. Instead of indulging an adolescent girl and encouraging her to explore the varied facets of her character, conservatives argued that a beautiful room counterbalanced a girl's experiments in adolescence; she would get through the phases of comics, boogie-woogie, and saddle shoes—supported by the backbone of beauty supplied by her room. When she grew through adolescence and emerged as a woman with a home of her own, this early training in taste would pay off.

Resourceful girls could also learn the virtues of economy by creating the rooms they desired. Girls often seemed to end up in a shabby bit of leftover square footage if they wanted their own bedrooms—a corner of the attic or other unused space. When architects had already created a girl's room in the design phase of house building, the girl still had to furnish her space, frequently with secondhand goods. Many articles from the 1920s through the 1940s promoted reusing old bed sheets or last year's dance dress to fabricate dressing table skirts, making worn draperies into new bed covers, appropriating an old packing box and turning it into a dressing table, cutting down an old kitchen table to become a desk, or shortening the legs of cast-off kitchen chairs to create more graceful seats in the girl's room. Repainting several pieces of old furniture in one color allowed the illusion of a proper suite of matching pieces. It is apparent that girls were willing to devote a great deal of both labor and economy toward producing workable spaces of their own. In furnishing their own rooms, girls learned to make homes of their own, through both understanding beauty and by mastering decorating on a shoestring.

After World War II. By the mid-1950s, girls' rooms had become less of a training ground for future married life and more of an exploratory space. Teenage girls of the 1950s who had their own rooms were encouraged to develop many sides of their personalities. Bookcases supported a girl's literacy practices; shelves for art supplies and an easel recognized her artistic talent; storage for records acknowledged her musical interests. An extra bed for entertaining friends encouraged her social side; she had her own telephone and privacy when she wanted it.

The Sixties. In the 1960s, a turn to nongendered language described rooms for children to help them develop into "worthwhile human being[s]" instead of boyish boys and girly girls. Decorator advice focused on a useful room—with desks, shelves, workspaces, and a bulletin board to express personal interests. Children should be encouraged to dream as well as do their homework. Yellow and green were popular choices for children's color schemes as parents strove to make settings that were more gender neutral than the pink and blue stereotypes of the past. Bold patterns, colorful paint, and natural wood replaced fussy effects; decorative schemes that instigated imaginative play were favored for both boys and girls. This turn toward thinking of adolescents as future human beings contrasted with the assumptions of gendered interiors in the 1910s, when girls were to have flowered fabrics and boys rough wood and leather to ensure their growth into men and women. Of course, there were still numerous articles that equated flower prints with femininity in the 1950s and 1960s, but a more wholesome, even holistic view of children began to play down gender difference and pay more attention to individual growth.

The Nineties. In the 1990s, the focus of decorating advice shifted toward the individualization of a girl's room. *Victorian Homes* magazine proposed that teens decorate their rooms in a Victorian style because that period offered variety and encouraged imagination and individuality. *Seventeen* magazine advised 1990 readers: "If you're into self-expression and your old 'flower power' linen set makes you restless, redecorate your room in your own image . . ." (Bed and Breakfast, p. 235). In April 1996, *Seventeen* published the results of a contest it had sponsored for the "Coolest Room." They invited readers to send in images of their rooms and noted how dedicated contestants had been in making their rooms into unique places. A preponderance of entries featured walls and ceilings plastered with hundreds of pictures (tacked up or glued on) representing personal obsessions—sports teams, bands, or beaux. Refurbished furniture was painted, glued, or upholstered with personal motifs. A popular theme was landscape vistas in wallpaper or painted murals—anything from a rain forest to the moon—suggesting a girl's travel ambitions. The girls who submitted their rooms did not have especially "girly" decorations—old-style femininity of the lace or pink variety was not much in evidence. Instead they gave their rooms a personal stamp, using a wide range of motifs that were valid as long as they were chosen by the girls themselves.

The New Millennium. Girls' rooms of the present continue to be furnished with many of the same pieces of furniture that were popular in the 1910s. A bed, of course, is central, although, in contemporary rooms, the bed may be a bunk bed or have a trundle component to make room for a guest. Dressers and shelves for storage are as essential today as ever. A chair or two and a table or desk are common and equally likely to be hand-me-downs or found in secondhand stores. Today's girls are more likely to get along without dressing tables than girls in the prewar era, probably because today's houses have more bathrooms with mirrors and makeup storage units to serve the purpose of dressing tables. Decorative schemes for girls' rooms have a much wider range than the flowery feminine décor that was preponderant before midcentury. The themes recommended in a recent book for girls on redecorating include the following: glamour, Victorian, Southwestern, industrial design, French flea market, modern, desert caravan, Japanese, and Indian. Entertaining friends in these self-decorated rooms gives pleasure to each girl because it represents her personal choices and, often, her own handiwork. Girls often state their future plans in the most open-ended way; one plans to become, for example, a teacher or a chef or a writer. None of these themes suggest constraints on what a girl can imagine for herself and her future, compared to boy's rooms where "masculine" Western, nautical, rustic and sports themes still prevail.

As in the early twentieth century, girls' rooms in the present take on personalities that can be far removed from the style of the rest of the house. However, today's girls are choosing their own expressive vocabulary and are much less likely to decorate with stereotypical "trifles." Covering the walls and ceilings with flattened-out Coke cans, as one *Seventeen* contestant did, gave a shiny and colorful interior to a teen girl's room, even as it detached the room from the taste and furnishings of the rest of the house. Such a dramatically personal statement allows girls of the 1990s to assert their independence of personality but still retain many of the physical, financial, and emotional needs that are met by living under a parental roof. Freedom in the decoration of their rooms allows girls to try colors and styles inexpensively and safely as they freely sample possible future identities.

See also Fan Culture

Further Reading

"Bed and Breakfast." (1990). *Seventeen* 49, 234–39; 235, 236.
Montano, Mark. (2002). *Super Suite: The Ultimate Bedroom Makeover Guide for Girls*. New York: Universe.
Ruhling, Nancy. (1990). "Decorating a Teen's Room." *Victorian Homes* 9, 44–47.
White House Conference on Child Health and Protection. (1936). *The Young Child in the Home*. New York and London: D. Appleton-Century Co.

ELIZABETH COLLINS CROMLEY

BENNING, SADIE (1973–). Born in Milwaukee, Wisconsin, Sadie Benning started making films at age 16 with a Fisher-Price Pixelvision movie camera. Challenging, personal, subversive, and contesting what being a girl and young woman means, Benning's work is an important contribution to the representation of girlhood in Western culture. Her tenet that "the most revolutionary thing is to just love yourself and love what you do" (Rigney 2003, para. 19) challenges girls and young women to step beyond a world of vacuous representations of girlhood to embrace their inner selves—no matter how different, awkward, or unadapted to the society at large.

Benning's father, experimental filmmaker James Benning, gave her the camera for Christmas. The Pixelvision was a small handheld camera made for children in the 1980s by Fisher-Price. Its pixilated black-and-white look quickly gained favor with experimental filmmakers, although it failed on the commercial market and was discontinued.

Benning's highly personal videos deal with issues of isolation, sexual orientation, violence, sexuality, representations of women, and her own identity as a lesbian. Her work takes seriously issues of homophobia, racism and sexism, while also exploring her own **coming of age** in an America fraught with violence and alienation. Ultimately, her films are not diagnostic, but they look to open up spaces in which gender, sexuality, and identity are amorphous, contextual, and under investigation. Gary Morris discusses the classic style of Benning's early diary-like films as "shot in her bedroom, starring an array of objects both culture-constructed (Barbie) and self-constructed (masks). Her main subject was herself, coming to terms with a pervasive 1980s culture of junk TV and mindless consumerism and finding some kind of comfort level there as a budding dyke-artiste" (Morris 1999).

In her films, Benning contests notions of childhood **innocence** in which girls are sheltered and unknowing. Rather, she presents girlhood as a space of sexual and cultural knowing, full of curiosity, pain, history, and selfhood. Her work had an impact on viewers in relation to its frank depiction of the actual realities of girlhood in the 1990s, a negotiated, difficult, and fraught terrain. *A Place Called Lovely*, unveils the violence of childhood as Benning recounts her own terror and, later, revenge on a school **bully**, Ricky. In that film, the playground, the school bus, and the neighborhood become the settings for childhood violence.

Recognizing her own helplessness in the face of the violence of childhood, Benning also recognizes the violence of the larger social environment: even the bullies are victims. *A Place Called Lovely* is a haunting reflection on child abuse, violence, the media, and the urban environment of girlhood. Through investigating her innermost self against a culture that often undermines women, especially young women, Benning presents us with a girl who is whole, contradictory, strong, and inquisitive.

In other works, such as *Jollies*, *If Every Girl Had a Diary*, and *Me and Rubyfruit* (all 1990), Benning focuses on sexuality and the negotiation of her identity as a teen lesbian. For example, *Jollies* documents her sexual awakening through a frank revelation of her own sexual experiences with both boys and girls before finally losing her virginity to a girl. Within the film, she bravely exposes her own process of negotiating emotion, sexuality, and desire as a girl coming to terms with her sexual self.

Sadie Benning's work has been shown at festivals around the world and was twice included in the Whitney Biennial. Benning is also a musician, playing for some time with the popular feminist post-**punk** band Le Tigre in the late 1990s.

See also Cuthand, Thirza; Filmmaking; Video Play

Further Reading

Morris, Gary. (1999). *Behind the Mask: Sadie Benning's Pixel Pleasures*. [Online March 2007]. Bright Lights Film Journal Web site http://www.brightlightsfilm.com/24/benning.html.

Rigney, Melissa. (2003). *Sadie Benning*. [Online March 2007]. Sense of Cinema Web site http://www.senseofcinema.com/contents/directors/03/benning.html.

SHANNON WALSH

BETTY AND VERONICA.   Owned by the Archie Comics publishing company, Betty and Veronica are characters in several titles aimed at young comic book readers. Perennial teenagers, Betty and Veronica have become icons of femininity, embodying dichotomous images of teenage girlhood.

The character of Betty Cooper was introduced in *Pep Comics* in 1942, when she appeared as the girlfriend of Archie Andrews. Veronica "Ronnie" Lodge, her best friend—and main competitor for Archie's affection—was introduced a few months later. Together with Archie and their friend, Jughead Jones, Betty and Veronica have been the main characters in the Archie Comic book family from 1942 through the present day. In 1950, Archie Comics launched a comic with the two girls as its focus, *Archie's Girls Betty and Veronica*. This title was on newsstands until 1987, when the publisher changed the title to *Betty and Veronica*, which is still presently published. Betty and Veronica have both enjoyed several of their own spin-off comics over the years. These include *Betty and Me* (1965–1992), *Betty's Diary* (1986–1991), *Betty* (1992–present), *Veronica* (1992–present), *Betty and Veronica Spectacular* (1992–present), and *Betty and Veronica Summer Fun* (1994–1999).

Betty and Veronica represent two distinct images of teenage girlhood. Blonde and charming Betty Cooper is typically referred to as the **girl-next-door**: middle-class, smart, athletic, friendly, and adept at stereotypically feminine duties such as cooking and taking care of children. As feminism and a more heightened social consciousness about women took hold in the latter half of the century, Betty's traits evolved to include an aptitude with auto mechanics and a passion for social and environmental issues. By contrast, brunette Veronica Lodge is fashionable and wealthy, and she possesses little talent for traditional feminine hobbies, although she loves **shopping** and is often depicted as a gossip. Although she can be vain and self-centered, Veronica can also be kind.

Betty, Veronica, and Archie form a classic love triangle that has persisted throughout the history of Archie Comics' storylines. While maintaining their close friendship, Betty and Veronica are very competitive for Archie Andrews's affections. Archie often chooses Veronica over Betty for dates and social functions, although he commonly proclaims his close friendship and trust to Betty. The friendship between Betty and Veronica presents a twist to the classic love triangle formula: instead of being bitter rivals, they maintain their close friendship, a representation of the possibility of relationships between girls that transcends social pressures and boy anxiety. However, both girls have continued to fight over Archie—even as he claims that he cannot make up his mind—making their friendship a complicated relationship. This love triangle, featuring a protagonist with two potential love interests, has become recognizable in many other comics, films, and television; it has become known as the "Betty and Veronica Syndrome."

The two contrasting images of girlhood offered by the characters of Betty and Veronica have become marketing tactics for several product lines aimed at young girls. In 2005, Archie Comics licensed the characters for a line of clothing and apparel aimed at girls. Products used the licensing theme "Are You a Betty or Are You a Veronica?" with different styles representing each girl. In 2005, **Mattel** also launched a series of "Are You a Betty or Are You a Veronica?" Barbie dolls with other products, including Magic 8 Balls that reflected each girl's personality and outlooks.

See also Compulsory Heterosexuality; Girls' Friendships; Nice

Further Reading

Robbins, Trina. (1999). *From Girls to Grrrlz: A History of Women's Comics from Teens to Zines.* San Francisco: Chronicle Books.

TAMMY OLER

BEVERLY HILLS, 90210.   Produced by Aaron Spelling and Darren Star, *Beverly Hills, 90210* was an hour-long teen drama that ran on FOX television network from October 4, 1990, to May 17, 2000. The show focused on a group of friends who attended West Beverly Hills High School, following them through their college years at California University and their subsequent careers. Although the show addressed common high school experiences such as bullies, bad boys, shopping, and driver's licenses, it also tackled difficult issues such as drug addiction, birth control, AIDS, and alcoholism. The creators of the show prided themselves on addressing real issues, but many critics saw the show as a teenage soap opera in which plot lines became more and more outrageous each season.

The first season of the show revolved around two teenaged **twins**, Brenda and Brandon Walsh (Shannen Doherty and Jason Priestley), who had recently moved from Minnesota to Beverly Hills because of their father's job transfer. As they adjust to life in posh Beverly Hills, they befriend numerous students at West Beverly High—Kelly Taylor (Jennie Garth), Donna Martin (Tori Spelling), Steve Sanders (Ian Ziering), Dylan McKay (Luke Perry), David Silver (Brian Austin Green), and Andrea Zuckerman (Gabrielle Carteris)—who become the main characters of the show. Originally, the show had low ratings, but it gained popularity when FOX ran new episodes of the show during

The cast of Fox's *Beverly Hills, 90210.* *Top row:* Ian Ziering (as Steve Sanders), Luke Perry (as Dylan McKay). *Middle row:* Brian Austin Green (as David Silver), Jennie Garth (as Kelly Taylor), Jason Priestly (as Brandon Walsh), Shannen Doherty (as Brenda Walsh). *Bottom row:* Tori Spelling (as Donna Martin), Gabrielle Carteris (as Andrea Zuckerman). (Courtesy of Photofest.)

the summer of 1991, when most other prime-time shows were on hiatus. The summer season focused on the group's adventures at the Beverly Hills Beach Club, involving Brenda's pregnancy scare, Brandon's attempts to get a summer job, Dylan's negligent parents and his alcoholism, and a burgeoning relationship between Kelly's mother and David's father.

The summer episodes began a *90210* frenzy, in which the show's popularity increased substantially, adolescent girls mobbed Luke Perry and Jason Priestley at malls, and *90210* merchandise such as bed sheets, T-shirts, perfume, and action dolls sold quickly. A series of books based on the series was also written by author Mel Gilden. By the summer of 1992, other networks tried to reproduce the popularity of the show by creating a variety of programs that had the melodrama of *90210*'s plotlines and the attractive look of its characters, such as NBC's *California Dreams*. Even FOX tried to duplicate the success of *90210* through programs such as *Melrose Place* and *Class of '96*. Although *90210* was the harbinger of the prime-time teenage soap opera in the early nineties, it was criticized for hiring twenty-something actors to play teenagers. In fact, Gabrielle Carteris was 29 years old when she started playing the role of Andrea in 1990.

As the main characters of *90210* graduated from high school, some moved on to attend California University; others—Brenda and Andrea—moved away and were replaced by new friends, such as bad girl Valerie Malone (Tiffani-Amber Thiessen) and intelligent Clare Arnold (Kathleen Robertson). After the college years, Brandon and Dylan also left the show, although Dylan returned in the final season. Kelly, Donna, Steve, and David were featured in all ten seasons. They were joined in the last seasons by the secretly rich Noah Hunter (Vincent Young); Kelly and Donna's roommate, Gina Kinkaid (Vanessa Marcil), who dates Dylan and later finds out she is Donna's half-sister; Kelly's lawyer fiancé, Matt Durning (Daniel Cosgrove), who cheats on Kelly under the influence of LSD; and Janet Sosna (Lindsay Price), who marries Steve and is the mother of his child, Madeline. In the last episode, Donna and David, who had an on-again off-again relationship since the beginning of the show, get married, and Kelly and Dylan reveal their love for one another.

See also Degrassi; The O.C.

Further Reading

McKinley, E. Graham. (1997). *Beverly Hills, 90210: Television, Gender and Identity*. Philadelphia: University of Pennsylvania Press.

JENNIFER MALOY

BEYONCÉ (1981–).   Born Beyoncé Giselle Knowles, Beyoncé rose to fame as a member of the R&B group Destiny's Child in the late nineties. She is also known as a solo artist, record producer, actress, and fashion designer.

Beyoncé was born in Houston, Texas. When she was 9 years old, she and her friend, LaTavia Robertson, formed the duo Girl's Tyme, which would later become Destiny's Child. Her father, Mathew Knowles, worked to make the group a success, and, in doing so, he placed his daughter as the group's lead singer. Their first big break was on *Star Search* as Girl's Tyme when Beyoncé was 10 years old. They did not win, but they continued to perform.

In 1995, Destiny's Child, which then had become a quartet, was signed to Electra Records. The band members were released from their contract by Electra before they could finish their first album but were then signed by Columbia. In 1998, Destiny's Child released its first album, *Destiny's Child*, and had a hit single, "No, No, No, Part 2," from the album. The single cemented the popularity of the group, who later went on to release several number 1 hits, including "Independent Women" from the soundtrack of the 2000 movie **Charlie's Angels** and, in 2001, "Bootylicious," both of which Beyoncé co-wrote. Destiny's Child became one of the most successful pop acts of the late 1990s and early 2000s.

Beyoncé began her solo career in 2002 as a featured vocalist on rapper Jay-Z's single "03 Bonnie & Clyde." She also remade the duet "The Closer I Get to You" with singer Luther Vandross in 2003, and the two won the Grammy for Best R&B Performance by a Duo or Group.

In 2003, Beyoncé also produced and released her debut solo album, *Dangerously in Love*. The album debuted at number one on the Billboard 200 and went Platinum in one month, with much help from its first hit single, "Crazy in Love," featuring Jay-Z. Beyoncé's album and single simultaneously topped the charts in the United Kingdom and the United States, making her the first act to accomplish this since Men at Work 20 years earlier and the Beatles, Simon and Garfunkel, and Rod Stewart in the 1960s and 1970s. Beyoncé was rewarded for her efforts by winning five Grammys in 2004, including Best Contemporary R&B Album and Best Female R&B Performance. Beyoncé was also awarded a Best R&B Performance for a Duo or Group Grammy in 2006 for her duet of Luther Vandross's "So Amazing," which she sang with Stevie Wonder. On her second solo album, *B'Day*, she is credited as executive producer. It was released on September 4, 2006, to coincide with her twenty-fifth birthday.

Beyoncé has also branched out into acting, making her debut in MTV's 2001 movie *Carmen: A Hip Hopera*. In 2002, she co-starred as Foxxy Cleopatra in the third of the Austin Powers films, *Goldmember*. The following year, she co-starred in *The Fighting Temptations*. In 2006, she took on the role of Xania in the remake of *The Pink Panther*. She also appeared in the critically acclaimed film *Dreamgirls*, based on the **Supremes'** rise to fame, which was also released in 2006.

In 2005, Beyoncé joined forces with her mother, Tina Knowles, to start House of Deréon, a clothing line named for Beyoncé's grandmother. The line includes edgy sporty and casual clothing, handbags, and shoes. Marketed to her older female fans, House of Deréon was introduced on the *Oprah Winfrey Show* in November 2005.

See also African American Presence in Popular Culture; Girl Bands; Hudson, Jennifer

Further Reading

Toure. (2004). *A Woman Possessed*. [Online May 2007]. *Rolling Stone* Magazine Web site http://www.rollingstone.com/news/coverstory/beyonce_a_woman_possessed.

REBEKAH BUCHANAN

BIKINI.   Although Minoan wall paintings dating to 1600 B.C.E. show women wearing abbreviated bandeau tops and matching bottoms, the modern bikini was introduced almost simultaneously in 1946 by two French designers, Louis Réard and Jacques Heim. Heim dubbed his creation the "atome" in honor of its brevity, but Réard countered with a model called the "bikini," after the Pacific atoll where the United States conducted atomic tests the same year. Looking best on young, firm flesh, the bikini has allowed generations of adolescent girls to experiment with their nascent sexuality.

When bikini-clad French showgirl Micheline Bernardini (hired after fashion models balked at appearing nearly nude in public) paraded poolside at a Parisian fashion show on July 5, 1946, the press went wild. The *Herald Tribune* alone ran nine stories on the tiny new bathing suit. Photos of the first bikini showed a **thong**-bottomed suit that would not be out of place on today's beaches (and a model whose pale buttocks precipitated the subsequent craze for all-over tanning). The scanty cut, which exposed the wearer's navel, scandalized Americans.

A more modestly cut bikini appeared almost immediately on French beaches, but Americans were slower to adopt the new fashion. **Midriff tops**, playsuits, and swimming suits (the latter two items featuring high waistlines that covered the navel) were already acceptable fashions, but the bikini was considered immodest. The general public left it to Hollywood starlets and beauty queens for film work or publicity photos. It also became a risqué staple of men's **magazines**.

When sales exploded in 1959, the *New York Times* called the suit's newfound popularity a "mystery," although it suggested both an increase in the number of home swimming pools (affording privacy to scantily clad sun worshippers) and passports issued (more Americans saw the bikini in action on European beaches) as reasons why the bikini caught on. Also, by that time, American connoisseurs of foreign film had been exposed to the tiny bikinis worn by French actress Brigitte Bardot in films such as *The Girl in the Bikini* (1952; originally titled *Manina, La Fille San Voiles*) and *And God Created Woman* (1956). Fashion photographs of red-headed top model Suzy Parker posed in a bikini against a Caribbean backdrop also helped the suit's ascent to mainstream acceptance in the United States when the photos ran in the January 1959 issue of *Harper's Bazaar*.

There is evidence to suggest that teenagers' opinions of the bikini originally mirrored those of adults. Of 1500 teens polled for an opinion survey in 1961, three-quarters purported to find bikinis "repulsive," "cheap," "vulgar," or "horrid" and felt that they should be worn only by film stars or individuals with private pools (Alden 1961, p. 44). Only a few years later, a follow-up survey would have received very different responses.

During the 1960s, children of the postwar baby boom began to hit puberty, in what *Vogue* editor Diana Vreeland later dubbed a "youthquake." Best suited to toned, youthful figures, the bikini not only dominated the decade's beach fashions, but also its popular culture. In August 1960, Brian Hyland's "Itsy Bitsy Teenie Weenie Yellow Polkadot Bikini" reached number 1 on Billboard's Hot 100 song chart. Later that year, the film *Where the Boys Are* showed bikini-wearing college girls frolicking on the beach at Fort Lauderdale, Florida during spring break. Actress Ursula Andress caused a sensation when she stepped out of the sea in a white bikini in the first James Bond movie, *Dr. No* (1962). Hot on the heels of the teenage surfing craze, Hollywood released a series of "beach party" movies, including *Bikini Beach* (1964) and *How to Stuff a Wild Bikini* (1965). From 1968 to 1970, a television comedy show, *Rowan & Martin's Laugh-In*, featured a young actress named Goldie Hawn go-go dancing in a bikini, with various slogans (e.g., "Make Love, Not War") painted on her body.

One girl who answered the 1961 opinion survey deemed the bikini acceptable unless worn "by girls who are too fat or too thin, by my mother or any other female relatives" (Alden 1961, p. 44) Her comment delineates what are still considered the parameters for bikini wear: body type and, to a somewhat lesser extent, age. A slender, fit mature woman in a bikini may be grudgingly congratulated for looking great "for her age," but a girl or woman whose body does not fit the ultra-thin norm espoused by fashion magazines is almost universally castigated. It also echoes swimsuit historians Lena Lencek and Gideon Bosker's contention that the bikini is "claimed by the young as a garment to which they have a natural right" (p. 150).

Indeed, the bikini is frequently a source of conflict between young women and their parents or other adults, who often have different ideas about how much of their bodies it is appropriate for teenagers to reveal. In 1963, a teenage girl explained to a reporter for the *Saturday Evening Post* that she rolled her bikini bottom down far enough to expose her navel only after she left the house and her mother's disproving gaze (Lencek and Bosker 1989). Forty years later, with the string bikini baring more flesh than ever, teacher chaperones assigned to check student luggage for alcohol before the Greenport (New York) High School senior class trip to Florida removed twenty-five bikinis that were deemed too small to wear on the beach. The school district superintendent eventually banned twelve suits— all of them string bikinis, leading one girl to condemn the decision in her local newspaper. She was, she maintained, old enough to make her own decisions about her body and her sexuality. Interviewed later, her father simply stated, "My feelings were different from hers" (Bellafante 2003, p. B9). Also in 2003, Daytona Beach (a popular spring break destination) effectively banned the thong bikini when it strengthened its public nudity laws by requiring that " . . . that portion of the buttocks which lies between the top and bottom of the buttocks, and between two imaginary straight lines . . ." must be covered (Clark 2003, p. D1).

Meanwhile, the movie *Blue Crush* (2002) and MTV's reality program *Surf Girls* show young women in tiny bikinis riding huge waves, conquering personal fear as well as their competitors on the women's pro-surfing circuit. They are simultaneously athletes and sex symbols, and their lean, muscular bodies present a new standard for young women to emulate. Indeed, as the bikini has continued to shrink, more and more girls are willing to do whatever is necessary to achieve the "perfect" bikini figure. Therapists suggest that, for those with patterns of **disordered eating**, the advent of spring break can act as a "trigger time" for obsessing about weight and body image. In 2006, young women participating in a blog ring called the "Bikini Coming Soon Challenge" shared tips for self-starvation and extreme exercise, the better to become what one **blogger** called the "tan, skinny girls, [who] looked perfect in their bikinis."

See also Go-Go Girl; Surfer Girls; The Thin Ideal

Further Reading

Alden, Robert. (1961, June 16). "Advertising Hints on Selling to Teen-Agers." *New York Times*, 44.
Bellafante, Gina. (2003, July 15). "More Itsy-Bitsy Teeny-Weeny Than Ever." *New York Times.*
Clark, Jayne. (2003, February 14). "Some Resorts Throwing Cold Water on Spring Break." *USA Today*, D1.
Lencek, Lena, and Gideon Bosker. (1989). *Making Waves: Swimsuits and the Undressing of America.* San Francisco: Chronicle Books.
Williams, Alex. (2006, April 2). "Before Spring Break, the Anorexic Challenge." *New York Times.*

LYNN PERIL

BIKINI KILL.   Bikini Kill was an indie punk band closely associated with the **Riot Grrrl** movement of the 1990s. Hailing from Olympia, Washington, Bikini Kill existed from approximately 1990 to 1998 and consisted of Kathleen Hanna on vocals, Kathi Wilcox on bass, Tobi Vail on drums, and Billy Karren on guitar. The band released three full-length albums: *Pussy-Whipped* (1993), *CD Version of the First Two Records* (1994), and *Reject All-American* (1996), as well as a collection of singles titled *The Singles* (1998).

The band began when Kathleen Hanna and Tobi Vail collaborated on a fanzine called *Revolution Girl Style Now*, which expressed their anger and frustration with sexism in the **punk** scene. This gave way to another **zine**, *Bikini Kill*, created with Kathi Wilcox. When the three women decided to form a band with Billy Karren, they took the zine's name as their own.

Bikini Kill's sound in the beginning was generally rough and loud, with plenty of distortion and screeching, although occasionally softer sung ballad-type songs were recorded. The lyrics expressed a sort of philosophy elaborated on in the *Bikini Kill* zines: they condemned violence against women, overt sexism, rigid gender roles, and the suppression of women artists and encouraged women to support each other rather than tear each other down with competition and jealousy. As the band progressed, its sound got noticeably cleaner, particularly on *Reject All-American*, but the message remained the same.

Bikini Kill and Kathleen Hanna in particular are often credited with the founding of the Riot Grrrl movement. In reality, *Riot Grrrl* was originally a zine created by Allison Wolfe and Molly Neuman of the band **Bratmobile**. When Bikini Kill moved briefly to Washington, D.C., in 1992, Hanna and Wolfe formed a loose group of punk feminist women who met to share ideas and who eventually adopted the name "Riot Grrrls." As a result, this group of young women formed bands, played shows, and wrote zines about their experiences on their own terms. Kathleen Hanna and Bikini Kill were involved in the group and contributed heavily to the general philosophy of the Riot Grrrl movement, but many others played an equal or even larger role in its creation and maintenance.

Bikini Kill was particularly notorious for its controversial stage performances. Hanna, wearing anything from underwear to vintage dresses to pajamas, bounced around the front of the stage, screaming at the top of her lungs about sexism, abuse, capitalism, and a myriad of other topics. In response, men often showed up at the shows to harass the band by throwing things and shouting lewd obscenities.

In the mid-nineties, things started getting out of control for Bikini Kill. The media had gotten wind of Riot Grrrl, and members of Bikini Kill were thrust into the role of spokeswomen for the movement. Articles began appearing in mainstream publications that misquoted and belittled the band, as well as the movement. In the popular media, Riot Grrrls were depicted as either man-hating lesbian psychopaths or silly little girls playing around on a stage. Many Riot Grrrl bands, including Bikini Kill, began simply refusing to speak to members of the mainstream press rather than have their members' statements distorted. This seemed only to fuel the fire, because more misinformation continued to be printed, and the Riot Grrrl label got stuck to any female in the growing "alternative rock" genre.

While Riot Grrrl was crumbling under the mass media's attention, the members of Bikini Kill were drifting in different directions. Hanna was involved in a band called The Troublemakers with Johanna Fateman while she was also working on a solo project, going by the name of Julie Ruin. The other members of the band sporadically released a number of singles with Molly Neuman as The Frumpies. Tobi Vail had also started a cassette label called Bumpidee, which released demo-style cassettes of unsigned bands as a low-cost

Kathleen Hanna, the vocalist with the band Bikini Kill, performs live on stage, ca. 1992. (© S.I.N./Corbis.)

"do-it-yourself" method of distributing music. Kathi Wilcox was involved for a while with a band called Star Sign Scorpio; Billy Karren played with Vail in Spray Painted Love.

By 1998, Bikini Kill officially disbanded. It was a peaceful parting, and all of the members continue to support each other and occasionally work together. In the aftermath of Bikini Kill, Kathleen Hanna's Julie Ruin project was released by the label Mr. Lady with some success. The Frumpies also gained some popularity with their releases *Frumpie One-Piece* (a compilation of all previous 7-inch recordings) and *Frumpies Forever*. To date, Hanna has reached new heights of fame with her band Le Tigre (also featuring Johanna Fateman), with three commercially successful full-length releases: *Le Tigre*, *Feminist Sweepstakes*, and *This Island*. Tobi Vail continues to run Bumpidee and has also helped found the Bands against Bush movement and the Ladyfest music and arts festival.

Further Reading

Baumgardner, Jennifer, and Amy Richards. (2000). *Manifesta: Young Women, Feminism, and the Future*. New York: Farrar, Straus & Giroux.

Raha, Maria. (2005). *Cinderella's Big Score: Women of the Punk and Indie Underground*. Emeryville, CA: Seal Press.

KATE ARTZ

BINGE EATING. Binge eating, also referred to as compulsive overeating, is one type of eating disorder that is prevalent among young girls and teens. It involves the ingestion of an excessive amount of food within a short period of time. A binge-eating episode is accompanied by the loss of control over food intake, followed by guilt or shame over the quantity of food consumed.

Binge eating is not synonymous with simply overeating. Overeating, or eating past the point of feeling comfortably full, is normal when it occurs infrequently and is fairly common in situations in which food tends to be an integral part of a social event, such as at family gatherings on special holidays. Occasional overeating does not involve the loss of control and negative self-judgment experienced by someone who engages in binge eating.

Recent research suggests that binge eating is fairly common among teen girls. One large, longitudinal study of adolescents, Project EAT (Eating Among Teens), suggests that approximately 16 percent of average weight girls and 21 percent of overweight girls engaged in binge-eating behavior in the past twelve months (Neumark-Sztainer 2005, p. 17). Approximately 3 percent of adolescent girls participating in Project EAT reported having been previously diagnosed by a doctor with binge-eating disorder (BED). New nationally representative estimates suggest that BED is the most prevalent eating disorder and that it is on the rise.

BED, although it is discussed in the *Diagnostic and Statistical Manual of Mental Disorders* (*DSM-IV*), is not yet an officially recognized psychiatric disorder. It has received an increasing amount of attention in recent years. In the *DSM-IV*, BED is characterized by five criteria. The binge-eating episodes involve (1) eating an amount of food much larger than most would eat during a discrete period of time under similar circumstances; (2) lack of control over eating during the episode; (3) and three or more of the following characteristics: rapid consumption of food, eating until uncomfortably full, eating large amounts of food when not physically hungry, eating alone because of embarrassment related to the amount of food consumed, and feeling disgust (with oneself), guilty, or depressed after the binge. Those with BED also (4) experience distress regarding the eating episodes and (5) binge at least two days per week over a period of six months.

The engagement in uncontrolled bouts of binge eating is also a defining characteristic of the eating disorder **bulimia** nervosa (BN). However, unlike BN, individuals with BED do not engage in compensatory purging behavior(s), such as extreme amounts of physical activity, laxatives, and vomiting immediately following the binge.

Direct references to binge eating in popular culture are rare. There are few discussions of binge eating in magazines, movies, or television shows targeting young girls. Although some young female celebrities have recently publicly disclosed struggles within binge eating (i.e., American Idol runner-up Katharine McPhee, American Idol judge and singer-choreographer Paula Abdul, and Brady Bunch star Maureen McCormick), it has often been in the context of BN. Some attention has been given to binge eating and BED on health-related informational clearinghouse **Web sites** for girls, adolescents, and young adults such as GirlPower.gov and KidsHealth.org.

Binge eating is a serious health concern in girl culture. Young girls face strong social pressure to conform to the **thin ideal**. Research suggests that, among adolescent girls, dieting, the pressure to be thin, appearance evaluation, body dissatisfaction, depressive symptoms, low self-esteem, and minimal social support can all increase a girl's risk for engaging in binge-eating behavior. Additionally, young girls without effective coping skills to deal with the many difficult emotional situations and negative mood states that often accompany adolescence, may inappropriately turn to food as a way to cope.

BED is associated with weight gain, overweight, and obesity, which increase the risk for numerous weight-related health complications, including Type 2 diabetes, hypertension, heart disease, and certain types of cancer. Additionally, given the negative emotionality and guilt that accompany binge episodes, girls with BED may also experience anxiety, mood, or substance use disorders. Unfortunately, the stigma associated with binge eating and BED may prevent some young girls from seeking help. However, several treatment options exist for those struggling with binge eating, including behavioral therapy, cognitive-behavioral therapy, interpersonal psychotherapy, self-help, medication (particularly SSRIs), or some combination of therapies.

The rising prevalence of BED and status of BED as the most common eating disorder may warrant its entry as a new diagnostic entity in *DSM-V*. As such, this may potentially elicit greater media and research attention to the subject in young girls, particularly related to etiology, prevention, and treatment.

See also Anorexia; Fat Girl

Further Reading

Binge Eating Disorder. (2006). [Online May 2007]. TeensHealth Web site http://www.kidshealth.org/teen/exercise/problems/binge_eating.html.

Marcus, Marsha D., and Melissa A. Kalarchian. (2003). "Binge Eating in Children and Adolescents." *International Journal of Eating Disorders* 34, S47–S57.

National Institute of Diabetes and Digestive and Kidney Diseases. (2004). *Binge Eating Disorder*. [Online May 2007]. Weight-control Information Network Web site http://win.niddk.nih.gov/publications/binge.htm.

Neumark-Sztainer, Dianne. (2005). *I'm Like, So Fat!* New York: Guilford Press.

LORI A. NEIGHBORS

BIONIC WOMAN.   The Bionic Woman was one of the first female protagonists to demonstrate her superhuman strength on the television screen. The show that ran from 1976 to 1978 (with a remake appearing in 2007) was a spin-off of *The Six Million Dollar Man*.

Audiences were introduced to Jaime Sommers (played by Lindsay Wagner) in 1975, as the perfect female companion and romantic interest of Steve Austin, the Six Million Dollar Man. As Jaime was preparing to embrace the traditional female role by marrying Steve, she nearly died in a skydiving accident. Steve pleaded with Oscar Goldman, head of the OSI (Office of Scientific Information) to save Jaime by giving her bionic parts.

Jaime was given two bionic legs, propelling her as fast as 60 miles per hour; a lifelike prosthetic right arm capable of bending steel or throwing an object for a mile; and a bionic device in her right ear, giving her the ability to hear a wide range of frequencies miles away. However, Jaime's body initially rejected the bionic parts, and she presumably died, leaving Steve grief-stricken.

Unanticipated popular interest in the character of Jaime Sommers prompted the network to find a way to bring her back. Through the removal of her cerebral clot using an experimental procedure, Jaime was revived. The procedure caused her to develop amnesia and forget her relationship with Steve. Any attempt to make her remember her life with Steve caused her disabling headaches, forcing Steve to let her go so she could live her own life. In 1976, Jaime was given a new life and her own TV series: *The Bionic Woman*.

Jaime Sommers as the Bionic Woman lived a dual life—between the socially acceptable role of a caring schoolteacher and less sanctioned activity as a tough secret agent for the OSI. Her missions frequently involved undercover work, in which she took on number of disguises, often typical female roles, such as a beauty pageant contestant, a governess, a nun, a flight attendant, and a singer. The disguises showed the flexibility of Jaime's character, but they also suggested that her tough image might be just another facade.

Bionic Woman paraphernalia had its share of the toy market. The popular Bionic Woman doll was 12 inches tall, an inch taller than Barbie (see the Barbie essay in Part 1) but an inch shorter than the Six Million Dollar Man doll. The doll came with a blue jumpsuit. Turning the doll's head from side to side created a sound to emulate the bionic ear. Panels in the thighs could be removed to reveal bionic parts. It also came with a vinyl red mission purse that contained a wallet, money, credit cards, a mission assignment, snapshots of Steve and Oscar, a comb, a brush, a cosmetic case with makeup, and a map case with two maps and Morse code.

At the time when girls were accustomed to playing house with their tea sets, baby dolls, and Barbies in **pink** dresses, the Bionic Woman doll represented a fresh new alternative, a shift in imagination, and an expansion of the gender roles and possibilities.

The Bionic Woman was a success partly because Jaime was a far more independent and central character than most women in television shows in the 1970s. She worked by herself, and she was confident, intuitive, and capable of meeting the demands of her many jobs and responsibilities. Her character, however, perpetuated gender norms and stereotypical notions of femininity. She was the combination of a radical female and a socially acceptable female. The show regularly emphasized her emotional and female attributes. The Bionic Woman was intentionally portrayed as a non-hero, a modest woman who used her bionic powers with great discretion and secrecy and rarely took credit for her own accomplishments. Perhaps the contradictory roles of the Bionic Woman made her even more appealing and accessible to so many young girls who struggled between tradition and resistance.

The Bionic Woman appeared on television screens around the globe in syndication. Like most female characters in popular culture, Bionic Woman was paradoxical in many ways, but she still offered a vision of female strength and independence that helped challenge the status quo.

See also Wonder Woman

Further Reading

Inness, Sherrie A. (1999). *Tough Girls: Women Warriors and Wonder Woman in Popular Culture.* Philadelphia: University of Pennsylvania Press.

TATIANA GARAKANI

BLOGGING.   A blog is a **Web site** that has diary-style entries that are date- and time-stamped and organized in reverse chronological order. The term "blog" is a contraction of the words "Web" and "log," and people who write blogs are referred to as "bloggers." Bloggers typically use their sites to serve one of two purposes: to inform the public and shape opinions about various news items or to share their personal experiences, thoughts, and ideas. It is this latter form that is preferred by adolescent girl bloggers, who have a significant presence on the Internet.

Blogs typically combine text, images, and links to other blogs or Web sites. The interactive design of blogs, which allows readers to post comments in response to the blogger's entry, is an important aspect of a blog. Most blogs consist mainly of text, although some blogs contain photographs (photoblog), videos (vlog), and audio files (podcasting). Because the software is relatively easy to use, it is easy to add new content to a blog.

Blogging is particularly appealing to girls because of its links to girls' popular practices: in many ways, a blog is a diary transformed to a new media format. It enables them to share their day-to-day lives with friends, posting about school and hobbies, experimenting with identity in public space. Unlike diaries, however, blogs are interactive media that enable readers and viewers to respond to the girls' entries. In these ways, blogging potentially creates a new public sphere, which provides girls with unprecedented opportunities for participation in an area to which girls have not traditionally had access. At the same time, there have been concerns expressed about the safety issues inherent in allowing girls to participate in online activities, because the nature of blogging requires revealing personal information in a public space.

Blogs are extensions of digital communities such as e-mail lists and bulletin boards. Blogs are web-like and interconnected through links, and, as a result, there is an online culture of blogging. The "blogosphere" is a term that refers to all blogs as an online community. Blogs have evolved into social networking spaces, which are basically sophisticated versions of blogs with added features; however, social networking spaces such as **MySpace** treat blogs as distinct and separate features.

Further Reading

Bell, Brandi. (2007). "Private Writing in Public Spaces: Girls Blogs and Shifting Boundaries." In Sandra Weber and Shanly Dixon, eds. *Growing Up Online: Young People's Everyday Use of Digital Technologies*. New York: Palgrave MacMillan, pp. 95–112.

Bortree, Denise Sevick. (2005). "Presentation of Self on the Web: An Ethnographic Study of Teenage Girls' Weblogs." *Education, Communication & Information* 5, no. 1, 25–39.

Scheidt, Lois Ann. (2006). "Adolescent Diary Weblogs and the Unseen Audience." In David Buckingham and Rebekah Willett, eds. *Digital Generations: Children, Young People and New Media*. London: Lawrence Erlbaum, pp. 193–210.

SHANLY DIXON

BLOSSOM.   *Blossom* is a half-hour sitcom that premiered on NBC in early January 1991. The show is a **coming-of-age** story in which Blossom Russo lives with her newly single studio musician father Nick and her older brothers Anthony, a recovering drug addict, and Joey, a teen heartthrob known for his catchphrase "Whoa!" Rounding out the main cast was Six LeMuere, Blossom's best friend. On the air from 1991 to 1995, *Blossom* became not only a cornerstone of NBC's Monday night block of comedy (airing directly after *The Fresh Prince of Bel Air*), but also widely noted as a show that offered a realistic representation of a strong, self-assured contemporary adolescent girl.

At 13, Blossom resembled more of what real girls were like, as opposed to the upper-class and highly sexual girls of **Beverly Hills, 90210**, which was just beginning to hit its first six-month peak when *Blossom* premiered. The main character, portrayed by newcomer Mayim Bialik, who was also 13 (unlike her *90210* actor counterparts, many of whom played characters 10 years younger than themselves), was not exceptionally pretty in the familiar media sense; she was a "normal" girl without the plastic surgeries, hair extensions, and other trappings that often make actors into representations of perfection. The friendship between Blossom and Six (Jenna von Oy) was easily recognizable to any teen girl who giggles with her best friend.

In the show, Blossom kept a diary. As a common literacy practice among adolescent girls, this aspect of the show linked strongly to established girl culture. Blossom's choice of a *video* diary, however, not only allowed viewers to share in Blossom's most intimate thoughts, but it also proved that, like *Doogie Howser, M.D.* (1989), which ended every episode with a journal entry by Doogie on his computer, Blossom was the contemporary teen, who was moving into spaces of familiarity with the digital media that was beginning to permeate this generation's lifestyle.

The writing on *Blossom* tapped into topics far beyond what had previously been addressed in sitcoms popular with adolescent girls. With her brother portrayed as a recovering drug addict and alcoholic, Blossom and her family dealt with the ongoing issue whether or not Anthony would slip back into addiction. Conversations of divorce were also common on the show, because Blossom was a child of divorce when the series premiered and Six's parents were divorcing by the end of the second season. Sex was the issue most often referred to, prompting the now familiar tagline: "Next week, on a very special Blossom . . ." Six's continual attempts to lose her virginity were commonly featured on *Blossom*; one episode arc included Six dating a married man 10 years her senior. Sex was also an issue for Blossom and her bad-boy boyfriend, Vinnie Bonitardi. *Blossom* dealt with a variety of sex-related issues, including date rape, homosexuality, safe sex, sexual harassment— topics that had never before been presented on television or, at least, not in relation to an adolescent girl. Although many of these issues had been prominent in after-school specials and prime-time dramas, very few representations of sexuality addressed the adolescent girl as the core audience. It is no wonder that *Blossom* became one of the top-ranked television shows for adolescent girls in the mid-1990s.

Blossom had a sizable impact on popular girl culture, particularly in girls' fashion. Many adolescent girls lived through the 1990s owning at least one flowered floppy hat, the signature *Blossom* look. Publicity photos often depicted both Blossom and Six in their floppy hats, and both girls frequently wore flowing baby-doll dresses over dark tights, often with heavy boots—clothes similar to those worn by girls in the **Riot Grrrl** movement, which was at its inception. *See also* Girls' Friendships

Further Reading

Douglas, Susan J. (1995). *Where the Girls Are: Growing Up Female with the Mass Media*. New York: Three Rivers Press.

Walkerdine, Valerie. (1997). *Daddy's Girl: Young Girls and Popular Culture*. Cambridge, MA: Harvard University Press.

MICHELE POLAK

BLUME, JUDY (1938–). Judy Blume is an American writer of books for children, especially girls, young adults, and adults. Blume's first children's book, *The One in the Middle Is a Green Kangaroo*, was published in 1969; since then, the author has published twenty-one titles for young readers and four books for adults.

She is simultaneously acclaimed and controversial: although she is the 1996 winner of the American Library Association's (ALA) Margaret A. Edwards Award for lifetime achievement in writing for young adults, she was also named by the ALA as one of the top ten most "challenged" authors between the years 1990 and 2004 (this designation of "challenged" implies that numerous documented requests have been made for the removal of her books from school or library shelves). In fact, five of her novels for young people have been placed on the ALA's list of the 100 most frequently challenged books between the years 1990 and 2000: **Forever** . . . ; *Blubber*; *Deenie*; **Are You There, God? It's Me, Margaret**; and *Tiger Eyes*.

Blume's novels feature characters that young readers are likely to recognize; the subjects of her books are curious, down-to-earth, and decidedly not romanticized. The appearance of Blume's novels on challenged booklists is likely the result of the author's willingness to address issues of sexuality and development; these topics emerge naturally in her work and are handled frankly. Her 1971 novel, *Then Again, Maybe I Won't*—about a young man whose family moves from a lower–middle-class city neighborhood to a more affluent suburb—acknowledges the narrator's nocturnal emissions without judgment, whereas *Deenie* (1973), the story of a young teen with scoliosis whose mother wants her to be a model, makes reference to the narrator's masturbation. Change is also a motif in many of Blume's books; she often uses a character's relocation to a new town, move to a new school, or change in family structure to introduce a character's more personal transformation from child to adolescent to young adult.

Although all of her novels stand on their own, Blume has devoted five books to the fictional Hatcher family and their friends and two books to a threesome of seventh-grade girls. *Tales of a Fourth Grade Nothing* (1972), *Superfudge* (1980), *Fudge-a-Mania* (1990), and *Double Fudge* (2002) are told from the point of view of Peter Hatcher, who, first as a fourth grader and later as a fifth and seventh grader, must suffer the antics of his younger brother, Farley Drexel, known as "Fudge." The weariness of his voice belies his younger years, as Peter recounts what he considers to be embarrassing crimes perpetuated by Fudge. *Otherwise Known As Sheila the Great* (1972) provides an outsider's perspective on the Hatcher family that is distinctly more sympathetic to Fudge. Although Sheila Tubman, the Hatcher's New York neighbor, tells her story from her family's rented summer home in the suburbs, her asides allude to the love-hate relationship that she and Peter enjoy. *Just as Long as We're Together* (1987) and *Here's to You, Rachel Robinson* (1993) address the best friendship of the narrators of each book, Stephanie and Rachel, respectively. Their bond is threatened when, first, Stephanie's parents divorce and a new friend joins their circle and, later, when Rachel's estranged brother returns to the family home and challenges Rachel's perfectionist ways.

Many of Blume's first readers have grown up with the author and her novels. Blume's most recent adult book, *Summer Sisters* (1998), owes much of its success to the continuing devotion of her readers. This book, Blume's first adult novel since the 1983 publication of *Smart Women*, covers familiar territory for Blume and her readers. *Summer Sisters* chronicles the friendship of Victoria (known as Vix) and Caitlin, who meet when Caitlin arrives as a new student at Vix's New Mexico junior high. When Caitlin unexpectedly asks Vix to accompany her on a summer trip to Martha's Vineyard (and thus, extends an invitation of best friendship), the two become a somewhat unlikely duo. The story is told in a series of flashbacks as Vix, who has arrived on Martha's Vineyard to act as the maid of honor in Caitlin's wedding, recalls the summers that the girls spent as "sisters" at the vacationers' haven. Despite what seems like a sentimental premise, the novel is a light but complex story of friendship between two very different women: hard-working Vix considers herself plain and strives to escape the lower-class existence her mother carved for their family; beautiful and wealthy Caitlin lives to break rules. It would be easy to imagine any of Blume's young female characters in the fictional roles given Vix and Caitlin, and this story could easily be the story of Margaret and Nancy from *Are You There, God? It's Me, Margaret* (1970) or Stephanie and Rachel from *Just as Long as We're Together* (1987) and *Here's to You, Rachel Robinson* (1993).

See also Girls' Friendships

Further Reading

Weidt, Maryann N. (1990). *Presenting Judy Blume.* Woodbridge, CT: Twayne.

AMY S. PATTEE

BLYTHE.   Blythe is possibly one of the most popular dolls of the first decade of the twenty-first century. Her original life as a child's toy lasted only one year. Marketed in 1972 by the Kenner Corporation of America, she had a mechanism that allowed her eyes to swivel on a drum, revealing different colored pupils and different positioning of the eyes. Her changing eyes gave Blythe a variety of moods. Kenner supplied Blythe with a wardrobe of twelve dresses in the styling of the late 1960s and early 1970s, with a strong hippie, ethnic, flea-market influence, and she had four hair colors and two hairstyles, a fringe and a center part. Wigs in crazy colors allowed for more transformative effects. Like many dolls, a special carrying case allowed for storage of dolls and clothes.

The doll actually resembles typical formats of popular culture and toy and doll design of the 1960s and 1970s. Her large eyes recall the sad-eyed or big-eyed children in prints from the 1960s and are frequently linked to the popular artworks of San Francisco artist Margaret Keene, in particular, among the overall genre of these prints. There were many big-eyed dolls in the 1960s and 1970s, such as Little Miss Noname by Hasbro 1965 and the Susie Sad Eyes brand, which covered a number of cheap dolls produced in Hong Kong in the 1960s.

The original Blythe dolls reveal some defects, particularly a tendency for the body to split and the legs to fall out of their sockets. The doll's moving eyes were her most notable feature, but it was perhaps not a device original to her: early trade journals suggest that dolls, possibly of porcelain, with changeable glass eyes of different colors were made in Germany in the early 1900s, but a century later none seem to have appeared in the hands of dealers, collectors, or museums.

Blythe's second life began in the 1990s. New York photographer and scriptwriter Gina Garan began to feature the doll in photographs, which were often taken in different locations around the world in 1997. At this point, Blythe was virtually unknown, except to some doll collectors. Garan's photography was published in an album, *This Is Blythe,* in 2000, which exposed Blythe to a new audience of young adult women. The same title has been used for Garan's Blythe **Web site** (http://thisisblythe.com), and she has published several more Blythe albums in subsequent years. Blythe was featured in 2001 in Nordstrom advertising campaigns, and Ashton Drake began producing Blythes in copies of the original packaging for the United States in 2004. Ever since, her likeness has appeared on various kinds of merchandise, including purses and handbags, boots, writing pads, and magnets.

Blythe culture abounds on the Internet: fan pages, photograph albums of dolls and makeovers, sales and auctions, and one popular knitting site that offers patterns for Blythe outfits. Unlike other collector dolls with high monetary values, such as Barbie or bisque dolls (see the essays on Barbie and Doll Culture in Part 1), for which total originality of components is prized, made-over and modified hairstyles and face paints and new clothing designs are happily accepted by Blythe fans.

One strong foundation of the current mania is Blythe's ironic combination of "high art" and "low art": artful photography that is typical of high culture and gallery shows is used to depict a doll, an artifact of girl culture that is usually celebrated by girls and doll collectors. As such, Garan and Blythe's fans encompass a diverse base of people, including young artists, girls, and doll collectors alike.

Fans in Asia are another support group that keeps Blythe to the forefront in North American girl culture. Garan's photography was the catalyst that set off the Asian Blythe mania. In 1999, at a New York exhibition opening, Garan showed her photographs to Junko Wong, a Japanese-American art curator, agent, and promoter, who is also an artist and performer in her own right. Wong negotiated a Blythe-themed Christmas promotion featuring Blythe in the Japanese Parco department store in 2000. Television advertisements featuring Blythe ensured that she gained a national audience of fans in Japan. A summer campaign with Blythe at Parco in 2001 witnessed the launch of a new line of Blythe dolls produced by Takara of Japan, whose most famous dolls are Jenny and Licca. These new dolls provoked signs of near hysteria as fans camped outside Parco stores the night before the dolls were to go on sale, and the new Blythes sold out within a day. As with manga, anime, **virtual friends**, and **Hello Kitty**, popular Japanese girl culture is often embraced by American girls and women. In this case, although Blythe was a product of American doll culture, her recent popularity in Japan influenced and reinforced her new-found popularity in North America.

See also Cross-Merchandising; Manga and Animé Fan Culture

Further Reading

Peers, Juliette. (2004). *The Fashion Doll: From Bébé Jumeau to Barbie.* New York: Berg.

JULIETTE PEERS

BOBBY SOX.   Bobby sox (also known as bobby socks or ankle socks) are commonly equated with an iconic teenage girl from the 1950s who wears a **poodle skirt** and saddle shoes. The significance of these socks in the history of American girls, however, comes from an earlier era.

In the late 1920s, female tennis players first adopted a "stockingless mode," wearing only socks. Despite negative media attention, the practice of wearing ankle socks spread. It was especially popular on college campuses, and high school students soon adopted the trend.

Female high school students primarily wore stockings to school in the 1920s and early 1930s. Socks appeared only as part of athletic uniforms, worn over tights. Over the next decade, however, the teenage fashion market emerged, and high school clothing grew less formal. Teenage girls began to trade their stockings for the less expensive, more durable ankle socks. By 1935, high school girls appeared regularly in yearbook photographs wearing ankle socks with saddle shoes (usually a white, flat leather shoe with a black strip wrapped across the upper of the shoe) or loafers. National marketers demonstrated some awareness of this trend, and, by 1938, the Sears catalog advertised ankle socks directly to girls age 10 to 16.

Bobby sox and saddle shoes provided a perfect palette for expressions of teenage culture and soon distinguished teenage girls from other age groups. Girls wore socks in bold or plain colors; folded, pulled up, or pushed down; decorated with gadgets and charms; over stockings; or held up with boys' garters. They decorated saddle shoes with drawings, friends' names, and favorite song lyrics.

Although high school yearbook photographs showed girls in ankle socks almost exclusively by the early 1940s and the term "sox" appeared frequently, the media—not the girls themselves—largely used the phrases "bobby sox" and "bobby soxer." In 1943 and 1944, national publications, such as *Life* and the *New Yorker*, described bobby soxers as hysterical, mindless worshipers of Frank Sinatra or crazed followers of adolescent fads (see, for example, *Life*, February 21, 1938, pp. 4–7, or the *New Yorker*, October 26, 1946, pp. 34–44).

Many teenage girls rejected the nickname and its associated stereotypes. Not all followers of musicians such as Benny Goodman or singers such as Frank Sinatra wore bobby socks and not all wearers of ankle socks were fans of Goodman or Sinatra. Even teenage music fans who danced in the aisles and wore bobby sox did not see this behavior as their defining characteristic. Although the term "bobby soxer" did not accurately represent all high school girls or music fans, it did demonstrate a media effort to grapple with an emerging social group, one increasingly recognized as a viable, even powerful, consumer market. Media continued to use the term into the 1950s to describe teenage girls.

See also Fan Culture

Further Reading

Kahn, E. J. Jr. (1946, November 2). "Profiles Phenomenon: II. The Fave, the Fans, and the Fiends." *New Yorker*, 35–48.

Nash, Ilana. (2006). *American Sweethearts: Teenage Girls in Twentieth Century Popular Culture.* Bloomington: Indiana University Press.

Palladino, Grace. (1996). *Teenagers: An American History.* New York: Basic Books.

Schrum, Kelly. (2004). *Some Wore Bobby Sox: The Emergence of Teenage Girls' Culture, 1920–1945.* New York: Palgrave MacMillan.

KELLY SCHRUM

BODY MODIFICATION.   Throughout history, individuals in many cultures have deliberately altered their bodies' natural appearance for aesthetic reasons. Piercing, tattooing, scarification, and inserting subdermal implants are the most common forms of permanent or semipermanent body modification practiced in contemporary North America. Piercing and tattooing in particular are of interest to girls who want to explore their identities by experimenting with their outward appearance.

It is an accepted notion that our physical appearance generally reflects our inner selves—our beliefs, values, and hopes. Body modification can therefore be seen as a tool for the realization of the inner self, as a vehicle to tell others what lies within. For some, body modification is considered purely decorative, much like fashion accessorizing. For others, it marks significant transitions in life, indicates group membership, or declares love. Some people get memorial tattoos to mark the death of friends and family members; for others, body modification offers a means to assert a sense of ownership over their bodies. For girls, body modification often signifies independence and assertive action, marking an attempt to undermine or challenge more traditional feminine attributes such as dependence and passivity.

Origins of Body Modification in North America.   Fakir Musafar, a white Californian who took his name from a nineteenth-century Muslim spiritualist, is credited with introducing body modification practices to North America. In the 1970s, Musafar began enacting rituals borrowed from African, Hindu, Native American, and Polynesian cultures. Piercing rituals, for example, were borrowed from Native American warriors who sought to gain spiritual powers through feats of self-torture, such as piercing and suspending the body from hooks. These practices, along with nose piercing and large tattoos drawn in thick black ink, challenged conventional American ideals of how the body should appear and be treated. The 1989 book *Modern Primitives* (a term that Musafar lay claim to in describing himself and his community) brought the more extreme forms of body modification to a mass audience.

Also in the 1970s, members of the British **punk** movement, who were mainly working-class youth frustrated by their marginalized social and economic standing, began using body and facial piercing to symbolize their alienation from mainstream society. Their dress and appearance were intended to be confrontational, and both girls and boys frequently pierced themselves with items such as safety pins and razors. Punk style and culture were soon adopted by American youth to express rebelliousness and to reflect a growing desire for independence. When the fashion industry later appropriated punk style, politics were turned into fashion and sold to middle-class suburban American youth. By the 1990s, the less extreme forms of body modification—primarily tattooing and body piercing—had become fashionable for both young boys and girls.

Piercing in Girl Culture. Piercing is the most widely practiced form of body modification, especially among females. Earlobes are generally the earliest body part that girls get pierced, and many parents endorse ear piercings or even expect their daughters to have pierced ears. Often, parents pierce their daughters' ears in infancy, perhaps as a way to feminize female babies, whose gendered physical appearance is still ambiguous. The usual method of ear piercing is accomplished with a small needle, although piercing guns are still commonly used in inexpensive retail stores. Their popularity has declined, however, because of their unhygienic nature—the same gun is often used repeatedly without thorough sanitization.

Although ear piercing has long been accepted in Western culture, ear projects—which involve either stretching the pierced earlobes or getting numerous cartilage piercings along the ear—have increased in popularity since the late 1980s. Earlobe stretching involves making an insertion in the ear, which is then stretched with increasingly larger and heavier jewelry over time to produce a permanently large opening. Eyebrow, lip, tongue, nose, and navel piercings have also become widespread in girl culture. Navel piercings are especially desired by teen girls and have been popularized by pop stars such as **Britney Spears** and **Christina Aguilera**, who rarely miss an opportunity to show off their flat, jewel-studded midriffs. Only the more extreme piercings, such as nipples and genitals, have retained the designation of "radical" among most teenage girls.

Tattooing in Girl Culture. Like body piercing, tattoos evolved from an anti-social activity in the 1960s into a fashion statement in the 1990s. Tattooing is a more permanent form of body modification than piercing, although it is not entirely irreversible. It involves injecting small amounts of permanent ink under the skin by piercing the epidermis (the top layer of skin) and depositing the ink into the dermis (the second layer of skin). The ink remains in the dermis, protected by the epidermis. Historically, tattooing has been linked to male-dominated cultures such as military groups, prisoners, street gangs, and motorcycle clubs, but, since the 1990s, it has become increasingly feminized. Recent estimates suggest that more women than men make up the newest generation of tattoo enthusiasts in North America. This is true of youth as well as adults; by September 2001, 55 percent of all tattooed adolescents across the United States were female (Collins 2001, p. 4).

The legal age for tattooing is generally between 16 and 18. Because some teens cannot legally or financially obtain a professional tattoo, they often get them from "scratchers," people who illegally tattoo others for money. This is often done in the home of a scratcher who has not apprenticed under a professional tattoo artist. Some teens tattoo themselves (do-it-yourself, or DIY). A common method of DIY tattooing, often referred to as "poke and stick," involves placing ink beneath the skin with a straight pin or sewing needle. Opening the skin increases chances of exposure to bloodborne pathogens, with hepatitis C being the most documented. However, this method also exposes the individual to other bloodborne pathogens, such as hepatitis B and HIV.

Tattooing practices are gendered in terms of the design that teens select, the size of the desired tattoo, and where it is placed on the body. Whereas boys tend get tattoos on their arms and shoulders, girls often choose to tattoo their lower back, hips, upper back, ankle, or other areas where the tattoo can be concealed. The derogatory term "tramp stamp" refers to the lower back tattoos popular among young women and reveals lingering stigmas associated with tattooed females. In general, girls tend to choose small tattoos of established images of femininity, such as floral designs, butterflies, ladybugs, and cartoons such as **Hello Kitty** or Betty Boop. Of course, trends in tattoo designs change over time, and currently, *kanji* tattoos are very common. *Kanji* are Chinese characters used in the modern system of Japanese writing: they are small, pictorial images. They were popularized by Julia Roberts's character in the 1990 film *Pretty Woman* and adorn the bodies of celebrities such as Britney Spears. For teenagers, *kanji* and other forms of writing (particularly foreign scripts such as Japanese, Arabic, Hebrew, or Celtic) are popular because their symbolism can remain a secret shared only between the tattooed person and a select group of her or his friends.

Although teens generally view their tattoos and piercing as objects of self-expression, adults often consider them to be signs of deviant behavior. Parents and teachers have often considered teenage body modification to be a sign of **disordered eating**, unsafe sexual activity, violence, low self-esteem, or school failure; multiple piercings have also been considered by some to be an act of self-mutilation. Much of the stigma attached to teenage piercing and tattooing stems from the impulsiveness of the decision, the visual messages in tattoo designs, and the exposure or flaunting of certain body parts.

Other Forms of Body Modification. Subdermal implants, which are popular in the extreme body modification community, involve implanting shaped objects under the skin to create a three-dimensional effect. **Breast enhancement** is the most common of these procedures, but it is generally reserved for women over the age of 18. Nonetheless, the number of teenage girls under the age of 18 who desire or undergo breast enhancement surgery is steadily increasing. Indeed, with television shows such as *The Swan* and *Extreme Makeover* showcasing breast implants on a regular basis, teens have come to view breast enhancement as a commonplace procedure.

Other forms of body modification are also reinforced through popular culture. Janet Jackson caused a media storm and a fashion trend when she exposed her sun-shaped nipple shield (a piece of jewelry worn to accentuate the appearance of a nipple piercing) during the half-time show at the 2004 Super Bowl. Other celebrities, including actress

Angelina Jolie and singers Mary J. Blige and **Pink**, exhibit their tattoos at high profile events. Because teenagers often hold actors, musicians, and professional athletes in high esteem, body modification is no longer associated with punks and gang members. The visibility of tattoos and piercings on female celebrities has led teens from all income levels and ethnic groups to embrace this popular form of self-expression.

Youth Marketing and Tattoo Appeal. Increasingly, body modification is marketed to children through temporary tattoos, airbrush tattoo kits, and vibrating tattoo pens with washable markers. In 1999, **Mattel** released Generation Girls dolls, including Butterfly Art Barbie, named for the butterfly tattoo on her stomach (see the essay on Barbie in Part 1). However, Mattel discontinued the dolls after receiving complaints from parents. The Internet also contributes to the growing popularity of body modification. Numerous **Web sites** have been created to allow individuals to post photographs of their tattoos or other body modifications, and communities of body modifiers continue to grow online. Body Modification E-zine (BME), for example, is an online resource covering a full spectrum of practices ranging from ear piercing

A young woman sports blue hair, tattoos, and piercings. (Courtesy of Shutterstock.)

to amputations. Increasingly, tattoos and other forms of body modification are regarded as legitimate art forms; art galleries now hold tattoo exhibits, and a growing number of professionally trained artists are beginning to make tattooing their career choice.

See also Midriff Tops

Further Reading

Atkinson, Michael. (2003). *Tattooed: The Sociogenesis of a Body Art.* Toronto: University of Toronto Press.

Caplan, Jane, ed. (2000). *Written on the Body: The Tattoo in European and American History.* Princeton, NJ: Princeton University Press.

Collins, Christopher. (2001). *Girls and Their Bodies.* [Online May 2007]. Girls Incorporated Web site http://www.girlsinc.org/ic/content/GirlsandTheirBodies.pdf.

DeMello, Margo. (2000). *Bodies of Inscription: A Cultural History of the Modern Tattoo Community.* Durham, NC: Duke University Press.

Jablonski, Nina. (2006). *Skin.* Los Angeles: University of California Press.

Mifflin, Margot. (1997). *Bodies of Subversion: A Secret History of Women and Tattoo.* New York: Juno Books.

Pitts, Victoria. (2003). *In the Flesh: The Cultural Politics of Body Modification.* New York: Palgrave Macmillan.

LORRIE BLAIR

BRA.   As a general rule, receiving her first bra is a milestone in a girl's life in North America. Many women vividly recall the style of their first girlhood bra, its color, its texture, and the feeling of its fabric against their skin. For many girls, going to a department store to select and purchase their first bra is a long-awaited rite of passage. A mother or female guardian is usually her chief companion. Many a dad has tagged along also, but a man's presence often raises a girl's nervousness. So significant is the initial bra-buying experience that girls who miss out on this special event may feel slighted.

Although the primary functions of a bra are to cover and support the breasts, the bra is also an icon of popular culture that eroticizes breasts as sexual objects. Therefore, girls often experience ambivalence (both positive and negative feelings) toward this item of apparel.

For some girls, the desire to wear a bra is especially fervent, even if only for decorative purposes. Many proudly put on a training bra or a starter bra while their breasts are still undeveloped. Coupled with this is a yearning to "fit in" with friends who are older or have ampler breasts. Having finally traversed the threshold into long-awaited womanhood, they are elated to be thought of as "grown up." New bras are admired with excitement, wonder, and awe. However, the new wearer of these badges of femininity is soon faced with an array of expectations, including insistence that she keep up to date with popular styles and color trends and that she conform to fashion's dictation of an idealized, average size.

Some girls dislike and avoid wearing a bra. Girls may bind their breasts in an attempt to hide their development. For many, puberty's breast buds and the impending bra represent a disheartening situation that signals the end of childlike freedoms, including going topless or engaging in active events. Some girls who behave in a manner that is usually considered boyish frequently dread the development of their breasts and the wearing of a bra, often interpreting the experience as the beginning of their being forced into typically feminine social roles and behaviors.

For some, the bra is embarrassing. Mothers and other caregivers are frequently blamed for coercing the young girl into wearing a bra when she doesn't want to, and bra-buying day can be a traumatic ordeal. Disliking or loathing the bra, some girls try to disguise it behind dark-colored shirts or sweaters. Other girls are proud of their new bras but may still be embarrassed.

Whether or not a girl reveals her new bra to others is a matter of individual preference. Some creatively announce the exciting news to the world that they have officially come of age. Secretly hoping to be noticed, they may pop questions here and there to solicit attention such as, "Is my bra showing?" Others are not so anxious for attention. Often family or friends draw public attention to a girl's new bra when she does not want them to. In addition to being humiliating and cruel, teasing of this kind can be disenchanting for girls who might otherwise be excited about their new bra experiences. A girl is often acutely sensitive to what boys and men might think of or comment about her bra. Many are mortified when bra straps are pulled and then snapped back against the skin with a noticeable slapping sound.

The age at which a girl begins wearing a bra can have social consequences. Girls who develop breasts at an early age are often teased by both male and female peers and are hypersensitive to these criticisms about their bust lines. As more girls develop breasts, wearing a bra becomes an accepted and expected norm. Ironically, the girls who don't yet require bras are teased.

Although girls' breasts evolve into many shapes and sizes, the fashion industry generally focuses on averages and mass production to maximize profits. Bras used to be sewn at home, where they could be adjusted to individual body types. However, in recent decades, bras are almost exclusively created in assembly-line factories according to standardized designs and sizes, which are then purchased in stores. When idealized averages do not fit a girl's unique breasts, instead of seeing the sizing scheme as the problem, she often self-consciously blames herself, thinking something is wrong with her body.

Girls continue to grapple with sizing issues today. Those with small or large breasts often exert great efforts to find correctly sized bras. Small-breasted girls frequently envy peers who develop faster or more fully or who have more average-sized busts. Some try to make their breasts appear rounded by stuffing material into the cups of larger-sized bras. The size of the bra can be linked to issues of **breast enhancement**. Girls on the large end of the breast size spectrum may have to request their bras through special mail-order arrangements, making the bras more expensive. Larger-breasted girls are often envious of their smaller-breasted peers, who seem to find correct sizes more easily, engage in more physical activities, or go without a bra more effortlessly. Issues of breast reduction may even be a concern.

Some have suggested that when a bra is used to mold a girl's breasts into an idealized shape and position that the fashion world promotes, the breasts symbolically change into sexual objects with erotic appeal. Whether or not a girl is aware of these implications, as she puts on the bra, she enters a world of adult behaviors and expectations, thus unwittingly marking her body.

Since World War II, a great deal of attention has been placed on a girl's first bra. The bra is accepted as a rite of passage, and girls have often been pushed to dress up (in such a way as to appear older) at an earlier age. Today, girls and **tweens** are encouraged by popular media to wear adult lingerie before or as soon as their breasts develop, to advertise their bodies sexually. Adolescent girls' bodies are big business for foundation garment industries (businesses that make undergarments for women and or girls to support or give shape to the curves of their bodies), but, as girls are consistently pushed toward a supposedly ideal bust shape, anxieties rise when girls feel they have fallen short.

Ultimately, when it comes to the bra in girl culture, much is dependent on the way that parents, teachers, and peers influence a girl's way of thinking. And whether she is excited or discouraged about the bra-wearing experience is largely a matter of her own perception.

See also Are You There, God? It's Me, Margaret; KGOY; Tomboys

Further Reading

Brumberg, Joan Jacobs. (1998). *The Body Project: An Intimate History of American Girls*. New York: Vintage Books.

Farrell-Beck, Jane, and Colleen Gau. (2002). *Uplift: The Bra in America*. Philadelphia: University of Pennsylvania Press.

JUSTIN BINGHAM

BRATMOBILE.   Bratmobile was one of the original girl **punk** bands formed in the first generation of the independent young feminist and gay-positive movement **Riot Grrrl**. Although Bratmobile and **Bikini Kill** are often credited with launching the Riot Grrrl movement, the claim is an oversimplification. Although the two bands were very important to the movement, the band members credit the collective energy of a number of women and girls, including but not limited to feminist punk bands, for generating the social movement. They were also part of creating and influencing the underground and independent music scene in the early 1990s, which included a surge of all-girl punk bands influenced by indie pop, surf rock, Britpop, and punk rock.

Bratmobile was informed by the regional influences of the thriving alternative music communities of both the American Northwest and Washington, D.C. As well known for their feminist critiques of culture as for their musical style, the members of Bratmobile were also responsible for two of the most influential feminist grrrl **zines** of the era, *Girl Germs* and *Teenage Gang Debs*.

Allison Wolfe and Molly Neuman created Bratmobile in 1991 when they were students at the University of Oregon. Their first collaboration was the publication of what would ultimately become the popular feminist fanzine *Girl Germs*, and their first show together was on Valentine's Day 1991. As a duo, Allison and Molly shared vocals, and both musicians played guitar and drums. They were later joined by Erin Smith, a Washington, D.C.–based co-writer of the popular culture fanzine *Teenage Gang Debs*. As a trio, Allison sang, Molly played drums, and Erin played guitar. Bratmobile's shows were known for their raw, high-energy punk style, sexiness, playful and political on-stage banter, and Allison's signature dance moves. They played together from 1991 to 1994 and then broke up on stage during what was their final show for five years.

During Bratmobile's break-up period, which later became known as a hiatus, each band member pursued solo work and played in other bands while remaining active in the underground scene and indie feminist politics. In 1999 they reunited and went on tour with Sleater-Kinney, another popular and influential band formed from the Riot Grrl movement. Their later albums included guest musicians such as John Nikki, Audrey Marrs, and Marty Violence, all of whom helped develop Bratmobile's sound. As a result, their formerly stripped down and raw minimalist guitar and drums style grew to a more dimensional sound that included keyboards and bass. Bratmobile toured from 2000 to 2003 and then officially broke up for the last time in January 2004.

Bratmobile records, T-shirts, buttons, and other paraphernalia, including copies of their respective zines, remain popular items to purchase and trade from official **Web sites** and auction or swap Web sites. Bratmobile's discography includes a number of titles, some of which are out of print, but all of which are still revered by those who identify with the Riot Grrrl movement.

Further Reading

Baumgardner, Jennifer, and Amy Richards. (2000). *Manifesta: Young Women, Feminism & the Future.* New York: Farrar, Straus & Giroux.

Fudge, Rachel. (2006). "Celebrity Jeopardy: The Perils of Feminist Fame." In Lisa Jervis and Andi Zeisler, eds. *BITCHfest: Ten Years of Cultural Criticism from the Pages of Bitch Magazine.* New York: Farrar, Straus, and Giroux, pp. 125–133.

ELIZABETH NELSON

BRATZ. Bratz is a successful line of fashion dolls released in 2001 by MGA Entertainment. Since their release, Bratz have enjoyed tremendous popularity with **tween** girls— which was a noteworthy trend in the toy industry, because the appeal of Barbie dolls had in recent years skewed toward much younger girls (see the essay on Barbie in Part 1). Unlike Barbie, Bratz dolls are ethnically indeterminate. Bratz are positioned as being particularly stylish, a feature emphasized by the Bratz slogan, "the girls with a passion for fashion." The Bratz girls are often outfitted in provocatively cut outfits that resemble those worn by pop stars. Therefore, parents and other concerned adults have criticized the attire of the Bratz dolls because of the sexualization. In 2004, parents were shocked to see that Bratz Babyz wore what looked like **thong** underwear. Other Bratz lines include Bratz Kidz, Bratz Petz, Big Bratz Babyz, and—to align with the direct-to-home-video Bratz movies—Bratz Rock Angelz and Bratz Genie Magic dolls. There is also a line called Bratz Boyz.

The 10-inch Bratz dolls are clearly differentiated from 11.5-inch Barbie dolls, not only by their smaller size and their more edgy clothing, but also by their physical features. The Bratz body type is markedly less curvy than Barbie's, featuring a nearly flat chest, a short torso, wide hips, and big feet, which must be removed in order to change the doll's clothing. The Bratz face is more cartoonish than Barbie's, with wide eyes and full lips.

The Bratz doll has had a dramatic impact on Barbie's sales in the United States. In response, **Mattel** has made changes to the Barbie brand. In 2002, Mattel released a new line of 11.5-inch dolls called **My Scene** that bear a striking resemblance to Bratz dolls. The My Scene dolls also have oversized eyes and lips, large shoes that serve as removable feet, and a more provocative wardrobe than typical Barbie dolls. In 2005, MGA Entertainment sued Mattel for copying Bratz. In November 2006, Mattel announced that it was seeking legal ownership of the Bratz line, alleging that the Bratz designs and prototypes were stolen from Mattel and brought to MGA Entertainment by a former Mattel employee.

Sara Morrison, 9, plays with Bratz Runway Disco by MGA Entertainment at the TIA & Toy Wishes Holiday Preview in New York, 2003. (AP Photo/Richard Drew.)

Because of the success of Bratz dolls, there are a number of Bratz spin-off media texts. These include *Bratz*, an animated television show, which debuted on Fox in 2005 and airs on Saturday mornings. The main characters on *Bratz* are Cloe, Yasmin, Jade, and Sasha, who look like their Bratz doll counterparts. In the cartoon, the characters are trendy teenagers with a "passion for fashion" who have started a fashion magazine called *Bratz Magazine*. Many plot lines revolve around the girls' conflicts with Burdine Maxwell, editor of *Your Thing* magazine, and the two teen girls who intern with her. Burdine, whose blonde hair and love of the color **pink** make her resemble a classic Barbie doll, is jealous of the hip young Bratz girls and their magazine's success. There have also starred in two feature-length movies: the 2006 animated film, *Bratz: Babyz the Movie*, and the live-action *Bratz: The Movie* of 2007.

See also Innocence; KGOY

Further Reading

BBC News. (2004). *Bratz Topple Barbie from Top Spot*. [Online September 2007]. BBC News Web site http://news.bbc.co.uk/2/hi/business/3640958.stm.

CBS News. (2005). *Barbie, Beware*. [Online September 2007]. CBS News Web site http://www.cbsnews.com/stories/2005/10/06/eveningnews/main924361.shtml.

Talbot, Margaret. (2006, December 4). "Little Hotties: Barbie's New Rivals." *New Yorker*, 74.

REBECCA C. HAINS

BREAST ENHANCEMENT.   The issue of breast enhancement surgery speaks to the emphasis placed on linking young women and their breasts. Breast enhancement surgeries, which have been primarily for adult women, have recently become more popular among teen girls.

Breast enhancements refer to surgical alterations that change the size or shape of a woman's breasts. Breast augmentation refers to a medical procedure that inserts silicone gel or saline implants into the breasts, thereby enlarging them. Although many women receive breast implants after a mastectomy (often called breast reconstruction), the most common reason for breast implants is cosmetic. Breast reduction diminishes the size of the breast by surgically removing glandular tissue, fat, and skin.

With society's emphasis on female breast size, it is no surprise that breast enhancements are a staple of tabloid conversation. This constant media attention has both reflected and partially fuelled a recent spike in breast augmentation for younger and younger women during the early 2000s. According to the American Society of Plastic Surgeons, in the early 2000s, there was a 24 percent increase in the number of teens having breast implant surgery; almost 4000 teens under the age of 18 had breast implant surgery in 2003 alone (Off Our Backs 2004). From morning news programs to stories in the popular press, people are debating the merits of breast implants—the new "it" high school graduation gift for presumably upper- and middle-class young women and their parents who can afford to pay thousands of dollars for this elective surgery.

Although the procedure is perhaps not perceived to be as sexy as breast enhancements, breast reductions are a welcome relief for many. According to the American Society for Aesthetic Plastic Surgery, more than 144,000 breast reduction surgeries were performed in 2004, which is an increase of 200 percent since 1997 (WebMd). For teens and adults with particularly large breasts, reductive surgery offers physical relief and lessens their feelings of self-consciousness. Although doctors are reluctant to augment the breasts of those younger than 18 and certainly younger than 16, doctors seem more willing to do breast reductions on teens this age because of patients' neck and back pain, their inability to play sports, and their improved quality of life (Mann 2001). Even so, surgery to reduce breast size usually occurs after the breasts are fully developed; the average age of those with breast reductions is 38.

Despite these benefits, questions about the safety of breast enhancement surgeries are significant. Both breast reduction and augmentation are major surgeries, which often require subsequent surgeries and pose potential difficulty for those who want to breast-feed. Perhaps the most publicized concerns about breast enhancements came from the series of class action law suits against Dow Corning, which developed silicone gel implants in the 1960s. Some of these silicone implants leaked, leaving women sick and debilitated. As early as 1977, these women sued Dow Corning (and won) for medical problems related to their implants. However, it wasn't until the 1990s, after hundreds of thousands of women worldwide were part of million-dollar settlements against Dow Corning and other companies, that the public, the government, and the medical establishment fully acknowledged the potential dangers of breast implants (Frontline).

Controversies surrounding breast enhancement surgery for teen girls extend far beyond medical concerns. Some argue that breast enhancements can empower young women by helping them improve their self-confidence. Others argue that instead of altering teens' breasts, parents and society more generally should be encouraging young women to pursue their talents and learn about how to resist the pressures of young women's image-obsessed culture. Situated within powerful economic and cultural trends, the topic of breast enhancements becomes a flashpoint for discussing not only what options girls and young women see available, but also how these options become naturalized in our culture.

See also Bra; The Thin Ideal

Further Reading

Chang, Louise. (2005). *Is Breast Reduction Right for You?* [Online May 2007]. WebMD Web site http://www.webmd.com/back-pain/features/is-breast-reduction-right-for-you.

Mann, Denise. (2005). *Is Plastic Surgery a Teen Thing?* [Online May 2007]. MedicineNet Web site http://www.medicinenet.com/script/main/art.asp?articlekey=51431.

National Research Center for Women & Families. (2007). *Teens and Breast Implants.* [Online May 2007]. National Research Center for Women & Families Web site http://www.center4research.org/teenimplants.html.

PBS. (1998). *Breast Implants on Trial: Chronology of Silicone Breast Implants.* [Online May 2007]. Frontline Web site http://www.pbs.org/wgbh/pages/frontline/implants/cron.html.

MARY P. SHERIDAN-RABIDEAU

BUFFY THE VAMPIRE SLAYER. In her film and television manifestations, Buffy the Vampire Slayer is representative of the **Girl Power** movement of the 1990s. *Buffy the Vampire Slayer* is a film that was released in 1992 by Twentieth-Century Fox and a prime-time drama that premiered on television's WB network in 1997, running seven seasons. *Buffy the Vampire Slayer* offered a unique twist on the standard teen horror fare. The story follows a seemingly vapid, blond California cheerleader named Buffy Summers, who learns that she is an incredibly strong vampire slayer. She is gifted with the power to fight and defeat evil forces. Buffy's creator, Joss Whedon, has explained that he was inspired by the fact that blond girls are always victims in horror films—a trope he sought to subvert.

As directed by Fran Rubel Kuzui, the 1992 *Buffy the Vampire Slayer* movie featured 86 minutes of over-the-top, tongue-in-cheek camp. The film's heavy-handed humor derived from the picture-perfect cheerleader taking on the previously unthinkable role of rough-and-tumble superhero. Taglines such as "Sometimes it takes more than just good looks to kill" and "She knows a sucker when she sees one" reinforced the comedic aspects of the film. However, the campy execution of the movie disappointed Whedon, who as creator and scriptwriter had no artistic control over its filming. He had envisioned *Buffy the Vampire Slayer* as a serious contribution to the horror genre. Moreover, Whedon is a self-described radical feminist, and he felt that his intended feminist message—that girls can be heroes, not just victims—was lost within the camp humor.

Whedon received a second chance when the new WB Television Network approached him to produce a weekly television show. Premiering on March 10, 1997, and running for seven seasons, *Buffy* targeted teenagers and young adults and was the network's first true hit, establishing the WB as a network for young people. The television incarnation of *Buffy the Vampire Slayer* was humorous, but it eschewed overt camp in favor of wittiness with a dark edge. Although *Buffy the Vampire Slayer*'s ratings were not as high as those of shows on other networks, it was a winner for the WB, securing a loyal, young audience. After renewals for four more years, *Buffy* moved to the fledgling UPN for seasons six and seven. During *Buffy*'s tenure on the WB and UPN, the core members of the cast—Buffy Summers and her friends Xander Harris and Willow Rosenberg—managed to survive high school and the adult world beyond it with the help of each other and their mentor,

Kristy Swanson (as Buffy Summers) stars in Fran Rubel Kuzui's 1992 film *Buffy the Vampire Slayer*. (Courtesy of Photofest.)

Watcher Rupert Giles, and a small circle of other friends and significant others. Buffy, her watcher, and her friends—also known as "the Scoobies"—frequently saved the world from destruction.

During *Buffy the Vampire Slayer*'s run, the show became a cult favorite and a darling of critics and scholars. Of the many academic papers written about *Buffy*, a sizable subset focuses on *Buffy* as a feminist text. Female empowerment was always an underlying and overarching theme of *Buffy the Vampire Slayer,* as was made clear in its May 2003 series finale when Willow, by that point a powerful Wiccan witch, uses her powers to change the slayer line: instead of there being one chosen vampire slayer at a time, every girl in the world who has the potential to be a slayer instantly becomes a slayer. Just prior to the finale's air date, Whedon commented, "I hope the legacy of the show would be that there's a generation of girls who have the kind of hero a lot of them didn't get to have in their mythos and a lot of guys who are a lot more comfortable with the idea of a girl who has that much power" (Hockensmith 2003, n.p.).

Buffy the Vampire Slayer continues to exist in different textual forms, as well as in reruns on specialty television channels. There is a series of video games and an ongoing series of books for young readers. *Buffy Season Eight,* which will exist in comic book form, is being overseen by Joss Whedon. From the outset of the show, Whedon supported a sophisticated Web site that encouraged fan feedback and content. After the show ended its run, Buffy lives on in the many fan sites, especially those devoted to **fan fiction**.

See also Cheerleading; Girl Power; Lesbians in Popular Culture; Valley Girls

Further Reading

Braun, Beth. (2000). "The X-Files and Buffy the Vampire Slayer." *Journal of Popular Film & Television* 28, no. 2, 88–94.

Hockensmith, Steve. (2003). *Dialogue with "Buffy" Creator Joss Whedon.* [Online May 2007]. Hollywood Reporter Web site http://www.hollywoodreporter.com/thr/article_display.jsp?vnu_content_id=1889839.

Nussbaum, Emily. (2002, September 22). "Must-See Metaphysics." *New York Times Magazine,* 56.

Wilcox, Rhonda V., and David Lavery. (2002). *Fighting the Forces: What's at Stake in Buffy the Vampire Slayer.* New York: Rowman & Littlefield.

Rebecca C. Hains

BULIMIA.   Bulimia nervosa, commonly referred to as bulimia, is an eating disorder in which an individual eats a large amount of food in a short period of time and then intentionally rids her body of the food through purging. According to estimates by the National Institute of Mental Health, 1.1 to 4.2 percent of females have bulimia in their lifetimes (NIMH 2001).

According to the *Diagnostic and Statistical Manual of Mental Disorders IV (DSM-IV),* those who have bulimia exhibit the following symptoms: The individual engages in frequent and regular episodes of out-of-control **binge eating**. The individual subsequently attempts to eliminate or minimize the fattening effect of the food consumed by compulsively exercising, fasting, inducing vomiting, or abusing laxatives, diuretics, or emetics. Typically, a bulimic engages in these behaviors at least once a week for three months. The individual's self worth is inextricably linked with her distorted perception of her body shape and weight. The bulimic's purging causes much damage to her body: frequent vomiting decays tooth enamel and can lead to the rupturing of the esophagus; laxative abuse can lead to chronic irregular bowel movements or constipation. Moreover, individuals with the disorder experience chemical imbalances that can lead to irregular heartbeats and possibly heart failure and death.

Several factors place a person at risk for developing bulimia: major life transitions, such as puberty, moving, or starting a new school, and the pressure placed on girls and women by American popular culture to attain the **thin ideal**. A group that is also particularly at-risk is female athletes who participate competitively in activities that place emphasis on thinness and body shape, such as **gymnastics**, dance, **cheerleading**, and figure skating.

With the exception of singer Karen Carpenter's struggle with **anorexia** in the 1970s, girls' media coverage of bulimia and other eating disorders became prevalent only in the early 1990s. In 1990, young television star Tracey Gold of *Growing Pains* publicly disclosed her long battle with both bulimia and anorexia. Gold later told of her struggles in her book, *Room to Grow: An Appetite for Life*. Also during that time, choreographer and pop singer Paula Abdul checked into an eating disorder clinic for bulimia. Since her recovery, Abdul has been very vocal about her disorder and her continued fight with the issue. Other famous stars who have admitted to struggling with bulimia include Justine Bateman of the television show *Family Ties*, **Spice Girls** member Geri Haliwell, and Jamie-Lynn Sigler of the television show *The Sopranos*, who has become the spokesperson for the National Eating Disorder Association.

Numerous television specials have focused on disordered eating and bulimia. Notably, CBS aired *Sharing the Secret* in 2000, a made-for-television movie that focused on one teenager girl's struggle with bulimia. The show was awarded a Peabody-Robert Wood Johnson Foundation Award for Excellence in Health and Medical Programming.

Further Reading

Mayo Clinic Staff. (2006). *Bulimia Nervosa: Risk Factors*. [Online May 2007]. Mayo Clinic Web site http://www.mayoclinic.com/health/bulimia/DS00607/DSECTION=4.

Nanda, Rita. (2006). *Bulimia*. [Online April 2007]. Medline Plus/National Institutes of Health Web site http://www.nlm.nih.gov/medlineplus/ency/article/000341.htm.

National Eating Disorder Association. (2002). *Bulimia Nervosa*. [Online March 2007]. National Eating Disorder Association Web site http://www.edap.org/p.asp?WebPage_ID=294.

ANDREA DUKE

BULLYING.   An American **Web site** devoted to a national anti-bullying initiative, "Stop Bullying Now" defines bullying for its young audience in the following way: "Bullying happens when someone hurts or scares another person on purpose and the person being bullied has a hard time defending himself or herself. Usually, bullying happens over and over" (Stop Bullying Now, para.1). It states that bullying often consists of several behaviors that can occur in the physical realm or on the Internet: punching, shoving, and other acts that hurt people physically; spreading bad rumors about people; keeping certain people out of a "group"; teasing people in a mean way; and getting certain people to "gang up" on others" (Stop Bullying Now, para. 2) In the past, bullying was a problem more commonly associated with boys or between boys and girls, but over the last decade the phenomenon of female bullying has become more apparent in the news, in popular films and books, and in research studies.

Female Bullying in the News. Real-life tragedies have fueled public interest in the phenomenon of female bullies. The suicide of Dawn Marie Wesley in British Columbia, Canada, in 2000 has been the subject of much public debate because she implicated three female bullies or friends in her suicide note. Her story has been included in several documentaries on bullying, including *Rats and Bullies: The Dawn-Marie Wesley Story* (2004) and *It's a Girls World* (2006). The hazing of a group of junior girls by senior girls in a Chicago suburb in May 2003 in the context of a "powder puff" football game also garnered much media attention. In January 2006 a group of five Texas **cheerleaders** known as "the fab five" were at the center of a media storm as a result of their public bad behavior and cruelty to other students and teachers in school.

Female Bullying in Popular Film. The reality of schoolyard cruelty between girls has been documented in the popular cinema for decades. For example, such films as **Carrie** (1976), based on Stephen King's 1974 novel, displayed the cruelties that outcasts experience everyday in high school. In the 1980s, John Hughes spent several years sharing the nuances of high school drama and social networks experienced by girls in his films **Sixteen Candles** (1984), *Breakfast Club* (1985), and **Pretty in Pink** (1986). Molly Ringwald played various roles in these films—from the invisible underclassman with a crush on a handsome, wealthy upperclassman, to a spoiled prom queen who is attracted to the school rebel, to a quirky and working-class social outcast who tries to date another handsome wealthy guy from the "in" crowd. These films showed how one's place in the hierarchy of the high school had a strong impact on each girl's experiences and relationships there. Later films such as **Heathers** (1989) and *Clueless* (1995) offered a more focused look at girl cliques and how they wielded their power in schools.

The 2004 film *Mean Girls* marked a high profile culmination of the recent wave of popular attention to the phenomenon of female bullying because the social hierarchies and cruelties that mark girls' relationships in high schools are the central focus. This film was based on the 2002 popular book *Queen Bees and Wannabes: Helping Your Daughter Survive Cliques, Gossip, Boyfriends, and Other Realities of Adolescence* by Rosalind Wiseman, based on her years of working with preteen and adolescent girls.

Another popular book on the subject was released that same year: *Odd Girl Out: The Hidden Culture of Aggression in Girls*, by Rachel Simmons. This was later made into a telefilm that aired on Lifetime in 2005. The effects of female bullying can have long-term impacts on girls' relationships and self-esteem. Simmons shares stories from adult women who, through memory work, reflect on how being subjected to this treatment in school had lasting effects on their lives as adults. Some girls turn to boys for friendship, others perpetuate the cycle by getting social revenge on their bullies, and others turn inward to avoid further harm from their relationships. Both of these books were on the *New York Times* best seller list, featured on episodes of *Oprah* (May 2003 and April 2002, respectively), and made into films. This demonstrates how strongly they resonated with girls' (and "older" girls') experiences.

Female Bullying as a Subject for Research. The phenomenon of female bullying centers around the notions of popularity in schools: who is cool and who is not. What is rarely discussed is how central standards of heterosexual attractiveness are in these hierarchies and that the girls who are shunned or targeted are those who somehow cross over the boundaries of "appropriate" femininity by being either too promiscuous, too strong, not fashionable or rich enough, or not thin enough. The main character in *Mean Girls* refers to the girls in the popular clique as "the plastics," which points to the perceptions of beauty that allow them to reign in the social hierarchy of the school. Neil Duncan, a researcher in the United Kingdom did important work with adolescent girls in asking them to note the qualities that make a girl "popular." In his article "It's Important to Be Nice, But It's Nicer to Be Important: Girls, Popularity and Sexual Competition," he explains that the items most strongly associated with being "popular" were the following: "Is very loud," "Is very popular with boys," and "Is very fashionable." He also makes the distinction between being well liked and being popular, "One could be popular in one's own clique, but to be known as one of *the* popular girls implied that you would be brash, aggressive, and involved in rumours and fights amongst the girls" (2004, p. 144).

See also Cyber-bullying; Meanness

Further Reading

Brown, Lyn Mikel. (2003). *Girlfighting: Betrayal and Rejection among Girls.* New York: New York University Press.

Meyer, Elizabeth. (2006). "Gendered Harassment in North America: School-Based Interventions for Reducing Homophobia and Heterosexism. In Claudia Mitchell and Fiona Leach, eds. *Combating Gender Violence in and around Schools.* Stoke on Trent, England: Trentham Books, pp. 43–50.

Simmons, Rachel. (2002). *Odd Girl Out: The Hidden Culture of Aggression in Girls.* New York: Harcourt.

U.S. Department of Health and Human Services. (2006). *Stop Bullying Now.* [Online September 2007]. Stop Bullying Now Web site http://stopbullyingnow.hrsa.gov/index.asp?area=whatbullyingis.

Wiseman, Rosalind. (2003). *Queen Bees and Wannabes: Helping Your Daughter Survive Cliques, Gossip, Boyfriends, and Other Realities of Adolescence.* New York: Three Rivers Press.

ELIZABETH J. MEYER

BUST.   *BUST* magazine has been published out of New York City since 1993 and provides a third-wave feminist perspective on popular culture. *BUST* reclaims the word "girl," a term that an older generation of feminists has cast off as demeaning, in a way that connotes a cheeky and exuberant type of feminine feminism. The magazine was founded by Michelle Karp, Laurie Henzel, and Debbie Stoller. Stoller is the magazine's current editor-in-chief. The magazine follows the format of more traditional **magazines** that are geared toward teens and young women, but its content is a departure from the standard fare.

The magazine contains a section in every issue called "Real Life: Crafts, Cooking, Home, and Hearth," but the advice found here focuses on do-it-yourself culture, which encourages the reader to create usable goods rather than purchasing them. This section contains practical yet trendy projects that are geared toward their readers' interests, such as accessories and housewares. The section also offers advice on other skill-based activities. These activities are typically domestic skills that a previous generation of feminists cast off, such as knitting and sewing. Interestingly, the patterns in *BUST* underscore both the functionality and the style possibilities of needlework and other craft projects. In past issues, these have included creating a skirt out of a Hawaiian shirt; a cross-stitched sampler that reads "Babies Suck"; and a disco ball made of old CDs. To this end, the magazine attempts to reconcile the previously opposing fields of domestic femininity and feminism. There is also a car maintenance and advice column written by Lucille Treganowan, an expert auto technician with over thirty years of experience.

The "Broadcast" section of the magazine gives information about noteworthy people, who are mostly young women, and activities in which young women are involved, such as fat-positive **cheerleading** troupes and all-girl breakdancing crews. Although this section of the magazine may seem reminiscent of the second-wave feminist concerns of women's consciousness raising ("Look, there are *girls* who can breakdance!"), *BUST* ensures that these columns are written with a mix of facts and tongue-in-cheek wit. For example, the June and July 2006 issue of *BUST* features an article entitled "Nothing But (Hair) Net: Granny Basketball Is a Slam Dunk." Granny Basketball is a group of women in Iowa, who are 50 years old and older, who play basketball competitively and whose game proceeds go to charity. One basketball granny says, "Lots of women make quilts or bake cookies for their hobbies . . . but nobody cheers. When you play basketball, people cheer" (McCombs 2006, p. 10).

BUST also moves beyond the second-wave feminist notion that sex-related industries such as pornography and prostitution are oppressive for women by nature. The magazine features sex-positive articles, including a recent one on young women who are "sex tourists," and an advice column by Betty Dodson, a renowned sexologist. There is also an erotic short story in every issue.

Rather than including clothing from big-name designers, *BUST* features clothing that is mostly affordable from stores such as H&M, Urban Outfitters, Target, and Claire's. They also showcase clothing produced by small (mostly female-headed) companies that sell their wares through boutiques or online sites. Although there is a strong emphasis on new clothing in these fashion spreads, this in not the only type of fashion seen in *BUST*: in addition to do-it-yourself fashion projects, the magazine also features a regular "Thrift Score" column, which suggests particular items to keep an eye out for in secondhand shops. Unlike many other magazines on newsstands, *BUST* uses both professional and nonprofessional models of various ethnicities and sizes in their fashion spreads.

In the "Fashion and Booty" section of the magazine, small collections of products are assembled under a theme that the readers might be interested in purchasing. Examples of themes include "Measure Pleasure," which features accessories that use measuring tapes for inspiration; "Up Against the Wallet," which shows various interesting wallets; and "Think **Pink**," which features pink technology, such as a pink **Hello Kitty** television. Consumerism is encouraged within the pages of *BUST*, but it is revamped to focus on unique and off-beat consumer goods. Similar to the fashion that is featured, the chosen "Booty Call" products are often manufactured by small independent companies.

Moreover, objects are not just things to be bought and sold in *BUST*; the regular "Museum of Femoribilia" column examines forgotten curiosities of women's lives that now appear ironic and kitschy. These items include old maid card games, novels about the misconduct of unwed pregnant single girls, and plastic **go-go dancer** dolls. Lynn Peril, the author of this column, uses these objects as a prism through which to tell the social history of women's lives in past eras.

The magazine is also supported by an extensive **Web site** (www.bust.com) that includes the "Boobtique," where readers can purchase *BUST*-related paraphernalia and other items. The site includes, as well as personal ads and e-postcards, the "Girl Wide Web"—a constellation of over 10,000 Web sites of interest to women and girls that cover culture, leisure, **blogs**, and journals, "she-commerce and services," or businesses of interest to women, as well as feminist and sex-positive resources.

Moreover, Stoller has published three Stitch 'n Bitch books—*Stitch 'n Bitch: The Knitter's Handbook, Stich 'n Bitch Nation,* and *Stich 'n Bitch Crochet*—which all feature lessons and patterns on how to produce hip homemade crafts that are aimed at a generation of young women and are relevant to their lifestyles. With her former co-editor Michelle Karp, Stoller also published and edited *The BUST Guide to the New Girl Order,* which is a collection of notable articles from the early years of *BUST.*

See also Sassy; Seventeen; YM

Further Reading

Karp, Michelle, and Debbie Stoller. (1999). *The BUST Guide to a New Girl Order.* New York: Penguin.

McCombs, Emily. (2006, June/July). "Nothing But (Hair) Net: Granny Basketball Is a Slam Dunk." *BUST,* 10.

McRobbie, Angela. (1994). *Postmodernism and Popular Culture.* London: Routledge.

MIRANDA CAMPBELL

C

CABBAGE PATCH KIDS. Cabbage Patch Kids are dolls that became enormously popular with girls in the early 1980s. Instead of depicting women or teenage girls, as do many other dolls that are popular with girls, Cabbage Patch Kids represent babies (including "preemies") and young children, both male and female. Marketed as coming from the "Cabbage Patch," the consumer "adopts" her doll: each comes with a predetermined name and an adoption certificate. The dolls have a distinctive appearance; they have molded plastic heads with soft, stuffed bodies and soft, yarn-like hair. They may be considered "ugly" baby dolls, with their large, round heads and small noses.

The dolls were originally devised by Xavier Roberts, who formed a company in 1978 called Appalachian Artworks. Through this company, he sold soft sculpture versions of the dolls at craft fairs. In 1982, Roberts teamed with the toy company Coleco to mass-produce the dolls, and soon afterward the company bought out his share. Cabbage Patch Kids became a phenomenon in 1983, when there was such a buying frenzy over the Christmas season in the United States that the toys sold out. By the end of 1984, 20 million dolls had been sold.

To foster the analogy to adopting a child, Roberts converted an old medical clinic in his hometown of Cleveland, Georgia, into the "Babyland General Hospital," where the staff made the dolls and offered them for adoption for the high fee of $125. Despite their high price, the huggable Cabbage Patch dolls were extremely popular with adults and children alike, similar to the teddy bear frenzy of 1906–1907. At the same time, groups devoted to protecting the rights of adopted children instigated some controversy about the pretend adoption procedure.

In 1986, Coleco diversified and created other "huggable" toys, such as Wrinkles and Furskins. These were not successful, and the company folded. Different versions of the

Cabbage Patch Kids are still available for sale on the World Wide Web, and handcrafted ones are still available for adoption at the original Babyland General Hospital.

Further Reading

Cross, Gary. (1997). *Kids' Stuff: Toys and the Changing World of American Childhood*. Cambridge, MA: Harvard University Press.

Goodfellow, Caroline G. (1998). *Dolls*. Risborough, Buckinghamshire: Shire Publications.

Hoffman, William. (1984). *Fantasy: The Incredible Cabbage Patch Phenomenon*. Detroit, MI: Taylor.

Seiter, Ellen. (1993). *Sold Separately: Children and Parents in Consumer Culture*. New Brunswick, NJ: Rutgers University Press.

JACQUELINE REID-WALSH

CADDIE WOODLAWN.   Caddie Woodlawn, the heroine of the children's book by the same name, is a spirited, 11-year-old pioneer girl. Her story takes place during the years when Caddie is transitioning from childhood to womanhood, and, unfortunately, the transition is not a smooth one. The opening paragraph of the book describes Caddie as a **tomboy** who "ran the woods of western Wisconsin." While such behavior was acceptable for a child, it was no longer tolerated as Caddie moved into adolescence. Her story illustrates the tensions girls face as they grow out of childhood, into girlhood, and beyond.

Caddie Woodlawn was written by Carol Ryrie Brink. It was published in 1935 and was awarded the Newbery Medal the following year. The book, which tells the story of Caddie and her six brothers and sisters, was based on true stories that Brink's grandmother had told her about life in the 1890s. Thus, not only is Caddie a captivating fictional character; she was also a real girl.

The book focuses on the Woodlawn family and farming life. Brink describes the everyday experiences of the Woodlawn family, ultimately providing the reader with a realistic insight into American pioneer life. The Woodlawns were part of a farming community, yet they also lived close to the wilderness in western Wisconsin. The family often interacted with the Native Americans who lived close by. Brink's sequel to *Caddie Woodlawn*, *Magical Melons*, continues the Woodlawn family's story.

Caddie's story involves adventures in the woods with her brothers and father. These activities ultimately put stress on the relationship she has with her mother: Caddie had been allowed to grow up side by side with her brothers, but as she approaches adolescence, her mother becomes less tolerant of her daughter's tomboyish tendencies. Caddie's parents want her to settle down, and her mother especially urges her to become a young lady. By the story's end, she accepts the gender-based expectations imposed on her.

Since the 1930s, many generations of girl readers have connected with Caddie's independence and freedom. However, many overlook the fact that Caddie's story actually ends with that independence and freedom being compromised. This central theme of a young, adventurous girl growing into a mature, more refined young woman is one commonly found in many classic girls' books. Caddie's transformation is quite similar to those of other popular girl characters, especially Laura Ingalls Wilder's main character Laura, of the **Little House on the Prairie** series, and L. M. Montgomery's Anne Shirley, of the **Anne of Green Gables** series. Like these characters, Caddie represents "girlhood"—the transitional, exploratory time in a female child's life.

See also Oakley, Annie

Further Reading

Agee, Jane M. (1993). "Mothers and Daughters: Gender Role Socialization in Two Newbery Award Books." *Children's Literature in Education* 24, no. 3, 165–183.

KATE ROBERTS EDENBORG

CALAMITY JANE.   Born Martha Jane Cannary Burke, Calamity Jane is one of the most famous cowgirls in American history. She was born in Missouri in 1852 and was the oldest of six children. The family moved to Virginia City, Montana, in 1865. The move took five months by wagon train, and, although only 13 at the time, Martha Jane learned to swear and drink whiskey along the way. Her mother died on the journey, in 1866. In the spring of that year, the family moved again, this time to Salt Lake City, Utah. When her father died a year later, Martha Jane took charge of the family, moving them to Piedmont, Wyoming. She settled in Deadwood, South Dakota, in 1876. Although it is not likely that she received any formal education, she was literate.

Many stories about Calamity Jane that are generally held to be true cannot be substantiated; for example, stories of her riding alongside General Custer at Fort Russell in the Indian Wars abound, but there is no proof that Custer was ever at Fort Russell. Even the origin of her nickname is in doubt: Martha Jane claimed to have been dubbed "Calamity Jane" by her superior, Captain Egan, after she rescued him through a daring feat of horsemanship. However, the *St. Paul Dispatch* once claimed that "she got her name from a faculty she has had of producing a ruction at any time and place and on short notice" (Lakewood Public Library 2005, para. 17).

In 1884 in El Paso, Texas, she met Clinton Burk. They married in 1885, although biographers argue over this date. She began her performing career in 1896 in Minneapolis and was booked as the "the heroine of a thousand thrilling adventures" and the comrade of famous cowboys Buffalo Bill and Wild Bill Hickok (Lakewood Public Library 2005, para. 34). She toured with Buffalo Bill's Wild West Show until 1901, when she was fired for drinking and fighting. A subsequent appearance in Buffalo, New York, ended similarly. Buffalo Bill had to lend her money to get home. She returned to Deadwood, where she died of pneumonia in 1903. Reportedly she requested, "Bury me beside Wild Bill, the only man I ever loved" (Lakewood Public Library 2005, para. 36). Her wish was granted.

Calamity Jane has been featured in several movies and television shows of the twentieth and twenty-first centuries. Notably, Doris Day starred in the 1953 musical film *Calamity Jane*, which plays up a romance between the cowgirl and Wild Bill Hickok. The film was produced in the wake of the hugely popular film *Annie Get Your Gun*, which was loosely based on cowgirl **Annie Oakley**.

See also Cowgirl Play; Evans, Dale; Jessie the Cowgirl

Further Reading

Flood, Elizabeth Clair. (2000). *Cowgirls: Women of the Wild West*. Santa Fe, NM: ZON International Publishing.

Lakewood Public Library. (2005). *Women in History: Martha Jane "Calamity Jane" Canary Biography*. [Online April 2007]. Lakewood Public Library Web site http://www.lkwdpl.org/wihohio/cana-mar.htm.

CATHERINE CAMPBELL

CAMP FIRE GIRLS.   Camp Fire Girls is a historic national girls' organization based in the United States. Developed in 1910, Camp Fire Girls, also known as simply Camp Fire, promoted a model of female citizenship that balanced traditional roles—especially domesticity and family service—with broadening opportunities in education, athletics, public reform, and employment. Now a coeducational endeavor called Camp Fire U.S.A., the organization is a pioneer in the field of girl-specific programming.

The founders, who intended Camp Fire to be the female corollary to the Boy Scouts of America, included youth workers, YWCA women, and progressive reformers. The most influential individuals in the development of Camp Fire were Luther and Charlotte Gulick and Ernest Thompson Seton. Originally designed to serve girls aged 12 to 21, Camp Fire added Blue Birds, a program for younger girls, in 1913. Camp Fire was the largest girls' organization in the United States until 1930, when **Girl Scouts** surpassed it.

Camp Fire founders subscribed to the notion that as mothers and homemakers, women's role was to provide care. Thus, Camp Fire's name symbolized the hearth and women's connection to the home. Girls participated in activities that were grouped into "honors," which included the required honor of fire maker and elective honors, including home craft, camp craft, handcraft, nature lore, business, and patriotism. Once a girl fulfilled the requirements for an honor, she was awarded rank and a distinctly colored bead, which was added to her ceremonial costume. This costume was adopted by Camp Fire from Native American culture.

Camp Fire promoted a national girls' culture. Although regional variations persisted, Camp Fire Girls across the United States shared common experiences and encountered the same ideals. Camp Fire lays claim to being America's "first . . . nonsectarian interracial organization for girls" (Buckler et al., p. 3). Early clubs formed in settlement houses and orphanages as well as schools, churches, and neighborhoods. Nonetheless, historically, Camp Fire membership was predominantly white and middle-class. Until the 1960s outreach was limited, which meant that clubs before that time were typically ethnically and racially homogeneous.

Extensive program changes came in the 1970s as Camp Fire, along with other traditional youth organizations, struggled to retain members. Seeking a distinctive niche and responding to the women's movement, particularly its demand that girls be prepared to live and work as equal partners with men, Camp Fire became committed to incorporating boys' involvement in their organization. In 2006, girls and women represented 54 percent of Camp Fire's 750,000 members. Most branches of Camp Fire U.S.A. have abandoned the system of honor beads. Today's flexible program allows local councils to respond within a national framework to community needs through day care centers, camps, after-school services, and other specialized programs.

Further Reading

Buckler, Helen, Mary F. Fiedler, and Martha F. Allen. (1961). *Wo-He-Lo: The Story of Camp Fire Girls, 1910–1960*. New York: Holt, Rinehart, and Winston.

Helgren, Jennifer Hillman. (2005). "Inventing American Girlhood: Gender and Citizenship in the Twentieth-Century Camp Fire Girls." Ph.D. diss., Claremont Graduate University.

Miller, Susan A. (2007). *Growing Girls: The Natural Origins of Girls' Organizations in America*. Camden, NJ: Rutgers University Press.

JENNIFER HILLMAN HELGREN

CAREER NOVELS. Career novels, also known as career girl novels or career romances, are a category of girls' **series fiction** featuring a young female protagonist making her way in the world in her chosen profession. Chiefly published during the 1930s through the 1960s, the novels were marketed as having both entertainment and instructional value for adolescent girls considering possible careers. This publishing trend reflected societal changes in the middle of the twentieth century, especially following World War II, as women experienced increasing opportunities to enter the workforce in a limited number of fields.

The genre's simple and formulaic plots played out in series such as Dodd Mead's *Career Books*, Avalon's *Career Novels*, and Julian Messner's *Career-Romance for Young Moderns* in the United States, as well as Bodley Head's *Career Guides* and Chatto and Windus's *Career Novels* in the UK. A typical scenario involves the heroine's graduation (from high school, vocational school, college, or graduate school) and subsequent relocation to a new town for a first job. This is followed by a sequence of professional and romantic trials, all of which are overcome for a picture-perfect ending, complete with a job promotion and a marriage proposal.

Earlier examples of the genre emphasized its educational role, allowing the reader to shadow the heroine during her interview and first few days on the job, and to listen in while a mentor figure lectures her on both the difficulties and rewards of the field. Some novels went a step further, such as a 1938 title, *Books on Wheels* by Mary Rebecca Lingenfelter from the *Kitson Careers Series*. It includes an appendix listing accredited library schools, areas of specialty within the profession, a bibliography, and a glossary of technical terms appearing in the novel. In contrast, later series such as Messner's *Career-Romance* books played up the love story angle in an attempt by the publisher to reach a wider audience.

Similarly, the types of careers represented in the novels changed over time, with mundane titles about bookkeepers and hairdressers increasingly giving way to escapist fare about models and actresses. Although a few of the series' heroines flouted convention in pursuit of careers as doctors, lawyers, or architects, far more common were those employed as nurses, secretaries, or teachers—traditionally female-dominated, low-paying professions.

Along with the genre's mandatory love story element, this focus on positions requiring nurturing and caretaking skills has prompted some feminist critics to suggest that the books were in fact preparing their young readership for their "true" roles as wife and mother—roles for which they would be expected to end or curtail their work outside of the home.

Career novels were obsolete by the 1970s, once women in the workplace had ceased to be a novelty and young adult fiction trends had shifted to more realistic fare about topics like puberty, teen sexuality, and divorce. The fictional career girl did spark another publishing trend beginning in the 1990s with the emergence of the **chick lit** phenomenon; however, those books focus almost exclusively on the heroines' pursuit of romantic rather than professional goals. Their prototypes, the mid-century career novels for girls, have become collectibles on the nostalgia market, generating a brisk trade in online auction and used book merchant sales.

Further Reading

Peril, Lynn. (2002). *Pink Think: Becoming a Woman in Many Uneasy Lessons*. New York: W. W. Norton.

Spencer, Stephanie. (2005). *Gender, Work and Education in Britain in the 1950s*. Hampshire, UK: Palgrave Macmillan.

JENNIFER WOLFE

CAREY, MARIAH. Known for her wide vocal range, Mariah Carey is an American pop musician. In the early 1990s, she was at the forefront of the female solo artist movement, which later included **Christina Aguilera, Beyoncé**, and **Jennifer Lopez**. In 2000, she became the top-selling female artist of all time.

Carey's career began in 1990 with an eponymous album released on Columbia Records, the company that released her next six studio albums. Her early sound relied on synthesizers, drum machines, and catchy melodies of pop music, but her vocal style has always been inflected with R&B style.

Although Carey has always participated in the writing, arranging, and production of her own music, during the mid nineties she successfully lobbied to gain more creative control over her work and public image. She also began writing for and producing other artists. During the late nineties, she infused more and more of her music with elements of **Hip Hop** through her collaborations with Sean "P. Diddy" Combs and **Missy Elliott**. Notably, she was the only artist who had a number 1 *Billboard* hit in every year of the 1990s.

After nearly a decade at Columbia, Carey made a heavily publicized move to Virgin Records for her eighth album—the soundtrack to *Glitter*, the 2001 film based partially on Carey's life, in which she starred. The album was released on September 11 and was a critical and commercial failure, as was the film itself, released ten days later. During the time of *Glitter*'s release, Carey suffered a nervous breakdown and was briefly hospitalized. After the failure of their first venture together, Virgin Records severed its contract with Carey, and critics began speculating that her career was over. Her next album, *Charmbracelet*, was released in 2002. Although it was more successful than *Glitter*, its sales and reviews were lukewarm, and it was seen by many as the death blow to her career.

Three years later, Carey's latest album, *The Emancipation of Mimi*, was released by Island. Carey collaborated with many well-respected Hip Hop artists to create the album: she coproduced songs with Kanye West, the Neptunes, and Jermaine Dupree, among others. The album also includes guest vocal tracks from rappers like Snoop Dogg and Nelly. The album is her most Hip Hop–influenced effort to date and earned Carey critical acclaim. It effectively put her back on the popular music map; the album was the best-selling album of 2005. Two of the album's singles ("We Belong Together" and "Don't Forget about Us") went to number 1 on the *Billboard* charts, while "Shake It Off" peaked at the number 2 slot—making Carey the first female solo artist to occupy the top two slots simultaneously. She also won the Grammy for Best Contemporary R&B Album of that year.

To date, Carey holds the record for having the most single-career number 1 hits by a female artist. With seventeen such hits, she is tied with Elvis Presley for second place (behind the Beatles) for most number 1 hits by a solo male or female artist or group.

See also Lil' Kim

Further Reading

Morgan, Joan. (2000). *When Chickenheads Come Home to Roost: A Hip-Hop Feminist Breaks It Down*. New York: Simon & Schuster.

Patterson, Sylvia. *High Notes, High Drama*. [Online May 2007]. Guardian Web site http://arts.guardian.co.uk/features/story/0,,1455242,00.html.
Roberts, Robin. (1996). *Ladies First: Women in Music Videos*. Jackson: University Press of Mississippi.

MARIANNA RITCHEY

CARRIE.   *Carrie* is a popular Stephen King horror novel and film adaptation that features the themes of adolescent girlhood, **menstruation**, and **bullying**. King's novel was initially published in 1974; the creative team of writer Lawrence Cohen and director Brian DePalma adapted it for the screen, and the film *Carrie* was released in 1976.

Told in the form of a series of letters using a collection of fictional news accounts, transcripts, and eyewitness testimony, King's novel tells the story of teenage girl Carrie White, a social outcast at her high school in Maine. Carrie has been emotionally and physically abused by her mother Margaret, a religious zealot.

As the novel opens, Carrie experiences her first period during a shower after gym class. Due to her cloistered upbringing, Carrie is unaware that she is experiencing menstruation, and she reacts with terror at the sight of her own blood. Carrie's female classmates, led by a very popular girl named Chris Hargensen, respond to Carrie's terror with cruelty: they tease her and pelt her with sanitary napkins and tampons. During this moment of humiliation, Carrie has her first experience with telekinetic powers. After the locker room incident, Carrie begins to practice and develop her telekinetic (and occasionally telepathic) powers in secret, which grow in power and ferocity over the course of the novel.

One of Carrie's classmates, Sue Snell, feels remorseful about her behavior in the locker room and attempts to become Carrie's friend. In an effort to make amends, Sue asks her boyfriend, Tommy Ross, who is also the father of her unborn child, to take Carrie to the **prom**. Viewing this as the start of a more normal adolescence for herself, Carrie defies her mother and accepts his offer. In a subsequent scene, Carrie uses her telekinesis to overpower her mother and assert her independence.

In the meantime, Chris Hargensen, the ringleader of the locker room incident, has been barred from attending the school prom for refusing to attend her detention. Her anger fuels a plan to embarrass Carrie that leads to the novel's prom night climax: Chris convinces her boyfriend to rig buckets of pigs' blood above the stage where the prom queen and king will be crowned. Chris then fixes the prom queen and king elections so that Carrie and Tommy are elected, and as they take the stage, Chris dumps the blood all over them. Tommy is knocked unconscious by one of the buckets, while Carrie is subjected to the laughter of all the students in attendance. In response, she uses her powers to lock the doors of the school gym and turn on the sprinklers, thereby inadvertently electrocuting several classmates. Carrie becomes gripped by her own power and growing madness, and sets fires in the school with the intent of killing everyone who has wronged her.

After destroying everything in her path, Carrie arrives at home. Her mother, believing that her daughter is possessed by Satan, tries to save her daughter from damnation by killing her, and she stabs Carrie in the shoulder with a kitchen knife. Carrie uses her powers to kill her mother before she is successful. When Chris and her boyfriend attempt to run Carrie over, she uses her powers to crash their car and kill them. Sue, who is one of the few students to escape the prom carnage, finds Carrie mortally wounded. Before dying, Carrie causes Sue to have a miscarriage, although Sue believes that she is simply having her period.

The film adaptation of *Carrie* remains faithful to the plot of the novel, with a few notable exceptions. The most striking of these is the marked increase in the violence of the prom sequence and the events that follow: Carrie's revenge at the prom is more willful, destructive, and chaotic; Carrie kills her mother by impaling her with kitchen instruments until she looks like the martyred figure of Saint Sebastian that Carrie keeps in a prayer closet; and Carrie then dies by bringing her house down upon herself.

In addition, there is no mention of Sue's pregnancy in the film, and there is no contact between Carrie and Sue at the end of the film. However, the film version of *Carrie* does offer a recurring and terrifying dream sequence: Sue dreams that she is placing flowers on Carrie's grave and Carrie's hand reaches out from the grave to grab her. In the final scene of the film, Sue is screaming in bed while her mother attempts to comfort her.

The film adaptation was immensely popular at the box office and received critical praise. *Carrie* became one of the few horror films to be nominated for multiple Academy Awards, including nominations for its female leads, Sissy Spacek (Carrie White) and Piper Laurie (Margaret White).

Historically, females who menstruate have been considered socially "unclean" or "cursed" within many male-dominated societies. While these labels have served to repress females, they also imbue menstruating girls and women with a certain mystery and power. In *Carrie*, the onset of the character's period coincides with the onset of her telekinetic powers and, consequently, Carrie is simultaneously terrifying and powerful.

The film *Carrie* is part of a horror film trend in the 1960s and 1970s that features narratives about adolescent girls who possess otherworldly powers, such as *The Exorcist* (1973), as well as adult females, often women who are pregnant with satanic or demonic babies, such as *Rosemary's Baby* (1968). The novel *Carrie* has spawned several other adaptations and sequels, including a Broadway musical, *Carrie: The Musical* (1988); a sequel to the film, *The Rage: Carrie 2* (1999); and a made-for-television remake, *Carrie* (2002). The popularity of horror stories like *Carrie* reflects the conflicted image of female puberty, sexuality, and power in popular culture.

See also Meanness

Further Reading

Clover, Carol. (1993). *Men, Women, and Chainsaws: Gender in the Modern Horror Film*. Princeton, NJ: Princeton University Press.

Oler, Tammy. (2003, Summer). "Bloodletting: Female Adolescence in Modern Horror Films." *Bitch* 21, 44–51.

TAMMY OLER

CATWOMAN.   Catwoman is a female character who first appeared in DC Comics' *Batman* #1 in 1940. An icon of female empowerment, she began as Batman's nemesis and over the years has shifted to become his ally. First called The Cat, Catwoman is revealed to have the secret identity of Selina Kyle, a woman who traded her life of prostitution for one of burglary. She continued to appear in Batman comics until a *Catwoman* comic series was published in 1993. While her cat suit and whip are the character's mainstay costume, the only constant in Catwoman's character is her ambiguity.

As comic book characters are rewritten, their history and relevance to contemporary social issues are often modified. Consequently, the story of Catwoman's origin has been told many times, but the themes of victimization and subsequent revenge feature prominently throughout and underscore the character's moral ambiguity. In *Batman* #62, Selina Kyle is portrayed as the victim of her abusive husband. When she decides to leave him, she breaks into her husband's vault to steal back her jewelry. The act of stealing back what was hers can be interpreted as a metaphor for regaining her independence and identity. It leads her to a life of crime, and she becomes Catwoman, Gotham's most notorious cat burglar.

In the 1993 *Catwoman* comic, the character is also portrayed as a victim and later as a morally sketchy thief: Selina's mother commits suicide when Selina is young, and after her alcoholic father dies a couple of years later, she is put into a juvenile hall. She runs away and becomes a child of the streets who resorts to thievery for survival. Her life of crime is very profitable and eventually leads her into the world of the social elite, where she mingles among the people from whom she would steal. As the series progresses, Catwoman becomes a Robin Hood of sorts, as she steals from the rich and gives to the poor.

Julie Newmar (as the Catwoman) in 20th Century Fox Television/ABC's television series *Batman*. (Courtesy of Photofest.)

Catwoman's character also frequently blurs the line between good girl and bad girl, especially in her interactions with Batman. While positioned as a villain, Catwoman's motivations in her relationship with Batman could be attributed to both desire and hatred. While Batman clings to the hope that Catwoman can be saved and turned into a heroine, she enjoys the challenge of using her sex appeal to manipulate the most powerful man in Gotham. For example, in *Batman* #610 (2002), Batman and Catwoman share a kiss after he saves her from a villain, Killer Croc. Batman then decides to reveal his secret identity to her as an act of trust. This challenges Catwoman's sense of morality, and she soon evolves into a character willing to devote herself to the greater good; she eventually partners up with Batman on different occasions.

In *Catwoman* #53 (2006), Selina Kyle's character gives birth to a baby girl and hands over the title of Catwoman to another character, named Holly Robinson. A childhood friend of Kyle, Robinson is also a former prostitute, and is in a relationship with another woman, Karon. She has no superpowers, though Kyle trains her in hand-to-hand combat.

Catwoman has been portrayed by a wide variety of actresses. In the 1960s *Batman* television show, Julie Newmar and Eartha Kitt played the role, followed by Lee Meriwether in the movie spin-off of the series. In the realm of animation, several actresses have voiced Catwoman, including Adrienne Barbeau (in *Batman the Animated Series* and *The New Adventures of Batman*) and Gina Gershon (*The Batman*). Recent movie portrayals include Michelle Pfeiffer in *Batman Returns* and Halle Berry, who starred in *Catwoman* in 2004.

See also Batgirl; Bionic Woman; Comics; Poison Ivy; Wonder Woman

Further Reading

Walton, Priscilla L. (1998). "A Slippage of Masks: Disguising Catwoman in *Batman Returns*." In Deborah Cartmell, I. Q. Hunter, Heidi Kaye, and Imelda Whelehan, eds. *Sisterhoods: Across the Media/Literature Divide*. London: Pluto Press.

KEVIN LETOURNEAU

CELEBRITY BAD GIRLS.   Celebrity "bad girls" such as Britney Spears, Paris Hilton, and Lindsay Lohan seem to provide a dangerous edge to girls' popular culture. They are continuously in the media and seem to be endlessly fascinating to the general public. This may be due to their expensive clothes, their hard-partying attitudes, and reported drug and alcohol use. It may be that girls and women have for centuries lived with two options—either good, innocent, and caring, or be dangerous, sexy, and self-centered—and that girls and women are fascinated by those who cross the boundary into "bad" in such spectacular ways. Some parents and educators worry that girls today, by being constantly exposed to media coverage of these "bad girls," are being encouraged to imitate the behavior of their tabloid role models. Another concern may be that by gossiping and fantasizing about celebrities' lives, we as a society "collectively define who we are and what we value as a culture" (Brooks 2004, p. 2).

Britney Spears is a pop singer from Kentwood, Louisiana. She has been an influential fashion trendsetter for **tween** girls, in that she has advanced the style of low-rise jeans, midriff shirts, and lower back tattoos. She went from being a member of the Mickey Mouse Club to playing a Catholic schoolgirl in the music video for her first hit single " . . .

Britney Spears and Madonna kiss during the opening performance of the MTV Video Music Awards at New York's Radio City Music Hall, 2003. (AP Photo/Julie Jacobson.)

Baby One More Time" to being videotaped attacking a photographer, shaving off her hair, and entering drug rehab. Other notorious moments include her 2000 MTV Awards performance, where she tore off a black suit to unveil a flesh-colored, skintight spandex outfit; her lip-locking kiss with **Madonna** at the MTV Awards three years later; partying without underwear; driving with her infant son on her lap; and engaging in troubled relationships with Justin Timberlake and Kevin Federline (the father of her sons), whom she married and later divorced.

Paris Hilton is the heiress to the Hilton Hotel fortune, with an expected inheritance of $30–50 million. The ultimate "famous for being famous" celebrity, Paris began appearing in gossip columns as a socialite in 2001 and earned the title of "New York's Leading It Girl." With her trademark expression "That's hot" and her eyes provocatively always half-closed, Paris is a tabloid favorite. She is also an actress in the reality television program *The Simple Life*, in which she and Nicole Richie play two city girls trying to make it in small rural towns, and she released a pop/reggae album titled *Paris* in 2006. In addition to misdemeanor charges for driving under the influence and **Web site** videos of her spewing racial slurs, Paris Hilton's "bad girl" title was forever etched into our culture with her infamous Internet sex video, which caused a downloading frenzy in 2003. In 2007, due to her repeatedly driving without a license, she was sentenced to a short time in jail.

Born in New York, **Lindsay Lohan** began modeling at 3 years of age and established herself as a child actress in the television soap opera *Another World*. She made her film debut in 1998 in *The Parent Trap*, and as an adult actress, her popularity climbed with the 2004 film *Mean Girls*. Like the other two celebrity "bad girls," she stepped into the music business, releasing her first album, *Speak*, in December 2004 and her second album, *A Little More Personal (Raw)*, in December 2005. Her party girl image is fueled by frequent tabloid photographs of her clubbing. Lindsay's "bad girl" claims to fame include paparazzi skirmishes, three car crashes in 2005, dramatic weight loss, and her father's jail stint for fraud and attempted assault. In 2007 she was admitted to rehabilitation for drugs.

Although Britney Spears, Paris Hilton, and Lindsay Lohan are examples of contemporary "bad girls," they are by no means the first. For example, **Courtney Love, Drew Barrymore**, Madonna, Marilyn Monroe, and Mae West, to name a few, may also be considered celebrity "bad girls." Paris Hilton recently garnered the unflattering title of Most Overrated Celebrity in the 2007 *Guinness Book of World Records*. As these young women age and the popular media moves on to new targets, there will be new celebrities that assume the roles of "bad girls."

Further Reading

Brooks, Carol. (2004, September 14). "What Celebrity Worship Says about Us." *USA Today*, 21A.
Gauntlett, David. (2002). "Representations of Gender Today." Chap. 4 in *Media, Gender and Identity: An Introduction*. New York: Routledge.

SANDRA CHANG-KREDL

CELL PHONES.   As an emblem of popular culture in general, and of girl culture in particular, the cellular phone has become one of the most ubiquitous items in contemporary North America. It has become both a necessary means of communication and a fashion accessory, and both of these functions are most prevalent in the social circles of young females. From films such as *Clueless* (1995) and *Material Girls* (2006) to celebrities like **Paris Hilton**, the cell phone functions on many levels, both literal and symbolic. Its cost and design, as well as when and how it is used, send important messages about a girl's identity and her place in the social order.

Cell Phones in Girl Culture: Communication Meets Fashion. If the primary symbol of teenage autonomy and status in the twentieth century was the car, in the twenty-first century it appears to be the cell phone. Although it was initially a symbol of wealth, largely associated with male business executives, the cell phone is now synonymous with contemporary youth culture. It is the primary means of communication between teenage girls, allowing them to be reachable anywhere and anytime. The ability to remain constantly "in the know" is also advanced by other forms of digital literacy that the cell phone inspires, such as text messaging and camera phone practices. Along with **social networking Web sites** like **MySpace** and Facebook, the cell phone—providing the option to have a conversation, send instant messages, and take pictures—has become an integral tool in facilitating a new form of virtual communication.

However, the cell phone does not only keep girls in touch; it also is a primary indicator of social status. Girls may take their cues about the importance of having a cell phone from such celebrities as Paris Hilton, who is almost always talking on her cell phone. In fact, it can be argued that in popular girl culture, the cell phone has come to upstage the fashion status of the handbag. By being constantly "connected," Paris and other celebrities demonstrate that they are popular and in demand, their ears and eyes always on what is current. Whether they actually use the phone or whether it operates as a prop, the cell phone remains a highly charged symbol of fashion and social status.

Many young women become attached to their individual phones, customizing them with faceplates and stickers that reflect a girl's interests, hobbies, favorite clothing brands, and so on. This customization further transforms the cell phone from a convenient communication device into a social and cultural object. The cell phone operates as an extension of the user's body, identity, lifestyle, and social groups. Telecommunications companies have been quick to seize on this trend within the burgeoning market of female teenagers. Phones are often branded and marketed as gendered through gimmicks such as pink faceplates on "slim" handsets. Often they will include functions such as calorie counters rather than calculators, and such gimmicks have inspired a great deal of debate about conservative gender stereotyping within advertising and the popular media (particularly television and **magazines**).

The "Where" and "When" of Cell Phone Use. While cell phone etiquette and patterns of use are informed by many factors—such as class, age, and cultural context—gender is undoubtedly fundamental among them. Many adolescent females conspicuously perform their conversations in public or text-message friends and view photos on public transportation or while waiting in lines. Many also view the cell phone as a security device; this is particularly the case when females are alone at night or in unfamiliar situations.

Cell Phone Dependence. Many girls' relationships to their cell phones are paradoxical. While cell phones provide freedom and mobility, particularly for teens who are trying to assert their autonomy, they can also become a "leash," to the extent that users feel compelled to answer them anywhere, anytime. Popular culture (especially Hollywood films) provides many examples of cell phones as both a vehicle for independence and dependence in girl culture. For example, in the film *Clueless*, the main character, Cher (played by Alicia Silverstone), is an independent and assertive Beverly Hills teenager, whose cell phone affords her autonomy in the forms of both physical and social mobility. However, this accessory, which rarely leaves her sight, also reflects her identity as an up-and-coming Beverly Hills socialite. Her excessive reliance on her cell phone is arguably a playful way for the directors to poke fun at the ubiquity of the cell phone in contemporary girl culture; however, it is also essential to the audience's understanding of what "type" of girl is being profiled in Cher's character. Incessantly talking to her best friend on her cell phone (even while they are in the same room), Cher would not be the same character without this ever-present accessory.

The pervasiveness of cell phones in contemporary culture, and the unrelenting enthusiasm for them among young females, has attracted much criticism. There are those who argue that cell phones represent a radical kind of individualism that can lead to the destruction of community values. Others believe that cell phones are introducing an element of instability in girls' lives in exchange for increased connectivity. One of the most passionate ongoing debates in regard to cell phones is the use of such technologies by minors. This relatively new debate represents a variation on previous debates concerning inappropriate or excessive television or video game use by children and adolescents. Many believe that cell phones are inappropriate for young users, who may take advantage of the freedom to communicate with friends at all times of day and night. Parents of some **tweens** and teens may also fear having to contend with their children's irrepressible need to be constantly connected to their friends.

Cell phone culture represents many forms of mobility—geographic, social, cultural, and economic. It is a complex consumer symbol, representing both a desire for independence and for community. The cell phone also shifts girls' and women's relationship to the once predominantly male terrain of technology, as it grows from a simple tool of communication into a comprehensive multimedia device—including an MP3 player, video and still camera, and Internet portal. More and more, technological spaces such as the Internet (which can increasingly be accessed by cell phones) are no longer just places to access information but sites for socializing and building relationships or communities.

Indeed, the transformation of the cell phone from a simple communication tool to a multimedia gateway has enabled young women to become active consumers and producers of mobile content. Consumer and producer have merged to become the "prosumer," who participates in both the give and take of online interactivity. As the twenty-first century unfolds, virtual spaces governed by prosumer practices continue to increase, led in no small part by girls and young women on their cell phones.

See also Web 2.0

Further Reading

Agar, Jon. (2003). *Constant Touch: A Global History of the Mobile Phone.* Cambridge, UK: Icon Books.

Castells, Manuel, Mireia Fernandez-Ardevol, Jack Linchuan Qiu, and Araba Sey. (2006). *Mobile Communication and Society: A Global Perspective.* Cambridge, MA: MIT Press.

Fortunati, Leopoldina, James E. Katz, and Raimonda Riccini, eds. (2003). *Mediating the Human Body: Technology, Communication, and Fashion.* Mahwah, NJ: Lawrence Erlbaum.

Glotz, Peter, Stefan Bertschi, and Chris Locke, eds. *Thumb Culture: The Meaning of Mobile Phones in Society.* Bielefeld, Germany: Transcript Verlag.

Katz, James. E., and Satomi Sugiyama. (2005). "Mobile Phones as Fashion Statements: The Co-creation of Mobile Communication's Public Meaning." In Rich Ling and Per E. Pedersen, eds. *Mobile Communications: Re-negotiation of the Social Sphere.* London, UK: Springer, pp. 63–81.

LARISSA HJORTH

CHARLIE'S ANGELS. *Charlie's Angels* began as a television series featuring three beautiful women who worked as crime-fighting private investigators. The show is particularly relevant to girl culture for its depiction of young women who are smart, sexy, and "taking action" as investigators, but it is also notable for the strong fan following of the "Angels" themselves. *Charlie's Angels* was the first show to ever cause such a craze over its stars, who were featured on the cover of *Time* magazine, accompanied by an article analyzing the impact of the show on popular culture.

The original television show aired on ABC from 1976 to 1981. The basic story line for the series is organized around the various Angels, who work for the Charles Townsend Agency. In each episode, Charlie calls his agency to give the Angels a new assignment. Charlie is never seen and communicates with them through telephone calls and his personal assistant, John Bosley. In these assignments, the girls go undercover; they assume new identities and use their charm, sexual wiles, and intelligence to solve various cases.

The cast changed numerous times during the duration of the show, as actresses left to pursue other acting or modeling jobs. However, for most of the show, Jaclyn Smith played Kelly Garrett, departing in 1979. Kate Jackson played the role of Sabrina Duncan until 1978, and Farrah Fawcett played Jill Munroe from 1977 to 1981. In supporting roles, Cheryl Ladd played Jill's sister, Kris Munroe, from 1979 to 1980; Shelley Hack played Tiffany Welles from 1979 to 1980; and from 1980 to 1981, Tanya Roberts was Julie Rogers.

As the original Angels, Jackson, Fawcett, and Smith generated an explosion of press coverage for the show. Over time, the show became known for the scantily clad attire that the Angels wore on their various stakeouts. As part of their job, the women would go undercover as **beauty pageant** contestants, maids, prisoners, roller girls, or **bikini**-clad beachgoers. By showcasing the characters' physiques, the show's ratings remained high. The Angels are also recognizable as silhouetted figures in fighting positions, an image that served as the show's logo.

Several television series were created as offshoots of *Charlie's Angels*, including *Angels '89*, a Telemundo version known as *Angeles*, and a German version (*Wilde Engel*) as well as a French version (*Anges de choc*). However, it was the two movie versions of the show that brought the Angels back to mainstream culture.

In 2000 **Drew Barrymore**'s film production company, Flower Films, produced *Charlie's Angels*. The director of the movie was McG, a director of music videos who went on to become an executive producer of *The O.C.* The stars of the movie included Cameron Diaz as Natalie Cook, Drew Barrymore as Dylan Sanders, and Lucy Liu as Alex Munday. The emphasis on the Angels' bodies remained, but in the movie the Angels engaged more physically and violently with their enemies. In the wake of the movie's commercial success, *Charlie's Angels: Full Throttle* was released three years later. The sequel featured Diaz, Barrymore, and Liu once again but introduced Demi Moore as a "fallen" Angel.

See also Nancy Drew

Further Reading

Inness, Sherrie A., ed. (2004). *Action Chicks: New Images of Tough Women in Popular Culture.* London: Palgrave Macmillan.

CYNTHIA NICHOLS

CHEERLEADING.   Cheerleading as an organized activity began from college sports fans chanting as a group for their teams. Combining loud cheers and physical movements inspired by dance and gymnastics, cheerleading is typically associated with American girls and **sports** events. There are currently 3.8 million American participants in the sport, 97 percent of whom are female.

Until the 1940s cheerleaders were primarily male, and the men who cheered were seen as embodying the best traits of masculinity. When men left high schools and colleges to fight during World War II, females took over the cheerleading squads. By the 1950s, particularly at the high school level, cheerleading had become the realm of teenage girls, and cheerleaders were often referred to as the "all-American good girls." With the feminization of cheerleading came a new kind of sexualization of the activity. This became particularly evident in 1972, when the Dallas Cowboys Cheerleaders became the first professional cheerleading squad. With performances more akin to those of Las Vegas show girls, the Dallas Cowboys Cheerleaders epitomized a standard male fantasy—the sexy and wholesome good girl.

Into the 1980s, cheerleading squads performed mostly for the benefit of male sports teams. However, in the 1990s competitive cheerleading was introduced. These squads, often called All Star squads, compete against one another in state, regional, national, and international championships. Typically sponsored by local gyms, they vie for prizes that include trophies, jackets, awards, and money. This remains the fastest-growing segment of cheerleading.

Cheerleaders are now considered athletes and participate in physical conditioning and grueling practices. Many state high school athletic associations acknowledge cheerleading as a

College cheerleaders prepare before a football game. (Courtesy of Shutterstock.)

sport. In 2003 the University of Maryland became the first university to recognize competitive cheerleading as a sport under Title IX. It is interesting to note that as participants in this sport, cheerleaders suffer more injuries than do female volleyball, soccer, softball, or basketball players. From 1982 to 2000, cheerleading accounted for 56.8 percent of the total number of catastrophic injuries to high school and collegiate female athletes.

Many girls are drawn to cheerleading because it provides a way to simultaneously be athletic and feminine: cheerleaders by necessity are muscular and strong, and they are frequently competitive and daring, but they are also highly sexualized. With cheerleading uniforms typically consisting of short skirts or shorts and **midriff tops**, the activity is a way to allow eroticism into places such as middle and high schools, which typically prohibit sexuality. Girls who cheer are able to simultaneously embody the identity of the all-American ideal girl and the sexually provocative heterosexual woman. Unlike girls who play football, basketball, or rugby, cheerleaders do not appreciably disrupt American society's preconceived notions of a girl's athletic capability.

See also Compulsory Heterosexuality; Girl Power; Girls and Sport in Contemporary Film; Nice

Further Reading

Adams, Natalie, and Pamela Bettis. (2003). *Cheerleader! An American Icon.* New York: Palgrave Macmillan.

————. (2003). "Commanding the Room in Short Skirts: Cheering as the Embodiment of Ideal Girlhood." *Gender & Society* 17, 73–91.

————. (2006). "Liberties and Lipstick: The Paradox of Cheerleading as a Sport." In Brian Lampman and Sandra Spickard-Prettyman, eds. *Learning Culture through Sports: Exploring the Role of Sports in Society*. Lanham, MD: Rowman & Littlefield Education, pp. 66–74.

NATALIE ADAMS AND PAMELA BETTIS

CHERRY AMES.   *Cherry Ames* is the name of a Stratemeyer syndicate book series with a protagonist by the same name. It was launched in 1943. At that time, it was one of several series for girls that featured a young female nurse and was based in part on an actual government project called the Cadet Nurse Corp, a program intended to recruit girls into nursing during World War II. The *Cherry Ames* series was comprised of twenty-seven books and continued until 1968. Perky, smart, adventurous, and astute, Ames poses as one of the early role models for girls indicating they can have a life that includes independence, glamour, and a career.

In the series, Cherry starts as a student nurse and then completes her training and joins the Cadet Nurse Corp. During her time overseas, she is promoted to Chief Nurse. Whereas most of the other nurses marry when the war ends, Cherry carries on without an enduring boyfriend. Ames is allowed a transition that many postwar women were not: the ability to keep working and not be forced back into the home. The story line then shifts and has her working as a traveling nurse-detective until the end of the series.

The *Cherry Ames* books were published for younger audiences, in part as a response to the growing number of other nurse series books, which included *Sue Barton, Nancy Naylor, Ann Bartlett, Penny Marsh,* and *Susan Merton.* Although it was not the first of these book series to appear on the market, *Cherry Ames* was the longest running. During the war years, the books were immensely popular, inspiring girls everywhere to serve their country in the name of freedom and reassuring them that all would be well if only they pitched in to help.

The creator of the first eight books was Helen Wells (born Helen Weinstock), who began her career as a social worker and then shifted to writing. She also penned the first three books in the *Vicki Barr* series, as well as a series called *Polly French,* which she published under the name Francine Lewis. Wells wrote other books for young people that were not series oriented. She quit writing the *Ames* series for a short period of time to try her hand at radio and television, leaving Julie Tatham to author at least six of the books. Tatham, too, wrote some of the *Vicki Barr* books, as well as some of the **Trixie Belden** and the **Ginny Gordon** series under her maiden name, Julie Campbell.

Writing for the *Ames* series after World War II, Tatham was at least partially responsible for moving the young nurse from the war zone into the role of traveling nurse-detective. She also gave her only a peripheral romantic life. While most of the protagonists in the other nurse series of the era marry when the war ends, Cherry remains single. The last *Cherry Ames* book Tatham wrote was *Country Doctor's Nurse.* In 1955 Wells resumed writing to finish out the series. She died in 1986. Tatham died in 1999.

Cherry Ames offered patriotism, adventure, and a bit of romance, all rolled into one. From war nurse to visiting nurse to sleuth nurse, she never lost her loyal following. Many a grown woman credits *Cherry Ames* with the decision to pursue nursing. In 2005, Springer Publishing reissued the first four books in the series. With the reissues, it seems she is on her way to impacting yet another generation.

See also Nancy Drew; Series Fiction

Further Reading

Authors and Books for Children. (2001). *Patriotism and Propaganda in Girls' Series: Fictional Nurses of World War II*. [Online February 2007]. Authors and Books for Children Web site http://www.elliemik.com/warnurses.html.

Mason, Bobbie Ann. (1995). *The Girl Sleuth: On the Trail of Nancy Drew, Judy Bolton, and Cherry Ames*. Athens: University of Georgia Press.

ELAINE J. O'QUINN

CHICK LIT.   Chick lit, loosely defined as a genre of popular fiction by, for, and about young women in the United States and the UK, can be hilarious, fanciful, and heart-breaking. "Chick lit" is usually associated with two icons of mid-1990s postfeminist girls' and young women's culture: Bridget Jones, the heroine of Helen Fielding's book *Bridget Jones's Diary* (1996), and Carrie Bradshaw, the main character of *Sex and the City* (1997), by Candace Bushnell. These heroines, despite surface differences, possess a number of similarities. Carrie Bradshaw is a popular downtown "scenester" who sets fashion trends in Manhattan, while Bridget Jones is more of an outsider who seeks invitations to glamorous galas while regrettably obliging bulge-control girdles in London. Yet both are loveable and reassuringly fallible 30-something professionals who spend more time on their personal upkeep than they do on traditional domestic upkeep. With a circle of female and gay male friends, cads and duds for dates, wicked bosses, and tender but daffy families, they both struggle to stay on top of their own unrelenting self-improvement regimens while operating under the pressures of a harsh world that just will not let up on them. These two "chicks" quickly became household names for chick lit by way of movie and television screens: the film *Bridget Jones's Diary* (2001) and the sequel, *Bridget Jones: Edge of Reason* (2004), starring Renée Zellweger, and *Sex and the City*, which aired on HBO from 1998 to 2004 and starred Sarah Jessica Parker. As Bridget and Carrie stepped off the page and onto the red carpet of cross-media success, chick lit expanded into an entire chick lit culture.

Chick Lit and Postfeminism: Contemporary Chick Lit. Today, many heroines of fiction and film seem to be modeled after these two original chicks. For example, the heroine of *Velvet Rope Diaries* (2006) by Danielle Brodsky is described on Amazon.com as a young, single woman living in a big city and working for a magazine with a female ogre for a boss. While there are differences between the characters and plots of chick lit, there is a certain formulaic quality to all of the books that invites the unflattering comparison to industrial mass production. "No doubt about it, publishers and filmmakers have identified a profitable audience for confessional-style stories among girls both growing and grown-up, and they're getting their products out before this trend, too, shall pass," writes Lauren Adams in "Chick Lit and Chick Flicks: Secret Power or Flat Formula?" (2004, p. 669). The distinctive appearance of chick lit's **pink** paperback covers and cursive titles defines it as a type of romance for women. "Since the mid-'90s, when Candace Bushnell and Helen Fielding wrote *Sex and the City* and *Bridget Jones's Diary*, millions of copies of chick-lit novels have come to represent a new force in publishing," writes Jami Attenberg online, in "A Girl's Guide to Writing and Publishing." "With the classics came a slew of imitators, some very well-written and enjoyable, and most formulaic: Girl meets two guys, one right and one wrong, and takes 300 pages to choose between them while introducing the sarcastic (often gay) friend, the wise (often dying) elder, and trouble at an unsatisfying job—all before delivering a happy, and the-oretically empowering, ending involving l-o-v-e."

Chick lit and chick lit flicks can be seen as narratives organizing young women after the so-called death of feminism. These not-so-fairy tales mostly feature savvy and stylish single, white females in their 20s and 30s, whose tribulations and elations lead them toward greater self-awareness and self-fulfillment. Often the anachronistic (and embar-rassingly hopeless) search for Prince Charming is translated to bargain hunting for a per-fect pair of shoes: Cinderella's glass slippers get updated as Jimmy Choo strappy sandals! Chick lit is contemporaneous with the rising number of educated, single, and professional young women in both the United States and the UK. And, in often silly and raunchy descriptions, many passages detail shifting sexual mores about dating, relationships, marriage, family, and the prospect of having children. In the pages of chick lit novels, ideas about femininity, sexuality, the perceived impact of feminism on mainstream society and women's lives, the strength of the tourism and fashion indus-tries in national economies, and the process and effects of globalization—such as global mass media—are engaged and responded to. On one level of analysis, chick lit manifests antiquated queries of what women should do, want, think, read, buy, and wear in order to be happy, healthy, and hip. On another level, chick lit seems to be a barometer for social, cultural, political, and economic issues that concern young women.

In most chick lit novels, where one starts out is not as important as where one intends to go, regardless of whether or not by the end of the book she actually arrives. Chick lit's origins are just as unconventional. Although critics typically credit Field-ing's novel with starting the chick lit craze, the original collection of short stories came out the previous year, in 1995, by editors Chris Mazza and Jeffrey DeShell—*Chick Lit: Postfeminist Fiction*. The experimental fiction in this collection flirts with surrealism and has themes of violence, psychosis, and perversion. Irked at getting passed over in the historiography of this still relatively young genre, Mazza, in "Who's Laughing Now? A Short History of Chick Lit and the Perversion of a Genre," explains why they chose "chick lit" and "postfeminism" for their title: "This was the ironic inten-tion of our title: not to embrace an old frivolous or coquettish image of women but to take responsibility for our part in the damaging, lingering stereotype" (2005, p. 18). A genealogy of the genre, then, will remind fans of its current incarnation as sexy-and-single-girls-in-the-city-looking-for-love-and-a-sample-sale that chick lit is neither monolithic nor vacuous.

Chick Lit and Pride and Prejudice: Early Chick Lit. Chick lit today is an amalgam of **coming-of-age memoirs** and stories, fairy tales, the traditional novel of manners, and, of course, romance novels. Chick lit has deep roots in American and British literature. The most immediate antecedents are autobiographical novels by young women in the 1960s and 1970s. Betty Friedan's *The Feminine Mystique*, Jacqueline Susann's *Valley of the Dolls*, Marilyn French's *The Women's Room*, Erica Jong's *Fear of Flying*, and Helen Gurley Brown's *Sex and the Single Girl* all helped to popularize feminist politics and foment the women's movement through fiction and frank discussions of femininity and sexuality. In fact, the introduction to a new edition of Sue Kaufman's *Diary of a Mad Housewife* (originally published in 1967), complete with a new pink cover and cursive lettering, claims that it "anticipated Chick Lit and its simple, uninhibited style and paved the way for future generations of relentless confessors, from Bridget Jones and the ladies of *Sex and the City*" (p. vi). Like their second-wave feminist predecessors, and behind all the exaltations of shopping, chick lit often addresses rape, family violence, and infertility.

Reaching farther back to somewhere between Jackie Collins and Jane Austen, chick lit is about today's young women. "Some writers and reviewers see Austen as the founder of chick lit, which in its best sense is literature written for women that shows women fulfilling themselves like Elizabeth, Emma, Elinor, and other Austen heroines do," writes former Jane Austen Society of North America president Joan Elizabeth Kingel Ray in the book *Jane Austen for Dummies* (2006, 291). Austen's Elizabeth, Emma, and Elinor share many of the same frustrations and anxieties as Fielding's Bridget and Bushnell's Carrie. Fielding readily admits that her book was inspired by Austen's *Pride and Prejudice*, and there are a number of references to Austen in *Bridget Jones's Diary*. For instance, the surname of the male hero in each novel is Darcy; Bridget works for Pemberley Press (the name of Darcy's estate in *Pride and Prejudice*); and Fielding's second novel, *Edge of Reason*, loosely parallels Austen's *Persuasion* (1816). Interestingly, all four novels were made into popular films in 2001 and 2004, and a number of actors—notably, Colin Firth—have appeared in both the television series and movies made from Austen's and Fielding's books. Amusingly, Austen's works are now reprinted and periodized as chick lit. *Flirting with Pride & Prejudice: Fresh Perspectives on the Original Chick-Lit Masterpiece*, by Jennifer Cruise (2005), also posits Austen as the mother of chick lit.

Writing about My Generation: Sense, Sensibility, and Sarcasm. The term "chick lit" is derived from the reclaimed slang word "chick" for a young woman and "lit" which is short for literature. (It is rumored that the term also nostalgically refers to the gum brand Chiclets, which this generation of young women writers would have been familiar with as girls.) This playful refashioning of outdated language and bygone cultural artifacts indicates an irreverent attitude toward the authority of the traditional literary canon and dominant culture in general. The light pink and hot pink covers of *The Guy I'm Not Dating* by Trish Perry (2006), *The Botox Diaries* (2005) by Lynn Schnurnberger and Janice Kaplan, and *Can You Keep a Secret?* by Sophie Kinsella (2005)—all with illustrations of high-heeled shoes or little handbags—are typical of this gender and age play. The color pink, the nearly universal color of Girl Power, is one way chick lit is seen as a brand itself. Chick lit emerged amid two powerful and mutually productive forces in the mid-1990s: the top-down marketing behemoth of **Girl Power** and the bottom-up desire of young women writers to tell and sell stories about young women while they themselves worked for publishing giants.

At the crossroads of girls' and women's culture, or possibly one reason for the collapse of any distinction between the two, chick lit is often criticized for its representation of girl-ified grown women. And chick lit is a product of Girl Power. Girl Power has been widely criticized for commercializing women's individuality and liberation as purchasing power while diminishing the need for broad-based social change to legally improve all women's lives (McRobbie 2004). In addition to showing young women working in mainstream media, like glossy magazines devoted to the fashion and beauty industries, chick lit constitutes young women's relationship to consumer culture in general. In many novels, descriptions of shopping sprees often include high-end designer labels such as Prada, Dolce & Gabbana, and Manolo Blahnik. These designers put the "chic" in chick lit, but the references could also be seen as product placement in the novels. And the Girl-Powered protagonists of chick lit often work on themselves (sometimes more than on their real jobs).

The "Shopaholic" series by Sophie Kinsella, including *Confessions of a Shopaholic* (2001), *Shopaholic Takes Manhattan* (2002), and *Shopaholic Ties the Knot* (2003), features the ironic situation of the main character, Becky Bloomwood, who is burdened with credit card debt as a compulsive shopper but has her own financial advice TV show. As a result, many have criticized chick lit for its overt commodification of girl culture.

"Perhaps the most insidious paradox of the new women's culture—from the Oxygen Network to *Bridget Jones's Diary* . . . is that its purveyors can make lots of money from women and simultaneously claim to be doing it for women's own good," writes Francine Prose in her scathing critique of the new Girl Power culture. "It is like having a best friend with her hand in your pocket" (2000, p. 66)

A case of (pop) art imitating life, chick lit also grew from young women writers' experiences working inside the profit-driven world of commercial media conglomerates, which are largely male owned but often woman dominated. By the late 1990s, Madison Avenue had become the new Wall Street for a generation of ambitious working girls. Lauren Wiesberger, who wrote *The Devil Wears Prada* (2006) and worked for Anna Wintour at *Glamour*, and Birdie Clarke, who wrote *Because She Can* (2007) and worked for Judith Regan at Regan Publishing, say they based the fictional editors Miranda Priestly and Vivian Grant in part on their real-life experiences working under duress for demanding bosses. Many protagonists of chick lit are columnists, publishing assistants, and aspiring journalists who become the pretty faces of the publishing houses, PR firms, and film distributors that produce them. As young urban women climbing the ranks of mass media companies, they aspire to smash the workplace glass ceiling, which is often, dishearteningly, upheld by older women bosses who assume the role of the wicked witches of the East Coast publishing world. After seeing the film *The Devil Wears Prada*, ex–*Harper's Bazaar* assistant Ali MacGraw called it "a documentary" (Reed 2006, p. 17). The generational issues in chick lit, from the viewpoint of the young protagonists, make a statement about the hypocrisy of the supposed sisterhood of women's personal and professional worlds.

Our Chick Lit/Ourselves: The Personal Is Popular Culture. With chick lit, to reformulate a 1970s political slogan, "the personal is popular cultural." Chick lit engages with and responds to the many contradictions and tensions between contemporary society and young women's lives. For example, Carrie Bradshaw's column "Sex and the City" in the fictional *New York Star* is the product of her personal and professional quest to assess contemporary cultural and sexual norms for young women in Manhattan; it is based on Bushnell's own columns for the *New York Observer* about the Big Apple's dating scene. Having grown up with *Tiger Beat* and **Sassy** before it was disbanded, grown-up writers and readers of chick lit might now read feminist independent media like *Bitch* or *Ms.* magazines while contradictorily embracing *Glamour* and *Cosmopolitan*. At the same time, publishers bank on women's identification with female protagonists in an era when identity politics and social movements are considered passé and unhip and as consumers are encouraged to alleviate what ails them with retail therapy.

"In pondering friendship with an ex or how many sexual partners is too many, the 'question of the week' device represents the desires and attempts of many real-life contemporary women to investigate the mysteries of modern sexual relationship and gender roles on their own terms and to determine their place within these relationships for themselves," writes A. Rochelle Mabry in her contribution "About a Girl" in *Chick Lit: The New Woman's Fiction*, the first academic collection about chick lit (Ferriss and Young 2006, pp. 199–200).

One of the ways chick lit blends the personal with popular culture is by both reflecting and re-creating sexual mores. "So where are we now, we post-hippie, Hip-Hop, shop-till-the-sale-stops young women who have been raised in this era of chick lit and third-wave feminism?" asks J. Love Calderon, co-editor of *We Got Issues! A Young Women's Guide to a Bold, Courageous, and Empowered Life*. "We've witnessed Ellen coming out on national TV and the government denouncing same-sex marriage. We've experienced the rise of raunch culture and its icons, like Paris Hilton. Cake sex parties—which bill themselves as 'feminism in action'—Internet porn, and live sex podcasting invite our generation's answer to the question: What does sexual liberation really look like?" (Goddess and Calderon 2006, p. 81).

Chick lit answers a number of questions surrounding the status of single women. For example, it has produced a new sexual vernacular, including the terms "singletons" and "smug marrieds" from *Bridget Jones's Diary*, which are used to describe the darned-if-I-say-I-do-and-darned-if-you-don't-propose conundrum of marriage prospects.

Most of the discourse about sex and sexuality in chick lit, however, fails to account for the range of novels and characters, and their social status vis-à-vis race, class, and citizenship. Although he praises some chick lit, like *Girls' Guide to Hunting and Fishing* by Melissa Bank (1999) and *Run Catch Kiss* by Amy Sohn (2000), for refusing to end "happily ever after" with a walk off into the sunset and the faint chimes of wedding bells, Andi Zeisler says other chick lit, like *Bridget Jones's Diary* and its "marketing hoodoo," offer a uniform conception of singleness as a lonely and desperate road "paved with empty bottles of gin and Slim-Fast" (Jervis and Zeisler 2006, p. 297).

To be sure, chick lit has shaken up the public discussion of young women's sexuality. Yet, often these debates about young women's desires and pleasures come at the expense of not noticing how such sexual freedom requires white privilege, class privilege, and a certain mobility and absence of physical bounds in a hypersexual, urban landscape where potential partners abound. In "Sistahs Are Doin' It for Themselves," Lisa A. Guerrero compares chick lit for white women with chick lit for black women: "Chicks are looking for love, because as white women they have been taught to believe in their preciousness, and the fact that they should be loved, even worshipped. . . . Having grown comfortable with the privileges these 'truths' provide, chicks seem to be seeking actualization of these promises" (Ferriss and Young 2006, p. 92).

Is Girls' Stuff Fluff? The Chick Lit Debates. To some onlookers it is amusing that something so pink (i.e., seemingly innocent) can be so controversial. First, chick lit seems to take the debates over women and writing to a new historic level. From Nathaniel Hawthorne's sexist screed about "the damned mob of scribbling women" to Virginia Woolf's seething proposal of a "room of one's own" as a requirement for women writers, women who have put pen to paper have always caused controversy. "At the bookstore it's chick lit versus regular ol' fiction," notes Lisa Jervis. "This is just one of the many cultural hangovers of the age-old notion that the concerns of mankind are universal but stories about women are just, you know, about women" (Jervis and Zeisler 2006, p. 50). Next, even though there has not yet been any qualitative study of chick lit readers for an assessment of what they think about the importance of chick lit in their lives and in the culture at large, the wide-ranging opinions of chick lit are increasingly publicized in print and online book reviews, news articles, and **blogs** and personal **Web sites**.

Literary scholars have name-called chick lit as "literature lite," and feminists have criticized the diminutive girlie representations of grown women. But others have responded that it is as empowering as it is entertaining. Maureen Dowd's criticism of chick lit inspired a downright chick lit catfight between the famous columnist and chick lit authors. "If imitation is the sincerest form of flattery, animosity is a close second," writes chick lit author Kyra Davis in response to Dowd on a blog called Beatrice.com. Jennifer Weiner posted this response to Dowd on February 12, 2007, on her own blog, Snarkspot: "Critics like Dowd deride and dismiss it, but it is undeniable that chick lit is important as a media phenomenon and social sensation. And judging a book by its pink cover underestimates how chick lit has unalterably changed the cultural imaginary by the end of the twentieth century."

The debates over chick lit are part of the struggle over the politics of representation, which examines media for inaccurate portrayals of women and girls and the effects of those misrepresentations on both the public at large (which already sustains sexist conceptions of females) and on the female consumers who buy, read, and enjoy chick lit. For example, Lisa Jervis, former editor of *Bitch* magazine, claims that chick lit is partly responsibility for the evacuation of feminist politics.

"Record producers, screenwriters, women's-magazine editors, chick lit publishers, and ad copywriters lift selections from movement rhetoric and use them to dress up their retrogressive pap" (Jervis and Zeisler 2006, p. 109). The question of whether chick lit is feminist or not (or postfeminist)—or whether one can be a fan of chick lit and still be a feminist, too—seems to imply a dubious dichotomy between literature that is feminist and literature that is not. Instead of asking, "Is chick lit feminist?" critics might reflect on their own investment in the opposition to a particular novel, flick, or the genre.

The titles of a number of new chick lit collections point to the increasing uncertainties over chick lit as a label for this genre. Some writers seem to scramble to have their work capitalize on this niche market, such as Lauren Baratz-Logsted's 1997 collection *This Is Chick-Lit*. One murder mystery novel, *Death by Chick Lit* by Lynn Harris (forthcoming 2007), ironically references the genre. However, other writers distance their work from what they must see as a diminutive moniker, like Elizabeth Merrick, editor of *This Is Not Chick Lit: Original Stories by America's Best Women Writers* (2006), who writes in the introduction, "Chick lit as a genre presents one very narrow representation of women's lives." In addition, Maggie Barbieri says her book *Murder 101* (2006) is "the perfect antidote to the oh-so-hip chick-lit protagonist." *The Bitch Posse* (2005) author Martha O'Connor alerts readers: "You Have Now Entered a Chick-Lit–Free Zone." Thus, these works seem to recall the authorial intent behind that original 1995 collection by Mazza and DeShell. Chick lit is full of tensions and contradictions. Collectively, disputes over chick lit may indicate instabilities in the dominant meanings of gender, sexuality, race, class, and citizenship that prop them up and make them profitable.

Conclusion. Ultimately, chick lit is more than one novel's guilty pleasure or even an entire genre's marketing campaign. Chick lit is a media empire that demands to be taken seriously. Over the past 10 years, hundreds of chick lit novels and anthologies of short stories have been published. Best-selling authors like Jennifer Wiener, Lauren Weisberger, Plum Sykes, Sophie Kinsella, and Candace Bushnell and Helen Fielding churn out multiple titles each, which are translated into many languages and sold around the world. Red Dress Ink (Harlequin), Strapless, Avon (Harper's), and Downtown Press were all created as separate imprints dedicated to the output of the genre. Sympathetic guides for becoming a media mogul include *Will Write for Shoes: How to Write a Chick Lit Novel* by Cathy

Yardley (2006) and *See Jane Write: A Girl's Guide to Writing Chick Lit*, by Sarah Mlynowski and Farrin Jacobs (2006).

The increasing number of titles has been the inspiration for news articles, magazine articles, movies, TV series, and global style trends. There are a number of personal blogs dedicated to chick lit. Major corporate booksellers' Web sites offer reader-sponsored links to "favorite lists" of chick lit to purchase. And product tie-ins are directly associated with chick lit—for example, daily tear-off calendars and self-help guides, such as *Becoming a Goddess of Inner Poise: Spirituality for the Bridget Jones in All of Us* by Donna Freita (2004), which pays homage to the original chick of chick lit.

Finally, the end of chick lit's reign might be signaled by its many new subgenres. "Latina Lit," like *Sex and the South Beach Chicas* by Caridad Pineiro (2006), and "Sistah Lit," such as *The Loves of a D-Girl: A Novel of Sex, Lies, and Script Development*, by Chris Dyer (2005), are both for women of color. "Mommy Lit," for women who disdain the term "soccer mom" and refuse to wear "mom jeans," and regional variations such as Southern chick lit—Mary Kay Andrews's *Savannah* series, for example—are also emerging on bookshelves. Christian chick lit (*The Guy I'm Not Dating* by Trish Perry, 2006), vampire chick lit (Mary Janice Davidson's *Undead* series), murder mystery chick lit (*Sex, Murder, and a Double Latte* by Kyra Davis, 2005), "suburbanista" chick lit (*Suburban Diva: From the Real Side of the Picket Fence* by Tracey Henry, 2006), and yoga chick lit, (Kimberly Wilson's 2004 *Hip Tranquil Chick: A Guide to Life on and of the Yoga Mat*) also share the marketing spotlight. The covers of these novels are not pink nor do they feature skinny white women; they feature an array of skin colors and background hues. Even Helen Fielding, in a sense transforming Bridget into Jane Bond, has turned to counterterrorism efforts with her chick lit spy novel, *Olivia Joules and the Overactive Imagination* (2005).

See also Crossover Literature; Junior Chick Flicks; Series Fiction

Further Reading

Adams, Lauren. (2004, November). "Chick Lit and Chick Flicks: Secret Power or Flat Formula?" *The Horn Book Magazine* 80, no. 6, 669–679.

Akass, Kim, and Janet McCabe, eds. (2004). *Reading* Sex and the City. London: I.B. Tauris & Co.

Attenberg, Jami. "A Girl's Guide to Writing & Publishing." [Online June 2007]. PRINT Magazine Web site http://printmag.com/design_articles/girls_guide_to_writing_and_publishing/tabid/94/Default.aspx.

Cavanaugh, Tim. (2005). "Bridget Jones, Super Spy: Chick Lit Goes to War." *Reason* 36, no. 9, 51–55.

Crusie, Jennifer. (2005). *Flirting with Pride & Prejudice: Fresh Perspectives on the Original Chick-Lit Masterpiece* (Smart Pop series). London: Benbella Books.

Davis, Kyra. (2007). *Thank you, Maureen Dowd!* [Online June 2007]. Beatrice Web site http://www.beatrice.com/archives/002044.html.

Dowd, Maureen. (2007, February 10). "Heels Over Hemingway." *New York Times*, A15.

Ferriss, Suzanne, and Mallory Young. (2006). *Chick Lit: The New Woman's Fiction*. New York: Routledge Taylor & Francis Group.

Goddess, Rha, and J. Love Calderon, eds. (2006). *We Got Issues! A Young Women's Guide to a Bold, Courageous, and Empowered Life*. Makawa, HI: Inner Ocean.

Hermes, Joke. (2005). "'Ally McBeal,' 'Sex and the City,' and the Tragic Success of Feminism." In Joanne Hollows and Rachel Moseley, eds. *Feminism in Popular Culture*. New York: Berg Press, pp. 79–95.

Jervis, Lisa, and Andi Zeisler. (2006, reprint). "Marketing Miss Right: Meet the Single Girl, Twenty-First–Century Style." In Lisa Jervis and Andi Zeisler, eds. *BITCHfest: Ten Years of Cultural Criticism from the Pages of* Bitch *Magazine.* New York: Farrar, Straus and Giroux, pp. 291–298.

Mazza, Cris. (2005, January/February). "Who's Laughing Now? A Short History of Chick Lit and the Perversion of a Genre." *Poets & Writers* 33, no.1, 31–37.

McRobbie, Angela. (2004). "Post-Feminism and Popular Culture." *Feminist Media Studies* 4, no.3, 255–264.

Negra, Diane. (2004). *Quality Postfeminism? Sex and the Single Girl on HBO.* [Online June 2007]. Genders Web site http://www.genders.org/g39/g39_negra.html.

Prose, Francine. (2000, February 13). "A Wasteland of One's Own." *New York Times,* 66.

Ray, Joan Elizabeth Kingel. (2006). *Jane Austen for Dummies.* Hoboken, NJ: Wiley.

Reed, Rex. (2006, July 2). "Devil's Delicious, Misses Hepburn." *New York Observer,* 17.

Smith, Caroline J. (2005). "Living the Life of a Domestic Goddess: Chick Lit's Response to Domestic Advice Manuals." *Women's Studies* 34, no. 8, 671–699.

Whelehan, Imelda. (2005). *The Feminist Bestseller: From* Sex and the Single Girl *to* Sex and the City. New York: Palgrave Macmillan.

Wiener, Jennifer. [Online June 2006]. Snarkspot blog. http://jenniferweiner.blogspot.com/ 2007_02_11_jenniferweiner_archive.html.

SARAH RASMUSSON

CHILDREN'S BEAUTY PAGEANTS.   Similar to adult beauty pageants, contestants in children's beauty pageants—young girls—are judged primarily on appearance. Children's beauty pageants became a subject for national discussion and concern following the 1996 murder of 6-year-old beauty queen JonBenét Ramsey. Pictures of Ramsey in competition gowns and makeup personalized the pageants for many Americans who had no previous exposure to these events. Children's beauty pageants, however, are not a recent phenomenon, but find their ancestry in nineteenth-century entertainment. From the beginning, critics have debated whether children's beauty pageants are used by parents to celebrate, entertain, and improve the children who participate in them, or to exploit them.

Early History: Beautiful Babies. Phineas T. Barnum, the founder of Barnum's Circus, held "Beautiful Baby" contests at his museum in the 1850s. Top prize for the "Most Perfect Baby" was $100, and awards were also given in the categories of triplets, fattest baby, and most handsome **twins**. In the early years of the twentieth century, increased attention to childhood and child rearing resulted in the formation of the U.S. Children's Bureau. As part of its Baby Week campaign in 1913, the Children's Bureau determined to convert "old-fashioned baby contests" into a mechanism for encouraging better health practices (Pub 1935, p. 15). In contests held all across the country, mothers brought their children in to be inspected by doctors who made recommendations and awarded prizes to the babies with the healthiest appearance. In some instances, such as the Baby Improvement Contest given by the Child Federation of Philadelphia in 1914, judging was a two-step process that took place over time, and a prize was given to the baby with the most-improved health.

Baby Contests were sponsored by various groups and commercial entities throughout the early decades of the twentieth century. The Borden Milk Company sponsored a mail-in contest in 1910 that awarded a gold locket to winners. The Mt. Beacon Incline Railway (Beacon, NY) offered $30 in prizes at a contest in 1919. Out of sixty-three entrants, a pair of twins was awarded first prize of $15 in gold. The National Association for the Advancement of Colored People (NAACP) also held contests for several years. In 1925 alone, the organization raised over $20,000 in seventy-eight cities (White 1998, p. 195).

Movie houses in the Midwest also used baby contests to boost ticket sales. Snapshots of babies were placed on slides and projected before the film, but only ticket-holders could vote. Devoted mothers would encourage all their neighbors to attend. The prizes on display in the lobby were useful household items, such as baby carriages, sewing machines, or dishes. During the Great Depression in the 1930s, the $10 prize awarded to a 5-month-old contest winner could buy groceries for her family for an entire month. The contests were enormously popular; a 1941 event sponsored by the Daughters of America in New Jersey drew over 1200 entries. Beautiful Baby contests were not, however, solely for infants or for girls. Alvah Bessie competed in a Beautiful Baby contest in 1907 when he was 5 years old, dressed as cupid with wings, bow, and arrows, and satin ballet slippers (Bessie 2000, p. 29).

In the early decades of the twentieth century, a variation of the Beautiful Baby contest format was used to promote health. In 1958, the America's Junior Miss Pageant began, as a scholarship program to recognize outstanding achievement in high school seniors. In the 1960s, children's beauty pageants emerged that fused elements of the old-fashioned Beautiful Baby contests with those of modern adult beauty pageants. These children's pageants emphasized glamour and physical attractiveness. While many commentators object to the sexualization of young girls, children's beauty pageants have become enormously popular, with hundreds of thousands of girls under age 12 participating every year in the United States.

Beauty Pageants for Girls and Young Women. The popularity of beauty contests for children was accompanied by popular adult **beauty pageants**. The Miss America Pageant was founded in 1921 in Atlantic City, and its popularity led to the creation of imitations such as the Miss Universe and Miss USA pageants, both of which focused primarily on the physical appearance of the contestants rather than the young women's talent and intelligence.

In 1958, possibly as an alternative to this approach, the America's Junior Miss pageant was instituted by the Jaycees (Junior Chambers) of Mobile, Alabama, as a scholarship program for high school seniors. The 1963 winner was Diane Sawyer, who would later become successful as a television journalist. Deborah Norville, who won a state-level pageant (Georgia, 1976), also went into a career in journalism. For many girls—such as Kim Basinger (Georgia contestant, 1971), Kathie Lee Gifford (Maryland winner, 1971), and Debra Messing (Rhode Island winner, 1986)—the award may have been a stepping-stone to an acting career. Other scholarship pageants for girls followed, including the Miss Teenage America Pageant in 1961 and the Miss Teenager Pageant 10 years later.

Pageants for younger girls emerged in the 1960s and have increased both in number and in popularity in the decades since. These contests often evoke the ethos of small-town America while copying the glamour and sexuality of adult pageants. The Miss Hemisphere Pageant, for instance, was established in 1963 for contestants age 3 years and up. The children were judged on beauty, charm, poise, and personality. Children's pageants proved as popular as the Baby Contest had decades earlier but were far more profitable. Hundreds of new pageants were created, with names ranging from Miss Catfish

Queen and Miss Baby Poultry Princess to Miss American Beauty Queen of Hearts and Miss American Starlet Fashion Model.

To increase participation, organizers expanded age divisions and categories of competition. For example, contestants in the Miss Hemisphere contest enter one of three divisions: Baby, Children, or Teen and Adult. Similarly, the Cinderella pageant, founded in 1976, created separate competitions for children based on age. Previously established adult competitions began opening children's divisions to capitalize on the trend. In addition to age divisions, pageants increased in revenue by offering different categories of competition, such as Partywear Modeling, Photogenic, and Talent, typically including vocal, dance, baton, gymnastics, theatrical, and instrumental activities.

Pageants were founded in all parts of the United States, with the majority in California, New York, and the Southern states. While some pageants are strictly local events, many others are organized for winning contestants to move up through local, state, and national tiers. Estimates of the number of children's pageants hover at about 3,000 per year, and they involve more than 100,000 contestants.

The Pageant Industry: Profit, Murder, and Controversy. Children's beauty pageants are supported both by corporate sponsors and by the families of the contestants, who together have made it a billion-dollar industry. The costs of participating tend to discourage those who are not affluent or at least middle-class. Contestants are generally charged an entrance fee, which can be as high as $175, with additional fees charged for each event or category in which they wish to compete. Families also sustain the many businesses that support the industry, including large-circulation pageant **magazines**, pageant jewelry, pageant journals, custom-made costumes, talent coaches, interview coaches, photographers, hair stylists, and makeup consultants. Promoters can make up to $100,000 per event.

National attention was drawn to the children's pageant industry in 1996 when 6-year-old JonBenét Ramsey was found murdered in her home in Boulder, Colorado. Television news stories showed film clips of dozens of pageant appearances by the little girl, who had won titles as National Tiny Miss Beauty, Little Miss Colorado, and America's Little Royal Miss, and whose mother was a former Miss West Virginia. Audiences watching the news of her murder were shocked to see the paraphernalia of the pageant circuit on her tiny body: fashion-model makeup, red **lipstick**, heavily mascaraed eyes, high heels, tight or off-the-shoulder dresses, and sophisticated, upswept hair.

In thousands of news stories, editorials, and documentaries, an examination of the world of children's beauty pageants almost eclipsed national interest in the murder, which remains unsolved. Most commentators focused on the premature sexualization and commodification of young girls as objects of an adult (and especially a male) gaze. Many labeled the pageants as inappropriate and near pornographic. Psychologists lectured that popular culture's beauty aesthetic was demeaning and harmful to young girls; news reports revealed intense, sometimes grueling preparations and contest procedures as children like JonBenét traveled each and every weekend to distant pageant locations. Through all of this, commentators questioned whether parents who started their children on the pageant circuit at very young ages were not vicariously pursuing their own ambitions or driving their children unreasonably.

Families involved in pageants defend the events as positive experiences in which their children learn social skills, gain self-confidence, and sometimes have opportunities to move into acting or modeling careers. However, prizes are also a motivating factor. While some pageants award only tiaras or certificates, others bestow cash prizes—a successful 6-year-old can accumulate enough winnings to pay for a college education. Parents insist that children participate of their own volition in what are generally wholesome community events, and the notoriety of the JonBenét Ramsay case did not seem to diminish the popularity of children's beauty pageants throughout America.

Innocence. The concept of **innocence** is central to the continuing debate over the value of children's beauty pageants. Some believe that the glamorous style required by many contests violates a child's naturally innocent nature, whereas others believe pageants to be harmless traditional rituals. Historians of childhood recognize that the idea of childhood innocence is itself a product of history, "primarily applied to children who are white and middle class" and upheld by "commercial and ideological structures within the broader society" (Giroux 1998, p. 35). Indeed, until the eighteenth century, children were primarily seen as potential contributors to the family by helping with chores, or as laborers and wage earners. Gradually this notion was replaced by a more romantic view of the child as naturally innocent, asexual, and fit only for protection and nurturing. Like the Victorian popular representation of women that denied their strength and sexuality, children's pageants flirt with a sexuality that is both hinted at and denied. Until the concept of childhood innocence is more fully interrogated, children's beauty pageants are likely to remain a contentious issue.

See also Asian Beauty Pageants; The Thin Ideal

Sofiani Murni Lestari, 12, demonstrates how to cover her head with a "kerudung," or head scarf, during the first round of the Abang None Youth beauty pageant in Jakarta, Indonesia, 2004. The pageant, which is run yearly in conjunction with other festivities celebrating Jakarta's 477th anniversary, judges youth age 5–16 on their attire, poise, and communication skills. (AP Photo/Suzanne Plunkett.)

Further Reading

Bessie, Dan. (2000). *Rare Birds: An American Family.* Lexington: University Press of Kentucky.

Giroux, Henry. (1998). "Nymphet Fantasies: Child Beauty Pageants and the Politics of Innocence." *Social Text* 57, vol. 16, no. 4, 31–53.

Gleick, Elizabeth. (1997, January 20). "Playing at Pageants." *Time.*

Heltsley, Martha, and Thomas C. Calhoun. (2003). "The Good Mother: Neutralization Techniques Used by Pageant Mothers." *Deviant Behavior* 24, no. 2, 81–100.

Higonnet, Anne. (1998). *Pictures of Innocence.* New York: Thames and Hudson.

U.S. Dept. of Labor, Children's Bureau. (1917, 1935). *Baby-Week Campaigns.* Miscellaneous Series No. 5, Bureau Publication No. 15 (rev. ed., No. 226). Washington, DC: USGPO.

White, Shane, and Graham J. White. (1998). *Stylin': African American Expressive Culture from Its Beginnings to the Zoot Suit.* Ithaca, NY: Cornel University Press.

Wonderlich, Anna, Diann Ackard, and Judith Henderson. (2005). "Childhood Beauty Pageant Contestants: Associations with Adult Disordered Eating and Mental Health." *Eating Disorders* 13, no. 3, 291–301.

SHAUNA VEY

COMICS.   For over 30 years, mainstream comic book editors and publishers, seemingly suffering from a collective amnesia, have insisted that girls do not read comics. Dirk Deppey, editor of the trade magazine *The Comics Journal*, quotes an unnamed comics retailer at a San Diego comics convention who went so far as to say, "Girls don't read comics, there's something in how their brains are wired that just doesn't respond to the way comics work" (Deppey 2006, p. 252).

In reality, girls have been reading comics as long as there were comics to read. Although no demographics have been found for the early years of the twentieth century, anecdotal evidence in the form of cartoons copied by teenage girls, cartoons cut out of newspapers then colored and pasted into scrapbooks, and letters from cartoonists to high school girls (many in the author's collection) shows that teenage girls were avidly reading the newspaper comics of women cartoonists Grace Drayton and Nell Brinkley, and the strip *Flapper Fanny*.

Nell Brinkley, whose delicate renditions of beautiful women known as "The Brinkley Girls" graced the pages of Hearst newspapers from 1907 to 1937, inspired later women cartoonists Hilda Terry (*Teena*), Marty Links (*Bobby Sox*), Marie Severin (Marvel Comics), Ramona Fradon (DC Comics), and especially Brenda Starr creator Dale Messick. In turn, high school girls of the 1940s and 1950s copied Messick's starry-eyed girl reporter in their school notebooks. Further proof that Brenda Starr was a predominantly female favorite can be found in the **paper dolls** that were printed along with the strip. Gladys Parker, who went from drawing Flapper Fanny to producing her own long-lasting strip, *Mopsy*, also included paper dolls with Mopsy. In fact, Parker was a well-known fashion designer in the 1930s, whose clothing was sold in such department stores as Best and Company, and who was featured in *Look* magazine.

Early Comic Books. Comic books, which started in the early 1930s, originally consisted of reprinted newspaper strips. This all changed in 1938, with the introduction of Superman to the pages of Action Comics, and soon caped flying men with fists of steel dominated the new industry. But in 1941 John Goldwater, publisher of Pep comics, called writer Joe Edwards and artist Bob Montana into his office and asked them to create a new and different comic character. He asked, "Why does every book have to be Superman?" (Robbins 1999, p. 8).

Archie, the character that Edwards and Montana came up with, was definitely not Superman. Along with his pal Jughead and his girlfriend Betty, the freckled, redhaired teenager made his debut in *Pep Comics* #22, in December 1941. Four issues later, Veronica joined the cast of characters, completing the eternal triangle that has been the basis of every Archie comic since then. By 1942, Archie and his pals had grown so popular that they got their own title. By the end of the war, Archie also had his own radio show and nationally syndicated newspaper strip. The majority of Archie's readers were girls, age 6 to 13, and demographics from the past 25 years show 60 percent female readership. Although no statistics for the earlier years have been found, ads in the books for such female items as charm bracelets, handbags, and women's belts suggest girl readers were in the majority.

The publishers of *Archie Comics* knew a good thing when they saw it. Perhaps reasoning that if one teenage boy comic was good, two would be even better, in 1944 they added blond Archie clone Wilbur to their line. And in 1944 they introduced Katy Keene in the pages of *Wilbur Comics*. By 1949, Katy had her own title and was wildly successful. Creator Bill Woggon not only included pages of paper dolls in his books, but he also came up with an entirely new gimmick: he invited his young readers to submit fashion ideas for his brunette movie star heroine, and he published the designs, crediting the designers. Although most of the designers were girls, some were boys. John Lucas, who sent in designs as a young fan, eventually drew Katy Keene when the title was briefly revived from 1984 to 1991.

This resulted in a devoted fan following, which, 20 years later, still put out *Katy Keene Fan Magazine*. In total, eighteen issues of *Katy Keene Fan Magazine* were published.

Other comic book publishers were quick to jump on the Archie bandwagon, producing comics with such titles as *Candy, Taffy, Mazie, Cindy, Sunny, Sorority Sue*, and *Suzie Q. Smith*. As suggested by the titles, these books starred—and were aimed at—girls. The protagonists of these books were plucky, peppy teenagers, and the stories dealt with light romance and funny misadventures. Some publishers, taking the success of Archie literally, experimented with comics starring boys instead of girls, but without as much success. *Dudley* (Prize Publications) and *Meet Merton* (Toby Press) both lasted only a year.

Besides *Archie Comics*, the biggest contender in the field of girls' comics was Timely Comics, also called the Marvel Comic Group, under the editorship of the same Stan Lee who later gave the world *Spiderman, The X-Men*, and *The Fantastic Four*. A 1947 ad for the Marvel Comic Group that ran in *Timely* comics shows nine titles with a girl's name (*Junior Miss, Patsy Walker, Miss America, Millie, Tessie, Cindy, Jeannie, Rusty*, and *Margie*), four titles with a boy's name (*Willie, Frankie, Georgie*, and *Oscar*) and three gender-neutral titles (*Teen, Joker*, and *Gay*). Not all of the Timely girls' comics were about teenagers. Career girl comics like *Millie the Model, Tessie the Typist*, and *Nellie the Nurse* provided positive images of working women in an era when most girls were expected to marry and raise a family rather than have a career.

During the 1940s, high school girls also found comics in girls' **magazines** such as *Junior Miss, Miss America, Calling All Girls, Keen Teens, Sweet Sixteen*, and, for younger readers, *Polly Pigtails*. These magazines combined chatty articles about fashion, crafts, and pop stars with comics about role models like Madame Chiang Kai Shek and Louisa May Alcott, or comics about girls who were reporters or had some other exciting profession. The circulation of *Calling All Girls*, which started in 1941, was over half a million by 1944, and it can be surmised that the other girls' magazines did as well. A 1946 graph in *Newsdealer* magazine showed that in the 8- to 11-year age range and also for ages 18 to 34, female comic book readers outnumbered male readers (Robbins 1999, p. 38).

The Postwar Period. In 1947, two young World War II veterans, Joe Simon and Jack Kirby, produced the first **romance comic**, *Young Romance*. It was a runaway success with older teens and even young housewives, selling 92 percent of its print run. Soon the team of Simon and Kirby added three more titles to their line: *Young Love, Young Brides*, and *In Love*. These comics were inspired by the success of romance magazines like *True Story, True Confessions*, and *True Experiences*, which had been around since the 1920s. Like their magazine counterparts, the comics often pretended to be true stories that were narrated to the writer. Despite suggestive titles like "Back Door Love" and "You're Not the First," the stories were comparatively tame and never mentioned sex. Nonetheless, they were racy enough for the high school girls of the late 1940s and 1950s, who gobbled them up in such numbers that a 1950 graph in *Newsdealer* showed that 17- to 25-year-old females were reading more comics than males (Robbins 1999, p. 54).

It did not take long after the 1947 publication of *Young Love* for other comic book publishers to come up with their own romance titles. *Girls' Love, Girls' Romances, Heart Throbs, Romantic Secrets, Lovers' Lane, Personal Love, My Confession, Sweethearts,* and *I Love You* were only some of the titles that crowded the newsstands. There were even variations of romance in other genres, such as *Wartime Romances, Career Girl Romances, Hi-School Romance,* and *Cowgirl Romances.* By 1950, over a quarter of the comic books published in America were love comics (Robbins 1999, p. 54).

It is no coincidence that love comics came into being after the end of the war. During the war, while the young men were overseas in the military, women stepped in to take their jobs. They worked in factories, made ships and planes, drove trucks and buses, and even flew planes. When the men came home after the war, they wanted their old jobs back. Women were encouraged to quit work, marry, and stay home to raise a family. This was the message in love comics: no matter who the heroine is, she will only find true happiness when she meets and marries the right man and starts having kids.

By the early 1960s, America had changed, and teenage girls changed along with their country. From 1961 to 1963, love comics were still one of the top two genres on the newsstands, but by 1964 they had been eclipsed by the fast-growing new superhero comics. The world, even for high school girls, had grown more sophisticated, and the simple stories in love comics seemed impossibly square. Comic book publishers attempted to keep up with the times by upgrading their heroines from high school girls and housewives to college students and stewardesses. They added the Beatles and Elvis to their covers, and produced stories like "His Hair Is Long and I Love Him" and "How Can I Love a Member of the Establishment?" But they had lost their audience, who were more interested in the new hippie lifestyle than panels featuring close-ups of pretty girls with tears rolling down their cheeks. Those panels, reproduced in pop art paintings by Roy Lichtenstein, had become clichés.

The Girl Comic Drought. Many love comics publishers had folded by the end of the 1950s, after the romance craze ran its course, and the remaining publishers limped on through the early 1970s. Marvel Comics published its last love comic in 1975, Charlton's romance line ended in 1976, and the last love comic, DC's *Young Romance,* ended in 1977. A similar fate had affected all those teen girl titles. Marvel's popular comic *Patsy Walker* folded in 1967, and its even more popular *Millie the Model* ended in 1975.

Except for the unsinkable *Archie Comics* line, from 1977 until the early 1990s girls were indeed not reading comics, because there were no comics for them to read. The phrase "comic book" had become almost synonymous with superheroes, and, with few exceptions, girls are generally not avid consumers of comics that feature hyper-violent male characters. Women and girls have also been turned off by the exaggerated poses, skimpy costumes, and large **bra** sizes they see on female characters—usually drawn by men—in superhero comics. Feminist fan **blogs** like Girl_Hero.com are full of angry comments on this subject, and in a June 8, 2000, issue of the *Wall Street Journal,* journalist Matt Phillips quotes Nicole Lewis, a 19-year-old sophomore at the University of Massachusetts, who says, regarding the image of women in mainstream superhero comics: "It's a little off-putting, especially to young girls who don't look like that at all" (p. B1).

There have been exceptions. In 1945 Timely's girls' magazine, *Miss America,* featured a teenage superheroine named Miss America, who sported cateye glasses and a cute skullcap. A few years later, editor Stan Lee came up with a group of superheroines aimed at girl readers: Sun Girl, Blonde Phantom, Venus (who was actually the Roman goddess herself, returned to Earth as a superheroine), and Namora, fishy cousin to the Marvel superhero, Submariner. While all of these female characters were beautiful, they had realistic figures and were decently clothed.

Meanwhile, DC Comics published **Wonder Woman**, the creation of pop psychologist Dr. William Moulton Marston (who also happens to be the inventor of the lie detector). Among the girls who devoured the adventures of the beautiful Amazon princess—who had left her perfect home on Paradise Island to come to our world and fight for truth, justice, and the American Way—was Gloria Steinem and most of the staff of Ms. magazine. Claiming that when they were girls, they had all been saved by Wonder Woman, they put her on the cover of their first issue in 1972.

And in 1942, Fawcett Comics came up with Mary Marvel, twin sister of their star superhero, Captain Marvel. Mary was a young teenager who said the magic word "Shazam" to be transformed into a flying, cape-wearing, short-skirted teenage superheroine. There was a Mary Marvel fan club for girls to join, and readers could even purchase Mary Marvel fashions—plaid blouses and dresses, dungarees and shorts—through the mail. The clothes were cute and fashionable, and the prices, at $2.98 for a blouse and $3.95 for dungarees, were right.

By the late 1960s, these characters, too, were gone or, in the case of Wonder Woman, greatly weakened, and of not as much interest to girl readers. In 1968, writer Dennis O'Neill demoted Wonder Woman from superheroine to an ordinary though mod young woman who ran a boutique. This unhappy state of affairs lasted until 1973, when the Amazon princess was restored with her special powers and her costume, in part due to the insistence of Ms. magazine editor Gloria Steinem. The late 1960s also saw the rise of the underground "comix" movement, and in 1972 a core group of eight women met in San Francisco to form *Wimmen's Comix*, the first and longest-lasting all-woman, feminist underground comix anthology. The 1970s and 1980s saw a proliferation of women producing underground comix, but because of their adult themes and often explicit sexuality, the books could not be sold to girls under 18. Nevertheless, it is entirely possible that underage girls managed to get their hands on these comix anyway, smuggling them into their houses and keeping them hidden.

During the 1980s, several unsuccessful attempts were made to bring back girls' comics. Inspired by the original *Katy Keene* comics, Barb Rausch and Katy Keene creator Bill Woggon produced a few issues of *Vickie Valentine*, published by Renegade Press. Trina Robbins drew six issues of a comic called *Meet Misty* for Marvel Comics, and went on to produce eight issues of another teen comic, *California Girls*, for Eclipse comics. At DC Comics, Barbara Slate produced nine issues of *Angel Love*, and in the early 1990s she produced six issues of *Sweet XVI*, a comic about a typical teen in the days of ancient Rome. Marvel even published *Barbie* comics for five years, but neither Barbie nor any of the other titles succeeded, because the managers of comic shops, now the home of superhero comics and adolescent boys, did not want to carry them, reasoning that "girls don't read comics."

The Return of Girls' Comics. The early 1990s saw the beginning of the end of the girls' comics drought when the Japanese comic character **Sailor Moon** arrived in America, in the form of animé (animated television cartoons) and manga (Japanese comics). By the 2000s, wave after wave of manga had arrived on American shores and ended the drought. Girls are now reading manga as never before, especially shoujou manga (Japanese girls' comics). The *Wall Street Journal* for June 8, 2007, reported that in 2006, total sales of manga books jumped 22 percent to 9.5 million units, up from 7.8 million in 2005, and that the manga category in 2006 accounted for about two-thirds of all graphic novels sold in American bookstores, up from a little more than half in 2004 (Phillips 2007, p. B1).

Shoujou manga, with beautifully drawn stories of teenage girls, involving romance and nonviolent adventures, represents a pleasant break from traditional violent superhero books. According to the *Wall Street Journal* article, Ms. Lewis, the college student quoted earlier, "says she likes the fact that female stars of manga are often girls without any special powers, who wear normal clothes, attend high school and are trying to resolve some life problems" (Phillips 2007, p. B1).

In 2007, inspired by the success of shoujou manga, DC Comics started the *Minx* comics line, aimed at young female readers. Today there are more girls and women both drawing and reading comics than ever before (Robbins 2001, p. 148). There is no longer any excuse for comics editors and publishers to claim that girls don't read comics.

See also Batgirl; Betty and Veronica; Catwoman; Manga and Animé Fan Culture; Poison Ivy

Further Reading

Deppey, Dirk. (2006, July). "Interview with Dallas Middaugh." *Comics Journal* 277, 248–256.
Phillips, Matt. (2007, June 8). "Pow! Romance! Comics Court Girls." *Wall Street Journal*, B1.
Robbins, Trina. (1996). *The Great Women Superheroes*. Northampton, MA: Kitchen Sink.
———. (1999). *From Girls to Grrrlz*. San Francisco: Chronicle Books.
———. (2001). *The Great Women Cartoonists*. New York: Watson-Guptill.
———. (2005). *What's Love Got to Do with It? The Education of a Comics Artist*. New York: Allworth Press.
Steinem, Gloria. (1972). *Wonder Woman*. New York: Bonanza Books.
Triggs, Teal. (2005). *Katy Keene: Forgotten Comics Icon. The Education of a Comics Artist*, New York: Allworth Press.

TRINA ROBBINS

COMING-OF-AGE MEMOIRS.   Coming-of-age memoirs are autobiographies that focus on the transition from girlhood to young womanhood. Some memoirs of girlhood, like Susanna Kaysen's *Girl, Interrupted* (1993), were written for an adult audience but are appropriated by adolescent girls. Other memoirs are created expressly by or for girls, including Zoe Trope's *Please Don't Kill the Freshman* (2003) and Ann Turner's *Learning to Swim* (2000).

While autobiographies follow a chronological pattern that tells an entire life story, memoirs usually center on certain periods in time or themes from an author's experience. Memoirs provide an opportunity for the author to be reflective and construct a particular representation of her life and identity. To create a retrospective account, authors use a range of familiar cultural materials. Writers may draw on literary or cultural narratives like traditional fairy tales or myths, use poetry or illustrations, and/or include official documents or photographs. In one of the most popular girlhood memoirs of the 1990s, *Girl, Interrupted*, Susanna Kaysen included excerpts from her psychiatric file to tell about her experience in a mental hospital as a young woman.

Memoirists frame their individual coming-of-age stories around larger social issues and practices that influence their own and other girls' opportunities and experiences. These include issues of race/ethnicity, class, and sexuality. Coming-of-age memoirs written by girls and women bring attention to concerns and issues that directly influence how girls come to understand themselves as female. Memoirists focus on how issues like mental illness, eating disorders, sexual abuse, and restrictive cultural norms about gender and sexuality define their female coming of age. In her book *Wasted: A Memoir of Anorexia and Bulimia* (1999), Marya Hornbacher explores how she lived with eating disorders from the age of 9 to 26. In so doing, she explores her relationship with her body: "My world as a child was defined by mirrors. . . . My face always peered back at me, anxious, checking for a hair out of place, searching for anything that was different, shorts hiked up or shirt untucked, butt too round or thighs too soft, belly sucked in hard. I started holding my breath to keep my stomach concave when I was five, and at times, even now, I catch myself doing it" (1999, p. 14).

Women write their stories of the self against specific social, political, and historical back-drops, and in the process they provide a context for and a critique about female coming of age at a particular moment and in a specific cultural location; for example, Maya Angelou's *I Know Why the Caged Bird Sings* gives the reader insight to Angelou's experience as a young black girl in rural segregated Arkansas. It can be argued that memoirs offer readers access to alternative story lines about girlhood that make underrepresented experiences visible.

See also Anorexia; Blogging; Bulimia; Fairy Tales, Traditional

Further Reading

Gilmore, Leigh. (2001). *The Limits of Autobiography: Trauma and Testimony*. Ithaca, NY: Cornell University Press.

Marshall, Elizabeth, and Theresa Rogers. (2005). "Writing Back: Rereading Adolescent Girlhoods Through Women's Memoir." *Alan Review* 33, no. 1, 17–22.

ELIZABETH MARSHALL

COMPULSORY HETEROSEXUALITY. "Compulsory heterosexuality" is a term first used in 1980 by poet and lesbian feminist Adrienne Rich (1929–). It is a theory that states that women are pressured or coerced into sexual and romantic relationships with men. It also states that, because of this pressure, women become competitive with one another.

For Rich, heterosexuality is not something that people are born to embody. According to her theory, heterosexuality is a political institution, one that is central to the mainte-nance of patriarchy, which is a form of social organization in which men dominate women.

Compulsory heterosexuality permeates girl culture by dictating the ways in which girls should behave. **Proms,** for instance, have "unwritten rules" that govern acceptable girl behavior: it is generally held that teenage girls are expected to attend their proms with male dates. If a girl attends her prom with another girl, it is considered outside of the heterosexual norm of proms and scandal often ensues.

In order for compulsory heterosexuality to be maintained, girls and women are encour-aged to personify "hegemonic femininity." Hegemonic femininity is the dominant or ideal way of "being female" in a given place and time. It codifies such things as girls' behavior, dress, and patterns of interaction. For example, until the mid-1960s, young women were encouraged to marry and have children at a young age. It was also held that a woman's place was in the home and that she was to dress demurely for her husband. This form of femininity was embraced wholeheartedly by American society up until that time, but it is no longer widely endorsed.

Western hegemonic femininity has perpetually idealized heterosexual romance and marriage. Evidence of this glorification can be found everywhere in popular girl culture: movies like **Dirty Dancing** and **Sixteen Candles** and dolls such as Wedding Barbie provide heterosexual models and scripts to which girls are expected to aspire. When these models are taken up by girls, compulsory heterosexuality is reinforced.

Another way that compulsory heterosexuality is enforced is by making female experiences invisible or unacceptable. This manifests in popular culture in many ways, including the popular dismissal of certain books as "mere **chick lit**." When girls internalize this attitude, they are **covering over** their own experiences.

Women-identified experiences are those that involve women seeking emotional, social, intellectual, political, and economic bonds with other women. Rich explains that these experiences exist along what she calls a "lesbian continuum." Rich identifies many behaviors across this spectrum that are empowering practices for girls and women that resist patriarchy; at one end of the spectrum, girls and women can support one another and become less competitive and catty; and at the other end of the spectrum, girls and women can live a lesbian existence.

Recently, scholars like Deborah L. Tolman have examined how teenagers experience compulsory heterosexuality. According to her studies, compulsory heterosexuality limits female teenagers' ability to explore women-identified experiences, which includes their sexual desire for other females. It also limits their experiences with heterosexual desire: when teenage females live out hegemonic femininity, they play out ideal narratives of love in which they are sexual *objects* for males, rather than sexual agents with their own sexual desires. Tolman argues that in order for positive sexual development to occur, girls must reject hegemonic femininity and compulsory heterosexuality.

There are some signs of resistance to compulsory heterosexuality in popular girl culture, particularly in teen television dramas, but they each have their limits. In the last few years, some shows have acknowledged lesbian existence by including storylines about females in same-sex relationships. Notable story lines have included the characters Willow and Tara on **Buffy the Vampire Slayer**; Anna on *One Tree Hill*; Marissa and Alex on **The O.C.**; Paige and Alex on **Degrassi**: *The Next Generation*; and Ashley and Spencer on *South of Nowhere*. However, despite these examples, overall there have been very few representations of lesbian relationships on television. Moreover, many of these characters are more often portrayed as bisexual, rather than lesbian.

There are also some examples of positive female nonsexual relationships on television. These include mother and daughter Lorelei and Rory on **Gilmore Girls** and crime-solving team Veronica and Mac on **Veronica Mars**. However, frequently female television characters are not portrayed as mutually supportive, but instead are pitted against one another, often in the context of competition over a male's affection. An example of this is Brenda and Kelly, who fought over Dylan's affections on **Beverly Hills, 90210**.

Although female teenager characters on teen dramas are often sexually active, there is little or no discussion of their enjoyment of sex. Female teenage characters are expected to be sexy and attractive to their boyfriends rather than express their own sexual desire.

In this way, female teenagers' desire is made invisible and even inappropriate, and compulsory heterosexuality is reinforced.

See also Lesbians in Popular Girl Culture; Romantic Relationships; Texts of Desire

Further Reading

Rich, Adrienne. (1986). *Blood, Bread, and Poetry: Selected Prose, 1979–1985.* New York: Norton.

Tolman, Deborah L. (2006). "In a Different Position: Conceptualizing Female Adolescent Sexuality Development within Compulsory Heterosexuality." *New Directions for Child and Adolescent Development,* 112, 71–89.

MAURA KELLY

COOTIE CATCHER.   The cootie catcher, while played internationally under different names, is a folded-paper game that is particularly popular with young American girls. The game is commonly used in two different ways: In its incarnation as a "cootie catcher," it is part of a larger system of negotiation of gender boundaries. As a fortune-telling game, it attributes the events of girls' lives to "luck," rather than to their own initiative.

The shape of the game can be attributed to the Japanese paper folding practice of origami. Girls were first observed playing with them as early as the 1600s in England, but it is unclear exactly when the game was taken up by American girls. The cootie catcher is created by making a series of folds in a square piece of paper, which results in a shape that has four outer surfaces and eight inner surfaces. The player can put her thumbs and forefingers underneath the form and use the paper shape as a pincer-type device (when it is used as a cootie catcher), or she may flip back and forth between two sets of four inner surfaces (when it is used as a fortune-telling game).

According to Barrie Thorne, a key scholar in the field of girls' games and their gendered implications, cooties are invisible "germs." While children can pass cooties among themselves, it is generally held that girls are the source of cooties (Thorne 1993). When a girl has cooties, she is treated as though she is contagious and her peers avoid her for a period of time. Sometimes, another girl will make a cootie catcher to get rid of her friend's cooties. A cootie catcher basic form is then made, and on one set of four inner surfaces, cooties are drawn (typically looking like small insects). The other set of four inner surfaces are left blank (i.e., clean). To remove cooties, a girl will touch the "afflicted" girl with the pincers of the catcher. The inner surfaces of the cootie catcher with the cooties drawn on will be shown to the "afflicted girl," then the clean inner surfaces will be revealed to her. This means that the cooties have effectively been removed for the moment. In a way, cootie catchers can reinforce female solidarity on the playground.

When the cootie catcher form is used as a fortune-telling game, the purpose of the game is completely different and the surfaces of the paper form are used differently. A color is put on each of the four outer faces of the cootie catcher, usually blue, green, yellow, and red. On the two sets of four inner surfaces, numbers are written (typically numbers 1 to 8). The inner surfaces are then flipped up, and underneath, fortunes are written. These can include friendly statements ("You will be rich"), **mean** statements ("You will live in a box"), and silly statements ("You will marry a goat").

To play the game, the holder of the game will ask a player, "Which color?" The player picks one of the four colors and the holder spells out the color (for example, R-E-D) while

The cootie catcher, a folded-paper game dating from the 1600s, is still enjoyed by many young American girls in a variety of contexts, including Ouija board–type fortune telling. (Drawing by Mike Trainor, 2007.)

flipping back and forth between the two sets of inner surfaces. The player must then select a number on one of the visible inner surfaces. The holder counts to that number while alternating between the two sets of surfaces. This is typically repeated two more times, after which the holder must flip open the cootie catcher to reveal the player's fortune that is written underneath that number.

This fortune-telling version of the cootie catcher is part of a group of girl games that deal with girls and the roles that luck and "destiny" play in their lives. Other "games," such as Ouija boards and Magic 8-Balls, rely on girls' questions about their present and future lives as a source of motivation for play. These games give answers to girls' questions as though the answers are completely independent of the girls' actions.

Mattel has taken the notion of cootie catcher as fortune-teller and created a hard-plastic toy that tells girls' fortunes. With the option of using pre-recorded fortunes or adding personalized ones, the Barbie Diaries Secret Fortune Teller is featured in the 2006 *Barbie Diaries* movie. There is also the **Bratz** Genie Magic Fortune Teller doll, which is a Bratz doll mounted from the waist up on a platform with her hand hovering over a crystal ball. Girls can ask the doll questions, and the doll will provide an answer from her bank of twenty responses.

See also Playground Games

Further Reading

Knapp, Mary, and Herbert Knapp. (1976). *One Potato, Two Potato: The Secret Education of American Children*. New York: Norton.

Opie, Iona, and Peter Opie. (1959). *The Lore and Language of School Children*. New York: Oxford University Press.

Samuelson, Sue. (1980). "The Cooties Complex." *Western Folklore* 39, no. 3, 198–210.

Thorne, Barrie. (1993). *Gender Play: Girls and Boys in School*. Piscataway, NJ: Rutgers University Press.

LINDSAY CORNISH

COVERING OVER.   Covering over is an important term in the study of girls' popular culture. It is a concept that deals with the popular devaluing that is typically attached to many aspects of girls' play and culture. It also accounts for the ways that adolescent girls and women may internalize this idea and subsequently dismiss, deny, or apologize for their girlhood play.

The term "covering over" was used in the early 1990s by the well-known girlhood psychologist Carol Gilligan. According to her theory, as girls move through adolescence toward womanhood, they begin to cover over their girlhood experiences by altering how and what they say about them. Adolescent girls no longer speak with openness and honesty of their girlhood experiences as they did when they were younger. Instead, they become reluctant to discuss their lives as girls and downplay or selectively "forget" certain experiences. An example of this is a teenage female stating that she "kinda read" **The Baby-sitters Club** books as a girl, when in fact she read them voraciously. Another example is that of an adolescent who vaguely remembers playing with her **She-Ra** dolls, but forgets the complex stories that she carefully crafted for her dolls to enact.

By covering over their girlhood experiences, female adolescents leave their "relational selves" behind, a process that Gilligan calls "revising girlhood." According to Gilligan, it is not healthy for adolescents to be disconnected from their girlhood pasts, and there is a need for adolescent girls and women to reclaim their voices.

Social science researchers have identified strategies that can be used to uncover girlhood. The field of memory work engages participants in three stages of remembering: recalling, questioning the memory, and working out what it means in the present. While these strategies have been applied to many kinds of girlhood play, such as playing with **paper dolls** and playing school, much has been learned about covering over in the context of playing with Barbie. When these strategies have been used by older adolescents and grown women in relation to Barbie, many women have recalled that, for them, playing with Barbie wasn't just about fashion and beauty, which are the popular associations with Barbie; for many participants, playing with a Barbie doll may have been their first doll play that wasn't about taking care of baby dolls and housekeeping, making it an almost rebellious act. Some researchers have noted that women remembering Barbie play recall how this experience turned them into cultural critics or political activists. (See the essay on Barbie in Part 1.) As several researchers have found, women may come to understand more about the pleasure of play but also about how it has informed their present personal and career choices. In recalling the pleasures of reading **Nancy Drew** books, for example, a police officer attributes her girlhood reading to her choosing to enter the police force. Similarly, an architect may recall her strong interest in Barbie **dream houses** as a girl.

See also Voice

Further Reading

Crawford, June, Susan Kippax, Jenny Onyx, and Una Gault. *Emotion and Gender: Constructing Meaning from Memory*. London: Sage.

Gilligan, Carol. (1991). "Women's Psychological Development: Implications for Psychotherapy." In Carol Gilligan, Annie G. Rogers, and Deborah L. Tolman, eds. *Women, Girls and Psychotherapy: Reframing Resistance*. New York: Haworth Press, pp. 5–31.

Mitchell, Claudia, and Jacqueline Reid-Walsh. (1998). "Mail-Order Memory Work: Towards a Methodology of Uncovering the Experiences of Covering Over." *Review of Education/Pedagogy/Cultural Studies* 20, no. 1, 57–75.

Rand, Erica. (1994). *Barbie's Queer Accessories*. Durham, NC, and London: Duke University Press.

Reid-Walsh, Jacqueline, and Claudia Mitchell. (2000). "Just a Doll? Liberating Accounts of Barbie-Play." *Review of Education/Pedagogy/Cultural Studies* 22, no. 2, 175–190.

CLAUDIA A. MITCHELL

COWGIRL PLAY.   Cowgirl play is a phenomenon of 1950s and early 1960s girl play. Inspired by such cowgirl heroes of television and movies in the 1950s as **Annie Oakley**, **Calamity Jane**, and **Dale Evans**, cowgirl play mirrored the popularity of children (especially boys) "playing cowboys and Indians" as represented in the various cowboy heroes of the day: the Lone Ranger, the Cisco Kid, Hopalong Cassidy, Zorro, Roy Rogers, and Gene Autry.

Cowgirl play was associated with dressing up in the typical cowgirl suit, consisting of a fringed vest, a cowgirl skirt (also often with fringes), cowgirl boots, and a Stetson hat. The costume may or may not include a toy holster with toy pistols. Appropriately garbed, no matter whether she was outside or in her **bedroom**, the girl could undertake imaginary heroic adventures set in the frontier world. In the well-known children's film *Toy Story 2* (1999), **Jessie the Cowgirl** features as a reincarnation of the fifties cowgirl and more than offsets the hero, Woody the Cowboy, with her energy, her openness, and the depth of emotion in the movie's plaintive song "When She Loved Me."

Cowgirl play is particularly important to a deepened understanding of girls' culture of the fifties because it serves as an example of play that is not solely about domesticity: playing with **dollhouses**, playing with tea sets, cooking in an **Easy-Bake Oven**, and looking after baby dolls. However, there is some debate about whether playing cowgirl represents non-traditional girls' play. On the one hand, cowgirl play can represent the girl player assuming the heroic lead role in imagined dramas. Scholars have also noted that girls have played out a variety of roles in their cowgirl play; some have, for example, donned a Davy Crockett coonskin cap and rifle, thereby challenging the conventional gender roles that adults have tried to prescribe for them.

On the other hand, playing cowgirl characters can just be an act of playing out the conventional female character in popular television shows and films, who served as an accessory to the main cowboy character. Some scholars have argued that the stories of such folk figures as Annie Oakley and Calamity Jane were rewritten after World War II to depict them as expressions of "femininity in Western garb," and that these depictions did not present "a challenge to male dominance" (Griffin 1999, p. 115). Dale Evans was able to ride a horse and manipulate a lasso, but she was still regarded as Roy's pretty wife.

Cowgirl play has led to the manufacturing of several cowgirl dolls. In addition to Jessie the Cowgirl, Barbie has been a cowgirl (Cowgirl Barbie). Other cowgirl representations include Cara the Cowgirl Sticker Paper doll, Fisher-Price's Cowgirl Dora (of **Dora the Explorer** fame), **Smurfette** Cowgirl, and, most recently, a **Bratz** doll: Bratz Wild Wild West Fianna.

Further Reading

Griffin, Sean. (1999). "Kings of the Wild Backyard: Davy Crockett and Children's Space." In Marsha Kinder, ed. *Kids' Media Culture*. Durham, NC: Duke University Press, pp. 102–121.

Mitchell, Claudia, and Jacqueline Reid-Walsh. (2002). *Researching Children's Popular Culture: Childhood as a Cultural Space*. London and New York: Routledge/Taylor & Francis.

CLAUDIA A. MITCHELL

CROSS-MERCHANDISING.   Girl-specific cross-merchandising or trans-media franchising occurs when numerous products are created that "tie in" to another girl-centered text or product (or sometimes even a girl culture celebrity). The term implies the repetition of a particular image, idea, or narrative by a commercial franchise across a range of affiliated media products and artifacts ranging from books to films to television presentations to dolls to clothing and home design and so on.

The **Olsen twins** and their media and product empire are a prime example of girl-specific cross-merchandising. Originally child stars on the popular television sitcom *Full*

House (1987–1995), in 1993 the Olsen sisters established Dualstar. They have starred in a number of television and video series, including *The Adventures of Mary-Kate and Ashley* (1994–1997), *Two of a Kind* (1998–1999), and *So Little Time* (2001–2002). These television and video series all have companion book series that are aimed at **tween** and younger girl readers. Over the years, Dualstar has expanded into a global trans-media franchise that includes DVDs, video games, books, clothing, accessories, fashion dolls, and beauty products, among much other merchandise that serves both to bolster the celebrity status of the Olsens and to turn a profit.

Also, the success of one product in the web of merchandise can affect the success of the others. For example, if a young woman buys **Gwen Stefani**'s *Love Angel Music Baby* CD, she may also go online and buy some of Stefani's Harajuku Lovers merchandise. Cross-merchandising influences and is influenced by brand loyalty, or the tendency of consumers to stick with the brands (and their affiliated girl culture celebrities) that they like best.

A Product for Every Girl (and Woman). Typically, when a brand is engaged in girl-specific cross-merchandising, the idea is not only to offer a wide range of girl products, but also to ensure that these products cover a range of prices. Sanrio's marketing of the **Hello Kitty** line is an example of this theory in action: from a collection of Kitty-themed stickers that cost only a dollar, to mobile homes and airplanes that are branded with Hello Kitty's likeness, there is a Kitty product for every girl. Another strategy that is used is the creation of products that appeal to both girls *and* women. Hello Kitty again offers great example: while there are Hello Kitty plush dolls for young girls, there are also Hello Kitty cars and even vibrators, which are intended for an older audience. Also, **Mattel** paired up with M.A.C. Cosmetics, a brand that is very popular with young adult women, to create a limited-edition line of cosmetics called "Barbie Loves M.A.C." Released in the spring of 2007, the cosmetics' packaging featured a ponytailed silhouette of the iconic doll, which was also imprinted into the blush and eye shadow compacts. Names of the colors in the line included "Malibu Barbie," "Springtime **Skipper**," and "Real Doll" (M.A.C. UK 2007).

Cross-Merchandising History: Disney, Strawberry Shortcake, and Girl Power. Many scholars have stated that contemporary cross-merchandising began in the 1930s, following the unprecedented popularity of Walt Disney's films and characters, including Mickey Mouse and Donald Duck (Kline 1993; Giroux 1999). Film producers and marketing specialists collaborated to create and market products for children, including character toys, clothes, watches, and other goods that bore the likeness of the popular characters. As Disney continued to produce films, the company also continued to create themed merchandise. (See the essay on Disney in Part 1.)

A specific kind of cross-merchandising that is rooted in popular girl culture emerged in the 1980s and set the tone for years to come. It is called "The **Strawberry Shortcake** Strategy" (Englehardt 1986). At that time, the Federal Communications Commission had strict regulations in place on how companies could advertise their products to children. Consequently, companies tried to come up with innovative ways of promoting their merchandise. A group called "Those Characters from Cleveland," which is part of American Greetings Inc., came up with a revolutionary approach to promoting their Strawberry Shortcake doll: create a cartoon television show based on the character and her friends. Thus, the cartoons became half-hour–long advertisements for the doll. Other companies quickly followed suit with their dolls (including **She-Ra** and **My Little**

Pony), and it is now standard industry practice to cross-merchandise products using television in this way.

Girl-specific cross-merchandising had a second boom with the popularization of **Girl Power** commercialism in the mid-1990s. Girls and specifically tweens were widely recognized as a distinct group of consumers seeking products that reflected their interests and preferences. Thus, when girls buy a **Powerpuff Girls** doll or a **Spice Girls** CD, they are not only sustaining popular girl culture, but by wearing and using the merchandise, they are also identifying themselves as "girls."

It is important to note that this strategy differs from the creation of "spin-offs." A spin-off is a completely different media text that branches off from another, which features a character, a setting, or another element that is taken from the original cultural text. Examples of this in girl culture are abundant: the television show *Dora the Explorer* features Dora and her cousin, Diego. When Nickelodeon understood the popularity of the Diego character among its audience, the television network created the spin-off show *Go, Diego, Go!*, which features Diego's own adventures.

Books as Launchpads for Cross-Merchandising. Books represent an important facet of popular girl culture, both in historic and contemporary contexts. Consequently, books aimed at tween girls are often at the root of wide-ranging trans-media franchises that may include film and television adaptations, affiliated music albums, online fan clubs, video games, clothing, and cosmetics.

The **Nancy Drew** series exemplifies the early commercialization of series books aimed at young female readers. First published in 1930, *Nancy Drew* is one of the most recognized book series for girls in the United States. *Nancy Drew* texts popularized fiction that depicted fantasy-infused adventures with female protagonists. Written by ghostwriters at the Stratemeyer Syndicate under the pseudonym Carolyn Keene, the commercialization of series books at this time set the stage for later developments in children's book publishing in the context of mass-market entertainment. Since its original publication, a number of adaptations and related merchandise have been developed, including feature films, a television series, a computer game, and, most recently, a graphic novel. *Nancy Drew* provides a model for the content, design, and commercialization of contemporary tween books and their cross-merchandising or trans-media franchises.

Recent Cross-Merchandising of Tween Girl Books. While the production and marketing of products affiliated with books has been a common practice in the history of children's book publishing, this trend has radically expanded in the last two decades. Many children's publishing houses that produce books for tween girls are directly connected to or exist under the auspices of larger entertainment companies and multinational corporations. The relationships between multinational entertainment corporations and children's publishing houses heavily influence choices in the way these print texts are designed, marketed, and distributed globally. Moreover, the branding or corporate mission of the companies that produce and distribute these texts may heavily influence the meanings promoted by the texts. The DVD editions of *The Princess Diaries* (2001) and *The Princess Diaries 2: Royal Engagement* (2004) include special features, advertisements, trailers, and music videos that make explicit links not only to the film-related merchandise but also to Disney's other princess products and tween-oriented programming.

Multimodal Design of Tween Girl Books. In recent years, digital culture has become central to tween engagement with books: the reflection on and discussion of books by tween girls are often mediated through **Web sites**, chat rooms, video games, and other, related texts and products. Consequently, many books aimed at tween girls are characterized by the inclusion of features from video games, **blogs**, and instant messaging in the design of the text itself. For example, both *The Princess Diaries* series and the Mary-Kate and Ashley Olsen *So Little Time* book series include representations of instant messenger conversations that are part of the written texts. This merging of the typical book format with elements of the layout and language of digital communication may be defined as a multimodal book design. "Multimodal" is a term used to define texts that integrate a several modes of communication in its representation (Kress and van Leeuwen 2001).

Some multimodal books are designed to include conventions from other print-based media, such as **comics**, **magazines**, and annuals. The Olsens' *So Little Time* books include photo-strip stories at the back of the written text, which follow the format of traditional comic strips.

When this complex overlapping of textual types and cross-merchandised products occurs in the context of one book, it can change how tweens read and interact with the book. Online **fan culture** is a prime example of this. For many of these books, the official Web site of the book, film, or television show is only one entry in a number of Web sites that relate to texts. Many girls produce fan trivia Web sites, photo collages, creative writing, soundtrack listings, and gossip sites that refer not only to the characters and the storylines of the books, but also to the related merchandise. For example, there are numerous fan sites dedicated to the Hermione Granger character in the *Harry Potter* series of books and films, but there are also several sites dedicated to Emma Watson, the actress who plays the character in the films. Fan communities of tween viewers and readers may illustrate an allegiance to a character that may not have been cultivated in response to the written text in isolation.

Empowering or Limiting? Cross-merchandising has its proponents and its opponents. On one hand, cross-merchandising can be seen as empowering for girls, especially when tween girls become active fans and producers of media texts based on their favorite products. However, some have criticized cross-merchandising because it reinforces the traditional positioning of girls as shoppers and consumers. Moreover, it reduces Girl Power to the ability to buy, read, and wear the latest "girl-specific" product and thus equates female empowerment with consumerism.

Further Reading

Banet-Weiser, Sarah. (2004). "Girls Rule! Gender, Feminism, and Nickelodeon." *Critical Studies in Media Communication* 21, no. 2, 119–139.

Cadogan, M., and P. Craig. (1976/2003). *You're a Brick, Angela! A New Look at Girls' Fiction from 1839–1975*. Coleford, Bath: Girls Gone By.

Englehardt, Tom. (1986). "Children's Television: The Strawberry Shortcake Strategy." In Todd Gitlin, ed. *Watching Television*. New York: Pantheon Books, pp. 68–110.

Giroux, Henry. (1994). *Disturbing Pleasures: Learning Popular Culture*. New York: Routledge.

Inness, Sherrie A., ed. (1997). *Nancy Drew and Company: Culture, Gender, and Girls' Series*. Bowling Green, OH: Bowling Green State University Popular Press.

Kline, Stephen. (1993). *Out of the Garden: Toys, TV, and Children's Culture in the Age of Marketing*. Toronto, ON: Garamond Press.

Kress, Gunther, and Theo van Leeuwen. (2001). *Multimodal Discourse: The Modes and Media of Contemporary Communication*. London: Oxford University Press.

Livingstone, Sonia. (2002). *Young People and New Media: Childhood and the Changing Media Environment*. London: Sage.

M.A.C. *UK. Barbie Loves MAC* [Online June 2007]. MAC Cosmetics UK Website http://www.maccosmetics.co.uk/barbielovesmac/index.tmpl?ref-577. Mackey, Margaret. (1998). *The Case of Peter Rabbit: Changing Conditions of Literature for Children.* New York: Taylor and Francis.

Mitchell, Claudia, and Jacqueline Reid-Walsh, eds. (2005). *Seven Going on Seventeen: Tween Studies in the Culture of Girlhood.* New York: Peter Lang.

Quart, Alissa. (2003). *Branded: The Buying and Selling of Teenagers.* London: Random House.

Van Fuqua, Joy. (2003). "'What Are Those Little Girls Made Of?' The Powerpuff Girls and Consumer Culture." In Carol Stabile and Mark Harrison, eds. *Prime Time Animation: Television Animation and American Culture.* New York: Routledge, pp. 205–219.

Watson, Victor, and Margaret Meek. (2003). *Coming of Age in Children's Literature.* London: Continuum.

NAOMI HAMER AND LINDSAY CORNISH

CROSSOVER LITERATURE.   "Crossover literature" is a term used to describe books that have both a child and an adult audience. This crossing over can happen in two ways: children can appropriate "adult" books, and adults can read "children's" books. The idea of crossover texts can also be extended to other forms of popular culture, such as film and television. In girl culture, crossover literature can provide a forum for sharing and connecting generations of adult women, adolescent girls, and even young girls.

Several factors influence whether or not a text is considered crossover literature. In terms of the author's intent, a crossover text may or may not be written expressly to reach both older and younger audiences (for example, Candace Bushnell wrote *Sex and the City* for an adult female audience, but it and its associated television show have nevertheless been appropriated by teenage females). This notion of intent also speaks to the publisher's role in publicizing and marketing a particular book to more than one audience. In terms of content, a crossover text typically addresses broad themes that are important to the female experience, such as one's coming of age and friendships; an example is Rebecca Wells's *The Divine Secrets of the Ya-Ya Sisterhood* (1996). In terms of the reader, a crossover text must be appealing enough to have a female reader transgress age-specific literacy practices.

Iconic female characters in popular crossover texts of the past have included the women of **Little Women** (1933), Alice of *Alice in Wonderland* (1865), Dorothy of *The Wizard of Oz* (1900), Anne of **Anne of Green Gables** (1908), Nancy of the **Nancy Drew** book series (1930), and Scout of *To Kill a Mockingbird* (1960). Adult crossover readers today may be intrigued by such unconventional characters such as Hermione Granger of the *Harry Potter* series (1997–2007), Lyra of the *His Dark Materials* series (1995–2000), Gatty of *The Arthur Trilogy* (2001–2006), and Daisy of *How I Live Now* (2004).

The recent trend of **chick lit** in adult literature is a prime example of books with crossover appeal. Chick lit books typically detail the lives of modern, cosmopolitan, single women in their 20s and 30s who place great emphasis on their dating relationships, careers, and shopping. Examples of these include Helen Fielding's *Bridget Jones's Diary,* Sophie Kinsella's *Shopaholic* series, and Emma McLaughlin and Kathe Mazur's *The Nanny Diaries* (2003), all of which have drawn in many younger readers. Publishers have since capitalized on girls' interest in these titles and created new brands specifically directed at their age level through copycat serials such as *Gossip Girls* (2000–), *The Nannies* (2005–), *The A List* (2003–), the *Princess Diaries* (2000–), and *The Sisterhood of the Traveling Pants* (2001–) books. Teen girls suggest through online booklists that they are also claiming "adult" titles such as *The Lovely Bones* (2000), *The Poisonwood Bible* (1998), and *The Red Tent* (1997) as their own.

In the shared reading of these texts, girls and women demonstrate continuity between life stages: girls look forward to future adult experiences, and grown women look back, nostalgically, to their pasts. When literature is passed back and forth, it can be seen as an act of endorsing certain depictions of girlhood. It can also be seen as a way to initiate dialogue about the female experience; for example, when young readers can share their understanding of teen literature with older women, such as through mother-daughter book clubs, there is a real potential for discussion of contemporary girl issues. Recognizing and evaluating the space that crossover readers inhabit together can lead to a better understanding of how girl and womanhood are constructed, and it can shed light on how both young girls and women make meaning and negotiate their identities through the reading of these texts.

Further Reading

Beckett, Sandra, ed. (1999). *Transcending Boundaries: Writing for a Dual Audience of Children and Adults*. New York: Garland.

Maija-Liisa Harju

CUTHAND, THIRZA (1978–).   Thirza Cuthand is a Saskatchewan-born Cree girl who started making films when she was 16. As a young filmmaker, she presented girlhood as a sexual space and girls as active agents in self-representation, who often challenge female stereotypes. In her **filmmaking**, Cuthand does not shy away from some of the more difficult aspects of exploring her identity: she presents herself, a "halfbreed dyke" in a world of violence, where colonization and racism have an impact on her artistic practice as a young woman.

In 1995 she produced *Lessons in Baby Dyke Theory: The Diasporic Impact of Cross-Generational Barriers*, which earned her critical acclaim. As the title implies, the film looks at how sexual relationships play out between generations. It led to the production of a series of other semi-autobiographical short films and videos, many of which explored issues surrounding ageism, sexuality, identity, race, and mental health. Using a simple low- or no-budget style, her work is highly personal and engaging. Cuthand's self-identification as a lesbian has been a major subject in her work and has allowed her to explore ideas surrounding female sexuality and homosexuality in a direct way, often turning insults like "dyke" into affirmations.

Cuthand's work provides a voice for girlhood subjects that are typically suppressed in popular culture, such as disability, gayness, sexuality, and depression. Working in a highly personal style, Cuthand uses the confessional mode to reflect on the fragmentation and fracturing that is caused by abuse, colonization, and growing up with multiple and contradictory identities. She is frank in exposing her own struggles within the medical system when she was misdiagnosed with bipolar disorder. She is also straightforward in discussing her negotiation of her own sexual desires and her lesbian identity.

Her work is significant for its contribution to making Native American girls' culture more visible. She has forgone the usual depiction of girlhood as a time of **innocence** and has opened up a terrain in which complex personal and social issues—sexuality, racism, depression, suicide, perversity, colonialism, gayness—are presented in an "in-your-face" manner. In the process, the audience is compelled to acknowledge these factors as a part of many girls' experiences of growing up.

See also At Twelve; Benning, Sadie; Video Play

Further Reading

Elwes, Catherin. (2005). *Video Art: A Guided Tour*. London and New York: I.B. Tauris.
Walsh, Shannon. (2005). "Losers, Lolitas, and Lesbos: Visualizing Girlhood." In Claudia Mitchell and Jacqueline Reid-Walsh, eds. *Seven Going on Seventeen: Tween Studies in the Culture of Girlhood*. New York: Peter Lang, pp. 191–205.

SHANNON WALSH

CYBER-BULLYING.   Cyber-bullying refers to the use of the Internet and **cell phones** to harass individuals. It has become an increasing problem among adolescents and **tweens**. While both boys and girls can be victims and perpetrators, it is sometimes seen in girls' culture as another manifestation of the "mean girl" phenomenon. There is a significant need to engage young people in understanding the impact of their jokes online because they do not perceive them to constitute cyber-bullying. Data from a 2006 study conducted by the University of Calgary shows that 53 percent of students reported that they knew someone being harassed online, while 15 percent of the students admitted to using electronic communication tools to bully others. Even though 25 percent of youths age 11 to 19 have been threatened via their computers or cell phones, only 16 percent of students say they talk to their parents about what they do online. This finding corroborates the findings in research conducted by Kids Help Phone (http://www.marchebell pourjeunessejecoute.ca).

Most recently, cyber-bullying has been represented in popular culture through the emergence of **social networking** media such as Facebook, **MySpace**, and YouTube. Although Facebook originated in university settings, where there seemed to be relatively few problems involving cyber-bullying, this medium of communication, in which all users identify themselves with a picture and personal information, has become immensely popular in high schools. Cyber-bullying in the form of cyber-libel on Facebook—where students put up pictures of their teachers or school principals and discuss their engagement in various sexual activities, such as masturbation—has flourished. Female teachers are especially victimized, and the impact of this very public libel is significant because it undermines their authority as teachers, causes embarrassment in the physical school setting, and destroys their reputations. And, as with other forms of sexual harassment, it often "filters down" to girls as well. The legal test involving cyber-libel in Canada is whether "an ordinary reasonable person would believe the expression" (Shariff and Gouin 2006). The difficulty with misogynist or sexual comments posted on Facebook is that the adolescents reading it may not be sufficiently mature to be considered "reasonable" adults, since they are still working out their sexuality and their social relationships, and are simply being kids that push the boundaries of authority.

Cyber-bullying is different from harmful graffiti written on bathroom walls because the walls can be scrubbed; online libel has a permanence and the possibility of reappearing over and over again. Moreover, it is open to an infinite number of viewers, so the harmed reputation of the victim can be spread. The Kids Help Phone survey found that approximately

70 percent of adolescents age 10 to 14 thought of Facebook as a private space where adults could not intervene, whereas in reality adults can monitor these sites, especially if they are used from within the schools.

See also Bullying; Meanness

Further Reading

Chu, Jeff. (2005). *You Wanna Take This Online? Cyberspace Is the 21st Century Bully's Playground Where Girls Play Rougher than Boys*. [Online April 2007]. Time Magazine Web site http://www.time.com/time/magazine/article/0,9171,1088698,00.html.

Shariff, Shaheen, and Rachel Gouin. (2006). "Cyber-Hierarchies: A New Arsenal of Weapons for Gendered Violence in Schools." In Fiona Leach and Claudia Mitchell, eds. *Combating Gender Violence in and around Schools*, Stoke-on-Trent, UK: Trentham Books, pp. 33–41.

SHAHEEN SHARIFF

D

DEBUTANTE. The term "debutante" is generally used to refer to a young adult woman who is being introduced to society. The word comes from the French word *début*, meaning "to lead off." The symbols associated with the debutante, such as a white dress, a bouquet of flowers, and a male escort, further identify the practice of "debuting" as a prelude to marriage. This social custom now transcends racial and ethnic lines and is one of the few remaining **coming-of-age** rituals for adolescent girls in the United States.

The Debutante in History. The concept of a young woman being formally introduced into society reaches far back in history. Anthropologists trace this tradition to ancient coming-of-age ceremonies, in which parents advertised their daughter's marriageability. In Mayan culture, 15-year-old girls were presented to their communities during elaborate religious rituals, and the Aztecs also celebrated young girls' nubility by formally acknowledging the onset of puberty. The Spanish colonists in North America incorporated Catholicism into Native American rituals, creating a hybrid of the earlier Aztec ceremonies. This is probably the origin of the modern **Quinceañera**, or coming-of-age ceremony, observed by **Latinas** in the United States. These celebrations reached their peak during the reign of the Spanish Emperor Maximillian and his wife the Empress Carlota, who introduced European influences to the events by holding lavish court presentations and balls.

The custom of being presented at the royal court began in Great Britain in the early seventeenth century, when the wives and daughters of the peerage and the landed class were formally introduced to the King and Queen. Court presentations were very elaborate affairs: everyone who was to be presented needed a sponsor to get on the presentation list, and the event required special preparation from its participants. For example, women underwent complex training for the "curtsy," a gesture at the heart of the court presentation. The curtsy was a very formal greeting and gesture that required a girl to lean forward on her front legs and lower her head until her nose almost touched the ground. The curtsy remains an important part of the debutante ritual today. In early British debutante rituals, a strict dress code was enforced at the court, prescribing even a particular type of headdress. While the style of this headwear changed throughout the years and included veils, tiaras, and jewels, its consistent feature was a plume of feathers. After World War II, court presentations were replaced by more informal garden parties and were ultimately abolished by Queen Elizabeth II in 1958.

The social debut was imported to the American colonies in the late seventeenth century by British aristocrats with strong links to those in the American aristocracy. By the eighteenth century, however, the American aristocracy had been replaced by more of a meritocracy, in which social position was founded in achievement, education, and service. Debuts were more modest and generally consisted of an afternoon tea or reception held at home, followed by an informal dinner party with dancing. At this time, debuts were simply a way of presenting a daughter to friends of the family, also signaling that a young woman now had permission to meet socially with young men if properly chaperoned. The average age of a debutante in the North was 18, but girls in the South "came out" as early as 14. Following their debut, girls were expected to marry.

The Modern Debutante Ritual. American society underwent still further changes in the nineteenth century when monetary wealth began to determine social standing. By the end of the century, members of the upper class were beginning to hold debuts outside their homes in order to make the events more public and grandiose. In 1870 Archibald Gracie King rented a large banquet room at Delmonico's for his daughter's debut, thus changing the nature of the ritual from a private to a public event. Soon after, other families followed suit, holding lavish balls. Debutante presentations became symbols of the materialism and ostentatiousness of the very rich during the nineteenth century. However, balls and assemblies had been held by men's organizations as early as the eighteenth century. The Philadelphia Assembly, founded in 1748, is considered the oldest debutante ball in the nation. After the Civil War, many other men's organizations began to invite debutantes to their assemblies for collective debuts. These organizations included the Bachelor's Cotillion of Baltimore, the St. Cecilia's Ball of Charleston, and the Mystic Order of the Veiled Prophet in St. Louis.

In the 1930s, the image of the debutante underwent another transformation. In their heyday, debutantes were treated like royalty by the American press, epitomized as the height of glamour and style for Depression-era America. Some of the most famous debutantes of the twentieth century were introduced during this period, including Doris Duke (heir to the American Tobacco Company) and Barbara Hutton, the heir to the Woolworth fortune. These were followed by the "glamour girls" of Café Society, such as Gloria "Mimi" Baker, as well as Brenda Frazier, whose debutante ball was so large that she was featured on the cover of *Life* magazine in 1938.

The advent of World War II curtailed the extravagant coming-out parties of the prewar years, and balls in honor of single individuals became rare. After the war, groups in various American cities began to organize black-tie events that combined debutante presentations with fund-raisers for local charities, such as the Desert Foundation Ball in Phoenix or New York's Infirmary Ball. Participation in the ritual of debuting declined drastically during the "Deb drought" of the 1960s, when the custom became viewed as irrelevant. Yet by the 1980s, debutante organizations began to proliferate once again. Whereas debutantes once came only from the ranks of the upper class, today such rigid social distinctions have been blurred in what might be regarded as the democratization of the debutante. In some communities, "Honor Cotillions" recognize young women for scholarship and social service. In the western and southwestern United States, a debutante ball serves as the culmination of many years of community service in the National Charity League.

Changing Values, Changing Faces. Traditionally, many debutante organizations have been characterized by exclusivity and religious or racial prejudice. This has resulted in the creation of a number of exclusive debutante balls, such as the Roman Catholic Fleur de Lis Ball in St. Louis, Missouri. Both religion and culture are incorporated in the *Quinceañera,* in which 15-year-old Latina girls attend mass and then throw elaborate parties that include "courts" of attendants and emphasize the responsibilities inherent in the transition to womanhood. Other immigrant groups have co-opted the custom, a trend exemplified by the Winter Blossom Ball in Los Angeles, which presents Chinese American girls to their families and communities. Hundreds of African American girls are presented annually by private organizations that include The Links, Inc.; Jack and Jill of America; Alpha Kappa Alpha Sorority; and the Delta Sigma Theta Sorority. Latina girls debut at the Hispanic Debutante Ball in Fort Worth, Texas, and in the Laredo, Texas, Colonial Ball and Pageant. Both ethnic and racial debutante organizations tend to highlight cultural tradition and civic involvement in their celebrations. Other organizations have further adapted the debutante ball to reflect specific values, as in the case of the evangelical Christian variation, the "Purity Ball." In this social rite of passage, teenage girls exchange rings with their fathers and publicly affirm a commitment to sexual **abstinence** before marriage.

For the most part, the debutante ball provides an important opportunity to demonstrate a family's social status and wealth. This tradition inextricably links status to ritual, using daughters to establish their families' social positions through the rite of passage that is the debutante ball.

See also Bat Mitzvah; Sweet Sixteen

Further Reading

Marling, Karal Ann. (2004). *Debutante: Rites and Regalia of American Debdom.* Lawrence: University of Kansas Press.

Vida, Vendela. (2000). *Girls on the Verge: Debutante Dips, Drive-bys, and Other Initiations.* New York: St. Martin's Griffin.

GEORGANNE SCHEINER GILLIS

DEE, SANDRA (1942–2005). Sandra Dee was an American film star who became famous in the 1950s and 1960s as the embodiment of the all-American girl. Dee is remembered as a virginal, perky adolescent and serves as a nostalgic reminder of a simpler time. However, in her films, Dee also embodied a kind of girl new to the late fifties: a teenager conflicted about her emerging sexuality.

Dee was born Alexandra Zuck in Bayonne, New Jersey, on April 23, 1942 (although for years her date of birth was given as 1944). Her parents divorced when she was 5. After the divorce, Dee's mother worked as a secretary until 1950, when she married Eugene Douvan, a real estate investor who was also her boss. Douvan began sexually abusing Dee when she was about 8 years old, something never acknowledged by her mother even after Dee went public with the story. When Dee began to menstruate and develop breasts at age 9, her mother had her bind her breasts and tried to deny Dee's sexual maturation. Dee became an anorexic the same year. Dee became a top model when she landed on the cover of *American Girl* magazine at 10 years old. In 1956, her stepfather died during heart surgery. A few days later, Hollywood producer Ross Hunter arranged a screen test for her after seeing her in a television commercial. She signed a seven-year contract with Universal and was immediately loaned to MGM for the film *Until They Sail*.

In her first year and a half, Dee made three more films: *The Reluctant Debutante*, *Stranger in My Arms*, and *The Restless Years*. In 1959 she made another three: **Gidget**, *A Summer Place*, and *Imitation of Life*. During those same years, she was hospitalized three times for **anorexia**. In 1960, at age 16, she met Bobby Darin during the filming of *Come September*, and they were married after a whirlwind courtship. They had a son, named Dodd, in 1961. She became an alcoholic during their turbulent marriage, which ended in 1967; Darin died in 1973 at the age of 37. Their relationship was the subject of the 2004 film *Beyond the Sea*. Dee's most famous film roles of the sixties include *Tammy Tell Me True* (1961); *Tammy and the Doctor* (1963); *Take Her, She's Mine* (1963); *I'd Rather Be Rich* (1964); and *That Funny Feeling* (1965).

Dee often played the part of a wholesome **girl-next-door**, a role commonly available to young actresses during the 1950s and 1960s. In fact, her squeaky-clean image was parodied in the 1972 Broadway show and 1978 Hollywood production *Grease*, in the song "Look at Me, I'm Sandra Dee." However, Dee's film characterizations did offer adolescent females an alternative to the chaste virgin model of sexual behavior so popular during that era. She was a "good girl," but she still had sexual desires of her own. The narratives of

Mary LaRoche and Sandra Dee (on surfboard) in Paul Wendkos's 1959 film *Gidget*. (Courtesy of Photofest.)

Dee's films involve conflicts that highlight adolescent females' sexual desire. Nevertheless, in many ways, Dee became a prisoner of her own image and will always be remembered as the archetypal adolescent girl.

By the late sixties, Dee disappeared from the public eye to battle her inner demons of incest, anorexia, depression, and alcoholism. Her career was virtually over by the 1970s except for scattered appearances on television, as in the pilot episode of *Fantasy Island* (1977), and film, as in *The Dunwich Horror* (1970). Dee made her last film appearance in the film *Lost* (1983). She died on February 20, 2005, from kidney disease and pneumonia.

Further Reading

Dodd, Darin, and Maxine Paetro. (1994). *Dream Lovers: The Magnificent Shattered Lives of Bobby Darin and Sandra Dee*. New York: Warner Books.

Scheiner, Georganne. (2001). "Look at Me, I'm Sandra Dee: Beyond a White Teen Icon." *Frontiers: A Journal of Women's Studies* 12, no. 2, 87–107.

GEORGANNE SCHEINER GILLIS

DEGRASSI.   *Degrassi* is a franchise of five television shows that have been enormously popular with adolescents, particularly teenage girls. Before *Degrassi*, most teen shows were actually family-oriented shows or educational programs that focused on parents and teachers as much as on young people. *Degrassi* started a trend in adolescent television programming by telling stories about young people from their perspective and focusing on peer groups instead of the family. It also dealt with many subjects—some of them taboo—that had never been talked about on TV before the 1980s, including abortion, drug use, suicide, teen parenting, AIDS, activism, sexism, and interracial dating.

Degrassi began in the 1970s in Toronto, Canada, as the brainchild of Linda Schuyler, originally a teacher, and Kit Hood, originally an editor and once a child actor. In 1976, they began a production company they called Playing with Time and produced the short film *Ida Makes a Movie,* based on the book by Kay Chorao. This became one of the episodes of their first series, *The Kids of Degrassi Street. Kids* was filmed in the Toronto community of Riverdale between 1979 and 1985. After *Kids* ended its run, Playing With Time developed a new series, and in 1987 *Degrassi Junior High* was born. It picked up where the previous show left off—some of the *Kids* actors simply took on the roles of new characters in *Junior High*. This iteration of the show ran for three seasons and then seamlessly transitioned into *Degrassi High* for another two. The two series are now often referred to as *Degrassi Classic*. *Degrassi Classic* was produced in partnership with the Canadian Broadcasting Corporation, a government-funded television channel, and was partially funded by the American Public Broadcasting Service.

After *Degrassi Classic* ended in 1992, Playing With Time produced a six-part documentary series called *Degrassi Talks*. Each episode dealt with a different social issue (sex, alcohol, abuse, depression, drug abuse, and sexuality) that affects teens. As the show traveled across Canada, each episode was hosted by a *Degrassi Classic* actor whose character had been affected in the course of the series by the particular issue addressed that week. Scores of young people were interviewed for the program.

In 2001, the newest installment of *Degrassi* premiered, titled *Degrassi: The Next Generation*. This version is produced by Linda Schuyler's new production company in conjunction with Stephen Stohn's Epitome Pictures, Inc. Its premise is ingenious. The

Degrassi Classic series featured a character named Spike, who gave birth to a daughter, Emma. In *Next Generation*, Emma is now enrolled in junior high at the Degrassi Community School. *Next Generation* features a whole new cast of characters, who have many of the same issues as the characters in the previous *Degrassi* incarnations. But more contemporary issues are also addressed, including date rape, adoption, mental illness, child abuse, cyber-stalking, and gay identities.

Degrassi Classic is often left out of discussions of the history of teen television, although it is probably one of the earliest examples of the genre, predating *Saved by the Bell* and **Beverly Hills, 90210**. Popular lore has it that noted producer Aaron Spelling tried to buy the rights to *Degrassi Classic* but was refused when the producers found out he wanted to change the style of the show and relocate it in Beverly Hills.

Unlike other shows of the 1980s, the characters of *Degrassi Classic* were relatively diverse in race, ethnicity, and class. The young actors on the series looked like regular kids: they had acne and weight problems, and they wore clothes that were not the latest styles. They were teens playing teens, unlike the adult who played teens in shows like *Beverly Hills, 90210*.

The writers of *Degrassi* have never provided easy solutions for their characters' problems, allowing them to face the consequences of their actions. Sometimes these consequences, which can be severe, do not disappear at the end of an episode or even a season. In the first episode of season 1 of *Degrassi High*, a character named Erica becomes pregnant. She is torn between the choice of delivering the baby, a responsibility with which she is not ready to deal, or having an abortion, a procedure to which she is morally opposed. This episode shows her struggle as she comes to terms with her situation and decides to have the abortion. In the episode, she walks through a line of pro-life protesters to enter the clinic where she will have her abortion. The scene was so controversial that it was recut before airing in the United States. Her choice to terminate her pregnancy was brought up in later episodes by her twin sister, Heather, who felt guilty about supporting her sister's decision and worried about her subsequent sexual behavior.

In *Degrassi: The Next Generation*, the producers have managed to reinvent the *Degrassi* franchise. It remains faithful to the original format, focusing on teens and their concerns, but it has updated its style. The teens on the show are more stylish than their predecessors. The show has a bigger production budget, so shooting occurs in a professional studio with permanent sets, rather than on location. The characters seem more firmly middle class.

In the United States, *Degrassi: The Next Generation* is broadcast on the cable network The N. The network has placed restrictions on the show and has asked for episodes to be reedited and new endings to be shot. In 2004, a three-episode story arc about abortion was never aired on The N. But, taking advantage of cross-border information swapping via the Internet, American teens found ways to access the episodes and created a petition, carrying thousands of names, that they presented to Viacom (parent company of The N). Recently, there has been less editing and scene cutting by The N. Some, though not all, of the controversial episodes were eventually rebroadcast on The N in their original format under the title *Degrassi: The Director's Cut*.

Further Reading

Byers, Michele, ed. (2005). *Growing Up Degrassi*. Toronto: Sumach Press.
Ellis, Kathryn. (2005). *Degrassi Generations*. Oakville, ON: Pocket.

MICHELE BYERS

DIRTY DANCING.   *Dirty Dancing* (1987) is both a classic **coming-of-age** story and a seductive tale of forbidden love. It recounts the summer of 1963 in the life of Frances "Baby" Houseman, a naïve but principled 17-year-old vacationing with her upper-class family in New York's Catskill Mountains. An aspiring member of the Peace Corps, Baby embarks on a journey that whisks her away from a life of childhood **innocence** into a deeper knowledge of love and desire, as she discovers the true nature of class divisions, family bonds, and protecting loved ones.

When Baby discovers the hidden world of dirty dancing—the sensual after-hours style favored by Kellerman's sassy entertainment staff—she becomes entangled (both physically and emotionally) in the world of Johnny Castle, the staff's venerated dance instructor. Johnny, the suave and sexy "bad boy" of Kellerman's Resort, is adored by women and viewed with both suspicion and disdain by the leading male characters in the film: Max Kellerman, the owner of the resort; and Baby's father, Dr. Jake Houseman.

The apple of her father's eye, Baby has always played by the rules, until a crisis emerges and Johnny's dance partner Penny cannot perform in a show at a nearby resort. When Baby steps in to fill Penny's shoes, she not only finds her rhythm, but becomes embroiled in a passionate affair with Johnny. The two come from opposite sides of the tracks, and though Johnny teaches Baby to dance, Baby ultimately teaches Johnny the greater lesson—that courage means standing up for what is right, being true to oneself, and pursuing love no matter the cost. In the end, Johnny sticks up for Baby and tells her father, "nobody puts Baby in a corner"—a line that would be quoted for decades to come in North American popular culture.

Though *Dirty Dancing* is an artifact from an earlier time and holds a special place primarily in the hearts of those who first saw it during their teenage years in the late 1980s and 1990s, its cultural value endures to this day. *Dirty Dancing* is arguably among the most popular American movies of the twentieth century. Produced on a budget of only $6 million, it has grossed $170 million, and 10 million copies of the DVD have been purchased worldwide (Clark 2007). The film's famous soundtrack, which sat at the top of the Billboard charts for eighteen weeks after its release, may have played a large part in the movie's sleeper success. Including tracks by several **girl groups** of the 1960s, such as the Ronettes and the Shirelles, the soundtrack went platinum eleven times, and the legendary song "(I've Had) The Time of My Life" won both a Grammy and an Oscar in 1988. On both its tenth and twentieth anniversaries, the movie was briefly re-released in theaters, to the great delight of fans both young and old, and a twentieth-anniversary special-edition DVD met with an enthusiastic response in 2007.

A second film, called *Dirty Dancing: Havana Nights*, was released in 2004 and was less a sequel than a wholesale transposition of the film's basic story line from 1960s upstate New York to 1950s Cuba. *Havana Nights* held little allure for original *Dirty Dancing* fans, and its success paled in comparison with that of the original. Nevertheless, it was a popular contribution to the genre of **junior chick flicks**, appealing chiefly to **tweens** and teens, especially those interested in dance movies such as *Center Stage* (2000), *Save the Last Dance* (2001), and *Step Up* (2006).

Dirty Dancing's success has not been limited to the silver screen. A stage version of the film was created in 2004 and debuted in Australia before traveling to London in 2006. Pre-premiere ticket sales soared to a London Theatre record of $11 million (CNN 2006), and the show is expected to continue in London until 2008, simultaneously playing in Toronto (2007) and Holland (2008).

Further Reading

Cable News Network (CNN). (2006). *The Insider's Guide to* Dirty Dancing. [Online June 2007].
CNN Web site http://edition.cnn.com/2006/SHOWBIZ/10/25/insider.dirtydancing/index.html.
Clark, Paul. (2007). *Dirty Dancing Marks 20 Years with Return to the Big Screen* [Online June 2007].
Citizen Times Web site http://www.citizen-times.com/apps/pbcs.dll/article?AID=200770429019.

LESLEY COHEN

DISORDERED EATING.   Although disordered eating and eating disorders sound similar, they are not synonymous terms. Eating disorders, such as **anorexia**, **bulimia**, and **binge eating**, are severe and have specific diagnostic criteria. The American Dietetic Association uses "disordered eating" to refer to a spectrum of behaviors, including restrictive dieting and bingeing, that occur less often or are less severe than full-fledged, diagnosed eating disorders. Restrictive dieting behaviors include severe caloric restriction, omission of specific types of foods or food groups, skipping meals, or fasting. Bingeing/purging behaviors include consumption of large quantities of food, followed by self-induced vomiting, excessive exercise, use of laxative/diuretics, or consumption of diet pills in attempt to suppress appetite or increase metabolic rate. Individuals with eating disorders exhibit disordered eating patterns, but not all those exhibiting disordered eating behavior necessarily have an eating disorder.

Disordered eating patterns tend to be symptoms of serious distress; food itself is rarely the essential problem. Extreme dieting methods can cause short-term weight loss, which makes them appealing to young girls. But the restrictive and extreme nature of these behaviors often induces a cycle of weight gain and loss, placing the individual at greater risk of developing an eating disorder.

In recent years, there has been an increasing prevalence of disordered eating behaviors, as well as eating disorders, in young girls, **tweens**, and teenagers in Western societies. Recent research suggests that approximately one-third of teenage girls engage in unhealthy weight control behaviors. Much research has explored the individual, sociocultural, and familial factors affecting a girl's likelihood to engage in disordered eating behavior. Adolescents and teens with dominantly negative emotions, low self-esteem, or intense body dissatisfaction, or who are experiencing the early onset of puberty are more likely to engage in disordered eating.

From a social perspective, exposure to the very thin ideal of womanhood in the media can lead to internalization of the **thin ideal**, increasing the likelihood of disordered eating. The content of many popular teen girl **magazines**, such as *Seventeen*, is appearance oriented and often includes topics related to eating and exercise strategies. Studies have shown that teen girls who often read magazine articles about dieting and weight loss are more likely to engage in extreme dieting practices, often in an effort to attain a similar body shape to that of ultra-thin female models and celebrities, such as **Lindsay Lohan**, Mischa Barton of **The O.C.**, and **Mary-Kate Olsen**, all of whom are portrayed in magazines of this type. The likelihood of disordered eating is also greater for girls who are more popular, have been teased about their weight, have been pressured to diet, or have friends who are dieting.

Even the family unit can increase the likelihood of disordered eating. This can occur if parents or caregivers show preoccupation with their own bodies, engage in disordered eating behaviors, comment on the girl's weight and encourage her weight loss, or if family relations are generally poor (for example, in cases of a lack of cohesion among family members, low parental expectations of children, or poor familial communication).

However, several factors can prevent girls from developing disordered eating patterns. One of the greatest protective factors is the development of positive family relationships between parents and children. Relationships (both peer and familial) that provide social support for coping with stress, engaging in activities that foster a positive identity and body image, and belonging to a cultural group accepting of a variety of body types all serve to protect young girls from practicing disordered eating patterns.

See also Fat Girl

Further Reading

American Dietetic Association's Public Relations Team. *Eating Disorders and Disordered Eating: How Do They Differ?* [Online December 2006]. American Dietetic Association Web site http://www.eatright.org/cps/rde/xchg/ada/hs.xsl/home_9079_ENU_HTML.htm.

Littleton, Heather L., and Thomas Ollendick. (2003). "Negative Body Image and Disordered Eating Behavior in Children and Adolescents: What Places Youth at Risk and How Can These Problems Be Prevented?" *Clinical Child and Family Psychology Review* 6, 51–66.

Neumark-Sztainer, Dianne. (2005). *I'm Like, So Fat!* New York: Guilford Press.

LORI A. NEIGHBORS

DJ CULTURE.   Girls' DJ culture refers to the growing phenomenon of girls acting as disc jockeys (DJs). While DJ culture has existed as part of **Hip Hop culture** since the 1970s, it became part of girl culture in the only mid- to late 1990s. It sheds light on girls' growing access to technology, as well as the establishment of a distinct female presence in the field of music. Girls today are being exposed to DJ culture and new forms of musical practice at younger ages than were previous generations of women. A strong feminist vision compels many female DJs—from older teens to adult women—to introduce younger girls to DJ culture and technology, something that may soon transform DJ culture into a truly egalitarian enterprise.

Several toys reflecting DJ culture are geared toward young girls. The DJ Barbie, or Barbie Karaoke toy, is a mini **pink** and blue boom box that plays sixteen preprogrammed melodies (see the essay on Barbie in Part 1). Complete with built-in speakers and volume controls, it comes with pretend CDs and tapes as well as "shout outs" (a series of greetings by DJ Barbie to her audience). Another DJ-themed toy designed for girls is the **Polly Pocket** Par-Tay Bus. This toy bus opens up to create the setting for a dance party, where girls can place their dolls in a DJ booth, complete with turntables and headphones. These toys, which appeared on the market within the last 10 years, signify a change in the marketing of technology-related toys. In the past, such toys were marketed solely toward boys and featured only boys in their advertisements (although non–gender-specific advertisements could be seen for toys such as the older Fisher-Price DJ set and the more recent CoolP3 DJ MP3 Player with Docking Station, by Tek Nek). Only recently have manufacturers of girl-oriented toys, including companies like **Mattel**, caught on to the real-world trend of girl DJ culture and begun to market DJ play in their toys. These toys also diverge from the long-standing trend of marketing only kitchen and housekeeping toys to girls (for example, the **Easy-Bake Oven**).

Girl DJ culture has also been fostered by DJing workshops. These workshops are typically run by female teachers who encourage girls to participate and learn DJing skills either as a hobby or in hopes of pursuing a career in the music industry. These workshops are held in many American cities. Some train girls to operate and repair DJ equipment such as turntables and speakers. Others also provide a history of Hip Hop culture and explore the many contributions female musicians have made to the field. Many provide practice space and opportunities for girls to perform. By making the technology accessible to girls, these workshops enable them to share a love for music and demonstrate their potential in ways previously impossible. Presently, limited access to the expensive, high-tech equipment used by DJs has greatly limited girls' involvement in DJ culture.

Older teens can attend events featuring all-female DJ lineups and DJ contests. By intentionally emphasizing female DJs, these events counter the all-male DJ lineups typical of mainstream clubs and events.

The emergence of female DJ collectives also encourages the involvement of older teenage girls. These collectives meet both face to face and virtually, providing supportive spaces for those females who are honing their DJing skills. Members of these collectives may include women active in other elements of Hip Hop culture, such as graffiti, breakdancing, and MCing, as well as those who work in the music industry, such as label owners and talent scouts. Some of these collectives have an activist component, encouraging female DJs to use their knowledge and skills to create positive changes in their communities.

See also Filmmaking; Toys, Kitchen and Housekeeping; Video Play

The popular Russian DJ Benzina performs at a rave in Moscow. (Courtesy of Shutterstock.)

Further Reading

Boston, Andrea. *Spin Sisters: Philly Female DJs Turn the Tables on a Traditional Boys Club*. [Online May 2007]. Philadelphia People Web site http://philapeople.temple.edu/spinsisters.htm.

Ostroff, Joshua. *The Chicks Dig It Crew Returns for More All-Female DJ Fun*. [Online April 2007]. Eye Weekly Web site http://www.eye.net/eye/issue/issue_01.03.02/thebeat/chicksdigit.php.

AMANDA CONNON-UNDA

DOLLHOUSE.   Dollhouses and girls have been linked for centuries. A long tradition exists of using wooden dollhouses as teaching tools for girls. Early dollhouses in seventeenth-century Europe were used to instruct girls in the details of household duties; in England and North America, dollhouses paralleled the history of dolls and became associated with children's play during the late eighteenth century

Many of these early houses were large enough for a child to crawl into, though not without destroying the expensive structure and its contents. Because of this, most play with dollhouses was carefully supervised. Traditional dollhouse play emphasized maturing girls' new association with the domestic sphere. The dollhouse was a space set apart for play so that girls would not be tempted to play outside. As a large, permanent structure, the dollhouse fulfilled a practical requirement for imaginative play, allowing a child to leave a complicated game and return to it at leisure.

Variations of both the furnished and unfurnished dollhouse have continued to be built until the present day. In the early twentieth century, a growing interest in providing children with practical, nurturing environments encouraged artists such as Claud Lovat Fraser, Jessie Marion King, and Roger Fry to design dolls' houses loosely modeled after homes of innovative design. Dollhouses began to reflect new trends in home design, expanding beyond the strict confines of traditionally styled homes to depict contemporary domestic architecture as well. In 1913, the wooden toy company Morton Converse offered a bungalow dollhouse that came complete with a car and garage. By the 1920s, professional architects were designing dollhouses for major toy companies; by the end of the decade, trends in dollhouse furniture reflected new developments in household technology, such as toy gas stoves by the Tappan company and toy refrigerators—even Maytag washing machines—sold by the Hubley company. Thus the dollhouse began to assume the function of a **dream house**, as would soon be produced by **Mattel** for Barbie in the 1960s. These toy houses were modeled on the homes that suburban, middle-class American families might actually inhabit, rather than the English or European traditionally styled dollhouses based on elegant townhouses owned by wealthy families.

In the 1980s, a fantasy element was introduced in dollhouse design with products such as the Bluebird teapot house and the highly successful **Polly Pocket** line of products. A Polly Pocket house is a miniaturized plastic toy so small and lightweight that a girl can now carry it in her pocket or backpack, in sharp contrast with the large wooden dollhouses of earlier centuries, which a girl could fit into. Each toy, however, encourages private, imaginative play. The current reversal may reflect a change in female societal roles, which now encourages girls to abandon the domestic realm for the public domain.

At the other end of the spectrum from today's miniaturized, inexpensive, prefabricated dollhouses is the dollhouse construction kit, which combines the construction play traditionally associated with boys with a traditional girls' toy. The most spectacular set of this type is the large Playmobil house produced by the Brandstätter company in 1989. Its house and occupants are constructed of nontoxic plastic and are elaborate playsets. In a return to tradition, or perhaps reflecting the European origins of the company, the house's traditional architecture style recalls those of the large dollhouses of earlier centuries—with the notable exception that the child assembles them herself.

Further Reading

Armstrong, Frances. (1996). "The Dollhouse as Ludic Space, 1690–1920." *Children's Literature* 24, 23–54.

Cross, Gary. (1997). *Kids' Stuff: Toys and the Changing World of American Childhood.* Cambridge, MA: Harvard University Press.

Pasierbska, Halina. *Dolls' Houses.* [Online March 2007]. Table and Home Web site http://www.tableandhome.com/education/polly-pocket.html.

JACQUELINE REID-WALSH

DORA THE EXPLORER.   Begun in 1999 as a pilot television series, and in 2000 turned into a regular program for the Nickelodeon children's network (based in the United States), *Dora the Explorer* is a show about a Latina girl that targets the preschool market. In addition to its cable distribution, the show is shown on the CBS network. As an example of girl-specific **cross-merchandising**, Dora has turned into an affordable but profitable brand including a broad range of products from toys, books, and DVDs to bed linen, clothing, gummy (Dora) bears, and backpacks.

Dora the Explorer is a 7-year-old girl whose first name is part of the Spanish word for explorer, *exploradora*. In each episode, she sets off on an adventure with her trusted pet monkey, Boots; her magic backpack; and a map. A sneaky fox named Swiper generally tries to distract Dora and her team from their quest. Nevertheless, by the end of the half hour, Dora and her helpers have completed their quest or solved their puzzle.

As an adventurous female protagonist of a preschool children's show, Dora is cutting edge. She works in an unspecified island-looking space without the help of adults or of many other humans. With the help of her magical team, she uses her active wits to solve problems. She can be seen as a role model and is a very popular character among both girls and boys. Accordingly, the nature of most of the Dora merchandise is gender neutral. The Dora scooter, inflatable chair, and ball and bat set can be used by any of her fans. However, some of the Dora merchandise is clearly intended for girls: her line of apparel includes ruffled tank tops, shorts with embroidered hearts, and a satin and fur jacket. The constant presence of the color **pink** on Dora merchandise further implies that it is girl centered. This may explain why a spin-off show called *Go, Diego, Go!* based on her male cousin Diego, was created in 2005. The Diego line features the same gender-neutral merchandise as the Dora line, but redone in blue.

Dora is inescapably Latina. Her use of the Spanish language, though in a very elementary form, is intended to introduce a few words of Spanish into the vocabularies of mainstream viewers. The language component of the television series is emphasized by offering viewers the opportunity to participate actively during the many pauses in the show for children to call out their responses to the characters in Spanish. Regardless of whether Dora was conceived as a character to appeal to ethnic audiences or as a way to infuse multiculturalism for the benefit of mainstream audiences, she is part of a larger trend that seeks to include diversity in girl-targeted products. Joining Dora in the doll market is the rising and ethnically indeterminate **Bratz** doll line, whose rapid rise in popularity—surpassing even that of Barbie—in conjunction with the **Muslim dolls** Fulla and Razanne, has doll manufacturers exploring the potential profitability of the ethnic doll market (see the essays on Barbie and Doll Culture in Part 1). Interestingly, Dora's rise to popularity coincided with the U.S. Census Bureau announcement that Latinas and Latinos form the largest minority group in the country.

Dora stands at the intersection of two understandings of the **Latina presence in popular culture**. Because she uses words that are indigenous to Mexican Spanish, and because her locales include such markers as a Mayan-looking pyramid, she is said to embody a Mexican Latina experience. On the other hand, because the show's soundtrack features mambo and salsa rhythms and its settings are filled with lush forests and palm trees, she could also be said to embody a Tropical Latina experience.

Overall, Dora's presence and popularity represent a recognition either that Spanish is likely to become a more important component of everyday American experience or that variety of ethnicity is an integral part of the fabric of American life. Many academics who focus on Latina or Latino studies and popular culture have noted that the state of being or performativity of Latina or *Latinidad* is permeating American popular culture through the presence of Latina females. Although a girl, Dora is part of this gendered incorporation of the Latina body into the mainstream popular culture that, through globalization, is circulated far beyond the national boundaries of the United States.

Dora and Monkey Boots star in CBS's children's series *Dora the Explorer*. (Courtesy of Photofest.)

Further Reading

Frenck, Moses. (2007). *Toy Treatment: Bilingual Playthings Mean Big Business for Industry Bent on Marketing to Latinos.* [Online September 2007]. Marketing y Medios Web site http://www.marketing ymedios.com/marketingymedios/magazine/article_display.jsp?vnu_content_id=1003546969.

ANGHARAD N. VALDIVIA

DREAM HOUSE.   Dream houses have been associated with postwar American culture since Cary Grant and Myrna Loy appeared in the movie *Mr. Blandings Builds His Dream House* (1948), based on Eric Hodgins's best-selling novel published two years earlier. Tapping into this dream of building an up-to-date suburban home, **Mattel** used the term in the 1960s to refer to a **dollhouse** for Barbie. Over the years, the house has been built of different materials and has had many different manifestations, from its modest beginnings to the elaborate structures sold today.

First manufactured in 1961, the house came in a flat cardboard form, and all of the pieces had to be punched out and put together. A studio home of modernist design, the entire construction folded into a small, light suitcase. As with Barbie's dream houses of today, the early versions were backdrops for Barbie's lifestyle of leisure and consumption of up-to-date goods. The house was filled with sleek, modern furniture, including a multimedia center. While relaxing in her "space," Barbie could watch herself on television or listen to record albums. Her house also had a closet to display her fashionable clothing. The Barbie dream house was intended to be different from a traditional dollhouse. In the past, dollhouses helped teach young girls to be good homemakers. In this context, Barbie was presented as a consumer instead of a homemaker—indeed, there was no kitchen in her house.

In terms of implied play patterns, the house appears to be more of a play set than a dollhouse, with its open plan and lack of interior walls. Unlike traditional dollhouses, which are accessible only through the hinged front walls, the dream house had was basically one room and no roof, allowing girls to easily manipulate the furniture. The colors of the walls and furniture were those that were fashionable during the period, such as blue and pumpkin as well as magenta; Barbie was not yet associated solely with the pervasive **pink** today's consumers are accustomed to. More recent and elaborate dream houses continued to function as play sets, allowing children multiple points of access to the structure.

From the 1970s on, the Barbie Dream House consisted of three movable modules and required adult assembly. One model, sold from 1977 to 1991, has features and furnishings composed of plastic that reveal what was considered desirable in a suburban home: French doors, a front balcony, casement windows, and so on. When assembled, it was a plastic pink and white structure about three feet high—the size of a small child. Other Barbie dream houses include Magical Mansion (1990), a two-story colonial house made of wood fiber, and Barbie Fold' n Fun House (1992), which was built of paper and plastic and came inside a bright pink suitcase that doubled as the roof of the assembled house. Around two feet high when built, it collapsed into a case the size of a small suitcase, allowing a child to carry the house around. The Barbie "three in one" house (1995) allowed children to create a town house, a beach house, or a ranch house from the same pieces. In 1997 controversy arose over issues of access when a new friend of Barbie with a physical disability was unable to access the elevator of the elaborate three-story dream house.

The idea of a Barbie dream house as not only a house but a mansion has crossed into other Barbie media as well, particularly digital media. The design of the activities portion of the official Barbie Web site resembles a celebrity house complete with a living room, bedroom, closet, garden, television studio, game room, and adjacent mall (http://barbie.everythinggirl.com/activities/fun_games/).

(See the essay devoted to Barbie in Part 1.)

Further Reading

Canedy, Dana. (1997). "More Toys Are Reflecting Disabled Children's Needs." [Online March 2007]. The New York Times Web site http://query.nytimes.com/gst/fullpage.html?res=9904E5DA113EF936A15751C1A961958260&sec=health&spon=&pagewanted=print.

Friedman, Alice, and Rosemary Haddad. (1995). *Dream Houses, Toy Homes*. Montreal: Canadian Centre for Architecture.

JACQUELINE REID-WALSH

DUFF, HILARY (1987–). Hilary Duff, a **tween** icon, is an American actress and singer famous for her leading role in the Disney Channel television series *Lizzie McGuire*. She also has a film career and has recorded four albums of pop music. Her trendy, affordable clothing line, *Stuff by Duff*, was launched in 2004 and is directed toward the tween girl market.

Duff was born in Texas, but when she and her sister became interested in pursuing careers as actresses, their family relocated to California. After acting in various commercials, Duff received her first major part as the young witch Wendy in *Casper Meets Wendy* (1998). She then acted in a supporting role in the television movie, *The Soul Collector* (1999), for which she won a Young Artist Award for Best Performance in a TV Movie or Pilot (Supporting Young Actress).

Duff's big break came when she landed the lead in *Lizzie McGuire* (2001–2004). She portrayed Lizzie, who, at the show's start, was in seventh grade. Lizzie was concerned about her friends, school, family, and fashion, all common preoccupations of pre-teens and teens. One of the Disney Channel's most popular shows, it spun off a movie in 2003, called *The Lizzie McGuire Movie*.

Duff also starred in the Disney Channel movie *Cadet Kelly* (2002), but her first major cinematic role was in the film *Agent Cody Banks* (2003). She has also appeared in the popular films *Cheaper by the Dozen* (2003), *A Cinderella Story* (2004), *Cheaper by the Dozen 2* (2005), and *The Perfect Man* (2005).

Duff has been nominated for numerous Young Artists Awards, Teen Choice Awards, and Kids' Choice Awards for her work in *Lizzie McGuire*, *Cheaper by the Dozen*, and *A Cinderella Story*. In 2005, she won The Kids' Choice Award for Favorite Movie Actress and the Teen Choice Award for Movie Actress: Comedy for her role in *A Cinderella Story*. She also won the Teen Choice Movie Breakout Star: Female Award in 2003 for *The Lizzie McGuire Movie*. Duff was also nominated for two Razzies for Worst Actress—in 2005 for *A Cinderella Story* and in 2006 for *Cheaper by the Dozen 2*.

In 2002 Duff launched her singing career with the release of a Christmas album, *Santa Claus Lane*, which sold over 500,000 copies. The album's title track was also included on *The Santa Clause 2* soundtrack. Her next album, *Metamorphosis* (2003), reached number 1 on the United States and Canadian charts and has sold over 3.7 million copies with the single "Come Clean," her first Billboard Top 40 U.S. hit. Her fourth non-Christmas album, *Most Wanted* (2005), debuted at number 1 on the Billboard 200 in the United States, where it has gone platinum (selling over one million copies). *Most Wanted* was her third number 1 debut in Canada.

Duff is also involved in charity work. She is an animal rights activist and is on the International Council of the charity organization Kids with a Cause, which focuses on work with children and the poverty-stricken.

See also Lohan, Lindsay; Olsen, Mary-Kate and Ashley

Further Reading

Krulik, Nancy. (2003). *Hilary Duff: A Not-So-Typical Teen (Young Profiles)*. New York: Simon Spotlight.

REBEKAH BUCHANAN

DUKE, PATTY (1946–).   Born Anna Marie Duke in New York in 1946, Patty Duke became one of the most celebrated actresses of the baby boomer generation. After several years of steady but minor work in television programs and commercials, she played the role of the young Helen Keller in the Broadway production of *The Miracle Worker* in 1959. The success of the play led to a film, released in 1962, in which Duke reprised her Broadway role. Only 14 years old when she played the deaf and blind Keller, Duke offered such a compelling, nuanced performance that she became the youngest woman at that time ever to have won an Academy Award for Best Supporting Actress (a record broken by Tatum O'Neal in 1974 at age 10 for her role in *Paper Moon*).

By the time of Duke's Oscar win, plans were already under way for *The Patty Duke Show*, which made Duke the youngest woman ever to have a television series named after her. Aired on ABC from 1963 to 1966, as part of the network's determined campaign to capture the teenage audience of the early 1960s, this situation comedy cast Duke in the improbable role of "identical cousins": Cathy Lane, a demure, mature Scottish lass living with her uncle's family in Brooklyn, and Patty Lane, an all-American fireball of madcap energy accustomed to acting first and thinking later. The series capitalized on predictable plots about mistaken identities and mirror opposites, and its famous theme song highlighted its producers' ideas of the difference between European and American adolescence, perpetrating stereotypes of high European culture and lowbrow American society: "Where Cathy adores a minuet, the Ballets Russes and crepes Suzette, our Patty loves to rock 'n' roll—a hot dog makes her lose control. What a wild duet!"

The Patty Duke Show was a popular sitcom and earned Duke an Emmy nomination in 1964. Merchandise bearing her name and likeness (including toys, games, books, fashion accessories, and even pop records featuring her singing) were popular with preteen and teenage girls. The series made Duke the best-known icon of the "all-American teenager" at a time when this was the most common representation of adolescent life.

Between seasons of *The Patty Duke Show*, Duke starred in *Billie* (1965), a film about an athletic girl who wants to run on her high school's all-male track team. This role further cemented Duke's popularity and her image as a girl who embodies paradox—**tomboyish** and impatient with traditional femininity, but still reassuringly "girlish" in the pursuit of her goals. Susan Douglas, in her book *Where the Girls Are* (1994), praised *The Patty Duke Show* for offering young viewers a model of "perky" femininity—a style that allowed for some of the aggression and incisiveness usually reserved for boys—while protecting the aura of "cuteness" that allowed girls to keep the approval of boys and men.

The image of girlhood Duke portrayed was meant to represent a topical "type," a snapshot of middle-class white teen life in the early 1960s. Ironically, the roles of Cathy and Patty Lane had little to do with anything specific to that time period; rather, they revived previous stereotypes of adolescent girlhood that had thrived during World War II, when comedies about teenagers were plentiful on Broadway and in Hollywood. Indeed, the pilot episode of the *Patty Duke Show*—written, as nearly all the episodes were, by series creator Sidney Sheldon—was based on Sheldon's own Oscar-winning screenplay for the 1946 **Shirley Temple** vehicle *The Bachelor and the Bobby-Soxer*, a similar comedy about a madcap high school student. That no one seems to have noticed Sheldon's recycling of his own screenplay testifies, perhaps, to the degree to which such stereotypes of girlhood had become naturalized and widespread.

Patty Duke (as Patty Lane/Cathy Lane) stars in ABC's series *The Patty Duke Show*. (Courtesy of Photofest.)

Like Cathy and Patty Lane, Duke lived a double existence, putting on the face of America's darling to mask a tormented private life. In her autobiography, *Call Me Anna* (1988), Duke revealed a story similar to those told by many child and teen stars, in which the adults who should have cared for her (her managers, the Rosses, who took control of Duke's upbringing from an early age but subjected her to extensive mistreatment) were more interested in profiting from her than in protecting her well-being. The book also reveals that Duke's adolescent struggles were exacerbated by undiagnosed manic depression, now known as bipolar disorder. In 1997 Duke published her second book, *A Brilliant Madness: Living with Manic Depressive Illness*.

Unlike some child stars' careers, Duke's continued steadily throughout her adulthood (primarily on television), garnering her numerous acting awards. She has also served as the president of the Screen Actors Guild (1985–1988). Duke has been married four times; the actor Sean Astin is one of her sons, by her third husband, John Astin.

See also Girls and Sport in Contemporary Film; Twins

Further Reading

Douglas, Susan J. (1994). *Where the Girls Are: Growing Up Female with the Mass Media*. New York: Random House.

Luckett, Moya. (1997). "Girl Watchers: Patty Duke and Teen TV." In Lynn Speigel and Michael Curtin, eds. *The Revolution Wasn't Televised: Sixties Television and Social Conflict*. New York and London: Routledge, pp. 95–118.

Nash, Ilana. (2006). *American Sweethearts: Teenage Girls in Twentieth-Century Popular Culture*. Bloomington: University of Indiana Press.

ILANA NASH

E

EASY-BAKE OVEN.   One of the most popular girl toys of the twentieth century, the Easy-Bake Oven was introduced to the general public at New York's Toy Fair in February 1964. Within the next twelve months, 500,000 units were sold (at a suggested retail price of $15.99); by 1968, total sales had exceeded $3 million.

Easy-Bake was not the first working toy oven. Louisa May Alcott's 1870 novel *Little Men* mentioned a play kitchen complete with wood-burning stove, and toymaker Lionel's 1930 catalog offered a plug-in electric range. However, what set the original Easy-Bake Oven apart from these earlier ovens was that it had an innovative "slide-thru" design that allowed young cooks to push a batter-filled pan into one side of the oven and remove a fully baked cake from a cooling chamber on the other. Another notable feature was its use of two ordinary 100-watt light bulbs as the heating source. As toy historian David Hoffman points out, despite the fact that the light bulb became hot enough to bake small cakes, it was nevertheless considered "safe" by parents. These features, combined with an advertising campaign aimed squarely at little girls that by 1967 saturated all three major television networks, helped the Easy-Bake Oven to surpass its domestic toy competitors, like Junior Chef and Suzy Homemaker.

The Easy-Bake Oven teaches the girl consumer simplified baking skills. Early models were packaged with an eponymous line of cake mixes (in addition to a cookbook, pans, and a special tool to guide them through the oven). After original manufacturer Kenner was purchased by General Mills in 1968, miniature boxes of its Betty Crocker brand became the cake mix of choice, and the company's logo was emblazoned on the toy. As of 2007, Easy-Bake (now owned by Hasbro) is again the name on the mixes, though a variety of food-related brands, such as Oreos and Chips Ahoy!, as well as cartoon character brand names, such as **Dora the Explorer** and Spongebob Squarepants, frequently appear on the packages.

The Easy-Bake Oven has gone through eleven stylistic upgrades in the 40 years since its introduction. Its colors have tended to reflect those popular in contemporary kitchen decorating style, including turquoise, avocado, harvest gold, orange, and white. In 1981 the Easy-Bake Oven was redesigned with an up-to-date microwave look that utilized a single 100-watt light bulb. In 2003 a grayish-beige Real Meal Oven was put on the market, but it was not as successful as the girl-oriented original. The 2006 makeover saw the Easy-Bake Oven redesigned to look like a range-style oven—in a garish shade of **pink**. The biggest change, however, was that it stopped using light bulbs as a heating source.

Historically, advertising for the Easy-Bake Oven is infused with stereotypical gender roles. Early advertising for the Easy-Bake Oven reinforced that era's popular belief that a woman's role is to be a nurturing cook and a happy homemaker. As a 1965 television commercial begins, a boy and girl stare in wonderment at the Easy-Bake Oven. Later scenes show only the girl cooking, while the boy eats cake and cookies, samples batter, and turns popcorn out of a special attachment. "It's the most beautiful oven I've ever seen!" coos a solo little girl in a 1972 TV spot. As late as 1989, a print ad for a New York City toy store told readers that "Every little girls [sic] dream of baking delicious treats comes true" when she uses the Easy-Bake Oven. Due to its enduring popularity, the Easy-Bake Oven was inducted into the Strong Museum of Play's National Toy Hall of Fame in 2006.

See also Toys, Kitchen and Housekeeping

Further Reading

Hoffman, David. (1996). *Kid Stuff: Great Toys from Our Childhood*. San Francisco: Chronicle Books.

LYNN PERIL

ELLIOTT, MISSY (1971–).   Widely regarded as the queen of rap music, Missy Elliott is an icon of girl culture because of her innovative style and ability to succeed in the music industry without objectifying herself. Elliott has surpassed all other women in rap music in terms of sales and has re-scripted the role of the female rapper: neither a sex kitten nor a gangsta, Elliott is a businesswoman and an eccentric performer.

Raised in the South, Melissa Elliott spent her childhood in fear of a father who was abusive toward her mother and occasionally toward herself. She credits the strength her mother had shown in finally leaving her husband—with just a fork, a spoon, and a blanket—as the basis for her own might and determination. Missy was always interested in music and spent her teen years writing songs and performing in groups. In 1991 she was signed to a recording deal with her group, Sista. Though both the group and the contract fell apart, Missy used her industry connections to get her songs into the hands, and eventually onto the recordings, of high-profile **Hip Hop** pop stars. Missy often wrote and produced music collaboratively with her friend Timothy "Timbaland" Mosley. In addition, Elliott recorded backup rap vocals for many songs by other artists, including "That's What Little Girls Are Made Of" on **Raven**'s first album, which was released in 1993. In 1996 she created her own record label, Goldmind Inc., under the Elektra name. She released her first solo album on the label, *Supa Dupa Fly*, in 1997. Ever since, she has continued to contribute her voice and production skills to the songs and albums of other artists, including **Spice Girl** Melanie B's first solo single, "I Want You Back" (1998), and **Madonna**'s single "American Girl" (2003). In the meantime, she has released five albums of her own: *Da Real World* (1999), *Miss . . . E So Addictive* (2001), *Under Construction* (2002), *This Is Not a Test* (2003), and *The Cookbook* (2005). She also released a greatest hits album, *Respect M.E.*, in 2006.

The winner of four Grammy Awards as a performer and another as a producer, Elliott is known for her innovation in rap music and the ways in which she has wielded control over her image and her art. Most notably, her 2002 song "Work It" includes portions played in reverse. Her lyrics are generally playful but occasionally offer poignant commentary on gender in rap music. "One Minute Man" pokes fun at the sexual prowess promised by many male rap artists, and "She's a Bitch" demands a revaluation of women and a reclaiming of the term "bitch."

Elliott's visual style is atypical for women in rap. Despite her reputation as being a serious businesswoman, her performance persona is comical and unique. Her first video, for the 1997 song "Rain," featured a spiky-haired Missy dressed in a garbage bag. She kept up the penchant for unusual outfits when she appeared in a video for 1999's "She's a Bitch" in a space-age jumpsuit, and she showed up at the 2003 MTV Video Music Awards in green and yellow plaid knickers with a coordinating pair of sneakers and a hat topped with a yellow pom-pom. Though the newly svelte Elliott began wearing more

Missy Elliott, ca. 2001. (Courtesy of Photofest.)

form-fitting and revealing clothing after a drastic weight loss in 2002, she has maintained her ability to be a musical powerhouse without resorting to using her body in a sexually provocative way.

Missy is popular among girl audiences because she represents a woman who has succeeded in the rap industry without adopting the ultra-feminine styling and formulaic musical approach of her peers. She has maintained control over her image, which is an effective combination of power and play.

See also DJ Culture; Lil' Kim

Further Reading

Perry, Imani. (1995). "Whose Am I? The Identity and Image of Women in Hip Hop." In Gail Dines and Jean M. Humez, eds. *Gender, Race and Class in Media: A Text Reader*. Newbury Park, CA: Sage, pp. 136–148.

Pough, Gwendolyn D. (2004). *Check It While I Wreck It: Black Womanhood, Hip-Hop Culture, and the Public Sphere*. Boston: Northeastern University Press.

Shaviro, Steven. (2005). "Supa Dupa Fly: Black Women as Cyborgs in Hiphop Videos." *Quarterly Review of Film and Video* 22, no. 2, 169–179.

EMILIE ZASLOW

EVANS, DALE (1912–2001). A singer, actress, songwriter, and author, Dale Evans is best known for popularizing the singing cowgirl as co-star to western film star Roy Rogers. Evans's persona was also projected through her own product line, which included coffee mugs and tin lunchboxes. Her **sassy** and strong-willed portrayals of cowgirls established her as a role model for young women of the 1940s, 1950s, and 1960s.

Born Frances Octavia Smith in Uvalde, Texas, Evans spent most of her youth in Texas and Arkansas. At age 14 she eloped to Memphis with Tom Fox and soon bore a son, Tom Jr. The couple separated and Evans enrolled in business school. While working as a secretary, her boss overheard her singing and arranged an appearance on Memphis radio. She left secretarial work to become a full-time vocalist, performing as Frances Fox.

After an unsuccessful move to Chicago and a period of recovery in Texas, she was hired as a vocalist for Louisville station WHAS, where she was renamed Dale Evans. In 1939 Evans gave Chicago another try and was hired by the Anson Weeks Orchestra. Performing on CBS radio affiliate WBBM, she caught the attention of a Hollywood agent, who offered her a screen test. Evans was initially not interested, but eventually traveled to Los Angeles to audition for a role in Paramount Pictures' *Holiday Inn*. Although she did not get the part, she signed a film contract with 20th Century Fox.

In 1942 she served as a vocalist on Edgar Bergen and Charlie McCarthy's radio program, *The Chase & Sanborn Hour*. In the same year, Republic Studios purchased her film contract, which led to her first major film role, in *Swing Your Partner*. After seeing the musical *Oklahoma!*, a Republic Studios executive decided that successful cowboy film star Roy Rogers needed a female counterpart. In 1944 Evans and Rogers made their first film together, *The Cowboy and the Senorita*. The partners went on to create twenty-eight films and a successful television and radio program, *The Roy Rogers Show*.

With two more unsuccessful marriages behind her, Evans cemented her partnership with Rogers in 1947 with a marriage that lasted until Rogers's death in 1998. In addition to Evans's son and Rogers's three children from previous marriages, the couple had one child and adopted four others.

The death of their 2-year-old daughter, Robin Elizabeth, provided the inspiration for Evans's first book, the best seller *Angel Unaware*. The early deaths of adopted children Debbie and Sandy inspired two more of Evans's numerous inspirational writings. She also penned several gospel and secular songs, including the theme for the couple's television show, "Happy Trails." In her later years, Evans hosted *A Date with Dale*—a religious program that aired on the Trinity Broadcasting Network—and continued to write inspirational books. She died of congestive heart failure in 2001.

In addition to three stars on the Hollywood Walk of Fame, Evans received numerous accolades during her life: the California Mother of the Year Award (1967), The Texas Press Association's Texan of the Year Award (1970), and the Cardinal Terrence Cook Humanities Award (1995). She was also inducted into the Cowgirl Hall of Fame in 1995.

See also Cowgirl Play; Horseback Riding; Jessie the Cowgirl; Oakley, Annie

Further Reading

Buwack, Mary A., and Robert K. Oermann. (2003). *Finding Her Voice: Women in Country Music, 1800–2000*. Nashville, TN: Country Music Foundation Press and Vanderbilt University Press.

Enss, Chris, and Howard Kazanjian. (2005). *The Cowboy and the Senorita: A Biography of Roy Rogers and Dale Evans*. Kingwood, TX: Falcon.

ELIZABETH HANSEN

F

FAIRY TALES, MODERN. From the publication of the first collection of European fairy tales, Giambattasta Basile's *The Pentamarone* in 1647, to the 1812 publication of the Jacob and Wilhelm Grimm's *Kinder und Hausmärchen*, to the immense success of Walt Disney's feature film debut of *Snow White and the Seven Dwarfs* (1937), fairy tales have been at the forefront of popular culture. People of the contemporary period are still intrigued by fairy tales. The cultural response to fairy tales and their conscious and subconscious meanings and effects on society has been overwhelming, particularly within the areas of psychology, sociology, and most notably, modern fiction.

Fairy Tales as Didactic Texts. Over the centuries fairy tales have been used in the same manner as Aesop's fables or fifteenth- and sixteenth-century morality plays—in short, to teach morals, and cultural and societal ideals of good and evil. In particular, fairy tales explore different virtues and transgressions that contribute to the idea of success in society. In fairy tales models of behavior are stressed; for example, the ideal child (often a girl) is shown to be generous, feminine, submissive, often in distress, and sometimes clever. Over the centuries these ideals have become ingrained or expected norms of behavior for females in particular.

In popular children's culture Disney and his creation of perfect **princesses** and damsels in distress came to overshadow the formerly well-known classic fairy tales of Perrault, Grimm, and Andersen. The Disney industry continually creates and invokes a culture of childhood and nostalgia by reproducing images of dazzling princesses, complete with tiaras, ball gowns, and glass slippers—products that seem to promise fairy-tale lives to any little girl who wears them, including being rescued by a handsome prince. (See the essay on Disney in Part 1.)

Despite these critiques, authors of the late twentieth and early twenty-first centuries continue to find fairy tales pertinent and interesting. Authors as well as readers remain enthralled with these stories and their memorable characters and events enough to update them, with modern political, cultural, and social concerns in mind. The concern with and interest in fairy tales has led to the rediscovery and re-creation of the form as a means to invoke cultural, social, and political analyses.

Among the major concerns of modern fairy tales remain the ideals of femininity and childhood and the specifically American and British cultural response to adolescence and maturation of young girls. While these concerns are in many ways culturally unique to modern Anglo-American audiences, they are also valuable objects of assessment in terms of ideals of girlhood as they contribute to the larger exploration of norms and stereotypes in a global society.

Whereas classic fairy tales reinforced acceptable social mores and sex and gender roles, modern fairy tales not only question cultural assumptions or the ideals that have been presented as models of behavior, they seek to question the creation of and subscription to any impersonally inscribed norms and ideals. In addition, modern fairy tales seek to expose just what classic fairy tale representations and their extreme popularity indicate about, for example, our perceptions and perpetuations of gender roles, particularly surrounding female physical, mental, and sexual maturation.

Contemporary fairy tales can be categorized into three distinct subtypes: politically correct, feminist, and postmodern. While each subtype is committed to responding to classic fairy tales, each has its own agenda in terms of what is critiqued and what form that critique will take.

Politically Correct and Feminist Tales. Politically correct fairy tales, often called politically correct bedtime stories, as seen in the 1998 collection by James Garner, seek to retell old tales by correcting the injustices of their classic versions. For example, in a retelling of "Red Riding Hood" the wolf and the title character may have a discussion on why it's not polite to eat your fellow creatures and how wolves, however fearfully they are characterized, are neither man-eating nor sinister, just creatures satisfying their natural hungers, after which the two go off to dinner with Grandmother together. While amusing, these tales have a tendency to sanitize the vivid characters and circumstances of their predecessors as they overcompensate for their glaring flaws, be they anti-Semitism or sexism, through excessive moralizing.

Similarly, feminist fairy tales have political views to uphold and often assimilate politically correct fairy tales into their rhetoric using, for example, role reversal to restore morality to those who have been demonized by history. At the same time they tend to be much less overt in their moralizing, allowing for a less sanitized and more creative retelling of old yarns. One example of this type of tale, Tanith Lee's "The Tale of the Apple," reverses the roles in the battle of the evil aging woman against the perfect and beautiful young girl. In this retelling, the evil queen is transformed into a pious Christian matriarch who wages war against the murderous onslaught of her vampiric stepdaughter, who is slaying the townspeople and is stopped only by being burned to death on the order of the Queen, who is anxious to save the souls of her village. Here, as in the politically correct fairy tales, she who was formerly evil becomes blameless. These role reversals function to cause readers to reconceptualize how they engage with the protagonists and antagonists of any story and to consider from what point of view history is often told, by presenting viewpoints that history has often ignored—here that of older, powerful women.

The Postmodern Fairy Tale. The third type of modern fairy tale is the postmodern fairy tale. Postmodern fairy tales are like their politically correct and feminist counterparts in theory: they begin with well-known characters from popular classic fairy tales, such as

Snow White (arguably the most popular subject of postmodern fairy tales), Cinderella, Rapunzel, Bluebeard, and Sleeping Beauty, and rewrite them in new roles, situations, and cultural meanings. This is where the similarities between the three main types of modern fairy tales diverge. Instead of using simple role reversals, the postmodern fairy tale seeks to explore the assumptions underlying the narratives. Instead of making an effort to make the old villains of classic fairy tales clean and blameless and to defame young heroes, or to instill new stereotypes in place of the old, postmodern fairy tales question the very institution of the stereotype and of the social norm, particularly in the realm of gender and sex roles.

Thus, evil stepmothers become sympathetic (though still evil) antiheroes, princes are impotent creatures who seek to own and destroy the princess, while princesses are volatile, monstrous creatures who are as terrifyingly beautiful as ever. Some of the best examples of these creatures come from Robert Coover, Neil Gaiman, Angela Carter, and Anne Sexton.

Postmodern fairy tales take the cultural assumption that everyone should love fairy-tale heroines such as Snow White, Cinderella, Little Red Riding Hood, or Rapunzel and turns it on its head. The cultural markers of successful girlhood and maturation as seen in classic fairy tales, particularly as rendered by Disney, consist of attributes such as **innocence**, child-like bodies and minds (most often lacking in secondary sex characteristics that belie womanhood), the ability to keep house and be a good caretaker, and above all, purity of heart and beauty, which are all traditionally used to enact and reinforce rigid notions of gender and sex roles for women. Postmodern fairy tales use them to a different end: to expose the social, political, cultural, and sexual consequences of stereotypes that are damaging and, in many ways, unattainable.

For instance, in "The Company of Wolves" Angela Carter retells the story of "Little Red Riding Hood." Instead of being a lesson in female propriety and safety, as in the Perrault and Grimm versions, this tale becomes an erotic exploration of the animal appetites found in human nature. Red Riding Hood is innocent and young, yet an intelligent, self-assured, and sexual being who is willing to sacrifice the life of her grandmother for a night of ecstasy with a ferocious wolf. Here our heroine, though still physically beautiful, displays desires that a girl at the height of puberty isn't usually shown to possess. She sacrifices almost everything for her passion, for her innermost desires, instead of killing her wolf-lover and proving her loyalty to family and social convention.

The metamorphosis from the pure child to the sexually dominant nymphet is seen most clearly and forcefully in retellings of Snow White. From an orgy scene with the prince and the seven dwarves in Robert Coover's "The Dead Queen" to the physical object of adulation, adultery, and death in Angela Carter's "The Snow Child," we find that Snow White is as sexual as she is silent. Indeed, in all of her retellings she hardly speaks a word. The epitome of our perverse desires, Snow White is a mute nymph, an object upon which we literally enact our desires.

The consequences of these desires are explored to their fullest in Neil Gaiman's "Snow Glass, Apples." In this retelling Snow White is a monster, a vampiric child with no heart, only an insatiable appetite for deviance, for sex and murder. This Snow White is the evil twin of the beloved Snow White of Disney and Grimm fame; her beauty is arresting, she speaks nary an unkind word, and she satisfies everyone she meets. Her silence and sexuality become an uncanny reminder of how our desires for the perfect, compliant, attentive child are in fact perversions, an embodiment of characteristics and actions that our society deems unacceptable yet continues to sell on every street corner magazine stand and television commercial. Society, it seems, has created this nightmare child and now must suffer the consequences. Snow White preys on whomever looks to her with this perverse desire, pleasuring them before she kills them.

Gaiman—and indeed, each modern fairy tale writer, whether politically correct, feminist, or postmodern—warns us that our creations have consequences and, in a return perhaps to the moral fable of Aesop, warns the reader that if we don't want a society of dead girls sucking the life out of everyone, we had better examine our assumptions or, better, do away with them altogether.

See also Fairy Tales, Traditional

Further Reading

Carter, Angela. (1979). *The Bloody Chamber and Other Stories.* New York: Penguin Books.
Coover, Robert. (1974). "The Dead Queen." *Quarterly Review of Literature* 8, 304–313.
Gaiman, Neil. (1998). *Smoke and Mirrors: Short Fictions and Illusions.* New York: Perennial.
Sexton, Anne. (1971). *Transformations.* Boston: Houghton Mifflin.

KL Pereira

FAIRY TALES, TRADITIONAL.   Fairy tales or wonder tales usually feature brief, fast-moving plots, stock characters such as beautiful princesses and evil stepmothers, and magic. Originally told as oral tales to a mixed audience of children and adults, fairy tales are now associated almost exclusively with childhood. Familiar stories, such as "Cinderella" and "Sleeping Beauty," were selected and written into literary tales by Charles Perrault (1697) in *Stories or Tales from Times Past with Morals: Tales of Mother Goose* and by Wilhelm and Jacob Grimm (1812 and 1857) in *Children's and Household Tales.* These authors adapted the tales to fit their particular historical and cultural location and selected and edited the tales in gendered ways. In these traditional variants, girls are punished for curiosity like the heroine in "Bluebeard," humiliated like Cinderella, or wait to be saved by a prince like Sleeping Beauty. Feminist scholars have argued that these tales offer girls lessons about heterosexuality, domesticity, and submissiveness to men. These traditional variants are regularly reproduced in picture book format for young readers.

In the twentieth century, the Walt Disney corporation made their adaptations of fairy tales accessible to a broad audience through film. Like Perrault and the Brothers Grimm, script writers and **filmmakers** at Disney altered the tales to fit contemporary ideas about girlhood. From *Snow White and the Seven Dwarfs* (1938) to more recent films, such as *Beauty and the Beast* (1991), Disney continues to reproduce fairy-tale variants in which girls' opportunities and roles are limited and defined by heterosexual norms. Even in the film *Beauty and the Beast,* where the heroine, Belle, is viewed by some as more assertive than her earlier counterparts, she sacrifices herself for her father and ultimately marries the abusive male beast. (See the essay on Disney in Part 1.)

Some rewritings of fairy tales, especially by female authors, challenge conventional ideas about romance and heterosexuality through parody, the recovery of less familiar fairy tales that feature strong female protagonists, or the creation of new literary narratives. For instance, writers Babette Cole, Francesca Lia Block, Emma Donoghue, Robin McKinley, Donna Jo Napoli, and Jane Yolen all create story lines told from the heroine's perspective that transform more traditional messages about heterosexuality, marriage, and victimization.

See also Compulsory Heterosexuality; Fairy Tales, Modern

Further Reading

Tatar, Maria, ed. (1998). *The Classic Fairy Tales: Texts, Criticism*. New York: Norton.

Zipes, Jack. (1986). *Don't Bet on the Prince: Contemporary Feminist Fairy Tales in North America and England*. New York: Routledge.

ELIZABETH MARSHALL

FAN CULTURE. Who can forget the televised images of Beatles fans swooning, screaming, and even fainting as the Fab Four made their first U.S. appearance in 1964? What about the thousands of **Madonna** wannabes appropriating the Material Girl's fashion statements during the 1980s? While fandom and fan culture can be traced back to the early twentieth century (notably, science fiction fandom), and while it transcends gender, race, class, and national boundaries, fan culture has been an integral part of the coming of age of **tween** and teen girls in Western culture.

While the objects of girls' fandom may have changed over the decades, the behavior associated with fandom has been fairly uniform and includes a range of cultural practices: adulation of teen idols, teen **magazines**, and the production of creative cultural artifacts such as **Web sites, zines,** and **fan fiction.**

Teen Idols. While in recent years the definition of teen idols has expanded to focus more on young female celebrities and characters that serve as role models for young girls coming of age—the **Spice Girls, Raven, Hilary Duff, Buffy the Vampire Slayer, Britney Spears,** and so on —girls' primary engagement with teen idols has taken the form of heterosexual romantic idolization of young male celebrities. Regardless of gender, a teen idol is a celebrity (usually a musician, actor, or actress) with a particular appeal to an audience of teens. Even though male teen idols themselves may no longer be teenaged, there tends to be an inherent romantic boyishness that defines their charm.

Many trace the origins of the teen idol phenomenon to the 1920s and Rudolph Valentino who, in the lead role in the film *The Sheik,* caused girls and women alike to swoon. However, the concept of the teen idol as we know it know it today is more aptly traced to the 1950s and Frank Sinatra, whose appeal to that decade's **"bobby-soxers"** (high school girls) generated rampant adulation. The 1950s, the decade that gave birth to the "teenager" as we know it and to the commercialized high school youth culture, also produced Elvis Presley, which further cemented the role of the teen idol in teen girl culture. Elvis was soon followed by the Beatles, David Cassidy, Donny Osmond, Boyz II Men, **New Kids on the Block,** Ashton Kutcher, and others.

A more recent phenomenon has been the manufacture of teen idols, notably "boy bands." While the genesis of prefab boy bands can be traced back to the Monkees in the 1960s (and some would even say the doo-wop groups of the 1950s), the modern boy band formula was pioneered in the 1980s by Boston-based music producer Maurice Starr (New Edition and New Kids on the Block) and in the 1990s by Florida-based entrepreneur Louis Perlman (**Backstreet Boys** and ***NSYNC**). The manufacture of these and other boy bands follows a standard formula: recruiters select a handful of boys and/or young men with some talent for singing and dancing, and a distinct image is carefully crafted for each member of the new group (the rebel, the sensitive soul, the hunk, and so on). More often than not, such boy bands perform a brand of "bubblegum" pop that has appeal to an age group described as "aspiring teenagers"—girls between 8 and 14. The formula became so entrenched during the 1990s that the latter part of that decade could be considered the heyday of boy bands, with 1998 being declared "the year of the boy band" by *Billboard* magazine.

Teen Idol Magazines. Boy bands, girl bands, and young actors and actresses are the staple for a distinct type of mass-produced teen idol magazine, the hallmarks of which are bold, colorful covers splashed with photos of the teen idols du jour; interior content that is more visual than textual (including dozens of pull-out celebrity posters and center-folds); and articles that may feature "questions and answers" (Q&A's) about an idol's favorite foods, first kiss, and ideal date. Some of the most popular teen idol magazines include *Tiger Beat*, *Teen Beat*, *Bop*, and *16*.

Like teen idols themselves, these magazines have been a staple of girls' fan culture for over 50 years. Beginning with the initial publication of *16* magazine in 1956 and contin-uing through the present day, generations of girls are linked by the shared experience of gently ripping out the magazines' archetypal glossy pictures and giant centerfolds, and then lovingly taping this visual evidence of their celebrity crushes to their **bedroom** walls. A mother today may remember pictures of David Cassidy and Donny Osmond taped to her walls, while her 20-year-old daughter's "crushes" may be Jonathan Taylor Thomas, Usher, and Joey Lawrence. Despite being a generation apart, the mother and daughter share this common cultural experience of adolescent girlhood.

Founded in 1965, *Tiger Beat* is perhaps the best known of these magazines. *Tiger Beat* and its sister publications, *Bop* (begun in 1983), *TeenBeat* (begun in 1975), and the pre-viously mentioned *16* magazine, provide a space for girls to gaze at their favorite male teen idols—typically boys and boyish-looking young men from the worlds of pop music, tele-vision, and film.

Like many artifacts linked with youth culture, teen idol magazines have gone high-tech. *Tiger Beat* and *Bop*, for example, now have high-energy Web sites replete with a wealth of interactive features, including reader "shout-outs," polls, and online **shopping** opportunities.

Production of Creative Cultural Artifacts. It's not only the magazines that have turned to the Web; girls themselves are using their technological savvy and creating their own Web shrines to honor their favorite teen idols. Although once most girls participated in fan culture by ripping pictures out of magazines and posting them on their bedroom walls, many now scan pictures into their computers and post them on their own personal celebrity fan Web sites for the entire world to see. The sites include various types of fan art, as well—poetry, drawings, and so on. Thousands of these Web shrines link like-minded female fans all over the world.

In creating such sites, girls are creating a space for themselves—a space in which to engage in a practice (fandom) that has been ridiculed, dismissed, and scorned by the dom-inant adult culture for decades. Until now, this activity, like many elements of girl culture, has been undertaken in the privacy of girls' bedrooms and only in the company of their inner circle of female friends. By moving their fandom out of the bedroom and onto the Web, girls proudly announce and celebrate their celebrity affiliation to an audience of potentially millions. Through the creation of an online fan community, the friendship cir-cle is widened. Moreover, the fact that anyone can access these Web sites shows that these girls are no longer willing to hide their fandom behind closed doors.

A major component of many fan Web sites created by girls is fan fiction. Fan fiction is a common, long-standing feature of fandom in which fans write new stories using preexisting media characters and settings. The stories are neither sanctioned by the creators of the original text nor published for profit. For example, tween and teen girl fans of the television program *Gilmore Girls* have created what some call "Trory" fan fiction—fiction related to two of the show's characters, Rory and Tristan. While these two teenage characters never engaged in a romantic relationship, Trory fan fiction authors believe they should have, and have written their own romantic stories using the characters and settings of the program.

Another aspect of creativity within girls' fan culture is the publication of zines, notably fanzines. Zines are self-published documents on any of a variety of topics, such as music, television programs, politics, literary genres, celebrities, and so on. Zines may include articles, essays, poetry, or simply personal ramblings. Some of the earliest zines were actually fanzines produced either by fan clubs or by individual fans. While the science fiction zine *The Comet*, published by a science fiction fan club beginning in 1930, is generally considered to be the first fanzine, the term itself was not coined until 1940. While many zines published by girls today are personal zines ("perzines"), many others are related to specific objects of fandom. Whether handwritten and photocopied, desktop published, or Web-based, fanzines are yet another means by which girls can actively engage in a broader, international network of other fans.

Girl-Based Fan Culture. With the exception of teen idol magazines, none of these elements of girls' fan culture are unique to girls. In fact, most began 60 or 70 years ago with science fiction fans and continue today across a broad range of demographic groups. However, it is the combination of these elements along with the specific objects of fandom that contributes to a unique girl-based fan culture. While many aspects of girls' fan culture are mass-marketed (magazines, boy bands, and so on), advances in technology have enabled girls to participate in a more active form of cultural production related to their fandom. Today, girls are appropriating or creating these cultural artifacts to create a fan culture that works for them.

Further Reading

Jenkins, Henry. (1992). *Textual Poachers: Television Fans & Participatory Culture*. New York: Routledge.

Lewis, Lisa A., ed. (1992). *Adoring Audience: Fan Culture and Popular Media*. New York: Routledge.

Mazzarella, Sharon. (2005). "'Claiming a Space': The Cultural Economy of Teen Girl Fandom on the Web." In Sharon R. Mazzarella, ed. *Girl Wide Web: Girls, the Internet, and the Negotiation of Identity*. New York: Peter Lang, pp. 141–160.

McRobbie, Angela. (1991). *Feminism and Youth Culture: From Jackie to Just Seventeen*. Boston: Unwin Hyman.

Sharon R. Mazzarella

FAN FICTION.   Fan fiction is amateur fiction based on the worlds and/or characters of preexisting texts. Most commonly, a fan fiction text is based on a popular book, film, or television show and published pseudonymously for consumption by a fan community. Fan fiction is usually written by females (Jenkins 1992, p. 1) and is organized by the particular source text it uses, such as *Star Trek*, *Harry Potter*, or *Lord of the Rings*. It comprises a set of different subcommunities with overlapping memberships on the sites of publication. Sections for review provide opportunities for reader feedback. With the dominance of Internet-based fan fiction, it is now harder to know the ages, socioeconomic and cultural backgrounds, family statuses, and sexual preferences of the writers, readers, and participants of fan fiction.

Women, Girls, and Fan Fiction. It has often been debated why it is mainly women who write fan fiction, but it is clear that the Internet has led to a dramatic increase in the participation of girls. One major reason for this increase is the availability of the Internet as a creative outlet that can be accessed from within the domestic constraints of many girls' lives; another is the community of engagement it provides with shared cultural forms.

Fan fiction is illegal in terms of its copyrighted source texts. However, legal action against fan fiction very often makes reference to its supposed moral threat in terms of promoting pornography and of endangering minors, particularly girls—both in what they circulate and how they circulate it. Fan fiction communities are also concerned about this possible impact on minors. It is standard practice for both fan fiction archives and individual stories to include a caveat that not only disclaims ownership of the source text but also warns readers about the presence of possibly inappropriate material and provides an age-based "rating" for the story in terms of its sexual and other adult content.

The Internet allows domestic spaces to contact a wider world, as the novel did in previous centuries. While the use of the Internet by women has not inspired the same kind of consternation that was raised with novel writing and reading, anxiety about exposure to inappropriate material does appear in discussions of how girls use the Internet. When concern over fan fiction is raised in the media, it is almost always with reference to its possible sexual content, and it is true that the dominant stylistic influences on fan fiction are romance fiction and pornography. The fear that fan fiction might be dangerous for girls assumes that they are interested in its romance and fantasy elements and will thus be, either unwittingly or eagerly, exposed to pornography. Within fan fiction communities, however, fan fiction is routinely distinguished from romance and porn. Fan fiction scholarship usually also distinguishes fan fiction from both romance and porn, but it does so in order to claim that porn (or "erotic" writing, depending on a scholar's preference) injects subversive potential into the field of romance.

Categories of Fan Fiction. The three overarching genres for fan fiction are generated by the communities themselves and explicitly categorize fan fiction as being about sex and gender. These categories are *het*, meaning stories featuring heterosexual relationships; *slash*, meaning stories featuring same-sex relationships (although in most communities *slash* means relationships between men, and lesbian stories are called *femslash*); and *gen*, which is variously defined but in practice means stories that are not predominantly based on romantic relationships and are thus neither het nor slash. While slash is very important to the histories of some fandoms (such as the British television series *Dr. Who*) and to the present practices of others (such as *Harry Potter*), most Internet-based fan fiction in the most popular fandoms is het. Under these general categories fall a range of more particular genres, like *angst*, for melodrama centered on a single character, and *drabble*, for a 100-word story.

Alongside the disclaimer and the rating, almost every fan fiction story is preceded by a *pairing*, which identifies the romantic or sexual couples in the story (sometimes more than one couple) or, for gen stories, names the character or characters on which the story centers. In fan fiction, pairing and rating function as more important distinctions than genre categories (such as comedy or angst) and are also the standard search categories for fan fiction archives. The most spectacular subcommunities within most fan fiction communities are formed around pairings. Pairings are the opposite of the phenomenon called *shipping*. *Ships* (short for *relationships*) support certain pairings, usually at the expense of others and with passionate antagonism towards pairings that would disrupt their own.

Girls and Fan Fiction. The participation of girls in fan fiction is characterized by a range of tendencies. Some describe the demographics of fandoms and subcommunities; for example, it is clear that the *Harry Potter* fandom and Harry-Ginny shipping within that fandom are populated more by younger girls than many other fandoms or fan fiction subcommunities. But other tendencies characterizing girls' engagement in fan fiction are not so clearly a reflection of demographics as of dominant perceptions of girlhood. Within and without fan fiction communities there is a perception that certain genres, writing styles, and reading practices are more likely to be preferred and performed by girls and that some are even "girlish" no matter who performs them. The most prominent examples of this are known as *Mary Sue*, a dismissive term used to identify a character or story that is excessively idealized and cliché. The actual "Mary Sue" is an original character—that is, one not part of the source text or so drastically changed from the source text as to be unrecognizable—and is judged to be a wish-fulfilling projection of the author's own self. Writing "Mary Sue" stories is widely dismissed as immature—the work of a girl not yet able to write fantasies that would be of interest to others.

Fan fiction requires a continual assessment of the relationship between fantasy and reality as it is established by both the source text and the experiences of community members. *Canon* is the name for material faithful to the source text and thus also identifies the agreed framework through which writers' and readers' experiences are translated for other members of the fan fiction community. Because it connects the diverse backgrounds and locations of community members, canon forms a common ground for the community, and despite allowances for interpretation, no narrative or characterization can be "bad" fan fiction if it is canon. Canon is also, however, used to identify its opposite: those things that are not really canon and are therefore more or less *fanon*. Fanon material is not faithful to the source text but is widely used and thus recognizable. Because fanon is less tied to knowledge of the source text or to effective original writing, it is also associated with the immature experimentalism often thought to characterize the writing and reading of young fan fiction writers.

Neither what counts as fanon nor what characters are considered Mary Sue is a constant for any fandom. Therefore, such internal dismissals often say more about the idea of girlhood that fan fiction draws from the world outside than about what girls objectively do in fandoms. However, the attraction of girls to fan fiction is clearly an attraction not so much to images of themselves as to the creative and communal opportunities that fan fiction brings into their personal spaces. Thus fan fiction emphasizes the self-assessment, self-representation, and peer relations that are central to girl culture more broadly.

See also Fan Culture

Further Reading

Busse, Kristina, and Karen Hellekson, eds. (2006). *Fan Fiction and Fan Communities in the Age of the Internet: New Essays*. Jefferson, NC: McFarland.

Jenkins, Henry. (1992). *Textual Poachers: Television Fans and Participatory Culture*. New York: Routledge.

Kustritz, Anne. (2003). "Slashing the Romance Narrative." *Journal of American Culture* 26, no. 3,
371–385.

Lamb, Patricia Frazier, and Diana L. Veith. (1986). "Romantic Myth, Transcendence, and Star Trek
Zines." In Donald Palumbo, ed. *Erotic Universe: Sexuality and Fantastic Literature*. Westport, CT:
Greenwood Press, pp. 235–255.

Penley, Constance. (1997). *NASA/TREK: Popular Science and Sex in America*. London: Verso.

CATHERINE DRISCOLL

"FAT GIRL."   Being an overweight or obese girl in contemporary culture can be viewed
as a health concern, but, more important in girl culture, it has profound social consequences. The designation "fat girl" is a derogatory one in Western culture. For many
young girls "fat" is a "four-letter word," meaning that it is as offensive as the more familiar obscenities. Current societal standards of beauty in North America emphasize the
importance of thinness, which drives many young girls to desire and attempt to develop
an impossibly thin body shape. If the **thin ideal** has not already proven harmful and unrealistic, it is becoming so with the current "obesity epidemic" sweeping North America. In
2005 the American Obesity Association reported that approximately 30 percent of children (age 6–11) and adolescents (age 12–19) are overweight (defined as having a Body
Mass Index, or BMI, in the 85th percentile or higher) and over 15 percent are obese (with
a BMI in the 95th percentile or higher). Despite the increasing health concerns associated with excess weight (particularly in childhood), the discrepancy between actual body
weight and the media standards of thinness leads many girls to believe that their bodies
are simply unacceptable.

Stigmatization of "Fat Girls." Stigmatization of overweight and obese girls is common in North America. Although body size is tied to many factors, such as genetics and
metabolism, many believe that one's body weight is simply a matter of self-control. This
belief, coupled with the pervasive notion that thinness is the only way to achieve beauty
and success, gives rise to the idea that being fat is a marker of laziness, **meanness**, stupid-
ity, and sloppiness. Within their social worlds, obese girls can face stigmatization from
peers, educators, health professionals, and even family members. Negative attitudes
toward overweight and obese people are seen in children as young as 3 years of age and
increase during early childhood when cultural norms first become understood and internalized. As a result, young girls who are overweight or obese often experience a host of
social and psychological consequences.

By adolescence, many overweight girls experience some form of social isolation. Being
overweight is often a barrier to being accepted into **girls' friendship** circles, and even with
friends around, body shape and size influence a girl's position in her social network.
Overweight adolescent girls are less likely to report having a best friend, feel more socially
isolated, and are often located on the periphery of their social networks. However, greater
participation in school sports and other activities may mitigate this social isolation.
Weight bias also extends to romantic relationships, particularly affecting young girls
entering the dating world. Overweight and obese girls are more likely to have never dated
and less likely to have a boyfriend than their slimmer peers.

Very high proportions of overweight adolescent girls report being targets of weight-
related teasing, jokes, and derogatory name calling, particularly in elementary and middle

school environments. **Judy Blume**'s popular fiction book *Blubber* (1974) portrays this sensitive topic in adolescent girl culture. While both boys and girls engage in overt teasing and cruelty toward overweight peers, girls are more likely to engage in subtler forms of discrimination by excluding overweight or obese girls from social activities or treating overweight peers in a hurtful manner within the context of supposed friendships. Teasing also often extends from public spaces into the home environment, as many overweight girls report being teased about their weight by family members. Well-intentioned comments made by parental figures encouraging weight loss may also be perceived as negative and hurtful.

As a result of weight stigmatization and the media's association of thinness with happiness, many overweight girls experience a range of negative psychological consequences, including loss of self-esteem, depression, eating disorders, self-mutilation, and suicidal thoughts. Many overweight girls feel ashamed of being fat and believe that the teasing and humiliation will cease if they lose weight. Although many slim girls often perceive themselves as fat and engage in dieting behaviors, the heavier a girl is, the more likely she is to diet. Those who diet are rarely successful in maintaining weight loss, as the cycle of restriction (i.e., skipping meals, eliminating food groups) and overeating often leads to even more weight gain. Extreme dieting behaviors can lead to nutritional deficiencies (e.g., iron, calcium, essential fatty acids), and this often means that dieting during adolescence could result in further weight gain in adulthood.

Other weight loss options available to overweight girls include fitness or weight-loss camps (also called "fat camps") and surgery. Although surgery is a controversial option for severely overweight teen girls, weight-loss camps have been a part of American culture for decades. They are immersion experiences in which daily activities focus on fitness and nutrition with the ultimate goal of weight loss. Personal testimonies suggest high levels of success in these programs, but the ability for girls to maintain their weight loss once they return to their home environment is not certain. Media portrayals of "fat camps" generally take a very comical perspective and include the movie *Heavyweights* (1995) and the MTV documentary *Fat Camp* (2006). Books on the topic include Daniel Pinkwater and Andy Rash's *Fat Camp Commandos* (2001) and Deborah Blumenthal's *Fat Camp* (2006). A notable exception to most comical popular books about overweight and obese girls is Wally Lamb's *She's Come Undone* (1992), which was enormously successful not only for its stunningly realistic portrayal of the complicated character of Dolores Price, but also because this young female character was developed so poignantly by a middle-aged man.

Representations of Overweight Girls in Popular Media. Popular media's representation of girls and women tends to promote thinness above all and endorse negative attitudes toward chubby, overweight, and (especially) obese girls. It is common to see depictions of thin girls who fear becoming fat (e.g., Regina in the film *Mean Girls*, 2004), those who fear regaining weight after having lost it (e.g., Monica Geller in the television show *Friends*), and the general promotion of celebrities' new "thinner" status (e.g., Nicole Richie, or the television show *Celebrity Fit Club*).

However, some recent movies such as *Real Women Have Curves* (2002) and *Phat Girlz* (2006) promote the acceptance of larger body sizes and illustrate ethnic variability in beauty. Celebrities like actress Kate Winslet and singer **Pink** (in her 2006 album *Stupid Girls*) have spoken out against the media's unrealistic focus on the thin ideal. Additionally, while the high-fashion industry has consistently doted on very thin models and offered a narrow range of size options that ultimately restrict access to fuller-figured girls, "big box" clothing retailers have increased the availability of larger-size clothing for young girls and teens (for example, Gap's Old Navy chain). **Magazines** like *BUST* showcase models of more realistic and heavier body sizes, and even "chic" clothing lines like **baby phat** are more oriented to voluptuous than to very thin girls. Clothing stores specializing in fashion for "curvy" and "fuller-figured" girls are becoming increasingly prevalent; these include Hot Topic's Torrid chain and B & Lu. Such companies and products provide over-weight girls with trendy fashion clothing like that of their thinner counterparts and thereby potentially contribute to a greater sense of belonging for large girls in their peer groups and social circles.

Community and Support. A growing number of Web-based support groups and online communities are available to overweight girls. These forums provide a sense of belonging and emotional support but also discuss fashion tips and generally provide an outlet to share experiences with other girls. National and international size acceptance organizations and advocacy groups, such as the U.S.-based National Association to Advance Fat Acceptance (NAAFA) and the International Size Acceptance Organization (ISAO), offer special-interest groups and support networks for overweight youth. ISAO, for example, has a division for youth called Big Beautiful Teenz.

The extension of the size acceptance movement into girl culture is one step toward promoting a healthy body image and potentially reducing the stigma related to being a "fat girl." While the health consequences of severe obesity should not be discounted, popular culture has a long way to go in promoting the message that healthy bodies can come in many sizes. Due to the negative psychological and social effects of being labeled a "fat girl" and the limited efficacy of dieting toward achieving a healthy weight, the topic of weight management must be approached with great caution, especially during the delicate years of female adolescence.

See also Anorexia; Bulimia; Bullying; Disordered Eating

Further Reading

Latner, Janet D., and Marlene B. Schwartz. (2005). "Weight Bias in a Child's World." In Kelly D. Brownell, R. M. Puhl, M. B. Schwartz, and L. Rudd, eds. *Weight Bias: Nature, Consequences, and Remedies.* New York: Guilford Press, pp. 54–67.
Neumark-Sztainer, Dianne. (2005). *I'm, Like, So Fat!* New York: Guilford Press.
Ogden, Cynthia L., M. D. Carroll, L. R. Curtin, M. A. McDowell, C. J. Tabak, and K. M. Flegal. (2006). "Prevalence of Overweight and Obesity in the United States, 1999–2004." *Journal of the American Medical Association* 295, 1549–1555.

LORI A. NEIGHBORS AND AMANDA LYNCH

FELICITY. *Felicity* is an American television show that aired on The WB network from 1998 until 2002. The show was created by producers J. J. Abrams and Matt Reeves, and it starred actress Keri Russell in the leading role of Felicity Porter. The drama series depicted Felicity's four years of college. Although she had planned to attend Stanford University, she impulsively changes her mind and follows her high school crush to the fictional University of New York. In New York City, far from home, Felicity embarks on a new chapter in her life. She experiences love and heartbreak, forms lasting friendships, navigates a conflicted relationship with her parents, and struggles to choose a career path that is right for her. Like its counterparts on The WB, *Dawson's Creek* and ***Buffy the***

Vampire Slayer, the show focuses on the lives of attractive young adults and presents issues that resonate with many teens, particularly young women.

The series offered a diverse group of characters and story lines that ranged from lighter, comedic fare to the treatment of serious issues, such as teen pregnancy, abortion, date rape, alcoholism, drug addiction, depression, and death. Because of the show's academic setting, it also addressed the typical struggles of a female college student and prominently features Felicity's uncertainty about whether she should study art or follow in her father's footsteps and become a doctor.

Central to the show were its depictions of romantic relationships, primarily Felicity's ongoing love triangle with Ben Covington (Scott Speedman), her high school crush, and Noel Crane (Scott Foley), her resident advisor and close friend. "Ben or Noel?" was a common discussion topic among fans and in media coverage of the show as people made their preferences known and debated which suitor Felicity should ultimately choose. Virtually unknown actors prior to *Felicity*, Speedman and Foley quickly became pinup material for many female fans.

Other key characters on the show included Felicity's friends, Julie Emrick (Amy Jo Johnson) and Elena Tyler (Tangi Miller); her mysterious and difficult roommate, Meghan Rotundi (Amanda Foreman); her gay boss and confidant, Javier Quintata (Ian Gomez); and Ben's quirky, entrepreneurial roommate, Sean Blumberg (Greg Grunberg). Felicity was also known for corresponding with an old friend and mentor, Sally, by recording her thoughts on audiocassette instead of writing letters. Sally was only heard, not seen, and was voiced by actress Janeane Garofalo. These "Dear Sally" letters were a recurring motif during the early seasons of the show and were often used as a form of voiceover narration.

Felicity never succeeded in attracting a large viewing audience, but its popularity among young women helped keep the show on the air for four years and contributed to the increasing visibility of The WB, which came to be known as the primary network for teen interest programming. The show also featured a fair amount of music that appealed to its young audience, which led to the release of two *Felicity* soundtrack CDs, one in 1999 and the other in 2002. Another factor in the show's resilience was the critical acclaim it received: in 1999, during its debut season, the show was nominated for a Golden Globe Award for Best Television Series—Drama, and Russell won the award for Best Actress in a Television Series—Drama. In 2001 *Felicity* was applauded by the National Organization of Women in its analysis of prime-time television programming, indicating that the show featured positive portrayals of women.

Even without a broad audience, *Felicity* made its way into American cultural consciousness. Most notably, the show made headlines during its second season when Felicity cut off her signature long, curly hair and there was a strong negative reaction from fans. When the show's ratings declined that year, rumors spread that it was because of Felicity's new haircut, though this was never proven to be the case. Felicity's hair grew back and the show survived for two more seasons, with the final episode airing on May 22, 2002.

See also Beverly Hills, 90210; *Degrassi*; Fan Culture; Hair, Stereotypes of

Further Reading

Meyers, Celina-Beth. (2006). "'Her Choice Changed Everything': Women and Love on *Dawson's Creek* and *Felicity*." Master's thesis, Bowling Green State University.

National Organization of Women. (2001, June and 2002, October) *Watch Out, Listen Up! Feminist Primetime Report Update 2000–2001*. [Online March 2007]. National Organization of Women Web site http://www.now.org/issues/media/watchout/watchout2.pdf.

Ross, Sharon. (2004). "Dormant Dormitory Friendships: Race and Gender in *Felicity*." In Glyn Davis and Kay Dickinson, eds. *Teen TV: Genre, Consumption and Identity*. London: BFI, pp. 141–150.

CELINA-BETH MEYERS

FILMMAKING.   Girls' filmmaking involves young females as directors, producers, and writers of films. This work generally centers on explorations of identity, though girl filmmakers have undertaken many themes representing a range of cultural, ethnic, and socioeconomic backgrounds. The culture of girls' filmmaking involves several components worthy of consideration—for example, historic barriers to girls' involvement in film production, reasons for the increase in young female directors since the early 1990s, and the primary forms of and themes in recent girl-made movies.

Barriers to Girls' Filmmaking.   Most female youth have not considered film production a practice worthy of their investment. The first and most obvious explanation for this is that filmmaking equipment has been quite expensive and therefore inaccessible to the vast majority of youth. This problem has been lessened somewhat in recent years by the introduction of relatively inexpensive video equipment. At the same time, however, a noticeable difference between the sexes is evident among contemporary youth who have direct access to filmmaking technology: boys who own film cameras significantly outnumber their female peers. Economics alone, therefore, cannot explain the relatively low number of girls who are actively involved in making movies today.

Most girls likely do not take seriously the option to engage in film production because they understand this practice to be closely affiliated with males and masculinity. Men have historically outnumbered women in virtually all areas of film production—screenwriting, directing, producing, and editing. Such male dominance has put interested females at a disadvantage, because the primary creative roles involved in filmmaking have been naturalized as masculine. This situation is made worse through both overt and covert forms of sexism within the field of film production. As a result of these dynamics, few women have received enough attention to be considered acclaimed filmmakers, much less role models for aspiring female directors.

Additional barriers to girls' involvement in film production include film critics' and the industry's privileging of traditionally male-oriented genres, such as westerns, gangster films, and action-adventure movies. In turn, even filmmaking equipment, the stores that sell such technology, and the media that promote it have come to be associated with males and masculinity. This has dissuaded many girls from engaging with such tools. Another factor in girls' disinterest in film production may be the traditional dominance of media education programs by male students and instructors. Since few women are formally trained in film production, there is a shortage of female instructors who might be able to help girls negotiate this traditionally male-dominated industry.

An equally significant barrier to girls' involvement in filmmaking is female socialization in a society structured by traditional ideas of sex and gender. Historically, girls have been encouraged to adopt "feminine" attributes and "female activities" over all other identities and behaviors, and this has diminished their potential interest and involvement in cultural practices associated with males and masculinity. Such messages are still directed to girls via primary social institutions in North America, especially commercial media. For example, teen **magazines**, the primary mass medium targeting female youth, rarely address female teens as cultural producers. Instead, they tend to affirm that a girl's place is in front of the camera, not behind it—a passive, objectified spectacle rather than an active, powerful agent with her own creative vision and voice.

Female Directors on the Rise: The 1980s and 1990s. Despite the numerous barriers that continue to prevent most girls from becoming seriously interested in filmmaking, recent transformations in technology, education, youth culture, and gender politics have contributed to a significant rise in the involvement of contemporary girls in film production. The introduction of the camcorder in the early 1980s was enormously important in this regard, for it freed young filmmakers from many of the expensive technologies and arduous practices traditionally involved in production. As a result of recent advancements in digital technology, most video cameras on the market today are small and lightweight enough to be operated by young children. Moreover, both image and sound editing can now be performed fairly easily on personal computers, allowing young people to engage in postproduction activities once dominated by adults.

Several toy manufacturers, including Lego and **Mattel**, have developed kid-friendly video cameras in the last decade, which has inspired many children to see filmmaking as a fun hobby from a young age. Guidebooks like *KidVid* by Kaye Black (1996), which offer aspiring directors knowledge in basic filmmaking skills, provide a service that is essential for youth who do not have access to media education programs. Numerous film festivals for youth-made movies have been introduced in the United States since the mid-1990s, and many films shown at these events are broadcast on local cable access shows, as well as on national series like HBO Family's *30 × 30: Kid Flicks*.

Another factor in the rise of girl filmmakers at the turn of the twenty-first century is the recent redesign of school-based media literacy programs, which now seek to combine media analysis with hands-on training in film production. Several private foundations and governmental agencies have also responded to the divide between rich and poor in U.S. society by investing in extracurricular, community-based filmmaking workshops for young people in disadvantaged neighborhoods.

The increase in girls' filmmaking has also been greatly facilitated by transformations in philosophies of sex and gender, which have in turn altered the experiences of girlhood. Although many contemporary female youth continue to adhere to traditional standards of femininity, many American girls are also encouraged to develop qualities conventionally associated with masculinity in order to be successful in school and work. These qualities include assertiveness, independence, and technical mastery. As a result, girls' interests in historically male-dominated activities such as filmmaking are no longer seen as abnormal or as challenging their female identity.

Recent transformations in youth culture, especially the increase in entrepreneurial countercultural communities, have also contributed to the recent increase in girls' investments in film. In particular, the **Riot Grrrl** movement has reconfigured the practices traditionally associated with girl culture by encouraging young females to be politically and culturally active through various forms of media production, including filmmaking. While these transformations have played major roles in increasing the number of girls involved in filmmaking today, female youth are still doubly disadvantaged as a result of their sex and their age. Therefore, the development of a broad support system has been necessary to sustain girls' interest and engagement in film production. Of primary importance to this infrastructure are girl-focused filmmaking workshops that have been introduced recently, such as Reel Grrls in Seattle, Washington, and Girls Film School in Santa Fe, New Mexico. The progressive work done in these programs has been supplemented by girl-oriented filmmaking guidebooks, such as Andrea Richards' *Girl Director* (2005), film festivals like the San Diego Girl Film Festival, and distribution services such as Joanie 4 Jackie, an independent movie distribution network developed by and for women.

Common Forms and Themes of Girls' Films. Girls' films appear in all forms that define the larger field of cinema, including narrative, documentary, and experimental, as well as live action and animation. In addition, many female youth have experimented with music videos, news magazines, and public service announcements. Most girls' films currently in circulation were shot in analog or digital video, and some are as long as thirty minutes. Most movies made by girls, however, are under five minutes in length, primarily due to their creators' limited filmmaking experience, access to resources, and available time to shoot.

The form a girl's film takes is often linked to her socioeconomic status and thus reflects the material conditions of her filmmaking education and practices. For example, middle-class girls and older female youth typically learn about media production in schools or workshops paid for by their parents and often have access to their own or their parents' filmmaking equipment. These girls tend to work individually or in very small groups that put the role of the director on a pedestal. This mirrors the traditional tendency to praise autonomous rather than community-focused artists and also reflects the hierarchical structure of the film industry. In contrast to middle-class girls, most working-class girls tend to learn about film production in free or low-cost community-based media workshops. Girl directors in this category typically share filmmaking equipment and work collaboratively. The difference in media education across socioeconomic lines often means that poorer girls create films that involve a large ensemble of characters, most of whom are friends and family, while middle-class girls tend to produce films that contain very few characters.

Class-based tastes seem to impact the style and content of girls' movies as well. For instance, many media programs designed for middle-class youth tend to steer their students toward narrative and experimental forms, which represent the individualistic perspective that has historically been privileged in upper-class culture and the fine arts. In contrast, community-based workshops for working-class or disadvantaged youth encourage students to represent themselves and their communities as authentically as possible in order to counter media stereotypes. Girls in these workshops typically co-produce documentaries and, to a lesser extent, narrative films. Their productions are often informed by social realism and reinforce the collective perspective valued by media activists and the working class.

While girls' movies can generally be categorized as documentaries, narratives, or experimental films, they have yet to evolve into distinct genres. Thematically, many contemporary girl directors seem interested in using their films to explore identity, especially experiences of girlhood. It is important to note, however, that most girl filmmakers are not interested in reproducing the media stereotype of female youth as boy-obsessed, appearance-oriented shopaholics, and often indicate their resistance to these clichés in their movies. In fact, many girl directors aim to reconfigure the representations of girls in popular media by exploring topics like female beauty standards, body image and the **thin ideal**, interpersonal relationships, and various markers of identity, including race, class, ethnicity, and sexuality. The range of topics and styles in girls' movies will undoubtedly expand as more female youth become engaged in film production.

Breaching the Gender Divide. Despite a dramatic increase in their numbers since the early 1990s, girl directors continue to receive less public attention than their male peers. Nevertheless, several young female filmmakers have been promoted in the U.S. media in the past 15 years. For example, **Sadie Benning** rose to much acclaim in the art world during the early 1990s after releasing several videos about her female adolescence, including *If Every Girl Had a Diary* (1990), *A Place Called Lovely* (1992), and the Riot Grrrl–inspired *Girl Power* (1992). Several years later Alyssa Buecker received some attention from the U.S. press for the award-winning short movies she made, including *Hazel, the Guinea Pig's Package* (1996) and *Carrot Wars* (2000), a *Star Wars* parody. Other girl filmmakers to receive public attention include Ashli and Callie Pfeiffer and Maggie and Sabrina Kelley, who joined forces in the late 1990s to form Ya Ya Productions. Like Buecker's films, several Ya Ya movies, including *Benny* (1998) and *Gimme Cookies* (2000), have appeared on HBO Family and have received awards at youth film festivals. The most recent U.S. girl director to appear in the news is Emily Hagins, who produced the first girl-made, feature-length film, *Pathogen* (2006), at the age of 12. Her story is chronicled in Erik Mauck and Justin Johnson's documentary, *Zombie Girl: The Movie* (2007).

See also Cuthand, Thirza; Girl Power; Social Networking

Further Reading

Kearney, Mary Celeste. (2006). *Girls Make Media*. New York: Routledge.

Richards, Andrea. (2005). *Girl Director: A How-to Guide for the First-Time, Flat-Broke Film and Video Maker*, 2nd ed. Berkeley: Ten Speed Press.

MARY-CELESTE KEARNEY

FLAVA DOLLS. Flava Dolls had a short but remarkable life. They were produced by **Mattel** for only two years (2003–2005). There were six fashion dolls in the series: P. Bo, Tika, Kiyoni Brown, and Happy D (females), and Tre and Liam (males). There were two differently costumed releases of the dolls, as well as some accessories, such as extra clothing, a **pink** car, and a motorbike.

The Flava dolls were one of several strategies that the somewhat embattled Mattel toy company launched to combat the **Bratz** dolls' relentless and seemingly inevitable assault on Barbie sales figures in the first decade of the twenty-first century. Bratz, produced by MGA Entertainment, had seemingly cornered an essential aspect of modern fashion culture—the close connection between fashion and celebrities, the music industry, and mainstream film—and thus highlighted the ubiquitous elaborate, sensuous, postfeminist, post-**Madonna** looks of the new millennium. The Flavas were inspired by another pervasive trend in contemporary fashion: **Hip Hop** and urban streetwear, an aesthetic that did not easily translate into a doll format. While the Flavas are more clearly naturalistic and human-like than Bratz—lacking the latter's anime-inspired and human-like characteristics—there are some strong borrowings from the Bratz concept. One example is the wide range of accessories offered with each doll, including a full extra outfit. Providing such a varied collection is a practice clearly derived from the Bratz dolls. Prior to the release of Bratz, standard Mattel packaging offered only a few bonus accessories. Likewise, the grouping of the dolls in a multi-ethnic crew, without the clear leadership of Barbie, also resembled the Bratz more than Mattel's traditional series of fashion dolls. However, many people saw a resemblance between the Happy D Flava doll and Barbie in terms of coloring and facial features, although Happy D was not identified as a "star doll" among lesser companions, as Barbie is.

The Flava dolls have a singular position in doll history: few doll products have been so universally and publicly condemned. Unlike **Blythe**, another doll once famed as a "failure," Flavas have not found redemption and a second life among adoring adult collectors. The Flavas did not blend non-polite styling, referencing popular music imagery, with the expected toy fantasy elements of pastel colors and shining surfaces as did **Jem and the Holograms**, whose "rocker" identity must have certainly made conservative parents uneasy. Moreover, the Flavas' detractors cover an extraordinarily wide social spectrum, suggesting that the dolls' potential capacity to offend went far beyond the expected demographic. Generally, girls' voices tend to be relatively silent or sidelined in the heated debates around the dolls. This relative silence suggests that, on the whole, the Flavas captured the attention of a predominantly adult or older audience, although the original marketing and Mattel press releases emphasized that the dolls were for a juvenile market. Their main function was to offer a creative, artistically literate, and empowering experience for contemporary girls: "the first reality-based fashion doll brand that celebrates today's teen culture through authentic style, attitude and values[.] Mattel has created a hot hip-hop themed line that allows girls to express their own personal flava."

The term "Flava," added Mattel—according to *Hip Hoptionary: The Dictionary of Hip Hop Terminology*, by Alonzo Westbrook—means "personal flavor or style." However, unlike the **My Scene** dolls, at least in Australia, the Flavas were rarely seen in the hands of girls in public space during their two years of commercial life.

Some parents found the Flavas offensive, believing that they were unsavory representations of urban underclass groups, and had no place inside a "proper" home because they offered potentially ambiguous social role models for future citizens. Others did not single out the Flavas in particular but condemned them as one of many modern dolls that imposed an inappropriate adult sexuality on girls. Schools and educational authorities suggested that the urban backdrops of brick walls and wire fences featured in the dolls' packaging and the graffiti-style graphics glamorized antisocial behaviors such as vandalism, graffiti, and gang membership.

Flava doll packages also included graffiti-style stickers that could be applied to the clothing or even the dolls themselves. These stickers were affixed with the aid of a plastic press, also supplied with the dolls, and glue that looked to some commentators like a tube of gynecological lubricant or a bag of glue, acetate, or gasoline for sniffing—none of which were suitable for girls' play activities.

At the same time, the Hip Hop audience found the dolls highly offensive because of their inaccurate representation of Hip Hop culture and personal styling. Thus the Flavas were rejected by even their intended audience, ensuring their short life. The dolls were ridiculed as white-inspired parodies of Hip Hop culture. It was noted that the darkest-hued Flava, Kiyoni, wore the most revealing clothes, reinforcing the assumption that African American women are highly sexualized. The high proportion of lighter-skinned Caucasians and Hispanic personas among the "crew" was also thought to be a white overwriting of Hip Hop culture. Some commentators interpreted the Flavas literally—as did white middle-class toy buyers—as semi-criminal members of society, pointing out that the dolls implied that African Americans and the urban poor did nothing more than hang out in graffiti-splashed streets and wear flashy, attention-seeking clothes. In contrast, the earlier, edgy Mattel series called the Generation Girls consciously emphasized the creative vocations and cosmopolitan lifestyles of the dolls.

Doll collectors have likewise failed to admire or accept the Flavas. This resistance is part of a larger relative indifference among collectors to many contemporary, "funky" new-generation play dolls, such as the Bratz. It also indicates a degree of hostility toward the permissive, audacious elements of contemporary fashion. This alienation from current fashion occurs frequently among collectors of dolls marketed to a mature audience who prefer the nostalgic and fantasy elements of "collector" dolls rather than dolls with a close relationship to current social trends. There are in some cases racist and classist overtones in collectors' lack of interest in Flavas; this was illustrated by the sound of collectors' groans when Mattel's "free gift" to collectors at a doll convention in 2004 was revealed to be Flava dolls—and the groans intensified when individual collectors received Tre, the darkest male of the Flava "crew."

Outside the United States—for example, in England—the Flavas had a more positive reception. When viewed by audiences who did not have intimate knowledge of North American Hip Hop culture, the Flavas appeared to be a compelling, fascinating documentation of North American urban style. "Fabulous creatures they are, too," said the *London Telegraph,* with no anxiety about the multi-ethnic social grouping of the Flavas (White 2003). For non-American commentators, the Flavas also documented the highly visible influence of Hip Hop on fashion, personal styling, adolescent behavior, dance, and contemporary music around the world. The doll format indicated how Hip Hop, a once outrageous and subversive art form, was now tamed and assimilated into mainstream consumption and the bourgeois home, not to mention conformist suburbia.

Elements of the Flava doll line have also been commended. With the Flavas, Mattel introduced some highly original and attractive face sculptings, of great charm and personable style, that were unlike any other dolls sold by the company. A sense of individuality within the group was achieved with small variations of height among the dolls. The clothing—even if rejected by Hip Hop purists and specialists—is far closer to popular garment formats and styles than much of Mattel's high-end doll fashion, such as the pastiches of the 1950s and 1940s devised by designers such as Robert Best. Likewise, the Flavas remain far closer to real-life fashion prototypes than, for example, the rock-inspired Jem dolls. In doll history relatively few dolls consciously represent "street smart," working-class, or outsider personas—if that is indeed what the Flavas are supposed to represent. Thus they should be worthy of note at least as an anomaly.

Part of the anxiety or **moral panic** caused by the Flavas reflects concern about definitions of girlhood and what types of art forms, aesthetics, and lifestyles are deemed appropriate for girl culture. These debates about the appropriateness of dolls tend to flatten the audience for dolls, ghetto-izing dolls in general to the simplistic and sentimental vision of the "world of a child" and invoking moral issues that can be both valid and exaggerated. In other words, making claims about the appropriateness of dolls' appearance and character ignores both the wide potential audience for dolls and the fact that in the past dolls have portrayed females and males of many age groups. The chubby little girl and the baby are merely two variations of doll formats and not the quintessential image of the "good" doll. The Flavas, which seem to portray women and men in their late teens or early 20s, like Barbie and her friends in the 1960s and early 1970s, contributed to the general tendency within the older teenage and **tween** market for dolls to shrink in recent years, leaving only a hard core of doll players who are very young and are less interested in the documenting of fashion and music culture than in relatively timeless fairy and fantasy images.

(See the essay on Barbie in Part 1.)

Further Reading

Arnold, James. (2003). *Tired Toys Try a Retro Relaunch.* [Online May 2007]. BBC News Web site http://news.bbc.co.uk/1/hi/business/3135378.stm.

Westbrook, Alonzo. (2002). *Hip Hoptionary: The Dictionary of Hip Hop Terminology.* New York: Harlem Moon.

White, Jim. (2003). "Hip Hop Isn't Hip Now That It's Hit Godalming." [Online May 2007]. Daily Telegraph Web site http://www.telegraph.co.uk/opinion/main.jhtml?xml=/opinion/2003/09/15/do1503.xml&sSheet=/portal/2003/09/15/ixportal.html.

JULIETTE PEERS

FOREVER . . .   *Forever* is the title of the eleventh teen novel written by acclaimed American author **Judy Blume**. Published in 1975, *Forever* is notable for its frank discussions of sexuality. The novel appeared at a time during which young adult novels featuring teen sex were primarily cautionary tales meant to discourage readers from "going all the way." Told as a first-person narrative, Blume's novel features characters who have sexual intercourse in the context of a loving relationship and who do not die, get pregnant, or become forced into bad marriages as a result of their sexual activity.

Seventeen-year-old Katherine narrates the story of her first adult relationship with Michael, a boy she meets at a New Year's Eve party. The two begin dating soon after their first meeting, and as their relationship progresses, they become more intimate. Because this is Katherine's first experience with physical intimacy, the novel includes detailed descriptions of the couple's sexual activities and grants readers the opportunity to observe Katherine's decision-making process as she contemplates losing her virginity with Michael. Once she decides to have sex with him, Katherine visits a branch of Planned Parenthood for a pelvic exam and to discuss birth control options with a doctor. Katherine and Michael are both certain that their relationship will last "forever"; however, when Katherine is sent to work at a summer camp and finds herself attracted to another counselor, she begins to wonder if her promise of "forever" is a terminal one.

Equal parts love story and information source, *Forever* delivers solid details related to sexuality and serves to fill in the gaps left by standard sex education curricula. The intimate passages are descriptive and at times erotic, as Katherine learns to achieve orgasm during intercourse.

Like another one of Blume's titles, **Are You There, God? It's Me, Margaret**, *Forever* has been named by the American Library Association as one of the top ten "most challenged" books—meaning that its removal from school or library shelves has been formally requested—between the years 1990 and 2000, because of its sexual content. The novel's history of challenges did not preclude the American Library Association from granting the author—citing this book as the reason—the Margaret A. Edwards Award for achievement in young adult writing.

The novel was written in 1975 when responsibility in heterosexual relationships referred mainly to preventing unwanted pregnancy, not preventing the spread of sexually transmitted diseases. In contemporary editions of the novel, the author has added a letter to the reader that explains the importance of condom usage.

Further Reading

Cart, Michael. (1996). *From Romance to Realism: 50 years of Growth and Change in Young Adult Literature*. New York: HarperCollins.
Sutton, Roger. (1996). "An Interview with Judy Blume: Forever . . . Yours." *School Library Journal* 42, 24–27.

AMY S. PATTEE

FUNICELLO, ANNETTE (1942–).   Child actor and recording artist Annette Funicello was a popular Disney television and movie actress in the 1950s and 1960s. Perhaps most famous for her first role as a Mouseketeer on the original *Mickey Mouse Club* television show, she is an iconic figure in 1950s entertainment. While Annette was adored by girls for her cute clothes and demure nature and admired by boys for her curvy figure and exotic eyes, her acting and singing abilities were panned by critics.

The daughter of first-generation Italian immigrants, Funicello was born in Utica, New York, on October 22, 1942. Seeking change, her parents relocated to Studio City, California, in 1946. It was in Southern California where Walt Disney discovered 12-year-old Funicello dancing lead in a ballet performance of *Swan Lake*. Disney cast her as a Mouseketeer in the innovative children's ensemble television program *The Mickey Mouse Club*. The twenty-fourth and final Mouseketeer to be cast, she was the only one hand-picked by Disney. Until Disney's death in 1966, he remained personally involved in the shaping of Funicello's career.

It has been said that Disney viewed television as a way to promote his other projects—like animated films and his theme park, Disneyland—and thus he did not intend to make stars out of the Mouseketeers; no child was to be featured more than the others or was to be considered the star of the program. However, the dark-haired, blue-eyed Funicello quickly became the most popular Mouseketeer among viewers. Within months of the beginning of the first season, she had received more fan mail than anyone else at the studio. In response, Disney carved out more airtime for Funicello and began marketing her as the star of the show.

By the second season she was featured in an unprecedented three series of ongoing soap opera segments aired during *The Mickey Mouse Club*. Funicello's serial work included the very popular "Spin and Marty," a series of vignettes set at a dude ranch camp for boys. Funicello played a camper from a nearby girls' camp who captured the heart of both title characters. Her character also turned heads in the "Annette" serial, in which she played a pretty orphan girl who moves from the country to the suburbs and struggles to fit in while facing jealousy and social class differences.

During an episode of "Annette," Funicello sang what would become her first Top 40 hit, "How Will I Know My Love?" After thousands of fans called in asking where they could buy a recording of the song, Disney decided that Funicello would begin a recording career. She was soon a regular on the pop music television show *American Bandstand*, and she toured the country singing with 1950s pop idols Frankie Avalon, Bobby Darin, and Connie Francis. Most of Funicello's songs were written by award-winning songwriters and brothers Robert and Richard Sherman, of *Jungle Book* and *Mary Poppins* fame. To

Undated publicity photo of Annette Funicello. (Courtesy of Photofest.)

strengthen her sound, the Shermans double-tracked Annette's voice and added an echo that can be heard on tracks such as "Tall Paul" and "Jo-Jo the Dog-Faced Boy."

When production stopped on original episodes of *The Mickey Mouse Club* in 1957, Funicello was the only Mouseketeer whose option was renewed by Disney. While her movie career was limited to a small role in *The Shaggy Dog* and a supporting role in *Babes in Toyland*, over the next three years she graced countless teen **magazines**, produced a steady stream of Top 40 hits, and was featured in several lines of Disney merchandise, including games, makeup kits, mystery novels, **paper dolls**, and **comic** books. Gossip columns and magazines thrived off pictures and stories of Annette's love life and her picture-perfect romance with fellow teen crooner Paul Anka.

By 1963 Funicello's bubblegum pop recording career had fizzled and, then 21, she had outgrown the role of the teenage **girl-next-door** that had marked her Disney film and television work. Disney kept her under contract but found a new, more grown-up vehicle for Funicello. He loaned her out to American International Pictures, known for producing lowbrow horror films, which cast her as Dolores (later Dee Dee) in the *Beach Party* movie franchise. Over the next two years, Funicello starred opposite Frankie Avalon in four films (Avalon had only a cameo role in a fifth film) about the prudent Dolores and her amorous boyfriend Frankie, set against the freewheeling beach scene. The films followed a common formula in which Frankie vies for romantic time alone with Dolores while she repeatedly rejects his advances, all the while wondering why he hasn't proposed yet. Each film features musical numbers by Avalon and Funicello. When American International Pictures neglected to release a soundtrack to the *Beach Party* films, Disney's Buena Vista record label released an album of Funicello singing songs from the movies.

By the time the final *Beach Party* film, *How to Stuff a Wild Bikini*, was released, Funicello was married to Jack Gilardi (her first husband) and had had her first child. She retired from show business and spent the next few years as a housewife and mother. Except for an endorsement deal with Skippy peanut butter, she enjoyed a low profile.

In 1978 Dick Clark produced a failed television pilot that reunited a now grown-up Frankie and Dolores (now called Annette), billed as *Frankie & Annette: The Second Time Around*. This was only the first attempt to resurrect the Frankie and Annette franchise. The reunion film *Back to the Beach* was shot in 1987 and featured the duo—now married, with children—deciding to return to their beach ways. The movie was a campy spoof of their earlier films and capitalized on a wave of nostalgia then sweeping popular culture. At this time Avalon and Funicello also staged a successful comeback concert tour.

During the late 1980s Funicello experienced the first symptoms of what would later be diagnosed as the debilitating nervous system disease multiple sclerosis. In 1992, after false reports that a struggle with alcohol was responsible for her apparent physical difficulties, she was forced to publicly announce her illness. She went on to campaign for multiple sclerosis awareness. Funicello's autobiography, *A Dream Is a Wish Your Heart Makes: My Story*, was published in 1994, and the next year it was turned into a made-for-television movie. Her health has continued to deteriorate, and since the late 1990s she has rarely appeared in public.

In her youth Funicello reflected the 1950s standards of morality, beauty, and sanitized fun. The height of her popularity came during the rise of a distinctive adolescent culture marked by a generation infatuated with rock 'n' roll and rebelling against the fashions and attitudes of their parents. In contrast, Funicello dressed and acted like a miniature adult. Through her role in the 1960s *Beach Party* films, Funicello may have represented a longing, in the midst of a changing social landscape, to cling to these values.

See also Beach Blanket Bingo; Dee, Sandra; Gidget; Surfer Girls

Further Reading

Lisanti, Thomas. (2005). *Hollywood Surf and Beach Movies: The First Wave, 1959–1969*. Jefferson, NC: McFarland & Co.

CLAIRE FOLKINS

G

GIDGET. The character of Gidget, a teenage girl surfer, appeared in American popular culture in 1957 and quickly became one of the defining images of teen girlhood for the baby boomer generation. She is derived from a real-life model: Kathy Kohner, a California teen who stumbled onto the male-dominated surfing subculture at Malibu Beach and fell in love with the sport. She set out to make herself a competent surfer and to win the respect of the male surfers, who, amused by her tiny stature, gave her the nickname Gidget (a contraction of "girl midget").

Kathy's father, Frederick Kohner, was a professional writer; when he heard his daughter's rapturous tales of the beach culture she had joined, he recognized their commercial potential. Salinger's novel *The Catcher in the Rye* had been published to great acclaim a few years earlier and initiated a trend toward teenage protagonists in popular literature and culture. With Kathy's permission, her father studied her peer group's habits and slang, and whipped them into a breezy, often humorous novel. Published in 1957, *Gidget* was quickly optioned by Columbia film studios. The resulting movie, 1959's *Gidget* (starring **Sandra Dee** in the title role), became an instant success with the first wave of baby boomer girls, who were just reaching adolescence and who saw in Gidget the perfect embodiment of the paradoxes of late-1950s girlhood: aggressively determined to achieve success and recognition, Gidget broke free of some of the confining gender norms of 1950s femininity. She did so even while she was portrayed as typically girlish in her naïveté and worshipful admiration of the older male surfers—especially one named Moondoggie, who becomes her love interest. Straddling progressive and traditional ideas of girlhood, Gidget allowed her audience the satisfying dream of breaking new ground without sacrificing the safety of conventional social girl patterns. (A stitched sampler in Gidget's **bedroom** reads, "To be a real woman is to bring out the best in a man.")

The combined popularity of *Gidget* as a novel and a film fueled the surf craze that characterized white teen culture in the late 1950s and early 1960s, a trend that influenced music (such as groups like Dick Dale and the Deltones and the Beach Boys) as well as films (e.g., American International Pictures' *Beach Party* series, starring teen icons Frankie Avalon and **Annette Funicello**). The popularity of this trend in turn led to multiple sequels of the *Gidget* tales in fiction, film, and television. Frederick Kohner published eight novels over the following several years, culminating in 1968's *Gidget Goes New York*, which showed its heroine working at the United Nations and, finally, marrying Moondoggie at the end.

Each new visual text brought a fresh actress to the franchise: in 1963 Deborah Walley played the lead in *Gidget Goes Hawaiian*, and in 1965 Cindy Carol assumed the role in *Gidget Goes to Rome*, the first version of the text that did not focus on surfing. Indeed, as the lifespan of the *Gidget* cycle lengthened, surfing became an increasingly marginal part of the action. The beach was replaced by the comfortable suburban milieu, which has become the predominant setting of white teen texts in American popular culture. The *Gidget* television series debuted in 1965, starring newcomer Sally Field, and references to surfing were few and far between. This series was also the first *Gidget* text in which the heroine's mother was absent, intensifying the father-daughter relationship and making Gidget a true "daddy's girl." A product of Columbia's Screen Gems division, the television *Gidget* aired on the ABC network. While it was popular with young girls, it did not receive high ratings because its time slot put it in direct competition with the hit series *The Beverly Hillbillies* on another network. *Gidget* thus survived for only one season before being canceled, despite a "Save Gidget" campaign spearheaded by some young female viewers, similar to that promoted by the fans of the television series **My So-Called Life** many years later.

Over the following 20 years, Gidget returned to television sporadically in a string of made-for-TV movies, including *Gidget's Summer Reunion* (1985), which spawned a second full series: *The New Gidget* (1986–1988). Frederick Kohner's original novel was published in a new edition in 2000, with a foreword by Kathy Kohner Zuckerman, the original Gidget herself. All three of the *Gidget* films are available on home video and DVD, and in 2006 Columbia released the entirety of the 1965 television series (thirty-two episodes) on DVD. Having kept her name recognition for nearly half a century, the Gidget character is now available for a new generation of consumers to enjoy, even while the novelty of the original story—the athletic adventures of a teen girl—has been eclipsed by the increasing frequency of girl athlete stories in popular culture.

See also Surfer Girls

Further Reading

Douglas, Susan J. (1994). *Where the Girls Are: Growing Up Female with the Mass Media*. New York: Random House.

Nash, Ilana. (2006). *American Sweethearts: Teenage Girls in Twentieth-Century Popular Culture*. Bloomington: University of Indiana Press.

ILANA NASH

GILMORE GIRLS.   *Gilmore Girls* is a television dramedy (a show characterized by a balance of comedy and drama) that first appeared on The WB network in October 2000. Now in syndication, the show has caught the attention of predominantly female viewers because it focuses on a single mother raising her only daughter in the fictional town of

Stars Hollow. The audience is predominantly teenage girls, young women, and their mothers. Many of the fans have grown up with the teen protagonist and continue to watch the show into young adulthood.

The story line focuses on Lorelai Gilmore (played by Lauren Graham) and her daughter, also named Lorelai Gilmore (played by Alexis Bledel) but better known in the series as Rory. Throughout each episode, they support each other through the ups and downs of both their shared and individual problems. Lorelai conceived Rory when she was 16 years old, and they seem more like best friends than mother and daughter. Lorelai is unable to have a healthy relationship with her own parents, who have never forgiven her for pushing them out of her life once she had Rory. The only relationship they have now, 15 years later, is a weekly Friday night dinner in exchange for their funding of Rory's education. Both Lorelai and Rory are plagued with difficult choices throughout the series, especially when it comes to love interests. However, what keeps them grounded is their constant love for each other and their sometimes-whacky friends in Stars Hollow.

Nielsen ratings, used in the United States to measure the number of people who watch particular television shows, ranked *Gilmore Girls* 121 out of 158 programs in the 2005–2006 television season—admittedly, not very impressive. However, the show's impact on youth culture is of immense importance because it reaches a coveted demographic sought by all major network shows. In 2002 *Gilmore Girls* received an American Film Institute Award and two Viewers for Quality Television Awards, and was named New Program of the Year by the Television Critics Association.

The show's creator and executive producer, Amy Sherman-Palladino, has been credited for creating a high-paced and witty dialogue that often references popular culture as well as other television shows and fictional characters. The references are at times difficult for audiences to grasp, which is why the official Warner Brothers Web site selling the DVD box set of seasons 1 to 4 (http://www2.warnerbros.com/gilmoregirls/dvd/) comes complete with a "Gilmore-isms" section in which viewers get a comprehensive guide to the references in each episode.

On April 20, 2006, Sherman-Palladino announced in a press release that she and her husband, Daniel Palladino, who acted as producer and writer for the show, would not renew their contracts for any subsequent seasons of *Gilmore Girls*. The show aired for one more season and, despite fans' petitions to keep it on the air (similar to those circulated by fans of **Gidget** and **My So-Called Life**), the last episode aired May 15, 2007.

Further Reading

Lotz, Amanda D. (2006). *Redesigning Women: Television after the Network Era*. Champaign: University of Illinois Press.

Say Goodbye to Gilmore Girls. [Online May 2007]. CNN Web site http://www.cnn.com/2007/SHOWBIZ/TV/05/04/tv.gilmoregirlscancel.ap/.

PHOTI SOTIROPOULOS

GINNY GORDON. *Ginny Gordon* is a Whitman Publishing Company book series that was purposely written for girls. Published between 1948 and 1956, it is a mystery series consisting of five books that feature a young adolescent detective. The main character and heroine of the series is 14-year-old Ginny, a budding entrepreneur who lives not too far from New York City in a place called Harristown, in the lower Hudson Valley. Like

Nancy Drew, Ginny's father, a newspaper publisher, holds a prominent position in town, affording Ginny the necessary safe and stable backdrop for her ongoing adventures and intrigues.

In the series, Ginny and her friends form a secret club called "The Hustlers." Their intent is to do good and set right any wrongs they discover. Over the course of the series, Ginny and her crew take on a jewel thief, a conniving stranger, a couple of out-of-town criminals, and a library thief. Their projects include founding a swap shop, establishing a hangout for local teenagers, and sponsoring a radio program for teens. Along the way, a number of predictable but somewhat interesting mysteries occur. Like other girl detectives before her, Ginny manages to save the day and win the respect and hearts of those who know her. Though the series is short, it was popular and remains a collector's item.

The series was conceived and written by Julie Campbell (Tatham). Campbell also wrote the first six books in the ***Trixie Belden*** series and several books in the ***Cherry Ames*** and the *Vicki Barr* **career novel** series. The first three books are illustrated by Margaret Jervis; Margaret Wesley is responsible for the art in the last two and also did the illustrations and cover art in the first three when they were reissued in 1954.

A post–World War II series, *Ginny Gordon*, much like *Trixie Belden*, represents the more "wholesome" side of the youth culture, complete with a real Main Street setting and feel and cast of characters. However, Ginny is a bit more sophisticated and the series was eventually dropped by the publishers in favor of the *Belden* series, possibly because of Ginny's more mature nature and slight tendency to take on some of the less popular issues of hometown life. Thieves, criminals, and other not-so-nice characters are readily encountered in the series. Additionally, astute readers will sense the romantic inclinations Ginny has toward a slightly older character, John Blaketon—a decided defect from the publisher's point of view, though a probable plus for young readers and an aspect that helped keep them reading.

See also Series Fiction

Further Reading

Dyer, Carolyn Steward, and Nancy Tillman Romalov, eds. (1995). *Rediscovering Nancy Drew*. Iowa City: University of Iowa Press.

Inness, Sherrie A., ed. (1997). *Nancy Drew and Company: Culture, Gender, and Girls' Series*. Bowling Green, OH: Bowling Green State University Popular Press.

ELAINE J. O'QUINN

GIRL BANDS.   Girl bands are musical groups in which girls and young women sing and play all the instruments. This is different from a **girl group**, in which women sing but do not play instruments. Although not popularized until the 1980s, with the commercial success of pop bands such as the **Go-Go's** and the Bangles, girl bands have a rich history dating to the 1960s.

Many young women played in garage bands during the 1960s, but only recently have collectors rediscovered these bands, which were signed to regional labels. One example of these bands is the Shaggs, a trio of three sisters from New Hampshire whose only release, 1969's *Philosophy of the World*, has since earned the admiration of rock and roll greats including Frank Zappa and Kurt Cobain—as well as the label "best worst" rock and roll band in the world by the *New York Times*.

The first girl band to gain some commercial success was the proto-**punk** heavy metal band the Runaways, the first group in which Joan Jett and Lita Ford played. All in their teens, the five-member band released their first album in 1976. Their biggest hit was the song "Cherry Bomb," which has been covered by a number of subsequent girl bands.

In the early and mid-1980s, the Los Angeles punk/garage scene produced two ground-breaking all-female bands. The first, the Go-Go's, formed in 1978 and became the first all-woman band to write their songs and to top the *Billboard* charts with a number 1 album (their 1981 debut, *Beauty and the Beat*). They had five Top 40 hits, and *Beauty and the Beat* is considered one of America's first new-wave albums. The Bangles debuted in 1984 with *All Over the Place*. Unlike the Go-Go's, who wrote all their own songs, the Bangles' major hit, "Manic Monday," which went to number 2 on the U.S. *Billboard* charts, was written by Prince. Later, in 1986, they had a number 1 hit with "Walk Like an Egyptian." Both bands broke up in the 1980s but have subsequently reunited and released new albums in the 2000s.

The late 1980s grunge and alternative rock movement brought girl bands 7 Year Bitch, from Seattle; L7, based in Los Angeles; and Minneapolis's Babes in Toyland. All of these bands were influential to the **Riot Grrrl** movement of the 1990s. This movement brought about bands such as **Bikini Kill** and **Bratmobile**, generally considered the two most popular Riot Grrrl bands. These bands were distinctive for their feminist lyrics and involvement in the do-it-yourself (DIY) punk subculture. The Riot Grrrl movement was begun to create women-friendly and female-centered spaces in the previously male-dominated punk subculture.

Other popular girl bands include folk duo and Grammy winners the Indigo Girls and country trio the Dixie Chicks, who are known not only for their music but also for their controversial views and outspoken criticism of George W. Bush's invasion of Iraq in the early 2000s. Also, the rock band the Donnas have made a name for themselves in mainstream music with the release of the 2004 album *Gold Medal*.

Further Reading

Carson, Mina, Tisa Lewis, and Susan M. Shaw. (2004). *Girls Rock! Fifty Years of Women Making Music*. Lexington: University Press of Kentucky.

Warwick, Jacqueline. (2007). *Girl Groups, Girl Culture: Popular Music and Identity in the 1960s*. New York: Routledge.

REBEKAH BUCHANAN

GIRL GROUP HISTORY.   A girl group is a musical group featuring several young female singers; it differs from a girl band, which features young women both singing and playing musical instruments. A popular music phenomenon associated with the early 1960s, girl groups engaged **tween** and teen girls as both performers and listeners. Most early girl groups included three to five adolescents who generally dressed alike and performed simple choreography while they sang songs about themes of importance to girl culture. For the most part, early girl group songs were written by professional songwriters, and the instruments were played by professional session players. The songs the girls sang treated such topics as crushes on boys, wedding fantasies, the strictness of parents, and the high drama of adolescent romance. The best-known early girl groups include the Ronettes, the Shirelles, the Crystals, the Marvelettes, and Lesley Gore (associated with the genre, although technically a solo artist). Although the **Supremes** and the ShangriLas are generally grouped into this category, their popularity came after the heyday of the girl group, in the mid-1960s.

Historical Dismissal of Girl Groups. Between 1960 and 1964, girl group music dominated Top 40 radio in North America, representing an unprecedented instance of teenage girls taking center stage within mainstream popular culture. Despite their enormous popularity, girl groups have been overlooked in most histories of music of the period. If they acknowledge girl groups at all, conventional histories of music in the 1960s tend either to dismiss girl groups as trite and politically irrelevant, or to mention them as an interesting, isolated fad that took place during the lull between Elvis Presley and the Beatles. Both of these positions are misleading. Girl groups had tremendous social and political significance, and their musical influence was an important one.

Doo-Wop and Pop: Girl Group Styles. The first girl group songs began to circulate in the late 1950s in New York, with ensembles such as the Chantels, the Bobbettes, and the Shirelles. These early artists had distinctly different styles, and their popularity was, on the whole, limited to African American communities in northeastern cities of the United States. Here they were not generally understood as representing a new style. Rather, these early girl groups drew from a variety of musical styles such as doo-wop, jump blues, barbershop quartet, light pop, and choral singing from school and church. These diverse influences led to songs such as the Chantels' "Maybe" (1957), the Bobbettes' "Mr. Lee" (1957), and the Shirelles' "I Met Him on a Sunday" (1958), all of which had success on the R&B charts.

In 1960 the Shirelles recorded a version of Carole King and Gerry Goffin's "Will You Love Me Tomorrow?" The record rose to the top of the *Billboard* pop charts early the following year and can be identified as the true start of the girl group phenomenon. The Shirelles' recording of "Will You Love Me Tomorrow?" has been called "revolutionary" by media scholar Susan Douglas, as it presents a teenage girl wondering whether she should surrender her virginity to her boyfriend. The voices heard on the record are clearly those of teenage girls; the musical language and vocal style suggest that they are respectable **"girl-next-door"** types rather than the womanly, raunchy blues queens of that time, who more often sang about female sexual desire. The clear and girlish voice of the lead singer, the demure backing vocals, and the orchestral accompaniment made "Will You Love Me Tomorrow?" stand out as the face of the new teen girlhood. Teenage girls from various race and class groups across North America responded enthusiastically to the song, as it addressed one of their most important and intimate anxieties. The Shirelles made it possible for "nice" girls to talk about sex without upsetting society's view of them as wholesome and respectable.

The musical style of "Will You Love Me Tomorrow?" set the standard for the girl group sound: a young, pleasant but untrained voice on lead vocals, supported by harmonies that suggested a community of friends and sisters in dialogue with the lead singer. This was set against a backdrop of pop instrumentation (dominated by piano and strings) and rock 'n' roll rhythms and grooves. Over the next few years, records such as the Marvelettes' "Please Mr. Postman" (1961), Little Eva's "The Locomotion" (1962), and the Crystals' "Da Doo Ron Ron" (1963) adhered fairly closely to this style of "good" girls discussing their feelings and fantasies in candid, yet polite, ways. Often, the backing vocalists responded to the lead singer's statements with encouraging remarks such as "Go ahead, girl!" Several songs also addressed themselves explicitly to female listeners, with phrases such as "Look here, girls, and take this advice." These aspects of the songs have led feminist scholars, including Susan Douglas, Charlotte Grieg, and Jacqueline Warwick, to identify girl group music as a crucial part of the consciousness raising of future feminists.

Girl Groups "Grow Up": The Ronettes. Different versions of girls' identity began to appear as the girl group phenomenon became more established. In 1963 a group from New York's Spanish Harlem, the Ronettes, experienced spectacular success with the song "Be My Baby," written for them by Ellie Greenwich and Jeff Barry. The song was produced by the notorious young producer Phil Spector. As a mixed-race singing group with towering beehive hairstyles, stiletto heels, and flamboyant makeup, the Ronettes signaled a new kind of girl altogether: she was a young woman demonstrating tremendous self-assurance and sexual confidence, yet retaining an unmistakably girlish sound. The trio was enormously popular in 1963–1964, heading the bill on a United Kingdom tour that included the Rolling Stones.

Lead singer Ronnie Bennett (later Ronnie Spector) had a powerful, sultry voice that was uniquely capable of making itself heard over Phil Spector's record production techniques. Spector's recording style was highly original for its day; his strategies involved using many more musicians than was customary, placing microphones in unusual places within the studio, and mixing layers of recorded sound. The result was a blurry soundscape that made individual vocal and instrumental lines difficult to discern. Teenage listeners were captivated by the high drama of the records, which were often compared to symphonies for their grandeur. Records by the Ronettes and the Crystals seemed to articulate all of the dramatic intensity and heightened emotional states of adolescence, and the singers provided new models of girlhood for their female listeners to experiment with.

Girl Groups Expand. In 1964 the ShangriLas introduced a tough, streetwise version of white girlhood. Songs such as "Leader of the Pack" (1964) were operatic in scope, presenting anguished tales of teenage death and tragedy. Listening to these records in the privacy and safety of her bedroom, a sheltered suburban girl could practice the defiant stance and seductive manner of the singers she heard, and could identify with the powerful emotions expressed in the music. Male adolescent listeners were equally enthralled and inspired by girl groups; Brian Wilson of the Beach Boys was moved to write a song for the Ronettes after hearing "Be My Baby." The Beach Boys also recorded their own version of a girl group song, transforming the Crystals' "Then He Kissed Me" into "Then I Kissed Her" in 1965.

Other male groups in the early 1960s also found that adapting girl group songs were the key to appealing to a female audience and earning mass popularity. Many British pop bands of the early 1960s based their first North American hits (marking what became known as the British Invasion) on girl group songs: Manfred Mann's 1964 hit "Do-Wah-Diddy" had been recorded earlier that year by the Exciters; "I'm Into Something Good," made famous by Herman's Hermits in 1965, was originally a solo effort by Ethel "Earl-Jean" McCrea in 1964; the Mindbenders' 1966 "Groovy Kind of Love" was first recorded that same year by the Bluebelles; and the Moody Blues earned their first number 1 hit in 1965 with "Go Now," originally recorded by Bessie Banks in 1964. Most significant, the Beatles performed numerous girl group songs in their stage and radio performances and included five of these songs on their first two albums. The songs they performed included the Cookies' "Chains," the Marvelettes' "Please Mr. Postman," and the Shirelles' "Boys." The famously appealing androgyny of the "Fab Four" derived in no small part from their ability to sing from the position of girls.

The widely accepted view that girl groups were wiped out by the British Invasion is flawed, because the songs, styles, and even listeners of the original girl groups were vital to the success of the new male bands in vogue. What is more, the only North American group to offer any serious competition to the British bands during these years was a girl group—the Supremes—who had eight number 1 hits between 1964 and 1966, compared with the Beatles' twelve.

Girl Groups as Racial Integrators. The influence of the music produced by girl groups on later music recorded by men is not the only reason to celebrate them. Early girl groups of the 1960s also gave a **voice** to teenage girls at a crucial point in North American history, providing important models of racial integration. In 1960 the Marvelettes' debut single, "Please Mr. Postman," was issued with a drawing of an empty mailbox on the record cover, because it was feared that a photograph of the black group would make it unmarketable to white listeners. By the mid-1960s, however, the Supremes were among the most visible African American groups in the United States and were adored by black and white fans alike. Girl group songs, created by teams of writers, musicians, producers, and singers from diverse ethnic backgrounds, were heard on Top 40 radio during the most revolutionary years of the civil rights movement in the United States (the mid- to late 1960s). It is tragic that in the fall of 1963, as four black girls were being murdered in the racially motivated bombing of a church in Alabama, four other black teenage girls—a musical group called the Chiffons—were being heard across North American radio with their number 1 hit "He's So Fine."

Early girl groups played more than a peripheral role in the agonizing struggle for racial integration in the United States. One particular African American female would soon become a sensation, through her own ambition and the vision of Motown Records founder Berry Gordy. Gordy's ambition was to create music that would appeal to his black, urban community and also cross over to top the white-dominated pop charts. He decided that the best performer to accomplish this would be a young and beautiful black woman who could conform to white middle-class standards of beauty and propriety. Gordy found his ideal in Diana Ross, who led the Supremes to fame throughout the mid- and late 1960s. Girl groups and their songs were the face of girl culture at a time when notions of identity—whether on the basis of youth, race, or gender—were in upheaval, and these groups played a central role in defining girlhood for decades to come.

See also Dirty Dancing

Further Reading

Clemente, John. (2000). *Girl Groups: Fabulous Females that Rocked the World.* Darby, PA: Diane.

Douglas, Susan J. (1994). *Where the Girls Are: Growing Up Female with the Mass Media.* New York: Random House.

Grieg, Charlotte. (1989). *Will You Still Love Me Tomorrow? Girl Groups from the Fifties On.* London: Virago.

Warwick, Jacqueline. (2007). *Girl Groups, Girl Culture: Popular Music and Identity in the 1960s.* New York: Routledge.

JACQUELINE WARWICK

GIRL POWER.   Girl Power encompasses a host of cultural phenomena for young women. The use of the term is usually traced to the early 1990s, when a group of mainly white and middle-class young women gathered in Washington, D.C., and Olympia, Washington. Largely identifying themselves as gay, these young women called themselves **Riot Grrrls**.

Like members of the American civil rights movement who used "Black Power" as a motto to re-articulate pride in being African American, Riot Grrrls used "Girl Power" as a strategy to reclaim the word "girl." They used it strategically, to distance themselves from the adult patriarchal worlds of propriety, class expectations, and hierarchy (Hesford 1999, p. 45). With their roots in **punk** music and the motto "Grrrls need guitars," Riot Grrrls celebrated Girl Power for its aggressive potential to change girl culture. Girl Power became the idea that drove self-expression through fashion, new attitudes toward femininity, and a do-it-yourself (DIY) approach to cultural production.

Girl Power as a Political Statement. Bands such as **Bikini Kill**, **Bratmobile**, and Heavens to Betsy exemplified the qualities of Girl Power by mixing a girlish aesthetic with some of the more threatening aspects of adult females: self-assertiveness, bitterness, and political insight. Many Grrrls used their bodies to convey this ironic merging of style with political expression: like punk girls, they juxtaposed feminine and masculine style by shaving their heads and wearing bright lipstick, or wearing the frilly dresses of 1950s homemakers with military boots (Klein 1997). They also made a conscious attempt to reclaim their bodies by writing politically loaded words such as "rape," "shame," and "**slut**" on their arms and stomachs (Japenga 1995, p. 30). Grrrls used the body itself as a performance text by taking the violent language used against them and instilling it with new meanings.

By most accounts, the early Girl Power movement was a response to the sexism, elitism, and violence of local male-dominated punk scenes, in which girls were considered less than full members. The Girl Power of the Riot Grrrls encouraged young women to see themselves not as passive consumers of culture but as producers and creators of knowledge. They became vocal dissenters; their critiques addressed both their own and others' experiences as women. However, the Girl Power movement was also concerned with experiences of race, class, and sexuality. As a result, the Girl Power movement is viewed by many who study girl culture as a prime example of what can be called youth feminism (Garrison 2000, p. 142).

Alternative Origins. An alternative origin of the concept Girl Power has been put forth by Laurel Gilbert and Crystal Kile, the authors of *Surfer Grrrls* (1996). They suggest that the idea of Girl Power came out of the phrase "You go, girl," which was popularized by young African American women as a statement of encouragement to each other in the late 1980s. Others suggest that it was not the white punk music scene but rather black **Hip Hop** music that spawned and continues to support the changing modes of femininity understood as Girl Power. Some have also claimed that Girl Power as a movement began much earlier than the 1980s or 1990s, in the call-and-response rhythms of the **girl groups** of the 1960s. From this perspective, it seems that the Girl Power phenomenon owes its longevity to a long history of relations between black and white women, particularly in music.

Mainstreaming and Consumerism. In the wake of the Riot Grrrls, T-shirts with expressions like "Girls Rule" and "Girls Kick Ass" began to show up in malls, and according to Jacques (2001), these messages were very similar to the words the Riot Grrrls wrote on their bodies. Ironically, though, while T-shirts are rather conventional ways of conveying political slogans, Riot Grrrls were strongly against consumer culture (Jacques 2001). In buying a trendy T-shirt—even if its slogan is meant to be ironic—any critique of capitalism is weakened by the fact that the article itself was mass-produced. With the proliferation of the term Girl Power, its meaning changed, and as the 1990s wore on, the term did not retain the political and social intentions of the original Riot Grrrls. Coverage of the Riot Grrrls began appearing in American mainstream magazines such as *Seventeen* (1992), the *New Yorker* (1992), *Newsweek* (1993), *Rolling Stone* (1993), and *Time* (1998).

Riot Grrrls often objected to this attention because it put pressure on their movement to become categorized, classified, and brought into the mainstream. Riot Grrrls and those who identified with the Girl Power movement resisted the imposition of strict definitions but could not stop the re-articulation and mainstreaming of the Girl Power message.

Feminism and Commercialization. While the Riot Grrrls clearly believed that their movement was attached to a liberating social and political agenda, the mainstream media presented a different message. For instance, a 1993 *Rolling Stone* article by Kim France concluded that the Riot Grrrls' "unifying principle is that being feminist is inherently confusing and contradictory, and that women have to find a way to be sexy, angry, and powerful at the same time." France positions feminism as the element of complication in what is assumed to be an otherwise easy transition from girlhood to womanhood. *Newsweek* took a somewhat different approach to dismissing the seriousness of the Riot Grrrls movement's politics by associating their youth with a time of natural—but temporary—rebellion. *Newsweek's* Farai Chideya and Melissa Rossi declared, "There is no telling whether this enthusiasm or the Riot Grrrls' catchy passion for 'revolution girl style' will evaporate when it hits the adult real world" (1992, p. 84).

Despite the objections of the Riot Grrrls, certain aspects of the Girl Power phenomenon became ubiquitous, entering mainstream culture through an incredible range of products and services. In the music industry, for example, Girl Power has been called the new buzzword to indicate the emergence of young female stars whose popularity can compete with and surpass that of their male counterparts. Girl Power has also become fuel for box office success; films such as **Charlie's Angels** and *Crouching Tiger, Hidden Dragon*, both released in 2000, feature empowered female protagonists and were hits with the public.

Diluted versions of the Girl Power message have spread to include products targeted at very young girls, such as a *Sesame Street* musical production entitled "When I Grow Up," the advertising for which reads, "Girl Power Takes the Stage." The success of television shows like **Buffy the Vampire Slayer**, **Xena Warrior Princess**, and **Sabrina, the Teenage Witch** can also be attributed to their representation of powerful, beautiful young women. Beyond cultural products, Girl Power has also been used to identify policy initiatives and education debates. For example, Girl Power was the name given to a 1997 U.S. Health and Human Services program for a public health initiative designed to help keep young females "healthy, smart, and strong."

Girl Power as a positive message about the strength and capabilities of females has been appropriated into a variety of children's, youth, and adult programming. However, it is perhaps the British all-girl band the **Spice Girls** that has been most closely associated with the Girl Power motto. The band was enormously popular in the mid-1990s, reaching their peak in 1997 and disbanding soon after. Their first album sold over 50 million copies worldwide in one year. In their lyrics, they call for equal rights and preach the power of sisterhood.

In contrast to the media response to the Riot Grrrls, the Spice Girls' message was celebrated by popular media outlets nationwide. Joy Press and Kelcey Nichols of New York's *Village Voice* applauded the Spice Girls for doing the "seemingly impossible: they have made feminism, with all its implied threat, cuddly, sexy, safe, and most importantly, sellable" (1997, p. 61). Although their comments may have sarcastic undertones, Press and Nichols nevertheless underscore the Spice Girls' success in manipulating the Girl Power message into a highly profitable commercial slogan.

Girl Power in Feminist and Academic Discourses. The hyper-sexualized and stylish Girl Power message popularized by the Spice Girls prompted cries of outrage from some feminists. Striking questions were raised about the relationship between feminism, girlhood, and commercialization: Can an authentic Girl Power message be preserved in mainstream pop music? Can girl-specific **cross-merchandising** ever be compatible with feminism? Such questions remain problematic in discussions of Girl Power, the audiences it draws, and the mainstreaming of feminism in the twenty-first century.

Some feminists in academic circles embrace popular forms of Girl Power messages because they have brought feminism into the lives of a broad range of young women through music, film, and television characters. For example, Debbie Stoller, editor of *BUST* magazine, argues that popular television characters Xena, Buffy, and Sabrina all have the incredible ability to "leap over sexist stereotypes in a single bound." She believes that these characters point to "a wellspring of untapped 'Girl Power' out there, with the potential to change the world if it could only be released" (quoted in Projansky and Van de Berg 2000, p. 15).

Other feminists, however, claim that the blatant commercialization of Girl Power has erased any feminist content it might have once had. Sociologist Jessica Taft, for example, strongly argues about the dangers of young women embracing Girl Power. She suggests that because it is presented as a gentle, nonpolitical, and nonthreatening alternative to feminism, it allows girls to think about girlhood in purely cultural ways rather than as a space for social and political action (2001, p. 4). Moreover, she argues that the popularity of Girl Power is credited to its very acceptance of the status quo. Many alongside Taft would argue that popular Girl Power reflects a white, middle-class society that prizes individualism and personal responsibility over collective responses to social problems. As a result, attention is redirected away from the widespread economic and social mistreatment of women.

Scholars like Catherine Driscoll lie somewhere in the middle, arguing for an understanding of Girl Power that does not position it on either extreme of feminism or antifeminism. Driscoll suggests that mainstream Girl Power's contentious message—"if you're with my sexiness, you're with my politics"—might have interesting effects on "feminism" as a political label (1999, p. 186). She argues that the Spice Girls' ability to generate dialogue about feminism in a massively popular field is actually constructive for girls and young women. Groups like the Spice Girls admittedly may not produce revolutionary change or challenge girls to participate differently in the larger mechanisms of society, but they do create a shift in the way media is marketed to young girls, and they signal the emergence of teenage girls as a powerful economic force.

The continuing debate over the multiple potential meanings of Girl Power—including what forms and articulations of the concept are authentic—guarantees there will be no obvious answers. Even the mainstream media have entered the debate. In *Time* magazine's July 1998 issue—the cover of which reads, "Is Feminism Dead?"—Girl Power is evoked in a number of the articles as both a marker of the successes of feminism and a sign of its demise. In an article that indirectly critiques girl-targeted marketing campaigns, Nadya Labi mentions Buffy, the Spice Girls, Alanis Morrisette, and others as examples of the lucrative success of Girl Power marketing (1998, pp. 60–62). What is not in question, therefore, is that Girl Power is a profitable concept that has been exploited for commercial gain. However, its popularity can be explained only by its social and cultural resonance within a culture of changing norms and expectations for girls.

Further Reading

Chideya, Farai, and Melissa Rossi. (1992, November). "Revolution Girl Style." *Newsweek*, 84–86.
Driscoll, Catherine. (1999). "Girl Culture, Revenge, and Global Capitalism: Cybergirls, Riot Grrls, Spice Girls." *Australian Feminist Studies* 14, no. 29, 173–193.

France, Kim. (1993, July). "Grrls at War." *Rolling Stone*, 8–22.

Garrison, Ednie K. (2000). "U.S. Feminism—Grrrrl Style! Youth (Sub)Cultures and the Technologies of the Third Wave." *Feminist Studies* 26, no. 1, 141–170.

Hesford, Wendy. (1999). *Framing Identities: Autobiography and the Politics of Pedagogy*. Minneapolis: University of Minnesota Press.

Jacques, Alison. (2001). "You Can Run but You Can't Hide: The Incorporation of Riot Grrrl into Mainstream Culture." *Canadian Women's Studies* 20/21, 46–50.

Japenga, Ann. (1995, November 15). "Punk's Girls Groups Are Putting the Self Back into Self-Esteem." *New York Times*, 30.

Klein, Melissa. (1997). "Duality and Redefinition: Young Feminism and the Alternative Music Community." In L. Heywood and J. Drake, eds. *Third Wave Agenda: Being Feminist, Doing Feminism*. Minneapolis: University of Minnesota Press, pp. 207–225.

Labi, Nadya. (1998, June). "Girl Power." *Time*, 54–56.

Press, Joy, and Kelcey Nichols. (1997, September). "Notes on Girl Power: The Selling of Softcore Feminism." *Village Voice*, 59–62.

Projansky, Susan, and Leah R. Van de Berg. (2000). "Sabrina the Teenage . . . ? Girls, Witches, Mortals, and the Limitations of Prime Time Feminism." In Elyce Ray Helford, ed. *Fantasy Girls: Gender in the New Universe of Science Fiction and Fantasy Television*. Lanham, MD: Rowman and Littlefield, pp. 13–40.

Taft, Jessica. (2001). "Defining Girl Power: The Culture Machine vs. the Girl Activist." Paper presented at A New Girl Order Conference, November, London.

U.S. Department of Health and Human Services. (1997). *Girl Power* (pamphlet). Washington, DC: U.S. Government Printing Office.

MARNINA GONICK

GIRL SCOUTS.   The Girl Scouts of the United States of America is one of the largest girls' organizations in the United States, with a current girl membership of 2.7 million and an adult membership of 986,000 volunteers. Since its founding on March 12, 1912, more than 50 million American women and girls have been members. Additionally, Girl Scouts U.S.A. is part of an international sisterhood of Girl Scouts and Girl Guides, which currently has more than 10 million members worldwide in 145 countries and comes together in the World Association of Girl Guides and Girl Scouts (WAGGS). From its inception, Girl Scouts has promoted both traditional gender norms of domesticity and new feminist ideals, most clearly illustrated by Girl Scouts' emphasis on physical fitness, outdoor activities, career preparation, citizenship education, and girls as leaders.

Founding of the Girl Scouts Movement. Girl Scouting was brought to America from England by Juliette Gordon Low (nicknamed "Daisy"). Low was born in Savannah, Georgia, on October 31, 1860; in 1886 she married William Mackay Low and moved to London, where she became active in British society, although her marriage was increasingly disappointing and unhappy. In 1905, in the middle of a bitter divorce, Willie Low died, leaving Juliette a widow who had to sue for her inheritance. In 1911 Low met Lord Robert Baden-Powell, a war hero and founder of the Boy Scouts, who was beginning to organize a girls' organization with his sister, Agnes. Called Girl Guides, the organization was dedicated to teaching girls skills, providing them with physical activities, and guiding them to womanhood. Low immediately began a troop near her home in Scotland, and the following year she brought the movement to America.

Within the first year of Girl Guiding in America, Low's troop demanded to be called Girl Scouts, because the name seemed more active and denoted America's frontier past. Although from then on the organization was known as Girl Scouts in the United States, that decision was never really embraced by Lord Baden-Powell, who felt that girls should be guiding and boys should be scouting (Jeal 1990). Thereafter the American and British movements began to differ somewhat in their programs.

Low worked tirelessly for the rest of her life to spread the news of Girl Scouting. The organization grew enormously. From the beginning, Low declared Girl Scouting was "for all the girls of America," and within a year of its founding, the first troop with African American girls was chartered in Massachusetts. By 1917, troops for disabled girls had been established in several state schools for the deaf and blind. Further, in many northern communities, within the first decade of Girl Scouting there were many racially integrated troops and troops that integrated able-bodied and disabled girls. Because of its early work with disabled girls, Girl Scouts became a model for mainstreaming children into other institutions decades later.

Girl Scout Programs. Girl Scouts focused on opening opportunities for girls with a program that mixed play, fun, skill building, physical fitness, and citizenship training. Based in the Girl Scout Promise and Laws, girls and women volunteers took seriously the importance of being "a sister to every other scout" and to do the best they could "on [their] honor" to help others, to serve God and country, and to live by the Girl Scout Law.

The Girl Scout program opened opportunities for girls to enlarge their world and to do things they had never dreamed of doing before. Girls loved the independence of running their own troops through the patrol system and making their own decisions about activities. Adult volunteers found themselves learning new skills and gaining confidence as public speakers and participants in the organization, which was especially notable for its emphasis on training leaders in skills they did not previously have. Fully eight years before women received the right to vote nationally, for instance, Girl Scouts were training girls and women how to vote and make citizenship decisions. But the world that was opened widest to girls and women was the world of physical activity, camping, and the outdoors. Nature, ecology, hiking, and physical fitness all were crucial to Girl Scouting.

When girls achieved a set of skills, they received a badge that showed what they had learned. Earning badges allowed girls to move up in the ranks of Girl Scouting, to the top honor, which was called the Golden Eaglet in the early years and is called the Gold Award currently.

Girl Scouts and the National Agenda. Girl Scouting has always responded to national crises, and these crises have often shaped the Girl Scout program as well. During World Wars I and II, Girl Scouts helped with the war effort and, especially in World War II, experienced a tremendous growth in membership. During the Depression, Girl Scouts expanded its program and organizing to poorer communities; for example, they set up a new program for Dust Bowl migrants.

As part of an international organization, Girl Scouts has always encouraged international cooperation and supported both the League of Nations and the United Nations, even when they were controversial in the United States. Several badges promote world knowledge and international understanding. Further, an American Girl Scouts benefactor, Mrs. Helen Storrow, funded the first permanent international camp—Our Chalet—in Switzerland, and there are now four around the world. High school Girl Scouts often plan trips to Europe, Mexico, or India to visit the international camps with their troops, raising money as a group and knowing that they will meet Girl Scouts and Girl Guides wherever they go. Ironically, during the McCarthy era, the American Legion called for Girl Scouts to be censured for their "one-world internationalism," which they saw as proto-communism.

Alice (Roosevelt) Longworth buying liberty bonds from Girl Scouts, ca. 1918. (Courtesy of the Library of Congress.)

Girl Scouts and Practical Feminism. Throughout its lifetime, Girl Scouting has emphasized both traditional feminine roles and a kind of practical feminism. At different times, one of these emphases has waxed and the other has waned, but neither has ever vanished from the program. Reflecting the reality of women's lives in America, Girl Scouting has in recent decades found itself stressing career preparation and more overtly "feminist" programs for girls. Although during the 1950s Girl Scouts was seen primarily as an organization supporting traditional women's roles and teaching girls to sell cookies door to door (the Girl Scouts' primary fund-raiser and most important cultural symbol to this day), even then it served as an avenue for girls to branch out from traditional roles.

Girl Scouts also represented an important career path for girls who wanted to work in a women's organization after their formal schooling. Professional Girl Scout work remains an important career option for young women and, as late as 1970, Girl Scouts was the largest nongovernmental employer of women in management positions in the United States.

In the late 1950s and throughout the 1960s, Girl Scouts worked quietly for racial change in America, and the organization began some integrated activities in the Deep South and throughout the North. In 1975 noted educator Dr. Gloria Scott became the first African American president of the organization, but the Girl Scouts still faced serious issues of full-scale multicultural inclusion.

By the late 1960s, Girl Scouts, like all other youth organizations in America, began to experience a membership decline, in part because of the "youth rebellion" and racial issues, as well as new challenges to the traditional roles of women and girls. Girl Scouts found itself embattled and worked on changing its program to respond to racial issues and new ideas about American girls and women.

Unlike **Camp Fire Girls**, which voted to become a coeducational organization, or the Boy Scouts, which voted to allow girls into a new coeducational senior high school program, Girl Scouts chose to remain single-sex and proclaimed in 1973 that it had always been a "feminist organization." The national Girl Scouts board also made its first political endorsement in the organization's history when it supported the ratification of the proposed Equal Rights Amendment.

While Girl Scouts experienced some significant backlash over its overtly feminist statements, the continuing reassessment of its program and its staunch commitment to remaining a girls' organization allowed the organization to withstand external pressures. Since 1980, membership has expanded and continues to grow, although it has increased the most in the youngest ages. Girl Scouts has changed considerably, with the Daisy program for girls as young as 5 years old, and with programs, badges, and groups that are

Vintage photo of Girl Scouts dressed in Red Cross uniforms. (Courtesy of Shutterstock.)

completely Web based. Girl Scouts has expanded its presence on the Web and now has a program for older girls on the Web entitled Studio 2B. Regardless of the changes, however, programs in the traditional areas of physical fitness, camping, ecology, outdoor activities, career training, and skill building remain at the heart of contemporary Girl Scouting. The organization continues to be strong and important to millions of American girls and women.

See also Girl-Centered Programs

Further Reading

Brown, Fern G. (1996). *Daisy and the Girl Scouts: The Story of Juliette Low*. Morton Grove, IL: Whitman.

Choate, Ann Hyde, and Helen Ferris, eds. (1928). *Juliette Low and the Girl Scouts: The Story of an American Woman*. Garden City, NY: Doubleday for the Girl Scouts.

Girl Scouts of the U.S.A. (1997). *Highlights in Girl Scouting, 1912–1996*. New York: Girl Scouts of the U.S.A.

Inness, Sherrie A. (1993). "Girl Scouts, Campfire Girls, and Woodcraft Girls: The Ideology of Girls' Scouting Novels, 1910–1935." In Ray B. Browne and Ronald Ambrosetti, eds. *Communities in Popular Culture: The Present in the Past and the Past in the Present and Future*. Bowling Green, OH: Bowling Green State University Press, pp. 229–240.

Jeal, Tim. (1990). *The Boy Man: The Life of Lord Baden-Powell*. New York: Morrow.

Schultz, Gladys Denny, and Daisy Gordon Lawrence. (1958). *Lady from Savannah: The Life of Juliette Low*. Philadelphia: Lippincott.

Tedesco, Lauren. (1998). "Making a Girl into a Scout: Americanizing Scouting for Girls." In Sherrie Inness, ed. *Delinquents and Debutantes: Twentieth Century American Girls' Cultures*. New York: New York University Press, pp. 19–39.

MARY LOGAN ROTHSCHILD

GIRL-CENTERED PROGRAMS. Girl-centered programs are gender-specific activities and projects aimed at addressing the needs and realities of girls. They consist of after-school programs, summer camps, one-time special activities, and weekly or daily activities; they are offered by a number of nongovernmental and community organizations, schools, and agencies. Girl-centered programs have a range of stated aims, including helping "at risk" girls to succeed in school, prepare for paid employment, delay sexual intercourse, and avoid pregnancy. Most empowerment programs are initiated in response to research or to specific requests from girls themselves. Girls can become involved in organizations such as the **Girl Scouts** of America as early as age 5, and many remain active for years to come, adopting leadership positions as teenagers until 17 or 18 years of age.

Early History of Girl-Centered Programming. The roots of girl-centered programming in North America date back to 1864, when a girls' club (later to become Girls Incorporated) was formed in Waterbury, Connecticut. Club activities were directed at young working-class women and their daughters, many of whom had migrated to city centers from the countryside to find employment. Programming was meant to break isolation; it focused on recreation and preparing girls to be future mothers and homemakers, and included lessons in sewing, cooking, dancing, and etiquette. This domestic emphasis was reflected in young girls' playthings of the time; kitchen and house-keeping toys dominated the sphere of girls' recreation throughout the majority of the early and mid-twentieth century. By the early 1900s, the Girl Scouts of America and the Girl Guides of Canada had begun to organize girl-specific activities. Their programming was similar; they both emphasized mentorship and involved girls in sports, outdoor activities, and community service. Such themes and activities remain central to these organizations to this day.

Girl-Centered Programming in the 1960s and Beyond. With the rise of the women's and civil rights movements in the 1960s and a heightened focus on social justice in the public sphere, girl-centered programming shifted its attention to dealing with juvenile delinquency, the erosion of moral values, and girls' sexual behavior. By the 1970s, Girls Inc. had adopted more progressive and educational programming, aiming to prepare girls for their new roles in a changing society. After navigating the sexual revolution of the 1960s and 1970s, Girls Inc. began to carve a role for itself as an advocate for girls' needs and rights. The group organized conferences, encouraged research on girls, and ran pilot projects. They developed a number of educational approaches in six main program areas: (1) careers and life planning, (2) health and sexuality, (3) leadership and community action, (4) sports and adventure, (5) self-reliance and life skills, and (6) culture and heritage. Whereas in the 1950s and 1960s the primary goal of girl-centered programming was to prepare girls for motherhood, such initiatives now worked to instill young girls with a sense of personal agency—to change the way girls thought and made decisions about their lives.

The early 1980s marked a period that researchers of female adolescent psychology identified as a time of crisis. With increasing pressures of social conformity and media-induced images of the **thin ideal**, girls were losing a sense of self-acceptance and confidence. Depression, **disordered eating**, and an inability to meaningfully relate to others were recognized as consequences of this trying time for young women in America. Through the work of psychologists and sociologists like Carol Gilligan and Lyn Mikel Brown, and because of the influence of popular books such as Mary Pipher's **Reviving**

Ophelia, the importance of single-sex social programming was given new articulation and reinforcement throughout North America.

New Interventions for a New Century. By the 1990s, scholarship on girlhood was increasing, as was interest in what has now been termed the "New Girls' Movement," focused on the particular needs, strengths, and interests of girls rather than on a particular set agenda. Girls Inc. adopted the slogan "We help girls become strong, smart, and bold." The Ms. Foundation released a report documenting a clear lack of girl-centered programming that addresses the root causes of inequality in the lives of girls. The report noted that most social programming of the time either responded to the needs of girls only when they showed signs of distress, or erased gender altogether under the umbrella of "youth programming." In response to this identified gap in single-sex services, the Ms. Foundation set up the Collaborative Fund for Healthy Girls/Healthy Women as a platform for promoting girls' health and social activism.

In November 2000, the Ms. Foundation released another report, "The New Girls' Movement: Charting the Path." The Ms. Foundation began work with various partners in building a movement of girls and young women. The idea was to support girls in becoming leaders who would work with other youth in their communities and across the country. Safe spaces, girls' leadership and activism, intergenerational relationships, and participatory research were put forward as the best ways to build this new movement.

The foundation financially supported organizations that involved girls in program development and allowed girls to take leadership roles in creating social change. Some of these partner organizations included the Young Women's Project (Washington, D.C.), Native Action (Lame Deer, Montana), the Center for Young Women's Development (San Francisco), and Mi Casa Resource Center for Women (Denver).

Canada has followed a similar path of providing research in support of girl-specific programs. In 1999 the Alliance of Five Research Centres on Violence (a coalition that was established in 1996) documented very few single-sex violence prevention programs in existence in Canada. Researchers noted some promising initiatives and interventions in the areas of youth prostitution, science-based education programs for girls, and healthy school environments, but concluded their report with a call for increased programming opportunities. More funding and programming was needed to thoroughly address the social, political, and economic realities that girls faced, especially Native American girls and young women who had experienced inequality in a predominantly white cultural landscape.

By 2005 girl-centered programming in the United States and Canada largely focused on similar objectives: creating safe spaces and communities for girls; initiating programs that make explicit connections to girls' families and traditions; taking seriously issues of accessibility, including disability; and ensuring opportunities for fun and lighthearted activities.

With the rise of new technologies, organizations that have existed since the late 1800s and early 1900s have had to adapt to changing social and economic circumstances for girls. Many organizations have developed a strong presence on the Internet, offering a range of online activities for girls, including games, chat rooms, quizzes, and opportunities to build personal Web pages. Girls Inc., Girl Scouts of America, Girl Guides of Canada, and a number of other organizations offering girl-centered programming have also included on their **Web sites shopping** links or product catalogs for items such as backpacks, T-shirts, and outdoor gear.

The online presence of organizations running girls' programming—and their need to fund their activities—creates an opportunity for corporations to contribute to girls' well-being.

Many corporations recognize the huge consumer potential of young girls and adolescents and are eager to become involved in girl-centered programming. A prime example of a partnership between corporate and girl-centered organizations is the *uniquely ME!* project, created by the Dove Self-Esteem Fund in partnership with the Girl Scouts of America. *Uniquely ME!* combines the Girl Scouts' mentoring message with messages about healthy body image, self-esteem, and inner beauty.

See also Toys, Kitchen and Housekeeping

Further Reading

Berman, Helen, and Yasmin Jiwani. (2001, November). *In The Best Interests of the Girl Child: Phase II Report*. Alliance of Five Research Centres of Violence.

Brown, Lyn Mikel, and Carol Gilligan. (1992). *Meeting at the Crossroads: Women's Psychology and Girls' Development*. Cambridge, MA: Harvard University Press.

Calhoun Research and Development and C. Lang Consulting, for the Canadian Women's Foundation. (2005, September). *Girls in Canada 2005*. [Online April 2006]. Canadian Women's Foundation Web site http://www.cdnwomen.org/newsite/PDFs/EN/CWF-GirlsCanada-Report05.pdf.

Gilligan, Carol, Annie G. Rogers, and Deborah L. Tolman, eds. (1991). *Women, Girls, and Psychotherapy: Reframing Resistance*. New York: Harrington Park Press.

Johnson, Norine G., Michael C. Roberts, and Judith Worell, eds. (1999). *Beyond Appearance: A New Look at Adolescent Girls*. Washington, DC: American Psychology Association.

Ms. Foundation for Women Collaborative Fund for Healthy Girls/Healthy Women. (2000, November). *The New Girls' Movement: Charting the Path*. [Online, January 2007]. Ms. Foundation for Women Web site http://www.ms.foundation.org/user-assets/PDF/Program/HCHW.pdf.

RACHEL GOUIN

GIRL-NEXT-DOOR.   The "girl-next-door" is a cultural archetype that has long been a fixture of romantic adolescent fiction. The girl-next-door can take many forms and through the years has been exemplified in different ways, but she is typified as a virtuous but unassuming adolescent female with a platonic relationship to a male protagonist who is initially indifferent to her modest charms.

The girl-next-door is particular in the sense that she is often defined by her association with a male protagonist. In essence, there must be at least one boy for her to be "next door" to. However, that is not to say that she is always "next door" in the literal sense. She can equally appear as a childhood acquaintance, a family friend, a best friend's little sister, a quiet schoolmate, the awkward **tomboy**, or even a distant cousin. The important elements are her sympathetic manner and portrayal as a sexless being (at least from the perspective of the male protagonist).

The girl-next-door in popular culture is commonly depicted as the overlooked "average girl" who, because of her familiarity and wholesome nature, is not viewed as a romantic prospect until an "awakening" occurs. This awakening usually takes the form of either a personal transformation on the part of the girl-next-door into sexual maturity, or an epiphany in the eyes of the male protagonist, who suddenly comes to appreciate her. In this way, the latent, "secret" sexuality of the girl-next-door can be seen as exclusive to the protagonist, as if he has "discovered" her hidden desirability. Hence, the girl-next-door has also become a fetishistic symbol of eroticized innocence and blossoming sexual availability. This latter interpretation has been frequently capitalized on by the adult entertainment industry, and in recent years this particular connotation for the girl-next-door has become especially prevalent.

It is also common for the girl-next-door to exist in contrast with a female counterpart, usually a more obvious and glamorous object of desire who overshadows the girl-next-door's prosaic appeal in the eyes of the protagonist. Sometimes this other female is an abstract or distant ideal that preoccupies the protagonist, and at other times she is a sexy sophisticate who pursues the male protagonist. Again, the girl-next-door archetype seems to be dependent on specific conditions or the presence of other types.

The character of Betty Cooper from Archie Comics can be seen as a girl-next-door. She is a dependable and hardworking girl with simple pleasures and an easygoing manner. She pines for her friend and schoolmate, the hapless "everyboy" Archie, but for the most part he has eyes for rich **debutante** Veronica Lodge. Veronica is Betty's best friend and her polar opposite; she is demanding, extravagant, exotic, and, in general, unattainable. As is often the case with the girl-next-door type, the audience is all too aware that Betty is an ideal match for Archie, even if he will be the last to realize it.

Often the girl-next-door's emergence from her peripheral role is transformative, very much like the proverbial ugly duckling that becomes the graceful swan. The story of Cinderella is a sort of girl-next-door story told from the girl's perspective. She is the unremarkable homebody who never gets noticed, overshadowed by her would-be socialite stepsisters. However, after a visit from her fairy godmother, she catches the eye of the handsome prince and lives happily ever after.

This story gets another twist in the film *She's All That* (1999), a teen-oriented remake of *My Fair Lady* (1964) in which a "klutzy," bookish, and sloppily dressed girl becomes the subject of a bet for one of the high school's most popular boys. He must "transform" her into a desirable beauty by the night of the **prom**. Naturally, at first he is concerned only with how to adapt her image to help him win his bet with the other boys, but by the end of the film he realizes that she is the one he truly loves. In this sense, the boy becomes both Prince Charming *and* the "fairy godmother," further increasing the strong male agency in the girl-next-door type.

Another common version of the girl-next-door is the "girl Friday" archetype. Usually this character is depicted as the colleague, sidekick, or pal of the male protagonist, always chipper and willing to help him in any scheme. Despite her obvious devotion to him, the male protagonist remains affably immune to her flirtations. A bespectacled Barbara Bel Geddes as Midge Wood plays an adult version of the girl Friday opposite James Stewart's John Ferguson in *Vertigo* (1958).

A literal incarnation of the girl-next-door appears in television's *Dawson's Creek*. Teenager Joey Potter (Katie Holmes) is the next-door childhood friend and constant confidant of Dawson (James Van Der Beek), who spends the early part of the series ignorant of the implications of her deep affection for him.

In recent years, the term "girl-next-door" has become increasingly associated with pornography. For example, *Playboy* magazine has published a series of special editions and calendars under the title "*Playboy*'s Girls Next Door" that feature models that are intended to resemble or espouse the "average, all-American good girl" characteristics, albeit in a highly contrived and eroticized fashion.

See also Betty and Veronica; Dee, Sandra; Funicello, Annette; Newton-John, Olivia

ZACHARIAH CAMPBELL

GIRLS AND SPORT IN CONTEMPORARY FILM.   Popular media representations of girls and sport have increased since the 1980s and 1990s. Virtually constant in these new representations is an effort to profile the female athlete as strong and resilient, while still emphasizing those aspects that mark her as feminine. Advertisements featuring "sporty" girls favor the more traditionally feminine athletic body rather than a body that might be considered masculine. Journalistic profiles of female athletes may emphasize traditional femininity by focusing on a female athlete's family, including spouse, children, and parents. Highlighting an athlete's caretaking activities often serves to feminize the activities she engages in outside of her sport.

Although the tendency to equate "athletic" with "powerful" and "feminine" with "attractive" can be subverted by female athletes who embody both athleticism and femininity, it also signals a media attempt to domesticate female athletes. This is particularly true in the film industry, where "Cinderella" stories of self-transformation abound. These fairy-tale adaptations often imply that in order to succeed on *and* off the playing field, female athletes must conform to a popular standard of beauty. Emphasizing a heterosexual romantic relationship is another means by which an athlete's feminine status is celebrated.

Female Athletes in Starring Roles.   The rise in media portrayals of girls and sport notwithstanding, few films have placed female athletes in leading roles. Scholar Timothy Shary calls this phenomenon the "invisible female jock" (2002, p. 70). The invisible female jock is possibly best represented by the 1992 film *Ladybugs*, a story about a girls' soccer team whose best player is in fact a male disguised as a female. Shary found only one example of an athletic female film protagonist prior to 2000, in *The Next Karate Kid* (1994). However, even this film's portrayal of female athleticism is problematic in its resolution. Whereas male athletes in the film prove themselves in scenes surrounded by an audience, providing instant fame to the victor, the heroine of *The Next Karate Kid* proves herself by fighting off an attacker on a dark and deserted pier; no one is around to witness her bravery. The end of the film also demonstrates that, along with her increased athleticism, the protagonist has become involved in a heterosexual relationship. She changes from her familiar martial arts training clothes into a sexy prom dress, and although she has become the victor, her success is linked to her new romantic relationship and ability to transform into a more conventionally feminine young woman.

Twenty-first–century films showcasing young, athletically gifted females in leading roles include *Bring It On* (2000), *Girlfight* (2000), *Love and Basketball* (2000), *Bend It Like Beckham* (2002), *Blue Crush* (2002), and *Stick It* (2006). The films represent a wide range, from small, independent pictures with limited releases and box office success, to major studio–backed productions with considerable budgets, resources, and receipts.

Bring It On tells the story of a coed high school cheerleading squad. While the squad cheers in support of the school's football games, their own cheerleading competitions are what really drive the plot. *Bring It On* emphasizes female cheerleaders as competitive athletes and places them above the weaker football team. However, the fact that there are both boys and girls on the cheerleading team indicates that the girls do not achieve success or higher status without the help of their male counterparts. *Girlfight* is a film that depicts the exact opposite of this dependence on and partnership with males. *Girlfight* is about the struggles of Diana, a social outcast who has lost her mother and is left to contend with her abusive father. Diana finds inner strength and a sense of self in becoming a boxer. She emerges victorious both emotionally and physically as she fights her new boyfriend in a title bout and wins.

Love and Basketball offers a similar coed athletic dynamic in which a girlfriend and boyfriend excel at the same sport. However, while *Love and Basketball* provides positive representations of young, female athletes—they are powerful, committed, physically capable, and empowered—these representations are compromised by the overt display of high femininity at the school dance. While the female protagonist wears her hair up or in braids for every basketball game, presumably to keep it out of her way while playing, she wears it long and straight (a much more conventionally female style) for the dance at the end of the film.

Bend It Like Beckham is a film about two 18-year-old girls in London who have their hearts set on playing professional soccer. Jesminder (Jess), the film's protagonist, rebels against her traditional Indian parents' expectations of her entering into an arranged marriage and living a traditional British Indian life. Her passion is not for settling down into a traditional relationship but for playing the sport she loves. Jess sneaks around to play soccer with a girls' team, in hopes of next playing for a college team and then possibly at a professional level in the United States. Her budding romance with her male coach, however, forms a subplot that places as much emphasis on heterosexual romance as it does on soccer. Much as in *Love and Basketball*, when the team goes out dancing, Jess engages in a self-transformation of sorts: she appears in a sexy dress with her hair sleekly styled and makeup that completes the narrative of transformation. This "Cinderella" moment in the film, and the budding relationship between Jess and her coach at the end of the film, are examples of **compulsory heterosexuality**.

A heterosexual romance is also at the center of *Blue Crush*, the story of a working-class Hawaiian surfer named Anne Marie. Anne Marie lives for riding the waves but struggles to raise her younger sister at the same time. The film depicts the daily struggles of Anne Marie and her three roommates to cover the rent, pay the bills, and also have time to surf, and Anne Marie's ability to overcome her fear of drowning is a moving subplot. Yet the film's athletic, competitive edge is overshadowed by the notions of compulsory heterosexuality that seem at times contrived; in the end, the protagonist and her love interest ride the waves into the sunset together, and the audience is left with the message that love—heterosexual love, in particular—conquers all. Furthermore, Anne Marie's younger sister depends on her as though she were her mother, effectively domesticating her into a traditional maternal role.

Stick It, the 2006 film about competitive **gymnastics**, may prove to be a turning point for popular media representations of girls and sport. The film tells the story of Haley Graham, a former elite gymnast who has gotten into trouble and must choose between spending time in juvenile detention and returning to the world of gymnastics she left behind. She chooses the latter, and brings her rebellious attitude and maverick spirit with her. Like many sports movies, *Stick It* explores the difficulty of harnessing natural talent; Haley's wild ways do not conform to the rigidity of training camp or the structured environment of competitive gymnastics. However, by the end of the film she becomes disciplined enough to contribute to the team, and what makes the story shine is her ability to share her renewed energy and enthusiasm with her teammates. The gymnasts in *Stick It* are portrayed as physically strong, capable athletes; Haley does not conform to the traditional prepubescent body type of female gymnasts. The team is coached by a male, but the girls' rebellion—and success—at the competition is all their own.

Themes of compulsory heterosexuality, traditional expectations of femininity, domesticity, and self-transformation occur within many representations of girls and **sport** on film. All of these themes can operate individually or simultaneously. However, when one or more of these themes are present, they can compromise the potentially empowering message of films driven by athletically gifted females.

Further Reading

Curry, Timothy J., P. Arriagada, and B. Cornwall. (2002). "Images of Sport in Popular Nonsport Magazines: Power and Performance versus Pleasure and Participation." *Sociological Perspectives* 45, no. 4, 397–413.

Shary, Timothy. (2002). *Generation Multiplex: The Image of Youth in Contemporary American Cinema.* Austin: University of Texas Press.

ALLISON WRIGHT MUNRO

GIRLS' FRIENDSHIPS.   Girl culture takes place within the context of girls' friendships: it is within friendship groups that the social practices and interactions central to the construction of gendered identities occur. As with all social networks, girls' friendship groups consist of different kinds of relationships, all of which affect the formation of individual and group identity. These identities are discovered through processes of belonging, inclusion and exclusion, and rules of conduct.

Best Friends and Friendship Groups. Predominantly, girls invest in two kinds of same-gender friendship: the one and only "best" friend and the larger peer group. Classic best friends in popular culture include Diana Barry and Anne Shirley in **Anne of Green Gables**, and **Betty and Veronica** in the long-running *Archie* **comic** strip. The dynamics of female peer groups are shown in movies such as *Now and Then* (1995) and *Divine Secrets of the Ya-Ya Sisterhood* (2002), both of which center on a group of adult women reminiscing about their girlhood friendships.

The prevalence and popularity of these movies demonstrate an interest in girls' friendships in popular culture. The movies themselves represent girlhood friendships as enduring over years and decades, and, indeed, girls often report intense emotional attachments to one another and place great importance on the longevity of these bonds. The popular saying "best friends forever" and the girl-oriented marketing of the "BFF" slogan on items such as necklaces, rings, and clothing is evidence of the importance that girls—and society at large—place on these intimate social bonds.

The desire to maintain intimate bonds with best friends while also being connected to a wider social network can lead to difficult and pressured situations as girls attempt to achieve balance in their friendships. Key tensions in the way girls relate are found between, for example, **niceness** and **meanness**, friendship and popularity, and closeness and competition (Frith 2004). Therefore, while the feeling of belonging is in some sense an individual psychological state, it is also—and perhaps more important—a social process. For this reason, it is often more important to understand girls and their friendships by looking at group dynamics rather than individual developmental processes. In particular, the way that girls use positions of power to define and navigate their peer relationships is a rich site of potential knowledge about girls' friendships.

Inclusion, Exclusion, and Belonging. It is primarily through practices of inclusion and exclusion that female friendship groups and positions of belonging are defined. Exclusion in particular highlights girls' negotiations and struggles over power by defining who is worthy of group membership and who is not. This dynamic is exemplified in the sleeper hits *Clueless* (1995) and *Mean Girls* (2004). In both films, the central characters wield a great deal of power and can single-handedly choose who is permitted into the group and who is not.

Central to these processes of inclusion and exclusion are factors such as social class, gender, and sexuality, as well as other material and symbolic differences that are used by girls to define their peer groups. Girls' processes of belonging do, however, change over time and in different places, particularly as they move through school and find new contexts for friendship formations (such as clubs, teams, and new classes). For instance, the final sequences of *Mean Girls* reveal that the four central characters have "grown up" by finding peer groups that are more closely aligned with their own interests and individual personalities. Equally significant determinants of inclusion and exclusion are biological transitions through life stages, from child, to **tween**, to teenager, to young adult.

What "Should" Girls' Friendships Be? Girls' friendships are different in many ways from the friendships of boys, but the rich and varied landscapes of girls' friendships have largely been ignored in research. This reflects prevailing sexist cultural notions that boys' friendships are of greater social character, interest, and importance than the friendships of girls. However, girls are now becoming the focus of many studies of youth culture that seek to critically assess the ways in which girls are represented both politically and in popular culture.

Often, **moral panics** about the state of contemporary society are reflected in media concerns about girls' friendships, and in this way female friendship has become an index of social change. These panics commonly play themselves out in concerns about mean girls, and embedded in them are powerful claims about girls' identities, relationships, and "correct" place in society. Some have argued that moral panics about mean girls clearly map onto stereotypical notions of respectable femininity, such that when girls' friendships disrupt common understandings of what girls are expected to be and do, this is seen as a measure of the moral degradation of society.

Romance or Conflict? Two clear themes emerge from representations of girls' friendships in the popular media: romance and conflict. The romance theme is characterized by sharing, support, intimate disclosure, and trust (in television friendships such as that of Anne and Diana in *Anne of Green Gables* or DJ and Kimmy in *Full House*), whereas the conflict theme is typified by exclusion, battles over status, and hierarchical cliques (such as the female dynamics in *Mean Girls* or 1989's **Heathers**). Arguably such polarized categories do not take into account the historical and cultural contexts that produce popular understandings of social categories like "girls" in the first place. Rather than inherently being "conflicted" or "romantic," as they mature, girls continually develop strategies and styles for dealing with the complexities of friendship groups (Ringrose 2006). Researchers who have talked with girls and young women note the deficits of the romance and conflict themes. When the accounts and experiences of girls themselves are prioritized, it is clear that their relationships at varying stages of adolescence and in varying social contexts do not conform to these polarized themes.

Defining Friendships, Defining Oneself. Many girls believe in the importance of sharing secrets as a way of defining "best" friends. Yet secrets also tend to be circulated throughout the larger peer group, highlighting their wide appeal and potential for creating scandal (Mellor 2007). This tension demonstrates how the collective nature of friendship can contrast with the desire for closeness and intimacy in girls' friendships. While young girls in particular may outwardly express their personalities as "good" or "nice," on another, highly self-conscious level, they may also experience anxiety about being disliked by others. Their acts of disclosure, then, are part of a wider process of gender identity maintenance, whereby best friends attempt to negotiate their friendship both on a one-to-one level and as part of a larger peer group. Tensions concerning closeness and popularity may result, and many girls experience this strain as they attempt to gain entry into a friendship group while maintaining a unique relationship with a best friend.

Girls' friendship groups are also defined by dominant cultural understandings of gender and sexuality. Renold (2005), for example, illustrates how girls attempt to make themselves attractive to boys, and how this performance is crucial to maintaining membership in popular circles. The social practices and statuses that define **compulsory heterosexuality** and the need for girls to define themselves as single, dating, or in a relationship (with a boy) are often important markers of feminine identity. They are also important in defining membership in a friendship group. Indeed, as girls enter their teens, their reputation with regard to boys takes on increased importance within their friendships (Lees 1993).

Girls must make and maintain their friendships in a world structured by masculine authority. Paradoxically, these male-dominated structures (and the naturalization of gender differences that result) are what create the space for girls' friendships to emerge and thrive, but they also contribute to the devaluing of girls' **social networks**. The **covering over** of books and films about female friendships as "mere **chick lit**" or "mere chick flicks" supports the minimization of female relationships and explorations of identity.

Social class is also an important determinant of friendship group membership, functioning much like gender and sexuality as a marker of identity. Class and socioeconomic status influence how girls produce accounts of their own identities and those of others. These factors also create different filters through which girls discipline and regulate themselves and one another. Middle-class girls, for example, may believe that working-class girls are overtly sexual, shamelessly flaunting their femininity and sex appeal, while working-class girls often view middle-class girls as lacking in femininity, for example, by being too academic (Hey 1997).

There is also a growing emphasis on the physical spaces in which friendships take place. Although the majority of youth research is carried out in schools (in classrooms and in the schoolyard), a large percentage of girls' interactions take place in nontraditional school spaces like bathrooms and changing rooms, or outside of school, in places like malls and homes. Within the home in particular, bedrooms are crucial sites for the practices of friendship. The spatial aspect of girls' friendships has meant that, historically at least, the friendship cultures of girls have often been sidelined by more general considerations of youth culture because girls' friendship practices are more often conducted in spaces deemed private. Boys' friendships, on the contrary, are more commonly viewed through displays and performances in public spaces, such as sporting events or on school playgrounds.

Further Reading

Frith, Hannah. (2004). "The Best of Friends: The Politics of Girls' Friendships." *Feminism and Psychology* 14, 357–360.

Hey, Valerie. (1997). *The Company She Keeps: An Ethnography of Girls' Friendships*. Buckingham, UK: Open University Press.

Lees, Sue. (1993). *Sugar and Spice: Sexuality and Adolescent Girls*. London and New York: Penguin.

McRobbie, Angela. (1991). *Feminism and Youth Culture: From Jackie to Just Seventeen*. London: Unwin Hyman.

Mellor, D. J. (2007). *Everyday and Eternal Acts: Exploring Children's Friendships in the Primary School*. [Online, October 2007]. Cardiff University School of Social Science Working Paper Series Web site http://www.cardiff.ac.uk/schoolsanddivisions/academicschools/socsi/publications/abstracts/workingpaper88.html?lang=eng.

Renold, Emma. (2005). *Girls, Boys and Junior Sexualities: Exploring Children's Gendered and Sexual Relations in the Primary School*. New York: Routledge Falmer.

Ringrose, Jessica. (2006). "A New Universal Mean Girl: Examining the Discursive Construction and Social Regulation of a New Feminine Pathology." *Feminism and Psychology* 16, no. 4, 405–424.

DAVID JAMES MELLOR

GIRLS GONE WILD.   *Girls Gone Wild* is a popular direct-to-video series whose signature images are of college-age women exposing their bodies in public settings. The brainchild of a young media entrepreneur, Joe Francis, the series originated from the unused footage of amateur porn producers, television news crews who shot displays of nudity during Mardi Gras or Spring Break assignments, and tourists who captured exposed bodies with handheld cameras. By 1998, Francis had produced his first *Girls Gone Wild* video by compiling the images on a single reel and launched the first of the series' ubiquitous infomercials on late-night cable television. The initial products were so successful that Francis launched his own production company, Mantra Entertainment, and began to deploy his own camera crews to capture gratuitous nudity on tape. Thanks to the quick production of dozens of videos and a successful marketing campaign of infomercials, within a couple of years the *Girls Gone Wild* brand became a household name.

The most common image associated with *Girls Gone Wild* is of a young woman (almost exclusively in her late teens or early twenties) exposing her breasts or other private parts on camera. A comparative look at the earliest videos and the most recent releases illustrates the evolution of the enterprise. The first few *Girls Gone Wild* videos feature a documentary-style aesthetic; they capture images from Mardi Gras and Spring Break, where young women were apparently already flashing their breasts in public in front of hard-partying crowds. Yet with each subsequent video release, the videos increasingly resemble a reality television format, complete with rough editing, calypso or techno music soundtracks, and direct conversation with the participants. In later videos, it became clear that the women are familiar with the *Girls Gone Wild* video franchise and often appear more than willing to take part in its production.

The majority of the series features women approached by an unseen male cameraman, whose disembodied voice offers these young women the opportunity to appear on the *Girls Gone Wild* video; or, in some cases, the videos feature young women who are supposedly seeking out the cameras for media exposure. Almost every scene of a *Girls Gone Wild* video features the consent process on camera, and most scenes conclude with the same routine: the cameraman asks the woman how old she is, and every participant makes the claim to be over the legal age of 18. Next, each woman is asked whether she knows what *Girls Gone Wild* is and whether the footage can be used; nearly all respond with an eager yes. In many cases, participants squeal with delight after successfully "earning" their tank top (silkscreened with the *Girls Gone Wild* logo), holding it up as if it were a trophy. In addition, more recent videos tend to feature not only gratuitous flashes of nudity, but also extended scenes of young women engaging in more salacious sexual acts by themselves or with other female friends, or participating in staged contests such as the "Girls Gone Wild Games."

The overarching theme of all of the *Girls Gone Wild* videos is that the featured participants are typically white, middle-class young women (i.e., not strippers, porn stars, or actresses) who are temporarily stepping out of their comfort zones, ostensibly having fun while on vacation or during a night out on the town. As a result, it could be argued that the emphasis on the reality television aesthetic and on the girls' voluntarily stepping out of the **girl-next-door** role helps the *Girls Gone Wild* enterprise elude classification as traditional pornography and secures its place in mainstream American culture. The franchise itself has been parodied on multiple American television programs—including *Saturday Night Live*, *The Simpsons*, *Chappelle's Show*, and *Arrested Development*—and *Girls Gone Wild* buses continually make pilgrimages to college bars, sporting events, and Spring Break destinations around the country.

Further Reading

Levy, Ariel. (2005). *Female Chauvinist Pigs: Women and the Rise of Raunch Culture*. New York: Free Press.

Mayer, Vickie. (2005). "Soft-Core in TV Time: The Political Economy of a 'Cultural Trend.'" *Critical Studies in Media Communication* 22, no. 4, 302–320.

McNair, Brian. (2002). *Striptease Culture: Sex, Media, and the Democratization of Desire*. New York: Routledge.

Pitcher, Karen. (2006). "The Staging of Agency in *Girls Gone Wild*." *Critical Studies in Media Communication* 23, no. 3, 200–218.

KAREN PITCHER

GO-GO GIRL.   In the late 1960s, the go-go girl was a hip-shaking, fringe-swinging queen of the American discotheque (a nightclub that played upbeat recorded dance music). The go-go girl became an important pop culture icon for girls of the period, associated with the sexual revolution, freedom, and independence of the 1960s.

Club History and Early Go-Go Dancers.   The go-go phenomenon had both French and American roots. In 1947, a discotheque called the Whisky á Go-Go opened in Paris. The name came from the whisky labels that lined its walls and the Parisian slang term *à gogo* ("more than enough" or "to spare"), which derived from the American jazz expression "Go, man, go." In January 1964, four businessmen opened a nightclub named after the Paris establishment on Los Angeles' Sunset Strip. In addition to its dance floor and stereo sound system, the club featured scantily clad young women who danced in a glassed-in booth over the crowd below. The women who entertained at these clubs were the world's first official go-go dancers, although during the height of the "twist" dance craze in 1961, enthusiastic young waitresses at New York's Peppermint Lounge were also known to leap on top of a wrought iron fence inside the club and twist the night away, to the crowd's delight.

Mainstream Americans were introduced to the go-go dancer in 1965, when the television music show *Hullabaloo* brought its mixed-gender and multicultural troupe of dancers into American households every week. What distinguished *Hullabaloo* from rival shows like *Shindig* was its special "Hullabaloo a Go-Go" segment: at the end of the program, musical guests danced on a nightclub set framed by go-go girls in fringed dresses who danced in elevated cages on either side. This allowed young people all over America

Go-go dancers perform the Watusi in a cage suspended from the ceiling at the Whisky a Go-Go night club in Hollywood, California, 1965. (AP Photo.)

to participate in the go-go craze, as they danced along with the televised dancers from the comfort of their own living rooms. It was the closest many teenage viewers would ever get to the Sunset Strip.

The Go-Go Girl's Influence on Pop Culture. Exposure to the go-go dancer aesthetic certainly created a demand from consumers for the short, vinyl go-go boots named after these famed dancers. The boots, which came in a variety of colors (some with a zipper up the back), were made available at stores like Sears and Montgomery Ward and were made to fit teenagers and even little girls. These became a fashion fad in their own right, along with the fringed skirts go-go dancers wore and other miniskirt styles of the period. Popular music and movies further promoted the go-go phenomenon. Gary Lewis and the Playboys sang about "Little Miss Go-Go" (1965), while the Miracles were "Going to a Go-Go" (1965) and Joanne Neel explored the trauma that resulted when "Daddy Was a Preacher; Mama Was a Go-Go Girl." One film, *Winter a Go-Go* (1965), even transported the beach party premise to a ski lodge.

Making a Living: Go-Go Dancers. A 1967 *Newsweek* article estimated that there were 8000 go-go girls in the United States at the time, most between 18 and 21 years old ("Go-Go Girls"). *Ebony* magazine told readers that "any girl who can dance to the big beat sound of rock 'n' roll can become a go-go dancer." All she had to do was "be willing to work long, hard hours and wear a variety of costumes from fancy slacks to frilly skirts or form-fitting tights and calf-high a-go-go boots" ("A Go-Go Girls" 1966, p. 143). Many believed go-go dancing to be good, clean fun that provided not only a way to express emotion and energy but also a way to keep a slim physique. For others, the decent money made by dancers was inspiration to take up positions. Whisky a Go-Go in Los Angeles claimed to pay the highest wages—in 1965, the bar shelled out $150 per dancer for about four hours of work a night. Two years later, going rates ranged from $2.50 an hour in Boston to $200 a week at the Swinging Door, a nightclub in Houston, Texas. Elsewhere some girls earned as little as $8 per night.

There were physical repercussions from go-go dancing: *Newsweek* reported that go-go girls were vulnerable to strained necks, dislocated ribs, and eyestrain (from squinting into the bright lights focused on them). The magazine also touched on some of the emotional strains to which go-go girls were subject. "The life of a go-go dancer is very lonely," noted a girl who worked at Whisky a Go-Go. "You don't know whether the boy you met likes you because of the way you dance or because he wants to go to bed with you. It bars you from finding a husband, almost" ("Go-Go Girls" 1967, p. 100).

Changing Norms of Nudity. Early go-go girls did not work topless. Most appeared in reputable discotheques where men and women came to dance to recorded music. The dancers were indeed part of the entertainment, but although their presence undoubtedly increased male attendance, they were not the featured attraction. Only after discotheques went out of fashion in the 1970s did go-go girls move on to perform in strip joints before all-male audiences, where nudity was often a requirement. Many young women hoped go-go dancing would be the starting point for a career in entertainment. While fame remained a pipe dream for most, go-go girls who went on to bigger things include actresses Teri Garr and Goldie Hawn, choreographer Toni Basil, topless queen Carol Doda, and convicted murderer and Charles Manson disciple Susan Atkins.

Further Reading

"A Go-Go Girls." (1966, April). *Ebony*, 143.
Dawson, Jim. (1995). *The Twist: The Story of the Song and Dance That Changed the World*. Boston and London: Faber and Faber.
"Go-Go Girls." (1967, March 13). *Newsweek*, 99–100.
Scott, John L. (1965, April 12). "At Whisky a Go-Go: Athletic Mayhem in Motion." *Los Angeles Times*.

LYNN PERIL

GO-GO'S, THE. The Go-Go's were the first **girl band** to emerge on the popular music scene. Debuting with 1981's *Beauty and the Beat*, which unexpectedly sold over 2 million copies, the Go-Go's were one of the first all-female bands to top the *Billboard* charts, and the album produced a number of hits, including "We Got the Beat," "Our Lips Are Sealed," "Vacation," and "Head over Heels." The group's beginnings were more **punk** than pop, and they started under the name the Misfits (which is also the name of the rival band on the 1980s animated television show ***Jem and the Holograms***). Changes in membership were followed by a change in name and sound, with their music becoming more of a sparkly California pop sound while still maintaining a punk/new-wave edge. Although the Go-Go's image was that of "wholesome clean fun," trouble with both alcohol and drug abuse, particularly cocaine, prevailed during their quick rise to fame.

The Go-Go's membership for *Beauty and the Beat* included Belinda Carlisle (vocals), Jane Wiedlin (guitar, vocals), Charlotte Caffey (lead guitar, keyboards), Kathy Valentine (bass), and Gina Schock (drums). The group released their second album, *Vacation*, in 1982, but the response and attention it received never approached that of their first record. In 1984, the group released their third album, *Talk Show*, with two Top 40 hits, including "Head over Heels" and "Turn to You."

The Go-Go's enjoyed a short-lived career, breaking up in 1985 and then reuniting for several concert tours in the 1990s, with new album releases that included mostly "greatest hits" and a few new songs. They produced a new original recording in 2001, *God Bless the Go-Go's*, which received only lukewarm reviews. The band continues to tour and perform in smaller venues.

Although Wiedlin was the one most set on a successful solo career, it was Carlisle who had the greatest commercial success. Carlisle's

The Go-Go's. *Shown:* Charlotte Caffey, Kathy Valentine, Belinda Carlisle, Gina Schock, and Jane Wiedlin. (Courtesy of Photofest.)

sound turned adult contemporary with her first album, 1986's *Belinda*, and the single "Mad about You." Her greatest solo success came with *Heaven on Earth* (1990) and the single of the same name, as well as "I Get Weak" and "Circle in the Sand." Her success continued but eventually began to wane, and she rejoined the Go-Go's in 1994. Her most recent release is *Voila* (2007), a collection of French pop songs.

Further Reading

Gaar, Gillian G. (1992). *She's a Rebel: The History of Women in Rock and Roll*. Emeryville, CA: Seal Press.

O'Brien, Lucy. (1996). *She Bop: The Definitive History of Women in Rock, Pop & Soul*. New York: Penguin Books.

ANN M. SAVAGE

GOTH GIRLS.   Goth girls represent a darker, alternative perspective on what it means to be a girl. Rejecting the bright, bubbly stereotype of the female image, goth girls steer clear of **pink** clothes, hair ribbons, charming laughs, and fluttering eyelashes. A typical goth girl outfit may include dyed hair (usually black but sometimes in bright and unusual colors, such as blue or fire engine red), black eye makeup, black **lipstick**, and black clothing in the form of a T-shirt, tank top, corset, dress, and/or pants, usually made from material such as satin, lace, or fishnet.

The "goth" in goth girls is short for "gothic," which begins to explain the origin of this look. Goth style was originally inspired by nineteenth-century gothic literature, which was the first of its time to employ the idea of "pleasing terror" (i.e., terror that both upsets and compels the reader). Aside from terror, some of the more prominent features of gothic

Goth girls display a unique fashion style and strong attitudes. (Courtesy of Shutterstock.)

literature include haunted areas, darkness, death, decay, castles, madness, and hereditary curses. Typical female characters in gothic literature were femmes fatales, madwomen, and persecuted maidens. This literature was also strongly anti-Catholic and included criticism of Catholic acts, such as the Inquisition. Goth influences continue into the modern day, as many horror movies have picked up and expanded on these themes and characters.

Goth subculture as it is known today began in the 1980s in the United Kingdom and branched off from the gothic rock scene, which was popular at the time. Today, music continues to inspire and be inspired by goth girls. Singer and performer Marilyn Manson has many female backup performers who express various versions of the goth girl ideal. Much contemporary music that is considered goth now comes out of Germany. German music events such as Wave-Gotik-Treffen, Zillo (which ceased to be active after 2004), and M'era Luna, as well as the Drop Dead Festival in the United States, promote the goth music scene and are attended by fans from all over the world.

In popular culture, goth girls are depicted with varying degrees of severity. *The Grim Adventures of Billy and Mandy* is a cartoon series that airs on the Cartoon Network. It depicts sullen, dark-humored Mandy, who is friends with the Grim Reaper. *Ruby Gloom* is a cartoon series set in Doomsville; the title character is a young girl with bright red hair, a black dress, a pet named Doom Kitty, a best friend named Misery who sleeps on a bed of nails, and a raven friend named Poe (descended from Edgar Allan Poe's pet budgie, Paco). The cartoon version of the movie *Beetlejuice* also contains a goth girl in the character of Lydia Deetz, who dresses in very typical goth girl outfits and enjoys "weird" things, such as spiders and horror movies. These versions of popular-culture goth girls are considered "perky goth," or "goth lite." These characters are generally dressed in a typical goth manner but do not reflect an entirely negative or dark perspective; they operate on the notion that dark does not always mean depressing.

A large range of goth girls are found in horror movies, and their image tends to be truer to goth girl origins. In *House of 1000 Corpses* (2003) and *The Devil's Rejects* (2005), the character Baby Firefly (played by Sheri Moon) is one of the darkest movie goth girls. She dresses more like a twisted **cowgirl** than a goth girl but has all the harder-edged traits of goth culture, such as an obsession with death, decay, and suffering. Other movie characters who enjoy the darker aspects of life and look the part of a goth girl are Lydia Deetz (played by Winona Ryder) in the 1988 movie *Beetlejuice* and Danica Talos (played by Parker Posey) in the 2004 movie *Blade Trinity*. These types of characters are portrayed as darker, more thoroughly solemn, and more depressed than the perky goth or goth lite characters often seen on television.

Further Reading

Baddeley, Gavin. (2002). *Goth Chic: A Connoisseur's Guide to Dark Culture*. London: Plexus.
Hodkinson, Paul. (2002). *Goth: Identity, Style and Subculture*. New York: Berg.

Kilpatrick, Nancy. (2004). *The Goth Bible: A Compendium for the Darkly Inclined*. New York: St. Martin's Griffin.

BROOKE BALLANTYNE

GUERILLA GIRLS.   Founded in 1985, the Guerilla Girls are a movement made up of feminist artists and activists. Their goal is to unveil the discrimination of the art world, which historically has been a white male–dominated institution. In so doing, they are advocating greater exposure of women and other marginalized artists in the art world. In an attempt to overcome stereotypes about classic femininity, they use the term "girl," and some embrace typically "girlish" clothing and colors as a means of reclaiming the power of oppressive labels.

Guerilla Girls formed in response to an exhibition at the Museum of Modern Art in New York entitled "An International Survey of Painting and Sculpture." The exhibition featured 169 artists, and of those only 13 were female. Moreover, that small group of women was composed only of white artists from North America and Europe. A group of female artists who were outraged by this lack of representation picketed in front of the museum. Their tactics did not garner much attention, so they opted for a very different approach to publicizing their grievance: they donned gorilla masks and used informational posters to get their message out.

One of their most widely recognized messages is a 1989 depiction of a famous nude female painting, *Odalisque*, re-created with a gorilla head. The caption reads, "Do women have to be naked to get into the Met Museum? Less than 5% of the artists in the Modern Art sections are women, but 85% of the nudes are female." This illustrates their primary goal of drawing attention to the specific galleries, museums, and benefactors who underrepresent and underfund female artists and artists of color.

Along with the gorilla masks, the Guerilla Girls use the names of deceased artists, writers, and scholars to protect themselves against repercussions from the individuals and institutions they expose, to keep the focus on the issues they are putting forth, and to pay tribute to pioneer female artists. In some ways, Guerilla Girls can be compared to **comic** book female heroes, such as **Wonder Woman** and **Batgirl**, in that they take on an alter ego and fight for a just cause. In accordance with their anonymity and growing global membership, their official numbers are unknown.

Although the Guerilla Girls were founded in New York City, they have spread to artistic centers across the United States and all over the world. One can encounter their posters and speaking events in many languages and in various media sources. The Guerilla Girls label themselves the "Conscience of the Art World" and use posters and advertisements as a means of achieving this role. Their activism is widely recognized, and they have been featured in such forums as the *New York Times*, *Ms. Magazine*, and CNN, and their work has been documented and analyzed in various scholarly journals.

Since 2000, the interests of the Guerilla Girls have spread to multiple arenas, including theater, visual arts, and Web-based media. Because of this expansion, there are now several individual groups that represent various interests of the Guerilla Girls.

See also Riot Grrrl

Further Reading

Guerilla Girls. (1995). *Confessions of the Guerilla Girls*. New York: Harper Perennial.
Guerilla Girls. (2003). *Bitches, Bimbos, and Ballbreakers: The Guerilla Girls' Illustrated Guide to Female Stereotypes*. New York: Penguin Books.

Hoban, Phoebe. (2004). *Masks Still in Place, but Firmly in the Mainstream.* [Online May 2007]. Guerilla Girls Web site http://www.guerrillagirls.com/tours/nytimes2004.shtml.

KATHRYN MURPHY AND MELODY BOYD

gURL.COM.   Launched in 1996, gURL.com is an online space specifically designated for girls. The name "gURL" takes the idea of location on the Web (URL) and feminizes it by placing a "g" in front of it. The **Web site** carries features similar to those found in the most popular **magazines** for adolescent girls, but by creating the site as a girl "community"— in which young girls actively voice their opinions and offer each other advice—the co-creators attempt to use the specific capabilities of the Internet medium to empower young women. The co-creators, Esther Drill, Rebecca Odes, and Heather McDonald, recognized that young girls respond to popular magazines about beauty, style, and pop culture, and they sought to create a girl-positive space for these concerns online with www.gURL.com, the product of a master's thesis project at New York University.

The design concept of gURL.com has not changed substantially since its inception. The basic design of the site is a black background with brightly colored text and drawings that look like sketches. The official gURL.com logo shows an arm that extends into a clenched fist, with polished nails visible on the hand. Site features include news updates, polls, message boards on selected topics, featured Web sites, games, and Web page hosting. To access some of these services, it is necessary to become a member, because gURL.com attempts to protect its community space by making chat available only to registered users. The membership registration includes the strong suggestion that members should establish a screen name alias. The relative anonymity that this provides facilitates discussion of controversial or difficult topics.

The individual "**voices**" present in the site are also a key part of the design. Drill, Odes, and McDonald decided to take advantage of the online format by allowing multiple opportunities for girl members to voice their opinions and respond to each other. While the site includes editorial content, it also includes multiple places for girls to respond to the content, ask each other questions, and offer each other advice. The advice section contains no editorial content; gURLs can send in queries, and other members of the community examine them and respond. Notably, gURL.com is considered to be one of the most popular online destinations for adolescent girls.

gURL.com often mimics and subverts the typical teen girls' magazine format. The site's style, fashion, and beauty pages are illustrated with sketches that make the topics appear fun and playful while simultaneously avoiding realistic photo images of young women that might spur negative comparisons between the user and the model. Quizzes and games (including "Dress Me Up" and "Paperdoll Psychology") take advantage of the interactive format by encouraging users to play again and again, a feature that also keeps the user from taking fashion and beauty too seriously.

Drill, Odes, and McDonald have published two spin-off books that integrate information from the Web site. *Deal With It! A Whole New Approach to Your Body, Brain, and Life as a gURL* (1999) and *The Looks Book: A Whole New Approach to Beauty, Body Image, and Style* (2002) are accessible, contemporary companions to the classic guide to women's health, *Our Bodies, Ourselves.* The books are popular and critically acclaimed, and they reiterate the site's philosophy of creating a healthy outlook for teenage girls. Both books include a large amount of chat samples from gURL.com. The authors enhance their credibility on every topic by including testimonials or advice from members of the gURL community.

gURL.com has had many owners during its brief history, partly because its appeal for young women has made it attractive in the corporate media landscape. By the late 1990s, gURL.com was part of the iTurf community of sites designed to target Generation Y. In 2003, Primedia Incorporated ran the site as a companion to its **Seventeen** magazine, featuring some *Seventeen* content on the site and a small section of gURL.com health information in the magazine. The crossover did not have much time to take off, because by fall 2003 Primedia sold the Web site to iVillage, an Internet content provider that targets women. Although iVillage continues to operate gURL.com, the entire company was acquired by NBC in 2006.

Overall, gURL.com presents issues of fashion and style as fun, expressive aspects of girls' personalities, but not as major or important concerns. The site emphasizes health over beauty, and individual substance over fashion and style. Drill, Odes, and McDonald no longer work with the site, but its original mission seems to have continued, despite multiple owners, through the steady influence and guiding voices of its teen girl community.

Further Reading

Drill, Esther, Rebecca Odes, and Heather McDonald. (1999). *Deal with It! A Whole New Approach to Your Body, Brain, and Life as a gURL*. New York: Pocket Books.

————. (2002). *The Looks Book: A Whole New Approach to Beauty, Body Image, and Style*. New York: Penguin.

Grisso, Ashley D., and David Weiss. (2005). "What Are Gurls Talking About? Adolescent Girls' Construction of Sexual Identity on gURL.com." In Sharon R. Mazzarella, ed. *Girl Wide Web: Girls, the Internet, and the Negotiation of Identity*. New York: Peter Lang, pp. 31–49.

Ivinski, Pamela. (2000, January/February). "Gurl Power." *Print*, 14–15.

CARYN MURPHY

GYMNASTICS.   Gymnastics is a sport requiring great physical agility, balance, and strength. It involves sequences of moves, often using props—such as balance beams, trampolines, and bars—and includes jumps, flips, somersaults, and handstands. Although it has long been practiced by both men and women, the world of female gymnastics has traditionally been defined by balletic choreography and celebration of the adult feminine form. Female gymnasts were therefore rarely expected to be as athletically competitive as their male counterparts.

In the 1970s, however, women's gymnastics established itself within the larger realm of competitive sports with great enthusiasm and pride. At the 1972 Munich Summer Olympics, Soviet Olga Korbut performed not only the first-ever backward release move in her bars routine but also the first back somersault on the balance beam in an Olympic competition. When Nadia Comaneci completed her bars routine at the 1976 Olympics in Montreal, she flew through the air toward her dismount and landed perfectly, resulting in a score of 10.0. The video of her performance reveals 14-year-old Nadia waving to the crowd, seemingly unable to register the first perfect 10 ever in Olympic gymnastics history.

Emergence of Women in Competitive Gymnastics. While the sport of gymnastics dates back to the era of ancient Greece, women did not enter the sport on a competitive basis until the 1936 Olympic Games in Berlin. Although gymnastics was designed to strengthen the body as well as the mind, women's roles as gymnasts were relegated to the aesthetics of performance rather than the athleticism of the female body. For decades the discipline of Women's Artistic Gymnastics (WAG) has focused less on the technical and more on the artistic. While much of male gymnastics history stemmed from the physical preparation for military service, women entered the sport by producing feminine dance moves to coincide with the few acrobatic movements allowed. The focus was on fluidity of movement with little effort or exertion.

Four different events structure Women's Artistic Gymnastics: uneven (or parallel) bars, balance beam, vault, and floor exercise. Each event has its own scale for judgment based on the gymnast's flexibility, strength, balance, and technique. A routine is choreographed according to the requirements involved for the particular apparatus.

Soviet Beginnings of Female Gymnastics. When Olga Korbut took to the bars for her Olympic debut in 1972, little was known about her in North America; Eastern Europe was at that time the spotlight for both male and female gymnasts. Russia (then the USSR) had carried the sport since the 1950s, producing champions at almost every Olympic and world competition. The Soviets built the foundation of gymnastic training, with children entering the gym as early as 4 years old, often leaving behind family to train six days a week in state-sponsored and state-maintained gymnasiums. Strength and agility training were balanced with acrobatics and ballet. For the girls, however, balletic choreography was the focus in most routines; it is easy to recognize the influence of intensive ballet training in Korbut's international debut.

Basic in their construction, floor exercises included traditional scores of classical music with a few acrobatic moves; walkovers, leaps, and splits added vigor to the routines, but graceful body movement remained the focal point. The beam held the greatest challenge for most competitors; with its width of only four inches, the key was to maintain balance while performing free-flowing dance movements, with only a few acrobatic moves, such as a backbend or walkover.

Olympic Successes and the New Female Gymnast. When 16-year-old U.S. gymnast Cathy Rigby first appeared at the 1968 Olympics in Mexico City, it was clear that a new generation of athletes was about to appear. Audiences saw something different in Rigby. She was small in stature, and while other competitors had the curvy bodies of adult women, Rigby was childlike. She wore her hair in pigtails as she bowed, hopped, flipped, and cartwheeled her way across the floor exercise and balance beam. Likewise, when Olga Korbut arrived at the Munich Olympics in 1972 at age 17, she also did not fit the mold of the traditional female gymnast. The new gymnast was extremely petite, and despite the fact that she was in the stage of late adolescence, she generally looked underdeveloped compared to the female gymnasts of less than a decade earlier.

Within months of the 1972 Olympics, the face of Women's Artistic Gymnastics had noticeably changed. The sport became popular as a televised event; when weekly sports shows began popping up on American television, audiences could track Korbut as she toured the world, including visits to the White House and Disneyland. Gymnastics no longer held a limited audience within Eastern Europe, and by the 1976 Montreal Olympics, many fans had followed several world competitions and were anticipating seeing their favorite competitors perform.

By the time Comaneci, a Romanian girl of 14, performed her first perfect 10.0 in Montreal, audiences had been primed by the appearances of Korbut and Rigby, and fans eagerly accepted the petite athlete, who became the darling of the Games. The vast difference in athleticism between 1972 and 1976, however, was astounding, and Comaneci's vigorous athletic routines far exceeded the expectations of her audience. She performed a large number of new moves with great skillful technique on each apparatus; many gymnasts are still performing several of her original moves today. Her popularity exploded, and gymnastics became a favorite of the Summer Olympic Games.

With Comaneci thrust into the public sphere, everything about the sport changed. The shift in audience was among the most marked changes. Whereas gymnastic enthusiasts were previously limited to attending live events or reading about competitions through sporting magazines, by 1972 the Olympics were being televised to a larger audience than were any previous games, and new fans began to emerge. When Comaneci stuck her landing after the final backflip on her floor routine in 1976, millions of young girls around the world not only were able to recognize gymnastics as an internationally respected sport, but could also see—in Comaneci's small physical frame, vibrant personality, and incredible athleticism—hope for themselves as potential gymnasts. Indeed, Nadia Comaneci became the face for the new female gymnast, and within years of her perfect 10.0, gymnastic training became increasingly popular across the United States and Canada. By the mid-1980s, Women's Artistic Gymnastics became a popular and highly lucrative sport.

Female Gymnasts in the Public Eye. A major contribution to the sport's burgeoning popularity was undoubtedly the media frenzy that followed the gymnasts. Comaneci appeared on the covers of major news magazines around the world and, as with Korbut, millions followed her career on television. The image of the female gymnast had become one of a small, preadolescent girl who grabbed the attention of audiences with a style and attitude of her own. Magazines with glossy color pictures of the sport became more popular among adolescent girls. Gymnastics terminology also came into fashion, with girls increasingly referring to acrobatic names, phrases, and athletic ranking. The goal for many gymnasts became elite status, that of an athlete competing at the highest possible level.

Competitive gymnastic clubs became popular across North America, and parents began to enroll their toddlers for basic tumbling classes, hoping to see their daughter become the next Nadia Comaneci. While boys' presence never wavered in the sport, girls became the focal point for both membership recruitment and audiences. Gymnastics fashion began to take shape, with elaborately designed leotards marking club teams. Club unity was fostered by adorning the girls with matching hairstyles and glittering cheeks that would catch the spotlight as they moved through their routines. Yet while the appearance of the gymnasts reinforced stereotyped images of girlhood—team hugging after a routine, a focus on fashion, and the shedding of tears for both good and bad performances—these female gymnasts never let their audiences forget that they were, first and foremost, serious athletes. When Mary Lou Retton received a perfect score on her vault routine at the 1984 Olympics in Los Angeles, she performed the routine a second time and again earned the flawless score of 10.0, proving to the audience that her first score was not a fluke but a product of intense, rigorous training.

The Popular Appeal of Gymnastics. Stars began emerging from this core group of elite gymnasts, and the audience reveled in the competition between athletes. Televised competitions of gymnastic events were often preceded by a story of two gymnasts training together, only to become competitors on the mat. Creating soap operas from sporting events, these video blurbs helped fuel dramatic interest in the gymnasts, and several athletes acquired very vocal and loyal fan bases as a result. Coaches also became a force of popularity, such as Romanian coach Béla Károlyi, who coached Nadia Comaneci in 1976. He immigrated to the United States in 1981 and began coaching a slew of Olympic gymnasts, including Retton, Kim Zmeskal, and Dominique Moceanu. His coaching style became the standard for many gyms across the country, and it produced results: parents consistently moved their daughters to his Houston-based gym to be coached by the best. At the 1996 Olympics in Atlanta, the women's team, dubbed "The Magnificent Seven" by the press, won the first-ever team gold medal for the United States and solidified the sport's popularity as the gymnasts became household names, even to people who were not gymnastics fans.

By the mid-1990s, there was no denying the popularity of women's gymnastics as a respectable and highly valued sport. However, with a growing rank of elite gymnasts around the world, stories about the dark side of the sport began to emerge. Many medical journals began publishing articles on the negative impact of gymnastics on young bodies. In 1995, sports columnist Joan Ryan published a book entitled *Little Girls in Pretty Boxes: The Making and Breaking of Elite Gymnasts and Figure Skaters*. The book exposed the hidden world of eating disorders, such as **anorexia** and **bulimia**, and the common practice of training while injured; these problems and pressures plagued both gymnasts and figure skaters, who were expected to remain agile, flexible, and strong, yet incredibly petite.

Many gymnasts have since come forward to discuss their lifelong battles with eating disorders. Ryan's research, while understandably not well received within the competitive gymnastics community, was a significant force in changing much of how the sport is now developed and taught. Coaching styles now include lessons in nutrition, and the age of acceptance to the Olympic team has risen from 14 to 16.

Gymnastics Audiences in the Twenty-first Century. Interest in gymnastics has recently acquired a new audience. With the emergence of video **Web sites** such as YouTube, young girls can now search for their favorite routines and watch them as often as they desire. More and more clips of the earliest gymnasts are popping up on these video sharing sites, so that hopeful gymnasts can see the most recent competitions while also learning about the history of the sport. Popular culture continues to feed the gymnastics frenzy; the recent film *Stick It* (2006) has virtually become part of the gymnastics canon. With a concern for healthier bodies for adolescent girls, and the move toward improving the sport with this aim in mind, gymnastics has yet to fully achieve its potential in a new generation of girls.

See also Girls and Sport in Contemporary Film; The Thin Ideal

Further Reading

Cogan, Karen D. and Peter Vidmar. (2000). *Gymnastics.* New York: Fitness Information Technology.

Comaneci, Nadia. (2004). *Letters to a Young Gymnast: Art of Mentoring.* New York: Basic Books.

Károlyi, Béla, and Nancy Ann Richardson. (1994). *Feel No Fear: The Power, Passion, and Politics of a Life in Gymnastics.* New York: Hyperion Books.

Kleinbaum, Nancy H. (1996). *The Magnificent Seven: The Authorized Story of American Gold.* New York: Delacorte.

Korbut, Olga, and Ellen Emerson White. (1992). *My Story: The Autobiography of Olga Korbut.* London: Century.

Ryan, Joan. (1995). *Little Girls in Pretty Boxes: The Making and Breaking of Elite Gymnasts and Figure Skaters.* New York: Doubleday.

MICHELE POLAK